ABOUT THE AUTHORS

For five decades, award-winning writer **Brad Steiger** has been devoted to exploring and examining unusual, hidden, secret, and otherwise strange occurrences. A former high school teacher and college instructor, Brad published his first articles on the unexplained in 1956. Since then he has written more than two thousand articles with paranormal themes. He is author or coauthor of more than 170 titles, including *Real Ghosts, Restless Spirits, and Haunted Places; The Werewolf Book; Mysteries of Time and Space;* and *Real Monsters, Gruesome Creatures, and Beasts from the Darkside.*

Brad is a veteran of broadcast news magazines, ranging from *Nightline* to the *NBC Nightly News,* and a wide variety of cable programs. He is also a regular radio guest on Jeff Rense's *Sightings, The Allan Handelman Show,* and *Coast to Coast* with George Noory. Brad has been interviewed and featured in numerous newspapers and magazines, including the *New York Times, Los Angeles Times, San Francisco Chronicle,* and *Chicago Tribune.*

For over forty-five years, **Sherry Steiger** has actively studied the mysteries of the paranormal, as well as the dynamic interaction between the body, mind, and spirit and the effects of environment and technology on health and wellness. Sherry has been the keynote speaker and addressed audiences and corporate groups from coast to coast.

Sherry has served as counselor to troubled youth, the homeless, migrant workers, and families in need of crisis intervention. In the 1970s she formed a nonprofit holistic research and education school, and in the 1980s she served as public relations director for astronomer Dr. J. Allen Hynek in the Phoenix branch of the Center for UFO Research. She has authored or coauthored more than forty-four books, including the best-selling "Miracles" series.

Together, the Steigers have researched mysteries and miracles throughout the globe and lectured and conducted workshops for over twenty years. They have been interviewed on many national radio programs and have guested on such television programs as *The Joan Rivers Show, Hard Copy, Inside Edition,* and *Entertainment Tonight,* as well as appearing in specials on HBO, The Learning Channel, Discovery, History, and A&E channels, among others. They were also featured in twenty-two episodes of the syndicated series *Could It Be a Miracle?*

Between them, Sherry and Brad have two sons, three daughters, and ten grandchildren. Information on their continuing research can be found at www.bradandsherry.com.

CONSPIRACIES

AND

SECRET SOCIETIES

CONSPIRACIES

AND

SECRET

SOCIETIES

BRAD STEIGER
AND
SHERRY STEIGER

VISIBLE
INK
PRESS

CONPIRACIES AND SECRET SOCIETIES

Visible Ink Press®
43311 Joy Rd. #414
Canton, MI 48187-2075

Visible Ink Press is a registered trademark of Visible Ink Press LLC.

Most Visible Ink Press books are available at special quantity discounts when purchased in bulk by corporations, organizations, or groups. Customized printings, special imprints, messages, and excerpts can be produced to meet your needs. For more information, contact Special Markets Director, Visible Ink Press, www.visibleink.com, or 734-667-3211.

Managing Editor: Kevin S. Hile
Art Director: Mary Claire Krzewinski
Typesetting: Marco Di Vita
Proofreaders: Sharon R. Gunton and Sarah Hermsen

ISBN: 978-1-4351-4993-9

Cover images: Shutterstock.

Library of Congress Cataloging-in-Publication Data

Steiger, Brad.
Conspiracies and secret societies : the complete dossier / by Brad Steiger and Sherry Hansen Steiger. — 2nd ed.
p. cm.
Includes bibliographical references and index.
ISBN 978-1-4351-4993-9
1. Conspiracies—Encyclopedias. 2. Secret societies—Encyclopedias. I. Steiger, Sherry Hansen. II. Title.
HV6275.S74 2013
001.9—dc23   2012009196

Printed in the United States of America

10 9 8 7 6 5 4 3 2

CONTENTS

Introduction [xi]

A

B

C

D

E

Contents

P

R

S

T

U

V

W

X–Y

Z

Photo Credits

AP/Wide World: pp. 117, 130, 179, 238, 308, 398, 405, 460, 490, 517.

Fortean Picture Library: p. 59.

Library of Congress: pp. 20, 144, 199, 257, 273, 276.

Mary Evans Picture Library: pp. 5, 7, 23, 29, 31, 37, 49, 78, 97, 106, 167, 186, 189, 195, 197, 209, 215, 222, 224, 233, 251, 254, 283, 284, 294, 299, 302, 323, 359, 407, 411, 422, 435, 450, 451, 457, 514, 522.

NASA: p. 134.

Ricardo Pustanio: p. 467.

San Diego State University: p. 372.

Shutterstock.com: pp. 3, 15, 42, 52, 56, 63, 70, 75, 103, 109, 115, 120, 127, 136, 142, 151, 153, 174, 193, 200, 248, 262, 345, 353, 364, 368, 371, 426, 433, 441, 486, 500, 505. 508, 520.

Wikicommons: 81, 268, 280, 305, 331, 337, 377, 394, 396, 415, 473, 497.

Photos of U.S. presidents are all in the public domain.

INTRODUCTION

In spite of his expressed reservations, on December 31, 2011, President Barack Obama brought in the new year by signing the National Defense Authorization Act, which gives the government enhanced powers to detain, interrogate, and prosecute its citizens. Under this new act, government agencies may order the indefinite imprisonment of American citizens without charges or trial, the possible military detention of ordinary citizens who would normally be outside of military control, and the transfer to the Department of Defense those law enforcement, penal, and custodial powers currently held by the Department of Justice. In the words of U.S. Senator Lindsey Graham, an enthusiastic supporter of the bill, "The homeland is part of the battlefield" in the global war on terror.

Since the end of the Cold War and the collapse of the Soviet Union in 1991, the American public has tended to believe that their government increasingly lies to them and conspires against them. Rick Ross, whose Ross Institute of New Jersey investigates conspiracies, has observed that more and more Americans see manipulative forces working behind the scenes of their own government.

Conspiracy theorists are quick to respond that they have many good reasons to suspect the government of dirty dealings behind the scenes. While only a few whistleblowers—officially dismissed as "kooks and dissidents"—tried to warn the general public about secret government agencies, it was later learned that in the late 1940s, 1950s, and 1960s the FBI's COINTELPRO really *did* have orders to defame, disgrace, and dispose of war protesters, radical political groups, and freedom marchers by any means necessary. The CIA's insidious, top-secret MK-ULTRA really *did* conduct ghastly brainwashing and mind-altering drug experiments that may have produced the perfect assassins, as well as the Unabomber.

In 1950, when nuclear weapons were still in their infancy, the Department of Defense detonated nuclear devices in desert areas, then monitored unsuspecting civilians in cities downwind from the blasts for medical problems and mortality rates.

In 1966, more than a million civilians were exposed to germ warfare when U.S. Army scientists dropped light bulbs filled with bacteria onto ventilation grates throughout the New York City subway system.

In 1977, Senate hearings revealed that between 1949 and 1969, 239 highly populated areas, including San Francisco, Washington, D.C., Key West, Panama City, Minneapolis, and St. Louis had been contaminated with biological agents.

In 1995, evidence surfaced that the biological agents used during the Gulf War had been manufactured in Houston and Boca Raton and tested on prisoners in the Texas Department of Corrections.

The years following the destruction of the World Trade Center on September 11, 2001, have seen what Mike Ward, writing in *PopMatters* (January 3, 2003) termed "probably the most staggering proliferation of 'conspiracy theories' in American history. Angry speculation—focused mainly on government dirty dealings, ulterior motives, and potential complicity in the attacks—has risen to a clamor that easily rivals what followed the Kennedy assassination."

Conspiracy theories are often replete with internal paradoxes, and some are easily dismissed by rational folks as completely weird and crazy. Often, the truth lies in the middle, and the task of the serious researcher is to make an intelligent discernment. To dismiss some conspiracy theories as too wild and off-the-wall to deserve attention may only result in the last laugh being enjoyed by those who seek to control and manipulate others.

Conspiracy theorists warn that Big Brother's eyes and ears are becoming increasingly active throughout the United States.

Cameras are showing up on street corners in cities across the United States, as well as other countries like England. Ostensibly, they are there to help police scan license plates on stolen cars and capture thieves and escaping killers, and many of the cameras have the capabilities of facial identification and can cross reference any citizen suspected of antisocial behavior of even the most minor of offenses with an extensive database.

Radio Frequency Identification (RFID) chips smaller than a grain of sand are being used to monitor the attendance and movements of children while they are at school, the sale patterns of retail merchandise, and the habits of factory workers. Plans are allegedly underway to place a chip in all newborns in the United States and Europe.

Government agencies can easily monitor both landline and cell phones, making a private call an anachronism. The FBI has been forced to admit that it regularly monitors Internet radio talk programs throughout the United States, as well as email and website browsing patterns.

Even the average American citizen who is more interested in sports and paying the bills, rather than politics and conspiracies, may become queasy at the idea that the power of the Patriot Act has become enhanced by the National Defense Authorization Act, and that three of the Republican candidates in the 2012 presidential race openly support waterboarding as a tool of interrogation. Just how far would the government extend its new powers to the process of making the unfortunate citizen suspected of treason or terrorism confess to those accusations?

America has been a cradle for conspiracies and secret societies from its earliest beginnings. Christopher Columbus, for example, held apocalyptic beliefs and claimed to have received a vision that the world would end in 1650 and that it was his divine mission to find a new land that would be the location of the new heaven and new earth promised by St. John in the Book of Revelation. In the 1600s, the master Freemason Sir Francis Bacon believed that America was the New Atlantis and that it would bring forth a New World Order that would restore all humankind to the earthly paradise that existed in that Golden Age of old.

Petty conspiracies that circulate about political or business rivals are as old as the human psyche, Daniel Pipes tells us in *Front-*

Page magazine (January 13, 2004). But fears about grand conspiracies, such as some secret society seeking to take over the world, go back only 900 years and "have been operational for just two centuries, since the French Revolution." While royal heads were being lopped off by Madame Guillotine, some citizens were blaming the revolution on the political manipulations of the Bavarian Illuminati and its hold on the Jacobins.

Fear of such conspiracies and shadowy societies have made American history replete with warnings of secret plots by the Freemasons, the Zionists, the Roman Catholics, the Communists, the World Bankers, the Bilderbergers, the Illuminati, the Secret Government, New Agers, and extraterrestrial invaders. Charges of conspiracy have grown to self-perpetuating histories of sinister cabals responsible for the assassinations of Abraham Lincoln, James Garfield, John F. Kennedy, Robert F. Kennedy, Martin Luther King, Jr., Malcolm X, and Princess Diana of Wales. Polls indicate that increasing numbers of Americans believe that they have not been told the truth about Pearl Harbor, the Gulf of Tonkin, the Oklahoma City Bombing, the fires that consumed Waco, or the Twin Towers on 9/11.

Sometimes, it seems these paranoid people are really on to something. When such conspiracies as those cited above prove to be true or partially true, the assertion that there is a kernel of truth in even the most far-fetched conspiracy theory appears also to be true. Michael Barkun, a political scientist at Syracuse University and the author of *A Culture of Conspiracy: Apolcalyptic Visions in Contemporary America* (2003), has identified what he believes to be three principles to be found in every conspiracy theory: Nothing happens by accident; nothing is as it seems; everything is connected. The essence of conspiracy beliefs, Barkun says, "lies in attempts to delineate and explain evil." Barkun also states that contemporary conspiracy theories have taken on a major new development, the joining of the occult, the heretical, and the unfashionable, such as spiritualism, alchemy, and theosophy.

With the advent of the Internet, anyone can become a conspiracy theorist and broadcast his or her unchecked, unquestioned, and unchallenged claims of government corruption, racist propaganda, or alien abduction all over the world. On Google alone, there are thousands of active websites devoted to conspiracy theories and dedicated to secret societies. Sharing stories about conspiracies and secret societies is very much like spreading sinister gossip, and one needs to develop a sense of what is true and what is merely a reflection of someone else's personal prejudices and beliefs.

For many years now, we have studied and evaluated the enormous influence of conspiracy theories on society and how people's beliefs can be manipulated for good or for evil by the promulgation of certain idea, theories, and beliefs. While this book may appear to document the more shadowy visages of human history, the images that appear in the dark mirrors that reflect portraits of chaos, confusion, and deceit down through the ages, we have tried our best to approach this work without any personal agendas. We do not subscribe to any particular conspiracy theory, and we do not belong to any secret society. It is up to each reader to decide whether this book presents a work of entertainment or enlightenment, a work of wonderment or of warning.

—Brad Steiger
Sherry Steiger

AIDS/HIV

Conspiracy theorists argue that AIDS did not come out of Africa, but out of secret government laboratories that created this and other terrible weapons of biological warfare.

The Kenyan ecologist Wangari Maathai, the first African woman to win the Nobel Peace Prize, took full advantage of the international attention that she received to state her claim that the AIDS virus was a deliberately created biological agent to be used in warfare. She disputed the theory that AIDS—acquired immunodeficiency syndrome—had come from monkeys, pointing out that Africans have been living around monkeys since time immemorial. But, she added, there was no disputing the somber fact that 25 million out of the 38 million infected with AIDS across the world are Africans, and the great majority of infected Africans are women.

The U.S. State Department congratulated Maathai on winning the Peace Prize but disagreed with her claims that the human immunodeficiency virus (HIV) believed to cause AIDS was invented as a bioweapon in some laboratory in the West for the purpose of mass extermination. While one might expect such a response of the State Department, conspiracy theorists are quick to remind us that one of the prime objectives of the New World Order and its agents who work in the shadows behind every government on the planet is to decrease dramatically the earth's population.

Credit for the discovery of the AIDS virus was settled by lawsuit in 1987 after Dr. Robert Gallo of the National Cancer Institute and Luc Montagnier of the Pasteur Institute in Paris both claimed to have isolated the virus sometime in 1984. The codiscoverers of the virus have never agreed about the origin of HIV or the birthplace of AIDS. Montagnier believed that the origin of the virus remains a mystery and that it was important to distinguish between its origins and the AIDS epidemic. Gallo, the more influential of the two scientists, insisted that the virus could have stemmed from a common viral ancestor found in animals and that it was passed to humans by monkeys. Gallo claimed that Ann Giudici Fettner, a freelance journalist who had lived in Africa, told him in 1983, a year before he discovered the virus, that AIDS came from green monkeys in central Africa. However, in her book *The Truth about AIDS,* Fettner never refers to green monkeys and emphasizes her opinion that AIDS began as an American disease. In spite of the paucity of scientific papers to substantiate Gallo's green monkey theory, the explanation remained a favorite of the media and the public and circulated widely until the late 1990s when another group of American scientists claimed that they had discovered the origin of the virus in a species of chimpanzee.

A large number of conspiracy theorists have never bought the "out of Africa" and green monkey or chimp or goat explanation for the origin of AIDS. In 1979 the first gay men began to come down with "immunodeficiency disease." For the first year of the epidemic, the victims were all young, predominantly white, previously in good health, well educated, promiscuous—and they all lived in Manhattan. By 1980 gay men in San Francisco, Los Angeles, Denver, St. Louis, and Chicago had developed the disease. An official AIDS epidemic was declared in June 1981. AIDS was unknown in Africa before this time, and the epidemic did not begin there until late in 1982. In 1984 Gallo discovered the green monkeys in Africa that had been incubating the disease for centuries before the epidemic, and he became world-famous for his work.

But now a problem of timing raises its puzzling head. If the first recorded cases of AIDS were reported to the Centers for Disease Control (CDC) in 1979, are we to believe that all those gay men in Manhattan who contracted the illness had recently traveled to Africa and been bitten by green monkeys? Or could there be a correlation between government-sponsored hepatitis B experiments that began with gay men in Manhattan in New York City in 1978, the year before the outbreak of the HIV epidemic in 1979? Interestingly, similar hepatitis B experiments were sponsored by the government in San Francisco, Los Angeles, Denver, St. Louis, and Chicago in 1980. Word was that the experimental vaccine injected into all those gay men had been developed in chimpanzees.

Early in the 1970s rumors had begun circulating about secret government research in bio warfare and about scientists who were conducting experiments in "species-jumping," mixing viruses and seeding them into animal and human cell cultures. In 1971 President Richard Nixon combined the U.S. Army's bio warfare department at Fort Detrick, Maryland, with the National Cancer Institute. Although the combination was explained to the public as part of the president's "War on Cancer," the program also united the army's DNA and genetic engineering programs with anticancer research and molecular biology projects. In addition, cancer research programs conducted by private companies were blended into anticancer research projects of the CIA, the CDC, and the World Health Organization. As research progressed, dozens of new laboratory hybrids, recombinant and mutant viruses, were engineered, and a few scientists with social consciences began to warn others that some of the newly designed viruses could be extremely dangerous if released from the laboratory. Because of the efforts of a few whistle-blowers, word got out that government scientists had achieved a synthetic biological agent that did not exist naturally and for which no natural immunity could be acquired.

Knowledge of what had been achieved spread rapidly to other government researchers throughout the world. In 1973 the Danish pathologist Johannes Clemmesen warned that the transmissibility of such genetically altered viral agents could cause a world epidemic of cancer if they ever left the confines of the laboratory. Then, in 1979, his dire prophecy began to come to pass with the outbreak of AIDS in Manhattan among the gay population.

Although most individuals are content with Robert Gallo's explanation that the AIDS epidemic is the result of a primate virus jumping species, conspiracy theorists have developed a number of their own explanations for AIDS/HIV. Here are some of the most persistent theories:

- Edward Hooper, author of *The River: A Journey to the Source of HIV-AIDS,* advances the theory that HIV evolved from SIV (simian immunodeficiency virus), found in the chimpanzee. Hooper outlines a scenario that has as its villain Dr. Hilary Koprowski, a virologist working for Philadelphia's Wistar Research Institute, who in the early 1950s used a hastily brewed chimpanzee kidney culture to concoct a million doses of oral vaccine for a mass experimental polio vaccination program in the Belgian Congo. Koprowski's urgency and haste in conducting the mass vaccination was fostered by the pharmaceutical company's putting pressure on him to beat Dr. Salk and Dr. Sabin to the market with the first commercially available polio vaccine.

- The World Health Organization, controlled by the New World Order, created the AIDS epidemic by deliberately administering contaminated vaccines to people in third world countries in the 1970s. Africa was targeted first, in a smallpox eradication program, so that a link could be subsequently made that AIDS had originated in Africa.

- Sometime around 1977, U.S. military scientists bioengineered HIV at Fort Detrick by splicing the Visna and HTLV viruses. It was tested on prison inmates who volunteered to be injected with the virus in exchange for an early release. From these released prisoners, the virus spread to a wider segment of the population, especially to the gay community.

- The Soviet KGB created the viruses, then planted disinformation that the CIA was behind the spread of the disease.

- AIDS was the product of bio warfare research conducted by the U.S. government for the express purpose of eliminating excess population among blacks, homosexuals, and other social groups.

A man protests budgets cuts for HIV/AIDS preventive care at a rally in Los Angeles in 2009. Is the AIDS epidemic a plot by the New World Order to exterminate homosexuals?

- Dr. Alan Cantwell (*AIDS and the Doctors of Death: An Inquiry into the Origin of the AIDS Epidemic* and *Queer Blood: The Secret AIDS Genocide Plot*) believes that HIV is a genetically modified virus that was introduced by U.S. government scientists into the gay and bisexual population under the guise of hepatitis B experiments between 1978 and 1981 in Manhattan, Los Angeles, St. Louis, Denver, and Chicago.

- Dr. Gary Glum (*Full Disclosure*) claims that he received top-secret intelligence that the AIDS virus was created at Cold Spring Harbor Laboratory in Cold Spring Harbor, New York. The World Health Organization and the Red Cross are complicit in the conspiracy to spread AIDS, which was released in 1978 as part of the overall population-control plan of the Illuminati and the New World Order. Glum warns that the virus is far more easily transmitted than medical reports have stated and can be spread through kissing, mosquito bites, and casual contact. Dr. Glum also maintains that Upjohn Pharmaceuticals has a number of medical cures for AIDS, but distribution of the substances has been suppressed by the government.

- Louis Farrakhan's Nation of Islam and the New Black Panther Party have accused Jewish doctors of creating AIDS as a means of destroying black people throughout the world.

- Dr. Leonard G. Horowitz (*Emerging Viruses: AIDS and Ebola—Nature, Accident, or Intentional?* and *Death in the Air: Globalism, Terrorism, and Toxic Warfare*) theorizes that such U.S. government defense contractors as Litton Bionetics engineered AIDS to target Jews, blacks, and Hispanics as the first to be eliminated in a massive population-control program.

AIRSHIP OF 1897

In 1897, years before any known terrestrial agency had accomplished heavier-than-air flight, members of a secret society in contact with extraterrestrials piloted a large airship, often described as resembling a cone-shaped steamboat, across the United States and later throughout the world.

In 1897 the world was poised confidently on the brink of the twentieth century. In 1893 Karl Benz and Henry Ford had built their first four-wheeled automobiles. In 1895 Auguste and Louis Lumière had invented the cinematograph, Guglielmo Marconi had invented radio telegraphy, and Konstantin Tsiolkovsky had formulated the principle of rocket reaction propulsion.

The Royal Automobile Club was founded in London in 1897, and cars on the ground were going faster every year. But there were no heavier-than-air vehicles racing across the skies—and a good number of brilliant scientists declared that it was aerodynamically impossible to build such flying machines.

And yet, on April 7, 1897, citizens of Wesley, Iowa, sighted a cone-shaped airship with brightly illuminated windows in its side. The witnesses were unable to determine how it was propelled or what sustained it in the air.

On April 15 the airship landed two miles north of Springfield, Illinois. The craft's occupants explained that they had landed to repair their electrical apparatus and searchlight equipment.

On April 17 the airship returned to Iowa and set down outside of Waterloo. One of the occupants brandished a rifle to keep the curious several hundred yards from the machine. Journalists described the airship as being about forty feet long and constructed like a giant cigar, with winglike attachments on the sides and a steering apparatus in the rear. The machine was surmounted by a cupola on its roof.

During April 21 and 22 the airship barnstormed Arkansas and Texas. In Harrisburg, Arkansas, it awakened a former senator after midnight. Members of the flight crew informed him that the builder of the craft was a brilliant inventor from St. Louis who had discovered the secret of suspending the laws of gravity. Nineteen years had been invested in building the airship, but because it was not quite perfected, the crew preferred to travel at night. Once they had accomplished a successful voyage to the planet Mars, they would put the airship on public exhibition.

On April 24 a prominent Texas farmer was awakened at midnight by a strange whirring sound and the brilliant lights of what he assumed were angels in a celestial vehicle. The visitors informed him that they came not from heaven, but from a small town in Iowa, where five such airships had been constructed. The craft were built of a newly discovered material

A newspaper artist's rendition of Walter McCann taking a photo of an airship over Rogers Park near Chicago in 1897.

that had the property of self-sustenance in the air. The motive power was a highly condensed electricity.

Throughout the following weeks, landing and contact reports came from areas all across the United States. During the summer months of 1897, sightings were reported from other parts of the world as well. In July and August mysterious aerial objects were seen over Sweden and Norway. On August 13 what appeared to be the same aerial craft was sighted off the coast of Norway and over Vancouver, British Columbia, on the same day.

In 1898 Count von Zeppelin announced his achievement of a dirigible, but the early models had such a restricted flying range that great difficulties were encountered in making successful flights from Germany to England. In 1903 Orville and Wilbur Wright accomplished the first flight with a heavier-than-air vehicle with a craft that managed to stay aloft for twelve seconds and travel 120 feet. But in 1897 no terrestrial agency had constructed an aerial vehicle that could traverse the globe with the speed and ease of the airship piloted by the mysterious inventors from Iowa or St. Louis. Because of this fact, many researchers believe that the builders of the 1897 airship belonged to a secret society, perhaps one that had been in touch with extraterrestrial intelligences—or their records and artifacts—for thousands of years.

Numerous European occult groups have been molded around the belief that a secret society centuries ago achieved a high level of scientific knowledge and has carefully guarded this dangerous learning from the rest of humanity ever since. A common theme is that certain men of genius in ancient Egypt and Persia were given access to the records of the advanced technologies of the antediluvian world. Many hundreds of years ago, these ancient masters learned to duplicate many of the feats of the Titans of Atlantis—and attracted the attention of extraterrestrials who had been monitoring Earth for signs of advanced intelligence.

The decision to form a society within a society may have reflected the members' highly developed moral sense and their recognition of the awesome responsibility that possessing this ancient knowledge placed upon them. They may have decided to keep their own counsel until the rest of the world became enlightened enough to deal wisely with such a high degree of technical accomplishment. Yet now and then the secret society may conclude that the time is propitious to make one of its discoveries known to the outside world. Such intervention in the affairs of the great mass of humanity is usually accomplished by carefully feeding certain fragments of research to "outside" scientists whose work and attitude have been adjudged particularly deserving.

On the other hand, the secret society's members may feel little or no responsibility of any kind to those outside the group. They may be merely biding their time until they turn most of humanity into their slaves. For hundreds of years, certain scholars have worried about global conspiracies being conducted by secret societies waiting until the right moment to achieve complete world domination.

The mysterious airship disappeared from the skies for twelve years. On March 24, 1909, a police constable in Peterborough, England, reported having heard a sound similar to a motorcar overhead. Looking up, he spotted an airship shining a powerful light and traveling as fast as an express train. By July the strange aerial machine was sighted in the skies over New Zealand, and it remained there for six weeks before it returned to the United States. There was one reported overflight in the New England area in August, then the airship disappeared until the night of December 12, when residents of Long Island heard a buzzing sound, resembling the rattle and hum of a high-speed motor, coming from the starlit skies above them.

The last reported airship sighting came from Memphis, Tennessee, on January 20, 1910. A number of witnesses saw a craft flying very high in the air and at a high rate of speed. It crossed the Mississippi River into Arkansas, veered slightly to the south, and disappeared.

Perhaps the secret society no longer felt that it was necessary to inspire the "outsiders" to pursue the science of aeronautics, for by 1910 there had already been an international aviation competition held in Rheims, France; a flight from the deck of a seagoing cruiser; a takeoff from water by a floatplane; and the first woman pilot had obtained her license.

ALCHEMY

Some medieval alchemists summoned demons to assist them in their discoveries. Others may have been contacted by extraterrestrials. The ancient demonic knowledge or alien science is passed on by certain secret societies today.

The essence of medieval alchemy lay in the belief that certain incantations and rituals could persuade or command angelic beings to change base metals into precious ones. The seven principal angels whose favor the alchemist sought were Michael, who supposedly could transmute base metals into gold and dissolve any enmity directed toward the alchemist; Gabriel, who fashioned silver and foresaw the future; Samuel, who protected against physical harm; and Raphael, Sachiel, Ansel, and Cassiel, who could create various gems and guard the alchemist from attack by negative entities.

Members of the clergy were skeptical that the alchemists were truly calling upon angels, rather than demons in disguise, and they recalled the words of the church father Tertullian (c. 160–240), who confirmed earlier beliefs that the "sons of God" referred to in Genesis were evil corrupters who bequeathed their wisdom to mortals with the sole intention of seducing them to mundane pleasures.

Some students of the history of alchemy have stated that crumbling, yellowed records of the alchemists remain in dusty libraries—more than 100,000 ancient volumes written in a code that has never been sufficiently deciphered. Evidence disinterred from the alchemists' libraries in Europe suggests that certain medieval and Renaissance practitioners conducted experiments with photography, radio transmission, phonography, and aerial flight, as well as the endless quest to transmute base metals into gold. If individuals of exceptional intellect, power, and wealth actually did achieve a high degree of technical accomplishment several centuries ago, perhaps alien life forms established an alliance with some of them as being worthy of receiving the benefits of extraterrestrial superscience. Perhaps we have early instances in which the mysterious Men in Black (MIB) visited a select number of Earth scientists.

On December 27, 1666, when Johann Friedrich Schweitzer, called Helvetius, was working in his study at The Hague, a stranger attired all in black appeared and informed him that he would remove all Helvetius' doubts about the existence of the legendary philosopher's stone that could serve as the catalyst to change base metals into gold. The stranger immediately drew from his pocket a small ivory box containing three pieces of metal the color of brimstone and, for their size, extremely heavy. The man proclaimed that with those three bits of metal, he could make as much as twenty tons of gold.

Helvetius examined the pieces of metal, taking opportunity of a moment's distraction to scrape off a small portion with his thumbnail. Returning the metal to his mysterious visitor, he asked that he perform the process of transmutation before him. The stranger answered firmly that he was not allowed to do so. It was enough that he had verified the existence of the metal to Helvetius. It was his purpose only to offer encouragement to alchemical experiments.

After the man's departure, Helvetius procured a crucible and a portion of lead into which, when the metal was in a molten state, he threw the stolen grain he had secretly scraped from the stranger's stone. The alchemist was disappointed when the grain evaporated and left the lead in its original state.

Some weeks later, when he had almost forgotten the incident, Helvetius received another visit from the stranger. This time the man in black transmuted several ounces of lead into gold. Then he permitted Helvetius to repeat the process by himself, and the alchemist converted six ounces of lead into very pure gold.

Later Helvetius demonstrated the power of the philosopher's stone in the presence of the Duke of Orange and many other prestigious witnesses. After repeated demands for such incredible demonstrations, Helvetius exhausted the small supply of catalytic pieces that he

An alchemist researching the Philosopher's Stone, a catalyst for transforming common metals into gold.

had received from the mysterious visitor. Search as he might, he could not find the man in all of north Holland or learn his name—nor did the stranger ever again visit him.

An increasing number of UFO investigators firmly believe that certain secret societies behind our terrestrial power structures have been communicating with alien intelligence and receiving guidance from them. Some theorists go so far as to declare that every major improvement in our culture, our science, our technology—literally every major turn humankind has taken throughout history—resulted from this behind-the-scenes alien manipulation.

Principal among these secret societies, and the group most often named as the conduit for alien control of world governments, is the Illuminati, founded in 1776 by a German law professor named Adam Weishaupt. Persistent researchers claim to have traced the history of the Illuminati back to the ancient Temple of Wisdom in Cairo.

Albertus Magnus (c. 1193–1280), bishop of Ratisbon, is said to have been another alchemist who achieved the transmutation of base metals into gold by means of the philosopher's stone. Magnus is also credited with other extraordinary accomplishments, including the invention of the pistol and the cannon. In addition, he reportedly was able to exert control over atmospheric conditions, once even transforming a cold winter's day into a pleasant summer's afternoon so he and his guests could dine comfortably outside. Tradition has it that Magnus bcqueathed the philosopher's stone to his distinguished pupil Saint Thomas Aquinas; but once the devout Aquinas had it in his possession, he destroyed it, fearful that the accusations of Magnus' having communed with Satan might be true.

Many other alchemists, although never witnessing the legendary philosopher's stone, achieved discoveries of lasting value to humanity. Ramon Llull (1235–1315) was credited with the discovery in about 1275 of ethoxythane (ether); Paracelsus (1493–1541) was the first to describe zinc and various chemical compounds in medicine; Blaise de Vigenère (1523–96) discovered benzoic acid. Discoveries increased during the Renaissance, when such men as Basil Valentine (fifteenth century) discovered sulphuric acid and Johann Friedrich Boetticher (1682–1719) became the first European to produce porcelain.

If an ancient secret society of alchemists and alien superscientists developed a technology that they have managed to keep hidden from outsiders, the matter in perpetual debate is whether the Secret Ones are benevolently guiding us to a time when they can share their accomplishments more openly or are merely awaiting the appropriate moment to conquer the entire world.

ALIEN ABDUCTIONS

Millions of men and women are being abducted by extraterrestrials and forced to endure medical examinations aboard spaceships in order to determine their eligibility for alien-human crossbreeding experiments. Preparatory to a global invasion of Earth, aliens are creating hybrids to serve as a fifth column within the human population.

Estimates presented at a conference held at the Massachusetts Institute of Technology in June 1982 suggested that from several hundred thousand to more than 3 million adults in the United States alone have had abduction experiences with UFO entities.

David Webb, an Arlington, Massachusetts, solar physicist and cochairman of the Mutual UFO Network, has stated that space aliens have abducted one out of every eight people who have reported seeing UFOs. In many cases, Webb said, the victims undergo some kind of examination, but they usually remember nothing of the on-board experience.

The case of Betty and Barney Hill, a couple then in their forties, has become the archetypal example of humans abducted, examined, and probed by aliens from another world. On September 19, 1961, Betty, a social worker, supervisor of the New Hampshire Welfare Department, and Barney, a mail carrier who was on the governor of New Hampshire's Civil Rights Commission, were returning to their home in New Hampshire from a short Canadian vacation when they noticed a bright object in the night sky and stopped to investigate with a pair of binoculars. Barney perceived what appeared to be windows—and strange beings looking back at him. The Hills got back in their car and began to race down the road. Suddenly unable to control their movements, they were taken from the car and, in a trancelike condition, led to the UFO by humanoids.

The Hills recalled the sensational details of their story only under hypnosis, for the couple had a complete loss of memory concerning the nearly two hours during which they were the chosen guests of the UFOnauts. When the Hills began weekly hypnosis sessions with

Benjamin Simon, a Boston psychiatrist, an astonishing pastiche of bizarre physical and mental examinations was revealed. Both told of being examined by aliens in much the same manner as human scientists might treat laboratory animals. Although they had been given hypnotic suggestions that they would forget their experience, their induced amnesia had apparently ruptured in rehypnosis.

Under hypnosis in 1964 Betty, with little or no understanding of astronomy, drew her impressions of a star map that she had seen aboard the alien spaceship. The map was interpreted by Marjorie Fish, an amateur astronomer, member of Mensa, and Ohio schoolteacher. Betty's map showed the location of two stars called Zeta 1 and Zeta 2 Reticuli, allegedly the home base of the space travelers, as well as several other stars in the same part of the sky. Interestingly, the existence of two of the stars on the map was not confirmed by astronomers until 1969 in the *Gliese Catalogue of Nearby Stars,* the standard reference work.

During the night of January 6, 1976, three Liberty, Kentucky, women were abducted by aliens and kept for more than an hour. When they regained consciousness, Louise Smith complained that her neck hurt. When Mona Stafford examined it, she saw a strange red mark like a burn that had not blistered, about three inches long and an inch wide. Elaine Thomas's neck had the same type of mark on it.

Although the peculiar burn marks disappeared in about two days, the three women still could not account for the missing time— nor could they recall more about that night than having seen a UFO overhead and Louise Smith screaming that she could not control her rapidly accelerating automobile.

Later, under hypnosis sessions conducted by Dr. R. Leo Sprinkle, Elaine Thomas remembered that she had been placed on her back in a long, narrow chamber. There were small, dark figures perhaps four feet tall standing near her. One of them placed a blunt instru-

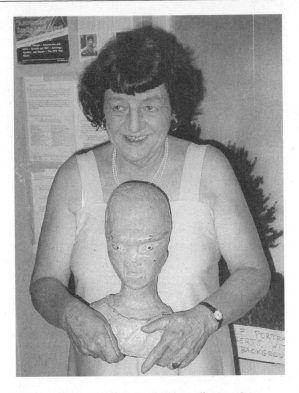

Betty Hill poses with a bust of her alien captor.

ment against her chest that caused her a great deal of pain.

Louise Smith recalled the frightening appearance of the humanoids and the bizarre environment in which she found herself.

Mona Stafford remembered lying on a table in what seemed to be some kind of operating room. At one point she felt as if her eyes were being pulled out of her skull. At another time, her stomach was blown up like a balloon. She also reported that a number of aliens pulled at her feet, then bent them backward and twisted.

There are numerous accounts in circulation of human-alien sexual interaction during abduction experiences. One of the earliest such reports came from Brazil and was originally published in the magazine *O Cruzeiro*. Dr. Olvao Fontes, one of the original investigators of the incident, stated that the abductee, Antonio Villas Boas, was a twenty-three-year-old farmer near the town of Francisco de Sales in the state of Minas Gerais. On the night of October 15, 1957, Antonio was plowing alone when an egg-shaped aerial vehicle hovered over his tractor. A few minutes later the object landed, and four occupants dressed in tight-fitting coveralls made of a thick, but soft, gray cloth emerged from it. One of the beings grabbed Antonio's arms, but he managed to wrench himself free. (The young, well-muscled farmer said later that his abductors were about his height—five feet four—and strength.) He had not gone far, however, when three other beings got hold of his arms and legs and lifted him off the ground.

> All of these abductees reported a basic progression of emotions, moving from uneasy, fragmented recollections to a clear memory accompanied by fear.

Inside the vehicle the aliens brought Antonio to a brightly lighted room. He later said that their speech sounded to him like a series of doglike barks. The young farmer was stripped naked and thoroughly examined. When the beings had finished their examination, he was left alone to rest on a couch. He had not lain there long before he became aware that gray smoke with a disagreeable, suffocating odor had entered the room. Antonio was forced to relieve his nausea by vomiting in a corner.

After a few more minutes, the door to the room opened and a well-proportioned and totally naked woman walked in to join Antonio on the couch. The alien seductress had large blue eyes that seemed to slant outward, a straight nose, high cheekbones, a nearly lipless mouth, and a sharply pointed chin. In spite of the stressful physical examination that he had just endured, Antonio found himself responding to the her frank sexual advances. Later he told investigators that the beings must have somehow dosed him with an aphrodisiac.

After the sexual act had been consummated, Antonio's clothing was returned, and an alien male indicated that he should get dressed. It was clear that his abductors were finished with him. The next day Antonio became ill. His eyes began to burn and a series of sores broke out on his arms and legs. In the center of each of the sores was a little lump that was very itchy. Two weeks later his face became speckled with yellowish spots.

Ever since the 1960s, alien abductions have been reported with alarming frequency. Many researchers maintain that the kidnappings and physical examinations are part of an alien program of interbreeding. In numerous instances, such as in the case of Antonio Boas, the aliens bring one of their women, whose egg is ready to be fertilized, to an earthman for insemination.

Some investigators argue that for pregnancy to occur during a sexual act, the male and female must be of the same species. Others counter that alien superscience might have evolved some remarkable method of DNA manipulation or cloning. Either thought is unsettling.

Many researchers say that if we were to read the creation story in Genesis from the historical perspective of our current awareness of genetic engineering, the interaction between the "sons of God" and the fair daughters of men assumes a rather different interpretation: "And it came to pass, when men began to multiply on the face of the earth and daughters were born to them, that the sons of God saw the daughters of men were fair; so they took them wives of all whom they chose. There were giants on the earth in those days; and also after that, for the sons of God came in unto the daughters of men, and they bore children to them, and they became giants who in the olden days were men of renown" (Gen. 6:1–4).

If the fallen angels of Genesis were actually extraterrestrials conducting experiments on female members of the developing strain of primitive humans, then rather than decadent heavenly beings sinning with Earth's daughters, they were scientists carrying out a directive to provide early humankind with a genetic boost.

In the apocryphal book of Enoch (7:12), we learn more of the nonterrestrial entities who desire the daughters of men for their own interests: "It happened after the sons of men had multiplied in those days, that elegant, beautiful daughters were born to them. And when the angels, the sons of heaven, beheld them, they became enamored of them, saying to each other: Come, let us select for ourselves wives from the progeny of men, and let us beget children."

Abductees speaking at the Mutual UFO Network's Washington, D.C., conference in June 1987 reported frightening and disorienting aspects of their experiences. They told of the frustration of being partially paralyzed and taken without their consent to undergo medical examinations. They said that they often remembered the events only in fragments and flashes until they underwent hypnotic regression.

Whitley Strieber admitted that when he first realized he had been abducted, he was suicidal. Then he began to investigate some UFO literature and discovered that others had endured similar experiences. He sought out the services of a hypnotist, thinking that perhaps that would alleviate his ordeal, and he wrote the book *Communion* hoping that the memories and the feelings would go away.

Strieber said that he had received thousands of letters from other abductees—people who do not welcome publicity, including en-

tertainers, political leaders, and members of the armed forces in high positions. All of these abductees reported a basic progression of emotions, moving from uneasy, fragmented recollections to a clear memory accompanied by fear.

R. Leo Sprinkle, formerly on staff at the University of Wyoming in Laramie, has speculated that hundreds of thousands of people may have undergone a UFO abduction experience but were not aware of it at the time. Sprinkle lists several characteristics common among people who have had such experiences:

1. An episode of missing time. They know that "something" happened between two points of consciousness, but they can't fill in the missing time.

2. Disturbing dreams about flying saucers, about being pursued and captured, then examined by doctors in white coats.

3. Daytime flashbacks of UFO experiences. While going about their normal daytime activities, abductees will flash back to some kind of UFO image or UFO entity.

4. Strange compulsions, such as a strong wish to travel to a certain location or to complete a certain task.

5. A sudden interest in UFOs. The abductee may suddenly want to read about UFOS, ancient history, or pyramids and crystals, without knowing why.

ALIEN AUTOPSY

If this film of an alien autopsy being secretly performed by U.S. government doctors is authentic, it is the most important footage ever made in the history of motion pictures.

London-based film producer Ray Santilli claims that he had never heard any of the stories about the crash of an extraterrestrial vehicle near Roswell, New Mexico, in June

1947, nor was he at all familiar with the rumors of dead aliens strewn near the wreckage. He happened to be in Cleveland, Ohio, in the summer of 1993 in search of some rare footage of Elvis Presley, never imagining that he would have an opportunity to purchase some even rarer film of a major cosmic event.

According to Santilli, an elderly freelance cameraman who had shot the footage of Elvis for Universal News in the summer of 1955 sold him the three-minute sequence of Presley, then offered to sell some very different material that he had filmed during his time in the military. The cameraman, now in his eighties, explained that the footage came from the Roswell crash site and that it included some incredible images of the autopsy of one or more aliens from the flying saucer.

Although ignorant of the Roswell incident, Santilli became interested in the alleged alien autopsy. The cameraman didn't appear to be a nut or a scam artist, so Santilli agreed to view the film. When they arrived at the man's home, the veteran cameraman put a reel on an old projector and projected the images directly on the wall.

What Santilli witnessed in the old cameraman's home in Cleveland in 1993 is allegedly what millions saw on their television screens on the evening of August 28, 1995, on the Fox network's "Alien Autopsy: Fact or Fiction?" At first the images are hazy, but then the viewer sees, lying on an autopsy table, what appears to be a smallish humanoid with a swollen belly (with no navel), huge dark eyes, a damaged right leg, a broken and swollen left leg, a cut-off right hand, and a bruise at the temple. Soon the pathologists are cutting the creature open and removing body organs that appear to be from an alien species. The entity resembles a human being in many ways, except for its innards—and its twelve fingers and twelve toes.

Santilli said later that he thought the footage incredible and offered immediately to

buy it. The cameraman told him that on June 2, 1947, he had received direct orders from General Clement McMullen informing him that there had been a crash in the White Sands area and that he was to go there immediately and film everything he could. Santilli came away with twenty-two reels of film, twenty-one safety prints, and one negative.

UFO researchers were arguing about the controversial film long before it was shown on Fox. Many condemned it outright as a hoax because the alien looked too human to be an extraterrestrial or in some way didn't fit their conception of how an alien Roswell crash victim should look. Others championed the footage and believed that it would convince millions—and most of all the scientific establishment—that UFOs from outer space were visiting Earth. Some UFOlogists argued that in their opinion the alien in the autopsy room could not have come from the Roswell crash, but had been retrieved from an early UFO crash site near Socorro, New Mexico. And then there were the purists who were offended by the very thought of commercially exploiting what could be the most important film of the century.

An analysis of the film confirmed the elderly cameraman's claim that the autopsy footage had been shot on vintage 16mm film and that it had likely been filmed with a Bell & Howell Filmo Camera, favored by the U.S. military in the 1940s. Samples cut from a number of leaders from the film and sent for analysis to Kodak labs in Hollywood, London, and Copenhagen revealed identifying symbols used by Kodak from 1947 to 1967. Bob Shell, editor of *Shutterbug* magazine, was given two segments of three frames each of the autopsy room footage. Shell, a photo technical consultant for the FBI, confirmed the snippets to be pre-1956 film.

As far as the props used in the autopsy footage, every artifact appears to date from circa 1947. The telephone is an AT&T model from 1946. The wall clock is a model popular since 1938. The instruments utilized in the autopsy itself were confirmed as standard for the time period by Dr. Cyril Wecht, a highly respected forensic scientist, ex-president of the American Academy of Forensic Sciences.

While the props check out as accurate, researchers have many problems with the alien corpse. In this time of remarkably realistic special effects in motion pictures, even the most earnest defender of the authenticity of the footage has to concede that it would be no problem for a Hollywood makeup specialist to create a realistic alien body. Is the badly mutilated corpse on the autopsy table that of an extraterrestrial space traveler, a young female human with polydactylism (having more than the normal number of fingers and toes), a young polydactylic female human who died of Turner's syndrome, or a foam rubber model of a young female with polydactylism, Turner's syndrome, and other anomalies?

Turner's syndrome affects about one in every 2,500 females, and a deceased victim of the syndrome was named by many physicians as a likely candidate for the "alien" on the table. The identifying characteristics of Turner's syndrome are short stature (a mean height of four feet seven inches); lack of secondary sexual characteristics; medical problems, such as ear, eye, thyroid difficulties; secondary features such as low-set ears, low hairline, webbed neck, and puffy hands and feet. Because of such characteristics being evident in the "alien body," many pathologists did not believe that they were seeing a dummy in the autopsy footage.

On the other hand, there were a number of pathologists who did not believe that they were seeing either a dummy or a human being in the autopsy film. Professor Christopher Milroy, Home Office pathologist, University of Sheffield, commented that although the close-up of the entity's brain was a bit out of focus, it did not have the appearance of a human brain. Professor M. J. Mihatsch of the University of Basel, Switzerland, admitted that he could not identify as human any of the organs the doctors in the footage removed from the alien. Wecht, famous for his testimony in such trials as those of O. J. Simpson and Scott Peterson, said that he could not place the organs in a human abdominal context and could not associate them in any way with the human body as he knew it. Professor Pierluigi Baima Bollone, University of Turin, concluded that there was not one single organ that in any way resembled any human organ. In general, there seemed to be a consensus among pathologists all over the world that the body on the table was not a dummy, but that of some biological being, extraterrestrial or not.

The controversy over the alien autopsy film is not likely to fade away. Some researchers consider it the most ingenious hoax of the century; others laugh and wonder that any UFO investigator could take the footage seriously. According to some investigators, Ray Santilli continues to make controversial statements about the origins of the film and has perhaps inadvertently done more damage to his own credibility than all the debunkers' efforts to prove him a scam artist combined. From his arrival on the UFO scene, Santilli demonstrated his ignorance of the field of research and his lack of respect for all the unwritten protocols of the UFO community.

The conspiracy theorists will always have the last word on any subject. For example, in the mid-1990s rumors circulated that famous Hollywood director Steven Spielberg had managed to acquire the Holy Grail of UFO research—actual U.S. military footage of the 1947 flying saucer crash outside of Roswell and the dead alien crew. According to the rumor, Spielberg purchased the film from a retired army cameraman who had kept it hidden for nearly fifty years. Spielberg intended to use the remarkable footage in a new motion picture, *Project X,* to be released in June 1997, the fiftieth anniversary of the Roswell incident. When no such film was forthcoming and June 1997 came and went without any blockbuster Spielberg UFO presentation, the rumors died.

Then at last it dawned on certain UFO researchers and conspiracy buffs: For some reason, perhaps due to the machinations of the New World Order or some shadow agency of the U.S. government, Spielberg had backed away from the project. Although blocked from informing the public about the extraordinary film, he had managed to get it to Ray Santilli, who, with the Fox network, revealed it to the world on August 28, 1995.

ALLIANCE DEFENSE FUND

The Alliance Defense Fund views homosexuality as the single greatest threat to religious freedom in the United States.

A coalition of thirty-five Christian Right groups founded the Alliance Defense Fund (ADF) in 1993. The principal architects of the ADF included Dr. D. James Kennedy of Coral Ridge Ministries, Rev. Donald Wildmon of the American Family Association, and Dr. James Dobson of Focus on the Family. Alan Sears, executive director of Attorney General Edwin Meese's Commission on Pornography during the Reagan administration, is president of the ADF, headquartered in Scottsdale, Arizona; Craig Osten, author of *The Homosexual Agenda: Exposing the Principal Threat to Religious Freedom,* is its vice president.

What the Alliance Defense Fund Believes

- Homosexuality creates pedophilia and other sexual crimes.
- The ultimate goal of the gay rights movement is to silence Christians by making prolife demonstrations illegal and censoring all religious broadcasting. When the courts of the land have made homosexuality acceptable, Christians will be forced to accept gays as teachers, preachers, and scoutmasters.

Activities: The ADF has actively challenged the legality of gay marriage, adoption, foster parenting, domestic partner benefits, and service in the military.

AL-QAEDA

Al-Qaeda issued a statement in 1998 that it is their duty as holy warriors to kill all U.S. citizens.

Al-Qaeda (sometimes spelled al-Qaida), Arabic for "the Base," is a terrorist group founded by Osama bin Laden in the late 1980s to unite Arabs who fought against the Soviet invasion in Afghanistan. Bin Laden, son of a billionaire Saudi family, is reported to have inherited approximately $300 million that he uses to finance the terrorist group.

Al-Qaeda may have several hundred to several thousand members in a loosely organized network of cells throughout the world. The terrorist group also serves as a kind of conduit for a worldwide network that includes many Sunni Islamic extremist groups such as Egyptian Islamic Jihad, al-Gama'at al-islamiyya, the Islamic Movement of Uzbekistan, and the Harakat ul-Mujahidin. Al-Qaeda also maintains moneymaking front organizations, solicits donations from like-minded supporters, and illicitly siphons funds from donations to legitimate Muslim charities. Although al-Qaeda was organized by Osama bin Laden, he was not its only leader. Dr. Ayman al-Zawahiri, an Egyptian surgeon from an upper-class family, is the group's theological leader and bin Laden's most likely successor.

Conspiracy theorists fear that the great terrorist acts of our time were openly planned in radical mosques in Hamburg, London, and Paris, offering Muslims the opportunity to become mujahideen (holy warriors) in a jihad (holy war) in which they might achieve holy martyrdom. According to many conspiracy researchers, the shadowy figures of the New World Order and a number of secret societies are behind it all, fanning the flames of planetary conflagration.

In February 1998 al-Qaeda issued a statement entitled "The World Islamic Front for Jihad against the Jews and Crusaders," declaring that it was the duty of all Muslims to kill U.S. citizens—civilian or military—and their allies everywhere. Some of the terrible acts of death and destruction sown by al-Qaeda are the following:

1992: Conducted three bombings that hit U.S. troops in Aden, Yemen.

1993: Al-Qaeda–trained Somalian tribesmen conducted ambushes of U.S. peacekeeping forces in Somalia. Downed two helicopters in Mogadishu and killed fifteen U.S. Army Rangers.

1994: Plotted to blow up the Israeli embassy in Washington. Planned to assassinate Pope John Paul II in Manila. Attempted to arrange the simultaneous bombings of U.S. and Israeli embassies in Manila and other Asian capitals.

1995: Planned to assassinate President Bill Clinton when he visited the Philippines. Bombed a military complex in Riyadh, Saudi Arabia, housing U.S. troops, killing five Americans and wounding forty-two.

1996: Truck-bombed a U.S. military complex near Dhahran, Saudi Arabia, killing nineteen U.S. airmen and wounding 515 people, including 240 Americans.

1998: Bombed the U.S. embassies in Nairobi, Kenya, and Dar es Salaam, Tanzania, killing at least 301 persons and injuring more than five thousand others. Attempted to bomb the U.S. embassy in Kampala, Uganda.

2000: Bombed the USS *Cole* while the ship was in port in Yemen, killing seventeen and injuring thirty-nine others.

Workers search for survivors in the wreckage of the World Trade Center in New York City, September 20, 2011.

2001: Crashed hijacked airliners into the World Trade Center and the Pentagon, killing nearly three thousand and igniting a new war on terrorism.

Al-Qaeda's long-term agenda is to establish a pan-Islamic caliphate (a *kalifah* is a great Islamic kingdom ruled by a caliph, following no laws outside of the Qur'an) throughout the world by working with allied Islamic extremist groups to overthrow regimes it judges "non-Islamic" and expelling Westerners and non-Muslims from Muslim countries.

After 9/11 the Bush administration tried desperately to establish links between Iraq and al-Qaeda in order to add another justification, besides Iraq's supposed weapons of mass destruction, for declaring war against Iraq. In late 2001 Vice President Dick Cheney said it was "pretty well confirmed" that in April 2000 in Prague, Czechoslovakia, the 9/11 mastermind, Mohamed Atta, met with a senior Iraqi intelligence official. In his speech aboard an aircraft carrier on May 1, 2003, President Bush told the cheering troops that the liberation of Iraq would be crucial in the war on terror because they had "removed an ally of al Qaeda and cut off a source of terrorist funding." Cheney also claimed the acquisition of Iraqi intelligence files that connected Iraq to al-Qaeda, the September 11 attacks, and the 1993 World Trade Center bombing in a relationship that went back to the beginning of the 1990s.

Despite such repeated assertions of a link between Saddam Hussein and Iraq and Osama bin Laden and al-Qaeda, subsequent FBI and CIA investigations found no direct relationship between the two, other than a possible agreement, spoken or understood, to keep out of each other's way.

Al-Qaeda's movements, plots, and attacks are greatly facilitated by the Internet. No matter how separated individual terrorists may be from any central authority or command, they need only go online to find out what their leaders are thinking and what they want done next. Muslim faithful need only listen to their radio or television to hear coded al-Qaeda threats, vows, and pronouncements that tell them when to act.

ALTERNATIVE 3

As early as 1962, the superpowers of Earth undertook a secret space program to transport an intellectual elite to bases on the moon, where, with the labor of ordinary humans serving as their slaves, they began to build a new world.

On June 20, 1977, Anglia Television broadcast "Alternative 3," the final program in its *Science Report,* a series of serious science documentaries. The program was simultaneously telecast in the UK, Australia, New Zealand, Canada, Iceland, Norway, Sweden, Finland, Greece, and Yugoslavia.

The script, by David Ambrose and Christopher Miles, declared that the superpowers have been working secretly together in space for decades, and their accomplishments in building bases and conducting interplanetary travel have advanced far beyond what they have officially released to the public. Ultrasecret joint U.S. and Russian conferences are held each month in a submarine beneath the Arctic ice cap.

Shortly after World War II the superpowers determined that Earth would soon be unable to support life and that our climate's recent strange behavior was only a preview of the tremendous cataclysms to come. High-level scientists and politicians viewed three possible solutions, alternatives, for humankind:

Alternative 1: Halt immediately all pollution and blast two large holes in the ozone layer to allow excessive ultraviolet light to reach the earth. While this might eventually restore plant life and reduce pollution, millions of humans would be likely to die of skin cancer.

Alternative 2: Immediately begin constructing underground cities for the elite and allow the billions of humanity on the surface to perish.

Alternative 3: Construct spaceships and transport the elite off the planet to the moon and Mars. The rest of humanity would be left behind to die.

The governments chose Alternative 3 and began devising a plan to preserve a tiny nucleus of human survivors to continue the species.

Since the early 1960s, government agencies around the globe have been kidnapping ordinary people for common labor and turning them into mindless automatons by advanced brainwashing methods. The few reports of NASA astronauts that leaked out concerning strange things sighted on the moon were suppressed by the secret agencies of the superpowers in order to keep the masses ignorant of the overall sinister plan.

Although the British television program and the later book version of the script, published in 1978, were both presented as science fiction with absolutely no basis in fact, the research of many UFO investigators has produced similarly frightening accusations that not only portray secret agencies of the superpowers working together on an overall clandestine master plan, but accuse the same superpowers of having made a deal with intelligences from outer space that have little regard for the average citizen of Earth.

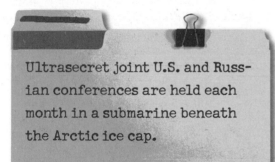

Ultrasecret joint U.S. and Russian conferences are held each month in a submarine beneath the Arctic ice cap.

In the opinion of many conspiracy theorists, the "Alternative 3" broadcast was a device created by whistle-blowers within various government agencies to leak details of a massive cover-up of disappearances of men and women throughout the world. Witnesses who claim top-level security clearances state that their consciences have compelled them to disregard their government oaths and reveal the use of abandoned U.S. military bases in creating "interdimensional tunnels" whereby aliens can enter Earth's atmosphere with greater ease. They report unspeakable experiments with abducted men, women, and children—for example, that large numbers of street kids and runaways have been used in certain experiments in teleportation of the physical body to established moon bases. And these same whistle-blowers point out that the mysterious "holes" in the ozone layer might very well make all three "alternatives" a grim reality.

AMERICAN FAMILY ASSOCIATION

The American Family Association condemns television as being a "trash land" as well as a vast wasteland.

Founded in 1977 by Rev. Donald Wildmon as the National Federation for Decency, the organization was renamed the American Family Association (AFA) in 1988. Wildmon, a former Methodist minister, has become well known as an effective force in removing advertisements on television that he has deemed trashy and objectionable. Appointed to Attorney General Edwin Meese's Commission on Pornography during the Reagan administration by the commission's executive director, Alan Sears, Wildmon in 1985 managed to persuade seventeen thousand convenience stores to remove such magazines as *Playboy* and *Penthouse* from their shelves. In 2005 Tim Wildmon, Donald Wildmon's son, assumed the AFA presidency and the overseeing of a two-hundred-station radio network, a monthly journal distributed to nearly 200,000 subscribers, and about a hundred employees.

What the American Family Association Believes

- A growing gay influence on the media is transforming the United States into a misshapen culture.

- Prominent gay leaders have publicly endorsed approval of pedophilia, incest, sadomasochism, and bestiality.

- Homosexuality must be opposed with the same fervor as murder, stealing, and adultery.

- The true originators of Nazism and Nazi atrocities were homosexuals.

- Procter & Gamble actively promotes Satanism and homosexuality.

Activities: Through its radio stations, flyers, and monthly journal, the AFA has convinced hundreds of thousands to boycott national advertisers of products or concepts it deems offensive.

AMERICAN NAZI PARTY

George Lincoln Rockwell decided that if he couldn't be president of the United States, he could still have people saluting him as founder of the American Nazi Party.

The American Nazi Party was founded in February 1959 in the residence of George Lincoln Rockwell in Arlington, Virginia. Rather than gathering in a crowded meeting hall with hundreds of men wearing swastika armbands and saluting their new leader with a chorus of "Sieg, heils," six people gathered in the Rockwell living room and voted to call their group the World Union Free Enterprise National Socialists. Later, they would change their name to American Nazi Party and, when Rockwell began his candidacy for the presidency of the United States, the George Lincoln Rockwell Party.

Rockwell wanted to be president, but he told his followers that first, in 1966, he would gain the governorship of Virginia. In another six years, by 1972, he would be elected president.

Rockwell's party platform was easily defined:

• Confiscate all property owned by Jews.

• Sterilize all Jews.

• Exterminate all Jews who are guilty of resistance or treason.

• Deport all African Americans to Africa.

• Amend the U.S. Constitution to comply with the governing concepts of the Third Reich.

Rockwell was fined and imprisoned several times. On August 25, 1967, he was shot and killed as he pulled out of a parking space in an Arlington shopping center. The assassin, firing from the rooftop of a beauty salon across the street, was a "captain" in the American Nazi Party, John Patler, twenty-nine. In December 1967 Patler was sentenced to twenty years in prison for Rockwell's murder.

The group was taken over by Matt Koehl, who renamed it the National Socialist White People's Party. In 1970 Frank Collin splintered the party and founded the National Socialist Party of America, which gained headlines around the world for its attempt to march through the largely Jewish community of Skokie, Illinois. In 1979 Collin's ambition to lead a new Nazi America was thwarted when he was arrested, convicted, and sent to prison on child molestation charges.

A reborn American Nazi Party, formerly known as the European American Education Association, is based in Eastpointe, Michigan, and is headed by Rocky Suhayda. In all its rallies and public appearances, the American Nazi Party recites the fourteen words of its motto: "We must secure the existence of our people and a future for White children."

AMERICAN PROTECTIVE ASSOCIATION

Responding to a perceived Roman Catholic conspiracy to take control of the United States, the APA formed a secret society to keep all Catholics out of public office.

The American Protective Association (APA) was a secret proscriptive society in the United States organized to prevent Roman Catholics from gaining political offices. The organization became an unsettling element on the political scene in most of the northern states during the 1890s but had little influence in the South, aside from a few members in Georgia and Texas.

Henry F. Bowers, a sixty-year-old lawyer originally from Maryland, founded the APA in Clinton, Iowa, on March 13, 1887. Bowers, a Mason, drew liberally from the rituals of that fraternal society and developed elaborate regalia, initiation rites, and a secret oath that bound members to endeavor at all times "to place the political position of this government in the hands of Protestants, to the entire exclusion of the Roman Catholic Church, of the members thereof, and the mandate of the Pope." The APA drew upon Protestant paranoia regarding Catholics for membership, and large numbers of Masons, who already excluded Catholics from their fraternal order, joined the movement to keep Catholics from gaining public office.

In 1893 the APA began the active distribution of anti-Catholic literature and arranged public lectures by men posing as ex-priests, who divulged the horrible secrets of the Catholic Church. Some of these imposters claimed to have seen a papal bull that called for the massacre of Protestants on or about the Feast of Saint Ignatius in 1893. By 1894 the APA had seventy weekly tabloids that printed defamatory stories about the Catholic Church. Chief among the reports was the claim that Terence V. Powderly, leader of the Knights of Columbus, was leading that Catholic organization in a massive conspiracy against all American institutions.

Bowers was reelected the national president of the APA in 1898, but the movement had failed to effect any new changes in the laws or policies of government, and it eventually dissipated, leaving only a legacy of distrust between Catholics and those Protestants susceptible to rumors of Catholic conspiracies.

AMERICAN VISION

Gary DeMar's vision of America is a country without homosexuality.

American Vision was created in 1978 by Gary DeMar, a prominent Christian reconstructionist, as an educational resource to assist in disseminating information designed to restore the biblical foundation of the United States. In DeMar's interpretation of history, the United States was established as a Christian nation and democracy should be replaced by a theocratic government completely dominated by Christians who will strictly enforce Old Testament prohibitions. DeMar is closely allied with R. J. Rushdoony, the founder of reconstructionism, Dr. D. James Kennedy of Coral Ridge Ministries, and Gary North, with whom DeMar authored *Christian Reconstructionism: What It Is, What It Isn't.*

What American Vision Believes

- Every social failure in American culture must be blamed on homosexuals.

- In an established theocratic America, homosexuality, gay marriage, and abortion would be strictly forbidden by law.

- Those found guilty of homosexuality would receive the death penalty. Executions of sodomites would serve society well and help drive underground gays back into the closet.

- A long-term goal of the theocracy would be the execution of convicted abortionists and those who seek their services.

Activities: American Vision works steadily to lobby state and local governments to pass antigay ordinances.

ANARCHISTS

Whether they are feared, admired, or misunderstood, there are always those individuals who oppose forms of government that they consider tyrannical, oppressive, and unjust.

Depending upon the historical period in which they conducted their protests, certain individuals have been called anarchists, libertarians, socialists, Marxists, syndicalists, and revolutionaries. Regardless of labeling, these men and women have opposed through pacifism, militancy, or civil disobedience actions of the government that they considered to be tyrannical, oppressive, and socially, politically, or economically unjust. Here some of the individuals who have been called "anarchists" and a summary of their beliefs:

William Godwin (1756–1836): Godwin, an English political philosopher and Calvinist minister, was the first writer to espouse anarchist ideals. Godwin's utopia was equalitarian and completely anarchistic. In his opinion, a sound education and proper social conditioning were the chief elements in forming good character. Godwin's *Enquiry Concerning Political Justice* argues that humans are capable of genuine benevolence. The French Revolution inspired his major work, *Political Justice,* completed in 1793. His novel *Caleb Williams* has a theme of social reform.

Max Stirner (1806–1856): A German social philosopher, Stirner is the spiritual forefather of individualistic anarchism. Stirner rejected all political and moral ties of the individual, emphasizing that the individual entity comprises the overriding reality. In his opinion, egotism determines everything. Stirner's concept of individualistic egotism was very democratic, and in *The Ego and Its Own* he encouraged everyone to become a liberated individualist.

Henry David Thoreau (1817–1862): Thoreau wrote the influential "Civil Disobedience" as a lecture for the Concord, Massachusetts, lyceum in January 1848. It has served as an inspiration for Tolstoy and Gandhi and for contemporary activists in the civil rights, antiwar, and radical environmentalist movement.

Mother Jones (1830–1930): After losing her husband and children to an epidemic, Mother Jones found an outlet for her love and compassion in the labor movement. Working with the steelworkers and the miners of West

American transcendentalist philosopher Henry David Thoreau was the author of *Civil Disobedience,* a book that inspired such people as Mahatma Gandhi.

Virginia and Colorado, she became a picturesque and forceful figure—a born crusader and a powerful speaker. Her work on behalf of child textile-mill workers was instrumental in reforming the child labor laws.

Lucy Parsons (1853–1942): Lucy Parsons was a Texas slave who claimed to be the daughter of a Mexican woman and a Creek Indian. After she married Albert Parsons, a Confederate Civil War veteran, in 1873, the couple moved to Chicago and became involved in the labor movement. Lucy also became a tireless champion for the rights of African Americans, maintaining that they were primarily victimized because they were poor. Racism, she argued, would disappear with the destruction of capitalism.

In 1886 Albert was implicated in the Haymarket Square bombing of police officers and sentenced to death by hanging. In 1892 Lucy published a short-lived journal called *Freedom.* She helped found the International Working

People's Association (IWPA), and in 1905 she participated in the founding of the Industrial Workers of the World. In 1939, fearing that anarchism could not effectively combat the advance of capitalism and fascism throughout the world, she joined the Communist Party.

Emma Goldman (1869–1940): As a young girl in Kovno, Russia, Emma Goldman witnessed the savage beating of a peasant by his master, a cruel memory that never left her and inspired her to become a social activist. In 1886 she came to the United States. She settled in Rochester, New York, experienced an unhappy marriage that ended in divorce, and relocated to New York City, where she became involved with anarchist circles. Emma, a gifted orator, also championed women's rights and, along with the pioneering Margaret Sanger, fought for freer access to birth-control methods. Her efforts on behalf of the anarchist movement caused her to be deported to Russia. Eventually she made her way back to America after spending a number of years in England, Canada, and Spain. Always agitating for her ideals, Emma was often imprisoned. Among her published works are *Anarchism and Other Essays* and *The Social Significance of the Modern Drama.*

Big Bill Haywood (1869–1928): William Dudley Haywood, known as "Big Bill," led the Western Federation of Miners from 1900 to 1905 and in 1905 helped found the Industrial Workers of the World (IWW), which sought to organize all laborers into one big union. In 1906 Haywood and other alleged conspirators were brought to trial for the murder of a former governor of Idaho. The famous trial lawyer Clarence Darrow was able to win their acquittal. In 1918 Big Bill and 165 other IWW leaders were convicted of sedition for opposing the U.S. involvement in World War I. In 1921 he jumped bail and sought refuge in the USSR, where he lived until his death.

Joe Hill (1879–1915): Hill, born Joel Hagglund in Sweden, became an American labor organizer for the radical Industrial Workers of

the World and a famous writer of union songs, such as "Casey Jones—The Union Scab," a parody of the popular ballad about the legendary train engineer. Charged, upon cloudy evidence, with murder in Salt Lake City, Hill was convicted and sentenced to death. Attempts by President Woodrow Wilson, the government of Sweden, and many prominent Americans could not win him a new trial. On the eve of his execution Hill telegraphed Big Bill Haywood the words that would later be immortalized in labor lore: "Don't mourn, organize." The next morning Joe Hill became a martyr for American labor upon his execution by a Utah firing squad.

Elizabeth Gurley Flynn (1890–1964): Born in New Hampshire to an Irish family passionate about union, socialist, and anticolonial struggles, Elizabeth would become one of the greatest of twentieth-century labor speakers and organizers. The inspiration for Joe Hill's union song "The Rebel Girl," Flynn stirred countless thousands of workers with her feisty spirit. In 1920 she helped to found the American Civil Liberties Union. During the anti-Communist witch hunts of the 1950s, Flynn served twenty-eight months in prison because of her membership in the Communist Party. Her published works include *Sabotage* and *My Life as a Political Prisoner.*

Nicola Sacco (1891–1927) and Bartolomeo Vanzetti (1888–1927): Sacco and Vanzetti are joined forever in the public mind as the principals in one of the most controversial and best-known cases in American jurisprudence. They were arrested on charges of murdering a shoe factory paymaster and guard at South Braintree, Massachusetts. Tried and convicted on July 14, 1921, in a time of antiradical fervor, they were sentenced to death. During the years of their imprisonment, worldwide protests were raised by those who doubted their guilt, but they were electrocuted August 23, 1927. Periodically pressure is brought to have the state of Massachusetts officially clear Sacco and Vanzetti of the charges against them, but this has not happened.

Noam Chomsky (1928–): "If we don't believe in freedom of expression for people we despise," Noam Chomsky has said, "we don't believe in it at all." Chomsky, a renowned linguistic expert who posits that the acquisition of language is part of the innate structure of the human brain, became well known to the nonacademic public as an anarchist and libertarian socialist who vehemently opposed the Vietnam War. Ever vigilant against any abuses of power, Chomsky remains a perceptive critic of U.S. foreign policy.

ANTHROPOSOPHY

Anthroposophy is a philosophy that subverts Christianity with occult beliefs and is a contributive factor to the rise of New Age heresies.

When he was in his late thirties, Rudolf Steiner (1861–1925), the founder of Anthroposophy (anthropos = man; sophy = wisdom), received a revelation of the incarnation of the divine being known as the Christ. Steiner said that sometime in the twentieth century humankind would begin to enter the "fullness of time" in which the Christ principle, cosmic consciousness, might once again become manifest.

Steiner defined "Christ consciousness" as a transformative energy that greatly transcends orthodox Christianity. In Steiner's view, the master Jesus became "christed" and thereby was able to present humankind with a dramatic example of what it means to achieve a complete activation of the spiritual seed within all human souls. The human intellect, Steiner insisted, can be trained to rise above material concerns and to perceive a greater spiritual reality. Human consciousness has the ability to activate the seed that the great Spirit Beings have implanted within their human offspring. When human consciousness rises to the spiritual level where it can experience the eternal element that is limited by

neither birth nor death, then it can comprehend its own eternality and its ability to be born again in subsequent existences.

Steiner was born at Krajevic, Austria-Hungary (now Yugoslavia), on February 27, 1861. Although he experienced encounters with the mystical and the unknown as a young child and was introduced to the occult by an adept he would refer to only as the "Master," Steiner's early academic accomplishments were in the scientific fields. His father wanted him to become a railway engineer, a goal that led Rudolf into a study of mathematics, which seemed only to whet his appetite for the material sciences. He went on to medicine, chemistry, and physics—as well as agriculture, architecture, art, drama, literature, and philosophy. Fascinated by the works of the famed German writer, philosopher, and scientist Johann Wolfgang von Goethe, Steiner began the extensive task of editing Goethe's scientific papers, and from 1889 to 1896 he worked on this project. It was also during this period that Steiner wrote his own highly acclaimed *Philosophy of Freedom.*

Steiner claimed to be endowed with the ability to read the "Akashic Records" and, from them, envision the true history of human evolution. He set forth the hypothesis that the people of our prehistory, the Atlanteans, were largely guided and directed by a higher order of beings who interacted and communicated with certain humans—the smartest, the strongest, the most intellectually flexible. Eventually these select humans produced what might be called demigods, semidivine human beings who, in turn, could relay instructions from higher intelligences. In effect, Steiner may have presented another version of the children of human mothers and the "sons of God" referred to in the book of Genesis, the hybrids that the ancient Hebrews named *Nephilim,* which does, in fact, mean demigods, men of "great renown."

Steiner went on to speculate that within the larger evolving human race were the descen-

Cover of the premier issue of *The Theosophist,* the journal by Helena Blavatsky.

dants of those divine-human hybrid beings, men and women who are animated by higher ideals, who regard themselves as children of a divine, universal power. He believed that what he termed the emerging "Sixth Post-Atlantean Race" would include children of the divine universal power who, having the "seed" within them, would be able to initiate those members of humankind who have sufficiently developed their faculty of thought to allow them to unite with the divine. People so initiated will be able to receive revelations and perform what others will consider miracles, and will go on to become the mediators between humankind and the higher intelligences.

At the turn of the century Steiner found his lectures well received by those in the audience who were members of the Theosophical Society, so he began to study their philosophy. In 1902 he became the general secretary of the

German Section of the society, but he eventually grew uncomfortable with what he perceived as a lack of enthusiasm about the place of Jesus and "Christ consciousness" in the society's overall scheme of spiritual evolution. Although he accepted many of their teachings, he came to believe that Helena P. Blavatsky and other high-ranking Theosophists were distorting many of the Eastern doctrines that they claimed to espouse.

In 1913 Steiner made a formal break with the Theosophical Society and set about forming his own group, Anthroposophy. In 1914 he married Marie von Sievers, an actress who had been secretary of the German Section of the Theosophical Society. Together they established a school for esoteric research near Basel, Switzerland, and developed new approaches to the teaching of speech and drama, which led to "eurythmy," an art of movement. Later Steiner originated the Waldorf School Movement, an innovative educational system that still maintains eighty schools in Europe and the United States. Rudolf Steiner died on March 30, 1925, at Dornach, Switzerland.

ANTICHRIST

For many Christians, the greatest conspiracy of all will be the one that the antichrist conducts against the followers of the returning Christ.

Although commonly associated with the apocalyptic New Testament book of Revelation, the word *antichrist* is nowhere to be found within that text. In 1 John 2:18 the epistle writer declares that the "enemy of Christ" has manifested and that many false teachers have infiltrated the Christian ranks. In verse 22, John names as the antichrist anyone who would deny Jesus as the Christ and the Father and the Son, and in 2 John 7 he declares that there are many deceivers already at work among the faithful.

In Matthew 24:3–44 Jesus speaks to his disciples at great length concerning false messiahs and prophets who will deceive many people with rumors about the end of the world. He makes reference to the prophet Daniel and his warnings concerning the endtimes, and he admonishes the disciples not to follow false teachers who will produce great miracles and signs to trick God's chosen ones. No one knows when the Son of Man shall appear again coming on the clouds of heaven, Jesus tells them, not even the angels.

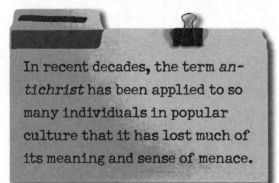

In recent decades, the term *antichrist* has been applied to so many individuals in popular culture that it has lost much of its meaning and sense of menace.

The earliest form of the antichrist is probably the warrior king Gog, who appears in the book of Ezekiel and reappears in Revelation along with his kingdom of Magog, representing those earthly minions of Satan who will attack the people of God in a final great battle of good versus evil. Jewish writings about the "end of days" state that the armies of Gog and Magog will eventually be defeated and the world will finally be at peace.

Throughout the Bible the antichrist bears many titles: Son of Perdition, Man of Sin, Man of Lawlessness, Prince of Destruction, and Beast. The prophet Daniel describes the man in great detail: He shall be an evil king who will "exalt himself and magnify himself above every god and shall speak outrageous things against the God of gods. But in his estate he shall (secretly) honor a god of forces and a god whom his fathers never knew. Thus shall he do in his fortress with a strange god, whom he shall acknowledge and increase with glory;

and he shall rule over many and shall divide the land for gain" (Dan. 11:36–39).

In the prophecies of both Daniel and John the Revelator, the evil king, the antichrist, is associated with ten rulers who give their power and allegiance to him in order to form a short-lived empire of bloodshed and destruction: "And the ten horns of this kingdom are ten kings that shall arise: and another shall rise after them, and he shall be diverse and speak great words against the most high God and shall wear down the saints of the Highest One and think to make changes in times and laws: and they shall be given into his hand for three and one half years" (Dan. 7:24).

Although Jesus makes it very clear that no one knows the hour or day of his Second Coming, Christian scholars have steadfastly viewed the rise of the antichrist to earthly power as a kind of catalyst that will set in motion Armageddon, the final battle between good and evil, the ultimate clash between the armies of Jesus Christ and Satan. Throughout the centuries, Christians have attempted to determine the antichrist from among the powerful and ruthless leaders of their day, such men as Nero, Napoleon, Hitler, Mussolini, and Stalin. Nominations for the role have often been influenced by politics or religious prejudices: ever since the Protestant Reformation, the pope has been a favorite of evangelicals for the ignominious title.

The association of the number 666 with the antichrist is derived from Revelation 13:18, which states that the number of the Beast is 666 and that this number stands for a person. In John the Revelator's world of the first century, the Beast who ruled the earth would have been the emperor, the caesar, of the Roman Empire, Nero. Using the Hebrew alphabet, the numerical value of "Caesar Nero," the merciless persecutor of the early Christians, works out to 666.

On May 1, 2005, scholars revealed that a newly discovered fragment of the oldest surviving copy of the New Testament, dating from the third century, indicates that later copyists got it wrong: the number of the Beast is 616. David Parker, professor of New Testament textual criticism and paleography at the University of Birmingham, England, says that the numerical value of 616 refers to another nemesis of the early Christians, the emperor Caligula.

However, those who maintain that the number 666 is still a potent predictor of the antichrist will continue to name their contemporary candidates for the role. The numerical value of Franklin Delano Roosevelt's name reportedly added up to 666, and since he held the office of president of the United States for twelve years—and during the Great Depression and World War II—many of his conservative Christian critics began thinking of him as the antichrist. And even Ronald Wilson Reagan, who in the estimation of many political analysts was one of our nation's most popular presidents, had certain dissenters calling attention to the fact that he had six letters in each of his three names—666.

In recent decades, the term *antichrist* has been applied to so many individuals in popular culture that it has lost much of its meaning and sense of menace. However, those fundamentalist Christians who believe strongly in the coming time of the Tribulation, the Apocalypse, the Rapture, and the great final battle of good versus evil at Armageddon firmly believe that the title of antichrist maintains its fear factor and that we must pay serious heed to those signs and warnings of the Beast as prophesied in the book of Revelation.

APOCALYPTIC MILLENNIALISM

The endtimes are coming. Beware of false messiahs, ranting prophets, and the antichrist—and prepare to be taken aloft by the Rapture.

To some Christians, the profound meaning of the New Testament is that Jesus Christ will return in the Last Days and prompt the resurrection of the dead and the Final Judgment. The heart of the gospels is eschatological, end-oriented. The essential theme of Jesus's teaching is that the last stage of history, the endtime, was being entered into with his appearance on Earth. In Matthew 24:3–44, Jesus speaks to his disciples at great length concerning false messiahs and prophets who will deceive many people with their rumors about the end of the world. He makes reference to the prophet Daniel and his warnings concerning the endtimes and the antichrist, and he admonishes the disciples not to chase after false teachers who will produce great miracles and signs to trick God's chosen ones.

No one knows when the Son of Man shall appear again coming on the clouds of heaven, Jesus tells them, not even the angels. However, the prophets of apocalypticism believe that they have received visions that allow them to see ahead to the endtime and predict when Christ will return.

Among the most famous of the endtimes prophets was William Miller, who founded the Millerite movement about 1831. Miller believed that he had discovered the exact date of Christ's return by calculating two thousand years from 457 B.C.E., when Ezra was allowed to return to Jerusalem to reestablish the Temple. Based on his studies, Miller concluded that the Second Coming would transpire in 1843, although he later revised this prediction to include the period between March 21, 1843, and March 21, 1844. When the latter date embarrassingly passed without notable event, he refined his calculations and finally settled on October 22, 1844, as the day that Jesus would return in all his glory. The Millerites, who numbered at least fifty thousand, were dealt the "Great Disappointment" when Christ failed to arrive on that date either. Then one of Miller's followers, Hiram Edson, had a vision revealing that the divinely inspired date had not been incorrect, merely misinterpreted. What Miller had seen, according to Edson, was the date when Jesus would begin to cleanse the heavenly sanctuary in preparation for the gathering of his earthly followers.

Another follower, Ellen G. White, author of *The Desire of Ages* and *The Great Controversy,* had visions which told the Adventists, as some of the Millerites were now calling themselves, that they were God's special endtimes remnant. She also concluded that they should begin to keep the original Sabbath, Saturday, as their day of worship. The Millerite apocalyptic revelations had evolved into the Seventh-day Adventists. Later, the Branch Davidian Seventh-day Adventists, seeking to reform the church, broke away and formed their own interpretation of Millerite doctrine.

In the Jewish tradition, apocalyptic thought presupposes a universal history in which the Divine Author of that history will reveal and manifest his secrets in a dramatic endtime that with finality will establish the God of Israel as the one true God. The "end of days" (*acharit ha-yamin*) is bound up with the coming of the Messiah, but before his appearance governments will become increasingly corrupt, religious schools will become heretical, the wisdom of the scribes and teachers will become blasphemous, young people will shame their elders, and members of families will turn upon one another. Then, just prior to the arrival of the Messiah, the righteous of Israel will defeat the armies of evil that have gathered under the banner of Gog and Magog, and the exiles will return to the Holy Land. The world will be at peace and all people will recognize the one true God. With the advent of the Messiah there will come the great Day of Judgment in which the dead shall rise from their graves to begin a new life. During the period known as the World to Come (*Olam Haba*), the righteous will join the Messiah in partaking of a great banquet in which all foods, even those previously judged impure, will be declared kosher. All the many nations

of the world will communicate in one language; the Angel of Death will be slain by God; trees and crops will produce fresh harvests each month; the warmth of the sun will heal the sick; and the righteous will be nourished forever by the radiance of God.

According to ancient Jewish teachings, only the ashes of a flawless red heifer could purify worshippers who went into the Temple in Jerusalem. The First Temple was destroyed by Nebuchadnezzar in 586 B.C.E.; the Romans demolished the Second Temple in 70 C.E. Without a flawless red heifer to sacrifice to purify the Temple Mount, the Third Temple could not be built and the Messiah could not come. In modern times, rabbinical law has forbidden Jews from setting foot on the Temple Mount and defiling the site where the Holy of Holies once resided.

Fundamentalist Christians believe that after Jesus Christ has returned and defeated the forces of evil at the great battle of Armageddon, he will begin his millennial reign from the Third Temple. Muslims revere the Temple Mount as the place where Muhammad ascended into heaven; and in 685, followers of the Prophet began constructing the thirty-five-acre site known as the Noble Sanctuary, which today includes the Dome of the Rock and the al-Aqsa Mosque. Muslims believe that Jesus will return as a Muslim prophet and conduct the day of final judgment in the valley just below the Noble Sanctuary.

A large number of Christians who believe in the endtimes also envision an event they call the "Rapture," in which born-again Christians will be taken up into the air to meet Christ. Many believe that the Rapture will happen unexpectedly. Those Christians of special merit will be lifted suddenly from their homes, their automobiles, even from their passenger seats on airliners. Most of humankind will be left behind, including those Christians whose faith requires strengthening. To fundamentalist Christians, the Rapture will be a literal, physical occurrence, rather than a spiritual transformation. Those who are taken up by Christ may leave their clothing on the streets and their cars crashing into trees, but they will be lifted body and soul into the sky.

In two of his epistles Saint Paul speaks of the return of Christ and what many Christians believe to be the Rapture. In 1 Thessalonians 4:16–18: "For the Lord himself shall descend from heaven with a shout, with the voice of the archangel, and with the trump of God: and the dead in Christ shall rise first: Then we which are alive [and] remain shall be caught up together with them in the clouds, to meet the Lord in the air: and so shall we ever be with the Lord." And in 1 Corinthians 15:51–53, the epistle writer tells of the mystery when "in the twinkling of an eye" those who believe in Christ shall be changed: "Behold, I shew you a mystery; We shall not all sleep, but we shall all be changed, In a moment, in the twinkling of an eye, at the last trump: for the trumpet shall sound, and the dead shall be raised incorruptible, and we shall be changed. For this corruptible must put on incorruption, and this mortal must put on immortality."

Although Christians who believe in the Rapture are certain that it will occur in association with the time of Tribulation (the seven-year period of disasters, famine, and illness during which the antichrist will be in power), opinions differ as to whether it will come about just before the Tribulation begins, midway through the seven-year reign of the antichrist, or at the very end of the Tribulation. There is, however, general agreement that when this awful time of lawlessness and corruption has passed, Christ will return to Earth with his army of angels and destroy the forces of darkness at Armageddon in the final battle of good versus evil. Babylon, the False Prophet, and the Beast (the antichrist) will be dispatched to their doom, and Satan, the Dragon, will be bound in a pit for a thousand years. With Satan imprisoned and chained, the Millenni-

A bas-relief of the Horsemen of the Apocalypse on a tomb at the Limoges cathedral, Paris, France. People have been predicting the end times for centuries—are we getting close to a time when the predictions will come true?

um, the thousand years of peace and harmony, will begin.

Not all Christians accept the scenario of the Rapture, but many Christians and non-Christians alike find the premise intriguing and read the books in the *Left Behind* series as exciting science fiction. Authored by fundamentalist minister Tim LaHaye and professional writer Jerry Jenkins, the twelve books in the series, based on the events of the Rapture, have sold an astonishing 65 million copies. In addition, a complementary *Left Behind* series of thirty-four titles for children has sold 10 million copies. Related computer screens, calendars, board games, and collectibles have also sold in the millions.

From 1958 until his retirement in 2011, Christian broadcaster Harold Egbert Camping (1921–) was president of Family Radio, a California-based radio group that broadcasts to 150 markets in the United States. Camping sometimes applied numerology to his interpretation of Bible passages that he believed predicted the endtimes. In 1988, Camping prophesied that the end of the world would occur on May 21 of that year. Undaunted by the sunrise on May 22, Camping went back to the Bible and his numerological computations, waiting until 1994 to make another doomsday prophecy that the world would end on September 6 of that year.

To fundamentalist Christians, the Rapture will be a literal, physical occurrence, rather than a spiritual transformation.

Somewhat chastened by another miscalculation, Camping was content to remain a fiery Christian broadcaster until his Bible interpretations moved him to receive another prediction for 2011. This time, he worked in some elements of the Rapture that were popular with certain evangelicals. On May 21, 2011, he predicted, Christ would return to Earth, elevating the righteous to Heaven. For all others, there would follow five months of terrible plagues on Earth, killing millions of people each day.

His predictions for 1988 and 1994 had come and gone without gathering too much notice, but Family Radio was more media savvy by 2011, and they launched a massive publicity campaign that brought international attention to Camping's prophetic utterances. Major media outlets carried stories that announced the approaching Judgment Day to believers and skeptics alike.

When May 21 left thousands of true believers disillusioned and even more unbelievers amused, Camping defended his power of prophecy by proclaiming his revelation that a great spiritual judgment did occur on that date and that the great physical Rapture would happen on October 21. But the responsibility of

serving as an Apocalyptic spokesperson proved too much for Camping and he suffered a stroke in June. On October 16, 2011, he retired from his presidency of Family Radio. When October 21 once again came and went without people rising to Heaven and the physical universe being destroyed, Camping conceded in a private interview that he guessed no one could know the actual time that the world would come to an end.

AREA 51 AND REVERSE ENGINEERING

The debris from the UFO crash site at Roswell was taken to a secret base and used in reverse engineering and the building of highly advanced technological aircraft.

In 1989 a physicist named Bob Lazar claimed that he worked at a secret base outside of Las Vegas, Nevada, where he had witnessed the reverse engineering of alien spacecraft and the testing of extremely advanced aircraft. The government officially denied the existence of the secret base, known as Area 51, but UFO investigators had long suspected that the installation, near Groom Dry Lake, was the site where a UFO that allegedly crashed near Roswell, New Mexico, in July 1947 was reverse-engineered to create such aircraft as the stealth bomber. For many years UFO buffs hid in the rugged terrain near the base and watched the night sky for the mysterious lights that they knew were engineered from an alien spacecraft.

The Groom Lake base, officially designated as the "Nellis Air Force Bombing and Gunnery Range" and located on the federally protected territory in Nye, Lincoln, and Clark Counties, covers an area equal to Rhode Island and Connecticut. It is in grid number 51 of the Nevada Test Site, thus, Area 51.

This inn in Rachel, Nevada, is a popular place for Area 51 investigators to stay the night.

The base has not really been secret since the March 1993 issue of *Popular Science* brought the reconnaissance aircraft Aurora out of the black and revealed that the Mach-6 spy plane was developed at the closely guarded air force facility at Groom Lake. Built in 1954 as a place to test the secret U-2 spy plane that flew reconnaissance missions over the Soviet Union, the base was later redesigned to accommodate the A-12 and SR-71 manned spy aircraft and the D-21 spy drone.

In his controversial book *The Day after Roswell,* Col. Philip J. Corso (U.S. Army, retired) claims that he was given "personal stewardship" of various extraterrestrial artifacts recovered from the crashed Roswell spacecraft of 1947. Corso states that he distributed the objects of alien technology to select government contractors and that despite official denials, the U.S. government has employed large numbers of scientists in secretly and ambitiously achieving reverse engineering from advanced alien technology. Among the results are fiber optics, light amplification devices, Kevlar (lightweight, heavily resistant material used in, among other things, body armor), and a large number of advances in laser weaponry.

Corso was on Gen. Douglas MacArthur's intelligence staff following the Korean War, and he was later assigned to President Dwight Eisenhower's Security Council, then to the Army Research and Development Department's Foreign Technology Desk at the Pentagon. According to Corso, when he moved into the Foreign Technology Division, he was given a file cabinet of artifacts from the Roswell crash and instructed to begin working on a plan of action and recommendations for their use. His superiors were enthusiastic about the artifacts' possible utility in building spaceships that would be impervious to radiation, cosmic activity, or gunfire.

One of Corso's first file-cabinet discoveries was a paper-thin piece of metal about the size of a postcard. Somehow the metal's atoms were aligned in such a way that government scientists all failed to back-engineer it. Next, according to Corso, the scientists moved on to an integrated circuit, the size of a microchip, that gave rise to the transistor.

In a government program called "Applied Engineering," Corso and his staff would find people in industry who were working in a particular area of scientific research and would then supplement these research-and-development efforts by introducing some of the alien technology. In some instances, the government agency would even fund the work.

Although Corso's claims remain controversial, they continue to keep alive the accusations that the government has hidden the truth about the alleged alien crash at Roswell from the public.

ARK OF THE COVENANT

The Ark of the Covenant that was given by God to the ancient Israelites contained great supernatural power that could annihilate entire armies and whole cities. Lost for centuries, the Ark, if found, could be used by its discoverer to conquer the earth.

As described in the Old Testament, the Ark of the Covenant served as the physical sign of God's presence to the Israelites. The design of the ark was expressed by God and was then made into a material object by skilled craftsmen. They built a chest about three feet nine inches in length and two feet three inches in height, using acacia wood overlaid with the purest gold. The outside of the ark had a gold rim and four golden rings, one on each corner. Two poles made of acacia and covered with gold ran through the gold rings on either side; the poles were used to lift the ark and were never removed from the rings. The ark had a cover of gold on which two cherubim faced each other, each with wings spread.

The ark is believed to contain numerous sacred relics, including the tablets of stone bearing the Ten Commandments that Moses brought back from Mount Sinai; Aaron's rod, a kind of rounded stick that miraculously grew leaves as a sign of God's trust in Aaron, brother of Moses; and/or a specimen of manna, the mysterious food that had provided nourishment to the Israelites as they wandered in the desert. Additionally, the ark possessed a supernatural power that awed and overwhelmed those who viewed it, and it served also as a means through which God communicated with the Israelites. The book of Genesis states that the commands of God would issue from a cloud between the ark's two cherubim. Some researchers have suggested that the "god" of the ark was really a benevolent extraterrestrial, who imparted both a communications device and a weapon before leaving in a fiery blast in a spaceship.

The ark provided safe passage to the Israelites in their journey to the Promised Land. Its power was manifested several times when Israelite warriors brought it to sites of battle and used its influence to destroy and scatter the enemies of God and Israel. At the famous battle of Jericho the ark was carried by a procession around the walls of the city for seven days, after which the walls came crashing down and the Israelites won the battle.

After losing a series of battles with the Philistines, the Israelites brought the ark to a battle site, hoping to strike fear into the enemy. However, the Philistines won the battle and captured the ark. The Philistines viewed their seizing of the ark as a victory over the Israelites and their God—but several disasters fell upon them, including the rapid spread of a plague and an invasion of mice wherever the ark was placed. The Philistines placed the ark on a cart pulled by two cattle and sent it away from them.

When David became king of Israel and established Jerusalem as the holy center of the nation, he ordered the ark to be moved there. The ark was then housed at a nearby site outside the city, where it was the object of veneration for several months before the journey to Jerusalem was completed. David took the ark from Jerusalem only once—to inspire his army in its battle against the forces of his son, Absalom.

The ark was later placed in the grand new Temple of Solomon in Jerusalem and only occasionally removed from the temple for battle. When Jerusalem was invaded and taken by the Babylonians led by King Nebuchadnezzar II, the whereabouts of the ark became a mystery and remain so to this day. Perhaps it was destroyed along with the city or, as suggested in Kings 4:25, taken to Babylon as one of the spoils of victory. Some biblical scholars theorize that those Israelites still faithful to God were forewarned about the fall of Jerusalem and moved the ark to safety. Jeremiah is said to have hid it in a cave on Mount Sinai, the mountain in Egypt where Moses first spoke with God. The Talmud, the ancient, authoritative history of the Hebrews, indicates that the ark was kept in a secret area of the Temple of

Solomon and survived the destruction and pillaging of Jerusalem. The temple was rebuilt on its original foundation after the Babylon captivity of the defeated Jews.

According to one account, the illegitimate son of Solomon and Sheba stole the ark about 1000 B.C.E. and hid it in Aksum, Ethiopia, where it was guarded by a monk. Other stories have the ark being transported during a Hebrew migration to Abyssinia (Ethiopia) that preceded the Babylonian captivity. There, according to this version of the story, the ark remained on an island in Lake Tana. With the spread of Christianity throughout the Roman world by 300 C.E., Abyssinia became largely Christian. Later, during the sixteenth century, fierce battles with invading Muslim armies caused much destruction in Abyssinia, including the razing of monasteries on Tana Kirkos, the island where the ark was believed to have been kept. A cathedral was built after the Muslim armies retreated, and there, according to popular legend, the ark remains safe.

Interest in the Ark of the Covenant has recurred through the centuries. In medieval times the Knights Templar supposedly came into possession of the ark. Some have theorized that Bernard of Clairvaux, founder of the Cistercian monastic order and mentor of the secret order of Knights Templar, may have been involved in building the magnificent Gothic cathedral that stands on the hill in the French town of Chartres. The Knights Templar, according to some theories, were sent on a crusade to the Holy Land by Bernard and discovered the remains of the Ark of the Covenant in the ruins of King Solomon's temple. The knights returned to France with the priceless treasure in 1128, and Cistercian scholars managed to decipher some of the ark's secrets regarding the principles of sacred geometry and the law of holy numbers, weights, and measures. Somehow, a Knight Templar or an enlightened scholar was able to employ architectural principles greatly in advance of the time. Those who visit the place

An artist's depiction of King David taking the Ark of the Covenant to Jerusalem.

today perpetuate the centuries-old claims that Chartres Cathedral has the power to transform individuals and to elevate them to a higher spiritual state.

The Spear of Destiny, also known as the Holy Lance, is in Christian tradition the spear that the Roman soldier Longinus thrust into the side of Jesus as he hung on the cross. The lance's power, though perhaps not the equal of the ark's, has been sought with almost equal fervor. Christian knights discovered the Holy Lance at Antioch during the First Crusade in 1098. The very sight of the sacred artifact so inspired the beleaguered Christian soldiers that they rallied and routed the Saracens from the city. From that time forth, according to legend, whoever claims the spear and solves its secret holds the destiny of the world in his hands, for good or evil.

There is an element of truth in Steven Spielberg's *Raiders of the Lost Ark,* in which a Nazi expedition under the directive of the führer seeks such holy relics as the ark, the lance, and the Holy Grail to assure their victory in World War II. According to Trevor Ravenscroft in *The Spear of Destiny,* a nineteen-year-old Adolf Hitler was first led to the lance in 1908—and from the moment of his first encounter it became "the central pivot" in his life and the "very source of his ambitions to conquer the world." Hitler found that as many as forty-five emperors, including Constantine, had owned the lance before the great Charlemagne had possessed it. Frederick the Great of Germany, who founded the Teutonic Knights on which Hitler allegedly based his SS, had also owned the Spear of Destiny at one time. Ravenscroft claims that Hitler would often visit the Weltliches Schatzkammer Museum (the Hapsburg Treasure House Museum) in Vienna, stare at the Holy Lance, and enter into a trance state in which he would view his future glory as the führer, the master of the Third Reich.

Thirty years later, on March 14, 1938, Hitler arrived in Vienna to oversee the annexation of Austria by the Third Reich. The führer also observed the transfer of the Hapsburg Crown Jewel collection, which included the Holy Lance, from Vienna to Nuremberg, the Nazi's favorite city. With the Spear of Destiny now safely ensconced in Germany, Hitler declared that the war could begin in earnest. The lance would be well protected in the hall of Saint Katherine's Church, where it had once rested for nearly four hundred years.

The Spear of Destiny fell into the hands of U.S. soldiers on April 30, 1945. A few hours after the Holy Lance passed from Nazi possession, Hitler committed suicide in his Berlin bunker. Today, the Spear of Destiny stands again in the Hapsburg Treasure House Museum in Vienna.

But no one really knows where the Ark of the Covenant resides. In December 2000 Erling Haagensen and Henry Lincoln published their thesis that the ark and the Holy Grail were both hidden on the Baltic Sea island of Bornholm about 830 years ago.

In December 2001 Reverend John McLuckie found a wooden tablet representing the Ark of the Covenant in a cupboard in Saint John's Episcopal Church in Edinburgh, Scotland. McLuckie, who had lived in Ethiopia, recognized the artifact as sacred to Ethiopia's Orthodox Christians and arranged to have the tablet returned in a special ceremony in 2002.

Those who revere the ark and all that it represents pray that the powerful holy relic never falls into the wrong hands.

ARMY OF GOD

The battle cry of the Army of God, "Death to the New World Order," has become a death sentence for abortion clinics and their staffs.

The Army of God is an extremist religious group that was organized about 1962 and has declared its objective to be the waging of total war on "the ungodly communist regime in New York" and the "legislative, bureaucratic lackeys in Washington." With the battle cry "Death to the New World Order," the Army of God targets homosexuals, abortion clinics, and all those who "preside over the death of children and issue policies of ungodly perversions that are destroying the American people."

In the early 1980s, while a women's clinic in Granite City, Illinois, was being mobbed by fundamentalist protesters, Dr. Hector Zevallos, the clinic operator, and his wife, Rosalee, were kidnapped by members of the Army of God. After being held for eight days in an abandoned ammunition bunker, the captives were released when Zevallos gave his pledge that he would perform no more abortions.

Don Benny Anderson and two other members of the Army of God, Matthew and Wayne Moore, were later convicted of the kidnapping.

Anderson's explanation that God had told him to wage war against abortion centers did nothing to convince the judge to cut him any slack, and he received a thirty-year prison term for the kidnapping and an additional thirty years when it was learned that he had torched two Florida abortion clinics.

In 1984 the Army of God took credit for the firebombing of a women's clinic in Norfolk, Virginia, and another outside of Washington, D.C. The year 1984 became the "Year of Fear and Pain" as militant abortion activists torched twenty-five women's clinics throughout the United States. At least seven firebombings were orchestrated by Rev. Michael Bray of Bowie, Maryland, who is often referred to as the "chaplain" of the movement. At the site of a Norfolk bombing, Bray left a note giving the Army of God credit for the act.

In the 1980s the Army of God generally took care that no one should be harmed in their bombings of women's clinics, but as the 1990s dawned, Bray began to advocate the murder of abortion doctors as part of a theocratic revolution to bring about biblical laws.

Rachelle "Shelley" Shannon, a.k.a. Shaggy West, an Oregon fundamentalist, prowled the western states launching butyric acid and arson attacks on women's clinics. She proclaimed that she was doing God's will when she shot and seriously wounded Wichita, Kansas, clinic doctor George Tiller in 1993. Investigating police officers found a copy of *The Army of God Manual* buried in her backyard. Shannon is currently in prison for attempted murder and arson.

On January 16, 1997, a women's clinic in Atlanta was firebombed. On February 21 a gay nightclub was torched in the same city. After the second bombing, a crude letter was sent to the Reuters news agency, giving the Army of God the credit and warning that any persons involved in abortion would "become victims of retribution" and that "sodomites" would always be one of the group's targets.

On October 23, 1998, James Kopp, a.k.a. Atomic Dog, murdered Dr. Barnett Slepian, a well-known abortion doctor in upstate New York. Hailed by his fellow Army of God members as a holy man who executed a wicked serial killer and saved the lives of innocent children, Kopp confessed to the murder but swore that he did not intend to kill Dr. Slepian. Kopp claimed that he had picked Slepian's name at random from a list of abortion providers and intended only to wound him. Kopp was on the run for more than two years and placed on the FBI's Ten Most Wanted Fugitives List until he was apprehended in Dinan, France, in March 2001.

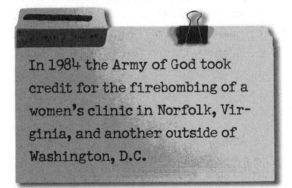

In 1984 the Army of God took credit for the firebombing of a women's clinic in Norfolk, Virginia, and another outside of Washington, D.C.

Vicki Saporta of the National Abortion Federation has called Michael Bray "one of the most well-known domestic terrorists." Bray went to prison for his participation in the bombings of ten mid-Atlantic abortion clinics in the 1980s and served two years of a six-year sentence after being convicted of conspiracy and explosives charges. Bray is the author of *A Time to Kill: A Study Concerning the Use of Force and Abortion,* an "ethical treatise on the use of force in defense of the child in the womb."

In 1997 a website sponsored by David Leach, whose newsletter *Prayer & Action Weekly News* supports the pro-violence abortion network, serialized *Rescue Platoon,* a futuristic novel that dramatizes the Army of God as emerging victorious after a bloodbath of epic and biblical proportions. That is the same ending that the real-life Army of God envisions.

ARYAN NATIONS

The Aryan Nations have issued a declaration of independence from the United States and declared Anglo-Saxons as the true "chosen people."

Aryan Nations is a paramilitary group that was founded in the mid-1970s by Rev. Richard Grant Butler and structured around his Church of Jesus Christ Christian, one of numerous churches associated with the Christian Identity movement. Originally headquartered near Hayden Lake, Idaho (the "international headquarters of the White race"), Butler preached the Identity doctrine that Anglo-Saxons, not Jews, are the Bible's true "chosen people"; African Americans are "mud people," more animal than human; and Jews are the offspring of Satan. Although Aryan Nations is primarily a Christian Identity group, Butler's anti-Semitism and his calling for the establishment of a white racist state undeniably reflected a Nazi-like philosophy.

During the 1980s a number of Aryan Nations members joined followers of the neo-Nazi National Alliance and some Knights of the Ku Klux Klan to form a secret organization called the Silent Brotherhood, also known as the Order, which plotted to overthrow the U.S. government. The Order planned to raise cash to fund the revolution by counterfeiting, robbing banks, and hijacking armored cars, but those drastic methods came to a halt with the death of its founder, Robert J. Matthews, in a shootout with federal agents in December 1984, and the subsequent imprisonment of many of its members.

As Richard Butler's health began to fail, the Aryan Nations Ohio chapter began positioning itself as a possible new headquarters for the group. On February 16, 1997, the Church of Jesus Christ Christian (also New Vienna Church of Christ) in New Vienna, Ohio, and the KKK organized a rally at the state capitol in Columbus to protest Black History Month. In September

1997 Ohio's Aryan Nations leader, Harold Ray Redfaeirn, was sentenced to six months in prison for carrying a concealed weapon.

Carl Franklin, chief of staff for Aryan Nations, whom Richard Butler had named as his successor, left the group in 1993 as a result of disagreements with Butler. Wayne Jones, security chief at the Aryan compound since the late 1980s, departed along with Franklin. Franklin, Jones, and two other members formed their own white-supremacist group called the Church of Jesus Christ Christian of Montana.

In steadily declining health, Butler underwent a crisis in his leadership after the departure of Franklin. In December 1995 Butler's wife's death added to his depression and inability to lead the group.

In August 1999 Aryan Nations member Buford Furrow shot and wounded four children and one adult at a Jewish community center in the Los Angeles suburb of Granada Hills. Not yet satisfied with his kill, Furrow drove to nearby Chatsworth and shot and killed a Filipino American postal carrier.

Aryan Nations was forced to sell its compound in Hayden Lake in 2000 after losing a civil suit brought by the Southern Poverty Law Center. Richard Butler died on September 8, 2004, and the number of active Aryan Nations chapters fell to fifteen. After the headquarters was relocated to Lincoln, Alabama, and Charles Juba assumed leadership, a splinter group, claiming to be the true Aryan Nations, led by August Kreis moved the base to Sebring, Florida, early in 2005. Kreis will not state how many members the Aryan Nations has at the present time.

Aryan Nations Declaration of Independence from the United States: In 1996 Aryan Nations published a "Declaration of Independence" that accused the "Zionist Occupied Government of the United States of America" of repeated injuries and of having "an absolute tyranny over these [United] states;

moreover throughout the entire world." The declaration continued:

> Therefore, the representatives of the Aryan people, in council, appealing to the supreme God of our folk for the rectitude of intentions solemnly publish and declare that the Aryan people in America, are, and of rights ought to be, a free and independent nation; that they are absolved from all allegiance to the United States of America, and that all political connection between them and the Federal government thereof, is and ought to be, totally dissolved, and that as a free and independent nation they have full power to levy war, conclude peace, contract alliances, establish commerce and to perform all other acts which independent nations may of right do.

The Aryan "Declaration" concludes: "We must secure the existence of our people and a future for White children."

Activities: In 2005 August Kreis offered sincere congratulations and best wishes to al-Qaeda and all Islamic terrorists groups who wage a holy war against the West. In addition, he has proposed an alliance with the neo-Nazis and Islamic radicals to fight their common enemies, the Jews and the American government.

ASIAN TSUNAMI 2004

Conspiracy theorists soon saw everything from a secret military operation to aliens correcting the Earth's rotation as a cause for the tragic tsunami.

E arly in the morning of December 26, 2004, a 9.3 earthquake shuddered the ocean floor off northwestern Sumatra, forcing billions of tons of seawater upward. Giant waves rolled toward the beaches of Sumatra, Thailand, and Sri Lanka, cascading downward on thousands of unsuspecting villagers, holiday celebrants, and foreign tourists. The massive tsunami claimed perhaps 300,000 lives and continued its destructive course until it spent the last of its energy on the beaches of Kenya.

Only a few days after the terrible catastrophe occurred, conspiracy theorists around the world were busy debunking the scientists' explanations of a natural disaster. An act of God was out of the question, these individuals argued: this was a deliberate act of cruel men. Among the most prevalent theories were the following:

- The U.S. military had secretly been testing a deadly ecoweapon whose electromagnetic waves caused havoc with the environment and triggered the earthquake that spawned the tsunami.

- One of the superpowers had tested an underwater nuclear device that proved more powerful than anticipated.

- The U.S. military and State Department had received advanced warning of the impending tsunami, but they did nothing to alert the Asian countries.

- All of the government agencies of the world knew of the coming monster tsunami but did nothing to alert the victims in its path in order to comply with the New World Order's plan to decrease planetary population.

- Benevolent aliens had noticed that the rotation of the earth had become irregular and wobbly and sought to correct its orbit. Scientists in India confirmed that the planet's rotation had become more stabilized after the tsunami.

ATLANTIS

Atlantis was a great lost civilization that possessed a technology superior to our own and a Golden Age that has inspired dozens of secret societies and thousands of dreamers, poets, mystics, and maverick archaeologists.

In 1882 Ignatius Donnelly (1832–1901) published *Atlantis: The Antediluvian World,* arguing that all civilization is an inheritance from Atlantis. Listing numerous parallels between ancient cultures spaced far away from each other, Donnelly argued that the traits they held in common resulted from contact with Atlanteans, members of the ancient civilization who escaped destruction during its catastrophic final days and managed to impart their knowledge to other peoples of the world, helping civilize primitive societies, passing on the secret of written language, and supervising construction of some of the world's grandest and most mysterious structures. The pyramids of Egypt and the Americas, the Sphinx in Egypt, and the megaliths of western Europe are among the structures attributed to the genius of the Atlanteans.

In the years since Donnelly published his controversial book, believers have credited the Atlanteans with having had the technology to generate electricity, build flying machines, and harness nuclear power for energy and warfare—all more than nine thousand years before such things came into being in modern society. Some claim that the Atlanteans were knowledgeable about a formidable death ray, secrets for levitation, and pure forms of energy through crystals. Many Atlantis enthusiasts firmly believe that the inhabitants of the lost continent had cosmic connections with extraterrestrials and may actually have been a colony established on Earth by alien explorers.

In the late 1960s undersea divers researching the region near Bimini Island in the Bahamas discovered what appeared to be roadways, walls, and buildings under the water in the exact location prophesied by Edgar Cayce (1877–1945), a widely admired psychic whose "life readings" for clients revealed that many of their present-life psychological traumas resulted from terrible incidents that the individuals had experienced in past lives. Many of their problems, according to Cayce, were due to the sufferings they had experienced as people who lived in Atlantis.

Cayce helped to popularize a modernized view of Atlantis as a superior civilization that had developed airplanes, submarines, X rays, antigravity devices, crystals that harness energy from the sun, and powerful explosives. He theorized that a terrible explosion in 50,000 B.C.E. split Atlantis into five islands; another rupture occurred in 28,000 B.C.E. and a third around 10,000 B.C.E. Cayce claimed that he himself had been an Atlantean priest around 10,500 B.C.E., had foreseen the coming destruction, and had sent some of his followers to Egypt, where they directed the building of the Sphinx and the Pyramids.

In 1940 Cayce predicted that remnants of Atlantis would rise again near the Bahamas in the late 1960s. In 1967 two pilots photographed a rectangular structure in the ocean off the coast of Andros, the largest island of the Bahamas. Another configuration of stone, in the shape of a "J," was found by divers off the island of Bimini. The J-shaped formation was believed to be a road of stone. Extensive diving expeditions became common in the area, and some divers claimed to have seen remnants of temples, pillars, and pyramids.

Atlantean enthusiasts insist that there is an organized cover-up on the part of the political, religious, and scientific establishments to keep proofs of Atlantis from the general population. If the existence of the ancient advanced civilization were officially acknowledged, they assert, the current hypotheses concerning the history and development of humankind would have to be completely revised. Acceptance of a prehistoric supercivilization would make the current understanding of history obsolete. To find irrefutable evidence of a great worldwide culture that thrived while the rest of humankind was struggling to exist on a

A 1933 map depicts the location of Atlantis during the time of the Ice Age, when the water levels of the oceans were much lower.

primitive level would demolish conventional knowledge of the progress of civilization.

Atlantis was first described in the works of the Greek philosopher Plato (427–347 B.C.E.), who depicted it as a world of perfect order, a model society. In two of his dialogues, *Timaeus* and *Critias,* he provides a description of the island continent and how Atlanteans conquered all the known world except for Athens. *Critias,* named after the primary speaker in the dialogue, Plato's great-grandfather, presents a history of Atlantean civilization and describes the ideal society that flourished there. Critias notes that the stories were originally passed on by an ancestor, Solon (615–535 B.C.E.), a politician and poet who traveled widely.

Solon was informed by Egyptian priests in the city of Sais, located in the Nile Delta, that there was once a land even older in history than Egypt, which the Greeks acknowledged as being centuries older than their own society. The priests described a large island continent called Atlantis that had prospered some eight thousand years earlier and was located beyond the Pillars of Hercules, the Greek term for the rocks that form the Strait of Gibraltar, the westernmost point of the Mediterranean Sea. Beyond the strait is the Atlantic Ocean. The primary city, also called Atlantis, was located in the center of a series of concentric rings that alternated between strips of water and land. The water rings served as canals for trade and helped form a series of natural defenses that made an invasion of Atlantis extremely difficult.

> In Plato's account, the people of Atlantis eventually became corrupt and greedy, putting selfish pursuits above the greater good.

Although Atlantis had a powerful army of professional soldiers, the culture promoted learning, through which advances in engineering and science made the land bountiful, beautiful, and powerful. In addition to magnificent architectural structures, a network of bridges and tunnels linked the rings of land, and clever uses of natural resources provided security and abundance. Many groves provided solitude and beauty, racetracks were used for athletic competitions, and irrigation systems ensured great harvests.

In Plato's account, the people of Atlantis eventually became corrupt and greedy, putting selfish pursuits above the greater good. They began invading other lands with the idea of world domination. Angered by these developments, the sea god Poseidon set about destroying the civilization, battering the continent with earthquakes and floods until Atlantis was swallowed up by the ocean.

The common description of the destruction of Atlantis has been linked by some to other cataclysmic events—stories of a great deluge in the Bible, the Epic of Gilgamesh and flood myths in other societies. Some contend that the end of the Ice Age between 12,000 and 10,000 B.C.E. likely resulted in rises of water levels in various parts of the world and that earthquakes, volcanic eruptions, and climate changes, either incidental or associated with the Ice Age, occurred during the time identified with the destruction of Atlantis.

Enthusiasts of the lost continent were tantalized in December 2001 when explorers using a miniature submarine to probe the sea floor off the coast of Cuba announced their discovery of stone structures deep beneath the ocean surface that were suggestive of ruins left by an unknown civilization thousands of years ago. Representatives of the Canadian-based Advanced Digital Communications, together with experts from the Cuban Academy of Sciences, said that the structures, at a depth of around 2,100 feet, were distributed as if remnants of an urban area. Estimates of the age of the ancient city under the sea were somewhere in the vicinity of 6,000 years, about 1,500 years earlier than the great Giza pyramids of Egypt. Whether this intriguing site proves to be Atlantis or evidence of a land bridge that once linked Cuba to mainland South America, it is certain to be controversial.

AUM SHINRIKYO (SUPREME TRUTH)

Asahara Shoko assisted the realization of his doomsday prophecies by having his followers release sarin nerve gas in Tokyo subway stations.

In 1987 Asahara Shoko (born Chizuo Matsumoto) established Aum Shinrikyo, a cult with several hundred members. Shoko/Matsumoto claimed to have received enlightenment while he was alone in the Himalaya Mountains in India in 1986. He was given the holy new name of Asahara Shoko, a new religion to be called Aum (Sanskrit for the powers of destruction and creation) Shinrikyo (teaching of the supreme truth), and a mission to teach the truth about the creation and destruction of the universe. In addition, the good deeds of Aum would prevent the time of the Apocalypse. In

1989, after some resistance, the group was approved as a religious entity in Japan.

Asahara Shoko was deeply influenced by the book of Revelation in the Christian Bible, the prophecies of Nostradamus, Tibetan Buddhist teachings of transmigration, and various Hindu motifs and deities. Shiva, the Hindu god of destruction, serves as the primary deity in Aum. Initially, Asahara taught his followers that they must strive to convert evil energy into positive energy. In order to avoid the mass destruction of nuclear war, thirty thousand disciples must achieve true liberation of spirit through his teachings.

Few outsiders understood that Asahara had a master plan to take over Japan and then the world. Aum created Shinrito (Supreme Truth Party), a new political party, and entered twenty-five candidates in the 1990 Japanese parliamentary election. Perhaps things might have been different if all twenty-five Shinrito candidates had not been defeated at the polls. Asahara now began to receive apocalyptic visions that emphasized the imminence of the end of the world. One of the most fearful messages from the spirit world stated that the United States would initiate Armageddon by starting World War III with Japan.

With such a cataclysm awaiting the world, Asahara told his followers that they must accelerate their schedule to seize control of Japan. One of the teachings in the Aum belief system held that believers might remove bad karma by enduring various kinds of suffering. Indeed, it seemed logical that nonbelievers might also be assisted in removing their bad karma if Aum should help them in their suffering—even in their death.

In 1994 Aum precipitated a number of mysterious chemical accidents in Japan. Clouds of sarin nerve gas killed seven people and injured hundreds of others in the Kita-Fukashi district of central Japan. On March 20, 1995, in the midst of morning rush hour in Tokyo, ten highly placed Aum disciples boarded five subway trains at different stations and, at a predetermined time, simultaneously released sarin, killing twelve persons and injuring up to six thousand. Placing the cult under close scrutiny, Tokyo police reported that between October 1988 and March 1995 Asahara may have ordered the murders of thirty-three Aum followers who disobeyed his commands or who wished to leave the cult. Japanese police arrested Asahara and 104 followers in May 1995.

The Japanese government revoked its recognition of the Aum as a religious organization in October 1995, but in 1997 a government panel decided not to invoke the nation's Anti-Subversive Law against the group, which would have outlawed the cult. A 1999 law gave the government authorization to continue police surveillance of the group due to concerns that the Aum might launch future terrorist attacks. In July 2001, Russian authorities arrested a group of Russian Aum followers who had planned to set off bombs near the Imperial Palace in Tokyo as part of an operation to free Asahara from jail and then smuggle him to Russia.

In January 2000, under the leadership of Fumihiro Joyu, Aum changed its name to Aleph ("to start anew") and claimed to have rejected the violent and apocalyptic teachings of its founder. However, early in 2005, Japanese police raided four sites connected with the cult. Inside one, they found a Geiger counter and a partially constructed concrete bunker with two stories underground. Many nervous Japanese could not help wondering whether the site was meant to take over the complex of buildings near Mount Fuji, where Aum Shinrikyo once made sarin gas and tortured and incinerated errant members.

B-25 GHOST BOMBER

The B-25 bomber is said to have been hauling some very mysterious cargo when it ditched into the Monongahela River. If the bomber was only on a routine training flight as the air force claimed, why has the entire aircraft disappeared?

The B-25 Mitchell bomber was one of World War II's most famous U.S. warplanes. On January 31, 1956, an aging B-25 ditched into the Monongahela River near Pittsburgh—and has never been seen again. Over the years, the "Ghost Bomber" has achieved legendary status in the area and spawned a number of conspiracy theories concerning its cargo. Depending on the theory, the B-25 was carrying an atom bomb, nerve gas, Las Vegas showgirls, or a fragment of the UFO crash at Roswell. Because of the bomber's clandestine cargo, some theorists contend, a top-secret crew of black-ops specialists arrived, hoisted the plane to the surface, then cut it into pieces and shipped the parts down the river in barges.

According to official air force records, the B-25 was hauling absolutely nothing of interest. The sole purpose of the flight was to give the six-member crew some air time before the bomber was retired. The plane took off from Nellis Air Force Base in Nevada, landed at Tinker Air Force Base in Oklahoma, then continued to Selfridge Air Force Base in Michigan before flying to Olmstead Air Force Base in Harrisburg, Pennsylvania. As the craft flew over western Pennsylvania, the pilot, Major William Dotson, thirty-three, of San Antonio, saw that his fuel was too low to make Olmstead, so he decided to head for Allegheny County Airport in West Mifflin. Then, realizing that he could not make the Allegheny airport either, he chose to ditch the B-25 in the Monongahela between the Glenwood Bridge and the Homestead High Level Bridge.

Hundreds of witnesses viewed the crash from the vantage points of the bridges. Major Dotson, a seasoned pilot, veteran of air campaigns in World War II and Korea, told the *Pittsburgh Post-Gazette* two days after the crash that he chose the river because he didn't want to hit anyone on the ground.

All flight personnel survived the initial impact of the crash. The pilot and five crew members managed to climb out onto the wings as the B-25 began to float downstream. One of the

A B-25 like this one disappeared after the pilot ditched it over the Monongahela River near Pittsburgh in 1956. The military claimed it had nothing in it of importance, but conspiracists assert the cargo included an atomic bomb.

crew members apparently slipped off the wings, and witnesses counted only five men on the rapidly sinking aircraft. About a half mile from Becks Run, the plane sank, and another crew member was lost. The four surviving crewmen were rescued, and the bodies of the two who drowned were found a few weeks later.

The day after the crash a Coast Guard cutter snagged what searchers believed may have been one of the plane's wings and dragged it to the surface. But the anchor slipped off and whatever it had nearly hauled to the surface sank. On a second try, the two-inch tow line snapped. On a third attempt, a smaller anchor was lost. Three days after the B-25 ditched into the Monongahela, an Army Corps of Engineers dredging barge swept the river 150 times and was unable to find any trace of the bomber. The Pittsburgh River Patrol and private vessels dragged the river repeatedly to find the plane. The water was high and running fast, making their efforts even more difficult. The Coast Guard tried once more, dragging the main channel with a specially made grappling hook, but located nothing. After fourteen days, according to official air force reports, the search for the B-25 was abandoned.

Air force spokespeople have commented that a common misperception in the popular mind is that a B-25 bomber is massive and that its wreckage should be easy to find. The B-25 is often confused with the B-17, the famous four-engine Flying Fortress. The B-25 has a wingspan of only 67 feet, compared with the B-17's 103 feet 9 inches.

The mystery of the Ghost Bomber of the Monongahela has grown over the years along with the conspiracy theories of Nazi gold, atomic secrets, and treasures of the Illuminati that have been nominated as possible cargoes of the aircraft. In the 1990s a sonar survey located only cars, trees, and an ancient paddle-wheeler. An image that seemed to have potential as a B-25's fuselage turned out to be a sunken barge.

Hundreds of witnesses saw the bomber crash into the river. Four of the six crew members were rescued. Is it possible that a World War II bomber could vanish almost immediately after it ditched? Or did the aircraft contain secrets so incredible that black ops scooped it up and hid it away?

LOUIS BEAM

Louis Beam became a lone-wolf terrorist against the government he believed had betrayed the white race.

One of the most influential and incendiary personalities on the far right, Louis Beam (1946–) is generally considered the first important practitioner of the "lone-wolf" or "leaderless resistance" model of activism. Beam became active first as a Klansman, later as a neo-Nazi with Christian Identity ties. For over three decades he has engaged in an active crusade against a government that he judges tyrannical and controlled by an international Jewish conspiracy.

Reared in the segregationist South, Beam grew up in Lake Jackson, Texas. After an eighteen-month tour of duty in Vietnam, he returned to Texas in 1968 and became a member of the Texas branch of United Klans of America (UKA), under the leadership of Texas grand dragon Frank Converse.

In 1976 Beam left the UKA and joined David Duke's Knights of the Ku Klux Klan (KKK), accepting the assignment of training Klansmen in guerrilla warfare.

Beam grew increasingly dismayed over the diminishing membership rolls of the white-supremacist movement, and it became his personal mission somehow to revitalize the Klan. During 1978 and 1979 he recruited Klan members among U.S. Army personnel at Fort Hood in Texas, and by 1980 Duke had promoted him to grand dragon of the Texas KKK.

In 1981 Beam ignited the explosive tensions between refugee Vietnamese shrimp fishermen and native fishermen sharing the Gulf Coast waters in the Galveston Bay area of Texas. With the battle cry "White Power! We will fight!" Beam brought in armed Klansmen in support of the Texas fishermen and harassed the refugee fishermen and other Vietnamese families residing in the area.

In concert with the Southern Poverty Law Center, the Vietnamese Fishermen's Association sought an injunction that would halt the Klan's harassment. In May 1981 a U.S. district court ruled in favor of the plaintiffs and ordered Beam and his men to cease engaging in unlawful acts of violence and intimidation.

Beam resigned as Texas grand dragon and became ambassador at large for Richard Butler's Aryan Nations. While living at the Aryan headquarters at Hayden Lake, Idaho, Beam established an elaborate computer network to more effectively promulgate racist and anti-Semitic propaganda. Beam also created the notorious assassination "point system," awarding scores to would-be assassins based on the importance of their victims. All indications were that Beam would ascend to the leadership of Aryan Nations when the ailing Butler decided to step down.

On April 24, 1987, Beam and thirteen others were indicted by a federal grand jury in Fort Smith, Arkansas, on charges that included the firebombing of a Jewish community center in Bloomington, Indiana, attempting to blow up a natural gas pipeline in Fulton, Arkansas, purchasing firearms and explosives in Missouri and Oklahoma, and stealing over $4 million from banks and armored cars in Washington State. Taking the code name "Lonestar," Beam disappeared in Mexico before the indictment was issued. After an encounter with Mexican federal judicial police in Guadalajara that left one officer critically wounded, Beam was captured and turned over to U.S. officials on November 6, 1987.

Beam chose to represent himself in court, with the assistance of Kirk Lyons, a lawyer known to be sympathetic to radical-right clients. On April 7, 1988, after seven weeks of testimony and twenty hours of deliberations, the jury acquitted Beam and his codefendants on all charges, dealing a major blow to the federal government's attempted policing of the far right during the 1980s.

Filled with new confidence in his cause and defiance toward the federal government, Beam announced the birth of the "New Right," a movement that married Christian Identity to "the creation of a national state for the white man, an Aryan republic within the borders of the present occupied country." At the same time, Beam linked America's far right with the "liberation movements" of Syria, Libya, Iran, and Palestine. In Beam's view, Palestinian leader Yasser Arafat was a particularly admirable figure.

In the first half of the 1990s Beam was recognized as one of the most influential figures in American extremism. He began slowly to fall out of favor with the radicals in the movement because he made anti-Semitism secondary to ridding the nation of the evils of the federal government. Beam had also been heard to make anti-Nazi comments.

In a letter to supporters in October 1996 Beam stated that it had been ten years since his arrest, trial, and subsequent release at Fort Smith, Arkansas. He had given the cause another ten years, and now he intended to give his family the next years of his life. In addition, he admitted for the first time, he had been exposed to Agent Orange while in Vietnam, and his health was declining.

Today, Beam focuses his efforts primarily on his website.

ART BELL

Broadcasting from a desert compound not far from the fabled Area 51, Art Bell keeps listeners up all night with accounts of UFOs, time travelers, and conspiracies.

Art Bell, the original host of *Coast to Coast,* one of the largest syndicated Monday-through-Friday talk radio programs in the United States, and its sister program, *Dreamland,* on Sunday nights, has said that his quest for wisdom began early in life. He claims that he makes no judgments about the stories that his listeners phone in regarding UFOs, monsters, government cover-ups, and Illuminati/Freemason conspiracies, but he espouses a personal theory he calls "the Quickening": namely, that time is speeding up and bad things are happening at an accelerated pace.

Bell operates his one-man show (he serves as his own engineer, producer, information director, and star) out of his ranch-style home in Pahrump, Nevada, sixty miles west of Las Vegas, not far from the fabled Area 51, the secret military base where, some of his guests swear, UFOs are being reverse-engineered. Bell and his wife, Ramona, are not reluctant to recount the UFO sighting they experienced one night as they were returning from his previous

job at radio station KBWN in Las Vegas. The Bells describe the object that hovered above their automobile as an enormous triangular craft, each side about 150 feet long, with two bright lights at each point of the triangle. Bell recalls that the UFO was silent and was barely moving as it floated directly over them.

After years of discussing alleged government conspiracies and the nefarious deeds of secret societies, Bell found himself embroiled in a conspiracy of his own when a scientist told him that a spaceship was surreptitiously following the Hale-Bopp comet. Bell repeated the story over the radio, and the airwaves reverberated with paranoia concerning the alien vehicle's mission. However, Marshall Herff Applewhite, a.k.a. Bo, the co-creator of the Heaven's Gate cult, *knew* why the spaceship was coming. Word of a UFO following close behind Hale-Bopp was just the message that Applewhite had been waiting for years to hear. The alien crew was coming from another dimension to take him and his thirty-eight followers home with them.

Bell insists that he discounted the story of Hale-Bopp and its tag-along alien craft on the air before the Heaven's Gate mass suicide, but several newspapers and national magazines slanted their reports so that it appeared Bell had been somehow responsible for the cultists' deaths. He was offended by what he considered a groundless attack on his credibility.

Soon after the Hale-Bopp UFO tumult, a fundamentalist Christian broadcaster accused Bell of being a child molester. Found innocent of all charges, which had been completely fabricated in an effort to discredit the radio personality, Bell next faced an Internet campaign claiming that he had openly declared his hatred of all Filipinos and condemned the Philippines as filthy and disgusting. The charge was totally unfounded and deemed absurd by Bell's listeners, who know that his wife is an Asian woman who is part Filipino. In 2001 the Philippine *Dail Inquirer* published a retraction and apologized to Bell after it had printed this slander as fact.

Bell was licensed by the Federal Communications Commission as a technician when he was only thirteen. He has worked in commercial radio for nearly forty years, but it was when he was at the 50,000-watt KBWN that he built a following over thirteen southwestern states for his brand of conspiracy/paranormal radio talk show.

Some conspiracy theorists have suggested that Bell is on the payroll of the secret government and is paid handsomely to spread disinformation about aliens and the extraterrestrial agenda on Earth. They suggest that black ops are able to keep tabs on some of Bell's more controversial guests by monitoring their statements on his radio program. Bell denies such accusations, stating that he is merely a radio host airing many differing and controversial views of the paranormal and the conspiratorial.

Over the years, Bell announced several retirements from radio programming, swearing each time that he was about to do his final broadcast. After a brief hiatus, Art Bell was back on the air at the request of his fans and the Premiere Radio Network, hosting Saturday and Sunday nights. On January 1, 2003, George Noory took over as host for the Monday through Friday *Coast to Coast* broadcasts.

On January 5, 2006, Ramona Bell (47), Art's wife of fifteen years, died of an apparent acute asthma attack while the couple was on a brief vacation in Laughlin, Nevada. During the January 22, 2006, broadcast of *Coast to Coast AM*, Bell told in detail the events of his wife's death and indicated that he would host C2C Saturday and Sunday evenings. By the end of the month, Bell was teasing his listeners about a major life decision that he was making, but he said that he was keeping it a secret for one year. By April 15, however, Bell ended the mystery by disclosing that, after several weeks of mourning, he had traveled to the Philippines and married a recent college graduate named Airyn Ruiz. Ac-

cording to Bell, the young woman had contacted the radio host to express her condolences upon learning of Ramona's death, and after the two had "dated" on the Internet for hundreds of hours, Bell had traveled to the Philippines to meet and to marry her.

> After years of discussing alleged government conspiracies and the nefarious deeds of secret societies, Bell found himself embroiled in a conspiracy of his own....

Bell relocated to Makati, Manilla, to begin broadcasting from the Philippines, but technical problems kept him intermittently off the air until July 23. On October 7, 2006, Bell announced on C2C that Airyn was expecting a child, and on December 28, he opened his program by stunning his listeners with the news that he and his bride had relocated back to Pahrump. On May 30, 2007, Asia Rayne Hall was born. On July 1, 2007, shortly after the birth of his daughter, Bell announced his wish to spend more time with his family. Effective that day, he retired as a radio host.

Bell did return sporadically in 2008 as an occasional host of *Coast to Coast.* But there were difficulties in obtaining a green card for Airyn Bell, and the family returned to the Philippines in March of 2009. On May 17, 2009, Bell hosted a program from Manila, hinting that his move to the Philippines might be a permanent one. His final turn at hosting was on what had always been his annual "Ghost to Ghost" Halloween program on October 31, 2010.

As of December 2010, Bell was no longer a host on the *Coast to Coast* website, but the weekly "Somewhere in Time with Art Bell" classic episodes remain. Sketchy information would seem to indicate that Bell and his family have returned to Pahrump and that the issues over Airyn Bell's immigration status have been resolved. Diehard Bell fans insist that an enigmatic message transmitted via Facebook in August 2011 indicates that Art Bell plans a return to broadcast radio.

DR. FRED BELL, A MYSTERIOUS DEATH

An expert on Remote Neural Monitoring and Synthetic Telepathy, Dr. Fred Bell was trying to reveal government research in which people could be tracked by satellite by reading their thoughts. He died mysteriously after talking about it on television.

Renaissance man, inventor, eclectic thinker, and controversial scientist and futurist Dr. Fred Bell died on September 25, 2011, within hours after Jesse Ventura interviewed him for the program *Conspiracy Theory with Jesse Ventura* on TruTv. Ventura told talk show host and conspiracy theorist Alex Jones that Bell "dropped several bombshells" during the interview (the program by press time has not yet aired), but did not elaborate on the specific topics discussed.

Some conspiracists familiar with Bell's work noted that he was considered an expert on Remote Neural Monitoring and Synthetic Telepathy, which is being used covertly by the government. Dr. Bell disclosed that secret government agencies had technology that had the ability to record people's electrical body impulses and upload them to a satellite. Using this method, a person under surveillance could be tracked anywhere and his/her thoughts could be read and even reprogrammed remotely.

According to Bell, the symptoms of electronic harassment include unusual forgetfulness, suicidal or homicidal thoughts, panic attacks, depression, and paranoia. "Confusion weaponry" uses frequencies or impulses to disrupt thoughts. Bell also warned about the advanced satellites that can knock things out of the sky with EMP (electromagnetic pulses) similar to what law enforcement is developing to remotely shut down the electronic ignition of cars they're chasing.

According to certain conspiracists, Bell's fiancée was with him in the hotel room the morning he died. He was carrying some coffee when he suddenly fell to the floor and began making odd noises. His fiancée called for help, and Bell was taken to a nearby hospital, where he was diagnosed with an enlarged heart. The doctors were unable to help him, and he was pronounced dead.

Dr. Fred Bell was born in Ann Arbor, Michigan, on August 10, 1943. According to his official biography, his father was a scientist who worked with the late Henry Ford, Sr. His great uncle on his father's side was Alexander Graham Bell, and on his mother's side he was a direct descendant of Ethan Allen, the folk hero of Vermont during the American Revolution. Bell speculated that, as a result of this "strange genetic gene pool," he had a tendency to be a "revolutionist with wild and crazy ideas … a bit of an eclectic eccentric."

Bell was propelled into science at a very early age. At age fourteen he was not only working at the University of Michigan on nuclear energy projects, but was also inducted into the U.S. government's project MK-ULTRA. This early mind control research covered such topics as past life regression and the popular remote viewing techniques used today by the CIA and other intelligence gathering factions worldwide.

At sixteen years of age he interned at the U.S. Army Biological Weapons Division in Little Rock, Arkansas. On his seventeenth birthday, he was transferred into the U.S. Air Force, where he began working on highly classified projects, several of which involved early warning radar defense systems and the detection and tracking of extraterrestrial craft.

After he left the defense sector, Bell began studying with Himalayan masters of ancient wisdom. During this time he became internationally known as a contactee to a Pleiadean group of extraterrestrial humanoids who claimed to have come here to help the people of Earth save themselves from their own destructive tendencies. This group of extraterrestrials allegedly came here from a star system five hundred light years from Earth. For this effort the Russian society of cosmonauts (astronauts) awarded Dr. Bell a distinguished scientific progress award.

Just prior to the 9/11 terrorist attacks, Dr. Bell was working with Dr. Steven Greer in decompartmentalizing the various agencies that work in concert with extraterrestrials on such projects as advanced propulsion systems and "star wars" weaponry. This project, known as the Disclosure Project, was being presented to the U.S. Senate on the very day of the 9/11 attacks.

Dr. Bell was also a practicing naturopath, environmentalist, and political activist who worked with programs worldwide that helped children with autism and other mental and physical problems. He spent twenty years with the National Health Federation, a U.S.-based group that has promoted the freedom of individuals to choose their own health care, as well as the various vitamins, minerals, and dietary supplements that work best for them.

Dr. Bell invented the famed and patented Nuclear Receptor, which he claimed improved the health and energy levels of the wearer. One of his most recent inventions, the Andromedan Holographic Projector, allows the operator to manipulate space and time conditions. Another of his latest inventions, the X-1 Healing Machine, allows the human body to heal itself in a matter of seconds, instead of taking several months. The concept of the X-1 Healing Ma-

chine was developed as an add-on to the original Depolaray Machine developed by Thomas Holson and Fred Hart in 1947. Furthermore, victims of electronic harassment can use one of his recent inventions, the QBAM (Quantum Biological Administrating Machine), a quantum healing device that employs counteraction technology to block energy or absorb microwave radiation.

> One of his most recent inventions, the Andromedan Holographic Projector, allows the operator to manipulate space and time conditions.

Dr. Bell also wrote several books, such as the bestselling *Rays of Truth—Crystals of Light,* and he is the subject of a number of others, including: *The Promise,* a novel based on Bell's life and work, written by Brad Steiger; *The Fellowship,* a nonfiction study of UFO contactees, written by Steiger and edited by Sherry Steiger; and *Starborn,* written by Brad and Sherry Steiger, also made reference to his work.

Dr. Bell was working on *The Inside Track,* a book to "pull the lid off" of everything currently held secret by "the Powers that be."

BIBLE CODE

The Hebrew Bible contains encrypted information that can be revealed by computers employing equidistant letter sequence (ELS). The Bible Code proves that the divine hand of God guided the ancient scribes and directed them to place certain prophecies within the texts. The code provides firm scientific proof of the existence of God and his direction of earthly events.

Eliyahu Rips, an Israeli mathematician and one of the leading experts on group theory, together with Doron Witztum and Yoav Rosenberg, discovered the secret Bible Code. Rips and Witztum entitled their original paper on the experiment "Equidistant Letter Sequences in the Book of Genesis." Although rabbis had discovered some parts of the code over the centuries, it was not until the advent of modern high-speed computers that the depth and intricacy of the coded information could be revealed.

To gain access to the mysterious code, the mathematicians first arranged the 304,805 Hebrew letters of the first five books of the Bible, the Torah, into a large array, removing all spaces and punctuation and running the words together one after another. Then a computer searched for matches in all directions for names, words, and phrases hidden in the text. Rips and his associates ran a test in which they set out to see if the code could pick out the names of the sixty-six rabbis who had the longest entries in various Jewish annals. The computer program found all sixty-six names embedded in the Hebrew text, together with either the rabbis' birth or death dates.

In test after test, the Bible Code found people, places, and inventions that did not come into being until three thousand years after the ancient Hebrew texts had been recorded. Months before the start of the Gulf War, the researchers found the message *fire on 3rd Shevat* (January 18), the exact date that Saddam Hussein chose to fire scud missiles at Israel. The words *Hussein, scuds,* and *Russian missile* were all found encoded in a close matrix in Genesis.

Control texts, such as the Hebrew translation of *War and Peace,* were searched, and nothing but random words were found. According to Rips, only the Hebrew Bible may be used, for according to tradition, God gave the characters to Moses one at a time, with no spaces or punctuation. However, in 1997 the mathematician Brendan McKay, among others, found countless "predictions" in *War and Peace* and several other books

In 1994 Rips and his colleagues published a paper in the *Statistical Science Journal* that passed three levels of secular peer review. Their work was later confirmed by mathematicians at Harvard, Yale, and Hebrew University. It was replicated and confirmed by Harold Gans, a senior codebreaker at the U.S. Department of Defense. Since publication, research has indicated that the hidden code exists throughout all the books of the Tanakh in the original Hebrew.

In 1997 Michael Drosnin's *The Bible Code* hit bestseller lists with its provocative claim that the Hebrew Bible contains a very complex code that predicted events which occurred three thousand of years after the ancient texts were first written. Among the startling examples given were the discovery of the name *Hitler,* and close by it, the terms *evil man, Nazi and enemy,* and *slaughter.* When *Eichmann*—Adolf Eichmann (1906–1962), the man Hitler named to mastermind the extermination of the Jews—was found, the words *ovens, extermination,* and *Zyklon-B* (the poison gas employed by the Nazi executioners of the Jews) were embedded nearby. The Bible Code also contained information regarding the assassinations of both John F. Kennedy and Robert Kennedy and their assassins. Drosnin also found word clusters with more positive connotations. For example, a test for *Shakespeare* found his name embedded with *presented on stage, Macbeth,* and *Hamlet* nearby. *Beethoven* appeared near *German composer, Wright Brothers* near *airplane,* and *Edison* near *electricity* and *light bulb.* Rips has since distanced his research from Drosnin's and emphasized the futility of attempting to predict the future from the code.

Drosnin, who says that he is an agnostic and an objective journalist, states that his belief in the Bible Code was confirmed when a fanatic's bullet killed Israeli prime minister Yitzhak Rabin in 1995. Drosnin states that he had seen the assassination forecast in the code a year earlier and had even warned Rabin of the danger.

BIG BROTHER

Conspiracy theorists say that the warning is no longer a literary allusion—Big Brother really is watching us.

The classic *1984* describes a gloomy scenario wherein a totalitarian government called "the Party" has complete control over its people at all times. Many refer to this novel as being a nearly perfect prophetic vision by the author, George Orwell, of a very bleak and dismal future, one that seems to be unfolding before our very eyes now in the twenty-first century.

Today we have the technology to dominate and track all citizens with brainwashing techniques, media (including television, movies, and computerlike devices that issue forth propaganda), tracking and spy systems that follow our every move, with the ability even to see and hear through walls. Yet in 1949 when Orwell wrote about these things, most were not yet in existence.

"Big Brother," the supreme leader of the Party in Orwell's novel, has come to be synonymous with a dictatorial society in which corporations and government take away our freedom, privacy, and ability to think for ourselves, ruling over us with total power and control. In the novel the Party's slogan, "Big Brother Is Watching You," is continually broadcast in and through all media. There is no place to hide as banners, posters, movie and TV screens, computers, stamps, coins, even thought transfer, all transmit the declaration of complete domination by Big Brother. By extension, Big Brother and "Big Brother Is Watching You" remain

In a 1956 film adaptation of George Orwell's novel, Edmond O'Brien played the part of Winston Smith, who tries to outsmart the oppression of Big Brother.

commonplaces in referring to any and all of the conspiracies involved in bringing about a One World Government.

BILDERBERGERS

The Bilderbergers, a powerful international secret society made up of six hundred wealthy and influential individuals, has an aggressive plan to achieve world domination.

The prestigious and influential secret society known as the Bilderbergers has a membership composed of six hundred very wealthy and very powerful individuals, drawn from the highest executive levels of international business, politics, education, finance, and the media. This elite group is governed by an even more secretive, almost entirely anonymous, inner circle of fifteen, known as the Incunabula.

The Bilderbergers got their name from the place of their first meeting in 1954, the Bilderberg Hotel in Oosterbeek, Holland. The event was hosted by Prince Bernhard of the Netherlands and a number of luminaries from the European branch of the Illuminati. Since 1954 the Bilderbergers, as they began calling themselves, have met secretly each year in a different geographical location.

Once, when asked the purpose for the international gathering of the global elite, their spokesman, Charles Muller, said that the group discusses issues that affect the Western world—issues such as China, Islam, energy management, the North Atlantic Treaty Organization (NATO), corporate governance, and the growth of certain nations. Journalists who observed the event from afar during the 1997 gathering said that they spotted General Colin Powell, Henry Kissinger, World Bank president James Wolfensohn, and David Rockefeller among the attendees.

Certain conspiracy theorists who have studied the makeup of the Bilderbergers insist that the group is controlled by the ten-man inner circle of the Illuminati. According to their claims, this secret cabal has painstakingly prepared an agenda for the masses of humanity. Such individuals as the Bilderbergers will become our masters, and the vast majority of the global population can look forward to a future existence as pawns, if not slaves, of the Illuminati.

According to certain sources who claim knowledge of the basic plan for world dominance set in motion by the Bilderbergers, the following are among their principal objectives:

- The United States must promptly pay its debt to the United Nations. In addition, the United States will be asked to contribute billions of dollars to the International Monetary Fund. U.S. taxpayers will be bled almost dry by such expenditures.

- NATO will be converted into a United Nations military force. U.S. troops will thereby come under the command of foreign officers.

- Corporate governance will dissolve national sovereignty and bring all of the earth's corporations under a single global order. Local control over businesses and corporations by nations and states will be terminated. The great giants of finance will be able to disregard the laws and dictates of all governments, including those of the United States.

- As the twenty-first century progresses, a new system of fascism will emerge under the guise of "free-trade" practices that will in fact be guided by the Illuminati.

- The Bilderbergers have approved the Red Chinese model of economics as the standard for the emerging European superstate and the United States. As in Communist China, all dissidents will be dealt with severely and placed in work camps.

- As soon as the program can be implemented, citizens in every nation will be issued the Universal Biometrics Identification Card.

- A Gestapo-like police force will enforce the dictates of the Illuminati's New World Order.

The 2011 meeting of the Bilderbergers was held at the Suvretta Hotel in St. Moritz, Switzerland on June 9. In attendance, by invitation only, were 140 prominent figures from politics, banking, business, and the military, who met behind closed doors. According to those who claimed to have received inside information regarding the topics that the global elite addressed were the following:

- How the unrest, suffering, and war in the Middle East might be prolonged so that they—the money masters—might increase their profits.

- How Internet censorship might be implemented to prevent liberty movements from succeeding in other Middle East countries as they did in Egypt and Libya.

- How the worldwide economic crises might be prolonged so that more countries will be forced to impose drastic austerity measures on their citizens.

- How to continue to provoke wars to reduce the world population—always popular on the New World Order agenda.

OSAMA BIN LADEN

The CIA's "Frankenstein monster" learned his lessons of terrorism so well that he was the most wanted man on Earth.

Osama bin Laden was the most wanted man on Earth. The Rewards for Justice Program of the U.S. Department of State was offering a reward of up to $25 million for information leading to his capture, and the Airline Pilots Association and the Air Transport Association were willing to throw in an additional $2 million. In 1988 bin Laden founded the terrorist group al-Qaeda ("the Base") and funded the terrorist bombings of U.S. embassies in Nairobi, Kenya, and Dar es Salaam, Tanzania, killing 224 people (August 7, 1998); the attack on the USS *Cole* in Yemen (October 12, 2000); and the coordinated plane hijackings and assaults on the World Trade Center and the Pentagon (September 11, 2001). In 1998 bin Laden established the World Islamic Front for Holy War against Jews and Crusaders and issued an edict that declared the killing of Americans, civilians and the military alike, "an individual duty for every Muslim" in order to "liberate the al-Aqsa Mosque and the Holy Mosque and in order to for their armies to move out of all the lands of Islam, defeated, and unable to threaten any Muslim."

Osama bin Laden was born in 1957 in Saudi Arabia, the son of a billionaire Saudi family. He inherited $300 million when his fa-

ther died, and he amassed a great personal fortune on his own, as a well-connected businessman in the construction trades and in retail merchandising throughout the Middle East. Standing six feet four or taller, he covered his very thin body with the clerical robes of a spiritual leader.

Conspiracy theorists see great irony in the bloody career of Osama bin Laden. In their view, he was the "Frankenstein monster" that the Central Intelligence Agency created. In 1979 bin Laden was recruited by the CIA to fight the Soviet invaders of Afghanistan as part of the largest covert operation in CIA history. The Agency utilized Pakistan's Inter-Services Intelligence (ISI) as go-betweens, for in order for this covert action to succeed, none of the CIA's efforts could be traced back to Washington. While there may have been some sympathy for the Afghanistan freedom fighters, the ultimate goal was to take a chunk out of the Soviet Union's military forces.

Bin Laden began funneling money to the mujahideen fighting the invaders and became closely associated with the Egyptian Jihad and other Islamic extremist groups. The CIA actively encouraged the rebel Muslims in Afghanistan to declare a jihad against the Soviets, and some 35,000 Muslim extremists from forty Islamic countries were drawn to fight the invaders of their brothers' homeland. The CIA and ISI set up guerilla training camps in which combat techniques were integrated with the teachings of Islam. In the early 1980s bin Laden was actively involved in the camps to train freedom fighters to engage the Soviets, and he enlisted thousands of recruits from Saudi Arabia, Algeria, Egypt, Yemen, Pakistan, and Sudan to continue the struggle against the enemies of Islam.

The CIA and ISI were rewarded for their covert efforts by eventually influencing over 100,000 foreign Islamic radicals to support the resistance to the Soviet invasion. In March 1985 President Ronald Reagan signed

Outraged Muslims protested the killing of Osama bin Laden in Quetta, Pakistan.

a National Security Decision Directive that increased covert military aid to the Muslim resistance.

The success of the covert operation can be gauged by the responses of Muslim extremists after the Soviets had withdrawn; many later said that they had no idea they were fighting the war on behalf of the United States. Although there were contacts at the upper levels of the intelligence hierarchy, the Islamic rebels in the field never suspected that it was the Americans who were supplying them with sophisticated weaponry and training them to become more effective warriors. Even the very clever bin Laden once admitted that he had seen no evidence of American assistance in the war against the Soviets.

The Soviet Union withdrew its troops in 1989, but the civil warfare in Afghanistan continued without missing a beat. The Taliban (the name translates simply and ironically as "students"), supported by various factions within Pakistan, eventually were able to install a hard-line Islamic government in Afghanistan. At the time, the Taliban Islamic State served America's geopolitical interests. The Afghan opium trade was financing and equipping the Bosnian Muslim Army and the Kosovo Liberation Army, so Washington turned a deaf ear to the cries for assistance from the reign of terror imposed by the Taliban.

In 1988 bin Laden founded al-Qaeda to unite Arabs who fought against the Soviet invasion in Afghanistan. It wasn't long, however, before he came to believe that al-Qaeda should be the champion for the over one billion Muslims in the world who feel that their complaints have not been heard by the West.

After a truck-bombing of a U.S. military complex near Dhahran, Saudi Arabia, in 1996 killed nineteen U.S. airmen and wounded 515 people, including 240 Americans, bin Laden reaffirmed his call for a jihad against Americans: "We have focused our declaration of jihad on the U.S. soldiers inside Arabia," he said during an interview with CNN, but he warned that other attacks were imminent because of the U.S. government's "extremely unjust, hideous, criminal acts" in support of the Israeli occupation of Palestine.

From bin Laden's perspective and the viewpoint of various Islamic extremist groups, the Arabs have many issues with the West, and especially the United States:

- The influence of Western decadence threatens Arab fundamentalist cultures in the Middle East and other heavily Islamic parts of the world.

- Americans have manipulated Arab politics and ignored nearly seventy years of demands for reparations for Zionist atrocities in Israel and the "theft" of Arab land in Palestine.

- The arrogance of some of those who took that land made Arabs feel unwelcome in their former homeland.

- The historic Western exploitation of Arab oil until Arabs formed their oil cartel.

- The prejudice against Arabs around the world for their religion and cultural beliefs.

- The desire of Arab fanatics to force the whole world to accept Islam and become an international Islamic theocracy.

In 1994, because of his opposition to the Saudi king, bin Laden was stripped of his citizenship and expelled from Saudi Arabia. He moved his operations to Khartoum, Sudan, where he had many prosperous businesses, but under pressure from the United States, he was expelled from that nation too. In 1996 he settled into mountain encampments in Afghanistan and established a number of training bases. At that time, he told Americans, through an interview with CNN's Peter Arnett, that if they seriously wished to cease the explosions inside their country, they should stop provoking the feelings of millions of Muslims. The "hundreds of thousands who have been killed or displaced in Iraq, Palestine, Lebanon," bin Laden warned, had "brothers and relatives" who would make Ramzi Yousef (convicted for the 1993 World Trade Center bombing) "a symbol and a teacher."

According to some students of bin Laden's evolution to the world's most notorious terrorist, the act that enraged him enough to put his threats into action might have been the August 19, 1998, U.S. missile strike in Sudan of a target that turned out to be an innocent aspirin, powdered milk, and baby food factory. The blast killed 167 Muslims praying in a nearby mosque, including at least one of bin Laden's relatives. Bin Laden then expanded his terror network and declared a *fatwa* (a religious opinion or judgment issued by a qualified scholar or a religious leader) decreeing jihad against America. He immediately gained 100,000 new volunteers.

Bin Laden was placed on the American Federal Bureau of Investigation's lists of Ten Most Wanted Fugitives and Most Wanted Terrorists for his involvement in the 1998 U.S. embassy bombings. After the 2001 bombing of the Trade Center, the FBI placed a $25 million bounty on bin Laden's head. Conspiracists offered proof that the secret government was watching over the bin Laden family by the fact that twenty-four American members of the bin Laden family, along with over one hundred other highly placed Saudis, were flown out of the United States just after the bombings on 9/11 without being questioned.

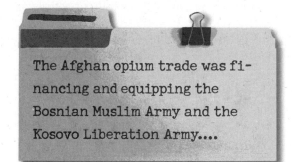

The Afghan opium trade was financing and equipping the Bosnian Muslim Army and the Kosovo Liberation Army....

On September 23, 2001, Osama bin Laden, commenting on the military strikes against al-Qaeda in Pakistan, said, "We hope that these brothers are among the first martyrs in Islam's battle in this era against the new Christian-Jewish crusade led by the big crusader Bush under the flag of the Cross...."

Osama bin Laden was able to evade U.S. forces during three presidential administrations. But on May 2, 2011, the fugitive leader of al-Qaeda was shot and killed inside a private residential compound in Abbottabad, Pakistan, by U.S. Navy SEALS and CIA operatives in a covert strike ordered by President Barack Obama. Within hours, bin Laden's body was prepared for burial according to Muslim religious laws, and he was buried at sea. Al-Qaeda acknowledged the death of their leader and spiritual mentor on May 6, 2011, and vowed to retaliate against Americans wherever they might be found all over the world.

Bin Laden had not been given last rites, and his body had been buried at sea for little more than a few days when conspiracy theorists began circulating their theories. They believed that the assassination of the master terrorist had not gone down the way the official U.S. report stated.

Some insisted that Osama was still alive, having escaped the raid on his home. Others repeated a theory that had been popular long before the SEALS dispatched the terrorist leader that stated that bin Laden had died of health issues many years ago. Top al-Qaeda personnel had kept alive reports of bin Laden sightings as a propaganda tool. Even alleged CIA agents had spread the rumor that bin Laden had died of marfan syndrome in Dubai in July 2001.

A big problem that the official reports of bin Laden's assassination had lay in the fact that no photographs of his body were made available to the media for distribution to the general public. Adding to doubts of bin Laden's death was his burial at sea. Skeptics around the world demanded to see the body as the ultimate proof that bin Laden was truly dead.

Conspiracy theorists also made much of the vast discrepancies in the reports of the shootout at bin Laden's mansion with the SEALS. Initial reports gave a play-by-play of a forty-minute gunfight with bin Laden's bodyguards before the SEALS seized the compound and killed the chief terrorist as he attempted to use his wife as a human shield. Later accounts mentioned only one man defending bin Laden when the SEALS stormed a rubbish-strewn compound rather than a multi-million dollar mansion.

Skeptics also made an issue of the interviews conducted with neighbors of the bin Laden compound in Abbottabad after the raid. The majority of the interviewees swore that they had never seen bin Laden in all the years that he was supposed to have resided there, and they were unaware of any evidence to prove that he had ever lived among them. It seemed especially strange that bin Laden could live undetected in the town for so many years when

Abbottabad serves as a staging ground for the Pakistani military, which is the Pakistani equivalent of West Point. For all the world knew, people argued, the White House could have selected nearly anyone to serve as a faux bin Laden for the SEALS to kill and bury at sea.

Conspiracy theorists have believed for many years that Osama bin Laden was very useful to elements of the secret government. When the world has had enough of fighting terrorists, so the conspiracists state, the populace will turn to the New World Order as their salvation from chaos. In the meantime, defense contractors are getting richer and richer, the military more and more powerful.

BIOCHIP IMPLANTS

The secret government, working together with the Illuminati and the New World Order, plans to chip-implant and track all Americans in order to make them subservient to the will of their rulers.

A July 2004 MSN poll revealed that 20 percent of those interviewed would experience no reluctance to receive an implantable microchip. Government workers in Mexico are informed that they must receive a chip or lose their jobs. Tech-loving members of the youth culture are unhesitatingly accepting chip implants in their arms as passes into exclusive nightclubs.

Over the past two decades propagandists for the New World Order have steadily eroded the revulsion and suspicion that the general public felt toward microchips implanted in their bodies. Initially, the chip was promoted as an effective means of tracing pets that strayed and of locating children who were lost or abducted. Because the microchip implants were successful, resistance and rational fears deteriorated on the part of many people.

In the 1950s and '60s, a large number of experiments in behavior modification were conducted in the United States, and it was well known that electrical implants were inserted into the brains of animals and humans. Later, when new techniques in influencing brain functions became a priority to military and intelligence services, secret experiments were conducted with such unwilling guinea pigs as inmates of prisons, soldiers, mental patients, handicapped children, the elderly, and any group of people considered expendable.

Rauni-Leena Luukanen-Kilde, former chief medical officer of Finland, has stated that mysterious brain implants about one centimeter square began showing up in X rays in the 1980s. In a few years, implants were found the size of a grain of rice. Dr. Luukanen-Kilde stated that the implants were made of silicon, later of gallium arsenide. Today such implants are small enough that it is nearly impossible to detect or remove them. They can easily be inserted into the neck or back during surgical operations, with or without the consent of the subject.

In May 1995 the *Washington Post* reported that Prince William of Great Britain was implanted at the age of twelve. If he were ever kidnapped, security agents explained, a radio wave with a specific frequency targeted to his microchip would be routed through a satellite to a computer in police headquarters. Employing such technology, the prince could be located anywhere on the globe.

According to many conspiracy theorists, within a few years all Americans will be forced to receive a programmable biochip implant somewhere in their body, most likely on the back a hand for easy scanning at stores. The implant will also serve as a universal identification card. A number assigned at birth will follow that person throughout life. Eventually, every newborn will receive such an implant.

Initially, people will be informed that the biochip is largely for purposes of identification. The reality is that the implant will be linked to a massive supercomputer system through which government agencies can maintain a surveillance of all citizens by ground sensors and satellites. Today's microchips operate by means of low-frequency radio waves that target them. With the help of satellites, implanted persons can be followed anywhere. Their brain functions can be remotely monitored by supercomputers and even altered through the changing of frequencies. Even worse, say the alarmists, once the surveillance system is in place, the biochips will be implemented to transform every man, woman, and child into a controlled slave, for these devices will enable outside intelligences to influence a person's brain cells and neurons. People can be forced to think and to act exactly as government intelligence agencies have programmed them to think and behave.

The technology exists right now to create a totalitarian New World Order. Secret government agencies are utilizing covert neurological communication systems in order to subvert independent thinking and to control social and political activity. The National Security Agency (NSA) has an electronic surveillance system that can simultaneously follow the unique bioelectrical resonance brain frequency of millions of people. NSA's Signals Intelligence group can remotely monitor information from human brains by decoding the evoked potentials (3.5 Hz, 5 milliwatt) emitted by the brain; similarly, stimulation signals can be sent to the brains of specific individuals, causing the desired effects to be experienced by the target.

A U.S. Navy research laboratory, funded by intelligence agencies, has achieved the incredible breakthrough of uniting living brain cells with microchips. Those who investigate this conspiracy contend that when such a chip is injected into a man's or a woman's brain, he or she instantly becomes a living vegetable and a subservient New World Order slave. And once this device is perfected, the biochip implant could easily be converted into a "Frankenstein-

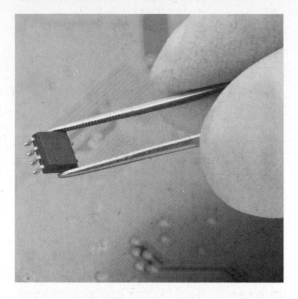

The New World Order plans on implanting microchips into all Americans so that they may track their every move.

type weapon," and the Defense Department can produce an army of killer zombies.

Various conspiracy journals recount the allegations issuing from a couple in Palo Alto, California, who are convinced that their teenaged son's psychological problems are the result of a biochip that was implanted in his head by a CIA agent during a tonsillectomy. According to the young man and his parents, he is constantly receiving threats and negative thoughts through a wavelength that is received by the biochip in his brain. They swear the device has shown up on X rays, but that the evidence was destroyed by CIA agents.

According to researchers, those who have been victimized by mind-control experiments are often diagnosed as mentally ill by doctors who are not privy to the secret research being conducted against the will of private citizens. Such claims that the individuals are being targeted against their will or being used as guinea pigs for electronic, chemical, and bacteriological forms of psychological warfare are assessed as paranoid delusions.

Experts have said that a micromillimeter chip placed in the optical nerve of the eye could draw neuroimpulses from the brain that embody the experiences, smells, sights, and voice of the implanted subject. These neuroimpulses could be stored in a computer and may be projected back to the person's brain, via the microchip, to be reexperienced. A computer operator could send electromagnetic messages to the target's nervous system, thereby inducing hallucinations.

Before his execution, convicted Oklahoma City Federal Building bomber Timothy McVeigh frequently stated his contention that federal agents were able to track him during the 1990s because of an electronic monitoring device that had been placed in his leg. McVeigh was not alone in his belief that the U.S. Army secretly implanted such devices in the legs of American soldiers during the Gulf War. Numerous veterans have made similar allegations.

BIOMAGNETIC WEAPONS

During the Cold War, the Americans and Soviets were both working on technology to control minds remotely.

In 1959, Saul B. Sells, a professor of social psychology, convinced the CIA that he would be able to build a very special electroencephalography machine that would be able to analyze brain waves. In other words, his machine could read minds.

The CIA received Dr. Sells's proposal with great enthusiasm, for the agency had amassed convincing intelligence that the Soviet spy masters had already developed an instrument capable of controlling minds at a distance. Some intelligence suggested that the Soviets were beaming a complex microwave signal at the American Embassy in Moscow from a building across the street.

Dr. Sells' project was approved by the CIA in 1960, and it was named "Subproject 119" in the agency's mind control program known as MK-ULTRA. Specifically, the objective of 119 was to develop "techniques for activating the human organism by remote electronic means."

By the late 1970s, the project had produced what writer Harlan Girard termed "the ultimate weapon ... a weapon system that operates at the speed of light, that can kill, torture, enslave, and escape detection." According to Girard and other investigators, electromagnetic weapons have been tested on humans since 1976. Whenever word has leaked out by whistleblowers concerning the heinous nature of such experiments, organized attacks on the credibility of the involuntary human test-subjects have proceeded with such viciousness that all criticism of the research has been effectively squelched.

In 1973, Dr. Joseph C. Sharp, an experimental psychologist at Walter Reed Army Institute of Research, was able to use equipment that had the capacity to convert sound waves into microwave radiation that enabled him to transmit threatening voices into a subject's head. In addition to inducing paranoid schizophrenia into a subject, the sound waves could block the normal processes of memory and supplant them with distorted pseudo-memories. As this project was developed, the researchers were able to produce electronic telepathy, transmit false memories, and induce visions, daydreams, and nightmares into the brains of involuntary test subjects.

The transmission of thoughts and fears would be effective on prisoners or on individuals subjected to brainwashing, but the apparatus truly becomes a weapon when the electronic frequencies are used to cripple people by limiting their range of movement or by prompting major organ failure, including heart attacks. Lessening the effects would cause severe pain, rather than death, and would be

an extremely painful instrument of torture. A number of conspiracy researchers firmly believe that such bioelectromagnetic devices were used in Iraq to gain information from prisoners of war.

In March 2001, the U.S. Marine Corps released information about their new non-lethal weapon, "active denial technology." According to those who had perfected such technology, the device causes the human skin to boil without damaging the skin itself.

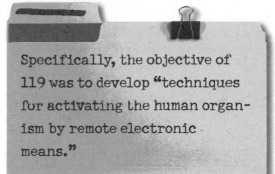

Specifically, the objective of 119 was to develop "techniques for activating the human organism by remote electronic means."

According to an evaluation of the Marine Corps claims published in *New Scientist,* the device produces "pulsed electromagnetic radiation at a frequency of 95 GHz with a range of about 600 meters." Volunteers testing the Active Denial System's effectiveness in crowd control said that the projected beam caused pain within two to three seconds. In less than five seconds, the pain was unanimously declared to be "intolerable."

MK-ULTRA was allegedly shut down in the 1970s, and all information regarding the CIA and military's research on Active Denial Systems are highly classified. Once again, the general public is hoping that those controlling the experiments possess a modicum of good will and compassion, given that these electromagnetic weapons can kill, torture, and enslave entire populations at the speed of light. Such machines would, indeed, be the ultimate weapons for tyrants, dictators, and New World Order despots.

BLACK HELICOPTERS

Since the 1980s, hundreds of men and women have reported being harassed and spied upon by mysterious unmarked black helicopters, which they believe to be the property of a clandestine national police force that will soon begin to wage incessant warfare against all Americans who oppose the secret government.

Many conspiracy theorists believe that individuals who are involved in the investigation of any suspected conspiracy or who are doing serious UFO research are certain to be under surveillance by hovering black helicopters without any identifying markings and flying at unsafe or illegal altitudes.

When the Federal Aviation Authority was asked by alarmed citizens' groups to investigate black helicopter traffic over the United States, the FAA stated that it had no investigations on file. However, many individuals reported that the FAA did have agents in the field taking depositions from witnesses to the activity of black, unmarked helicopters.

The pilots who fly the mystery helicopters, as well as the black-uniformed agents within the craft, are thought to be the minions of the secret government that has signed a document turning over control of our nation's military forces to greedy and power-hungry international bankers, the Secret Brotherhood of the Illuminati, and their various allies. In a few ground sightings, the occupants of the helicopters have been described as men wearing black uniforms and carrying automatic weapons. They may shy away if law enforcement officers try to approach, but there are also numerous accounts of aggressive behavior on the part of the helicopter crews.

According to some conspiracy researchers, the crews of the black helicopters are veterans of a highly classified CIA project, which involved the training and indoctrination of selected, multiple-personality assassins. These agents were not only programmed to kill, but after repeated torture and hypnotic brainwashing sessions they were given selective "memories" of new and fictitious lives. Such insidious and reprehensible experiments in mind control were conducted by the CIA in the 1950s and 1960s under the code name MK-ULTRA, and the assassins produced by the program were considered a kind of secret weapon against the Soviet Union.

MK-ULTRA crews aboard the black helicopters are assigned to seek out those researchers and investigators who are becoming too much of an annoyance to the secret government. If these individuals do not desist in their investigations of the international conspiracy headed by the New World Order and the Illuminati, they will be abducted and undergo experiments in biochemical research, psychosurgery, and electrical stimulation of the brain. After repeated torture and hypnotic brainwashing sessions, they will be given selective "memories" that may include intense recall of UFO sightings and abduction experiences, causing them to be discredited by any civil authorities to whom they might later report their claims of having been abducted by agents of the secret government.

Many of the black helicopters patrol the area above underground bases constructed for use by government agencies in the event of nuclear war. Entities associated with such underground facilities include the Pentagon, CIA, Federal Emergency Management Agency, and National Security Agency. According to some informants, at least ninety-six underground centers have been secretly funded by the U.S. government.

BLACK MADONNA

Tradition says that the portrait on display in the church in Czestochowa, Poland, is that of Mary, the mother of Jesus, painted from life by Saint Luke. Others argue that the portrait is of Mary Magdalene.

According to tradition, Saint Luke, the "beloved physician," painted a portrait of Jesus's mother on the cedar wood table at which she took her meals. More than two centuries later, during her visit to the Holy Land, Helena (c. 247–c. 330), the mother of Emperor Constantine (c. 288–337), is said to have discovered the portrait and brought it to Constantinople. In the eleventh century, Saint Ladislaus (1040–1095), determined to save the image of the Madonna from the repeated invasions of the Tartars, took the portrait to Opala, Poland, the city of his birth, for safekeeping. Regrettably, not long after this move, a disrespectful Tartar's arrow managed to find its way to the Madonna's throat, inflicting a scar that still remains visible. In 1430, Hussite thieves stole the portrait and broke it into three pieces.

Of the more than four hundred images of the Black Madonna or Black Virgin known worldwide, the image of Our Lady in Czestochowa, Poland, has received the most contemporary recognition because of the personal devotion displayed toward this religious icon by Pope John Paul II (1920–2005). Pope John Paul, a native of Poland, prayed before the Madonna of Czestochowa in 1979, several months after his election to the chair of Peter, and he made subsequent visits in 1983 and in 1991. The reports of miracles and healings attributed to Our Lady of Czestochowa (also known as Our Lady of Jasna Gora) down through the centuries are numerous, and they include greatly enhancing the ability of a small group of Polish defenders to protect her sanctuary from an army of Swedish invaders in 1655 and her apparition's appearance dispersing an invading army of Russians in 1920. Records of such spectacular acts of intervention and dramatic cures are kept in the archives of the Pauline Fathers at Jasna

Images of the Black Madonna have existed in Europe since the Middle Ages. They may be the result of African influences, or the blending of Virgin Mary images with such Pagan gods as Isis and Artemis.

Gora, the monastery site in which the portrait was housed for six centuries.

An aspect of the painting that has puzzled many individuals upon viewing Our Lady of Czestochowa, as well as all the other portraits of the Black Madonna, is why she has such dark skin tones. Some scholars suggest that it wasn't until the onset of the Renaissance in the fourteenth century that artists began to portray Jesus, Mary, and Joseph as having pale skin, blue eyes, and blond or reddish-blond hair. Before then, the holy family and the apostles were most often depicted as Semitic people with the dark skin tones characteristic of the Middle East. If the Black Madonna of Czestochowa was truly a portrait of Mary painted from life by the apostle Luke, he would surely have captured a woman with olive or dark brown skin and black or brown hair.

Other researchers, commenting upon the mystique of the Black Madonna, state that the Roman Catholic Church has not warmly embraced such depictions of the Virgin Mary because it regards such representations as actually paying tribute to the ancient goddesses and earth mothers, and thus perpetuating strains of pagan worship. Church scholars point out that Saint-Germain-des-Prés, the oldest church in Paris (*Par-Isis,* the Grove of Isis), was built in 542 on the site of a former temple dedicated to Isis, the Creatress, the "Giver of Life" in the Egyptian and Roman mysteries. Isis had been the patron goddess of Paris until Christianity replaced her with Saint Genevieve. Within the church of Saint-Germain-des-Prés, however, parishioners worshipped a black statue of Isis until it was destroyed in 1514.

Diana/Artemis, together with the other two preeminent goddesses of the East, Isis and Cybele, were represented as black madonnas. And before the people of the East bent their knees to Diana, Isis, and Cybele, they had worshipped the Great Mother in Sumeria as Inanna, as Ishtar in Babylonia, and as Astarte among the Hebrews. Most scholars agree that among the first images of the Black Madonna and her divine son were Egyptian representations of Isis and Horus.

The Black Madonna may also refer to Mary Magdalene, who in the traditions of some early Christian sects, such as the Gnostics, was the wife of Jesus. In one version of the events after Jesus's death on the cross at the hands of the Romans, Mary Magdalene brought the cup used at the Last Supper—the Holy Grail—from Palestine to southern France, where it would eventually be guarded by the Knights Templar.

There is also a belief that Mary arrived in France carrying within her womb a child fathered by Jesus of Nazareth, and that this child became the progenitor for the royal family of France. For those who hold such beliefs, the Holy Grail is a metaphor for Mary Magdalene's womb, which carried the true blood of Jesus in the person of his unborn son. Therefore, many of the depictions of the Black Madonna and Child throughout the regions of southern France and Spain may be regarded as images of Mary Magdalene carrying the infant son of Jesus, rather than the Virgin Mary carrying the infant Jesus.

BLACK SUN

This German secret society was developed to prepare the Aryan race to meet the supermen who live in the earth's interior.

*T*he Coming Race (1871), a novel by the occultist Edward Bulwer-Lytton, was set in the earth's interior, where an advanced civilization of giants thrived. The giants had built a paradise and discovered a form of energy so powerful that they outlawed its use as a potential weapon. This force, the Vril, was derived from the Black Sun, a large ball of "Prima Materia" that provides light and radiation to the inhabitants of the inner earth.

Persistent legends in nearly every culture tell of an elder race that populated the earth millions of years ago. The Old Ones, who may originally have been of extraterrestrial origin, were an immensely intelligent and scientifically advanced species who eventually chose to structure their own environment under the surface of the planet's soil and seas. The Old Ones usually remain aloof from the surface dwellers, but from time to time throughout history they have been known to visit certain of the upper world's more intelligent members in the guise of alchemists or mysterious scientists in order to offer constructive criticism and, in some cases, to give valuable advice in the material sciences.

According to certain occult traditions, Agharta is a subterranean empire of underworld supermen who periodically surface to oversee the progress of the human race. According to one source, the underground kingdom of Agharta was created when the ancestors of its present-day denizens drove the Serpent People from the caverns during an ancient war.

By the 1840s the legend of Agharta and its underworld capital, Shambhala, had circulated widely among the mystically minded in Germany. According to this ancient tradition, the Master of the World already controlled many kings and rulers of the surface world by exercising his occult powers. Soon this master and his superrace would launch an invasion of the surface nations and subjugate all humans to his will. Various secret societies formed in Germany in the late nineteenth and early twentieth centuries wanted desperately not only to prove themselves worthy of the superhumans who lived beneath the planet's surface, but also to control the incredibly powerful Vril force. This ancient force had been known among the alchemists and magicians as the Chi, the Odic force, the Orgone, and Astral Light, and they were well aware of its transformative powers to create supermen of ordinary mortals.

The secret society of the Black Sun coexisted with the Vril and the Thule societies in Germany prior to and during World War I, and it blended with the other groups after the war. Although these societies borrowed some concepts and rites from Theosophists, Rosicrucians, and various Hermetic groups, they placed special emphasis on what they believed to be the innate mystical powers of the Aryan race. Madame Helena Blavatsky had listed the Six Root Races—the Astral, Hyperborean, Lemurian, Atlantean, Aryan, and the coming Master Race. The Germanic/Nordic/Teutonic people were of Aryan origin, and Christianity had destroyed the power of the Teutonic civilization.

The Black Sun, like the swastika, is a very ancient symbol. While the swastika represents the eternal fountain of creation, the Black Sun is even older, suggesting the very void of creation itself. The symbol on the Nazi flag is the Thule *Sonnenrad* (sun wheel), not a reversed good-luck swastika. The Black Sun can be seen in many ancient Babylonian and Assyrian places of worship. In its German incarnation, it perhaps also suggests the Norse myth in which the great wolf Fenrir will swallow the sun at the beginning of the Wolf Age.

BOHEMIAN GROVE

Sealed off by black helicopters and a private security force, the wicked men of the Bohemian Grove are free to perform supreme acts of vile debauchery while they plan the fate of the world.

Sealed off from the public by helicopters and armed guards, some 2,500 of the world's wealthiest, most influential, and most powerful men meet each year for seventeen intense days in a private 2,700-acre retreat on the Russian River in Sonoma County, California. The rites and rituals of the San Francisco Bohemian Club are held in secret in a grove of ancient redwood trees, but the decisions made there shape international policies that influence people throughout the world. Conspiracy theorists state that the principal theme of the annual meeting is celebration of patriarchy, racism, and class privilege.

The membership roll of this elitist group of men—no women members—is kept in strictest confidence, but it includes superwealthy, blood-dynasty family members of the Illuminati, corporate chieftains, and high government officials. According to a number of conspiracy theorists and several fundamentalist Christian evangelical ministers, one might find among the rich and politically powerful gentlemen cavorting about in the Bohemian Grove former U.S. presidents George H. W. Bush and Gerald Ford; Supreme Court justice Antonin Scalia; former secretary of defense

Caspar Weinberger; the mayors of Los Angeles, San Francisco, and other major cities; astronauts Wally Schirra and Frank Borman; former FBI and CIA directors; former secretaries of state George Shultz and Henry Kissinger; international bankers; and the heads of big oil companies. Many of the world's media chiefs are Bohemian Grove members, including the leading representatives of *Time* magazine, *People* magazine, CNN, and many other information outlets.

The former German chancellor Helmut Schmidt is alleged to have commented that his weekend as a guest at the Bohemian Grove encampment was one of the most astounding experiences that he ever had in the United States.

According to an informant for the conspiracy theorists, Great Britain's Queen Elizabeth made a stunning cameo appearance at the Bohemian Grove in 1983. Her Majesty was honored with a wild, ecstatic pagan dance ceremony, complete with stage props such as Egyptian pyramids and Babylonian artifacts.

In the allegations of certain researchers, the Bohemian Grove hierarchy exercises considerable control over the U.S. presidency. President Ronald Reagan once confided to friends that it was his acceptance by the men of the Bohemian Grove, following his "coming out" at one of their conclaves, that sealed for him the high office of president of the United States.

In 1995 House Speaker Newt Gingrich attended the meeting in the grove and was given instructions to cooperate with President Bill Clinton in building the New World Order.

One of the main rituals performed by the Bohemian Grove participants involves their bowing down before a forty-foot statue of an owl. Walter Cronkite on tape is said to be the voice of the carved-wood owl, the mascot at Bohemian Grove that opens the ceremonies. Members proudly display owl figurines, statues, and images in their homes and in their corporate and government offices.

The Bohemian Grove represents the eternal mystery cults of Babylon, Rome, and Greece. Scottish Rite Masonry is part and parcel of the Bohemian Grove. Most important, this is where diabolical satanic powers congregate each year to plan and to execute their grotesque hidden agenda for the world.

On August 3, 2011, more than 2,000 guests of the conservative elite of North America and Britain left the annual Bohemian Club's redwood retreat. According to some sources, special guests included actor Tom Cruise, former baseball star Mark McGwire, and former President George H. W. Bush, who reportedly stripped down to his underwear and played in a drum circle. Conspiracy theorist and radio host Alex Jones learned that the agenda of the Bohemian Grove was much the same as that of the Bilderberg Group's: the Arab Spring, the overthrowing of Middle East dictators, and Internet security and spying.

BRITISH PETROLEUM OIL SPILL

On April 20, 2010, Deepwater Horizon, the semi-submersible exploratory offshore drilling rig in the Macondo Prospect oil field in the Gulf of Mexico, exploded and sank after two days. A partially capped oil well one mile below the surface of the water began releasing 35,000 to 60,000 barrels per day into the Gulf, eventually contaminating the coasts of Louisiana, Mississippi, Alabama, Texas, and Florida.

Of the 126 crew members on board the rig at the time of the explosion, 79 were employees of Transocean Ltd., seven of British Petroleum, and the rest of various companies, including Anadarko, Halliburton, and M-I Swaco. Eleven of the crew were killed as a result of the blowout. The U.S. government named British Petroleum (BP) as the responsible party and held the company liable for all

Workers clean up globs of oil on the coastline near Pensacola, Florida, after the disastrous BP oil spill in 2010.

clean-up costs and other damages. Deep-sea robots were unable to stop the approximately 60,000 barrels of oil from gushing into the Gulf until July 15, 2010.

BP is a global oil and gas company head-quartered in London, England. It is ranked as one of the six "supermajor" oil and gas companies and is the third-largest energy company and fourth-largest company in the world, as measured by revenues. BP has operations in over eighty countries, produces approximately 3.8 million barrels of oil a day, and franchises 22,400 service stations around the world. The largest division of BP is in the United States.

Although British Petroleum assumed responsibility for the clean-up at an estimated $7 million a day, established a $20 billion spill response fund, and willingly dealt with individual lawsuits, all of which cut into its profit margin, some conspiracy theorists argued

that BP had destroyed the rig in the Macondo Prospect oil field itself in order to profit from higher gas prices.

Other conspiracists argued that BP and the citizens of the Gulf Coast region were the victims of such insidious plots as:

- North Korea, a nation whose leaders seem intent on prodding the United States and South Korea to declare war, launched a small suicide submarine from Cuba with the mission of blowing up a significant number of oil rigs off the coast of the United States. Although the destruction of Deepwater Horizon was successful, the submarine was also destroyed when it ventured too close to the rig. U.S. officials declared a blackout of the identity of the submariners in order to prevent a national panic about an attack in U.S. waters, and North Korean involvement was covered up.

- Rush Limbaugh, who has never met a disaster that he couldn't blame on Liberals and Democrats, expressed his suspicions that left-wing saboteurs blew up the Deepwater rig on the eve before Earth Day, thus signaling that the Cap and Trade Bill was an important deterrence to the evil of drilling for oil off the coast of the United States.

- Republicans, who are unashamedly in favor of drilling for oil in any and all parts of the United States, sent a demolition squad to blow up the Deepwater Horizon rig, figuring they would somehow come up with a plan that would blame President Obama for the disaster.

RON BROWN MURDER

Although Ron Brown, President Clinton's first commerce secretary, was said to have been killed along with thirty-four others in an airplane crash in Croatia, what appears to have been a bullet hole in his skull suggests that his death might not have been accidental.

In August of 1997, sixteen months after he died in a jet crash, Ron Brown, President Bill Clinton's first commerce secretary, was once again in the Washington spotlight as congressional investigators examined allegations that he had misused his agency to aid Clinton's reelection campaign. Principal among the accusations were those suggesting that Brown had sold his influence with the president to the highest bidders among U.S. business executives and foreign interests.

FBI agent Jerome Campane testified that restauranteur Charlie Trie, a Clinton friend from Little Rock, escorted Chinese arms dealer Wang Jun to a White House coffee with the president in February 1996. After the amenities at the coffee party, according to Campane, Trie and Jun went across Pennsylvania Avenue to meet with Ron Brown at Commerce.

Accusations of campaign abuses continued to be thrown at the Democratic National Committee, which Brown had headed before he joined Clinton's cabinet. Getting the goods on the crew who helped reelect the president was made difficult by Brown's sudden death and the fact that as early as the summer of 1997, nearly all of the twenty-one senior officials or lower-level employees who worked under Brown had left the agency. According to former Commerce aide Robert Atkins, political documents bearing the logo of the Democratic National Committee and the Executive Office of the President were frequently shredded at Commerce—so much so, Atkins said, that the shredder was repeatedly broken from overuse.

Ron Brown was the Democratic National Committee chairman from 1989 to 1992. He headed the Commerce Department for three years, from January 1993 until his death in April 1996. Perishing with him in the Croatian air tragedy were twenty-eight other passengers, including senior officers of the Commerce Department, corporate chief executive officers, financial experts, journalists, and photographers. In addition, the aircraft's six crew members were killed.

One of those crew members, Tech. Sgt. Shelly Kelly, steward, who was riding in the tail, is said to have survived the crash itself with only minor cuts and bruises. However, she died en route to the hospital. An autopsy later revealed a three-inch incision over her femoral artery. According to some sources, the incision was made at least three hours after the injuries sustained in the crash. Strangely enough, there were no further autopsies. An official order called for all the bodies to be cremated. This was considered by most people to be a thoughtful act because so many of the bodies were terribly shattered. It is also impossible to conduct autopsies on ashes.

Although the majority of U.S. officials denied even the possibility of foul play in regard to the crash, a number of investigators wondered why co-captains Ashley J. Davis and Tim Shafer were ordered to take off in such bad weather. Many news publications pronounced the storm in which the military plane had taken off as the worst in ten years, with visibility of only a hundred yards.

Villagers at the base of Sveti Ivan, one of the highest mountains in the area, said that they heard a plane fly directly overhead into the clouds, rev its engine briefly, then, two or three seconds later, crash into the mountain with an earth shattering explosion. Investigators later deduced that the plane's left wingtip had grounded, spinning the aircraft and slamming it into the mountain.

The jet, a military version of the Boeing 737, left Cilipi Airport at 2:48 P.M. and vanished from the screens of the main regional radar station at 2:52 P.M. Davis and Shafter piloted the craft over Cilipi's first beacon, 11.9 miles from the airport, at 2:54 P.M. If the aircraft had not strangely vanished from the radar screens, Cilipi control tower could have warned the pilots that they had begun to veer slightly off course. The jet was now heading straight for Sveti Ivan.

At 2:58 P.M. the plane flew over the tiny village of Velji Do at the base of Sveti Ivan and crashed a few seconds later. Official investigators wondered how a beacon light that tests had shown to be extremely accurate could have misled the pilot. When they sought to view the tapes at the control tower in the hope of gaining a clue to the mysterious misdirection, they discovered the tapes had somehow disappeared. When persistent investigators sought to interview the air traffic controller to gain his interpretation of the events leading up to the accident, they found, to their great concern, that he had committed suicide.

That left the plane's black box, the cockpit voice recorder, to provide whatever clues might exist to explain the reasons for the tragic crash. Local Croatian journalists were informed that U.S. Marines had recovered the black box.

However, the Pentagon later denied that there was a black box on board the aircraft. The box that the marines had taken was designed only to hold soda and toilet paper for the pilots.

When civilian investigators from Pratt and Whitney, the manufacturer of the engines that powered the jetliner, arrived to conduct their own research into the reasons for the crash, they were told to return stateside. The air force had officially canceled the usual safety investigation in favor of a quick legal investigation.

> Principal among the accusations were those suggesting that Brown had sold his influence with the president to the highest bidders among U.S. business executives and foreign interests.

But the biggest bombshell of all in regard to the crash was the statement by Lt. Col. Steve Cogswell that there was a wound on the very top of Ron Brown's head that looked suspiciously like a bullet hole. Cogswell, a member of the Armed Forces Institute of Pathology (AFIP), had participated in the investigation of the crash, and according to his allegations, when Brown's body was examined by military medical personnel, they discovered a wound that could have been caused by a gunshot.

Cogswell's startling assertions were seconded by Lt. Col. David Hause, who later examined the suspicious head wound on Brown's corpse at Dover Air Force Base, Delaware. Hause said that a "commotion" erupted when one of the medical examiners exclaimed that the wound looked like a "punched out .45-caliber entrance hole."

In December 1997 Cogswell expressed his opinion that the wound on the top of Brown's head was "as close to a perfectly circular hole as you can get." Hause, one of the AFIP's leading experts on gunshot wounds, agreed with his colleague that the wound appeared consistent with a high-velocity impact caused by a bullet. Cogswell, who had taken part in more than a hundred plane crash investigations, and Hause, who had been involved in such examinations for five years, went on record as stating that neither of them had ever before seen a similar wound in a plane crash victim's head.

According to purported sources close to the commerce secretary, Brown threatened to finger the Clintons as his partners in wrongdoing....

Cogswell took issue with Col. William Gormley, the assistant armed forces medical examiner, who contended that the hole was not a bullet wound and therefore did not order an autopsy. Cogswell argued that as a member of the cabinet, Brown would have been covered under the Presidential Assassination Statute, and his corpse should have been autopsied. Hause stated that he understood the "political and administrative" factors that were likely to have prohibited an autopsy on Brown, but he believed that "by any professional standard" one should have been conducted.

Cogswell went on to charge that initial X rays of Brown's head revealed tiny metallic fragments, which he said could be consistent with a disintegrating slug from a .45. Furthermore, Cogswell alleged that these damning X rays were later replaced by others that did not indicate the possible bullet fragments. Once

again, Hause backed up Cogswell's charges. When he and Dr. Jerry Spencer, the AFIP's chief medical examiner, were asked to review the Brown case, they retrieved all the photographs and X rays that had been taken of Brown at the time of the initial medical examination. They were surprised to discover that there were no X rays of the commerce secretary's head. They had all disappeared.

When it was learned that the only existing evidence of the X rays were slide images in the current possession of Cogswell, he received a letter from the AFIP informing him that he was under internal investigation and could not leave the area of his office without permission. At about the same time, it came to the AFIP's attention that Cogswell had expressed his concern over the possible murder of Brown and that he had projected slides of the wound in Brown's head during public lectures. A military police officer arrived and accompanied Cogswell to his home to retrieve all slides and photos in his possession that related in any way to any AFIP cases in which he had served as an investigator.

Based on the AFIP's actions toward Cogswell, investigators of the Ron Brown mystery ask themselves three basic questions:

1. Are government officials disturbed because the AFIP botched the medical examination of Brown?

2. Are high-ranking officials upset that the American public might learn that the AFIP botched the case?

3. Are officials of the highest rank in the government worried that the American public might learn that Ron Brown was murdered?

Of course, these questions raise one more: Why would anyone want to murder Ron Brown?

Before Brown left for Croatia/Bosnia-Herzegovina, he was up to his neck in numerous scandals. He was under investigation by the Justice Department, the Federal Deposit Insurance Corporation, the congressional Reform and Oversight Committee, the FBI, the Energy Department, the Senate Judiciary Committee—and even by his own Commerce Department's inspector general. In addition, evidence was mounting that the government of Vietnam was able to get the United States to drop a trade embargo against their country by paying Ron Brown $700,000 to swing the deal. The cash was deposited in a Singapore bank account, and the embargo fell. Although the FBI began an investigation of this alleged purchase of political influence by a foreign power, President Clinton allegedly ordered the agents to cease and desist. Later, a federal grand jury probe was neutralized.

It was well known that Brown sold plane seats on trade trips such the one that made the fatal flight to Croatia. Corporations that made large contributions to the Democratic Party or the Clinton Victory Fund were able to buy seats for their CEOs on board the prestigious special flights.

Just four days before the crash, FBI and IRS agents subpoenaed as many as twenty witnesses for a grand jury hearing regarding Brown's various activities in Washington. The *Washington Post* reported that Brown had hired Reid Weingarten, a former high official in the Justice Department, as his criminal attorney. Attorney General Janet Reno appointed Daniel Pearson as Brown's special prosecutor and gave him carte blanche to carry the investigation wherever it might lead. Before he left on his overseas junket, certain sources claim, Brown angrily demanded that Clinton force Reno to withdraw Pearson or to limit his powers. When Clinton told him that such a move was impossible because the Republicans had backed both Reno and him into a corner, Brown allegedly completely lost his temper and told the president in no uncertain terms that he was not about to become the fall guy for the multitude of the administration's scandals. According to purported sources close to the commerce sec-

retary, Brown threatened to finger the Clintons as his partners in wrongdoing and tell all that he knew about Whitewater unless Clinton used his power to call off the various investigations.

Clinton knew that he was between a rock and a hard place. A cover-up would be obvious if he interfered with the House Government Reform and Oversight Committee. On the other hand, if Brown told all he knew and revealed all the smoking guns that he had previously concealed, the campaign for reelection would be over.

It is against this background that certain of those investigating the death of Ron Brown make the most serious charge of all: A decision was made at the highest political levels that there was no time to arrange a "Vince Foster–type" suicide. It was unfortunate that all those Commerce Department officials and high-ranking U.S. businesspersons had to be traveling with Brown, but there was no choice other than to order a "mysterious crash" in Croatia. How convenient that the area was undergoing the worst snowstorm in ten years. That would make an airplane crash seem all the more believable.

Many serious questions regarding Ron Brown's death remain to be answered, and persistent investigators vow to keep chipping away at the case until the true story is revealed to the American public.

MAE BRUSSELL

Years of intensive research convinced Mae Brussell that the Kennedy assassination, the CIA, and Nazi Germany were all linked to an international network of secret societies.

After seventeen years of feisty and fiery radio broadcasts in which she warned her listeners that the United States was secretly controlled by a shadow government, Mae

Brussell became known to her many admirers as the queen of conspiracy theorists.

Born in Beverly Hills in 1922, Mae was the daughter of the prominent Wilshire Boulevard Temple rabbi Edgar Magnin and the great-granddaughter of Isaac Magnin, founder of the I. Magnin clothing stores. In 1963 Mae was married with five children and living in Southern California. After she became convinced that there was no way that Lee Harvey Oswald could have accomplished the John F. Kennedy assassination as a lone wolf, her interests broadened from being a housewife and mother to tracking down clues to the Kennedy and Oswald murders and becoming a conspiracy theorist. Mae purchased the twenty-six-volume Warren Commission report on the killings and began reading, filing, and cross-indexing information from a wide variety of books, articles, and government documents.

After years of intensive research, Mae discovered that the Kennedy assassination revealed links not only to the CIA and Nazi Germany, but to many other contemporary and historic institutions and events throughout the world. It seemed clear to her that the international network of secret societies and conspiracies that had created the Axis powers during World War II—and had supposedly been defeated—had merely gone underground and very effectively continued their campaign to control governments worldwide. In document after document, Mae recognized many of the same names and the same devious tactics that had been used to transform Germany from a cultured and scientific nation in the 1920s and 1930s into a barbaric and malicious machine of racism and hatred.

In June of 1971, after seven years of research, Mae was invited to appear as a guest on KLRB, a local FM radio station, to discuss her views on political assassinations. The audience response was good, and she soon had her own show, *Dialogue: Conspiracy* (later changed to *World Watchers International*).

Nearly every week for seventeen years, Mae shared information with her audience from her files of raw data, covering everything from the assassination of the president in Dallas to the Iran-Contra investigations to what she considered the atrocities and high crimes of the Reagan administration.

From time to time when Mae had no host station for her show, she recorded her broadcasts at home on a small cassette tape recorder and personally mailed out copies to a list of subscribers. In 1983 her radio program was picked up by KAZU in Pacific Grove, California, but in 1988 she was forced off the air by death threats. She continued sending out tapes detailing her research and investigations until June 13, 1988. Mae Brussell died of cancer on October 3, 1988. Her work continues on the website http://www.maebrussell.com.

GEORGE H. W. BUSH

The Bush family tree reveals their descent from a reviled traitor and a ruthless warlord who took delight in invading other countries. Which is stronger, heredity or environment? Or does it matter?

According to an Irish artist working on a tapestry to commemorate Ireland's Norman heritage, the Bush family is descended from a line of traitors and ruthless warlords. Ann Griffin Bernstroff was researching the history of Richard de Clare, Earl of Pembroke, when she discovered the genealogical link to the George H. W. Bush family in the United States. Pembroke, known as Strongbow for his skill as an archer, was a power-hungry warlord who led an invasion of old Ireland. The Bush lineage can also be traced to Dermot MacMurrough, who is reviled in Irish history books as Ireland's worst traitor for collaborating with the Normans. MacMurrough was said to be so vicious a warrior that he severed the heads of his victims and tore at the flesh of particularly hated victims with his teeth.

With President George H. W. Bush having led the United States in the Persian Gulf War and his son President George W. Bush declaring war on Iraq in search of nonexistent weapons of mass destruction, many U.S. citizens are left to ponder how much of that ruthless warlord blood surges through the veins of the Bush dynasty. Behaviorists and social psychologists have argued for decades about whether it is our genetics or the environment in which we are reared that has more influence on our character and who we really are. Perhaps it is equal parts of both that shape our destiny.

The pathway to the White House for the Bush dynasty may have begun in 1918 when George H. W. Bush's father, Prescott Bush Sr., stole the Apache leader Geronimo's skull for the Skull and Bones secret society at Yale. All the connections he made through this elite brotherhood no doubt paid off in many ways.

George H. W. Bush's maternal grandfather, George Herbert "Bert" Walker, moved his St. Louis banking and investment firm to the prestigious address of 1 Wall Street in the early 1920s and was one of Hitler's most powerful financial supporters. Bert Walker's sponsorship of the Nazis went back to 1924 when Fritz Thyssen, the wealthy German industrialist, was financing the fledgling Nazi Party. Averell Harriman's W. A. Harriman & Company sold more than $50 million of German bonds to American investors, and Walker's Union Banking, located in the offices of Harriman's firm, became a virtual Nazi money-laundering machine.

In 1934 Bert Walker arranged to have his son-in-law Prescott Bush placed on the board of directors of Union Banking. About the same time, Walker took over the North American offices of the Hamburg-Amerika Line, which was smuggling German agents into the United States to bribe politicians to see things Hitler's way. Just prior to the Nazi invasion of Poland in September 1939 that ignited World War II, Prescott Bush's investment firm arranged for Hitler's Luftwaffe to obtain tetraethyl lead for their airplanes.

A great source of revenue for Bush was terminated in 1942 when three firms with which he was associated were seized under the Trading with the Enemy Act. All of the shares of Union Banking were seized, and major sections of other companies were confiscated when it was determined that they were being operated on behalf of Nazi Germany. One of Bert Walker's employees had been a double agent for Naval Intelligence and had blown the whistle on the shipping company's deals with the Nazis. William S. Farish, one of Prescott Bush's partners in business deals with Adolph Hitler, was grilled so intensely by the Senate about his Nazi dealings that he collapsed and died on November 29, 1942.

Seeing clearly the ominous handwriting on the wall, eighteen-year-old George H. W. Bush gave up his plans to enter Yale and entered flight school in October 1942, perhaps in an effort to salvage the family's honor, for he was quite aware that his father was under investigation for running Nazi front groups in the United States. George H. W. Bush returned from World War II a hero, awarded the Distinguished Flying Cross, the youngest pilot in the Navy, who endured great risk bailing out of his torpedo bomber over the Pacific when it was hit by Japanese anti-aircraft fire. Years later Chester Mierzejewski, a turret gunner on a bomber flying near Bush's plane, claimed to have had an unobstructed view of the incident and stated that Bush's aircraft was never on fire and that Bush never attempted a water landing, which was standard procedure and which would have given his crew, Jack Delaney and Ted White, a chance to survive.

After the war Bush entered Yale and in 1948 became a member of Skull and Bones. By 1955, he had formed Zapata Petroleum with

George H. W. Bush campaigns in Connecticut in this 1992 photo.

the Liedtke brothers, Hugh and Bill, then bought them out and set up Permago, a Mexican drilling operation, through a front man to hide his ownership. Unfortunately for Bush's go-between, he was convicted of defrauding the Mexican government and fined $58 million.

Some investigators are convinced that George Bush spent part of 1960 and 1961 in Miami organizing anti-Castro Cubans on behalf of the CIA. CIA official Fletcher Prouty has said that he delivered three navy ships for use in the Bay of Pigs invasion to a CIA agent named George Bush, who subsequently named the vessels the *Barbara,* the *Houston,* and the *Zapata.* The ill-fated Bay of Pigs invasion of Cuba became a black eye for the Kennedy administration with 115 men lost and another 1,100 imprisoned.

Many researchers place George Bush in Texas when John F. Kennedy was assassinated on November 22, 1963. An article in the *Na-*

tion in 1988 quoted a memo from J. Edgar Hoover, the late former FBI chief, stating that "Mr. George Bush of the CIA" was briefed on November 23 about the reaction of anti-Castro Cubans to news of the assassination. Bush admitted that he was in Texas at the time but said that he couldn't recall exactly where, and he stated firmly that Hoover must have been referring to "another" George Bush.

George H. W. Bush entered politics in 1964, running for Congress as a Goldwater Republican campaigning against the Civil Rights Act. He served two terms as a representative from Texas and ran twice unsuccessfully for the Senate. In 1971 President Richard Nixon named him ambassador to the United Nations.

In 1973 Bush was named the Republican Party national chair, and he brought into the GOP the Heritage Groups Council, a group with a number of Nazi sympathizers. After serving as chief of the U.S. Liaison Office in the People's Republic of China, Bush was named director of the CIA by President Gerald Ford in 1976. Bush claimed that this is the first time that he had worked for the Central Intelligence Agency and once again denied that he was "that George Bush" associated with either the Bay of Pigs disaster or the JFK investigation. While serving as CIA chief, Bush provided special training for the Saudi royal family's palace guard.

Bush met with Manuel Noriega and guaranteed him a stipend of $100,000 a year, even though the Panamanian dictator was known to be working for Fidel Castro as well. It was at this time that Bush established Team B within the CIA, a group of neoconservative special agents and generals.

In 1978 Bush, Robert Mosbacher, and Jim Baker became partners in an oil firm, Arbusto Energy. In 1980 Bush was named Ronald Reagan's vice presidential candidate. Mosbacher, as chief fund-raiser for Bush, developed a millionaires' club of 250 contributors, each of whom was assessed $100,000 for membership fees. In 1981 the Reagan-Bush team was inaugurated.

Some investigators state that after Bush became vice president and drug czar, cocaine flow into the United States increased by over 2,000 percent. Through the militarization of a phony drug war, the researchers claim, Bush declared war on the American people and the Bill of Rights.

In 1988 Bush campaigned for the presidency and assigned Stuart Spencer to improve the image of his running mate, Dan Quayle, who always seemed to be suffering from "foot in mouth disease." A drug dealer who claimed to have sold marijuana to Quayle was put in solitary confinement by the head of federal prisons.

In the midst of a heated presidential campaign, Bush had to contend with the uncomfortable circumstances of his son Neil getting caught up in the savings and loan scandal. Neil's Silverado Savings and Loan in Denver was shut down after receiving 126 cease and desist orders in four years at a taxpayer cost of $1 billion.

Political pressure was placed on Bush to disassociate himself from the GOP Coalition of America after many of the leaders were accused of anti-Semitism and Holocaust denial. Fred Malek, a former Nixon aide, was asked to leave the presidential campaign when it was revealed that he was compiling a list of Jews in the Labor Department and investigating a possible "Jewish cabal" on orders from former president Nixon. The offensive Willie Norton political ad was telecast, suggesting that Bush's opponent, Michael Dukakis, would be soft on rapists, drug pushers, and child molesters.

In 1989 Bush was inaugurated as the forty-first president of the United States. He denied knowing that Noriega was a drug dealer and authorized CIA support to the dictator's opposition, thereby providing Noriega with an opportunity to annul Panama's elections. In Operation Just Cause, Bush sent troops to Panama with orders to overthrow the corrupt regime. Noriega was brought back to the United States to stand trial as a drug trafficker. He was imprisoned in 1992 and remained in a federal prison in Miami until he suffered a minor stroke in December 2004 and was removed to an undisclosed hospital.

Bush also claimed executive privilege to escape testifying in the Oliver North trial, thereby becoming the first U.S. president to seal his former activities as a vice president. William Casey, CIA director during the Reagan-Bush administration, died two days before he was to testify. Banker Edmond J. Safra, whose banks had been used for laundering money for the Iran-Contra affair, died mysteriously when a fire swept through his Monaco penthouse apartment.

George Bush signed the savings and loan bailout bill, and in 1990, federal regulators gave Neil Bush a seemingly impossible mild penalty, overlooking the fact that he, as Silverado's director, voted to approve over $100 million in loans to his partners. Neil soon formed Apex Energy with a personal investment of $3,000, receiving $2.7 million from a small business loan program. Apex failed, and Neil ducked out after receiving a $320,000 salary. The entire savings and loan industry was said to be losing investors' money at the rate of $3 million a minute. Estimates for the total cost for a federal bailout exceeded $500 billion. Bush's son Jeb convinced the federal government to pay off the $4 million he owed to a failed Florida thrift. George's brother Jonathan's brokerage firm was fined in two states for violations and barred in Massachusetts.

In August 1990, Saddam Hussein invaded Kuwait, and Bush was determined to turn the dictator of Iraq away from the oil fields and keep him from obtaining an even stronger control of world oil markets. Osama bin Laden urged the Saudi royal family to fight Hussein on their own and to raise a mighty Arab army.

Already uncertain of bin Laden's motives, the Saudi royals requested that the United States assume the task of driving Hussein's million-man army back to Iraq. Bush received UN approval to free Kuwait, and the 425,000 American troops were joined by 118,000 soldiers from allied nations. After several weeks of air and missile strikes, the hundred-hour land battle called Desert Storm turned Hussein's army conquest of Kuwait into a rapid defeat. Conspiracy theorists believe that Bush and the leaders of Kuwait tricked former ally Hussein into attacking Kuwait so Bush could declare war under a UN mandate, strengthen the UN, and hike up petroleum prices in order to protect his own oil investments.

> Through the militarization of a phony drug war ... Bush declared war on the American people and the Bill of Rights.

In 1992 George H. W. Bush lost his run for another term in the White House to Bill Clinton. After a time Bush became an adviser to the powerful Washington-based investment firm known as the Carlyle Group. Among his duties, Bush set about strengthening Carlyle's defense ties to the Saudi royal family. Bush visited the bin Laden family compound and solicited their investment in the Carlyle Group.

In 1993 the first attack on the World Trade Center in New York occurred. Osama bin Laden and al-Qaeda have been linked to the initial bombing of the WTC, as well as to the destruction of the WTC and the attack on the Pentagon on September 11, 2001.

With all the theories accusing the George W. Bush administration of having known in advance that the September 11 attacks would occur, it only throws fuel on the fire to learn that as the World Trade Center was collapsing and thousands of lives were being lost, the news interrupted a Carlyle business meeting that was being held at the Ritz-Carlton in Washington, D.C. Attending that conference was former president George H. W. Bush and a brother of Osama bin Laden, a fellow Carlyle investor. Neither claimed to have any advance information about the attacks on the World Trade Center or the Pentagon.

GEORGE W. BUSH AND THE MISSING WMDS

Conspiracy theorists maintain that George W. Bush's invasion of Iraq was not about pursuing a war on terror, but about securing oil fields and obeying the directives of the New World Order.

In March 2004 President George W. Bush prepared a set of slides that he thought would make for a hilarious spoof at the annual dinner of the Radio and Television Correspondents' Association. The photographs showed him in the Oval Office searching for the weapons of mass destruction that had not been found in Iraq. Bush peered under the desk, behind curtains, looking in vain for the WMDs. As the audience roared in laughter, the president read such captions as, "Those weapons of mass destruction have to be somewhere. Nope, not here. Maybe under here?"

Millions of Americans fail to find anything funny about the grim fact that President Bush led the United States and its allies into war on the basis of "faulty intelligence" about a supposed link between al-Qaeda and Saddam Hussein and about Hussein's alleged willingness to use weapons of mass destruction on his Middle East enemies unless the United States ousted him. And there is definitely nothing humorous about thousands of Americans in the military services killed or wounded—or the tens of thousands of Iraqis who have died and the thousands of men, women, and children severely wounded.

Conspiracy theorists state that they knew all along that Bush was absolutely correct when he insisted that Hussein *had* chemical and biological weapons of mass destruction in Iraq—because it was the U.S. government that gave Hussein both the technology and the means to acquire as many WMDs as he thought he needed to maintain his dictatorship. Once Hussein had received those terrible weapons from the U.S., he used them effectively and mercilessly against the Kurds in Iraq's war with Iran. In the Anfal campaign in the late 1980s, as many as 150,000 Kurds were shot or killed in poison-gas attacks. In March 1988 a chemical weapons attack on the town of Halabja killed an estimated 5,000. To repress a Shiite rebellion in southern Iraq in 1991, Saddam's elite troops are thought to have killed at least 150,000. In each instance of these mass murders, the U.S. government chose to look the other way.

There are unlikely to be any theorists who doubt that Saddam Hussein was a ruthless, cruel tyrant, a megalomaniacal dictator who believed that he was the reincarnation of Nebuchadnezzar, the king of ancient Babylon (605–562 B.C.E.), or that he committed horrific crimes against the Kurds, Iranians, Kuwaitis, and his own Iraqi people. But it should not be forgotten that when Hussein was committing his most heinous crimes, the U.S. government was supporting him materially and politically.

Many researchers will not be shaken from their belief that George W. Bush's insistence that the United States go to war with Iraq is all about nothing but oil and that GWB is only following up on the master plan devised by his father, former President George Herbert Walker Bush (GHWB). Here, according to numerous conspiracy theorists, is a timeline of the New World Order of the Bush dynasty and their

links with the Saudi royal family and the bin Laden family in the oil business.

1942: The U.S. Congress seizes the Bush family's banking assets by enforcing the Trading with the Enemy Act. Prescott Bush and his father-in-law George Herbert Walker made their fortunes supplying Nazi Germany and the other Axis nations with money, steel, ships, munitions, and formulas for synthetic gas.

1953: George H. W. Bush (GHWB), a World War II hero and 1948 graduate from Yale in the Skull and Bones fraternity, becomes an owner of Zapata Off-shore Oil, which controls a large fleet of oil tankers off the coast of Kuwait.

1968: George W. Bush (GWB) joins the Texas Air National Guard, exempting him from duty in Vietnam, and becomes friends with Jim Bath, a former air force pilot. In that same year, GWB joins Skull and Bones at Yale.

1976: GHWB is named director of the CIA by President Gerald Ford. During his tenure Bush works to cement relations with the Saudi royal family, and he privatizes some CIA assets.

GWB's friend Jim Bath, recruited for the CIA by GHWB, enters into a trust agreement with Salem bin Laden, older brother to Osama, which enables Bath to act as the bin Laden family's financial representative in the United States. Later, Bath will also represent Khalid bin Mahfouz, a member of Saudi Arabia's preeminent banking family, owners of the National Commercial Bank, the bank favored by the Saudi royal family.

1978: GWB starts an oil company in Texas called Arbusto 78. Jim Bath invests well over $1 million from Salem bin Laden and Khalid bin Mahfouz in Bush's fledgling company.

1987: GWB's oil companies fail, but Harken Energy, a company that has absorbed them, receives a $25 million stock offering underwritten by Bank of Credit and Commerce International (BCCI), a Middle East banking concern.

1989: As the forty-first president of the United States, GHWB authorizes a top-secret directive that orders closer ties with Iraq and provides $1 billion in new aid for Saddam Hussein. GWB assembles a group of partners who purchase the Texas Rangers baseball franchise.

1990: Bahrain grants exclusive offshore drilling rights to Harken Oil. GWB sells two-thirds of his Harken stock at top dollar for $850,000 but fails to make a report to the Securities Exchange Commission until March 1991. One week after Bush's coup on the market, Harken stock plummets 60 percent. Bush pays off his bank loan for the Texas Rangers.

In August, with the help of the leaders of Kuwait, Saddam Hussein is tricked into invading that country by GHWB. Zapata Oil's slant drilling from Kuwait is invading Iraqi territory, and Bush does not want Hussein to control world oil markets. The U.S. ambassador assures Hussein that America is neutral in the battle over oil drilling rights between Iraq and Kuwait. Then, after the invasion, GHWB declares that the world would suffer if all the world's oil reserves fell into the hands of Saddam Hussein.

GWB is asked to serve on the board of directors of Caterair, a company supported by the Carlyle Group, a powerful investment group with strong ties to the bin Laden family.

1991: GHWB is able to declare the Gulf War under a UN mandate, strengthen the UN, and hike up oil prices. GHWB compares Hussein to Hitler but stops short of toppling the dictator's regime. Hussein agrees to destroy all chemical and biological weapons.

John Sununu, former aide to the White House chief of staff, leaves the Bush administration to work for BCCI.

George W. Bush spends three nights in a Houston hotel so he can claim Texas residency.

1992: The first of Harken Energy's wells off Bahrain comes in dry.

GHWB loses the presidential election to Bill Clinton but becomes an adviser to the Carlyle Group and continues his ties to the bin Laden family.

BCCI, which bailed out George W. Bush's oil company failures, is exposed as a massive international criminal enterprise, laundering money for Panamanian dictator Manuel Noriega, Hussein, many terrorist leaders, and the Medellin drug cartel.

1994: George W. Bush is elected governor of Texas.

1998: GWB becomes the first governor in Texas history to be elected to consecutive four-year terms.

1999: GWB executes his ninety-ninth prisoner and announces that he will run for president of the United States.

2000: Democrat Al Gore receives more popular votes than George W. Bush, but the U.S. Supreme Court declares GWB the victor in spite of a public outcry about voting irregularities.

September 11, 2001: The terrible tragedies of the destruction of the World Trade Center in New York City, the attack on the Pentagon, the hijacking of airliners, and the loss of nearly three thousand lives changes America forever.

GHWB is in a business meeting with one of Osama bin Laden's brothers at the Ritz-Carlton Hotel in Washington when the attacks occur.

Soon after the attacks, GWB and Defense Secretary Donald H. Rumsfeld begin focusing on Iraq and planning an invasion to oust Saddam Hussein.

January 29, 2002: GWB makes his famous "Axis of Evil" speech in which he links Iraq, Iran, and North Korea and suggests that the clouds of war might be forming. Some theorists note that in addition to being "evil," the three nations mentioned are, interestingly, also great oil producers.

On January 31, 2002, the head of the UN's International Atomic Energy Agency reports that Iraq has cooperated fully and that there are no weapons of biological and chemical mass destruction.

In March the Bush administration begins to raise publicly the possibility of engaging Iraq. About March 14 Britain's chief foreign policy adviser, David Manning, meets with U.S. national security adviser Condoleezza Rice, who expresses gratitude for the UK's support in bringing about regime change in Iraq and assures him that it will be very carefully done.

In April British prime minister Tony Blair meets with Bush at the ranch near Crawford, Texas, and gives GWB a conditional commitment to support U.S. military action to remove Saddam Hussein.

In late May and early June, U.S. and British forces begin a covert combination of air strikes and raids on Iraq. (The chief Allied air force commander, Lieutenant General Michael Moseley, revealed on June 27, 2005, that between June 2002 and March 2003, before the official declaration of war was made, U.S./British aircraft flew 21,736 sorties over the southern no-fly zone. Moseley reported 600 bombs dropped on 391 targets.)

In July Hans von Sponeck, a UN humanitarian aid coordinator, returns from Iraq and says that all facilities the UN inspectors had previously destroyed are still disabled.

Former UN inspector Scott Ritter conducts a personal media campaign to alert Americans that Iraq does not possess WMDs.

Hans Blix, an expert nuclear weapons analyst, insists there are no WMDs and asks for just one more inspection to prove it.

The *New York Times* reports that the CIA has no evidence that Iraq has any links to al-Qaeda or any weapons of mass destruction.

Was President George W. Bush merely carrying out the directions of the New World Order when he invaded Iraq?

In August U.S. forces quietly move heavy armor into the region and increase air strikes.

2003: GWB authorizes the invasion of Iraq in March. Although the intense bombing raids are called "shock and awe," the numbers of raids actually decreases after the "coalition of the willing" invades the nation.

In June 2005 Michael Smith, the British reporter who broke the now infamous "Downing Street Leaks" that revealed the grand deception of the U.S. plans to use military force against Iraq over a year before declaring war, stated that he had further learned that on June 8, 2002, roughly one hundred U.S./British aircraft had engaged Iraq's major western air defense installation. The number of days per month in which allied warplanes attacked installations in Iraq went from six to nine between July and August 2002, then increased to thirteen from December to February 2003.

On October 15, 2005, Richard Norton-Taylor writing in the *Guardian* (UK), reported that on January 30, 2003, shortly before the invasion of Iraq, Bush told Blair that he intended to go beyond Iraq and target other countries, particularly Saudi Arabia, Iran, and North Korea. According to British international lawyer Philippe Sands, the memo was drawn up after a telephone conversation between the two heads of state by one of the prime minister's foreign policy advisers in Downing Street and delivered to the Foreign Office.

Conspiracy theorists insist that the war was never about weapons of mass destruction or an Iraqi link to al-Qaeda. The war was not even about regime change or removing Saddam Hussein from power. The United States simply feared that the world's largest oil reserves would fall into the control of anti-American, militant Islamists. Vice President Dick Cheney once remarked, "You've got to go where the oil is." Under the cover of fighting terrorism, removing an evil dictator from power, and making Iraq safe for democracy, the U.S. government could be viewed as a global savior, instead of an imperialist conqueror.

Noam Chomsky, professor of linguistics at the Massachusetts Institute of Technology, author of *Hegemony or Survival: America's Quest for Global Dominance,* commented on July 7, 2005: "If the United States can maintain its control over Iraq, with the world's second largest known oil reserves that will enhance significantly its strategic power and influence over its major rivals in the tripolar world that has been taking shape for the past 30 years: U.S.-dominated North America, Europe, and Northeast Asia, linked to South and Southeast Asia economies."

In his June 28, 2005, speech, President George W. Bush tried once again to assure Americans that the invasion of Iraq was the right thing to do as a significant aspect of a "global war against terror." In reality, many theorists assert, the invasion of Iraq may have significantly increased the threat of terror, for many terrorists from all over the Muslim world have found in harassing the occupation forces in Iraq the perfect training ground for schooling in assassinations, kidnappings, car bombings, and a host of other ghastly techniques.

CATHARS

The Cathars were a secret society of Satanists who sought to destroy the medieval church in France.

The Cathars, also known as the Albigensians, were largely centered in Albi, the town in the French province of Languedoc in which an ecclesiastical Roman Catholic Church council condemned the group as heretics in 1208. Most of the Albigensian communities were first sacked, then burned, along with their records and their libraries, and testimony as to exactly what the Cathars believed was wrung out under extreme torture. Contemporary research now indicates that far from being the evil monsters that Pope Innocent III (c. 1161–1216) decreed should be exterminated, the Cathars were devout, chaste, tolerant Christian humanists who loathed the material excesses of the medieval church. Beliefs similar to theirs can be found in the Gnostic gospels, in the Essenic teachings discovered at Qumran, and in the Egyptian mystery schools. The Cathars called themselves the True Church of God, but they had no fixed, codified religious doctrine. Most of the few manuscripts that survived the flames of the Inquisition were written in Provençal, the old language of southern France, the rest in Latin.

The cultural life of the Albigenses far outshone that of any other locality in the Europe of their day. In manners, morals, and learning, objective historians state, the Albigenses deserved greater respect than the orthodox bishops and clergy. It is now generally conceded that the court of Toulouse was the center of a higher level of civilization than existed anywhere else in Europe at that time.

In the opinion of Pope Innocent III and many of the church hierarchy, the Cathars were teaching the rudiments of witchcraft. Although they centered their faith on Christ, they perceived him as pure spirit that had descended from heaven on the instructions of the God of Good to liberate humankind from the world of matter. According to the Cathars, because Christ was pure spirit, he did not die on the cross and the teachings of the church were false. The Cathars rejected all the Catholic sacraments, and they taught that the God of the Old Testament was the lord of matter, the prince of this world—designations that the

The Cathars (Albigensians) were falsely accused of mistreating their enemies, as this anti-Cathar illustration issued by the Catholic Church depicts.

Catholic Church reserved for Satan. Not only was the God revered by the church as the Creator really the devil, but the Cathars also instructed their followers that most of the patriarchs and prophets mentioned in the Old Testament were really demons. They also believed that it was Satan who created the material world after his expulsion from heaven when God the Father, taking pity on his once bright star Lucifer, allowed him seven days to see what he might create. The bodies of Adam and Eve were animated by fallen angels and directed by Satan to beget children who would follow the ways of the serpent.

To counter the lust of the flesh inspired by the devil, the Cathars preached chastity, vegetarianism, and nonviolence. They believed in a progressive doctrine of reincarnation, with the spirits of animals evolving into humans. In their view, it was a dualistic universe, with good and evil having equal strength, and they considered their time in the world as a struggle to resist Satan's power.

In 1208 Innocent III declared the Cathars to be heretical and condemned the citizens of the Albigensian towns of Béziers, Perpignan, Narbonne, Toulouse, and Carcassonne to death as "enemies of the Church." Simon de Montfort (c. 1160–1218), an accomplished military leader, was appointed to conduct a crusade against fellow Christians, cultured men and women of what is today southern France, whom the pope had deemed a greater threat to Christianity than the Islamic warriors who resisted the Crusaders. Although it took him nearly twenty years of warfare against the beleaguered Albigenses, de Montfort managed to exterminate 100,000 men, women, and children before he himself was killed during the second siege of Toulouse.

In 1244 Montségur, the last center of Albigensian resistance, fell, and hundreds of Cathars were burned at the stake. The headquarters of the Inquisition was now established in the once highly cultured city of Toulouse, and the few Cathars who had managed to escape death during the bloody decades of the crusade that had been launched against them were at the mercy of the relentless witch and heretic hunters.

CATTLE MUTILATIONS

Extraterrestrials are mutilating cattle and removing their tongues and sex organs in order to obtain enzymes to enable them to survive on Earth.

According to many forensic pathologists who have examined mutilated cattle with their tongues, eyes, ears, anuses, udders, and genitalia removed without shedding a drop of blood, traditional surgical instruments had not been used. The incisions appeared to have been the result of an advanced laser technology.

A number of veterinarians and forensic scientists who have investigated the mysterious mutilations have described the blood as appearing to have been drained with no resultant vascular collapse. The known technology that could process such an accomplishment does not exist on Earth, and even if it did, it would require large, heavy equipment to manipulate animals often weighing well over 1,500 pounds.

According to most accounts of cattle mutilation, tracks or markings of a conventional nature, such as tire imprints or human or animal tracks, have never been found near a carcass; however, many farmers and ranchers have reported the indentations of a tripod nearby. And there have been numerous reports of UFOs or unmarked black helicopters in the immediate vicinity prior to the incident.

It seems that this same type of animal mutilation occurs worldwide, with the same kinds of animals selected as the victims. Reports from Argentina in July 2002 stated that beginning with the first detected mutilation in April, over two hundred cattle had been found with their blood drained and their tongues, organs, flesh, and skin removed by angular, neatly curved, cuts. Argentine ranchers often named crews from UFOs as the most likely mutilators of their cattle herds.

In the opinion of many skeptical veterinarians, livestock association officials, forensic pathologists, chemists, and a host of county, state, and federal officers and agents, such alleged mutilations are simply the result of Mother Nature fulfilling one of her primary responsibilities, that of keeping the countryside clean. The true perpetrators of the mutilations, according to these investigators, are predators and scavengers.

UFO researchers reject the possibility that predators or scavengers could so neatly incise and remove select organs from their victims. And the obvious problem with blaming predators and scavengers is the fact that all the rest of the animal remains intact.

The most prominent researcher of animal mutilations is Linda Moulton Howe, author of *Glimpses of Other Realities* (1998). Howe has documented hundreds of abnormal, inexplicable deaths of animals, mostly cattle and horses on the open range—all of which exhibited bloodless excisions of eyes, organs, and genitals.

When she began her intensive research in the fall of 1979, Howe suspected that there was some sort of contamination in the environment, and that some government agency was secretly harvesting tissue and fluids for examination. But she could not fathom why any government agency working in secrecy would be so careless as to leave the carcasses of the cattle lying in the fields or ranges, thereby creating alarm and anger among the owners of the animals. Howe's early interviews were with ranchers and law enforcement officers, who reluctantly informed her of sightings of glowing disks in the vicinity of the mutilations. Some witnesses even told her of having seen nonhuman entities at the scene. Her continuing research has convinced her that something very strange is going on, which may, indeed, involve alien experimentation with Earth's animals.

About 1954, some UFO/conspiracy theorists assert, a shadow group within the U.S. government made a deal with extraterrestrial intelligences that permitted mutilation of animals and abductions of humans in exchange for advanced alien technology. Regarding the cattle mutilations, the aliens explained that their own evolutionary ascent had left their digestive systems severely dysfunctional. The extraterrestrials would best be able to sustain themselves on Earth by ingesting an enzyme, or hormonal secretion, most readily obtained from the tongues and throats of cattle.

CENTRAL INTELLIGENCE AGENCY

Name almost any conspiracy and chances are you'll find that the CIA is involved in some way.

Only die-hard supporters of the Bush administration were surprised when the CIA released a number of classified reports revising its prewar intelligence assessments of Iraq's weapons of mass destruction (WMD). Any American who had a pulse clearly recalled the president telling the nation after the horror of September 11, 2001, that "intelligence reports" claimed that Iraq possessed large stockpiles of chemical and biological weapons and was attempting to acquire nuclear capability. CIA intelligence reports formed a main justification for the 2003 invasion of Iraq and validated the need for the United States to make a preemptive strike. According to journalist Bob Woodward's book *Plan of Attack,* CIA director George Tenet told President Bush that finding WMDs in Iraq would be a "slam dunk."

"The CIA has finally admitted that its WMD estimates were wrong," Representative Jane Harman of California, ranking Democrat on the House Intelligence Committee, said in a statement to Reuters. She also called on CIA officials to conduct vigorous intelligence on Iran and North Korea, "where active WMD programs are known to exist."

The Central Intelligence Agency was formed in 1947 and supplanted the OSS, the Office of Strategic Services, which had served the United States during World War II. The Agency was designed to gather intelligence, which meant stealing the Soviet Union's secrets, and to counteract the plots of Soviet spies. It was the time of the Cold War, the iron curtain, brainwashing techniques, insidious Communist propaganda, and a Soviet leader's threat that they would bury us.

The CIA statement of purpose and mission is designed to inspire confidence in the integrity and the righteousness of the Agency: "*Our Vision*—To be the keystone of a U.S. Intelligence community that is pre-eminent in the world, known for both the high quality of our work and the excellence of our people. *Our Mission*—Conducting counterintelligence activities, special activities, and other functions related to foreign intelligence and national security as directed by the presidents. *How We Do Our Work*—Accepting accountability for our actions. Continuous improvement in all that we do."

Conspiracy theorists aren't buying any of the flag-waving, high-minded statements of the CIA's "vision and mission." According to whistle-blowers within the government and elsewhere, ever since the early 1950s the U.S. government has funneled hundreds of billions of dollars through the Agency to fund the nation's wars, black operations, and secret military projects. This is the dark underbelly of the shadow government. The only way these secret programs can obtain the funding they require without creating a national budget shortfall that would rouse public outcry is to engage in illicit operations. A good part of the reason that our government fought in Southeast Asia, defeated the Taliban in Afghanistan, and invaded Panama to oust Manuel Noriega was to protect its substantial interests in the drug trade in these areas, from which the CIA extracts hundreds of billions of dollars a year that is spent on secret programs. The CIA is involved in drug operations in the Golden Triangle and Golden Crescent in Southeast Asia and Asia Minor and in countries south of the U.S. border, such as Panama and Colombia. The rogue portion of the CIA stays just under the radar. It is ostensibly carrying out these programs to protect America's prosperity and strength.

Conspiracy theorists are aware that the U.S. government, through the CIA, has manipulated and controlled many foreign governments for decades. It has often assassinated or disenfranchised foreign leaders of sovereign nations and installed puppet governments friendly to our interests.

The CIA has also conducted secret chemical and biological experiments on the American public for fifty years, injecting individuals, spraying areas of cities, infecting unsuspecting citizens. As many as half a million people have served as guinea pigs for the government without their knowledge. Soldiers, minorities, drug addicts, prison populations, homosexuals, and the entire populations of major U.S. cities have been wantonly used without their consent. Since 1998, conspiracy theorists have accused the secret government of spraying "chemtrails" across U.S. skies, permitting unidentified chemicals to fall on the population.

Perhaps the most consistently named black project of the CIA and rogue elements within the Pentagon, together with members of the Mafia and anti-Castro Cubans, is the assassination of President John F. Kennedy, who was planning to shut down the Vietnam War and declaw the CIA. But conspiracy theorists have a long list of other nefarious projects and dark dealings that they believe rogue elements within the CIA conducted, arranged, helped plan, or at least had prior knowledge of. The evil enterprises most persistently named by conspiracy theorists include the following:

- the assassination of Martin Luther King Jr.;
- the assassination of Robert Kennedy;
- the assassinations of most of the Black Panther leadership;
- the attempted assassination of George Wallace;
- extensive domestic surveillance of U.S. citizens;

The new CIA headquarters in Washington, D.C., was completed in 1991. Not surprisingly, many conspiracists consider the CIA to be at the heart of subversive plots that harm American citizens.

- control of opium shipments in Laos and Vietnam;
- allowing mass murders of thousands in Vietnam and Indonesia;
- igniting revolutions and wars in small nations around the globe;
- Iran-Contra;
- the clandestine arming of Iraq in its war against Iran;
- billions of dollars ripped off from savings and loan banks;
- hundreds of thousands of murders committed by death squads acting as U.S. proxies.

In his *Dirty Truths: Reflections on Politics, Media, Ideology, Conspiracy, Ethnic Life, and Class Power*, Michael Parenti notes that the CIA is by definition conspiratorial. The CIA may use "covert actions and secret plans, many of which are of the most unsavory kind. What are covert actions if not conspiracies?"

Conspiracy theorists remind us that the ultimate goal of the most elite and exclusive secret societies has always been to consolidate all economic and political power into a new global network wholly controlled by the New World Order. In order to accomplish this goal, they need to bring down the United States from its present position of economic and political power. Currently, their agenda is to destroy us from within.

CHALCEDON FOUNDATION

As the father of Christian reconstructionism, Rousas John Rushdoony called upon fundamentalist Christians to take control of American and world governments.

Rousas John Rushdoony (1916–2001) was a formidable scholar. For twenty-five years he read and annotated a book a day, six days a week. Such a voracious reading program by no means occupied his every waking hour. Rushdoony earned a master's degree in English from the University of California at Berkeley, attended the Pacific School of Religion, and entered the Presbyterian ministry, serving a mission to the Chinese in San Francisco and, later, the Western Shoshone tribe in Idaho. He also wrote a number of books on politics, education, law, philosophy, and conservative Christianity. In 1965 Rushdoony moved to the Los Angeles area and founded the Chalcedon Foundation, recalling the Council of Chalcedon in 451, which proclaimed that the political structure of the state must be subservient to God.

In 1973 Rushdoony published his magnum opus, *The Institutes of Biblical Law,* an eight-hundred-page wake-up call to Protestants to begin to apply biblical legal principles to the real world around them. With this massive call to fundamental Christians to take control of American and world governments, Rushdoony became the "father of Christian recon-

structionism." In 1981 he served alongside Beverly and Tim LaHaye, Rev. Donald Wildmon, and Dr. D. James Kennedy in the Coalition for Revival, a group dedicated to "reclaiming" America.

What the Chalcedon Foundation Believes

- The Ten Commandments must be the ordering principle applied to civil government in order for the free market and voluntary social action to flourish. Christians must take control of the U.S. government and impose strict biblical laws.

- The death penalty should be applied to practicing homosexuals.

- There should be no interracial marriages permitted or any kind of enforced integration allowed.

- The Bible recognizes that some people are by nature meant to be slaves. Slavery in the pre–Civil War United States was really benevolent, in spite of contemporary efforts to make whites feel guilty.

- The Holocaust did not happen in the manner that the Jews who "bear false witness" portray the alleged death camps.

CHRISTIAN IDENTITY

Viewing Anglo-Saxon and Nordic people as the true chosen people, Christian Identity's members believe Christ will not return until the world has been cleansed of Satan's children.

Michael Barkun, one of the leading experts on the Christian Identity movement, has labeled as virulently racist and antisemitic its theology that the Anglo-Saxon, Celtic, Scandinavian, and Germanic peoples are the true racial descendants of the tribes of Israel. By anointing essentially white, Nordic people as the chosen ones, Christian Identity denies the Jews their biblical roots and accuses them of being children of Satan. Small, extremely conservative fundamentalist Christian denominations in the United States have embraced this interpretation of history and scripture and extended their loathing of blacks and Jews to include gays and lesbians. As Barkun states it, Christian Identity is the "glue" that binds the racist right together.

Traditionally, the largest segment of the movement has been the Ku Klux Klan, which was reorganized in 1915 by Williams Simmons, a pastor who had been inspired by the racist film *The Birth of a Nation,* which depicted the Klan of the post–Civil War era as heroic defenders of white civilization. By the early 1940s and World War II, the Klan had begun to fade into obscurity, but the movement was born again in reaction to federally enforced racial integration in the South.

Larry Brown, a professor at the University of Missouri, has studied the Christian Identity movement in an effort to determine how its members could read the sacred Hebrew and Christian texts in a manner that supports racism and hate crimes. Brown found the movement prevalent in rural, isolated areas, such as the Appalachian and Ozark Mountains and parts of Iowa and Oregon. In Brown's opinion, Christian Identity appeals to individuals who feel marginalized by modern society and who are trying to find a personal connection to the cosmos. As these individuals perceive the many different ethnic groups coming to the United States, bringing with them multiculturalism and different ways of thinking, they see only threats to their own lifestyle and beliefs. These people need to explain a rapidly changing society by sustaining the hope that they are the ones who will survive a massive destruction of the old world. "It's the story of power that's given to people who otherwise are just people," Brown has said.

The psychologist Mark Stern observes that those in the Christian Identity movement believe that they are the true representatives of how Christianity should have been from the beginning. Stern comments that the many groups that are part of the movement reject the label of "cult," preferring to call themselves "holiness groups."

Among current groups who follow the principles of Christian Identity are the American Nazi Party, Aryan Nations, Church of Jesus Christ Christian, National Association for the Advancement of White People, Scriptures for America, and White Separatist Banner. Essentially apocalyptic groups, most of their leaders see Armageddon, the final battle between good and evil, Jesus and Satan, right around the corner. Although Christian Identity groups insist that they do not promote violence of any kind, many of their leaders flatly state that Christ cannot return until the world has been cleansed of all satanic influences, including Jews, homosexuals, and those who mix races.

CHURCH OF SATAN

Anton Szandor LaVey brought in the dawn of the Age of Satan with the creation of the First Church of Satan in San Francisco, April 30, 1966.

On April 30, 1966 (Walpurgisnacht, a night legendarily favored by the disciples of darkness), Anton Szandor LaVey (1930–1997) shaved his head, donned black clerical clothing, complete with white collar, and proclaimed himself Satan's high priest. This was the dawn of the Age of Satan, LaVey boldly announced. It was the morning of magic and undefiled wisdom, and he thereby established the First Church of Satan in San Francisco.

There was nothing new about a belief in magical powers or in worshipping Satan. What was new was LaVey's use of the term *church* as part of his organization's title. In addition to ceremonies and rituals devoted to the Prince of Darkness, there were weddings, funerals, and children baptized in the name of Satan.

When LaVey, high priest of the Satanic Church of America, united the socialite Judith Case and the freelance writer John Raymond in the bonds of matrimony, he performed the rites over the naked body of a woman who served as the living altar. Later, when LaVey explained the ritual significance of the living altar to reporters, he remarked that an altar shouldn't be a cold, unyielding slab of sterile stone or wood. It should be a symbol of unrestrained lust and indulgence.

It was quite a wedding for the first public marriage ceremony ever held in the United States by a satanic cult. The bride shunned the traditional white gown to appear in a bright red dress. The groom wore a black turtleneck sweater and complementary coat. The high priest stole the show, however, in a black cape lined with scarlet silk and a close-fitting blood-red hood from which two white horns protruded.

In 1969 LaVey published *The Satanic Bible,* affirming the teachings of the Church of Satan and proclaiming Satanism as being "dedicated to the dark, hidden force in nature responsible for the workings of earthly affairs for which science and religion had no explanation." He explained that he was moved to establish the Church of Satan when he saw the need for a church that would "recapture man's body and carnal desires as objects of celebration." The First Church of Satan does not recognize the existence of Satan as an actual being, but as a symbol representing materialism. The church emphasizes that the figure of Satan stands for an inner attitude and is never to be regarded as an object onto which human powers are projected in order to worship what is only human in an externalized form.

The Satanic Bible is divided into four sections, or books, each corresponding to one of the four hermetic elements: fire, air, earth, and water. The first section, the "Book of Satan," advises the reader that the "ponderous rule books of hypocrisy are no longer needed" and

that it is time to relearn the Law of the Jungle. The second section, the "Book of Lucifer," explains how the Roman god Lucifer, the light bearer, the spirit of enlightenment, was made synonymous with evil through Christian teachings. The "Book of Belial" is a basic text on ritual and ceremonial magic expressed in Satanist terms. The fourth section, the "Book of Leviathan," stresses the importance of the spoken word in successful magic.

> The First Church of Satan does not recognize the existence of Satan as an actual being, but as a symbol representing materialism.

Satanist doctrine celebrates man the animal. It exalts sexual lust above spiritual love, claiming that the latter is but a sham. Satanism declares that violence must be met with violence and that to love one's neighbor is a utopian unreality. Satanists condemn prayer and confession as vain, futile gestures, believing that the way to achieve what one wants is through magic and aggressive effort—and that the best method of ridding oneself of guilt is not to assume it in the first place. If Satanists make a mistake, they recognize sincerely that to err is human; and instead of involving themselves in efforts to cleanse themselves, they examine the situation in order to determine exactly what went wrong and how to prevent its happening again. They believe that the way to greater levels of personal perfection and an exploration of the deeper mysteries of life is through study and the performance of rituals emphasizing the sensual nature of humankind and directing this power toward the release of psychic or emotional energy.

Because Christian churches, especially the Roman Catholic, are considered anathema to the Prince of Darkness, Satanists parody Christian rituals and symbols in their ceremonies. For example, the cross is used, but it is displayed with the long beam pointing downward. Satanists may on occasion use the pentagram or five-pointed star, traditionally favored by the practitioners of Wicca or witchcraft, but as with the cross, it is inverted, resting upon a single point, rather than two. Satanists insist that their parodying and inversion of other religions' rites and symbols are not done strictly for purposes of blasphemy; rather, such use appropriates the power inherent in the rite or symbol and inverts it for Satan's purposes.

The Satanic Bible lists nine criteria that define Satanism for a new age. Satan represents:

1. indulgence, instead of abstinence;

2. vital existence, instead of spiritual pipe dreams;

3. undefiled wisdom, instead of hypocritical self-deceit;

4. kindness to those who deserve it, instead of love wasted on ingrates;

5. vengeance, instead of turning the other cheek;

6. responsibility to the responsible, instead of concern for psychic vampires;

7. man as just another animal more often worse than those that walk on all fours, who because of his divine spiritual and intellectual development, has become the most vicious animal of all;

8. all of the so-called sins, as they lead to physical, mental, or emotional gratification;

9. the best friend the Church has ever had, as he has kept it in business all these years.

LaVey became immediately popular in the media, often allowing reporters to attend certain rituals that he conducted over the living altar of a woman's naked body in his church, the famous "Black House," said originally to have been a brothel. In a sudden rush came attention from movie stars, work as a technical adviser on such motion pictures as *Rosemary's Baby*—and the enmity of millions of devout Christians, who saw in LaVey a kind of antichrist. After a few years, the death threats and harassment had become oppressive, and LaVey went underground, ceased all public ceremonies, and recast his church as a secret society.

In 1991 LaVey lost ownership of the "Black House" when a judge ordered him to sell it, along with such mementos as a shrunken head and a stuffed wolf, and split the proceeds with his estranged wife, Diane Hagerty.

LaVey died on October 30, the day before Halloween, 1997, and soon after his death, what remained of his estate became the object of a legal struggle between his oldest daughter, Karla, and Blanche Barton, his long-time consort and the mother of his son Xerxes. (LaVey's younger daughter, Zeena, renounced the Church of Satan in 1990 and became a priest in the Temple of Set.) The First Church of Satan continues today under the direction of High Priestess Blanche Barton and the Magister (High Priest) Peter H. Gilmore.

Recently, when Magister Gilmore was asked about the revelation of New Testament scholars that the long-feared number of the Beast of Revelation might be 616, rather than 666, he replied that Satanists will always use something that frightens Christians. It matters not if the number is 616 or 666, the Satanist will use whatever is most detested.

CHURCH OF THE LAMB OF GOD

Murderous Mormon sects have conducted a bloody, secret religious war, wreaking vengeance on individuals judged wayward in the eyes of God.

The Mormon historian Tom Green believes that over twenty killings of members of polygamous sects have been motivated by religious beliefs and by the desire to gain rival prophets' financial assets, their congregations, and their multiple wives. And it may be that the killings noticed by the police and the public are only some of the deaths. At least a dozen other disappearances of sect members have gone unreported since 1981.

The web of murders centers on the now-deceased Ervil LeBaron, an excommunicated polygamist who declared himself to be God's prophet on Earth and assumed the title of the "One Mighty and Strong." In a book of "New Covenants" that he wrote while he was in prison, LeBaron drew up a blueprint of death for "traitors"—members of feuding sects in Utah, Arizona, Texas, California, and Mexico.

Ervil was so ruthless that he had his pregnant daughter killed for disagreeing with him, and he ordered his brother Joel shot down to clear the path for his own bid to become God on Earth. In October 1987 the man accused of Joel's execution, Daniel Ben Jordan, was himself gunned down. He had committed the fatal error of straying away from the protection of nine of his wives and twenty-one of his children while deer hunting. Utah detective lieutenant Paul Forbes revealed that Jordan's body was found in the southern part of the state. Jordan had been shot in the head and chest with a 9-mm handgun. Someone was waiting for him when he left his hunting camp.

The murder of Jordan, self-styled prophet apostle of the Church of the Lamb of God, was only one in a string of mysterious slayings that remain wrapped in a cloak of secrecy.

The Mormons practiced polygamy until the late 1800s. At the time when Utah was trying to become a state, the church decided to discontinue the practice of multiple wives. However, a number of groups broke off from the original Church of Jesus Christ of Latter-day Saints and established their own versions of Mormonism. Each sect was led by an individual who claimed to have the keys of authority. Many of the groups left Utah and went to Mexico, Arizona, or California.

One such group of fundamentalists settled in Chihuahua, Mexico, and titled themselves "Colonia Juárez." Ervil LeBaron was reared in this colony of polygamists, the son of a farmer excommunicated from the mainstream faith in 1924 because of his bizarre beliefs and teachings. Ervil and his six brothers were, in turn, excommunicated in 1944.

Joel LeBaron, upon his father's death, announced that he possessed the Key of Power, and he founded the Church of the Firstborn of the Fullness of Time. Joel declared himself God's prophet and demanded that all of his wishes be carried out and obeyed without question.

Ervil wasn't so certain that Joel was correct, and since Ervil was in the enviable position of writing most of the sect's literature, he could set down the facts as he perceived them. He decided that Adam was God and that Joseph Smith, the founder of Mormonism, was the Holy Ghost. Ervil also declared that the doctrine of blood atonement demanded that all sinners be put to death. Furthermore, he envisioned that the One Mighty and Strong had supremacy over all Mormons.

Detective Forbes said that Ervil sent out notes announcing that he was the final authority and that all group members must pay tithes to him. In 1970 Joel had suffered enough of such insubordination. He assessed Ervil as unstable and stripped him of his leadership in the sect. Undaunted, Ervil quickly founded the Church of the Lamb of God and announced that he was the genuine One Mighty and Strong. In short order he took thirteen wives and embarked on his crusade of blood.

Police authorities have established that from this point onward in the secret war, gory events occurred very rapidly:

August 1972: Joel LeBaron is murdered in Mexico by order of his brother.

December 1974: A squad of men and women on a commando-style raid firebomb the Mexican village of Los Molinos, a Mormon community. Two are killed, fifteen others wounded. Ervil LeBaron is said to have led the attack.

January 1975: Ervil decides that Naomi Zarate, the wife of one of his followers, is disobedient. Shortly thereafter she disappears and is never seen again.

April 1975: Robert Simons of Grantsville, Utah, disputes Ervil's claim and declares himself the One Mighty and Strong. Simons vanishes and is presumed to have been executed.

June 1975: Dean Vest, one of Ervil's military chieftains, becomes sickened by the executions and murders and prepares to defect. He is murdered in his sleep.

March 1976: Ervil is arrested in Mexico for complicity in Joel's death. His twelve-year sentence is abruptly reversed after eight months, and he is released. While in prison, however, he converts new followers, including drug smuggler Leo Peter Evoniuk.

April 1977: Ervil announces to his followers that his daughter Rebecca has rebelled against him. He orders her strangled and buried in a hole in the mountains.

May 1977: Dr. Rulon Allred, leader of the largest polygamist sect in Utah and Ervil's principal rival for the title of God's Prophet, is murdered in Murray, Utah. LeBaron boldly dispatches a hit team to Allred's funeral, but the gunmen withdraw when they spot heavy police protection. They flee to Texas to escape Ervil's wrath for their failed mission.

May 1979: Ervil is arrested by Mexican police, extradited to Utah, and tried and convicted for the murder of Allred and for a machine-gun attack on his brother Verlan LeBaron.

August 1981: Ervil LeBaron is found dead in his cell at Utah State Prison. The official report lists the cause of his death as a heart attack.

August 1981: Verlan LeBaron is killed in a mysterious car crash in Mexico.

July 1984: Brenda Lafferty and her baby daughter, Erica, are found dead, victims of a ritual killing at their home in American Fork, Utah. Their throats are found to be so deeply slashed that their heads were almost severed.

May 1987: Leo Peter Evoniuk, fifty-two, presiding patriarch of the Millennial Church of Jesus Christ, vanishes while making a business call near Watsonville, California.

October 1987: Daniel Ben Jordan, fifty-three, prophet apostle of the Church of the Lamb of God, is ambushed while deer hunting in southern Utah.

Lieutenant Forbes clarified that the individuals conducting the bloody secret war should be regarded like clan chieftains, rather than like most of the polygamous Mormons, generally law-abiding and low-key people who do not wish to make waves of any kind.

Law enforcement officers have estimated that in the southwestern states and Mexico, there are about are thirty thousand people in ten groups like Ervil LeBaron's. These groups engage in power struggles to take over one another's financial bases. If they kill rival prophets, then a lot of the deceased's followers are likely to come to them. Some of the groups are quite wealthy. Some, like the remains of Ervil's, are destitute. But they are all very secretive, very close.

CLINTON BODY COUNT

Some conspiracy theorists say that as many as a hundred unfortunate individuals paid a tragic price for getting on the wrong side of the Clinton administration.

Some conspiracy theorists and Clinton watchers have set the body count of those who somehow irritated the administration of William Jefferson Clinton and paid the ultimate price from perhaps eighty-five to more than a hundred. As with all of the body counts or death lists that we include in this encyclopedia of conspiracies and secret societies, we add our disclaimer that many of the individuals that we find on such lists may have been elderly, suffered from long-term illnesses, were killed in the line of duty, met their demise in accidents totally devoid of nefarious circumstances, or committed suicide of their own free, albeit troubled, will. Conspiracy researchers remind us that the CIA and other secret government agencies have developed means of making murders appear to be deaths due to natural causes or accident. Some of these methods are designed to be able to avoid detection in autopsies and postmortem examinations. Various insidious techniques involve the injection of cancer cells, heart attack inducements, and absorption of deadly, untraceable poison. There are some deaths on these lists that do seem quite suspicious, and that is why we include them for your own assessment.

Among those associates, friends, or foes of Bill Clinton who met what many investigators believe to have been a "convenient" or "highly coincidental" death are the following:

Susan Coleman, February 15, 1977: Susan Coleman allegedly had an affair with Clinton when he was a law professor in Arkansas. Her death from a gunshot wound to the back of the head was ruled a suicide. No autopsy was performed, and persistent rumors maintain that Coleman was nearly eight months pregnant with Clinton's child.

Paul Tully, September 24, 1992: Tully, Democratic National Committee political director, was found dead in a hotel room in Little Rock, Arkansas, of unknown causes.

Paula Gober, December 9, 1992: Gober was Clinton's speech interpreter for the deaf,

and she traveled extensively with him until her death. She was killed in a one-car accident with no known witnesses.

John Wilson, May 18, 1993: Former Washington, D.C., council member John Wilson claimed to have important information on the Whitewater scandal. He was found dead from suicide by hanging.

Paul Wilcher, June 22, 1993: At the time of his death, Wilcher, an attorney, was investigating drug smuggling and gunrunning out of Arkansas and the Bureau of Alcohol, Tobacco, and Firearms assault on the Branch Davidians at Waco, Texas. Wilcher was found dead on a toilet seat in his Washington, D.C., apartment.

Vincent Foster, July 21, 1993: Foster, White House counsel and Hillary Clinton's longtime friend, was found dead in a public park of a supposed suicide by gunshot.

Jon Parnell Walker, August 15, 1993: A Whitewater investigator for Resolution Trust Corporation, Walker mysteriously fell to his death from an apartment balcony.

Jerry Luther Parks, September 26, 1993: Parks, head of Clinton's gubernatorial security team in Little Rock, was shot three times in his car at a deserted intersection.

Ed Willey, November 1993: A Clinton fund raiser, Ed Willey was the husband of Kathleen Willey, who claimed to have been groped by Clinton in the Oval Office. Willey was found dead of a gunshot wound to the head in the woods near his Virginia home. His death was ruled a suicide.

Gandy Baugh, January 8, 1994: Baugh represented Clinton's pal Dan Lasater, a convicted drug distributor, in a case concerning financial misconduct. Baugh allegedly committed suicide.

Herschel Friday, March 1, 1994: Attorney and Clinton fund-raiser Herschel Friday, seventy-three, died when he was landing his plane on a poorly lighted airfield. According to various accounts, the plane suddenly crashed and exploded.

Kathy Ferguson, May 1994: The ex-wife of Arkansas state trooper Danny Ferguson, who is said to have escorted Paula Corbin Jones to the hotel room for her alleged sexual harassment by then-governor Clinton, Kathy Ferguson died of an alleged gunshot suicide in her living room.

Bill Shelton, June 1994: Bill Shelton, an Arkansas police officer and fiancé of Kathy Ferguson, was found dead of a gunshot wound at Kathy's gravesite. His death was ruled a suicide, supposedly brought on by grief over his fiancée's taking her own life. Fellow officers reported that Shelton was extremely dissatisfied over the manner in which Kathy's death was investigated.

Barbara Wise, January 29, 1996: Barbara Wise, a Commerce Department staff member, was found dead, partially nude, in her locked office at the Department of Commerce.

Ron Brown, April 3, 1996: Ron Brown, Clinton's secretary of commerce and former Democratic National Committee chairman, died with thirty-four other people in an airplane crash in the Croatian mountains. A pathologist reported finding a hole resembling a bullet wound in the top of Brown's skull.

Charles Meissner, April 3, 1996: Assistant Secretary of Commerce for International Economic Policy Meissner died in the same plane crash as Ron Brown.

Mary Mahoney, July 1997: A former White House intern working as an assistant manager at a Georgetown Starbucks, Mahoney was shot five times with bullets from two different guns. Her two co-workers were taken to a back room and killed.

Sandy Hume, February 22, 1998: Sandy Hume, twenty-eight, son of the well-known journalist Brit Hume, was found dead in his Arlington, Virginia, apartment, an apparent suicide.

President Bill Clinton was a popular American leader, but was there a darker side to the president as some conspiracists believe?

He had just joined the staff of Fox TV news and had been a reporter for *The Hill* magazine.

James McDougal, March 8, 1998: President Clinton's convicted Whitewater partner died of an apparent heart attack while in solitary confinement, serving a three-year sentence for bank fraud.

Christine M. Mirzayan, August 1, 1998: A Clinton intern who was about to go public with her story of sexual harassment at 1600 Pennsylvania Avenue, Christine M. Mirzayan was shot dead as she entered a Georgetown Starbucks.

Eric Fox, March 1999: Fox, who had served on Air Force One, was discovered shot in the head after his car swerved off the road. His death was ruled an apparent suicide.

And one who got away.

Gary Johnson, June 26, 1992: An attorney who lived next door to Clinton paramour Gennifer Flowers, Gary Johnson had security videotapes of Clinton entering and leaving Flowers's apartment. Johnson was beaten and the incriminating tapes were taken from his apartment. Left for dead from a beating so severe that his spleen had to be removed, Johnson survived.

COINTELPRO: THE FBI'S COVERT WAR AGAINST AMERICA

In our innocence, we believed the FBI always stood for truth, justice, and the American way. But then Director J. Edgar Hoover gave his agents carte blanche to go after certain radical movements.

To counter the growing radical movements of the 1950s, 1960s, and 1970s, the FBI and the police pushed back the borders of their legally authorized powers in what they believed were justified violations of constitutionally guaranteed individual freedoms. FBI director J. Edgar Hoover ordered his field agents to "expose, disrupt, misdirect, discredit and otherwise neutralize" specific target groups. Among the groups deemed disruptive to the fabric of American society were the American Indian Movement, the Communist Party, the Socialist Workers Party, black nationalist groups, Students for a Democratic Society, and a sweeping range of antiwar, antiracist, environmentalist, feminist, and lesbian and gay groups. Martin Luther King Jr. came under special attack, as did any organization that sought social or racial justice, such as the NAACP, National Lawyers Guild, American Friends Service Committee, and many others.

Covert operations were employed in the extreme. The assigned purpose of the field agents were not merely to spy on organization leaders and to report any "un-American activi-

ties," but to discredit them personally and attempt to smear their reputations.

For those individuals who have always regarded the FBI as following the highest of standards and steadfastly defending truth, justice, and the American way, it will come as a deep disappointment to learn that FBI agents acting on Hoover's orders carried out such foul and illegal activities as the following:

· regularly planted false and libelous stories about radical leaders in the media;

· forged signatures on personal correspondence and public documents;

· published and distributed bogus leaflets in the names of their target groups;

· made anonymous telephone calls and inflammatory calls to important individuals claiming to be the leaders of the targeted groups seeking social or racial justice;

· advertised meetings of various groups, publishing incorrect dates and times;

· posing as members of radical or civil rights groups, set up phony cells in order to get information on the kinds of individuals attracted to such organizations;

· made false arrests in order to establish criminal records for the leaders and members of the targeted groups;

· gave perjured testimony and provided fabricated evidence in courts, resulting in wrongful convictions.

· In order to frighten some targeted groups —especially black, Puerto Rican, and Native American activists—FBI agents and police officers threatened physical violence, conducted break-ins and destruction of groups' headquarters, and administered vicious beatings.

Early in 1971 the Citizens Committee to Investigate the FBI accomplished the removal of secret files from an FBI office in Media, Pennsylvania, and released them to the press. The FBI's domestic counterintelligence program

(COINTELPRO) was exposed. In that same year, the Pentagon Papers, the top-secret government files on the Vietnam War, were brought into the light of public scrutiny. A number of FBI agents began to resign from the bureau and reveal additional distasteful details of COINTELPRO. High-ranking government officials were made uncomfortably aware that the FBI had employed "dirty tricks" on American citizens solely because they espoused antiwar views or conducted marches and sit-ins for social and racial justice. The organized attacks on individuals' rights, reputations, and lives were denounced as acts of official terrorism.

Senate and House committees conducted rigorous and extensive inquiries into the methods of government intelligence-gathering and covert activities. These hearings revealed far-reaching illegal programs involving the FBI, CIA, U.S. Army Intelligence, the White House, the attorney general, and state and local law enforcement against groups of citizens who opposed domestic and foreign policies.

Although the exposure of COINTELPRO brought about a period of temporary reform of government abuses in the 1970s, government secrecy has been restored. The Freedom of Information Act that was so useful in uncovering such programs as COINTELPRO was basically eliminated through administrative, judicial, and legislative actions taken under the Reagan administration. Civil rights attorneys warn that many of the covert illegal activities conducted under COINTELPRO were legalized by Executive Order 12333 on December 4, 1981. And, chillingly, that which was legalized is probably still being performed.

CONTRAILS
AND CHEMTRAILS

We've all grown used to seeing those white vapor trails left in the sky by jet aircraft. We've *been told that those wispy lines are nothing but the natural by-product of exhaust fumes. Lately, though, conspiracists insist that a black-ops agency working with the New World Order is systematically releasing a chemical spray that spawns disease and mind control upon the U.S. population.*

Contrails are the thin, smoky-looking white streams left in the wake of aircraft flying at high altitudes. Contrails (short for "condensation trails"), also known as vapor trails, result from natural chemical and physical reactions in the wake of an aircraft. They vary greatly in length and duration, depending on atmospheric conditions at the flight altitude. Contrails can be miles long and last for many minutes or they can vanish almost immediately a short distance behind the airplane. The key to their formation and behavior is that they are made largely of ice crystals.

Surprisingly, given the potential dangers, as of today the U.S. Environmental Protection Agency reports having no regulations addressing contrails and their atmospheric effects.

The basic two types of engines used in planes are piston engines, powered by petro/gasoline, and jet engines, normally fueled by paraffin/kerosene. Both jet and piston engines draw air from the surrounding atmosphere to combine with the fuel in order to create the combustion that powers them. Air contains water vapor in some relative concentration, varying from dry to saturated, at which point rain, snow, or sleet may result. Taking in the moisture with the air, an airplane's engine heats the vapor, which then emerges as superheated steam in the exhaust. There will be more steam or less, depending on the amount of moisture in the air to begin with and on the fuel-to-air ratio. Typically, for every gallon of fuel burned, one gallon of steam is produced.

Aircraft exhaust also contains countless microscopic solid particles produced during combustion. When the surrounding air is cold enough, the ejected steam almost instantly condenses on these particles and freezes. These ice-coated particles are what constitutes a contrail. The air must be very cold for this to happen, which is why contrails generally form only at fairly high altitudes. In fact, contrails were rarely observed until the end of World War I, when aircraft first began to reach altitudes of thirty thousand feet or more.

Records dating from the 1940s in World War II state that contrails gave away the position of U.S. bombers to the German fighter pilots hunting them, and many pilots and planes were lost as a result. Hundreds, if not thousands, of cold war pilots complained that contrails pinpointed their exact location and made them obvious targets.

This vulnerability provides an obvious reason for military involvement in experiments regarding contrails and the like: what causes them, what their properties are, and how to make them invisible. This military interest is most likely the springboard for the many conspiracy theories about secret government projects involving contrails, chemtrails, HAARP, weather manipulation and control, bio warfare, and a whole gamut of other classified experiments and operations.

According to some scientists, the environmental effects of flying aircraft had not been accurately measured from the time the Wright brothers took flight in 1903 until September 11, 2001. In the aftermath of the 9/11 attacks, commercial flights were grounded for three days. The Climate Impact Experiment sponsored by NASA was able to gauge the impact that flying has on the environment. The results definitively show that the air we breathe is changed by the exhaust from aircraft.

Dr. Cheryl E. Merritt, a researcher and professor at Yale University, is one of many scientists who take note of the wonders of flight yet also warn of the growing harmful consequences of atmospheric pollution from aviation. Dr. Merritt is especially concerned that very-high-altitude supersonic transport planes could engender stratospheric air pollution with "consequent changes in climate." Besides the water vapor that forms contrails, jet exhaust contains carbon dioxide, oxides of nitrogen, and particulate matter including substances known as aerosols. Merritt notes that "it is speculative just how harmful these pollutants can be."

Surprisingly, given the potential dangers, as of today the U.S. Environmental Protection Agency reports having no regulations addressing contrails and their atmospheric effects. Some observers believe that this lack of regulation is itself part of a conspiracy—a conspiracy centering less on contrails than on their sinister cousins, chemtrails.

As opposed to contrails, which are the relatively natural product of high-altitude airplane-engine combustion, chemtrails consist of man-made chemicals deliberately sprayed from aircraft. There are legitimate reasons to dispense chemical in this manner: *crop dusting* over farm fields to destroy weeds or insects harmful to crops; *cloud seeding* to bring rain to areas of drought; *firefighting* by dumping fire extinguishing chemicals on forest fires or other large blazes; and the release of *smoke trails* in air shows or to create advertising messages. The chemtrails that have caused great concern are none of these, but rather the artificial clouds that conspiracists are convinced are raining down influenza and other diseases on an unsuspecting populace.

Chemtrails have become the focus of one of the most popular of the conspiracy theories of late, thanks to frequent discussions over the airwaves by popular radio talk show hosts such as Art Bell, George Noory, and Ian Punnet on *Coast to Coast* and Jeff Rense on the *Jeff Rense Program*. With worldwide audiences numbering in the millions, these programs broadcast the concerns of scientists and laypersons who call in to report the accumulating data regarding chemtrails. Many theorists believe that a secret government project is in effect to alter the thought processes of people and render them powerless to resist New World Order dictates. Others believe that our own government is engaged in a massive depopulation effort so calculatedly subtle and dangerous that potentially millions will die. The methodical and deliberate poisoning of the air we breathe is being manipulated by the spraying of chemicals from aircraft.

Within the last few years the fear of chemtrails has become so intense that thousands of websites devoted to the topic have appeared on the Internet. Many call for action to stop this effort, which they believe to be a methodical program of the New World Order to sicken and kill off the weak and indigent, then manipulate the healthier citizens remaining.

To the average person, contrails and chemtrails in the sky may look to be of the same origin, but there are key differences. Chemtrails are usually thicker, extend farther across the sky, and are arranged in patterns of X's, tic-tac-toe grids, and cross-hatched and parallel lines. Rather than dissipating in a few minutes, as contrails generally do, chemtrails expand and drip "feathers" and "mare's tails." In about half an hour they spread into wispy formations that come together to form a thin white veil or a pseudocirrus-type cloud that can persist for several hours. It is this false cloud that will rain down various highly contagious diseases and/or mind-control hallucinogens.

Conspiracists began reporting suspicious chemtrail or aerosol spraying in the late 1970s. In the late 1990s chemtrail spraying

We see contrails in the sky all the time, sometimes many of them criss-crossing each other. Might those harmless-looking whisps contain something sinister? And what about chemtrails?

appeared to increase, and sightings of unmarked white planes diffusing chemicals into strange cloud formations soared worldwide.

Skeptics endeavor to squelch paranoia by pointing out that such a massive program of chemtrail spraying as conspiracists suggest would require an extensive cover-up involving thousands of aviation employees and military personnel. Conspiracy theorists see no problem in black-ops or New World Order agents achieving such a cover-up of the participants in spraying chemicals on a populace that has already been deceived about the truth on innumerable prior secret government operations.

Skeptics also dismiss such a plot by pointing out how ineffective it would be to release a cloud of spray above 30,000 feet and leave it to the vagaries of high-altitude winds. Conspiracy buffs say that such an objection might have value if the chemtrails were targeted for a specific area. As it is, however, the sinister agencies simply wish to disperse the chemicals as widely as possible.

As reports of chemtrails continued to raise the ire of citizens across the nation into the twenty-first century, an increasing number of serious-minded individuals took offense at establishment scientists' arch dismissal that only paranoid conspiracy theorists were experiencing the unidentified fallout. Some claimed they became seriously ill as a result of being drenched by the chemicals that were released into the skies above them. The mysterious Morgellons disease is often mentioned as a result of exposure to chemtrails.

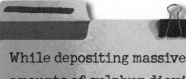

While depositing massive amounts of sulphur dioxide into the atmosphere might filter out sunlight and contribute to the cooling of patches of earth, the chemical also results in acid rain....

Some conspiracists are adamant in their claims that HAARP, a secret weapon system that taps into the limitless plenum of energy surrounding Earth, uses chemtrails as frequency reflectors from its ground and space bases so that it might direct its binary weapons system against whatever segment of the human population is designated as a target.

In 2009, some scientists admitted that certain vapor trails from airplanes had been doused with chemicals to create artificial clouds that could block out the sun's rays, thereby helping to decrease the effects of global warming. Climate scientist Ken Caldeira of the Carnegie Institution in Stanford, California, recommended that jumbo jets deposit clouds of tiny particles of sulphur dioxide to reflect away sunlight from the earth. Nobel Prize winner Paul Crutzen suggested that 747s should release huge quantities of sulfur particles into the stratosphere to cool down the atmosphere. Scientist Tom Flannery also predicted the eventual need for humanity to disperse large amounts of sulphur into the stratosphere to shield Earth from the sun. The U.S. Department of Energy's Savannah River National Laboratory in Aiken, South Carolina, began shooting huge amounts of porous-walled glass microspheres into the stratosphere.

While depositing massive amounts of sulphur dioxide into the atmosphere might filter out sunlight and contribute to the cooling of patches of earth, the chemical also results in acid rain and the acidification of lakes, streams, forests, and croplands. Acid rain also causes the erosion and decay of buildings, bridges, painted surfaces, statues, and sculptures. Environmental Protection Act scientists also warned that exposure to sulphur raining down on humans could bring about such deleterious health conditions as neurological and behavioral changes, disturbance of blood circulation, heart damage, stomach and gastrointestinal disorders, damage to liver and kidney functions, reproductive failures, and damage to the immune system.

Even those scientists who in the beginning were enthusiastic about their experiments with chemtrails have begun to express concern that acid rain and increased weather pattern disruptions could also trigger droughts, famines, and ozone depletion, thereby defeating the purpose of dispersing chemtrails. Secretive attempts to bioengineer the natural cycles of the planet were beginning to be reassessed as outlandish and dangerous.

On November 29, 2011, a 300-member group in Mohave Country, Arizona, calling itself the "Chemtrail Geo-Engineering Lawsuit," began actively testing individuals who have suffered heavy metal toxicity in their blood and hair follicles. The group claims that a federal geo-engineering program has been using jet planes to spray a solution of barium, aluminum strontium, and other elements into the skies above the United States in an effort to reflect sunlight and cool the planet.

Al DiCicco, of Golden Valley, Arizona, who spearheaded the group, said that they found a woman in Bullhead City who showed levels of barium in her blood that were 28 times normal levels. DiCicco accused the federal and state governments and environmental agencies of being unwilling to properly investigate the geo-engineering projects being conducted. DiCicco's group plans to seek a law firm that will represent their claims in a class-action lawsuit.

DiCicco said that he was in contact with people all over the world who were concerned about the reality of geo-engineering and the harm being done to humans, animals, plants, and food production. DiCicco also stated that the group had established contact with film-maker Michael J. Murphy, whose film *What in the World Are They Spraying?* examines the phenomenon of chemtrails.

WILLIAM COOPER

Milton William Cooper: UFO expert? Conspiracy theorist? Navy Intelligence operative? Controversial radio personality? Militia leader? Survivalist? Patriot? Fanatic? The most dangerous man in America?

William "Bill" Cooper (1943–2001) was a leading conspiracy advocate—a patriot, by his own definition—who was outspoken about the Constitution, the JFK assassination, the Trilateral Commission, the Bilderberg Group, the Illuminati, the New World Order, UFOs, and the One World Government.

Cooper's intense research into information he "stumbled on," along with his top-secret clearances in the military, fueled what he came to believe was his purpose. For over ten years he lectured and taught in every state in the nation, and worldwide, all the while creat-

ing as many ways and means as possible to keep his discoveries in the public eye. His drive to get the facts out, to "disseminate the truth" as he saw it, became his life mission.

Along the way, Cooper achieved international recognition as a radio personality with *The Hour of the Time* (or *HOTT),* a WBCQ worldwide shortwave radio program he founded and maintained for one hour Monday through Thursday nights. He often announced that the high risks he took in speaking out would be lessened by going public with as great an audience as possible. That way, he stated, if he ended up being "taken out permanently," folks would have to suspect that he'd been a deliberate target to be silenced. The more people who heard his radio broadcasts, watched his video productions, listened to his tapes and lectures, or read any or all of his many publications, including newspapers, newsletters, and books, the better—even if it cost him his life. "Wake up, people, don't believe me or anyone else, research it for yourself," was his constant urging for his audience to check things out and make up their own minds.

Speaking incessantly about the overall plans of the secret One World Government, Cooper warned that any kind of registration, whether it involves products, social security, or gun control, is a method contrived to gather information on humans in order eventually to subjugate them. Further asserting that credit cards, driver's licenses, bank accounts, and the like are all part of the overall design that will lead to the forthcoming cashless society, he passionately urged listeners to be aware that virtually *all* data—even medical—will be encoded into a mandatory computer chip or similar tracking device and implanted in each and every individual so that all citizens will be completely dependent upon and subject to the secret government. All monetary transactions, including income, purchases, and even taxes, will be coded through these chips, so that without one implanted, no one will be able to earn a living or to buy or sell anything.

Cooper maintained that if our society and every person in it acted honestly and with purity, such a Big Brother system might not be threatening; but because of the malicious intentions, desires, and greed of some elitists, the ultimate manipulation and total rule over the masses would be devastating.

Supplementing his lectures with documents, diagrams, and massive research, Cooper repeatedly drummed one of his most inflammatory arguments: that it is against the law to make people pay taxes. Citing the Declaration of Independence and the Constitution as proof that from its inception the United States of America has been a republic, he argued that it is illicit to declare it mandatory for citizens to pay taxes. This was one of his main causes and perhaps his most dangerous. "We Americans have blindly and dutifully submitted ourselves to this and it is wrong," he would yell.

Reared in an air force family with the requisite moving from town to town and country to country, Cooper was educated in, lived in, or traveled in most of the major countries of the world and gained a broad perspective. In his adult years he achieved a proud service record in the military, holding many top-secret clearances, which would later prove to be instructional in ways he did not anticipate. He entered into the Strategic Air Command of the U.S. Air Force, where he held a secret clearance working on B-52 bombers, refueling aircraft and Minuteman missiles for a time, and received an honorable discharge. His dream of joining the navy had been thwarted earlier because of motion sickness. Having overcome that condition, after leaving the air force he did enlist in the navy, serving some of the most intense years of the Vietnam War in submarine duty. He also participated in harbor patrol and river security missions in Vietnam and was awarded medals for his heroism and leadership during combat.

Cooper was also on the intelligence briefing team for the commander in chief of the Pacific Fleet and was petty officer of the watch at the Command Center at Makalapa, Hawaii, where he held a Top Secret, Q, SI security clearance. Receiving an honorable discharge from the navy in 1975, he pursued additional education. Achieving an associate of science degree in photography and serving as executive director of Adelphi Business College, along with several other positions, he also was marketing coordinator for *National Education and Software.* These endeavors provided him with the background and skills he developed and used later in producing and marketing his own documentaries, when his *real* career became evident to him.

Cooper's bold declarations and allegations served as a magnet for government authorities. Knowing this to be so, he always maintained that he'd rather go out in a blaze of glory than to maintain silence. Apparently sensing that a major confrontation was eminent, in March of 1999 Cooper sent his family out of the United States for their security. He remained in his Eagar, Arizona, home to continue his work, alone except for his "guard geese," two dogs, one rooster, and one chicken. There, during a raid on his home by the Apache County Sheriff's Department on November 5, 2001, Cooper was shot and killed.

One can always find differing reports of any given incident, and this one is no different. Several reports from the sheriff's office claimed that the episode did not involve a planned SWAT raid on Cooper's property but a simple "confrontation" between the police and Cooper that resulted in an exchange of gunfire. Also critically wounded was one of their own: Robert Martinez, an Apache County deputy. Other reports claim that the gunfire took place during an attempted arrest. Whatever the case, many of Cooper's listeners and followers believe that the episode was simply the murder of one of the first men to expose the government for what it truly is. Although conceding that Cooper may not have been an easy man to get along with, these adherents hold a mounting belief that the authorities concealed evidence about the shootout, and claims along these lines have ever since served as provocative fodder for those screaming that his "murder" was itself a conspiracy—to silence Milton William Cooper for once and all.

FATHER CHARLES COUGHLIN

The famous "radio priest" Father Coughlin, pastor of the Shrine of the Little Flower, became one of the most virulent anti-Semites of the 1930s.

Born in Hamilton, Ontario, on October 25, 1891, Charles Coughlin was ordained a Catholic priest in 1916 and became the pastor of the Shrine of the Little Flower in Royal Oak, Michigan, in 1926. Coughlin accepted the role of a "radio priest" in 1930 and slowly gained a following until shortly before the presidential election in 1932. On the CBS network Father Coughlin railed against Herbert Hoover and became an ardent supporter of Franklin D. Roosevelt. Coughlin became the voice of the common man when he vented his frustrations over the machinations of bankers and the uneven distribution of wealth. Far from being a socialist or Communist sympathizer, however, the priest used his electronic pulpit to blast liberalism and socialism in the government.

Because he had become such a vocal and enthusiastic endorser of the candidacy of Roosevelt, many among Father Coughlin's radio constituency expected that the outspoken priest would receive a high post in the new administration. Although he may not have admitted it openly, Coughlin harbored such expectations himself. He confided to certain friends that if Roosevelt should so reward him, he would quit the church and become a positive force within the government. When the rumored post did not materialize, Coughlin became openly disgruntled. By 1937 his at-

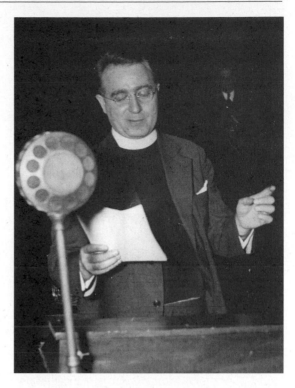

Father Charles Coughlin began spouting anti-Semitic comments on the radio in the 1930s.

tacks on Roosevelt had grown so virulent that he received a rebuke from Pope Pius XI.

Dropped by CBS, Father Coughlin was certain that NBC would welcome him and his radio parish of millions. Unwilling to rile the Roosevelt administration, NBC informed Coughlin that they had a policy of not accepting commercial religious broadcasting. Incensed, the volatile cleric used WOR New York and WJR Detroit as his flagship stations and then, with the thousands of dollars of voluntary contributions from his radio audience, bought time on individual stations throughout the United States.

Coughlin developed a magazine called *Social Injustice* to supplement in print his rants over the airwaves. He continued to fulminate against the Roosevelt administration, but his invective now included Jews. To the horror of many of his steadfast listeners, he became perhaps the foremost preacher of anti-Semitism in the nation. He was an embarrassment to Catholics, and prominent leaders within the church fomented a movement to remove him from the airwaves. In I942 *Social Injustice* was banned from the mail by enforcement of the Espionage Act invoked during World War II.

In that same year, yielding to pressure from both the secular and religious establishments, Coughlin left his bully pulpit on the radio and returned to the Shrine of the Little Flower. He remained active as pastor until 1966. He died on October 27, 1979, at the age of eighty-eight.

COUNCIL FOR NATIONAL POLICY

Some conspiracy theorists say that the ultrasecret Council for National Policy is the right-wing conservative version of the Bilderbergers.

When U.S. Senate majority leader Bill Frist (R-Tennessee) received the Thomas Jefferson Award from the Council for National Policy (CNP) in August 2004, the media was not invited. In fact, one of the cardinal rules of the CNP is that the media should never know, before or after an event, who participates in its programs. The membership of the CNP is kept so confidential that guests can attend only with the unanimous approval of the executive committee, and the group's leaders are so secretive that members cannot refer to them by name even in emails.

In October 1999 George W. Bush addressed the CNP. Due to the group's policy of strictest secrecy, Bush's campaign leaders refused to release the full text of his remarks. Other speakers whose words were meant only for CNP members have included Vice President Dick Cheney, Defense Secretary Donald Rumsfeld, and Supreme Court justice Clarence Thomas.

Just prior to the Republican convention in New York City in 2004, the *New York Times* reported that several Bush administration representatives spoke at a CNP meeting. Also scheduled to speak were Undersecretary of State John Bolton, Assistant Attorney General Alexander Acosta, and Dan Senor, an aide to Paul Bremer, presidential envoy to Iraq.

Just who are the Council for National Policy and why are they so powerful? In 1981, right-wing leaders were encouraged by Ronald Reagan's election to the U.S. presidency and decided that they must somehow capitalize on the administration's popularity. Tim LaHaye, a fundamentalist Baptist preacher and author, president of Family Life Seminars; Richard Viguerie, a conservative fund-raiser; Paul Weyrich of the Free Congress Foundation; and about fifty other far-right conservatives met at Viguerie's McLean, Virginia, home to plan strategies by which they might maximize the power and influence of the ultraconservative movement. The Council for National Policy was fashioned out of that meeting as a tax-exempt organization for conservatives who were concerned about the social/religious issues of abortion, gay rights, and school prayer.

Back in 1981 the CNP was far less secretive in declaring its goals and its potential power when it united the theocratic religious right with the low-tax, antigovernment segment of the Republican Party. Congressman Woody Jenkins of Louisiana, the CNP's first executive director, told *Newsweek* that "one day before the end of this century the Council will be so influential that no President, regardless of party or philosophy, will be able to ignore us or our concerns or shut us out of the highest levels of government."

During the 1980s and 1990s some very influential right-wing and conservative leaders were affiliated with the CNP. Among those attracted to the movement have been televangelists Jerry Falwell and Pat Robertson; antifeminist crusader Phyllis Schlafly; right-wing talk show host Oliver North; North Carolina Republican senator Jesse Helms; former House majority leader Dick Armey; Attorney General John Ashcroft; Tommy Thompson, secretary of the U.S. Department of Health and Human Services; Beverly LaHaye (wife of Tim LaHaye), founder of Concerned Women for America; and Christian Coalition head Ralph Reed.

> Today the CNP continues to be made up of powerful members of the religious right who strive to turn the United States to their conservative agenda.

Today the CNP continues to be made up of powerful members of the religious right who strive to turn the United States to their conservative agenda. Interestingly, this "Christian" organization has definite ties to Rev. Sun Myung Moon's openly anti-Christian movement, to the controversial and cultic Church of Scientology, to the ultraright John Birch Society, and to the intelligence community. Donald P. Hodel, former executive director of the Christian Coalition, is the current president of CNP; T. Kenneth Cribb Jr., vice president, was a domestic policy adviser to President Reagan. Among CNP's current members are James C. Dobson, founder of Focus on the Family; Wayne LaPierre, National Rifle Association; Grover Norquist, Americans for Tax Reform; and Stuart W. Epperson, owner of a chain of Christian radio stations.

The goals of the CNP remain the same as those set forth in 1981:

- Scale back the size of the federal government.
- Restructure the United States in a Christian fundamentalist image.
- Pass censorship laws against popular culture.
- Vote liberals and progressives out of office.
- Bring back prayer into the public schools.
- Fund private Christian schools with tax money.
- Prevent gays from achieving full civil rights.
- Make abortion illegal.

CREATIVITY MOVEMENT

The Creativity Movement is a religion that doesn't believe in God, heaven, hell, or eternal life—only in the white race.

Although the Creativity Movement, whose motto is "RaHoWa" (*Racial Holy War*), proclaims itself a religion of race, Creators, as members of the group call themselves, do not believe in God, heaven, hell, or eternal life. If you are a member of the white race, according to the Creators, then you already have everything. You are, in fact, "nature's highest creation." The Creators' version of the Golden Rule is: "What is good for the white race is the highest virtue; what is bad for the white race is the ultimate sin."

The Creativity Movement was originally founded by Ben Klassen in 1973 as the Church of the Creator (COTC). Klassen, born in the Ukraine, reared in Canada, joined a number of far-right organizations, including the John Birch Society, which he later denounced. He served as Florida chairman of George Wallace's 1968 presidential campaign and worked on a book, *Nature's Eternal Religion,* which he envisioned would depose the Judeo-democratic-Marxist values poisoning contemporary life and supplant them with a new concept of race as a transcendent embodiment of absolute truth. By contrast, Christianity was a suicidal religion. That particular denouncement became ironic when Klassen committed suicide on August 6, 1993, at the age of seventy-five, by swallowing four bottles of sleeping pills.

Things had not gone well for Klassen toward the end of his life. He had gained a few converts to his new religion, but on May 17, 1991, one of the COTC ministers, George Loeb, murdered a black Gulf War veteran and was sentenced to life with no possibility of parole for twenty-five years. In 1992 the murdered sailor's family, represented by the Southern Poverty Law Center, filed suit for $1 million against the COTC for vicarious liability. Klassen desperately attempted to divest himself of all personal assets and to dissociate himself from the COTC. His first choice for someone to take his place as leader of the group was serving a six-year sentence for selling tainted meat to public school cafeterias. Choice number two was a pizza delivery man in Baltimore, but at the last minute, the position fell to a Milwaukee skinhead who ran COTC until January 1993. Shortly before his death in August 1993, Klassen replaced the skinhead with Richard McCarty, a telemarketer.

The COTC floundered under McCarty's leadership. Less than a year after Klassen's suicide, the Southern Poverty Law Center sued for dissolution of the Church of the Creator, and McCarty quickly rolled over.

Matt Hale discovered COTC in the early 1990s when he attended Bradley University in Peoria, Illinois, but he exhibited no real interest in joining the movement until he saw an opportunity to assume leadership in 1995. Hale had become fascinated with Hitler and National Socialism when he was just a boy and had read *Mein Kampf* and racist organizations' literature since he was in the eighth grade. On Hale's twenty-fifth birthday, July 27, 1996, a group of COTC elders, known as the

Guardians of the Faith Committee, named him pontifex maximus, "highest priest," of the organization, which he renamed World Church of the Creator (WCOTC). Hale gave the group new energy and brought many young male followers to the WCOTC to become dedicated members.

In 1999 Hale earned a law degree from Southern Illinois University and passed the bar exam. The state bar denied him a license to practice due to his highly publicized bigotry. Subsequently Hale used this denial as another ploy in gaining publicity. He appeared on numerous radio talk shows and tabloid television programs, such as those hosted by Ricki Lake, Leeza Gibbons, and Jerry Springer. Tom Brokaw profiled him on an NBC report entitled "Web of Hate."

In 1999 Benjamin Smith, one of WCOTC's members, went on a two-state killing spree, beginning on July 4, that left two dead and nine wounded—all members of racial and religious minorities, including African Americans, Asian Americans, and Jews. At first Hale denied knowing Smith, but then, reflecting upon the carnage wrought by Smith, commented that the overall loss was only one white man.

In November 2002 the WCOTC lost a copyright infringement lawsuit brought against it by Te-Ta-Ma Truth Foundation, which had trademarked "Church of the Creator" many years earlier. Hale refused to comply with U.S. district court judge Joan Humphrey Lefkow's order to cease using the name Church of the Creator on websites and all printed matter, and in January 2003, when he appeared in court for a contempt of court hearing, he was arrested for conspiring to have the judge murdered.

On March 7, 2005, Judge Lefkow returned home from work to find her husband, attorney Michael F. Lefkow, and her mother, Donna Humphrey, lying dead in pools of blood, seemingly executed with bullet wounds to the head. Immediately Matt Hale was suspected of orchestrating and ordering the murders from his jail cell as an act of revenge against the judge. Hale protested his innocence, and in this matter he was found not guilty when Bart Ross, who had been angry with Judge Lefkow for dismissing a malpractice suit that he had brought, left a suicide note confessing to the murders. But in the matter of conspiring to have Judge Lefkow assassinated in 2003 Hale received a forty-year prison sentence on April 6, 2005.

In 1981 Ben Klassen wrote *The White Man's Bible,* required reading for all Creativity Movement members. Among the beliefs outlined in Klassen's "Bible":

- Nonwhites, the "mud races" are subhuman and the natural enemies of the White Race.

- Jews are the mortal enemy of the white race, seeking to "mongrelize" it and achieve their ultimate historic goal of totally enslaving all the races of the world.

- Christianity is actually a "concoction" of Jews that is used to frighten the childishly gullible with the concept of hell and to terrorize them into submission.

- White people are the creators of all worthwhile culture and civilization.

- Every issue, whether religious, political, or racial, must be viewed through the eyes of the White Man and "exclusively from the point of view of the White Race as a whole."

CRÉDIT MOBILIER

The ambitious project of linking East to West via the Union Pacific Railroad provided the fruits for one of the biggest congressional scandals of the 1870s.

The building of the Union Pacific Railroad in the 1870s is one of the dramatic, and often romanticized, chapters in the taming of the West. It took a great expenditure of raw human energy in tough, brutal labor to lay thousands of miles of tracks across what had been a great wilderness in order to link the eastern with the western states; and, of course, it also took a great amount of financial energy to supply the lumber, steel, food, and other necessities required by such a vast undertaking. Throughout history we see only a few truisms that remain constant. Unfortunately, one of the eternal constants is that when there is an opportunity to make a lot of money, some participants in the project will find a way to steal more than their rightful share.

On the eve of the 1872 presidential election the *New York Sun* broke the story of the scandal behind the Union Pacific Railroad. Major stockholders in the railroad had formed the Crédit Mobilier, a company that would receive most of the contracts to build the Union Pacific. The greedy stockholders gave or sold shares in the construction of the railroad to equally greedy congressmen, who surreptitiously increased the conspirators' profits greatly by approving large federal subsidies for the project. By approving federal funds for inflated expense budgets, the congressmen and the other stockholders were essentially stealing government money.

The Speaker of the House, James G. Blaine, a Maine Republican, set up a committee to investigate the extent of the congressional abuses—though he himself was implicated in the scandal. The investigation sullied the ending presidential term of Ulysses S. Grant and darkened the political careers of his vice president, Schuyler Colfax, and the incoming vice president, Henry Wilson. Oakes Ames of Massachusetts and James Brooks of New York were censured by the House. Representative James A. Garfield was implicated in the scandal, but enough voters accepted his protestations of innocence to elect him president in 1872.

CROP CIRCLES

Mysterious nonhuman intelligences are leaving strange geometric designs in fields of cereal crops around the world. Whoever unlocks the key to these bizarre circular markings will discover if the unknown artists are here to help or to hinder humankind.

Strange geometric designs have appeared in stands of cereal crops around the world, even in the rice paddies of Japan. The designs are often hundreds of feet in width and length and may cover many acres. Controversy rages over how these "crop circles," as they are generally known, originate, as they are usually formed overnight and involve downed, not cut, swaths of grain stalks.

Although many people believe that crop circles are a comparatively recent UFO-related phenomenon that began in the late 1970s or early 1980s, the mystery is hundreds of years old. Unexplained geometric designs occurred in fields of wheat and corn in Scotland in 1678, and rural residents of England speak of the "corn fairies" that made similar designs in the fields in the late 1800s. Researchers have discovered accounts of the discovery of so-called fairy circles in fields and meadows dating back to medieval times throughout the British Isles, Germany, Scandinavia, and France. Recent evidence indicates that Chinese farmers found crop circles as much as three thousand years ago. In those cases of crop circles that have appeared since the 1980s, investigators have determined that the crops were biochemically or biophysically altered.

Cerealogists (experts in this bizarre field of research) state that since 1989 there have been in excess of two hundred formations in the UK each year. The so-called golden years of crop circle appearances seem to have been 1990 and 1991, in each of which there were between three hundred and four hundred formations.

In 1991 Doug Bower and Dave Chorley, two retired artists in England, confessed that they were responsible for making the crop circles that had baffled the world for so long and that they accomplished the most intricate of designs by using a simple board pulled by a length of rope. While the confession of Bower and Chorley satisfied a good many skeptics and journalists, serious crop circle researchers asked how these two elderly gentlemen could have accomplished their hoaxes throughout the world in such great numbers.

While admitting that there have been hoaxes, cerealogists point out that pranksters have been unable to create crop circles with the same precision and undisturbed nature as those thought to be of alien or unknown origin. Some suggest pranksters and tricksters far older than the retired artists as the perpetrators of the enigma. Why deviate, they ask, from the suspects who were originally named as culprits? The creators of the crop circles might be found among that group of beings commonly called fairies, elves, or devas—entities that have played a significant role in the myths and legends of every planetary culture for centuries.

Regardless of general dismissal of the crop circle phenomenon by conventional scientists, it would appear that there is a genuine mystery in the formation of many of the incredible designs that suddenly appear in fields around the world. Four principal theories regarding the origins of crop circles are the following:

1. extraterrestrial entities offering clues to their identity and intentions toward earthlings;

2. natural phenomena, ranging from insects to lightning, from plasma vortices (a kind of ball lightning) to electromagnetic anomalies;

3. hoaxers, such as the duo of Doug and Dave;

4. an ancient nonhuman intelligence indigenous to this planet that is utilizing

archetypal designs in order to warn contemporary humankind to be more responsible and more respectful toward Mother Earth.

Various scholars have focused on the fourth possibility and suggested that many of the designs appear to be bound by the laws of sacred geometry. Sacred geometry, these experts state, embodies harmonic waves of energy and universal proportions. Some mysterious intelligence could be attempting to communicate geometrical and proportional wave forms—veritable keys to the cosmos and symbols of the archetypal world.

The English researcher Lucy Pringle believes that many crop circle formations are due to natural causes, such as the discharge of some electromagnetic energy, but she also notes that a particular design formed around April 21, 1998, appeared very close to the prehistoric mound of Silbury Hill. She likened the double-ringed circle with thirty-three scroll-like bands between the rings to a Beltane wheel, an ancient symbol used at Celtic fire festivals on May Day.

In July 2002 a three-day conference of leading crop circle investigators was held in Somerset, England. Andy Thomas, an organizer of the meeting, commented that his eleven years investigating the enigma had convinced him of one thing—that not all the circles were made by pranksters. Other than that, he stated, it was hard to say whether the phenomenon was caused by extraterrestrials, some kind of superconsciousness, collective psychokinesis (mind over matter), natural forces, or some other thing currently beyond human awareness. Most cerealogists in attendance insisted that it is relatively easy to tell the difference between circles made by hoaxers and those made by what appears to be some kind of superior intelligence.

The first crop circle of 2005 appeared in the Netherlands, and cerealogists predicted that the strangely designed circles would

Crop circles in a field near Wiltshire, England.

soon be manifesting primarily outside the United Kingdom, the nation previously most associated with the phenomenon.

University of Oregon physicist Richard Taylor summed up his opinion about the mystery of crop circles in the August 2011 issue of *Physics World* when he attributed the remarkable geometric designs in farmers' fields to the work of unknown artists practicing "the most science-oriented art movement in history." The "art," according to Taylor's assessment, is accomplished by GPS, microwaves, and lasers.

While nearly everyone who has looked into the mystery of crop circles admits that a good number of them are hoaxes, Jeffrey Wilson, director of the Independent Crop Circle Researchers Association, told journalist Lee Speigel of the *Huffington Post* that there were many cases in which eyewitnesses observed the designs forming during the daytime. Other circles had formed after a storm front or a severe weather front had passed.

Putting hoaxsters aside, Wilson remains open-minded about the identity of the mysterious force that forms the circles, suggesting that there may well be more than one source involved in their creation. While the majority of crop circle buffs believe that the complex geometric designs are hidden messages left by extraterrestrial visitors or some hidden terrestrial intelligence, Wilson stated that he is not completely convinced that there is any intelligent source responsible. There may be natural processes that could fashion such designs, he said.

Linda Moulton Howe, author of *Mysterious Lights and Crop Circles,* recalled that the first time that she walked into a crop formation, she seemed to feel a "residual electrostatic field around it," as if she were "walking into Jell-O along the edges." Since she began researching crop circles in 1991, Howe has ex-amined and been inside 250 formations. She stoutly takes issue with those debunkers who claim that all the crop designs are created by artistic hoaxsters with lasers or other electronic devices.

Howe said that she had often observed small, unidentified lights moving over crops and subsequent formations in England. She cited her work with Italian astrophysicist Massimo Teodorani in which they studied mysterious plasma in the mountains of Hessdalen, Norway. Teodorani expressed his opinion that there appeared to be intelligence in the plasmas that created the crop circles, but he was baffled as to what kind of intelligence was behind the phenomenon.

D

THE DA VINCI CODE

The Vatican called Dan Brown's novel a "sack full of lies." While there is no question the book is a work of fiction, millions are left pondering which of the many controversial "facts" are lies and which are truths hidden for centuries.

In March 2005, in an interview from Vatican City with the Reuters News Service, Cardinal Tarcisio Bertone called upon all Roman Catholics to shun *The Da Vinci Code* by Dan Brown as if it were rotten food. "The book is a sack full of lies against the Church, against the real history of Christianity, and against Christ himself," Cardinal Bertone proclaimed. He condemned the novel as "the latest in a series of devastating attacks against Christianity."

In 1982, when Michael Baigent, Richard Leigh, and Henry Lincoln published *The Holy Blood and the Holy Grail,* it was regarded as a controversial, albeit skillful and well-researched, nonfiction account of the centuries-old tradition that Jesus of Nazareth and Mary Magdalene were man and wife, that Jesus might have escaped death on the cross, and that their descendants intermarried with the family that later formed the French Merovingian dynasty. The book became a bestseller in Europe and the United States, creating a bit of a stir with its theory that there might well be people in France walking around with Christ's blood coursing through their veins. As the book encouraged discussion of previously off-limits and sacrosanct topics, it roused a number of clergy to defend the faith as it had been cherished for nearly two thousand years, and there were resounding official denials that Jesus was married to Mary Magdalene or anyone else. Then things settled back to normal in church pews across the world, and such topics as the Knights Templar, the Holy Grail, Gnosticism, Rosslyn Chapel, and the bloodline of Jesus and Mary became subjects discussed only by scholars and men and women with esoteric and arcane interests.

When *The Da Vinci Code* was published in 2001, the book rose almost overnight to number one on the *New York Times* bestseller list and quickly attained comparable ratings on charts around the world. Printing after printing pushed the sales to nearly 20 million. The book has been translated into forty languages, and some estimates place Brown's financial

Dan Brown's book *The Da Vinci Code* was adapted as a movie starring Tom Hanks.

take somewhere in the neighborhood of $390 million. For a time, it seemed that one could not go anywhere with hearing people discussing the startling new and never-before-known revelations that Brown had made in his book. Could Jesus and Mary really have been married? Has the church been hiding knowledge of their children all these centuries? What about the Dead Sea Scrolls, the Nag Hammadi codices, and all the other gospels and books that got left out of the Bible?

It has been often noted that there is nothing so powerful as an idea whose time has come—and in writing and all the other arts, timing is everything. In the 1980s the prevailing spirit of the time, the mass acceptance of ideas and concepts that would challenge age-old dogmas and ecclesiasticisms, had not yet been infused with the Internet, an increasingly aggressive mass culture, and the scandals that the church brought on itself by hiding for hundreds of years the sins of the fathers. With the dawning of a new millennium, millions of men and women not only were ready to ask

questions, they were ready to get some answers of their own.

At the same time that some previously very orthodox Christians, inspired by the novel, are preparing to venture forth on some rather iconoclastic quests, a number of scholars, both religious and secular, urge a bit of caution. The problem with Brown's book, argues a kind of academic and ecclesiastical consensus, is that too many people regard it as a scholarly nonfiction treatise, rather than a story, a work of fiction, a novel.

Among the flashing yellow lights of caution issued by scholars are the following:

• Brown writes that the Council of Nicea in 325 C.E. established the divinity of Jesus, and until the council's decision, Jesus was regarded by his followers as a mortal prophet. Theologians counter this assertion by explaining that one of the principal reasons the council was called was to deal with the heresy of Arius, an Alexandrian theologian who argued that

Jesus was not God in the flesh. Throughout the epistles and in the canon, rules, and practice of most early Christians, Jesus was Lord (Greek *kyrios*), divinity.

- Brown's characters maintain that the figure to the right of Jesus in Leonardo da Vinci's painting of the Last Supper is Mary Magdalene, rather than an effeminate apostle John. This controversial identification was first made in *The Templar Revelation: Secret Guardians of the True Identity of Christ* by Lynn Picknett and Clive Prince. If the figure at the Last Supper is not John, the disciple most loved by Jesus, the disciple to whom he entrusted the care of his mother, then where is John in the painting?

- Brown's hero, Robert Langdon, cites the absence of a chalice in da Vinci's painting as proof that the great artist knew the truth about the actual identity of the Holy Grail and was a member of a secret society protecting that truth from being declared heretical and stamped out by the Inquisition. Biblical scholars point out that da Vinci based his painting on John 13:21, where Jesus prophesies, "One of you will betray me." The Catholic scholar-journalist Sandra Miesel further states that there is no institution of the Holy Eucharist in the gospel of John.

- The albino Opus Dei monk who murders the curator in the Louvre in Paris and begins the action of the novel is said to operate out of Opus Dei headquarters on Lexington Avenue in New York. Brown claims that he worked very hard to create a fair and balanced depiction of the group. Although conceding that the organization has been a very positive force in the lives of some people, Brown states that "for others Opus Dei has been a profoundly negative experience."

- One of the novel's central storylines defines the Holy Grail as the bloodline descended from Jesus and Mary Magdalene, rather than the cup or drinking vessel used by Jesus at the Last Supper. Traditional clergy say that in this and other respects, the novel consistently depicts the church as suppressing the role of women. Cardinal Bertone countered this charge by stating that the role of women in the church is "a primary one, starting from Mary, the mother of God."

In December 2004 Michael Baigent and Richard Leigh announced that they were suing Random House and Dan Brown for theft of intellectual property and charged that there were clear links between their book *Holy Blood, Holy Grail* and Brown's *Da Vinci Code.* Baigent told the *New Zealand Herald* that having his and his colleagues' research "lumped" into Brown's fictional work degraded the historical implications of their efforts. Baigent and his coauthors, Leigh and Lincoln, set forth a hypothesis in *Holy Blood,* and they "managed to establish that a certain amount was shown to be correct; the rest was plausible."

Dan Brown, for his part, has never claimed to have come up with ideas that were never before in circulation. On his website he admits that most of the information is not as "inside" as it seems: "The secret described in the novel has been chronicled for centuries, so there are thousands of sources to draw from."

DEAD SEA SCROLLS

Discovery of additional "lost" scrolls promises more controversy as texts reveal hints of biblical treasures and direct interaction with angels and gods.

Information gained from the Dead Sea Scrolls, which were discovered near Qumran, Israel, in 1945 and are slowly being translated and released to the public, may have a revolutionary effect on both the Jewish and the Christian religions. These scrolls, believed by many scholars to have been written by a sect known as the Essenes, refer often to a great Teacher of Righteousness and a great warfare between the Sons of Light and the Sons of Darkness. The sect forms a definite link between Judaism and Christianity, and many scholars have suggested that Jesus was a member of the Qumran group.

The author, editor, and scholar Herschel Shanks disagrees that the scrolls contain data that foreshadows Christian teaching. "Jesus is not in the scrolls," Shanks writes in *The Mystery and Meaning of the Dead Sea Scrolls.* The scrolls are not Christian, he contends, and their value lies in what they reveal about the state of Judaism between roughly 250 B.C.E. and 68 C.E. The scrolls, Shanks says, call into question "the naive notion that Jesus' Jewishness was accidental or incidental and the belief that his message was wholly new, unique and unrelated to anything that had gone before, astonishing everyone who heard it."

Shanks and other scholars have pointed out that the concepts of what would come to be known as Christian doctrines are to be found in Jewish mystical trends that were in circulation decades before the birth of Jesus. Among the subjects thought to be unique to Jesus and to Christianity that are found in the scrolls are the beatitudes of the Sermon on the Mount, the idea of the Messiah, and the apocalyptic prophecy of a final battle between the forces of good and the forces of evil.

Shanks finds evidence in the Dead Sea Scrolls that there were several factions of Judaism at the time when Christianity was being formulated. One of these schools of Jewish theology taught a far more apocalyptic doctrine than many Jewish scholars have wished to believe. Eschatology—the study of the so-called endtimes—has usually been associated with the teachings of early Christianity and the beliefs of modern-day evangelical Christians.

After the Roman destruction of Jerusalem and Judea in 70 C.E., Shanks says, only two of the many splinter groups survived—Christianity and Rabbinic Judaism, which dropped its apocalyptic remnants and evolved into the major Jewish doctrines that exist to this day.

Shanks's book contains a chapter on the Copper Scroll, which was discovered in March 1952 by a team of Jordanian and French archaeologists. The ancient, engraved copper sheet had been broken into two parts and hidden in a cave in Qumran, and the contents translated thus far have puzzled scholars by seeming to provide hints about the location of buried biblical treasure. The examining scientists found the scroll too fragile to unroll, so they sliced it into twenty-three segments. The scroll was not quite a foot wide and about eight feet long. Scholars concluded that the text, engraved down twelve columns and listing sixty-four caches of treasure from gold bars to silver ingots, was in Hebrew, but they were baffled by the figures of twenty-five tons of gold and sixty-five tons of silver, which would have totaled more than the entire amount of those precious metals mined worldwide at the time of the engraving.

In March 2002 Ronald Feather, a metallurgist and a member of both the Jewish Historical Society and the Egypt Exploration Society, argued that the copper document had not been written by a member of the Essene monastic sect. Feather believes the engraved scroll, which lists the proverbial treasures of Solomon buried in the Holy Land, is written in Egyptian, not in Hebrew. In Feather's carefully derived opinion, the scroll can be traced back to the monotheistic court of the Egyptian pharaoh Akhenaten and Queen Nefertiti in Amarna, six hundred miles south of the Dead Sea and halfway down the Nile between Cairo and Luxor.

In October 1999 another "lost" Dead Sea Scroll was unearthed that has the possibility of setting off another theological firestorm. If the Angel Scroll, as it is known, proves to be authentic, Jews and Christians will be presented with a new understanding of how the ancient Israelites viewed God, the angels, and humanity's place in the universe.

According to researcher Barry Chamish, the Angel Scroll is one thousand lines long and had been purchased in Jordan by Benedictine monks and taken to their German monastery in 1970. In 1977 one of the group, Father Gustav Mateus, died and bequeathed his photographs and transcriptions of the scroll to an unnamed Jerusalem college administrator who, in turn, handed the material over to Stephan Phann, a member of the team of scholars translating the scrolls held by the Israeli government. Subsequently, Phann's findings were published in the news magazine *Jerusalem Report.*

In presenting the information, Phann admitted that some scholars were skeptical, but he said that most experts were in agreement that the text of the Angel Scroll "felt" genuine. The bits of the scroll that were released for the public's examination deal with "divine chariot-throne themes with elaborate details of angels ascending heaven's multiple gates." Such references may be of great interest to those who take a literal view of the biblical accounts reporting encounters with extraterrestrials/angels.

Mordechai Spasser, an Israeli UFOlogist who is also a student of Kabbalah, cautioned researchers about taking the UFO viewpoint without more study. Spasser stated that from what he had read, the scrolls appear to refer to the "astral plane" and other aspects of Jewish mysticism.

Chamish, however, quotes a number of passages from the Angel Scroll and follows them with his literal interpretation. Here is one, describing a visionary's (or UFO contactee's) "heavenward visit above the high places of the clouds" with an angel:

According to the plan of that day, the Voice went forth to me and directed me

The Qumran Caves, where the famous Dead Sea Scrolls were discovered.

and he drove me by the Spirit. And a vision was revealed to me from the Most High, and [the] Prince of Angels lifted me up in the Spirit and I ascended heavenward above the high places of the clouds and he showed me the great world and the image of the gods. And I pondered the appearance round about and there was no time and no place and their appearance from the dwelling places of light was like a rainbow in the clouds. And they had no bodies and no bodily structure and the dominion of darkness was over all of the earth round about.

Chamish concludes that this is an accurate description of a trip in a space shuttle. "First the traveler passes above cloud level. Then he sees the earth from space and it is surrounded by darkness. He is shown 'images of the gods' and their homes on a control monitor and marvels at the fine color quality and at the bizarre fact that there is no firmament to the images on the screen."

It seems very apparent that the Dead Sea Scrolls have only begun to yield sources of inspiration and controversy, to believers and nonbelievers alike.

DECIDED ONES OF JUPITER

An errant Catholic, Annunchiarico should have known better than to leave the priesthood of one religion to become the wrathful, murderous deity of another.

In 1816 a man named Ciro Annunchiarico became southern Italy's greatest nightmare when he claimed the power of Jupiter, father of the gods of Imperial Rome, and successfully brought a number of bandit gangs into a single striking force, leading them to rob, pillage, and burn under the banner of the skull and crossbones and the motto "Sadness, Death, Terror, and Mourning."

By 1817 Annunchiarico commanded twenty thousand members of the secret society of the Decided Ones of Jupiter the Thunderer. The men were divided into camps of three hundred to four hundred members, and squadrons of forty to sixty. The society was structured along military lines, and strict discipline was enforced. If Annunchiarico had so wished, he could easily have led an open revolution against any state government in southern Italy. But despite his claim that the might of the great god Jupiter flowed through his body, he was more interested in personal aggrandizement and a life of luxury than in political opportunities.

Annunchiarico, the son of wealthy parents, had entered the priesthood and seemed destined for a fruitful career in the church. However, he much preferred the life of a country gentleman on the family estate—and the vow of celibacy didn't appeal to him, either. He seduced a young woman who was engaged to Giovanni Montolesi, the son of a wealthy merchant. When Montolesi learned of the affair, he sought out Annunchiarico and reproached him for bringing shame to the priesthood and dishonor to his fiancée. Without a word, Annunchiarico drew a dagger from his belt and stabbed Montolesi in the heart. He later swore a blood-feud against the entire Montolesi family, declaring that the man whom he had murdered had insulted him and the entire Roman Catholic priesthood. Over the next few months he ambushed and murdered thirteen members of the Montolesi clan. Pursued by the authorities, he then fled with some friends into the mountains.

As the leader of a small band of brigands who favored a life of luxury above that of living in spartan hideouts, Annunchiarico developed a plan to combine the people's love and respect of the priesthood with their fear of secret societies who plundered and murdered them. Boldly summoning the other bandit chiefs in the mountains to a meeting, Annunchiarico eloquently convinced them that they should unite as one to resist the soldiers who were constantly sent to hunt them down.

While the outlaw leaders were deciding just who among them should be in charge of the newly united force, Annunchiarico appeared in the full regalia of the priesthood and announced that he would celebrate the Mass. As the chiefs all kneeled to receive his blessing, such an attitude of obeisance signaled their acquiescence to his leadership. At the same time that he was celebrating Mass, Annunchiarico informed all of the assembled outlaws that the spirit of Jupiter, the ancient father of the gods, had passed into his person and commanded him to form a new order, the Decided Ones of Jupiter.

In a remarkably brief time, numerous independent bands of thieves and murderers became a single secret society. As word spread of the alleged supernatural powers of their leader, Annunchiarico, now known as Jupiter the Thunderer, men flocked to the mountains to join the Decided Ones.

In order to spread accounts of his legendary abilities, Annunchiarico secretly used men who resembled him to serve as his doubles, dressed in priestly robes exactly like his, so it would appear that Jupiter the Thunderer could lead raids in several different places at the same time. He also had his personal bodyguard outfitted in devilish costumes, complete with horns and tail, to perpetuate the belief that he had the power to command and control demons. And then, of course, there were reports of his terrible thunderbolts, which he was said to be able to hurl at his enemies just as Jupiter had flung the deadly bolts in ancient times.

Small troops of soldiers sent against the Decided Ones were quickly annihilated. Early in 1818 when a force of a thousand regular troops under the command of a General d'Octavio marched into the mountains to arrest Annunchiarico and destroy his band of outlaws, the superstitious soldiers were so fearful of the mighty Jupiter that they permitted Annunchiarico to enter their camp at night and to place a dagger at the throat of their general as he lay on his cot. Annunchiarico decreed mercy but warned the general and the thousand men that if they ever dared again to violate his mountains, his thunderbolts would be certain to kill them all. General d'Octavio and his troops were gone at first light the next morning.

When the authorities realized that any army conscripted from southern Italy would hold Annunchiarico in the same kind of superstitious awe as the local populace, they hired a force of 1,200 German and Swiss mercenaries under the command of an Englishman, General Church. Strangely enough, the very approach of these veterans of the Napoleonic

Wars affected Annunchiarico in ways that astonished his men. Their god was visibly nervous, even frightened, by the movement of the battle-hardened professional soldiers toward the mountains. Suddenly the person who harbored the spirit of Jupiter seemed like an ordinary mortal—and not a very brave one at that. When word reached the camps of the Decided Ones that the mercenaries were very well-equipped and experienced fighting men, thousands deserted. Within a matter of days, Annunchiarico had only a few hundred of his most loyal disciples remaining out of what had been a fearsome band of twenty thousand.

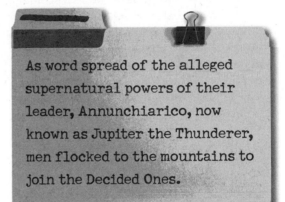

As word spread of the alleged supernatural powers of their leader, Annunchiarico, now known as Jupiter the Thunderer, men flocked to the mountains to join the Decided Ones.

Annunchiarico and his remnant of followers retreated to the small village of Santa Marzano, choosing this location because of the wall that encircled the town. Hoping that the local populace would join in their defense, Annunchiarico prepared for siege. But the citizens of Santa Marzano could also see that the mighty Jupiter the Thunderer was, after all, just another bandit, and nothing about his person persuaded any of them to risk their lives defending him against the professional Swiss and German soldiers. After a few days of siege, General Church's mercenaries entered the village, killed those Decided Ones who offered resistance, and arrested the others. Annunchiarico and three of his lieutenants managed to escape but were captured four days later.

As he was being led to the firing squad, Annunchiarico's boastful arrogance returned. He bragged that he had killed sixty or seventy men with his own hands, and he mocked the priest who came to administer the last rites. Many of the villagers who had gathered on the day of execution murmured that the Thunderer would call down one of Jupiter's lightning bolts and escape from the mercenaries who had captured him.

Incredibly, after the twenty-one-member firing squad shot a volley into him, Ciro Annunchiarico remained alive and somehow managed to get to his knees to begin a prayer to Jupiter. The astonished General Church ordered that the Thunderer's own musket be loaded with a silver bullet and that a soldier discharge the weapon directly into Annunchiarico's head, making certain that the legendary leader of the secret society was truly dead.

DEISTS

Deists believe in the existence of a God, a supreme being, but deny the revelations claimed by organized religions and are content to follow what they maintain is a common sense approach to spirituality. A Deist believes that nature and reason reveal the design of a creator throughout the universe.

Frequently accused of being atheists, Deists counter such criticism by pointing out that they believe in God as an eternal entity, whereas atheism teaches that there is no God.

Another charge leveled by conventional religionists is that Deism is a cult. Deists answer this indictment by emphasizing their teaching of self-reliance. Deism cannot be a cult if it teaches its adherents to question authority and to use reason at all costs.

The Deist definition of God can perhaps be glimpsed in the following quotation from Albert Einstein: "My religion consists of a humble admiration of the illimitable superior spirit who reveals himself in the slight details we are able to perceive with our frail and feeble minds. That deeply emotional conviction of the presence of a superior reasoning power, which is revealed in the incomprehensible universe, forms my idea of God."

DEPARTMENT OF THE UNORTHODOX

Posing as researchers from the Scientific Engineering Institute, the CIA's Office of Research and Development scoured the country for practitioners of black magic and the occult arts.

In 1969 the Central Intelligence Agency's Office of Research and Development (ORD) became known as the "Department of the Unorthodox" when they became intrigued by some of the ideas suggested in earlier years by Dr. Donald Ewen Cameron, whose experiments explored the farthest reaches of the human psyche. Some of the behavior modifications achieved by Dr. Cameron seemed to some members of the ORD to tread somewhat warily into the world of the supernatural. When Cameron had worked for MK-ULTRA, the secret group had 150 subprograms involving biology, drugs, psychology, sexual activities, and even motion pictures. Many Hollywood films of the 1950s were influenced by MK-ULTRA operatives who suggested storylines about the threat of Communism, brainwashing, or invasion from monstrous aliens from outer space.

Cameron had begun his career in psychology assisting the Office of Special Services (OSS, the forerunner of the CIA) in interrogating Nazi prisoners during World War II. Cameron, a Canadian, became intrigued by the experiments conducted on concentration camp prisoners by German doctors, and he contracted to work for the OSS, then the CIA, in the field of behavior manipulation. He continued this specialty in Projects Bluebird and Artichoke, which became MK-ULTRA in 1953.

According to those who knew Dr. Cameron, he was a man driven by a need to understand the workings of human behavior and an obsession to find the methods to modify and control it. He conducted numerous experiments in sensory deprivation, sensory overload, and drug inducement. He also performed a great number of prefrontal lobotomies and oversaw electroconvulsive shock treatments.

In 1957, when Cameron's experiments in effectively creating potential "Manchurian Candidates" became known, he relocated his work to the Allen Memorial Psychiatric Institute in Montreal with the help of his friend CIA director Allen Dulles and the Canadian government. The Allen Institute soon became known as "the brain butchery" due to Cameron's excessively harsh experiments with electroshock, LSD, bright lights, sounds, lobotomies, and drug-induced comas that sometimes lasted for months. Many of his experiments proved far too extreme for his "patients," and many of them died.

Fortunately, most in the ORD were not inspired by Cameron's work to become "brain butchers," but they were fascinated by the notion of expanding the parameters of MK-ULTRA into this uncharted territory. Agents traveled across the United States searching for practitioners of black magic and the occult arts—fortune tellers, palm readers, clairvoyants, and psychic sensitives. The operatives introduced themselves as researchers from the Scientific Engineering Institute.

By 1971 Operation Often, as this subproject was code-named, had three full-time astrologers on its payroll whose specific assignment was to predict the future. Two Chinese American palm readers were added to the staff in 1972. Extensive research was conducted into black magic and witchcraft, and an analysis was formulated concerning the number and locations of covens in the United States and the effectiveness of fertility rites and rituals conducted to raise the dead. A Spiritualist medium was assigned to walk the halls of the United Nations to detect any evil or potentially evil ambassadors.

What results came of this remarkable research funded by the CIA? There are stories indicating that many agents continued to infiltrate covens of witches and Satanists. There are accounts of black magic rituals being used in brainwashing and mind-control techniques. While many conspiracy theorists swear to the truth of these allegations, all records of any of MK-ULTRA's projects, operations, and subprojects were ordered destroyed in 1972 by the then-director of the CIA, Richard Helms.

DIANA, PRINCESS OF WALES

It doesn't matter what the official reports say. The people know that there was evil afoot the night of August 31, 1997, when Diana, Princess of Wales, was murdered.

The incredible spectacle of worldwide mass mourning over the loss of Diana, Princess of Wales, eventually quieted to an orderly exploitation of her final resting place on a small island surrounded by a tranquil pond on the ancestral mansion of the Spencer family. However, the lovely, tragic lady has not been able to rest in peace as tourists are charged admission to view her burial site and conspiracy theories continue to swirl about her death and that of her lover Dodi al-Fayed.

According to one poll taken in the United Kingdom in 2004, 27 percent of the British public still believed that Diana was murdered. Official denials from French police, who insist that they conducted an exhaustive investigation and discounted all the conspiracy rumors and hypotheses, have done little to quell the doubts of those who insist that Diana was killed by secret agents, who were ordered to assassinate her for a variety of reasons. Fayed's father, Mohamed al-Fayed, who owns Harrods department store, is certain that the crash was not an accident and has been fanning the flames of the theories with a variety of lawsuits.

Among the most common allegations that there was bloody work afoot on that tragic night are the following:

Princess Diana Was Assassinated by Angry International Arms Dealers

Princess Diana became the target of international munitions manufacturers and arms dealers because of her high-profile global campaign against the use of land mines.

Those men on motorcycles who, according to some witnesses, forced Fayed's limousine to crash were not wild and crazy paparazzi who became tragically overzealous in pursuit of sensational photographs, but cold and cruel hired assassins who accomplished exactly what they set out to do: provoke the driver into dangerous speeds and cause the vehicle to crash. Although they were fully prepared to administer a bullet in the back of Diana's head to be certain she was dead, a rapid appraisal of the crash scene convinced them that their job of assassination had been completed successfully.

Diana Was Assassinated by British Intelligence on Orders of the Royals

An equally pervasive theory insists that Diana was offed by British intelligence agents on the orders of the royal family.

Why would the British royals want to take out one of their own?

Conservative Queen Elizabeth and her consort, Prince Philip, were extremely upset by the whole nasty business of the divorce of Prince Charles and Lady Di. They recoiled in humiliation at the manner in which the royal laundry was scrubbed in full view of the world press.

All the gossip about Diana and a string of clandestine affairs became all the more sordid when the princess declared that her infidelities were in retaliation for the lurid fact that marriage to Prince Charles had not caused him to give up his mistress, his true love, Camilla Parker-Bowles. And now, after all the disgraceful embarrassment of the divorce, Diana, thirty-six, had taken up with Dodi al-Fayed, forty-one, a Muslim playboy. What was worse, it appeared that Diana was really quite taken with the bounder, and after leaving her sons, William and Harry, with their father, Prince Charles, she was openly carrying on with Dodi in a romance that was meticulously covered by the world press. Scandalous photographs of the princess in various stages of undress, cavorting aboard the Fayed yacht near the Italian island of Sardinia, made a mockery of the staid House of Windsor.

As if these tasteless goings-on were not enough, it was said that Dodi had presented Diana with a diamond-studded, star-shaped ring to seal their vows of engagement and their intention to wed.

The British press frequently reported that Prince Philip, in particular, made no effort to keep his dislike of Diana's suitor a secret. Philip had been heard to refer to Dodi as an "oily bed-hopper," and he made it very clear that he considered him completely unworthy of becoming the stepfather of William and Harry.

On August 31, 1997, the day of Diana's tragic death in Paris, London's *Sunday Mirror* newspaper quoted a friend of the royal family as saying: "Prince Philip has let it rip several times frequently about the Fayeds—at a dinner party, during a country shoot and while on a visit to close friends in Germany. He's been banging on about his contempt for Dodi. Diana has been told in no uncertain terms about the consequences should she continue the relationship with the Fayed boy."

Among those "consequences" were possible exile—even though she was the mother of the future king of England—or social ostracism from all association with the royal family. Earlier, when such a threat had been made to her, Diana's attitude had seemed to be that if social ostracism meant she no longer had to deal with the royals and their stuffy kind, then she would be delighted. Certain observers of the war of nerves between the Princess of Wales and the royal family suggested that Diana had grown past caring what Charles and his parents thought about her or her romances or her charitable deeds. She was now in a relationship with a man who could afford to keep her in the lifestyle to which she had become accustomed.

Theorists maintain that when rumors began to circulate that Diana might be pregnant with Dodi's child, the royal family had had enough and ordered her death. Even if she were not currently pregnant with Fayed's seed, if they ever married—as it appeared they might—then she might one day bear an unsuitable stepsibling for William and Harry.

And, of course, a bonus for Prince Charles, once Diana was out of the way, was that he could now have full control over his sons, continue his adulterous relationship with Camilla, and one day ascend unencumbered to the throne of England.

Diana Paid the Price for Dabbling in the Dark Arts

Prince Charles has often been characterized as a bit off-the-wall for his interests in the supernatural, the paranormal, alternative medical practices, and environmental concerns. It was also well known that Princess Diana and Sarah Ferguson, the ex-wife of Prince Andrew, sought the counsel of spiritualist mediums and psychic sensitives. Knowledge of Diana's dependency on New Age healers and psychics and her tendency to air sometimes bizarre paranoid fears with friends, servants, and therapists keep the assassination theories alive.

Simone Simmons, a New Age therapist, said that she was hired by Diana in 1993 to

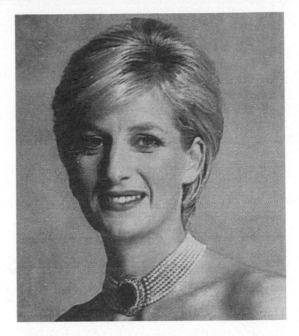

Was Princess Diana's death in a car crash really an accident, or a successful assassination plot by secret British agents?

rid Kensington Palace of "negative energy." Ms. Simmons said that the princess felt vulnerable and persecuted. In 1994 Diana was convinced that the Saudi royal family wanted to kill her. Another time, she thought the CIA wanted to assassinate her.

Some theorists have claimed that they have evidence that Diana became deeply involved with the occult and adept at certain techniques of sorcery. Others have said that a rather large number of her close friends joined her in her forays into witchcraft, astrology, magic, and the commanding of dark forces.

Could it be, as some have suggested, that the death of Diana and Dodi was a result of occult practices that backfired? Is it possible that curses directing the dark forces against her enemies somehow boomeranged and unleashed their malignant energy upon Diana and her lover?

Some say that is exactly what happened and that evil and mysterious forces were at work that fatal night of August 3l, 1997—demonic forces that took the life of one who too carelessly opened a door to a dark dimension of a reality far more sinister than she could have guessed.

Diana Was Killed because She Offended a Powerful Secret Society

Closely related to the theory that dabbling on the dark side of the force did Diana in is the ancient allegation that there exists a powerful inner circle of men who operate in secrecy behind the scenes in Great Britain, certain European nations, and the United States and who fervently believe that the royal family of England is in direct lineage to the Throne of David, the House of Jacob, and the actual bloodline of Jesus. Some theorists firmly insist that this secret society did not approve of the public and private actions of Lady Di and pronounced her death sentence before she further embarrassed the royals.

The conspiracy theories concerning Princess Diana's death show no signs of abating and grow even more sinister—and sometimes facetious. Perhaps, as an exasperated Simon Hoggart of the *Guardian* wrote on January 8, 2004, with tongue firmly in cheek, maybe Diana, Princess of Wales, died because "Prince Charles, together with various gay courtiers, shot at the car from a stealth helicopter just as it entered the tunnel."

In February 2009, CBS News' *48 Hours* interviewed Argentinean businessman Roberto Deverik, a friend of Diana's, who told correspondent Erin Moriarty that the princess had often spoken to him about her concern that "murderous plots" were being formulated against her and that she feared that she would be blown up in a car or in a helicopter.

Although it had been seven years since his son Dodi's and Diana's deaths, billionaire Mohamed Al-Fayed had not relented in his accusations that the British government had carried out a well-orchestrated hit on the two

lovers. It was Fayed's contention that Dodi and the princess were murdered to prevent Diana from marrying a Muslim and bearing a child. In fact, Fayed insisted, Diana was pregnant at the time of the crash in Paris.

The emphasis of the CBS program *Diana: Secret Documents Revealed* was to make public for the first time a 4,000-page report that had been produced by the French government that proved that the fatal crash was an accident and not the fault of the paparazzi, foreign agents, or British intelligence. According to exhaustive examinations conducted by a number of top French scientists, the responsibility for the accident must be placed on Henri Paul, Diana's driver, who was severely impaired that night by a combination of alcohol and prescription drugs. Paul had been driving at nearly twice the speed limit and had clipped a Fiat Uno; he then lost control of the car and crashed into a tunnel pillar. Forensic tests of Paul's body indicated that he had imbibed three times the legal limit for alcohol. Tests of Diana's body testified that she was not pregnant at the time of her death.

In spite of the extensive report produced by the French probe of Princess Diana and Dodi's deaths, conspiracy theorists hold fast to the many scenarios that, in their opinion, reveal a plot to murder the two colorful and controversial figures. Al-Fayed continues to insist that British intelligence or some rogue military group carried out an assassination of Diana and Dodi, and he weaves elaborate fictions that would remove the blame from Henri Paul, his head of security. In a CBS poll conducted in 2009, more than seventy-six percent of those surveyed believed wholeheartedly that the public will never learn the complete truth about the deaths of Princess Diana and Dodi.

LOU DOBBS

CNN television host Lou Dobbs had been a respected broadcaster for decades before he sur-

prised everyone by accusing President Barack Obama of not being a U.S. citizen.

With his mellifluous voice and warm, expansive smile, Lou Dobbs was the genial host of "Lou Dobbs Tonight" on CNN for nearly three decades. There he discussed current business affairs with an expertise that made his cable program one of the most popular of its kind on television. Dobbs had been with CNN since its founding in 1980 and had served as an anchor, managing editor, and executive vice president. He was the last of the original anchors on the network. Then, unfortunately, he got bitten by an extremely virulent conspiracy bug.

On July 15, 2009, he questioned the validity of President Barack Obama's birth certificate while on the air. Many of his loyal viewers listened and watched in disbelief as Dobbs became a "birther" before their very eyes. He continued on subsequent programs to question the president's fitness for office, and he went so far as to suggest that Obama might be an undocumented, illegal alien. And while he was on the topic of illegal aliens, Dobbs began a systematic series of attacks on Latinos that soon had civil rights groups calling for him to cease and desist. It was one thing to hear Dobbs openly defending the Minutemen, the vigilante militia who patrolled the Mexico–U.S. border hunting down illegals, but then his rants became much worse—and less supported by facts.

Among Dobbs' vitriol against Latino illegals was the following:

- From 2006 to 2009, Latino immigrants brought over 7,000 cases of leprosy into the United States. (Dobbs's source for this untruth was a right-wing radical author, and it was quickly debunked.)

- Illegal immigrants make up a third of the U.S. prison population and cost the nation a hundred billion dollars a year in depressed wages, social costs, and the

CNN television host Lou Dobbs shocked his loyal fans when he attacked President Obama on his birth certificate issue.

cost of incarceration. (The U.S. Department of Justice statistics indicate that immigrants make up a very small proportion of the U.S. prison population.)

- Dobbs often sought to stoke fear of Latinos by using evidence from a white supremacist group that claimed Mexican immigrants were dedicated to a subversive organization called La Reconquista, whose goal was to return the southwestern states to Mexico.

- Dobbs inflated the old standby conspiracy theory that influential politicians in Mexico, Canada, and the United States were working clandestinely to create the North American Union.

On November 11, 2009, Dobbs announced to his audience that that evening's broadcast would be his last on CNN. In explaining his departure from the network that had been his home for nearly thirty years, Dobbs said that he needed "to engage in constructive problem solving, as well as to contribute positively to a better understanding of the great issues of the day, and to continue to do so with the most honest and direct language possible."

Scores of offended viewers and civil rights groups were unanimous in their rebuttal that for many years during his tenure at CNN, Lou Dobbs had been neither constructive nor positive in dealing with the nation's more delicate issues.

On November 10, 2010, the FOX Business Network announced that it had signed a multi-year contract with Lou Dobbs to host a daily program beginning in 2011. *Lou Dobbs Tonight* is currently telecast each night at 7:00 Eastern Time.

DOMINION THEOLOGY

Dominion theologians want to establish an Old Testament theocracy in the United States—but they can't agree among themselves on how to do it.

There are many ideological differences among advocates of the Christian Right. Those who endorse Reconstructionism would like to see the United States become an Old Testament theocracy that would mete out capital punishment for blasphemy, homosexuality, and adultery. Supporters of Dominionism would like to bring into effect a political structure in which Christians alone are biblically mandated to control all secular institutions.

In *A Christian Manifesto* (1981), Francis Schaeffer, an evangelical philosopher who had been allied with Rev. Carl McIntire, head of the fundamentalist American Council of Churches, argued that the United States originated as a nation established in biblical principles. As the generations passed, America

became more pluralistic, more multicultural, and more secular. God was moved out of the center of American life, and American society steadily grew more atheistic, hedonistic, and decayed. Legalized abortion, the removal of prayer from public schools, the absence of crèches in front of the courthouse during the Christmas season—all these factors contribute to the downfall of American society. In the closing pages of *A Christian Manifesto,* Schaeffer called for Christians to use civil disobedience to bring back biblical morality throughout the United States.

Schaeffer died of cancer in 1984, and Jay Grimstead, who had been greatly influenced by *A Christian Manifesto,* founded a group called the Coalition on Revival (COR) for the purpose of unifying Christians on the questions of the endtimes and when Christ will return. COR's position is postmillennial, taking the view that Christ will return only after Christians have been in charge of the earth for a thousand years. While more-liberal Christians feared that COR might engage in various conspiracies to take over the nation, only a few of its members turned out to be committed to extremist principles.

Dominion theologians have an inability to focus on any one approach to bringing about a theocracy in the United States. Evangelical Christians include in their number Pentecostals, charismatics, and Calvinists. Some believe that salvation comes by the grace of God and the faith of believers. Others maintain that the saint and the sinner have predestined roles. Some assert that all the Founding Fathers—with the possible exception of Benjamin Franklin—were evangelical Christians who intended to build a Christian nation. Secular historians counter that, at best, most of the Founding Fathers were Deists.

IRA EINHORN

Was the "Unicorn" set up for murder by a secret government agency as he insists—or is Ira Einhorn just a New Age con man?

Although his surname, Einhorn, means "one horn" in German, Ira quite likely named himself the Unicorn because the image of the mythical silver-white creature with the single horn rising from its skull would suggest an aura of mystery and magic to his New Age followers and benefactors. However, the fact that the unicorn is also an ancient symbol for Christ has made former hippie guru Ira Einhorn's crimes of murder and deceit seem all the more offensive to millions of the more conventional members of society.

For twenty-two years, one of the leading icons in the peace-and-love counterculture movement of the 1960s managed to avoid being the star figure in a trial for the murder of his lover, Holly Maddux. Einhorn insists that he is innocent, that an ultra-secret group within the FBI or the CIA murdered his lover and framed him for the crime.

For the flower children of the late 1960s, the days and nights of the dawning of the Age of Aquarius were occupied with free love, antiwar protests, and experimental exercises with recreational drugs. Einhorn, Philadelphia's "official hippie," stressed that he was a lover, not a fighter, that he espoused harmony and understanding rather than violence. Those residents of the City of Brotherly Love who did not hail him as their guru knew Einhorn as the pacifist who organized the city's first "be-in," the environmentalist who established the nation's first Earth Day, and the publicity-grabbing hippie mystic who never bathed or groomed himself.

In October 1972 Einhorn began a stormy, star-crossed relationship with Helen "Holly" Maddux, a romance that to those who were not under the spell of Einhorn's New Age charms had to look like a real-life version of *Beauty and the Beast*. On the one hand, Holly was the all-American girl: a cheerleader in her Texas high school, a Bryn Mawr graduate, and a talented dancer whom many described as possessed of an "ethereal beauty." On the other hand there was the scruffy, wild-haired, bearded, unbathed hippie high priest preaching peace and love and regaling his disciples with tales of psychic powers. Obviously Holly, like so many others, had been enthralled by

Einhorn's charisma and had seen something in his musky animal magnetism that completely escaped those who perceived him only as a New Age con man.

Holly was certainly not alone in her idolatry of the boisterous hippie. The Unicorn seemed always to live well, the recipient of generous gifts from wealthy benefactors—and even from members of influential corporate structures who believed that the great unwashed master of the flower children, the self-styled "planetary enzyme," had secrets that they could exploit into big bucks.

Then came the day in September of 1977 when the sensible Texas girl who had been inside Holly all along wanted to leave the chaotic life she had been sharing with Einhorn. Friends of the couple remember noisy quarrels, attempts on Einhorn's part to reconcile, and more heated arguments. But Holly stood firm. She told the shaggy, unkempt counterculture potentate with the offensive body odor whom she had once found so charismatic that she was leaving him.

Einhorn's closest associates knew that he was furious that the beautiful blonde had dumped him. Friends of Holly's knew that she had yielded to his pleas to come visit him in his apartment on some pretext or other that they judged to be bogus. They had warned her to stay away, not to give in to his alluring promises. In hindsight, they had been correct, for from that day forward she was never seen again.

For eighteen months Holly's parents, three sisters, and brother in Texas were desperate. They felt certain that Einhorn had played a major role in her mysterious disappearance, and they hired a private investigator to find out the truth.

Meanwhile, Einhorn was busy, as always, cultivating new contacts among the local politicians and corporate executives. Socialites invited him to their parties; businesses hired him as their counterculture consultant.

For the Flower Children of the 1960s, the Age of Aquarius meant a time of free love, drugs, and war protests.

He was sorry, he told investigating authorities. He had absolutely no idea where Holly might have gone after she left him—and he was simply too busy to worry about her. Right now he was involved in so many really important humanitarian projects for the city of Philadelphia that Holly was the farthest thing from his mind.

In March 1979 Einhorn's downstairs neighbors were finding it difficult to tolerate the foul smell that had begun to permeate their apartment. When a sickening brown stain appeared on their ceiling and a strange fluid began leaking down, they called the police.

When the investigating officers arrived at Einhorn's apartment, the unperturbed, quintessential hippie answered the door in the nude. He offered no resistance as the officers began to search for the source of the offensive odor and the mysterious brown stain. In a closet off Einhorn's bedroom they found a large steamer trunk. Inside the trunk was the mummified body of a woman whose skull had been crushed. The wretched odor and the brownish fluid were coming from her decomposing corpse. A coroner's report was hardly necessary to confirm that the body was that of the missing Holly Maddux and that she had been bludgeoned to death.

Although Einhorn was arrested, on the day of his bail hearing an impressive number of high-profile character witnesses appeared in court to vouch for him. Einhorn's attorney, future senator Arlen Specter, managed to get a bail set that required only $4,000 cash. After all, a high priest of peace, love, and harmony could certainly be trusted to remain in Philadelphia so that he might clear things up at his trial.

Einhorn had plenty to say to his supporters to "clear things up": According to one of his stories, he didn't know Holly's body was decomposing there in the steamer trunk in his bedroom closet. He hadn't seen her after she had told him their relationship was over and had left him. She had obviously been murdered by agents of a secret government conspiracy and her body brought to his apartment and hidden there to frame him.

And then there was another oft-told story: He had returned to the apartment one day and found her murdered. She had been killed by either the FBI or the CIA and left there to frame him. Fearing that no one could believe him and accepting the sad fact that it was too late to help Holly, he hid her body in the steamer trunk and hoped that it would never be found.

Einhorn reminded his supporters that the Feds considered him an agent provocateur and that they were still furious with him for his participation in the antiwar movement and his communications with peaceniks behind the iron curtain. He claimed that they also wanted him out of the way because of his pioneering work on the Internet and his desire to make it international in scope, beyond the control of the federal government.

Mike Chitwood, later the police chief in Portland, Maine, was the detective who opened the steamer trunk that day in Einhorn's apartment and made the shocking discovery of Holly Maddux's corpse. Nearly two decades later he recalled that as soon as the judge set bail, he knew that Einhorn would skip the country: "I told the other homicide detectives, this guy will never come to trial, he'll take off."

Chitwood was right. Two months before his trial was to begin in January 1981, Einhorn fled the country.

For seventeen years, a Philadelphia district attorney's investigator, Richard DiBenedetto, tracked Einhorn from Ireland to England to Sweden, and finally to France. There were three occasions—twice in Dublin, once in Stockholm—when DiBenedetto missed his man by only a matter of hours. The persistent investigator commented to the press that it had always disgusted him that wealthy benefactors—many still under Einhorn's spell from his days as the hippie guru—continued to support the fugitive. DiBenedetto stated that it was consistently apparent to him that Einhorn was always living very well in his exile.

In 1993 a Philadelphia court tried Einhorn in absentia for the murder of Holly Maddux. The defendant was represented by an empty chair placed next to his lawyer. The unusual proceeding reflected the prosecutors' concern that a number of witnesses might die before Einhorn could be apprehended and brought back for trial in person. They also believed that an official trial could help bring closure for the Maddux family. Unfortunately, however, the guilty verdict against the Unicorn turned out to be an unforeseen obstacle in finally bringing him to justice.

A year or so later, DiBenedetto received a tip from a wealthy Canadian socialite who had been generously funding Einhorn's program of evading capture. It seems that during a time of serious introspection, the woman had come to believe no longer in Einhorn's innocence in Holly Maddux's death. She told DiBenedetto to look for Einhorn with a wealthy Swedish woman named Annika Flodin.

In 1997 a Swedish Interpol officer turned up the name of Annika Flodin Mallon on an application for a French driver's license. DiBenedetto knew that Einhorn had assumed the name Eugene Mallon, "borrowed" from a Dublin bookseller. Apparently Annika Flodin was now Mrs. Eugene Mallon, a.k.a. Mrs. Ira Einhorn.

On May 15, 1997—Einhorn's fifty-seventh birthday—DiBenedetto secured the fugitive's address in Champagne-Mouton, a village in the wine country of southwestern France. The investigator feared that someone would once again warn Einhorn of impending capture and that he would flee once more into obscurity. But finally, for once in the seventeen years of pursuit of the murderer, Einhorn received no tip that the noose was about to tighten around his neck. The French police arrested him in June, and it appeared that he was at last on his way back to Philadelphia for long-overdue justice.

But that was when the fact that the prosecutors had tried and convicted Einhorn in absentia became a giant international sticking point. France has a law which firmly states that defendants tried in absentia must receive a new trial when they appear so that they can speak in their own defense. The state of Pennsylvania has no such law. So, in December 1997, a French court denied the request to extradite Einhorn.

In 1998, according to Philadelphia district attorney Lynne Abraham, the Pennsylvania legislature "turned on a dime" to pass a law granting courts the power to offer new trials in special cases such as Einhorn's. Abraham was the judge who in 1979 had signed the warrant that allowed investigators to search Einhorn's apartment and led them to the gruesome discovery of Holly Maddux's body in the steamer trunk.

At last authorities in France agreed to extradition for Einhorn with the proviso—also following French law—that he not be given the death penalty. On October 17, 2002, twenty-five years after he was accused of the crime, Ira Einhorn, sixty-two, received an automatic sentence of life in prison without parole on the first-degree murder charge. He still maintained his innocence and his accusations of secret government agencies' having committed the murder of Holly Maddux, but District Attorney Abraham declared it a "sweet day for the Maddux family and for Holly's memory."

EISENHOWER AND THE EXTRATERRESTRIALS

In 1954 President Dwight D. Eisenhower inspected a variety of alien space vehicles on a U.S. Air Force base.

The story of President Eisenhower and the "Etherians," an extraterrestrial species, finds its origin in a letter from Gerald Light, Los Angeles, California, to Meade Layne, San Diego, the director of Borderline Sciences Research Associates, dated April 16, 1954. Light writes that he had just returned from Muroc (Muroc Dry Lake, located at Edwards Air Force Base, California) and that he made the trip in the company of Franklin Allen of the Hearst newspapers, Edwin Nourse (President Truman's financial adviser) of the Brookings Institution, and Bishop McIntyre of Los Angeles. Light asks that these names be kept confidential.

Then Light discloses the shocking sight that met those assembled at Edwards Air Force Base when "Etherians" appeared with their alien craft:

When we were allowed to enter the restricted section. I had the distinct feeling that the world had come to an end. For I have never seen so many human beings in a state of complete collapse and confusion, as they realized that their own world had indeed ended with such finality as to beggar description. The reality of otherplane aeroforms is now and forever removed from the realms of speculation and made a rather painful part of the consciousness of every responsible scientific and political group.

During my two days' visit, I saw five separate and distinct types of aircraft being studied and handled by our Air Force officials—with the assistance and permission of the Etherians! I have no words to express my reactions. It has finally happened. It is now a matter of history.

I will leave it to your own excellent powers of deduction to construct a fitting picture of the mental and emotional pandemonium that is now shattering the consciousness of hundreds of our scientific authorities and all the pundits of the various specialized knowledge that make up our current physics. In some instances I could not stifle a wave of pity as I watched the pathetic bewilderment of brilliant brains struggling to make some sort of rational explanation which would enable them to retain their familiar theories and concepts. I shall never forget those forty-eight hours at Muroc!

Light believed that President Eisenhower would soon go directly to the people via radio and television and make an official statement that the aliens had landed. That official announcement of aliens among the human population was never made. Conspiracy theorists assert that either the president reconsidered informing the American public or Majestic-12 and other secret government agencies persuaded him to keep the nation in the dark concerning the aliens.

In the 1990s the Earl of Clancarty, a member of Great Britain's House of Lords, repeat-

President Dwight Eisenhower is said to have been well familiar with the presence of alien vehicles and the Etherians on our planet.

ed the testimony of a British pilot who had been vacationing in Palm Springs in February 1954 and was summoned to Edwards Air Force Base by military officials. According to the pilot—a man Lord Clancarty respected as a gentleman of the greatest integrity—the aliens disembarked from their space vehicles and approached Eisenhower and a small group of political and military figures.

The ETs seemed able to breathe the air of Earth without the need of a helmet or other apparatus, and the pilot described them as basically humanlike in appearance, about the same height and build as an average man. However, their features were, in his opinion, somewhat misshapen. The aliens spoke English, and the thrust of their dialogue centered on their wish to begin a program of education that would make all of humanity aware of their presence. The British pilot recalled that Eisenhower was not in favor of this plan. In a very forthright manner he told the aliens that he didn't believe the people of the world were ready for the sudden revelation that extraterrestrials were on the planet. Such an announcement, in Eisenhower's assessment, would only cause widespread panic.

The aliens appeared to understand the president's point of view, and they agreed not to institute their proposed program of widespread education about their presence. Instead, they informed Eisenhower, they would continue to contact isolated humans until more people got used to their being here. The president agreed with a program of limited contact, but he urged the aliens not to do anything that would create panic and confusion among the people of Earth.

The ETs next demonstrated a number of their incredible technical advances. (Eisenhower reportedly was very uncomfortable when they displayed their ability to become invisible.) The aliens then boarded their craft and left the air base. Those who had witnessed the historic meeting were sworn to maintain complete secrecy.

Lord Clancarty clarified that although the pilot had kept his vow and had not previously disclosed word of the remarkable events at Edwards Air Force Base, he believed that all the principals who were present in 1954 were now deceased.

In 1993 Dr. Hank Krastman of Encino, California, revealed in *Unexplained* magazine that he had been present that day in 1954 at Edwards Air Force Base as a young sailor in the Royal Dutch Navy. Krastman was trained for internal services dealing with matters concerning the NATO pact and CIA affairs, and at nineteen years of age he was serving as an adjutant to his ship's commander. Krastman remembered that on February 19, 1954, they were briefed about a top-security meeting that would take place the following day. The next morning they left Long Beach Navy Base in a

van with a military police escort, and they arrived at Edwards Air Force Base at 10 A.M.

Escorted to a hangar at the far west side of the base, Krastman recognized President Eisenhower and, among others, the great physicist Albert Einstein, the German scientists Wernher von Braun and Victor Schauberger, and the American billionaire and aviation innovator Howard Hughes. Krastman wondered what the "two Nazi war criminals" von Braun and Schauberger were doing there. To the young Dutch sailor, von Braun, with his wartime work on the German V-1 and V-2 rockets, and Schauberger, who was involved in Hitler's secret V-7 flying discs, were enemy scientists who had been responsible for the deaths of many of his countrymen.

Krastman heard his commander being told that there were five alien ships in another hangar and that some of the ETs would demonstrate the capabilities of the craft. Krastman was not allowed to enter the hangar that contained the aliens and their spaceships. When his commander returned, he was very pale and would not give any information regarding what he had seen.

The next day, Krastman said, various large crates were loaded onto their ship for the return voyage to Holland. He later found out that the crates were destined for a secret underground NATO base—a converted coal mine of great depth—in Limburg, Holland.

In 1959 Krastman returned to the United States as an immigrant, and he has continued to dig into the true meaning of his peculiar experience in February 1954.

Some researchers continue to believe that Eisenhower never called the press conference that Gerald Light had been so certain would take place because the truth about flying saucers would have created "a state of complete collapse and confusion" a "mental and emotional pandemonium," and "pathetic bewilderment."

ELECTRONIC SPYING, TRACKING, AND HARASSMENT

From wiretaps and Internet monitoring to implanted microchips in our children, the government has many tools available to watch our every move.

The late Dr. Fred Bell often warned that electronic harassment can come in a variety of forms—it can be imposed by the surveillance of people's belongings or surroundings, by sabotaging computers, by directing high energy devices at targets, and by using voice data imaging in which voices are beamed into a person's head. The symptoms of electronic harassment often include unusual forgetfulness, suicidal or homicidal thoughts, panic attacks, depression, paranoia, and even death.

Warrantless Wiretapping

Before the Patriot Act, which was signed into law in 2001 by President George W. Bush, the use of electronic devices to track, spy on, or harass individuals constituted a violation of U.S. citizens' Fourth Amendment rights to privacy. Law enforcement agencies seeking to justify the interception of private communications in a private environment had to obtain a court order or warrant showing probable cause before they were permitted to "tap" someone's tools of electronic communication. Conspiracy theorists insist that such rights for individuals were being completely ignored by dozens of government and secret agencies using highly sophisticated techniques of electronic surveillance—without seeking court orders—even before Homeland Security violated previous rights to privacy.

In the warrantless telephone "bugging" of today, human agents are no longer required to sit long hours monitoring the calls of suspected criminals or terrorists. Speech-to-text software quickly creates machine-readable text from intercepted audio calls, which is then processed by automated call-analysis programs. Human agents are assigned the task of monitoring the suspect only when certain trigger words or phrases are detected by the electronic programs.

High on various watchdogs' lists is the National Security Agency (NSA), whose agents secretly conduct warrantless wiretapping on anyone they please. Conspiracy theorists maintain that the scope of the NSA's infrastructure is so vast and comprehensive that its range of abilities is as unknown to the average NSA employee as it is to the average U.S. citizen.

The Internet as an Instrument of Terrorism and Revolution

The Internet has become increasingly important as an instrument of terrorism—both foreign and domestic—as well as of civil unrest aimed at overthrowing governments. There is far too much data being transmitted on the Internet for human investigators to manually sift through all of it, so automated Internet surveillance computers search through an unimaginable cacophony of sounds and images seeking certain trigger words or phrases. In the United States, according to conspiracists, the Communications Assistance for Law Enforcement Act monitors all phone calls and broadband Internet traffic, including emails, Web traffic, instant messaging, and so forth. Billions of dollars per year are spent by the Information Awareness Office, the FBI, and the NSA in this pursuit.

The NSA has allegedly developed a supercomputer known only as A.I. (for Artificial Intelligence), or "Mr. Computer." A.I. is capable of forming a "hive mind," a kind of collective consciousness that can stretch across continental links. A.I.'s wiretapping program is able to copy verbatim every piece of data that travels across the Internet, send it to various data analysis stations, and provide a real-time analysis of the information packets.

The NSA also taps into the global wide-band radio listening system. By combining its numerous listening devices, the agency manages to detect nearly every expression of human thought. Through its advanced satellite network, supported by a remarkable network of ground stations throughout the world, it can identify all radio stations and their individual broadcasts. With its incredible wide receiver, it can also pick up WIFI, RFID, cordless telephones, cell phones, GPS, and satellite uploads and downloads.

As such conspiracy theorists as Dr. Fred Bell warned, the NSA's "Mr. Computer" can transmit ELF transmissions that can reduce enemies in specific geographical targets to quivering individuals suffering intense emotional duress. In extreme attacks, the transmissions can even kill target individuals by interfering with neuronal firing patterns and nerve impulses.

The FBI's Digital Collection System

In addition to the NSA's massive computer network, the FBI has built a nationwide computer system called the Digital Collection System (DCS), which is connected by fiber-optic cables and designed to collect and analyze wiretaps of all manner, including those utilized in ultra-secret terrorism investigations.

Increasingly, the U.S. government seems to believe that its citizens have no right to privacy in their public movements. With their growing access to invasive technologies, the police, the FBI, the Drug Enforcement Administration, and numerous other agencies are authorized to engage in covert 'round-the-clock surveillance over as long a period of time as the investigating agency deems necessary. The Justice Department has authorized law enforcement agencies to use warrantless GPS tracking devices to any suspect who drives a vehicle, for instance.

No Such Thing as a Private Telephone Call

There was a time when people became well aware of the warrantless wire-tapping of their telephones on landlines and believed that at least their cell phones were safe from others eavesdropping on their private conversations. That time of freedom and privacy no longer exists on the cell phone. Anything you say on your smart phone can easily be sent to the carriers, who keep a wealth of information regarding text messages, call-location data, and PINS. None of the carriers reveal to anxious and concerned customers how long they store such private and privileged information. Neither do they make it known that law enforcement and security agencies may easily obtain such data.

Intelligence and law enforcement agencies in the United States and the United Kingdom possess the technology that can activate the microphones in cell or smart phones by accessing the phones' diagnostic/maintenance features and listening to any conversation occurring near the person holding the instrument.

DARPA, Our Semi-Secret Agency

The Defense Advanced Research Projects Agency (DARPA) is the agency that conspiracy buffs term a "semi-secret" anti-terrorism security group. It is officially an agency of the U.S. Department of Defense and is responsible for the development of new military technology. DARPA is independent of other military units and reports directly to the senior management of the U.S. Department of Defense. It employs approximately 240 personnel and is given a $3.2 billion budget (conspiracists say the budget has been boosted dramatically).

The agency's original name was the Advanced Research Projects Agency (ARPA), and it was established in 1958 in response to the Soviets' launching of *Sputnik* in 1957. The mission of ARPA was to upgrade U.S. military technology and be always at least one step

The UAV Global Hawk is a high-altitude military drone. Could drones like this one also be spying on the American people?

ahead of the nation's potential enemies. It was renamed DARPA in March 1972, then retitled ARPA in February 1993, then redesignated DARPA in March 1996.

ARPA's Network (ARPANET) was the world's first operational packet switching network and the core network of what became the global Internet. The network was originally funded by DARPA for use by its projects at universities and research laboratories in the United States. In retrospect, it seems that DARPA was working for Big Brother from its very inception.

In October 2011, DARPA let slip word about its "Narrative Networks" project. The first part of the program would involve the analysis of what happens to people when they hear or see a message. Is it possible that certain messages or images actually cause alterations in the brain to accommodate new ideas? The second part would involve a means of taking advantage of those individuals who are vulnerable to such messaging and to bombard them with messages that would overwrite any undesirable brain changes that might have occurred to people susceptible to bad messages so their behavior could be moderated.

Interesting. But what if an agency of the U.S. government used such technology to reprogram those individuals who object to certain programs that the government might wish to implement, such as declaring war or raising taxes or sending protesters to FEMA camps?

Combat Zones that See

DARPA is also developing a project called "Combat Zones that See," which would utilize all the video security cameras in a city and link them up to a centralized monitoring station. With thousands of cameras at strategic places, the centralized station could track individuals and vehicles as they moved through the city. Any activities assessed as "suspicious" could be reported to law enforcement and intercepted or investigated.

While city governments usually claim that the cameras are intended for traffic control, they are also used for general surveillance. Chicago's government has openly declared that it will have a surveillance camera on every street corner by 2016. Washington, D.C., recently had 5,000 "traffic" cameras installed.

Drones, the Eyes in the Sky

DARPA also developed the Heterogeneous Aerial Reconnaissance Team program that employs large teams of drone planes that pilot themselves and have the technology to automatically make decisions about who looks suspicious and how best to monitor them. Such judgments are shared with other drones, and human operatives can be notified if their suspicions prove to be justified. A squadron of these automated, self-directing drones can patrol a city or any designated area, tracking suspicious individuals and reporting their questionable activities to a centralized monitoring station.

Disconnecting Unwanted Telephone Calls

The London Metropolitan Police recently purchased a suitcase-sized device that can remotely disable phones, intercept communications, and track individuals in real time. All the police need to do is to arrive on the scene of a protest or a scene of civil unrest, turn on their suitcase device, and instantly no one is able to record the demonstration on their cell phones or call for help.

The device, called "ICT hardware," is produced by Datong in the UK. Datong was awarded $1.6 million in contracts from the U.S. Secret Service, Special Operations Command, and the Bureau of Immigration and Customs Enforcement. In February 2010, they were awarded another $1.2 million to deliver tracking and location technology to the American defense industry.

The suitcase device can intercept text messages and telephone calls, which allows law enforcement agencies to track the caller's movements in real time. It can also prevent outbound communications from reaching a cell tower, which would be most effective in preventing crowds from being able to organize during demonstrations and protest rallies. In addition, cell phone signals that can set off bombs can be blocked.

Someone Is Looking over Your Shoulder at the Supermarket

The innocent act of visiting a supermarket can place entire families on a massive tracking system. Almost any physical item purchased— from a toothbrush to a bottle of aspirin—carries its own information in the form of an embedded chip. This chip contains a consumer goods tracking code, an EPC (Electronic Product Code) that sends out an identification signal permitting it to communicate with reader devices and other products embedded with similar chips. The consumer goods tracking system is known as Radio Frequency Identification (RFID), and it signals the death of consumer privacy. The UPC bar code, with which every consumer has been familiar for decades, simply identifies the product. There is nothing wrong with that, people think, because it helps the merchant keep track of his stock. But the EPC does far more by assigning a unique number to every single item produced by every company in the United States—from soda to cream cheese. The RFID tags, hardly larger than a speck of dust, are planted directly into the product during the manufacturing process. Everything from soup to nuts, and from razor blades to automobile parts, is tracked as products move from warehouses to retail outlets. Every company is aware of the whereabouts of its products at all times. The eventual goal is for RFID to spawn a totally linked world wherein every item produced is numbered, identified, catalogued, and tracked.

As Katherine Albrecht writes in "Supermarket Cards: The Tip of the Retail Surveillance Iceberg," RFID would be able to "monitor individuals' behavior to undreamt of extremes. With corporate sponsors like Wal-Mart, Target, the Food Marketing Institute, Home Depot, and British supermarket chain Tesco, as well as some of the world's large consumer goods manufacturers ...

it may not be long before RIFD based surveillance tags begin appearing in every store-bought item in a consumer's home."

RIFD Chips in School Kids

In 2008 the Middletown School District in Rhode Island put in place a pilot program to monitor student movements at the Aquidneck School by implanting RFID chips in their schoolbags. The chips would be read by an external device installed in the school buses, which would also be fitted with GPS instruments. The American Civil Liberties Union (ACLU) argued that the school was entitled to track its buses, but it was "a quantitative leap to monitor children themselves."

Monitoring school children with RFID chips has been going on since at least 2005, when a grade school in California began handing out RFID badges. In 2001 a preschool in Richmond, California, installed an expensive high-tech system to track the attendance of its students. The system was heralded as a pilot program for others to come.

RIFD Chips in Workers … Next, Everyone!

Workers in the United Kingdom have gone on strike to protest being tagged with RIFD chips by their employers. Conspiracists believe that it may not be long before all employees are injected with chips to ensure against thefts. Conspiracists also worry that a day might come when everyone will be tracked and scanned wherever they go.

The Verichip, produced by Applied Digital Solutions, is only slightly larger than a grain of rice and is injected under the skin. The Verichip Subscriber Number allows a scanner to access personal information that is on the Internet. from Verichip's database. Thousands of people have already had such chips inserted. The Attorney General's office in Mexico required all 160 of its workers to have such a chip inserted for identity and access control purposes.

ELF

Conspiracy researchers are convinced that ELF has been used for mind control and has been responsible for many alleged suicides and mysterious deaths.

Extremely low frequency (ELF) is the band of radio frequencies from 3 to 300 Hz. The U.S. Navy has used ELF very successfully in communicating with their submerged submarines. Submarines are blocked from most electromagnetic signals because of the electrical conductivity of salt water. However, communications in the ELF range are able to penetrate much more deeply.

ELF is quite limited in its use in ordinary communications for the very reason that it is useful to signal submarines. Its extremely low transmission rate would require enormously large antennae in order to communicate over long distances or internationally. The government constructed and maintained two sites, in the Chequamegon National Forest, Wisconsin, and the Escanaba State Forest, Michigan, each utilizing power lines as antennas stretching from fourteen to twenty-eight miles in length. Ecologists became concerned about environmental conditions and human health problems resulting from the great amounts of electricity generated and emitted by ELF, and in 1984 a federal judge ordered construction halted until further studies could be made and evaluated. In spite of the U.S. Navy's protesting that they had invested over $25 million in studying the effects of ELF and had found their frequencies no more harmful to the environment and humans than standard power lines, the antennae were ordered dismantled beginning in 2004.

Conspiracy theorists don't buy into the abandonment of any government ELF program. They warn that the human brain can be controlled, even at a distance, by the utilization of ELF carried by pulse-modulated mi-

Located in the Chequamegon National Forest in Wisconsin, this satellite receiver was part of the ELF project. According to the U.S. Navy, this and other receivers were shut down in 2004. Conspiracy theorists have their doubts.

crobeams. Shadow government or New World Order agencies have the technology to broadcast mind-control commands directly into the brain by use of microwave beams.

Secret Russian neuromedical research discovered that there are specific brain frequencies for each mood, thought, and emotion that humans experience. An extensive catalog of these brain actions with their distinctive frequencies was established by Russian scientists and psychologists. An agent can beam ELF waves for anger, suicide, hysteria, lust, paranoia, or whatever he chooses at a potential victim and control that individual's actions from the room next door or from a car parked across the street.

Conspiracy researchers are convinced that the transmission of ELF has been in-strumental in the alleged suicides and mysterious deaths of scientists, UFO investigators, and witnesses to secret New World Order machinations. If the suicide brain frequency should be beamed at a victim, he or she would enter severe bouts of depression that would quite likely result in suicide. Researchers see this as an explanation why a scientist, a researcher, or a government official who was reported by his or her friends and family to have been positive and happy might suddenly become depressed and commit suicide after a few hours or days of ELF beams.

EXOPOLITICS AND OBAMA'S TRIPS TO MARS

"Exopolitics may turn the dominant view of our universe upside down. It reveals that we live on an isolated planet in the midst of a populated, evolving, and highly organized interplanetary, intergalactic, and multidimensional universal society. It explores why Earth seems to have been quarantined for eons from a more evolved universal society. Exopolitics suggests specific steps to end our isolation by reaching out to the technologically and spiritually advanced civilizations that are engaging our world at this unique, challenging time in human history." — Alfred Lambremont Webre, J.D., M.Ed.

Exopolitics is the creation of Alfred Lambremont Webre's groundbreaking work as a futurist at the Stanford Research Institute, where in 1977 he directed a proposed extraterrestrial communication study project for the Carter White House.

In 2011 Webre revealed that he had learned from two former participants of a secret space project that the CIA had developed a visitation program to the planet Mars in the early 1980s. As if it were not astounding enough to learn that humans have already traveled to the red planet, the two whistle-blowers told Webre that young Barry Soetoro, whom we know today as Barack Obama, teleported to Mars on at least two flights.

Andrew D. Basiago, currently a lawyer in Washington state, who served in the Defense Advanced Research Projects Agency's (DARPA) time travel program, Project Pegasus, in the 1970s, and fellow "chronometer" William B. Stillings have confirmed that young Barry was enrolled in their Mars training class in 1980 and that they each saw him during visits to the early U.S. facilities on Mars from 1981 to 1983. Barry's mother, Stanley Ann Dunham, was on assignment for the CIA in Kenya and Indonesia while her son was tutored for travel to Mars.

Ten teenagers were enrolled in the Mars training program, which was held at the College of Siskiyous, a small college near Mt. Shasta in California. One of the select ten was Regina Dugan, who in later years Obama would appoint as the nineteenth director, and first female director, of DARPA in 2009. When the students attained a certain degree of proficiency, they teleported to Mars via a "jump room" located in a building owned by Hughes Aircraft adjacent to the Los Angeles International Airport.

Basiago has stated that the U.S. facilities on Mars in the early 1980s were rudimentary, appearing much like the construction phase of a rural mining project. The infrastructure supporting the jump rooms on Mars were also in the beginning stages of constructing buildings that could serve as a permanent base. Among the personnel on the early base whom Basiago encountered was Courtney M. Hunt of the CIA. Basiago learned that the Mars program was created in order for the United States to be able to establish a claim of territorial sovereignty over the planet. In addition, the planetary pioneers were to familiarize the Martian humanoids and lower life forms with the appearance of humans.

For those who doubt Basiago's and Stilling's stories, Alfred Lambremont Webre lists others whom the two say were seen on Mars while they were on the planet: Michael Relfe, a U.S. serviceman who spent twenty years on Mars as a member of the permanent security staff; and Arthur Neumann, a former Department of Defense scientist who has testified publicly that he teleported to the facility on Mars.

Laura Magdalene Eisenhower, great-granddaughter of U.S. President Dwight D. Eisenhower, has stated that in 2006 she was approached by a government agent who informed her of the bases on Mars and attempted to recruit her to travel there. In 2007 she gave her final refusal to become a member of the secret U.S. colony on Mars that allegedly has a population of 500,000.

FACE ON MARS

The government is covering up proof of an ancient civilization that once thrived on the planet Mars, for fear that the shock of such a discovery would destroy Earth's own civilization.

Brian O'Leary, author of *Mars 1999* and *Exploring Inner and Outer Space,* worked with Carl Sagan at Cornell University and was an Apollo astronaut. O'Leary is supportive of the Mars Pathfinder probes but disappointed by what he regards as NASA's lack of vision—especially the agency's failure to investigate adequately the Cydonia region and its mile-wide structure that very much resembles a human or humanoid face.

Richard Hoagland, author of *The Monuments of Mars,* has studied and gathered scientific data on several provocative photos of the surface of Mars taken by NASA's Viking probe in 1976. These photos show certain formations that appear unusual compared with the rest of the geologic features on the Martian surface, and he contends that these formations are artificial, not unlike the Egyptian pyramids or Sphinx. He goes so far as to say

that these features may have been constructed by some alien race thousands or even millions of years ago. He also claims that the same possibility exists for Europa, a moon of Jupiter, as seen in Voyager mission photos.

Hoagland was a consultant to NASA's Goddard Space Flight Center from 1975 to 1980. During the historic Apollo missions to the moon, he served as science adviser to CBS news. The first time that Hoagland saw the mysterious Sphinx-like face in the Martian landscape known as Cydonia (not to be confused with Sedona, the New Age mecca in Arizona) was the summer of 1976, when NASA's *Viking* had taken 100,000 pictures of Mars.

When a group of reporters and scientists were shown the initial image of the "face," they were told that the spacecraft had taken another frame a few hours later in which the whole image did not appear. It was all a trick of the light. When the project scientist at NASA made a joke of the preposterous thought that it could really be an artificial structure, everyone laughed with him, Hoagland says, because, after all, everyone knew that NASA's highest objective was to find evidence that we are not alone in the universe.

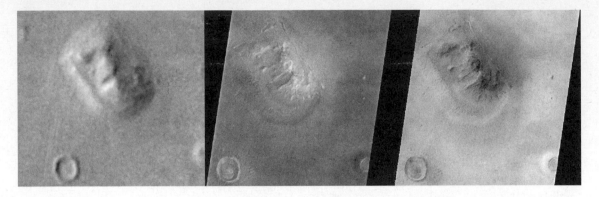

Three views of the Face on Mars that many believe to be evidence that there was once a civilization on the Red Planet.

Hoagland's subsequent investigations have yielded what he believes to be evidence not only of the mysterious face, but of several five-sided and four-sided pyramids. In his firm and educated opinion, no natural force could have fashioned such regularly repeated geometric structures. It is as if an unknown ancient alien culture had left a message for those who would discover the objects in an undetermined future. Perhaps the message of Cydonia is that a code has been laid out for those intelligent enough to figure it out, astute enough to determine the mathematics and the geometry that can open new gateways to the universe.

Hoagland was undaunted on April 7, 1998, when NASA's Mars Global Surveyor sent back photographs of the Face on Mars that were clearly expected to debunk any theories that an ancient Martian or other extraterrestrial civilization had carved the mysterious feature. After twenty-two years of waiting for clearer photographs that would confirm the handiwork of intelligent life on Mars, the new pictures showed only eroded landscape and a pile of rocks.

While other researchers fulminated about NASA's having "erased" the face, Hoagland stated that he was really far more interested in the ruins of what has been called the City of Cydonia. And now he could only wonder if NASA had missed obtaining better pictures of

the city on purpose. "This is ancient, ruined architecture we're seeing," he told *USA Today* in May 1998. Hoagland went on to accuse NASA of having obtained photographs that could confirm his theory but were refusing to release them because they would so shock humankind that civilization might collapse.

Tom Van Flandern, former head of celestial mechanics at the U.S. Naval Observatory, who currently runs a Washington, D.C., group called Meta Research, states that because the Martian region photographed by NASA has so many odd patterns and shapes, he would place the odds at a billion to one against all of them having occurred naturally. According to Van Flandern, the fact that the desert surrounding the Face on Mars is flat and featureless is of great significance in contrast to this sudden four-hundred-meter object rising at a regular height all around with perfectly straight sides. Ninety-degree angles are common; the bottom is symmetric. He claims that even in the new images the eye sockets and forehead are well defined and match up well with the original photo of the face.

Continuing with his analysis, Van Flandern told Art Bell on the *Coast to Coast* radio program that before seeing the new image sent back by the Mars Global Surveyor, "we knew that a fractal content implied a natural origin, while regularity, angularity, and symmetry implied artificiality. I see almost no fractality with the exception of the nose bridge, the feature least protected from wind erosion. I do see smooth lines and curves, right angles and corners (including one in the 'furrowed' eyebrow) and lots of symmetry, especially detailed symmetry in the headdress enclosure."

In 1984 Richard Hoagland organized the Independent Mars Investigation (renamed the Enterprise Mission) and has been a fierce advocate of the position that NASA has been withholding knowledge concerning structures and artifacts discovered on Mars and the moon that would yield proof of extraterrestrial civilizations. Hoagland has come to believe that there are two space programs in existence: one to appease the taxpayers, and another conducted by a top-secret group with a hidden agenda.

FALUN GONG, THE WHEEL OF LAW

Li Hongzhi says that his cult Falun Gong battles evil aliens that come to Earth to undermine its spirituality. The Chinese government pronounced the Falun Gong itself to be evil.

Falun Gong means the "Practice of the Wheel of Dharma." (Dharma is a complex Hindu and Buddhist concept that translates in a broad sense to "law," especially to the natural order of personal ethics and principles of conduct, equivalent to what is commonly referred to as "religion.") The founder of the movement, Li Hongzhi, a former Chinese government grain clerk who now lives in the United States, claims to have been born on May 13, the supposed birthday of Siddhartha Gautama, the Buddha, but government records list his birthday as July 7, 1952. Li also claims that Falun Gong, which he founded in 1992, has 100 million members worldwide, 80 million of whom are in China. The Chinese gov-

ernment insists that the number in their country is more like 2 million.

Although Falun Gong incorporates many Buddhist and Taoist concepts and terms, Li insists that it is not a religion and that its exercises and techniques complement all religious expressions. He says that Earth has been quietly invaded by evil extraterrestrials who want to undermine human spirituality by contributing to the rapid expansion of technology. Humankind would be much better off without computers and all other machines that replicate human activity and supplant human productivity.

The movement's sacred texts, *Revolving the Law Wheel* and *China Falun Gong,* were both written by Li. The Falun Gong symbol is a spinning swastika (from the Buddhist and Taoist traditions) surrounded by four smaller spinning swastikas and four twirling yin-yang symbols. Five daily exercises activate the higher abilities of mind, body, and spirit and contribute to an individual's self-examination and self-knowledge. Through proper and conscientious practice, the student will be able to attain enlightenment and to master many supernatural powers, including levitation, psychokinesis, and telepathy.

For thirteen hours on April 25, 1999, fifteen thousand members of the Falun Gong's Qigong sect, standing five or six rows deep along more than a mile of the Avenue of Everlasting Peace in central Beijing, protested their negative treatment in the state media and demanded official recognition for their sect and the freedom to publish their texts. The protest, held only six weeks before the tenth anniversary of the arrest of dissidents on Tiananmen Square and the infamous events of June 4, 1989, managed to get the State Council of China to agree to negotiate with the Falun Gong. However, in July 1999, Chinese officials branded the Falun Gong an evil cult, claiming that it had caused the deaths of fifteen hundred of its members. The

Members of the Falun Gong celebrate Chinese New Year in Flushing, New York.

Chinese government banned the practice of the cult and sent more than fifty thousand adherents to prisons, labor camps, and mental hospitals. The relationship between the cult and the government continues to be uneasy.

FEDERAL EMERGENCY MANAGEMENT AGENCY

According to some conspiracy theorists, FEMA has a very nasty secret agenda.

Certain watchdogs of the freedoms of U.S. citizens see the Federal Emergency Management Agency as having a secret agenda very different from FEMA's own portrayal of itself as rescuer and benefactor when disaster strikes.

Among the concerns of many serious-minded guardians of American's freedoms and liberties is an executive order signed into existence by President George H. W. Bush in 1989. This document authorized FEMA to build forty-three primary camps, each of which would have the capacity of housing 35,000 to 45,000 people, and hundreds of secondary facilities, some of which could accommodate 100,000 individuals.

Have these camps been constructed in preparation for some great future cataclysm that will deprive millions of people of their homes and force them to take shelter in the barracks-style housing thoughtfully prepared for such an emergency by the benevolent FEMA? Or are the camps designed by the federal government to hold prisoners of the state? Rather than refugee camps, are they concentration camps constructed to isolate those citizens who dare to oppose a new political order in the United States?

There are executive orders that grant frightening powers to FEMA and actually permit the government agency to suspend the Constitution and all the rights and liberties of U.S. citizens, as those rights are now known. These orders are in the Federal Register located in Washington, D.C., where they can be examined by concerned citizens who may wish to judge for themselves the awesome potential control of FEMA over all Americans and over every aspect of American life.

Executive Order 12148 stipulates that FEMA is in charge during national security emergencies, such as national disasters, social unrest, insurrection, or a national financial crisis.

Executive Order 11051 empowers FEMA to put the following orders into effect in time of increased international or domestic tension:

Executive Order 10995 authorizes FEMA, if the agency deems it necessary to accomplish its goals, to seize all communications media in the United States.

Executive Order 10997 provides for the seizure of all electric power, petroleum, gas, fuels, and minerals, both public and private.

Executive Order 10998 allows the seizure of all food supplies and resources, public and private—and all farms, lands, and equipment.

Executive Order 10999 provides for the seizure of all means of transportation, including personal cars, trucks, or vehicles of any kind, and total control over all highways, seaports, and waterways.

Executive Order 11003 allows the government to take over all airports and aircraft—commercial, public, and private.

Executive Order 11005 provides for the seizure of all railroads, inland waterways, and public storage facilities.

Executive Order 11000 allows the government to seize all American people for feder-

ally supervised work forces. If the government deems it necessary, it may even split up families.

Executive Order 11002 empowers the postmaster general to conduct a national registration of all persons. Under this order all U.S. citizens must report to their local post office to be registered. It is at this juncture that families might be separated and individual members assigned to new areas.

Executive Order 11004 allows the Housing and Finance Authority to relocate entire communities and to designate areas to be abandoned and new locations to be repopulated.

Executive Order 11001 permits the government to seize all functions of health, education, and welfare.

All of the orders listed above were combined by President Richard Nixon into Executive Order 11490, which permits the government to take control if a national emergency should be declared by the president. Should citizens of the United States be growing a bit nervous when we consider all the "national emergencies" that are declared each year? Should we worry that FEMA might one day decide that it is time to exercise the extraordinary powers that have been granted to it?

After the summer of 2011, when the Occupy Wall Street (OWS) protesters had established a presence in many cities, Oakland, California mayor Jean Quan called for a crackdown on the OWS protesters in her city in early November 2011. When word of Oakland's action became known, conspiracists warned that the Department of Homeland Security and FEMA might well be preparing to begin the occupation of some of the dissident camps first established by FEMA in the 1960s and 1970s. At that time, according to those concerned with our freedoms, FEMA was alerted to detain as many as 20 million African Americans in anticipation of a black militant uprising in the United States, as well as those members of all ethnic groups who protested the Vietnam War.

Mayor Quan disclosed in an interview that she had been on a conference call with the mayors or civic leaders of 18 U.S. cities prior to the raids on the Oakland OWS protesters. Shortly after the Oakland police dispersed the encampment of OWS in that city, raids scattered OWS groups across the nation. With a number of civic leaders and government officials portraying the OWS as homegrown terrorists in the making, the likelihood that those protesting for any cause that the establishment deemed threatening might be packed off to detention camps seemed a real possibility.

Oakland, California mayor Jean Quan called for a crackdown on the OWS protesters in her city in early November 2011.

When New York Representative Peter King, head of the House Homeland Security Subcommittee, expressed his concerns that the federal government had to be cautious concerning the OWS gaining any legitimacy with the general public, conspiracy researchers became worried. Especially, perhaps, when Rep. King said that he was old enough to recall what happened in the 1960s, when left-wing protesters took to the streets.

King warned that the government must be alert to this new movement being glorified by the media because it might attain enough public acceptance to actually shape policy. When other government officials vowed not to allow the OWS movement to gain power, conspiracists heard echoes of COINTELPRO, the FBI's unconstitutional secret police who menaced protesters in the 1960s and 1970s.

The National Defense Authorization Act, which was passed by the Senate immediately after 9/11, allows all military branches to be used to quell civic disturbances and to round up political activists. In addition, regarding those active protesters who might lead troublesome demonstrations, the NDAA allows any American suspected of civil disobedience to be snatched off the streets and confined.

In 2006, KBR, a global engineering and services company that is a subsidiary of Halliburton, was contracted by Homeland Security to build detention camps that could hold large numbers of people. The ostensible reasons given for such camps was that they were to be used as places to hold an emergency influx of immigrants; they were also to be made available for unnamed "new government programs" that would need to house large numbers of people.

In 2008 troops returning from duty in Iraq were put on notice that they could be called to serve on homeland patrols to deal with crowd control. The *Washington Post* reported that as many as 20,000 U.S. military troops could be called to assist in squelching civil unrest and terror attacks set in motion in the event of complete economic collapse.

On December 31, 2011, President Barack Obama expressed his reservations about his signing into law the bill that Congress placed on his desk extending the powers of the NDAA. It would allow even a U.S. citizen detained on U.S. soil to be placed in military custody. In spite of such reservations, the president did sign the law.

Such a seemingly unconstitutional and dangerous act reinforced fears initially instigated by the revelation that in early December 2011 KBR was hiring subcontractors to staff and outfit "emergency environment" camps in five regions in the United States. It seems to conspiracy theorists that the risk of protesters being thrown into FEMA camps is now a grim reality.

FISH AND BIRD KILLS ON MASSIVE SCALE

In early 2011 reports flooded in from all over the world about massive fish and bird die-offs. Theories multiplied as to the cause, from freak weather events, to disease, to the effects of HAARP on wildlife.

On New Year's Day, 2011, residents of Beebe, Arkansas, awoke to find the bodies of over 5,000 red-winged blackbirds strewn over 1.5 square miles. Blackbirds do not fly at night. What were they doing flapping around after dark? What caused this mass killing of birds that would normally be roosting after dark? Theories ranged from people shooting fireworks on New Year's Eve to lightning, thunder, or hail that sent the birds into a panic. Necropsies ruled out poison.

John Fitzpatrick, director of Cornell University's ornithology laboratory in Ithaca, New York, suggested that the most likely explanation was that the birds were nesting in a single tree that got caught up by a thunderstorm that fatally soaked and chilled them. Violent weather had invaded much of Arkansas that New Year's Eve, including a tornado that killed three people, so lightning might have frightened the birds into taking flight.

Perhaps the thousands of dead blackbirds found in Beebe might be explained, but a deadly and mysterious plague that killed millions of birds and fish seemed to be just the beginning of events striking all around the world.

December 20, 2010

Reports were received that 100 tons of sardines, croaker, and catfish began washing up in Brazilian fishing towns.

January 4, 2011

- 500 blackbirds were found dead in a region of Louisiana about 300 miles south of Beebe.
- Dozens of dead blackbirds were reported in Kentucky.
- Hundreds of dead birds were found in central Sweden.
- Millions of dead fish surfaced in Maryland's Chesapeake Bay.

January 5

- 100,000 dead drum fish were found in the Arkansas River, 100 miles away from the site of the dead blackbirds in Beebe.
- 40,000 bodies of Velvet swimming crabs, lobsters, sponges, and anemones were found on the beaches of England.
- Hundreds of dead snapper fish were washed up on the beaches of Coromandel Peninsula in New Zealand.

January 6

- 10,000 dead birds were found in Manitoba.
- Thousands of dead birds and fish were reported in the St. Clair River, Ontario.
- Hundreds of dead fish appeared in Lincoln Park, southeastern Michigan.
- Pelicans died at terrible rate in Topsail Beach, North Carolina.
- East Texas was alarmed by deaths of hundreds of birds.

January 7

- Mass deaths of petrels and other seabirds were discovered in New Zealand.
- One hundred tons of dead fish were found floating on Lake Buhi, Philippines.
- Tons of farm fish were found dead in Vietnam.

January 8

- Thousands of turtle doves fell dead from the sky in Italy.
- Flocks of dead birds were found in Wilson County, Tennessee.

January 10

- Hundreds of dead sealife of several varieties washed ashore in South Carolina.
- Thousands of dead barramundi fish floated up on shore in Australia.
- Millions of dead fish, alligators, and turtles floated on Bolivian rivers.
- Two thousand five hundred tons of fish died in China.
- Thousands of small fish washed ashore in southern Cuba.
- Hundreds of dead birds fell from the sky in Germany.
- Numerous dead whales washed ashore on the Ghana coast.
- Thousands of dead fish were found in India's Yarmuna River.

January 11

- Mass deaths of birds occurred in areas of Brazil, Thailand, Sweden, and the United States.

January 12

- Thousands of bird deaths were reported in Karacabey, Turkey.

January 14

- Three hundred dead birds dropped from the sky in Alabama.

January 15

- Fifteen hundred dead birds fell to earth in Ukraine.
- In the United Kingdom, carcasses of dozens of seals were found off Norfolk Coast; 100 dead birds fell on a British home; 40,000 dead devil crabs found on a beach.
- Mysterious deaths of puffer fish were reported in Hawaii.
- Large numbers of dead birds were found in Southern Illinois.
- Unexplained whale deaths, the highest on record, were reported having occurred off Argentina.

Throughout the month of January, bizarre mass deaths of fish and birds continued to occur around the world. Here are even more examples:

- Twenty-four pilot whales were found dead in northern New Zealand.
- Ten thousand cattle died mysteriously in Vietnam.
- A million dead fish filled a Los Angeles area marina.
- Thousands of dead fish washed ashore in Florida, followed by the bodies of over a million jellyfish.
- Hundreds of dead birds were found near Lake Charles, Louisiana.
- Twenty dead horses died suddenly on a farm in Virginia.
- Two hundred dead cows were found in Portage County, Wisconsin.

Many suspects were named as the possible assassins in these strange mass deaths of birds and fish. Pollution was named as a likely possibility, followed by various types of poisons. When these possibilities were ruled out by scientists and environmentalists, the general public was quick to voice a number of candidates:

- Monsanto's genetic engineering program.
- The endtimes—God is coming for His people and Judgment Day is near. The mass killing of birds and fish was a warning sign of what certain errant humans had in store.

- Chemical dispersants thrown into the Gulf to cover up the BP oil spill in the Caribbean.

- The Bush family working with the Bilderbergers.

- Earth movements causing the release of methane gas.

While conspiracy buffs could embrace one or more of the above as possible causes, number one on most of their lists was HAARP or some other weather modification instrumentation. The many flocks of birds struck down from the sky and the hundreds of tons of fish killed in bodies of water around the world were simply collateral damage from experiments conducted to fine-tune advanced mechanisms for controlling world weather.

FLUORIDATION

For over half a century fluoridation has been touted as one of the most beneficial means of preventing tooth decay, especially when the process is started and maintained from childhood on. Conspiracy theorists advise that new research reveals the opposite to be true. In fact fluoridation is literally poisoning us, young and old.

Fluoride is the ionic form of fluorine, and although elemental fluorine is rare (because it combines so readily with other elements), in the ionic form it is the thirteenth most common element in the earth's crust. Manmade fluorine compounds have become grossly abundant since the invention of weapons of mass destruction used in World War II. Fluoride and uranium are key components in the atomic bomb, and fluoride is a key ingredient in fluorinated organophosphate nerve agents, such as sarin.

Drinking water containing fluoride was first utilized in Nazi prison camps, in a deliberate effort to sterilize and subdue prisoners into calm submission. In the 1930s Hitler and Nazi scientists envisioned world domination through mass medication of water supplies. A report submitted to the German general staff indicated findings that repeated doses of very small amounts of fluoride would gradually decrease people's ability to resist domination, slowly narcotizing a certain region of the brain and rendering the individuals submissive to the will of those who wished to govern them.

Charles E. Perkins, an expert in biochemistry, physiology, and the pathology of fluorine, said that when the Nazis invaded Poland, the German and Russian general staffs exchanged scientific and military ideas, including the scheme of mass control through water medication. Perkins declared, "with all sincerity and earnestness," that "any person who drinks artificially fluorinated water for a period of one year or more will never again be the same person mentally or physically."

In 1945, select cities across America added the chemical sodium fluoride to the water, and eventually most U.S. cities followed suit—thinking it was the healthful thing to do. The "wonder-working" benefits of fluoride were taught not only to dentists and dental hygienists, but also to children in elementary-school health classes. Soon families across the United States spent money and time making dental appointments for their children and themselves in hope of having strong, healthy, and cavity-free teeth. In order to enhance the entire process, dental fluorination treatments began offering a vast variety of flavors, such as bubblegum, mint, or cinnamon. In the 1960s and 1970s guidelines issued by the Centers for Disease Control suggested that schoolchildren's drinking water should be fluoridated at approximately *4.5 times* the amount of municipal water, for "greater benefit" to the children.

The fluoride contamination of our environment comes from all the following things: coal combustion, cigarette smoke, pesticides (such as roach and rat poisons), animal feeds, fertilizer, plastics, nonstick cookware, soft drinks, juices and other drinks (both

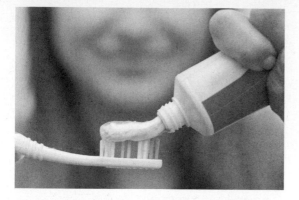

Fluoride in our toothpaste is meant to prevent cavities, and it has also been placed in American water supplies, but is it actually poisoning us?

canned and bottled), and, unfathomably, in an astounding number of pharmaceutical products. Antibiotics, steroids, anesthetics, vitamins, antidepressants, hypnotic psychiatric drugs, and, of course, military nerve gas, all contain fluoride. Even molecular imaging and tracking agents contain fluoride.

Conspiracy researchers maintain that current research reveals that fluoride does not prevent cavities or slow gum disease—in fact, the opposite is true. Many studies indicate that fluoride *causes* cavities and gum disease. Research on toddlers living in regions where the water is 100 percent fluoridated now have twice the rate of cavities as those in regions that have banned fluoridation. Many are asking if there is a conspiracy involved in suppressing this and other information about possible adverse effects of fluoride.

Going all the way back to 1954, doctors have suspected and reported fluoride to be harmful. Dr. George L. Waldbott observed that his fluoridation patients became forgetful, drowsy, lethargic, and incoherent. His testimony does not stand alone. Comparable cases of "impaired cognition and memory" have been reported to the government by many other dental professionals. Government reports themselves indicate similar findings of "impaired cognition and memory."

So well known is the impact of this chemical on the human brain and mental function that fluoride continues to be incorporated in a variety of popular, well-known psychiatric drugs. Because of its toxicity, fluoride-containing pharmaceuticals require a prescription when administered by medical professionals, yet fluoride is still administered en masse to the general public, ignorant of its mind-altering and hazardous side-effects, by industry, city officials, government officials, or some mastermind/minds.

There is a growing awareness among researchers, scientists, doctors, physiologists, neurosurgeons, and other professionals of an increasing presence of fluoride within the human brain. Since fluorides are known to have effects on the right temporal lobe, the hippocampus, and the pineal gland, some of these same professionals are asking a similar question: Could fluoridation explain some strange societal behavior in recent years? People observing odd behavior often say, usually with a laugh, "There must be something in the water." Could it be that this old adage is at least partially true?

Some who are concerned about fluorides in the environment claim that an exponentially growing number of children—in particular, but people in general as well—have been acting in an unpredictable manner, strangely and sometimes violently, often with memory impairment while and after doing so. Does this have anything to do with fluoride poisoning? If so, is fluoridation simply something done in ignorance over the years, more or less accidentally? Or is fluoridation a sinister plot?

A list of what some scientists are calling definitive links to fluoride is emerging. In addition to mental impairment, possible effects include heartburn, acid reflux disease, GERD (gastroesophageal reflux disease), bone disease, acute toxicity (especially in those with impaired kidney function), reproductive organ effects (especially in men), and cancer—all increasing in colossal numbers.

Researcher, dentist, and doctor Jennifer Luke released a startling disclosure. While doing postmortem examinations, Dr. Luke detected a recognized neurotoxin, one that is known to cause nerve cell degeneration and "outright disruption of motor coordination" in human brains. Luke found this neurotoxin in "extremely high concentrations" centered within the pineal gland. A normal and healthy pineal gland controls the following functions:

- produces serotonin and melatonin;
- catalyzes serotonin to melatonin;
- regulates circadian rhythm;
- helps regulate gonad hormone secretion.

This neurotoxin is none other than fluoride. Does this harmful accumulation provide a clue about a potential relationship between fluoride poisoning and disease? Even if we assume that the true reason behind launching fluoridation/fluorination on the American public in 1945 was belief in the promise of its medicinal benefits, how many people realize that fluoridation has *never* been approved by the Food and Drug Administration?

And as a capper, just try to find a toothpaste in *any* brand that does not contain fluoride. Most likely what you will notice is that fluoride is a listed ingredient, added to make the toothpaste "better" or "improved." In fact, 99 percent of all name-brand toothpastes contain dosages of fluoride so lethal that a special POISON label must be included specifically warning against ingestion of the product.

HENRY FORD AND HIS GREAT JEWISH CONSPIRACY

An engineering genius who didn't like to read, Henry Ford claimed that he really didn't know what his newspaper was printing.

There seems little doubt that Henry Ford (1863–1947) was a genius. He didn't invent the automobile when he built the Model T in 1908, but by 1913 he had created the assembly line, a process of mass production that revolutionized the way that the world lives—and with the advent of the rugged and reliable Model T, he began Americans' great love affair with the motorcar.

Ford grew up on a farm in Dearborn, Michigan, the oldest of six children, and received his education in a one-room schoolhouse. When he was sixteen he went to work as an apprentice machinist in nearby Detroit and for three years divided his time between repairing steam engines and machinery and helping out on the family farm. In 1893 he became chief engineer in the Edison Illuminating Company in Detroit, and by 1896 he had invented the Quadricycle, a self-propelled vehicle with two forward speeds and no reverse, steered by means of a tiller, like a boat. With the advent of the Model T, motorists had a vehicle that was reasonably priced, efficient, and easy to handle on rough country roads, and by 1918 half of all the automobiles in the United States were Model T's.

By the age of sixty Henry Ford was regarded as a great hero of industry and was so popular with the people of America that he briefly considered running for the presidency. However, if the general public had ever encountered the private and personal Ford, they would quite likely have been turned off by an authoritarian, prejudiced, and rather antidemocratic despot who tolerated few views other than his own. He grew to hate unions, and any move toward unionism at Ford motor company was discouraged by his own strikebreakers. Cherishing the values and traditions of his nineteenth-century rural rearing, Ford was against any signs of dramatic social change in manners and mores. He fiercely opposed any kind of government interference with business and industry, and as early as 1927 he warned against the influence of Hollywood on old-fashioned virtues and values. Ford disliked paperwork and wouldn't even read his mail. It was Ernest Liebold, Ford's private secretary and one of the few individuals that he trusted, who read Ford's mail for him and who handled most of the paperwork that accrued in his office.

From 1910 to 1918, as the Ford Motor Company was rising to power, Ford became increasingly agitated by the number of Jewish immigrants flooding into the United States from Eastern Europe. Such individuals, he worried, could take jobs away from native-born Americans and could easily be persuaded to join unions.

In 1919 Ford purchased a newspaper, the *Dearborn Independent,* and hired William J. Cameron, an experienced journalist, to listen to his views about a Jewish conspiracy that had instigated World War I in Europe and was now attempting to take over the automobile business in America. Cameron was to write a weekly column, "The International Jew" in Ford's name, expressing anti-immigrant, anti-labor, anti-Semitic thoughts. The editor of the *Dearborn Independent* refused to run the column regardless of the fact that it was "written" by Henry Ford, who was not only one of the wealthiest men in America, but the owner of the newspaper. When the editor told Ford that he would quit before he ran such bigotry in his newspaper, Ford accepted his resignation and made Cameron the editor of the *Dearborn Independent.*

After "The International Jew" had been running for a few months, Henry Ford was introduced to Paquita de Shishmareff, who brought him a copy of *The Protocols of the Learned Elders of Zion,* the notorious Tsarist forgery, the mother of all anti-Semitic literature. Mme de Shishmareff told Ford that the book outlined the conspiracy by Jewish bankers to overthrow all European governments and enslave the world. An English-language edition of the *Protocols* had been translated by Victor Marsden of the *Morning Post* in London, and copies of the book were being distributed in the U.S. by Boris Brasol, a former Tsarist prosecutor. In his intro-

Most Americans remember industrialist Henry Ford as the man who successfully developed the assembly line process for making cars that the public could afford. Was he also an anti-Semite who backed Adolf Hitler?

duction to the book, Marsden had warned that the Jewish conspiracy was being carried out "with steadfast purpose, creating wars and revolutions to destroy the white Gentile race, that the Jews may seize the power during the resulting chaos and rule with their claimed superior intelligence over the remaining races of the world." In 1920 the *Dearborn Independent* published an American version of the book in a series entitled "The International Jew: The World's Foremost Problem." Later the columns were published in book form with half a million copies in circulation in the United States.

For nearly seven years the *Dearborn Independent* ran anti-Semitic articles. Liebold hired private investigators who came up with all sorts of "evidence" about the international Jewish conspiracy to control world finance, create radical political movements, and foster wars that would cause Christians to be killed and Jews to profit from the bloodshed.

A number of Jewish businessmen had tried to sue Henry Ford to cease and desist publishing and disseminating anti-Semitic propaganda and hate literature, but with Ford's influence, none of the charges ever came to trial. However, in 1927 the target of a defamatory series, Aaron Sapiro, a California farm cooperative organizer, sued for libel and made the charges stick. A trial was ordered, but Ford refused to testify. As the years passed, he had become increasingly reclusive. The thought of appearing in a public trial for libel terrified him. The fear that he might lose and face public humiliation was even more frightening. And then came the news that Jewish leaders across the nation had called for a boycott of all Ford cars and trucks—and sales were steadily decreasing at Ford dealerships throughout the United States. With pressure on him to appear in court to testify, Ford had a car accident and was confined to a hospital. Most people assumed that the accident was staged, but whatever the circumstances, Henry was able to hide out in a hospital room for a while. It was here, in reflection and semi-solitude, that he and his attorneys decided to settle with Aaron Sapiro out of court.

Leaders of the American Jewish Committee and B'nai B'rith Anti-Defamation League wrung a public announcement out of Ford that articles derogatory to or "reflecting" on the Jews would never appear again in the *Dearborn Independent.* Ford claimed that he was mortified and incredulous when he learned that *The Protocols* was well known by scholars and historians to be a forgery. Once again, Ford claimed that he hated paperwork and was too busy to read the book himself, so he had entrusted Cameron and Liebold to study the contents of *The Protocols*—and he put the blame on them for printing the columns. But he was publicly humiliated by the incident, and in 1927 he shut down forever the presses of his newspaper.

Silencing the presses of the *Dearborn Independent* hardly ceased Ford's animosity toward Jews, for in 1922 he had become Adolph

Hitler's first foreign backer. Hitler quoted sections of Ford's *The International Jew* verbatim when he was writing *Mein Kampf*. In 1928 Ford merged his German assets with the I.G. Farben chemical cartel and transferred forty percent of Ford Motor A.G. of Germany to the company. Carl Bosch of I.G. Farben was named head of Ford in Germany. Simultaneously, in the United States, Edsel Ford joined the board of American I.G. Farben.

> Hitler quoted sections of Ford's *The International Jew* verbatim when he was writing *Mein Kampf*.

In August 1938, after Hitler had gained complete power with the aid of the cartels, the Führer awarded Henry Ford with the Grand Cross of the German Eagle. When criticism arose in Jewish circles, Ford attempted to quell anger by emphasizing that the medal presentation was a gift from Hitler to celebrate the automobile pioneer's seventy-fifth birthday. In no way, Ford stressed, was the medal a reward for being sympathetic toward the Nazi Party.

Ford-Werke A.G. essentially became a German company in the late 1930s; it badly needed raw materials, such as rubber and nonferrous metals, which were funneled from the United States into Germany. When war broke out, Ford-Werke placed itself at the disposal of the Wehrmacht for armament production. Ford-Werke was able to bring additional valuable supplies into Germany from the Ford plants in Amsterdam, Antwerp, Budapest, Bucharest, and Copenhagen. There is very strong evidence to support the charge that Ford Motor Company worked on both the Allies' and the Nazi's sides during World War II.

Ford died in 1947, long after he had created his Jewish conspiracy out of an inflammatory forged manuscript. It is unlikely that he passed on very repentant, however. Before he died, he was known to have accused "Jewish bankers" of causing World War II.

VINCENT FOSTER: MURDER OR SUICIDE?

An affair with the First Lady may have cost the White House deputy counsel his life.

One of the most troubling questions in the mystery surrounding White House deputy counsel Vincent Foster's alleged suicide is why, in his final days, Foster behaved so unlike a man contemplating suicide. Foster gave no indication to those closest to him that he was so terribly distraught about his new life in Washington, D.C., that he wanted to kill himself. The very evening that he was found dead, he had enthusiastically set aside time to take his children on an outing. With the anticipated arrival of his sister and niece flying in from Arkansas on the following day, he had promised them that he would escort them personally around the nation's capital, with a bonus of a special lunch at the White House.

Yet according to students of the mystery, there is no question that Vincent Foster was a troubled man and was uncomfortable working with the president as deputy counsel. Foster's association with the President Bill Clinton was primarily through Hillary, with whom he had been partners at a law firm in Little Rock, Arkansas. For years, Clinton insiders were aware that Hillary and Foster had shared a romantic relationship in Arkansas and that they maintained the affair when the Clintons moved to the White House. Because of the tense situation between himself and the Clintons and because of his knowledge of the facts of the Whitewater scan-

dal, conspiracy theorists maintain that Foster intended to resign on July 21, 1993.

On the morning of July 20 Foster attended the White House announcement of Louis Freeh's appointment as the new director of the FBI. Foster had scheduled a private meeting with President Bill Clinton for the next day, a meeting at which many believe Foster intended to resign as White House Deputy Council.

At midday on July 20 Foster told his secretary, Deborah Gorham, that he would be "right back." On the way out of his office he offered his co-worker Linda Tripp the remainder of the M&Ms from his lunch tray. That was the last time that Foster was seen alive.

The White House is equipped with the most sophisticated entry-control and video surveillance systems in the world, yet there is no video record of Foster leaving. Neither does there exist any logbook entry to show that he signed out of the building. Students of the circumstances surrounding Foster's alleged suicide are convinced that he was somehow taken out of the building undetected and against his will.

Several hours after Foster told his secretary that he would return shortly, his body was found in Fort Marcy Park, in a Virginia suburb outside of Washington. He appeared to have committed suicide by placing the barrel of a .38 pistol in his mouth and pulling the trigger.

The U.S. Park Police were the first to investigate, but according to conspiracy theorists, they neglected the protocol mandating that all suspected suicides first be investigated as homicides. In addition, they failed to retain such evidence as Foster's beeper and were remiss in not conducting a thorough search of the crime scene and the surrounding area. Overexposed photographs of the scene were considered worthless by subsequent investigators, and later the X rays of Foster's skull, along with the ineffective crime scene photographs, disappeared.

The timeline of Foster's death becomes greatly jumbled. Some witnesses stated that

Foster's office was being cleaned out before the Park Police arrived to seal it. Several boxes of documents were allegedly removed by Hillary Clinton's chief of staff, Margaret Williams, and carried to the private residence area of the White House.

The Park Police supposedly arrived on the scene of Foster's death at 6:00 P.M. and had identified the body by 6:30 but delayed notifying the White House until 8:30. The staff was allegedly not told of Foster's death until at least 9:00 P.M., and the official identification of Foster's body by Craig Livingstone, former White House security director, did not take place until 10:00 P.M.

Arkansas state trooper Roger Perry later said that he felt the FBI tried to pressure him into changing his testimony about when the White House was notified of Foster's death. Perry says he was at the Governor's Mansion in Little Rock when he answered a call from Chelsea Clinton's nanny, a close Foster family friend, alerting him to Foster's apparent suicide. Perry says he's positive the call came in between 6:30 and 7:30 P.M. (CST; 7:30–8:30 Washington, D.C., time). The nanny testified before Congress that she herself did not learn of the tragedy until about 10 P.M. and did not place the call to Little Rock until 10:30.

Back in Little Rock, none of Foster's friends and former associates accepted his death as a suicide. Former Arkansas state trooper and Clinton confidant L. D. Brown said on October 31, 1998, that he didn't know how Foster had died, but he did know that both investigations by independent counsels Robert Fiske and Kenneth Starr were cover-ups. Brown went on to say that the most relevant fact about Vince Foster was that he and Hillary Clinton were in the middle of a "long torrid affair." Brown said that he ought to know, he was there: "Hillary and I talked about it often during late-night chats in the Governor's mansion. This affair started in Little Rock and drew Vince Foster to Washington and to his death. Without putting the affair between these two people at its center, without interviewing Hillary, any investigation into the death of Vince Foster will be totally compromised."

Among conspiracy theorists' contentions that Foster's death was murder, rather than suicide, are the following:

- The positions of Foster's arms and legs were extremely inconsistent with suicide.

- The almost total lack of blood and brain tissue at the site indicates that Foster was killed elsewhere and carried to the park.

- Foster was not wearing gloves, yet neither of the revolver's handgrips yielded any of his fingerprints.

- If Foster had truly placed the barrel of the .38 revolver in his mouth and pulled the trigger, the blowback would have coated the pistol and Foster's hand and white shirt sleeve with a spray of blood and powder residue. No blood or gunpowder residue was found on the barrel, cylinder, or grips, and very little blood was found at the site.

- Foster must have already been dead when the pistol was placed in his mouth, for the head wound would have continued to bleed for some time even after death.

A Zogby poll of the American public five years after Vincent Foster's alleged suicide revealed that 70 percent rejected the official story of his death.

FOUNTAIN OF THE WORLD

In the 1950s Krishna Venta convinced his followers in the Fountain of the World cult that he was the present incarnation of Jesus Christ.

Krishna Venta gave birth to himself as a new incarnation of Jesus Christ in 1951, after long, arduous troubles with the law and a long string of failures in other more mundane endeavors. The messiah had been born in San Francisco in 1911 under the "earth name" of Francis Pencovic, and it was under that name that he had studied theology. In 1941, while living in Phoenix, Arizona, he was held and questioned by the police for allegedly writing a threatening letter to President Franklin Delano Roosevelt. Later, he transformed himself to "Frank Jensen" and committed a number of petty thefts and burglaries. It was sometime after he had been placed in a hospital for psychiatric evaluation that he received the supernatural word that he should metamorphose himself once again—this time into Krishna Venta.

Once he had convinced himself that he was the Son of God, it didn't take him long to convince others of his divine credentials. The mystic, resplendent in his yellow robes, persuaded his followers that in 1932 he had teleported himself to the United States from the Valley of the Masters below Mount Everest. He had lived in Nepal for centuries, having originally arrived on Earth in a spaceship from the planet Neophrates. He told his disciples that he was ageless.

It seemed that in no time at all he had ordained a priesthood composed of donors to the cause of the Fountain of the World, as he called his enterprise, refusing admittance only to those who did not come bearing gifts. Beautiful women, however, could enter by virtue of their physical attributes.

A benefactor's large donation enabled the Fountain of the World to purchase twenty-six acres in beautiful Box Canyon, about forty-five miles northwest of Los Angeles. In the early 1950s a nonprofit corporation was formed in California with Krishna Venta as president. Under him were twelve disciples. All applicants were technically required to bequeath to the Fountain of the World all earthly wealth that they possessed.

From the beginning, Krishna Venta was determined not to be run out of the state by the authorities. He earnestly set about creating good public relations, training his followers in disaster aid and other socially helpful fields. Of special note was the skill of the Fountain of the World cultists as firefighters. Timber fires in that section of California were a menace, and when one was reported, Krishna Venta, at the command of his brigade, would speed to the scene in his station wagon to supervise the construction of firebreaks and trenches to combat the blaze.

As noble as all this might seem, what probably caused the messiah's downfall was his penchant for racing to the fires in the company of young, beautiful female disciples. He had the back of his station wagon outfitted with a mattress, and whenever there was a break in the firefighting, Krishna Venta would steal away with a lovely disciple.

The doctrine of the Fountain of the World allowed its members the unrestrained use of tobacco or alcohol, but it ordered a tight rein on their sexual desires. It was not, of course, that Krishna Venta was against sex, but he did most heartily wish to keep the cult's personal expression of sexual activity away from the unfavorable scrutiny of the public eye. He did not want rumors of orgies and free love to excite his more conservative neighbors.

Most of the true believers went along with the cult's rules and got married before they engaged in any serious or regular sexual intercourse. As one might suppose, as the spiritual master of the Fountain of the World, Krishna Venta reserved the right to dally with whichever women he chose. On occasion, his sexual indulgence was cloaked under the guise of various subterfuges, some religious and some therapeutic. Most often, however, he simply willed into bed a host of mistresses.

Krishna Venta's image as a perfect savior began to melt. He went to Las Vegas and lost a great deal of money at the craps tables, claiming that he had done so only to see how the sinners conducted themselves in that city of glaring neon lights and clattering slot machines. He traveled to London on a missionary tour, but reports reached his followers that even though the British had given him a cool reception, he stayed in expensive hotels and lived in the grand style, as if he were a visiting rajah. Once back home in Box Canyon, he continued to eat nothing but the finest foods while his disciples were left to scrounge for themselves.

Finally, his annoyed followers began to question the validity of his messiahship. As is too often the case with cult leaders, Krishna Venta had failed in his relationships with his own subjects. Greed and sexual promiscuity had ensnared him, and he had come to believe his own pronouncements that he was truly what he proclaimed to be and just as invincible.

The spiritual straw that broke the faithful's back was the discovery by two disciples, Ralph Muller and Peter Kamenoff, that their wives had been summoned to their guru's private orgies in the back of the infamous station wagon. Such knowledge proved to be more than they could endure, and it became the catalytic element that brought them to the door of the Fountain of the World's administration building on the fateful evening of December 10, 1958. When the bundle of dynamite borne by Muller and Kamenoff was detonated, the two-story administration building disintegrated along with Krishna Venta, his two assassins, and seven other members of the cult.

FREE AND ACCEPTED ORDER OF FREEMASONS

Servants of their Supreme Architect of the Universe, Lucifer, the Freemasons have plotted to

take over the world since they labored on Solomon's temple.

As the Freemasons enter the new millennium, the order's membership in the United States is about two million and the average age is well over sixty. It seems that younger men are no longer attracted to an organization whose members receive such grandiose titles as Master of the Royal Secret, Knight of the Brazen Serpent, or Worshipful Master. As for being a secret society, the telephone numbers of Masonic lodges are in the directory and many of their oaths have been made public— for example: "You agree to be a good man and true; you agree to conform to the laws of the country in which you reside; you promise not to be concerned in plots and conspiracies against the government." Each year the Masons give millions of dollars to charities.

In 2005, as a wit has observed, the Masons are Laurel and Hardy heading for the Sons of the Desert convention to get away from their wives and party up; the secret rituals are Ralph Kramden and Ed Norton shaking their tails at the Raccoon Lodge; the reenactments of ancient traditions are Amos and Andy at the Mystic Knights of the Sea; the secret handgrips are Fred Flintstone greeting Barney Rubble with the secret word of the Water Buffalo, *ak-ak-a-dak.*

But there are those conspiracy buffs who see beyond the innocuous public image of the Freemasons and discern their true identity as a powerful secret brotherhood of darkness that is planning to take over the world. According to some scholars of the occult, the Masons' "Supreme Architect of the Universe" is none other than Lucifer, who cloaks himself in Masonic literature as Zoroaster, Shiva, Abaddon, and other pagan-god disguises. The so-called holy writings of Freemasonry, as well as their secret rites, passwords, initiations, and handshakes, have their origins in the Roman mystery religions, Egyptian rituals, and Babylonian paganism. Often linked to the Illuminati, Freemasonry is said to have exerted its influence on every aspect of American society—including its currency.

On the front of a one-dollar bill there is a portrait of George Washington, an avowed Mason, who donned his Masonic apron and presided over the dedication of the U.S. Capitol. The flip side of the bill displays both faces of the Great Seal of the United States. The front of the seal depicts the spread eagle, arrows in one claw, olive branch in the other, and a banner proclaiming *E Pluribus Unum* ("Out of many, one") in its beak. On the seal's other side is an incomplete pyramid with an eye floating in a glowing triangle where the capstone should be. Above the eye is the caption *Annuit Coeptis,* commonly translated as "He has favored our undertaking," and in a scroll beneath is the slogan *Novus Ordo Seclorum,* "New Order of the Ages." Historians of the Masonic order state that the establishment of such a "new order" is an integral part of the ancient plan of the Freemasons, the Illuminati, and other nefarious groups to control the world. Former president George H. W. Bush's Masonic connections influenced his decisions in the Oval Office. Russia's premier Mikhail Gorbachev is a secret Mason who worked with Bush to institute a New World Order.

Most scholars agree that the pyramid represented on the bill is the Great Pyramid of Cheops at Giza, which, to a Mason, is emblematic of the continuity of the craft of Freemasonry from the dawn of civilization in Egypt. It is also a reminder of the legend that Egyptian civilization was founded by survivors from Atlantis and that the United States is the New Atlantis foretold by the great master Mason Sir Francis Bacon. The pyramid with the all-seeing eye represents the Great Architect of the Universe guiding the Founding Fathers of the United States to establish a nation that might one day reveal itself as the heir of the ancient mysteries of Atlantis and restore all humankind to the earthly paradise that existed in that Golden Age of old.

The central mythos of Freemasonry centers on the building of the great temple of King Solomon and Solomon's securing the services of the most accomplished architect in the world, Hiram Abiff, who designed the magnificent temple according to the precepts of the Great Architect of the Universe. Although Hiram is mentioned in biblical accounts as a master of the arts of construction, the rites of Freemasonry extend beyond the Bible and fashion a parallel myth, portraying Hiram as a primary figure in the creation of the temple. According to Masonic tradition, the ancient builders of Solomon's temple created the rites still practiced in modern lodges, with the various degrees of initiation and their secret symbols and handshakes.

While the Free and Accepted Order of Freemasons may claim to be the oldest fraternity in the world, historically it does not date back to the masons working on Solomon's temple—nor does it date, as some Masons vow, to those who labored on the Egyptian pyramids. Freemasonry evolved from the guilds of stonemasons who traveled from city to city in Europe in the fourteenth century looking for work on the great cathedrals being constructed at that time. The secret passwords and handshakes were unique ways by which a newcomer to a city might prove that he was a true member of the guild. Although there are references to Freemasonry as early as 1390, the structured fraternity as such did not come into being until 1717 when four London lodges united.

The Freemasons were nondenominational, asking only that members recognize a Supreme Being and seek somehow to better humanity through the course of their own lives. Because men of low rank could join and no religious philosophy was deemed superior to another, the lodges of Freemasonry became champions of the emerging concepts of democracy that were suffusing the Enlightenment. Such freedoms of thought and spirituality did not endear the organization to certain facets of established society, particularly the

Roman Catholic Church, who condemned the fraternity as anti-Christian.

By the mid-1700s Freemasonry had established its lodges throughout Europe and had been carried across the ocean to the New World by numerous immigrants. George Washington, Benjamin Franklin, John Hancock, Paul Revere, and many other of the Founding Fathers of the United States were Masons. A freed slave, Prince Hall, who was initiated into Masonry by a British soldier in Boston, later founded an African lodge, which became the still-extant Prince Hall Masons.

After the Revolution, Freemasonry became extremely powerful in the United States. Lodges sprang up in the smallest of villages, and it became an undeniable sign of prestige in any community to be a member. For businessmen who wished to succeed, it was almost a requirement to join the Freemasons.

It was the tragic death of one of its members in 1826 that led to the near-annihilation of the Masons in the United States. William Morgan, a disillusioned Mason from Batavia, New York, let it be known that he was writing a book that would reveal all the secrets of Freemasonry to the world. The printer's shop that was going to publish his manuscript was torched, and a few days later Morgan was arrested on trumped-up charges that he was in arrears on a two-dollar debt. That night, a stranger arrived to pay Morgan's bail, and the dissident Mason was then seized by a group of his fellow lodge members and forced into a carriage. Neither Morgan nor his remains were ever found.

One of the cornerstones of Masonry is loyalty to its members, but the entire nation was offended by the manner in which juries were stacked in favor of the Masons accused of having murdered William Morgan. The general population was shocked by the power of a secret society that could stonewall three special prosecutors. After twenty trials for murder and kidnapping, the local sheriff, who was a Mason and obviously an integral element in Morgan's

The symbol of the Freemasons chiseled into a nineteenth-century gravestone. The Masons and their beliefs have become more public in recent years, it seems, but conspiracists claim they are still a secret brotherhood with designs on world domination.

abduction and disappearance, received the most severe judgment of all the defendants when he was sentenced to thirty months in jail.

Anti-Mason sentiment swelled throughout the country, and an Anti-Mason Party was founded that elected governors in Pennsylvania and Vermont and won seven electoral votes in the 1832 election. It was no longer prestigious to be a Mason. In state after state, lodges closed. Overall, the fraternity lost more than half its members.

By 1845 Freemasonry began to revive in the United States, but it never again achieved the social status it had once enjoyed. In 1872 two Masons formed a kind of parody of the Masons and named it the Ancient Arabic Order of the Nobles of the Mystic Shrine, a.k.a. the Shriners. By 1897 the Masons had about 750,000 members and societal pressures had lifted as numerous other fraternal organizations, such as the Knights of Columbus, the Benevolent and Protective Order of Elks, the Odd Fellows, and the Loyal Order of Moose sprang into being. In the 1950s the Masons reached their numerical peak in America with more than 4 million members. Depending upon the prejudices of the beholder, the Freemasons remain a fraternal group that donates generously to charities—or an insidious secret society bent on world conquest.

FUKUSHIMA AND HAARP

People were shocked all over the world when a huge 9.0 earthquake struck Japan, resulting in a devastating tidal wave that hit the eastern coast, wiping out entire towns. Worst of all was the damage to the Fukushima Daiichi nuclear power plant, which caused a radiation leak that forced the evacuation of nearly a quarter million people.

On Friday, March 11, 2011, the world watched in horror as a 9.0-magnitude undersea earthquake struck the northeast coast approximately 81 miles east of Japan's Oshika Peninsula of Tohoku near Sendai just minutes before 3:00 P.M. (local time). With its epicenter about 20 miles under the earth's surface, within a few minutes the quake had triggered 33-foot high waves. Entire towns and villages were swept away by the massive tsunami, and fears immediately arose concerning the power supply and cooling systems at Tokyo Electric's (TEPCO) reactors at the Fukushima Daiichi nuclear power plant.

Initial reports attempted to assuage global concerns by stating that damage was minimal and there was no cause for alarm. However, by Sunday the government disclosed that 230,000 people had been evacuated from the area near the nuclear reactors. The power plant had suffered damage from the tsunami, and, on Saturday, an explosion had occurred in a building that housed one of the reactors. Prime Minister Naoto Kan admitted to the

world that Japan now faced its greatest crisis since World War II. Millions of residents were without power or water.

During the decades after World War II, as people in the United States and Europe had become more familiar with Japan and its thriving global economy, it had seemed that earthquakes were commonplace; rumbles occurred so frequently that the citizenry had become inured to feeling the earth move under their feet. However, the 9.0-magnitude quake on March 11 was the most powerful ever recorded in Japan.

On Monday, March 14, a second explosion occurred at the damaged Fukushima plant, where courageous employees attempted to make the surrounding area safer by doing what they could to repair the damage. On March 15, when two more explosions and a fire shook the Fukushima plant, the radiation levels rose to such dangerous levels that authorities strongly recommend that people who lived as far away as twenty miles from the reactor stay indoors.

On March 17, a radioactive plume entered western North America and was moving toward the North Atlantic, where it was detected on monitoring sites. In Japan, the U.S. State Department recommended the voluntary departure of the families of the U.S. embassy staff. Other nations quickly followed suit and began to bring home the families of their embassy workers.

The core of the Number Three reactor was found to be damaged, and on March 18, the Japanese nuclear safety agency elevated the Fukushima radiation danger from 4 to 5 on the international 0 to 7 scale of gravity.

By Saturday, March 19, abnormal levels of radiation were detected in dairy and garden products in the Fukushima area, and traces of radioactive iodine were found in tap water in Tokyo, 155 miles away from the damaged nuclear plant. By March 21, abnormal radiation levels were detected in food products in four

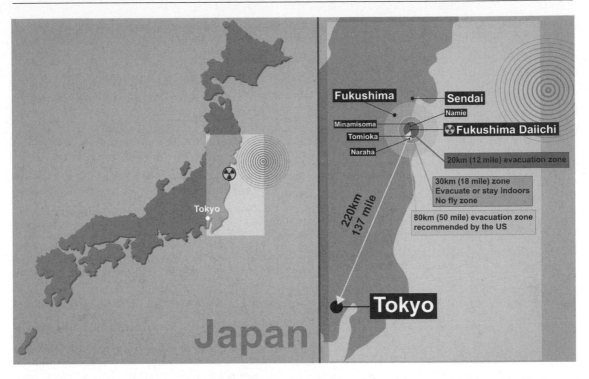

This diagram shows the location of the damaged Fukushima nuclear plant and the extent of the evacuation zone.

prefectures. In a few more days, tap water in Tokyo yielded high readings of radiation levels, and officials warned that the levels were not safe for babies.

The London *Guardian* opined that Japan appeared to have lost the fight to save the nuclear reactor: "The radioactive core in a reactor at the crippled Fukushima nuclear power plant appears to have melted through the bottom of its containment vessel ... raising fears of a major release of radiation at the site." (Ian Sample, March 29, 2011).

By the end of March, the area of Fukushima went on maximum alert after high traces of plutonium were discovered in the soil. At least nineteen selfless workers at the site were exposed to high levels of radiation.

An estimated total of 28,000 dead or missing was attributed to the tsunami, and about 25,000 Japanese and U.S. soldiers were de-

ployed to the northeast coast of Japan to search for victims of the disaster. The nation of Japan soon announced the beginning of an official rehabilitation and reconstruction phase.

International experts began speaking of Fukushima as being worse than the nuclear disaster in Chernobyl, which rocked the Ukraine in 1986 and is still contaminated today. They predicted radiation releases that would spread catastrophically across wide parts of Japan and the entire Northern Hemisphere. Some areas would be permanently contaminated, and millions of people could perish from deadly cancers.

By the close of 2011, radiation levels had reached fifty million times the normal levels in the ocean water off the coast of the Fukushima Daiichi facility. The alternative press was detailing such information and proclaiming the event as the worst radiological accident in the history of nuclear research, while the mainstream media largely reported that the radiation at Fukushima had been contained. TEPCO, according to whistleblowers, had repeatedly and deliberately lied to the public. In December 2011, TEPCO admitted that alarming quantities of radioactive strontium had leaked into the ocean and that the leaks were still continuing.

The London *Guardian* opined that Japan appeared to have lost the fight to save the nuclear reactor.

The Pacific Ocean provides the main source of protein for about one billion people in Asia alone. Ken Buesseler, senior scientist at the Woods Hole Oceanographic Institution in Woods Hole, Massachusetts, reported that Fukushima released ten to one hundred times more radiation into the ocean than the 1986 Chernobyl catastrophe.

The first debris from the tsunami began washing ashore on the West Coast of the United States in December 2011, a year earlier than predicted. Residents of the Pacific coastal cities have found large quantities of bottles, cans, lumber, and other trash, the forerunners of the estimated nineteen million tons of debris from the Fukushima area floating across the Pacific, an "island" of assorted debris thought to be the size of Texas. The huge mass should reach Hawaii by February or March 2012.

Almost from the day it happened, conspiracy theorists had begun to question whether the Fukushima disaster was the result of natural or technically engineered causes. Whenever the discussion occurred between conspiracists, the High Frequency Active Auroral Research Program (HAARP) was named as the most likely villain that might have caused such a tragedy.

Based in Gokona, Alaska, HAARP is a jointly managed U.S. Air Force/Navy weather warfare program that has been operating since 1992.

On its official website (www.haarp.alaska. edu), HAARP acknowledges its ability to induce "a small, localized change in ionospheric temperature so that resulting reactions can be studied by other instruments located either at or close to the HAARP site." Such researchers as Rosalie Bertell, president of the International Institute of Concern for Public Health, insist that HAARP can accomplish far more than "localized changes in temperatures." Bertell describes HAARP as a "gigantic heater that can cause major disruptions in the ionosphere, creating not just holes, but long incisions in the protective layer that keeps deadly radiation from bombarding the planet."

In Bertell's opinion, while HAARP is presented to the public as a device for repairing the ozone or as a space shield against incoming weapons, it has the ability to "deliver very large amounts of energy, comparable to a nuclear bomb, anywhere on earth, via laser and particle beams."

Conspiracists have long claimed that HAARP has the power to trigger floods, droughts, hurricanes, tsunamis, and power blackouts over major cities and surrounding areas. To control the weather to cause an earthquake and tsunami like the Fukushima disaster would be well within its capabilities.

A television documentary on HAARP by the Canadian Broadcasting Company in 2010 reported on the international discomfort over what appears to be a secret weapon used for electromagnetic warfare: "It isn't just conspiracy theorists who are concerned about HAARP. The European Union called the project a global concern and passed a resolution calling for more information on its health and environmental risks. Despite those concerns, officials at HAARP insist the project is nothing more sinister than a radio science research facility."

If HAARP was responsible for the worst nuclear disaster since Chernobyl and a great loss of life and terrible economic suffering, why was Japan a target?

Some conspiracy theorists suggest that it was an awful miscalculation of the power of the electromagnetic mechanisms employed by HAARP. An experiment that was intended to test power on an area of open sea was misdirected to eighty-one miles east of Japan's Os-hika Peninsula of Tohoku. More cynical conspiracists say that HAARP doesn't make mistakes—especially now that it has been taken over by agents of the New World Order. Japan may be only the first of the new high-tech nations to feel the power of those who have mastered electromagnetic warfare. Who will be the next example made for the egomaniacal satisfaction of those shadowy figures who seek world domination?

G

GARDUNA

In 710 a hermit's vision of the Virgin Mary that appointed him savior of Spain and gave him the command to raise an army of holy warriors, the Garduna, was later transformed into a thriving criminal organization that still exists today.

According to tradition, around 710 C.E. a holy man named Apollinario, who lived a hermitlike existence in the hills above Cordova, had a vision in which the Blessed Virgin Mary appointed him to be the savior of Spain and drive the Moors out of the land. At first the holy man was stunned by the very suggestion, but when the Holy Mother presented him with a button that she said had been taken from the robe of Christ, Apollinario knew that he had been given the power to raise a band of holy warriors.

The hermit was blessed with a charisma that caused the common people to flock to his leadership. He told them that those who followed him in the Garduna, his sacred army, would be licensed by God and the Holy Virgin to destroy the invading heathens. There would be open warfare, of course, but they would also be free to plot murders and practice any kind of secret treachery. Those who joined the Garduna would be absolved of all wrongdoing as long as their violence was committed only against non-Christians. Thousands joined the holy man in his crusade against the Moors, and his ragtag army of peasants, beggars, and bandits fought so fiercely under the standard of the Holy Virgin of Cordova that no Moorish force could repel them.

While the Garduna may have harassed the powerful Muslim armies and conducted a guerrilla-type warfare against them, by no means did they drive the invaders from Spain, as legend tells. After about 714, the Gothic monarchy of Spain had been replaced by the conquering Arabs, and a short time after Spain had fallen to the Moors, it became the most prosperous and civilized country in the West. Within a few more years, the Arabs had extended their European empire north of the Pyrenees Mountains into the south of France and from the mouth of the Garonne to that of the Rhone. What remained of Gothic Spain had fallen into decay, deteriorating into a patchwork of petty princedoms, woefully ineffectual against the powerful Moors who had conquered most of the land and established their royal seat in Cordova.

In 732 Charles Martel of France stemmed the Muslim tide of conquest at the battle of Tours, and the Arabs retreated back to Spain, where they retained a peaceful possession of the country for many centuries. Cordova became a highly respected seat of art and learning, and the Arab philosophers became the sages of the West.

With the passage of time, the Garduna degenerated into a loosely knit criminal network controlled by the descendants of the mountain bandits who had followed Apollinario in his crusade against the Moors. Deception and murder were still practiced on a large scale by the Garduna, and they maintained the old dictum that only the blood of non-Christians was to be shed. Perhaps the Garduna would have vanished completely into legend if fifteenth-century Spain had not become a Christian nation and King Ferdinand V (1452–1516) and Queen Isabella I (1451–1504) had not so avidly supported the mission of the Inquisition and that of its chief heretic hunter in Spain, Tomás de Torquemada (1420–1498).

Until the Inquisition, Moors, Jews, and Christians had for centuries lived quite peacefully in Spain. But Ferdinand reasoned that the Moors and the Jews had grown too powerful and too rich. He wondered how much farther he could extend the Spanish Empire if he were to acquire their wealth. Ferdinand recalled the stories of the Garduna, who killed only non-Christians, and he summoned their leaders to meet with high officers of church and state. These officials told the bandit chiefs that they must once again become holy warriors and a weapon of terror against all heretics. All their sins would be forgiven. All their crimes would be pardoned. They were to become a secret society of murderers with the full approval of church and state.

For over a hundred years, the Garduna murdered, raped, and looted on the orders of the Inquisition. Their victims were always non-Christians or those suspected of being heretics. By 1670 the Inquisition withdrew its support from the Garduna, but the holy warriors became a secret cult within the church and continued their attacks against all those who held beliefs contrary to the teachings of Christianity. When the church itself withdrew its recognition of the Garduna, they became a secret society, maintaining always that everything they did was an expression of God's will and any alleged crime they might commit was free of any taint of sin.

During the eighteenth century the Garduna expanded its profile of potential victims to include Christians, as well as unbelievers, and they began selling their services of murder, kidnapping, robbery, and so forth to anyone who could afford them. They became so powerful and daring that if any member of the society should be caught and imprisoned, the others thought nothing of attacking the prison and freeing him.

At the height of its powers in the eighteenth century, the Garduna instituted ranks within the society which could only be attained by acts of merit. At the head of the Garduna was the "Great Brother" or "Grand Master," who ruled the society from its headquarters in Seville. Following his orders were the commanders, the district chiefs, and the chiefs, the leaders of individual bands. Under the chiefs came the swordsmen, well-trained men who were responsible for planning the criminal operations of the Garduna. The true fighting men of the society were called the "athletes," tough and ruthless individuals who were very often escaped convicts, galley slaves, and vicious criminals. Below the athletes in rank were the "bellows," elderly men who were regarded by their cities and villages as men of good character and who could serve as the disposers of stolen goods for the society. The lowest rank in the Garduna was held by the "goats," new recruits who had yet to prove their abilities. There were also two female ranks: the "sirens," young, beautiful women whose task it was to seduce state officials, and the "covers," whose assignment lay in luring unsuspecting victims into ambushes where they could be robbed or murdered.

In 1822, in a era of social reform in Spain, police entered the home of the Grand Master in Seville, arrested him, and confiscated all his documents. Remarkably, the Garduna had kept meticulous records of all of their various criminal activities from 1520 to that date. The Grand Master and sixteen district chiefs were publicly hanged in the main square of the city. Members of the other ranks of the Garduna scattered and resumed a life of banditry in the mountains.

The Garduna gave evidence of their survival as a secret society throughout the Spanish Civil War (1936–39) when their battle cry of "Remember the Virgin of Cordova!" was heard. Some historians say that the Garduna established their own church, blending their concept of unorthodox Catholicism with a kind of "holy socialism." With branches allegedly in Portugal and South America, as well as Spain, the Garduna continues to flourish as a criminal secret society nearly thirteen centuries after its conception by the hermit Apollinario.

The legend of the Garduna's origins resembles that of El Cid (c. 1040–1099), the heroic knight who defended northern Spain from the invading Moors in the eleventh century. No longer legend, the secret society continues to this day in a criminal organization not dissimilar to the Mafia.

JAMES A. GARFIELD, ASSASSINATION OF

President James A. Garfield had barely begun his term in office when he was assassinated by an occultist from a free-love community who received his orders to kill directly from God.

The assassin was armed and waiting when President James A. Garfield and his entourage arrived at the Baltimore and Potomac Railroad station in Washington, D.C., on the morning of July 2, 1881. Garfield planned to attend a commencement program at his alma mater, Williams College, then journey to the summer White House on the New Jersey shore for a brief vacation. The president left his carriage, walked into the station, and settled back wearily on a wooden bench.

The Secret Service was not so security conscious in those days, and no one paid any attention to a slight, bearded man who had walked up behind the presidential party. No government agent appraised the almost glassy stare of the stranger, and no alert eye saw him slip his trembling right hand into the inner pocket of his worn suit coat and withdraw a snub-nosed British Bulldog pistol.

Forcing a crooked smile, the assassin fired a bullet into Garfield's back. As the president was slammed forward off his bench and onto the floor of the railway station, the bearded man leveled his weapon at arm's length and fired again. The second bullet plowed into the fleshy portion of the president's arm.

As the assassin walked deliberately toward an exit, a doctor in the station dashed to Garfield's aid. Hastily the physician probed the wounds, and the president's face twisted with pain. "Thank you, doctor," he gasped. "Thank you, but I am a dead man."

The escaping assassin was apprehended as he left the station. He was identified as Charles J. Guiteau, an attorney, religious fanatic, pamphleteer, and vociferous advocate of the occult sciences who had become incensed when his application to be the U.S. ambassador to France was denied.

Later, in his jail cell, Guiteau was without remorse. He was, quite the contrary, wonderfully relieved. Guiteau had experimented with offbeat religious expression and various occult ritualistic practices. In reference to his fascination with otherworldly communication, he stated that such etheric intercourse brought into a man a "spirit" that could inspire him to do great things.

President James A. Garfield was assassinated in 1881 by an occultist.

Death came slowly to the mortally wounded president. Garfield lingered near death throughout a long summer, then he died in Elberon, New Jersey, on September 19 when complications developed.

James Abram Garfield, born in Cuyahoga County, Ohio, November 19, 1831, was the last U.S. president to be born in a log cabin. Before he became involved in the Republican Party, Garfield taught school, and in 1858 he married Lucretia Rudolph. In spite of a promising military career in which he rose to major general of volunteers during the Civil War, he resigned in 1863, after having been elected to the House of Representatives. Garfield was known for a compelling oratorical style and keen parliamentary skills, which soon made him the leading Republican in the House. His reputation was tainted by his acceptance of a fee in a paving contract case and by suspicions of his involvement in the Crédit Mobilier scandal.

Garfield weathered the criticisms against him and was elected to the Senate in 1880.

Then, as a result of a deadlock in the Republican convention, he became the party's presidential candidate. In the election, he defeated the Democratic choice, Winfield Scott Hancock. Garfield had been in office only one hundred days when he was shot by Guiteau.

"It was the Deity who inspired me to remove the President," Guiteau insisted when he was notified of Garfield's death. "I had to use my ordinary judgment as to the ways and means of accomplishing his will, but I was acting according to orders."

Guiteau had always marched to a different drummer, but the Deity, whom he affectionately called "Lordy," had never seen fit to play the little man a tune of success. Guiteau had failed miserably at every enterprise that he had ever undertaken. When he arrived in the nation's capital in 1881 to seek his fortune, he was recently divorced, physically and emotionally exhausted, yet at the same time obsessed with a sense of destiny and personal infallibility. Such seemingly disparate psychological elements may have inclined Guiteau toward an attitude of receptivity when he heard the disembodied voices speaking to him from the shadows of his room in a rundown Washington boardinghouse. "The President must be removed," the voice whispered. Whether it was some inner voice speaking to him from an obscenely darkened portion of his own psyche or whether it was some independent malignant entity, the effect of those words would soon accomplish the same outrageous deed. When the voice proclaimed, "You are the man to do this," Guiteau accepted the bloody charge with grave responsibility.

Guiteau did confess, however, that his immediate reaction had been one of shock and revulsion. He had never been a violent man. Was this a true revelation from the Deity or a temptation from Satan? Guiteau prayed for many weeks until the voice was revealed to be the Divine Presence.

Few neighbors in Freeport, Illinois, would have suggested that any kind of holy dispensation was to be found around the Guiteau residence when Charles was born in 1841. Luther Guiteau, Charles's father, was a temperate, hard-working bank cashier, but it was also true that the senior Guiteau had most unusual beliefs for that place and time. He attempted to heal his neighbors with his "God-given" powers, he was an avid student of the occult, and he was an avowed follower of the cultist John Humphrey Noyes, a controversial figure who had founded the Oneida Community in New York State. Oneida was organized on what Noyes termed "Bible Communism," with all property owned by the commune. Noyes was convinced that the Second Coming of Christ had occurred in 70 C.E. with the destruction of Jerusalem. Since man was, therefore, on a kind of spiritual probationary period, Noyes required absolute moral perfection in his followers.

Noyes's detractors took issue with his definition of "absolute moral perfection," for in their estimation the Oneida Community was the epitome of free love, unlicensed sex, and the unrestrained practice of organized perversion. When Charles Guiteau entered the Oneida Community as a young man, he was informed that all members should love each other equally. Fidelity between couples was considered bad social form and was evaluated as the sin of selfishness. Sexual relations were permitted at Oneida between any consenting couple who desired them.

In spite of—or perhaps due to—the commune's unusual sex code, Guiteau was hard pressed to find a consenting female adult. After a humiliating session wherein he sat upon a chair in the center of a room while the other members of the commune assessed his personal faults, he left Oneida to wander about the nation in search of his individual destiny.

Guiteau practiced as an attorney in New York until a newspaper published a story about his misappropriation of a client's funds. For a time he traveled as a stumble-tongued evangelist and moved from town to town in a continual effort to stay a few minutes ahead of county sheriffs and the outraged tradesmen he had bilked. In Philadelphia he sought guidance from a fortune-teller and consulted a phrenologist who claimed to delineate character from the information of the skull. Throughout his adventures as a fast-traveling religio-occult follower, Guiteau developed irrational grandiose schemes that he swore would make millions for any person who financed his enterprises. When asked about the source of these ideas, he explained: "The spirit speaks to me."

During his trial for Garfield's murder, Guiteau on numerous occasions had to be restrained from launching into shouting attacks against the prosecution, the trial judge, and even his own defense attorney. Sentenced to death, the bearded little man calmly walked up the steps of the gallows on the morning of June 30, 1882. He dismissed the solace of the prison minister and announced that he would read a selection from the tenth chapter of Matthew. Next the condemned assassin read an original poem entitled "I Am Going to the Lordy, I Am So Glad." Upon completion of the last stanza of his poem, Guiteau stood erect as the hangman placed the noose over his neck and fitted the traditional black hood over his head. Guiteau dropped his manuscript and the trap was sprung.

To the end, the demented little man maintained that he had assassinated the president because he was compelled to do so by the voice of God.

JIM GARRISON

Jim Garrison stubbornly maintained that there was a conspiracy to kill JFK.

Three days after President John F. Kennedy was assassinated in Dallas on November

22, 1963, New Orleans district attorney Jim Garrison arrested David Ferrie as a possible associate of the alleged assassin, Lee Harvey Oswald. Word had reached Garrison that the FBI had found Ferrie's library card in Oswald's wallet. Law-enforcement officers in New Orleans were quite familiar with the mysterious Ferrie and suspected him of having several links to the city's crime scene. Garrison turned the case over to the FBI, and on December 6, 1963, two weeks after the assassination, Director J. Edgar Hoover abruptly closed the investigation of David Ferrie.

Born Earling Carothers Garrison in Denison, Iowa, in 1921, Jim was still a child when his family moved to New Orleans. He joined the U.S. Army in 1941 and was commissioned as a lieutenant in the field artillery in 1942. He received tactical flight training at Fort Sill, Oklahoma, and served during World War II as a pilot in France and Germany. After the war, Garrison earned bachelor of laws and master of civil laws degrees at Tulane Law School. Shortly after graduation he joined the FBI as a special agent, serving in the Seattle and Tacoma region. Soon dissatisfied with his assignment of investigating the loyalties and associations of applicants for defense plant employment, Garrison returned to New Orleans and accepted the post of assistant district attorney in 1954. After working as a trial lawyer from 1958 to 1961, he won the office of district attorney of New Orleans in a runoff in 1962.

Some time after the findings of the Warren Commission were released in September 1964, Louisiana senator Russell Long confided in Garrison that he could not accept the commission's findings that Oswald had acted alone, that there was no connection between Jack Ruby and Oswald, and that there was no conspiracy of any kind. In the fall of 1966 Garrison began an independent inquiry based on the assumption that the assassination of Kennedy had been the result of a conspiracy.

When Garrison announced in February 1967 that one of his chief suspects was David Ferrie, he placed Ferrie in protective custody. Soon thereafter Garrison made the connections among Ferrie, Oswald, former FBI agent Guy Banister, and Clay Shaw, the director of the New Orleans International Trade Mart, who allegedly had links to the CIA. On February 22 Ferrie was found dead in his apartment with two strange typed messages that appeared to be suicide notes. The New Orleans coroner officially ruled Ferrie's death due to cerebral hemorrhage.

In March 1967 Garrison arrested and charged Clay Shaw with complicity in the assassination of President Kennedy. It took exactly two years for Garrison to shepherd the case against Shaw through an exhausting legal marathon of motions, continuances, and appeals—but it took a jury less than an hour to acquit Shaw of all charges.

Garrison retained the office of district attorney of New Orleans until 1973. He wrote a number of books, including *A Heritage of Stone, The Star-Spangled Contract,* and *On the Trail of the Assassins,* which was used as the basis for the Oliver Stone motion picture *JFK.* From 1978 to 1988, Garrison was judge of the Court of Appeals in New Orleans. He died on October 21, 1992.

GERM AND BIOLOGICAL WARFARE

Although some form of germ warfare has been used by opposing armies for thousands of years, conspiracy theorists believe the new batches of laboratory designed "superbugs" are being created on orders from the New World Order.

Germ warfare, also known as biological warfare, is not a new concept. Centuries before anyone knew anything about bacteria or viruses, germ warfare was employed as a weapon of death and annihilation. History tells us that the Assyrians of the sixth century B.C.E. routinely poisoned their enemies' wells with a fungus that caused hallucinations. In the Middle Ages opposing armies would catapult diseased animal and human corpses into their foes' encampments or over their city walls. When the Black Death, the bubonic plague, decimated Europe's population in the fourteenth century, attacking armies flung excrement and bits of diseased corpses over castle walls. And American history texts generally neglect the biological warfare used against Native Americans—the distribution of blankets infected with smallpox.

As may be noted by reading about the use of excrement, rotting corpses of animals, diseased portions of humans, and the microscopic agents of smallpox and other diseases, biological warfare is the utilization of any organism or toxin found in nature in an attack against one's fellow humans. While some advocates have issued hollow arguments that germ warfare might be a benign method of disabling one's enemies, the cold hard truth is that bio warfare—and most certainly bioterrorism—intends to kill its victims.

Use of biological weapons was outlawed by the Geneva Protocol of 1925, but barely a decade later reports that the Japanese Imperial Army was employing such weapons against Chinese soldiers and civilians begin to filter out of Asia to Great Britain and the United States. During the war years of 1937 to 1945, the infamous Japanese Unit 731 conducted gruesome experiments that resulted in the deaths of an estimated 580,000 victims.

In 1941, in response to the bioweapons developed in Japan and Nazi Germany in the late 1930s, the United States, the United Kingdom, and Canada established their own biological warfare program and produced an-

thrax, brucellosis, and botulinum toxin that could be used in war.

1942: British tests with anthrax spores so contaminated Gruinard Island, Scotland, that it was quarantined for forty-eight years.

U.S. Chemical Warfare Services began mustard gas experiments on approximately four thousand servicemen.

1950: In an experiment to determine how susceptible an American city would be to a biological attack, the U.S. Navy ships sprayed a cloud of bacteria over San Francisco. Many residents became ill with pneumonia and other illnesses.

1951: The U.S. Department of Defense began open-air tests over many U.S. cities, using disease-producing bacteria and viruses.

> In an experiment to determine how susceptible an American city would be to biological attack, the U.S. Navy ships sprayed a cloud of bacteria over San Francisco.

1969: The Department of Defense requested $10 million from Congress to develop a synthetic biological agent for which no natural immunity existed. Funding for the synthetic biological agent was granted under H.R. 15090. The CIA supervised the Special Operations Division at Fort Detrick, Maryland, the army's top-secret biological weapons facility.

1972: The Biological and Toxin Weapons Convention reinforced the prohibition of all chemical and biological weapons. The international ban pertained to nearly all production, storage, and transport of such biological agents; however, numerous researchers believe that the secret production of such weapons actually increased.

1977: Senate hearings on Health and Scientific Research confirmed that 239 populated areas had been contaminated with biological agents between 1949 and 1969. Some of the cities included San Francisco, Washington, D.C., Minneapolis, St. Louis, and Key West and Panama City, Florida.

1984: The cult of Bhagwan Shree Rajneesh conducted the first act of bioterrorism in U.S. history the old-fashioned way when they attempted to influence a local election by infecting restaurants and salad bars with salmonella. Over nine hundred people became ill as a result of ingesting food laced with salmonella.

1986: A report to Congress stated that the new generation of biological agents included modified viruses, naturally occurring toxins, and agents that were altered through genetic engineering to prevent treatment by all existing vaccines.

1987: The Department of Defense admitted that regardless of treaties banning research and development of biological agents, it operated 127 research facilities throughout the nation.

1991: The U.S. military was frequently accused of using various biological and chemical weapons in the Gulf War. Often mentioned was the charge that "BZ," a hallucinogenic, was sprayed over Iraqi troops, causing them to surrender as passive, drooling zombies with vacant stares.

1994: It was revealed that many returning Desert Storm veterans were infected with an altered strain of *Mycoplasma incognitus,* a microbe commonly used in the production of biological weapons.

1996: The Department of Defense admitted knowledge that Desert Storm soldiers were exposed to chemical agents.

2001: In September and October, the U.S. experienced a number of well-publicized anthrax attacks on government buildings and politicians and one photo editor through mailed envelopes. Five deaths resulted from this domestic terrorism.

2004: Dangerous "superbugs" began popping up out of nowhere. Suddenly there were cases of flesh-eating bacteria, fatal pneumonia, and life-threatening heart infections—seemingly all caused by mutating strains of *Staphylococcus aureus* that shrugged off penicillin as a duck shakes off rain. Conspiracy theorists were quick to denounce government experimentation in such labs as those in Fort Detrick as being responsible for these new drug-resistant viruses.

Conspiracy theorists believe that biological weapons continue to be manufactured in response to the New World Order's mandate to decrease global population, and they point out the links between Litton Bionetics, the CIA, and Germany's I. G. Farben Company, an extensive chemical and pharmaceutical cartel that came to international prominence in the early 1900s. Some researchers name I. G. Farben as one of the prominent sponsors of Hitler's rise to leadership in the Nazi Party. It was primarily Rockefeller money that built the Kaiser Wilhelm Institute for Eugenics, Anthropology, and Human Heredity in pre-Nazi Germany, and it was Rockefeller cash that installed Ernst Rudin, Hitler's chief racial hygienist, as the institute's director.

Operation Paperclip, the secret project that brought thousands of Nazi scientists to the United States at the close of World War II, included Erich Traub, a world-class virologist who had served as Hitler's biological weapons chief. U.S. Navy and CIA biological warfare laboratories made good use of Traub and other Nazi experts on germ and chemical warfare.

Kanatjan Alibekov (Ken Alibek) was second in command at the Soviet Union's Biopreparat bio warfare section when he defected in

1992. Now a key researcher at a U.S. biodefense contractor, Alibek has stated that even after the USSR signed a treaty banning such research, Biopreparat employed ten thousand scientists at forty sites.

With the advent of genetic manipulation, deadly designer viruses can be created. Through the sorcery of recombinant engineering, the highly contagious influenza virus could be spliced with botulism or the toxin from plague. The Soviet bio warfare scientists were attempting to combine the venom-producing genes from poisonous spiders with ordinary bacteria.

The smallpox virus is said to be particularly amenable to genetic engineering. The deadliest natural smallpox virus is *Variola major,* and an outbreak of it would be especially deadly now because the disease was eradicated from the planet in 1977. The smallpox vaccine dissipates after ten to twenty years, so unless someone has had a reason to be vaccinated against the disease recently, no one today is immune. The last known human case of smallpox appeared in Somalia, but no one can guess how many canisters of the lethal virus reside in government laboratories awaiting deadly use in biological warfare.

Conspiracy researchers name the Ebola virus as the ideal biological weapon, because it has the potential of killing nine out of ten infected humans within three weeks of contact. Conspiracists state that the virus first emerged in three European vaccine-production laboratories virtually simultaneously in 1967 (one strain is named "Marburg" because one of these labs is in Marburg, Germany). Scientific consensus has it that this virus arrived in Europe in a shipment of nearly five hundred African monkeys from Kitum Cave near the West Nile region of Central Africa. Kitum Cave, conspiracy theorists state, is really a Litton Bionetics research lab where NCI scientists experimented on nonhuman primates and African villagers, as well.

In April 2005 the World Health Organization (WHO) reported an Ebola-like virus spreading rapidly through seven of Angola's eighteen provinces. The initial outbreak appeared to have spread from a pediatric ward in Uige, about 180 miles north of Luanda. Most of the victims of the virus were children. Over a dozen health-care workers had died from the disease, and those who remained were deserting hospitals and clinics. In one village, terrified people had attacked WHO workers out of fear of catching the disease.

Again, conspiracy theorists recall the plan of the New World Order to greatly reduce Earth's population, leaving the majority of those who survive to toil as servants to the financial and political elite. The delivery of combinations of biological and chemical agents, if conducted properly and secretly, cannot easily be traced to its source. If a population of an "undesirable area" should be subjected to multiple exposures and infections over time, they would perish—and save the New World Order the trouble and expense of conducting a conventional military campaign.

GHOST DANCE

Wovoka, the Paiute messiah, taught the tribes a dance from the spirit world that would bring back the buffalo. Unfortunately, the U.S. Cavalry interpreted the drums as beating out a war dance.

On January 1, 1889, Jack Wilson, a Paiute who worked as a hired hand for a white rancher near Mason Valley, Nevada, came down with a terrible fever during a solar eclipse. His sickness became so bad that for three days he lay as if dead.

When he returned to consciousness, Wovoka, as he was known in his tribe, told the Paiute who had assembled around his "dead" body that his spirit had left his body and had walked with God, the Old Man, for those three days. The Old Man had given him a powerful vision that revealed that Jesus lived again upon the Earth Mother and that the dead of many tribes were alive in the spirit world, just waiting to be reborn. If the native people wished the buffalo to return, the grasses to grow tall, the rivers to run clean, they must not injure anyone; they must not do harm to any living thing; they must not make war. On the other hand, they must lead lives of purity, cease gambling, put away the white man's strong drink, and guard themselves against all lusts and weaknesses of the flesh.

The most important part of the vision that God gave to Wovoka was to revive the Ghost Dance first taught by his grandfather, the Paiute prophet Wodziwob, and spread by his father, Tavibo, during the 1870s. The Old Man had stressed that this was the dance of the spirit people of the Other World. To perform this dance was to ensure that God's blessings would be bestowed upon the tribe, and many ghosts would materialize during the dance to join with the living in celebration of the return of the old ways. The Old Man had spoken to him as if Wovoka were his son and had assured him that many miracles would be worked through him. He promised Wovoka that the dead from many tribes would soon be born again in a restored world that would once again be filled with plentiful game. All those whites who interfered with this rebirth would be swallowed up by the earth, and only those who practiced the ways of peace would be spared. All the nation would once again belong to the tribes.

Wovoka had spent his time in imitation of death, lying in a trancelike state for three days, receiving his spiritual initiation in the Other World. Wovoka had emerged as a holy man and a prophet, and history would forever know him as the Paiute Messiah.

Soon, representatives from many tribes visited the Paiute and saw them dance Wovoka's vision. They saw the truth of the Ghost Dance, and they began calling Wovoka "Jesus." His fame spread so far that newspaper reporters from St. Louis, New York, and Chicago came to see the Ghost Dance Messiah and record his words. The white people were pleased that Wovoka did not speak of war, only of the importance of all people living together in harmony.

Kicking Bear, an Oglala-Brule Sioux who, through marriage with Chief Big Foot's niece, had become acting chief of the Miniconjou Sioux, traveled from South Dakota to Nevada to see the Ghost Dance. He was impressed with Wovoka, and he saw the scars left on the Paiute's hands and feet where the whites had crucified him in another life. Kicking Bear was a warrior, sick of the unfulfilled promises of the whites, but he and the Sioux delegates accepted Wovoka as the true Messiah, and they returned to tell Big Foot and Sitting Bull about the Ghost Dance.

Sitting Bull, the great Sioux prophet and holy man, was impressed by Kicking Bear's report, but rather noncommittal toward the teachings of the Paiute Messiah. While he did not wholeheartedly endorse the Ghost Dance, neither did he prevent those Sioux who wished to join in the ritual from doing so.

In spite of his reservations about following only the path of peace with the whites, Kicking Bear introduced the Ghost Dance to the Miniconjou and other bands of Sioux. Within a few months, most of the Sioux regarded Kicking Bear as the founder of their own version of the Ghost Dance.

Sometime during the fall of 1890 the Ghost Dance spread through the Sioux villages of the Dakota reservations with the addition of the Ghost Shirts, special shirts that could resist the bullets of the bluecoats, the soldiers who might attempt to stop the rebirth of the old ways. As the Sioux danced, sometimes through the night, believing they were hastening the return of the buffalo and their many relatives who had been killed in combat with the pony soldiers, the settlers and townsfolk in the Dakota Territory became anxious.

"Ghost Dance of the Sioux Indians," by Amedee Forestier, *Illustrated London News*, 1891.

And when the Sioux at Sitting Bull's Grand River camp began to dance with rifles, it became apparent to the white soldiers that the Ghost Dance was really a war dance after all.

After a nervous Indian agent at Pine Ridge wired his superiors in Washington that the Sioux were dancing in the snow and acting crazy, it was decided that Sitting Bull and other Sioux leaders should be removed from the general population and confined in a military post until the fanatical interest in the Ghost Dance religion had subsided. Sitting Bull was killed by Sioux reservation police on December 15, 1890, and Big Foot and 350 of his people were brought to the edge of Wounded Knee Creek to camp.

On December 28 Col. James W. Forsyth led a force of cavalry, infantry, and Sioux police against the Wounded Knee camp and surround-

ed it. Their weaponry included Hotchkiss multiple-firing guns and mountain howitzers. A shot rang out. The encamped Sioux scattered to retrieve rifles that had been discarded or hidden. From all around, fire from the automatic rifles, violent eruptions from the exploding shells, and volleys of grapeshot destroyed the village. As they were being slaughtered by two battalions of soldiers, the Sioux sang Ghost Dance songs, blended with their own death chants. Within minutes, approximately three hundred Sioux had been killed, Big Foot among them, and twenty-five soldiers had lost their lives.

Angered by the senseless massacre at Wounded Knee, Kicking Bear and his warriors donned their Ghost Shirts to make them impervious to the whites' bullets and began to attack small columns of cavalry and to raid ranches and small settlements. As Kicking

Bear's warriors eluded the cavalry and continued to attack supply trains, Colonel Forsyth realized that he was no longer confronting a "hostile" force composed largely of elderly men, women, and children. Kicking Bear's men were seasoned fighters who skillfully planned ambushes and employed guerrilla tactics.

On January 15, 1891, Kicking Bear's 3,500 Sioux, cold, starving, and surrounded by 8,000 soldiers, surrendered. Fully expecting to be executed for crimes against the whites, an amazed Kicking Bear and the other Ghost Dance leaders spent two months in prison— then were pardoned to tour Europe as part of Buffalo Bill Cody's Wild West show. Some years later, after Kicking Bear returned from his foray into show business, he became a Presbyterian minister.

The massacre at Wounded Knee and Kicking Bear's seventeen-day campaign of revenge ended the Native American tribes' widespread practice of the Ghost Dance religion and brought the last of the Indian Wars to a close. It was said that Wovoka wept bitterly when he learned the fate of the Sioux at Wounded Knee. The Paiute messiah died in 1932.

GLOBAL WARMING

The United States alone disputes the evidence for global warming while its average citizen consumes as much as twenty-four times the resources as those in some nations.

The global average temperature in 2004 was the fourth warmest since systematic measurements began in the nineteenth century. Scientists noted that temperatures were particularly high in Alaska, the Caspian Sea region of Europe, and the Antarctic Peninsula. The highest global average was recorded in 1998, when a strong El Niño cycle in the Pacific Ocean boosted temperatures. The 2010 average temperatures tied the 1998 record as warmest, fol-

lowed by 2005, 2003, 2002, and 2009 in that order, from highest to lowest.

The United Nations International Panel on Climate Change predicted in 2001 that the world could warm up by between 1.5 and nearly 6 degrees by the end of the twenty-first century. In their opinion, it was clear that human activities are to blame for most of the temperature rise.

Almost alone in the developed world, the United States disputes the human element in climate change. President George W. Bush failed to participate in world energy or global warming conferences, and U.S. delegates who did attend were accused of blocking key initiatives on energy use, biodiversity, and corporate responsibility. The administration's failure to cooperate with other nations was especially ironic in light of the World Wildlife Fund's finding that the average U.S. resident consumes almost twice as much resources as a citizen of the United Kingdom and more than twenty-four times as much as some Africans.

Conspiracy theorists claim that the U.S. government is not doing enough to protect its citizens from the effects of global warming and other geophysical dangers, such as the caldera (below-ground-level volcano) in Yellowstone. Up to fifty-two miles long, twenty-eight miles wide, and six miles deep, the Yellowstone caldera has been heating up for some time and, according to many observers, might blow at any time. The blast would be at least a thousand times more powerful than Mount St. Helens and shower seven inches of ash over a diameter of up to six hundred miles. It would blacken the world's skies for years and pollute the atmosphere sufficiently to drop world temperatures, ruin agriculture, and annihilate a great deal of life on land and sea. Mount Rainier, Mount Etna, and numerous other volcanoes in the United States and the world are also ripe for eruption.

Other researchers worry that without proper preparations solar ejections of energy rays could destroy us. A massive solar flare direct-

168

ed toward Earth would demagnetize the binary codes of all computer technologies, totally disrupt the planet's natural magnetic field, and cause global superstorms that would dwarf anything Earth has ever experienced.

Although they don't receive much media attention, professional astronomers have warned us about asteroids, comets, and even planetary bodies in our solar system that could threaten Earth's existence. Astronomers from nearly every nation traveled to observatories at the South Pole in 2004 to assess the cosmic influx and the danger to Earth.

A study by the World Wildlife Fund (WWF) warned that we are plundering the planet at a pace that outstrips its capacity to support life. More than a third of the natural world has been destroyed by humans over the past three decades. In order to support Western society's high consumption levels, two additional planets the size of Earth would be required by the year 2050. Or, to put it another way, the earth will not be able to support its population and may simply call it quits by 2050.

Based on consumption of grain, fish, wood, and water, along with emissions of carbon dioxide from industry and internal combustion engines, the WWF derives an ecological "footprint" for each nation by estimating how much land is required to support each of its residents. The USA's consumption footprint is about 30 acres per individual, while the UK and Western Europe as a whole stand at about 15.5 acres. In Ethiopia the figure is not quite 5 acres, falling to just 1.24 acres for Burundi, the country that consumes the least resources.

Some scientists, such as Bill Hare of the Potsdam Institute for Climate Impact Research, Germany's leading global-warming research institute, have projected a detailed timetable of the destruction and distress that is likely to face the world in the next few years.

By the middle of the present century, global temperature is likely to move up to 2 degrees Centigrade above the preindustrial level. There will be substantial losses of Arctic sea ice, and species such as polar bears and walruses will be threatened. In tropical regions, marine animals that live in the coral will be forced out by high temperatures and the reefs may die. Mediterranean regions will be hit by more forest fires and insect pests, while in parts of North America, such as the Rockies, rivers may become too warm for trout and salmon. In South Africa, the world's most remarkable floral kingdom will start to lose its species. Alpine areas from Europe to Australia will dry up. The broad-leaved forests of China will die. The numbers at risk from hunger will increase and another billion and a half people will face water shortages.

The United Nations International Panel on Climate Change predicted in 2001 that the world could warm up by between 1.5 and nearly 6 degrees by the end of the twenty-first century.

Early in the second half of the century, the global average temperature will rise to 3 degrees Centigrade above preindustrial levels. There is likely to be irreversible damage to the Amazon rainforest, leading to its collapse. There will be a rapid increase in populations exposed to hunger and water shortages. About 2070 the Arctic sea ice will disappear, and animal and marine species will disappear with it. Water stresses for humans will worsen, and whole regions of land will become unsuitable for producing food.

Although some scientists argue that the present global trend toward warming is but a cyclical phenomenon and point out that there have been many such trends in the past, conspiracy theorists exclaim that the handwriting is on the wall. If some measures are not soon taken, famine, droughts, and diseases will occur at previously unseen rates due to global warming. And they wonder why their government seems to be doing nothing to stop the rise of global temperatures or to prepare for its deleterious effects.

GNOSTICISM

Gnosticism has been an enemy of the church since early Christianity. One of the Gnostics' greatest sins in the eyes of the church fathers was their belief that Jesus and Mary Magdalene were married.

Several cults with widely differing beliefs but all bearing the label of "Gnostic" arose in the first century, strongly competing with other versions of early Christianity. The term *Gnostic* is derived from the Greek *gnosis,* meaning "knowledge," and the adherents of Gnosticism unabashedly declared that they "knew" from firsthand experience the truths that other beliefs had to accept on faith. Many of the Gnostic sects blended elements of Christianity with the Eleusinian mysteries, combining them with Indian, Egyptian, and Babylonian magic, bringing in aspects of the Jewish Kabbalah as well.

Nearly everything that was known about the Gnostics prior to the discovery of the Nag Hammadi library in Upper Egypt in 1945 was taken from the highly prejudiced writings of such church fathers as Irenaeus, Hippolytus, and Epiphanius, who condemned the Gnostics as heretics and devil worshippers. The Nag Hammadi library consists of twelve books called codices, plus eight leaves removed from a thirteenth book and tucked inside the front cover of the sixth. These eight leaves make up the complete text of a single work

that was taken out of a volume of collected works. Each of the codices, except the tenth, consists of a collection of brief works, such as *The Prayer of the Apostle Paul, The Gospel of Thomas, The Sophia of Jesus Christ, The Gospel of the Egyptians,* and so on.

Although the Nag Hammadi library is written in Coptic, the texts were originally composed in Greek and contain many references to Egyptian sites and beliefs. And although the work is ascribed to Christian Gnostics, there are many essays within the library that do not seem to reflect very much of what is today regarded as Christian tradition. While there are references to a Gnostic Savior, his presentation does not seem to be based on the Jesus found in the New Testament. On those occasions when Jesus does appear in the texts, he often seems to be criticizing those orthodox Christians who have confused his words and his teachings. By following the true way and thus achieving transcendence, Jesus says in *The Apocalypse of Peter,* every believer's "resurrection" becomes a spiritual reality.

Throughout the Nag Hammadi library there are admonitions to resist the lures and traps of trying to be content in a world that has been corrupted by evil. The world created by God is good. The evil that has permeated the world, although alien to its original design, has risen to the status of ruler. Rather than perceiving existence as a battle between God and the devil, the Gnostics envisioned a struggle between the true, most high, unknowable God and the lesser god of this earth, the "Demiurge," whom they associated with the angry, jealous, rule-giving deity of the ancient Hebrews. All humans have the ability to awaken to the glorious realization that they have within themselves a spark of the divine. By attuning to the mystical awareness within them, they can transcend all earthly entrapments and regain their true spiritual home. Jesus was sent by the most high God as a guide to teach humans how to free themselves from the control of the Demiurge and to understand that the kingdom of God is within, a transcendental state of consciousness, rather than a future reward.

The theology of the Gnostics often utilized feminine imagery and symbology. Especially offensive to the patriarchal church fathers was the Gnostic assertion that Jesus had close women disciples as well as men. In *The Gospel of Philip,* it is written that the Lord loved Mary Magdalene above all the other apostles and sharply reprimanded those of his followers who objected to his open displays of affection toward her.

The first Gnostic of importance was Simon Magus, a Samaritan sorcerer, a contemporary of the apostles, who was converted to Christianity by the apostle Philip. Although he was a highly respected magus, Simon was impressed by the remarkable powers of the apostles and their ability to heal and to manifest miracles. When he saw the apostles Peter and John performing wonders, Simon offered to pay them a fee to teach him how to manifest the Holy Spirit. Peter strongly rebuked him for attempting to buy this profound spiritual gift (Acts 8:9–24). The term *simony* to describe the purchasing of ecclesiastic blessings has come down through the ages.

According to tradition, Simon fell back on his old ways of sorcery and began to traffic once again with demons. To prove his power, he announced to all of Rome that he would soar into the sky and ascend to heaven, just as Jesus had done. Supported by demons, Simon began to rise skyward. Peter, fearful that many innocents would be attracted to this false prophet, prayed for God to end Simon's flight. Frightened away by the apostle's prayers, the demons fled, and the magus crashed to the ground, breaking both legs.

The story of Simon Magus fueled the belief that a secret oral tradition existed, passed down from Jesus, that had much greater power and authority than the scriptures and epistles

offered by the orthodox teachers of Christianity. The Gnostics, like the initiates of the Greek and Egyptian mysteries, sought direct experience with the divine, and they believed that this communion could be achieved by uttering secret words of wisdom that God had granted to specially enlightened teachers.

> On those occasions when Jesus does appear in the texts, he often seems to be criticizing those orthodox Christians who have confused his words and his teachings.

The Gnostics continued to be regarded as heretics by the church down through their spiritual descendants in the Cathars and the Knights Templar. In turn, the Gnostics considered themselves much more spiritually advanced than the larger community of Christians, whom they regarded as ignorant plodders and easily led sheep.

Gnosticism ceased to be a threat to the organized Christian church by the fourteenth century, but many of its tenets have never faded completely from the thoughts and writings of scholars and intellectuals. Elements of the various creeds of the Gnostics surfaced again in the so-called New Age movement of the twentieth century, and an impetus to study the writings of the Gnostic texts was provided by the psychologist Carl Jung (1875–1961). In Jung's opinion, Gnosticism's depiction of the struggle between the most high God and the false god represented the turmoil that exists among various aspects of the human psyche. The most high God, in the psychologist's interpretation, was the personal unconscious, the Demiurge was the ego (the organizing principle of consciousness), and Christ was the unified self, the complete human.

GOTHS AND NEO-NAZIS

Neo-Nazis are infiltrating the Goth lifestyle through the Goth's music and their fascination with Hitler and occult Nazi symbols.

In the United States, "Gothic" or "Goth" is a choice of clothing, a particular taste in music, a lifestyle that many assess as dressing up for Halloween all year long. However, in parts of Europe, especially in Germany, the extreme fringe element of Goth has become the point at which Satanism and neo-Nazism come together. Some conspiracy researchers with a keen sense of history are quite aware of the links between occultism and Nazism and see shadows of the Thule, Vril, and Black Sun societies being reborn in many young people who affect Goth style and satanic philosophy.

According to authorities, Germany's neo-Nazis have attempted to penetrate several youth scenes since the mid-1990s, but it seems that with Goths they have had their greatest success. The Goth movement may be on the wane in the United States, Britain, and many other European countries, but in Germany, where Goths are known as "Gruftis" (meaning "crypt"), their numbers constitute a large group. Some experts estimate that between 5 and 7 percent of all Germans between the ages of twelve and twenty-five are Goths, an overall population of at least 650,000. The areas in which the neo-Nazi ideas have had the greatest success is in "neo-folk" music and in black metal, the dark variant of heavy metal. In the past five years, neo-Nazi ideas and symbols have merged with the Goth music scene.

It must be emphasized that many of these young Goths are doing little more than making a fashion statement or protesting against the conformity they must face as they morph into adults. True Satan worshippers exist only on the extremist fringe, but experts estimate that there are as many as seven thousand Satanists in Germany, with many of them embracing Nazism as well.

On January 31, 2002, two Satanists in western Germany were sentenced for the gruesome murder of a friend. The prosecutor in the case called the murder of Frank Hackert by the husband and wife Daniel and Manuela Ruda "a picture of cruelty and depravity" such as he had never seen. On July 6, 2001, before they left the bloody scene in their home in the town of Witten, the Rudas had killed Hackert with a hammer and sixty-six knife stabs. There was evidence that Manuela had drunk some of the victim's blood before the couple carved a pentagram in his chest and left a scalpel protruding from his stomach. Acting on an anonymous tip, police broke into the Ruda home on July 9 and discovered a poster of hanged women in the bathroom and a collection of human skulls in the living room. Blood-stained scalpels littered the house, and there was a coffin in which it was later determined that twenty-three-year-old Manuela sometimes slept. Near Hackert's mutilated body was a list of names that police theorized were those of the couple's next intended victims.

During the Rudas' trial, a great deal of the prosecution's case focused on Manuela, who had had two of her teeth replaced with fangs to look more like a vampire. Manuela testified that she had been initiated into Satanism at a Gothic club in London, where she claimed to have met real vampires and drank the blood of living people.

There was testimony at the trial that Daniel Ruda had once been active in the far-right/skinhead movement and had even canvassed for the National Democratic Party of Germany (NPD), a far-right party that the government tried to ban. Daniel had eased out of skinhead activism and plunged heavily into the Goth scene and black metal music after he found his "princess of darkness" in Manuela. Upon conviction Manuela was sentenced to thirteen years in a secure mental facility, Daniel to fifteen years.

German officials state that the neo-Nazi constituency does not make much of an impression at the polls at election time, but the far-right movement is disturbing because its members are more ready than those of other fringe movements to resort to violence. Experts suggest that the reason the neo-Nazis have little impact on election days is that most of them despise the democratic process and abstain from voting. Herein lies another similarity between the neo-Nazis and occult societies: both are secretive and have only a few members in their individual cells, with a wider circle of like-minded allies spread throughout the nation.

Germany has passed laws making both Holocaust denial and the use of symbols from the Third Reich criminal offences. In January 2005, during the observance of the sixtieth anniversary of the liberation of the Nazi death camp at Auschwitz-Birkenau, the current president of the European Union, Luxembourg justice minister Luc Frieden, proposed a ban on all Nazi symbols in the twenty-five-nation bloc that was later shelved.

GREAT PYRAMID OF CHEOPS

The nine or more secret rooms in the Great Pyramid on the plateau of Giza contain proof that the ancient monuments of Egypt are thousands of years older than previously believed and quite likely constructed with the help of extraterrestrials.

Rising up on a plateau called Giza, ten miles west of present-day Cairo, Egypt, the Great Pyramid, its two companions pyramids, and the Sphinx are probably the world's oldest and best-known mysteries. The Pyramid of Cheops stands 481 feet high, measures roughly 756 feet on each side, and covers 13 acres of land. For more than four thousand years, it was the tallest architectural structure on earth. It has been estimated that more than 2,300,000 stone blocks of an average weight of two and one-half tons went into the construction of this last resting place for the pharaoh Cheops (also known as Khufu) circa 2550 B.C.E. The Pyramid of Khafre, near Cheops, stands 442 feet high and covers 12 acres. The third pyramid in the massive triumvirate, Mycerinus, is 215 feet tall and 346 feet wide on each side. The pyramids are situated at cardinal points on the compass and indicate knowledge of astronomy and mathematics in advance of other civilizations.

Among the questions swirling about the pyramids are the following:

1. Where was the immense amount of rock forming them (11 million cubic yards of stone for the Great Pyramid alone) quarried, and how was it moved and then erected into such an astonishingly precise structure?

2. What kind of surveying methods and equipment did the ancient Egyptians use to ensure that the landscape was level and their measurements were accurate?

3. How could the vast number of workers required for such an undertaking be mobilized, housed, and fed?

4. All three of the pyramids at Giza were supposedly erected as tombs. Why has not a single body been found in any of them?

A baffling series of chambers, tunnels, shafts, blocked passageways, corridors leading to empty spaces, and false leads confront pyramid explorers. Numerous Egyptologists and researchers of the mysteries of antiquity

The Pyramid of Cheops was built around 2589 to 2550 B.C.E. as the burial place for one of Egypt's great kings. Some archeologists estimate it would have taken 100,000 slaves to construct it, but there are those who believe the ancient Egyptians had extraterrestrial help.

have announced the discovery of nine or more secret rooms in the Great Pyramid, but the contents of those fabled hiding places remain unknown to all but a few privileged insiders who wish to keep their treasures from the world. Some researchers contend that the secret rooms hide solid proof of the ancient lost civilization of Atlantis.

Others insist that the dusty corridors house undeniable evidence of extraterrestrial colonies that thrived on Earth in our prehistory. Proponents of the ancient astronaut theory maintain that such massive works as the Pyramids were built by intervening extraterrestrials, who used the power plants of their flying saucers to hoist such tonnage into place. Spaceships of vast proportions may have brought extraterrestrial colonists to various parts of Earth before returning to the home planet.

Edgar Cayce, the famous "Sleeping Prophet" of Virginia Beach, Virginia, predicted the existence of secret rooms in the Great Pyramid and beneath the right paw of the Sphinx.

According to Cayce, who made his prophecies in the 1930s and '40s, the fabled Atlantean Hall of Records would be discovered in Giza before 1998. It is known that the presence of such secret chambers was confirmed in 1994 by classified high-tech radar photographs taken by the NASA shuttle.

In 1996 much fuss was made over a video that had reportedly been made of one of the secret rooms. Although a network television presentation ballyhooed a peek inside the legendary chambers, millions of disappointed viewers were able to see only a shaky film produced by a videocam attached to a small, four-wheeled robot as it crept down a corridor in the Great Pyramid. Allegedly the tunnel had never before been opened for the eyes of modern humans, and an audience of millions were teased into believing that they were about to behold a revelation of earthshaking importance. But the tunnel and the supposed secret chamber showed us nothing.

In 1997 the archeologists Mark Lehner and Zahi Hawass excavated a grid of rooms near the Great Pyramid, and Lehner believes that an entire additional complex might be unearthed, providing more answers, and probably more questions, about the pyramids of Giza. Lehner, associated with the Oriental Institute of the University of Chicago and the Harvard Semitic Museum, first traveled to Egypt during the 1970s, inspired by the theories of Edgar Cayce, who believed that the pyramids were actually thousands of years older than they were credited.

A great number of researchers believe that at least one of the hidden chambers in the Great Pyramid will contain a full-sized aerial vehicle of ancient terrestrial or extraterrestrial design.

Khalil Messiha, physician and aeromodeller, believes that he has found evidence to indicate that the Egyptians had flying machines as early as the third or fourth century B.C.E. Messiha's brother, a flight engineer, agrees with him and adds that the aerofoil shape of the models discovered among some ancient bird figures demonstrates a "drag effect" evolved only recently after many years of aeronautical engineering research.

Khalil Messiha first found the model glider or airplane in 1969 when he was looking through a box of bird models in one of the Cairo Museum's storerooms. The relics had first been unearthed at Saqqara in 1898. The glider, made of sycamore wood, bears a striking resemblance to the American Hercules transport plane, which has a distinctive wing shape. Messiha is certain that it is no toy model. It is too scientifically designed, and it required a lot of skill to make.

Most of the bird figures that have been found at excavations in Egypt are half-human, half-bird in design, but this object is very different. It seems to be a model of a high-winged monoplane with a heart-shaped fuselage, which assumes a compressed ellipse toward the tail.

Dr. Messiha was quoted in the May 18, 1972, *Times* of London as saying, "It is the tail that is really the most interesting thing which distinguished this model from all others that have been discovered." The tail, it seems, has a vertical fin. No known bird flies equipped with a rudder. In addition, as Messiha learned from his several years' study of ancient Egyptian bird figures, all other models were lavishly decorated and fitted for legs. The glider has no legs and only very slight traces of an eye painted on one side of the "nose," together with two faint reddish lines under the wing. Messiha and several researchers are convinced that it is a scale model of a full-sized flying machine of some kind that was actually flown by the ancient Egyptians.

The discovery of such an aerial vehicle in the Great Pyramid would completely revolutionize the way that academics and scientists view the ancient Egyptians and other forgotten cultures of human prehistory. Lost civilizations, such as Atlantis, would have to be taken very seriously. Some researchers believe that many scholars and others in authority simply do not want such information made available to the masses. The religious and scientific establishments fear that the great majority of men and women would not be able to deal with irrefutable evidence that there was a world civilization before our own.

GUN CONTROL

Each year Congress fails to pass antigun legislation. Conspiracists figure that in a participatory democracy, the people who want to ban guns should learn to take no for an answer.

The seemingly endless debate over gun control in the United States means only one thing to most conspiracy theorists: another plot by the New World Order, the globalists, who know that it would be more difficult to subdue an armed population than one deprived of its right to bear arms. The conspiracists cite the U.S. Constitution's Second Amendment, which protects the right of citizens to keep and bear arms, as one of the best ways to keep the New World Order under some kind of control and cause them to think twice before trying to conquer America.

Although most gun-control advocates recognize that right, they argue that the arms that citizens have the right to bear should not include assault rifles. And what could be the harm in laws that require mandatory childproof gun locks, a ban on semiautomatic rifles, and a limit on the number of firearms that a person can buy? And what about a waiting period before someone can walk out of a sporting goods store with a Glock pistol?

The National Rifle Association answers by stating that even these laws infringe on the constitutional rights of law-abiding citizens and that no laws, however strict, would keep firearms out of the hands of criminals.

In the January 2005 issue, *Police Times* magazine released the rather surprising results of a survey of police chiefs and sheriffs across the United States. In regard to gun control, 93.6 percent supported civilian gun-ownership rights; 96 percent believed that criminals obtain firearms from illegal sources; 92 percent said they hadn't arrested anyone for violation of "waiting period" laws; and 63.1 percent answered "yes" when queried if citizens' concealed-weapons permits would reduce violent crimes.

In 1929, the Soviet Union established gun control. From 1929 to 1953, approximately 20 million dissidents, unable to defend themselves, were rounded up and exterminated.

"If a person kills someone with a shovel, should the shovel manufacturer be held liable?" asks writer Jim Marrs. "As silly as that may sound, this is precisely the argument being expounded in cities where suits have been filed against gun manufacturers seeking damages for the misuse of their products." Marrs also comments on how the antigun ac-

tivists lobby each year to get restrictive laws passed, and year after year Congress fails to pass antigun legislation: "You would think that in a nation that prides itself on being a participatory democracy, the folks who want to disarm America would take no for an answer and yield for a while."

Pressure a conspiracy theorist on restrictive gun laws and you are likely to get a copy of "Facts on Gun Control" similar to the one compiled by Daniel Lopez of Texas:

- In 1929, the Soviet Union established gun control. From 1929 to 1953, approximately 20 million dissidents, unable to defend themselves, were rounded up and exterminated.

- Germany established gun control in 1938, and from 1939 to 1945, 13 million Jews, gypsies, homosexuals and others, unable to defend themselves, were rounded up and exterminated.

- China established gun control in 1935. From 1948 to 1952, 20 million political dissidents, unable to defend themselves, were rounded up and exterminated.

The list goes on until Lopez has totaled approximately 56 million dissidents or otherwise government-condemned individuals who have been killed.

When a conspiracy theorist is asked if he or she is in favor of gun control, don't be surprised if the reply is, "Which group of citizens do you wish to have exterminated?"

H

HAARP

U.S. Air Force and Navy scientists assures us that the goal of the High Frequency Active Auroral Research Program (HAARP) is only to gain greater knowledge of the Earth's ionosphere. Conspiracy theorists warn that the true purpose is to gain control of all communication and navigation systems, as well as the weather.

The High Frequency Active Auroral Research Program (HAARP) is jointly managed by the Air Force Research Laboratory (AFRL) and the Office of Naval Research (ONR) and had as its goal the achievement of greater knowledge of the physical and electrical properties of Earth's ionosphere, which can affect military and civilian communication and navigation systems. The program, begun in 1990, has its observatory located approximately eight miles north of Gakona, Alaska. The site location, according to the official HAARP website, is perfect on two accounts:

1. The Alaskan ionosphere over HAARP can be characterized as mid-latitude, auroral or polar depending on how active the sun is at any given time and day. This gives a wide variety of ionospheric conditions to study.

2. The HAARP research facility consists of two major subsystems: 1) the HF transmitter, and 2) the other scientific, observational instruments that have been designed and built and which are also being installed at the site. The two subsystems are equal in research importance. The scientific observation instruments require a quiet electromagnetic location away from cities and built up areas.

Currently, there are forty-eight active antennas in the array. The HF transmitter produces 960 kilowatts of power and has an operational range of 2.8–8.2 MHz. When the HAARP antenna array is completed, it will consist of 180 antennas on approximately thirty-three acres of land and will have a total transmitter power of about 3,600 kilowatts.

The official website is very forthcoming in its section of "Frequently Asked Questions." In spite of the reassuring responses, many conspiracy theorists see HAARP quite differently than do the staff members who work there. Nick Begich and his coauthor Jeane Manning (*Angels Don't Play This HAARP*) are outspoken about the dangers and hazards of the AFRL and ONR developing and deploying a system based on the pioneering work of the genius Nikola Tesla. Many other scientists, environmentalists, and conspiracy researchers have taken up the warning cry first sounded by Begich and Manning. If we could conduct an interview with representatives of the AFRL, the ONR, and a couple of conspiracy theorists, the discussion might go something like the following:

Is HAARP capable of affecting the weather?

AFRL/ONR: HAARP will not affect the weather. The energy transmitted will be negligible and easily absorbed in the troposphere or the ionosphere, the two levels that produce the planet's weather. The ionosphere is continuously replenished as the sun's radiation interacts with the highest levels of Earth's atmosphere.

Conspiracy Theorists: HAARP will boil the upper atmosphere. It is an advanced model of an "ionospheric heater." HAARP is a test run for a super-powerful radio-wave-beaming technology that raises the temperature of areas of the ionosphere by focusing a beam and heating those areas. Electromagnetic waves then bounce back to Earth, penetrating everything, living and dead.

How long do the effects of ionospheric heating remain?

AFRL/ONR: The ionosphere is a turbulent medium that is always being either stirred up or renewed by the sun. Artificially induced effects are quickly eliminated—depending on the height of the ionosphere where the effect is produced—in less than a second to ten minutes. Visualize a fast-moving stream in which you drop a stone. The momentary ripples are quickly lost in the rapidly moving water and within a few feet are undetectable.

Conspiracy Theorists: Plumes of atmospheric particles could act as a lens or focusing layer and scorch some areas of the planet. Ozone levels in the atmosphere could be artificially increased and concentrated in specific areas.

Is it true that HAARP can create a hole in the ionosphere?

AFRL/ONR: Absolutely not. Any effects created by HAARP are insignificant compared with the normal and natural day/night variations that occur in the ionosphere every day.

Conspiracy Theorists: In a burst lasting only a few minutes, HAARP will not burn a hole—it will produce a long tear, slicing through the ionosphere like a gigantic knife. HAARP pumps tremendous energy into the very delicate molecular configuration that constitutes the multilayer of the ionosphere.

Can HAARP interfere with radio communication?

AFRL/ONR: While some interference has been noted in the area near Gakona, the program is committed to achieving compatibility with all other users of the electromagnetic spectrum.

Conspiracy Theorists: HAARP can be used to wipe out communications over a very large area. Specific beams can be established to form a network of communication to serve shadow-government or New World Order agencies even though the rest of the world's communications are disrupted or shut down.

Are there any health hazards posed to humans by HAARP?

AFRL/ONR: None. The electromagnetic fields measured at the closest public access to the site are lower than those existing in many urban environments.

Conspiracy Theorists: A system could easily be developed for manipulating and disturbing human mental processes through pulsed radio frequency radiation. The potential applications of artificial electromagnetic fields are enormous. HAARP is the most versatile and largest radio-frequency-radiation transmitter in the world. Electromagnetic systems can provide coverage over large areas. They are silent and can produce mild to severe physiological disruption or perceptual distortion or disorientation.

Completed in 2007, the High Frequency Active Auroral Research Program (HAARP) near Gakona, Alaska, is supposedly merely a high-tech physics experiment. Conspiracists believe HAARP has a much more nefarious purpose.

Will HAARP be used to generate ELF?

AFRL/ONR: No. Previous experience at other facilities has demonstrated that it is possible to generate a small, useful ELF signal through ionospheric heating, but any ELF produced in the ionosphere at around 100 km altitude would be 11 million times weaker than the earth's normal background field and 1 million times weaker than the level at which researchers have noted biological effects.

Conspiracy Theorists: It is likely that HAARP's high-frequency emissions will be coupled with ELF to replace the submarine communication system in use today. The combination will also be utilized to transmit specific brain frequencies to urban areas to undermine the mental health of the population. New World Order agencies could use HAARP to beam ELF waves for anger, suicide, hysteria, lust, paranoia, or depression in order to make any population easy prey for an invasion.

Will HAARP be used for military purposes?

AFRL/ONR: HAARP is not designed for military purposes. A consortium of universities has declared that HAARP meets the requirements of a world-class research facility. Because the Department of Defense (DoD) operates numerous communication and navigational systems whose signals depend on reflection from the ionosphere and/or must pass through the ionosphere to satellites, there is obvious DoD interest in the program.

Conspiracy Theorists: Nick Begich and Jeane Manning state that HAARP publicly gives the impression that the program is primarily an academic project with the goal of changing the ionosphere to improve communications for everyone's good. But the DoD is seriously investigating the uses of HAARP for weather control, climate disruption, polar ice cap melting, earthquake engineering, and brain wave manipulation.

In the overwhelmingly unanimous view of conspiracy theorists, HAARP is, plain and simple, a weapon of mass murder and destruction that has been used often in recent times. These theorists are convinced that HAARP weather and tectonic attacks caused the Myanmar Cyclone on May 3, 2008, which left as many as 80,000 dead and 60,000 missing; the China Earthquake of May 12, 2008, which had a death toll of 68,000; the Haiti Earthquake of January 12, 2010, which left an estimated 92,000 dead and 1.8 million homeless; and the Fukushima Earthquake and Tsunami on March 11, 2011, which left 16,000 dead, thousands missing, and 770,000 buildings destroyed or partially destroyed.

According to conspiracy theorists, HAARP has three major weapon-system components: space-based, which weaponizes the Earth's ionosphere; air-based, which uses chemtrails as a frequency reflector from its ground and space base; and ground-based, which energizes the stations in Alaska, Greenland, Norway, and Australia.

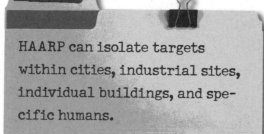

HAARP can isolate targets within cities, industrial sites, individual buildings, and specific humans.

The HAARP arsenal of weapons is prepared for Strategic Defense Initiatives, which utilizes powerful radiofrequency weapons to bring about weather and earthquake warfare. HAARP can isolate targets within cities, industrial sites, individual buildings, and specific humans. Its ELF weapons can launch electromagnetic harassment and mood manipulations on target population groups or individuals within those groups.

HANGAR 18

An alien life form that crashed in the New Mexico desert in 1947 has been kept alive in a highly secured area of Hanger 18 at Wright-Patterson Air Force Base in Dayton, Ohio.

According to UFO researchers, on July 2, 1947, an alien spaceship crashed during a violent thunderstorm in a remote area of the desert northeast of Corona, New Mexico. Personnel from Roswell Army Air Base in Roswell were immediately dispatched to clean up the area. When they arrived, they discovered alien bodies in the wreckage, one of whom was still alive. The surviving alien was treated and taken to Hangar 18 at Wright Field (now Wright-Patterson Air Force Base) in Dayton, Ohio. In some variations of the report, all the aliens were dead, and it is only their refrigerated corpses that are kept in Hangar 18.

In recent years, accounts from both civilian and military eyewitnesses to the 1947 events in the New Mexico desert speak of five alien bodies found at the impact site and state that four corpses were transported to Hangar 18 at Wright Field, the fifth to the air force's mortuary service at Lowry Field in Denver. Two years before his death in the late 1990s, pilot Oliver "Pappy" Henderson swore at a reunion of his World War II bomber crew that he had flown the remains of four alien bodies out of Roswell in a C-54 cargo plane in July 1947.

In their book *UFO Crash at Roswell* (1991), Don Schmitt and Kevin Randle include an interview with Brig. Gen. Arthur Exon in which he states that, in addition to debris from the wreckage, four tiny alien cadavers were flown to Wright Field: "They [the alien bodies] were all found, apparently, outside the craft itself. The metal and material from the spaceship was unknown to anyone I talked to. [The event at] Roswell was the recovery of a craft from space."

In his subsequent research Randle has determined that most eyewitness accounts speak of five alien bodies found at the impact site. His investigations confirm the claims made previously by other researchers that four corpses were transported to Wright Field and the fifth to Lowry Field. Numerous secondary accounts, however, maintain that one of the aliens survived the crash and was still alive when the retrieval unit arrived on the scene. Some UFO researchers believe that as late as 1986 the alien entity was still alive and well treated as a guest of the air force at Wright-Patterson. It became known to many investigators that the extraterrestrial being's favorite flavor of ice cream was strawberry.

HASHSHASHIN

The Hashshashin, a cult of highly trained Muslim assassins, were one of the deadliest of all secret societies.

Regarded as one of the most fearsome of all secret societies, the Hashshashin seemed capable of striking down any victim or penetrating any security. They moved as if they were deadly shadows and struck with a fury that shattered the nerves and the resolve of their most stalwart foes. Because the Hashshashin had been indoctrinated to believe that death in the pursuit of orders guaranteed an immediate transference to Paradise, they fought with a fury untouched by the normal fear of dying in combat.

Most of the early members of the secret society were followers of the Nizari branch of the Isma Iliyya sect of Shiite Muslims and were located primarily in Syria and Persia. In 1090 Hasan ibn Sabbah seized the mountain citadel of Alamaut in northern Persia and made it his "Eagles' Nest," a center where he, as grand master, could live in relative safety and direct his forces throughout Asia. Hasan became known as the "Old Man of the Mountains," and he set about creating a fanatical organization composed of devotees, known as *fedayeen,* who did whatever he commanded with blind obedience.

The very name of the secret society of killers has given us the word *assassin,* one who kills for fanatical or monetary reasons, and its offshoots *assassinate,* the act of killing suddenly and treacherously, and *assassination,* the murder of a prominent person. Their name, Hashshashin, is derived from the Arabic *hashish* (the concentrated, intoxicating resin of the Indian hemp plant) and the accusation made by European Crusaders that the fierce warriors made liberal use of the narcotic effects of hashish to achieve their courage and to eliminate their fear of death.

Hasan ibn Sabbah frequently bought boys from poverty-stricken parents and reared them in camps where he trained them to be skilled murderers, leading them step by step to higher levels of killing proficiency. At the same time that he was shaping them into deadly warriors, he indoctrinated them spiritually, convincing them that as they advanced under his leadership they would come closer to the sacred and ultimate mystery that only he could reveal. Hasan told them that the conventional teachings of Islam had misled them. Paradise could not be attained by following the preachings of Muhammad, but only by complete obedience to Hasan ibn Sabbah, who was the true incarnation of God on Earth.

Hasan supplied his young soldiers with generous amounts of hashish, then hypnotically guided them in a visual meditation to the lavish gardens of heaven, where they were allowed to witness the beauty of the afterlife. When the youths regained full consciousness, they believed unequivocally that they had been allowed a glimpse of their future dwelling place in Paradise.

Although the Hashshashin came to be feared by kings, princes, sheikhs, sultans, and Christian Crusaders, their membership probably never included more than two thousand *fedayeen* at any one time. Masters of disguise and fluent in many languages and dialects, they might one day appear as simple peasants working around a castle wall and the next emerge as deadly warriors springing on their victims from the shadows.

The assassins inveigled themselves into the services of all the surrounding rulers, posing as loyal soldiers or servants, but always awaiting the bidding of their grand master. A powerful sultan who defied the orders of Hasan might suddenly find himself mercilessly attacked by men he had regarded for many years as trusted servants. As the power of Hasan's secret society became known throughout the East, a monarch never knew which of his seemingly faithful retinue was really an assassin only awaiting orders to murder him.

Between 1090 and 1256 there were eight grand masters who ruled the society of assassins. In 1256 and 1258 the Mongols virtually destroyed the sect in Iran and in Syria. Although the Hashshashin scattered throughout the East and into Europe, in 1272 the Mamluk sultan Baybars brought about their downfall as an organized sect.

HAYMARKET BOMBING

The Haymarket bombing remains one of the largest acts of terrorism committed on U.S. soil.

On May 1, 1886, the International Working Peoples Association (IWPA) called a strike throughout the United States in support of an eight-hour workday. On May 3 the IWPA in Chicago held a rally outside the McCormick Harvester Works, where 1,400 workers were on strike. Soon, 6,000 strikers from other manufacturers joined the crowd to hear a speech by August Spies, one of the IWPA's leaders. Chicago police arrived and fired into the crowd, killing four men.

On May 4 Spies published a leaflet in English and German entitled *Revenge! Working-*

men to Arms! in which he called upon the striking workers to show courage and not meekly accept the supreme will of their employers. If they were men, Spies challenged, they would rise up in their might and destroy the hideous monster that sought to destroy them. Later that day Spies distributed another leaflet calling for a mass protest that evening at Haymarket Square.

Over three thousand people came out for the labor protest and enthusiastically cheered speeches by Spies, Albert Parsons, and Samuel Fielden. When Captain John Bonfield and 180 policemen arrived on the scene, Bonfield order the crowd to disperse immediately and peaceably. Before the mass of protesters had an opportunity to comply or resist, someone threw a bomb into the police ranks from one of the alleys that led into Haymarket Square. The blast killed eight men and wounded sixty-seven others.

If the police had been looking for a pretext to make some arrests, the terrible crime that had just been committed more than provided a reason to retaliate against the protesters. In the carnage that followed, two hundred people were injured. The exact number of those killed has never been disclosed.

Numerous witnesses identified Rudolph Schnaubelt as the assailant who had thrown the bomb. In spite of the number of individuals who swore to Schnaubelt's guilt, he was arrested, held for a brief time, then released without any charges being filed against him. After his release, the authorities took seven leaders of the revolutionary and libertarian socialist movement into custody: Samuel Fielden, who was English, and six German immigrants—August Spies, Adolph Fisher, Louis Lingg, George Engel, Oscar Neebe, and Michael Schwab. There was also a warrant for Albert Parsons, Chicago head of the IWPA, but he had gone into hiding. Although dozens of witnesses swore that none of these men had thrown the bomb, the case against them was that they had made incendiary speeches and written inflammatory articles that had led the unnamed bomb-thrower to attack the police at Haymarket Square.

During the trial, Parsons emerged from hiding to stand alongside his comrades. The jury heard testimony from various reporters who had attended IWPA meetings and claimed to have heard the accused urge their followers to use violence to obtain political change. A detective from the Pinkerton agency testified that he had infiltrated the group and heard the leaders of IWPA advocating violence to overthrow the system. State's Attorney Julius Grinnell instructed the jury to convict the eight men and make an example of them.

In spite of the number of individuals who swore to Schnaubelt's guilt, he was arrested, held for a brief time, then released without any charges being filed against him.

Parsons, Spies, Fisher, Lingg, and Engel were given the death penalty and ordered to be hanged. Neebe, Fielden, and Schwab were sentenced to life imprisonment. On November 10, 1887, Lingg committed suicide by exploding a dynamite cap in his mouth. Parsons, Spies, Fisher, and Engel were hanged the following day.

Many people in Chicago believed that the leaders of the IWPA had not received a fair trial. Several investigators who made a serious study of the case claimed that Rudolph Schnaubelt had been hired to throw the bomb by representatives of the businesses under strike restrictions. In 1893 John Peter Altgeld, newly elected governor of Illinois, issued pardons to Oscar Neebe, Samuel Fielden, and Michael Schwab.

HEAVEN'S GATE

Bo and Peep gained worldwide attention in 1975 when it was feared that their Human Individual Metamorphosis cult had abducted twenty Oregonians in a spaceship. Twenty-two years later, they gained even greater notoriety when the UFO cult committed mass suicide.

Bo (Marshall Herff Applewhite) and Peep (Bonnie Lu Trousdale Nettles), the founders of the Heaven's Gate cult, achieved national media attention after a UFO lecture in Waldport, Oregon, on September 14, 1975, when they were said to have taken away twenty members of the audience aboard a flying saucer. Concerned family members of the vanishing Oregonians were not convinced that extraterrestrials had kidnapped their relatives. They feared that their missing kin had been murdered. Law enforcement officials tried to squelch rumors that satanic sacrifice was involved in the mysterious disappearances. However, it would soon be revealed that a good number of the UFO enthusiasts who had attended the lecture had chosen of their own free will to join Bo and Peep on their spiritual pilgrimage.

The theology of Heaven's Gate was born in the cosmic revelations received by Applewhite and Nettles sometime around 1972 when they formed the Christian Arts Center in Houston for the declared purpose of helping to make humans more aware of their spiritual potential by sponsoring lectures in comparative religion, mysticism, meditation, and astrology. Applewhite, the son of a Presbyterian minister, had served with the U.S. Army Signal Corps in Salzburg, Austria, studied sacred music at Union Theological Seminary in Richmond, Virginia, directed musicals for the Houston Music

Theatre, and from 1966 to 1971 taught music at the University of St. Thomas in Houston. Nettles, an astrology enthusiast, was a graduate of the Hermann Hospital School of Nursing in 1948 and worked as a nurse in the Houston area. Although they had each been previously married to others, in 1974 Applewhite and Nettles, while creating their philosophical blend of apocalyptic Christianity and UFOlogy, said that they were not married but were living together "by spiritual guidance." Espousing the highest principles, the couple stated that they had renounced sex in preparation for their journey to the "Father's Kingdom," and they invited others to join them in the process that they called Human Individual Metamorphosis (HIM).

Applewhite and Nettles began to refer to themselves as "Bo" and "Peep" or "the Two," and they proclaimed that they had awakened to their true extraterrestrial origins. As benevolent aliens, they had come to Earth to demonstrate how the human body could undergo a dramatic metamorphosis, just as the chrysalis changes from caterpillar to butterfly.

Bo and Peep claimed to have originated from the same level as Jesus, asserting that they were the two witnesses referred to in the book of Revelation as the harbingers of a great harvest time for humanity:

And I will give power to two witnesses, and they shall prophesy. And when they have finished their testimony, the beast that ascendeth out of the bottomless pit shall overcome them and kill them. And their dead bodies shall lie in the street of the great city three days and a half. And after three days and a half the spirit of life from God entered them and they stood upon their feet. And they heard a great voice from heaven saying to them, Come up hither. And they ascended to heaven in a cloud and the remnant were affrighted and gave glory to the God in heaven. (Rev. 11:3–13)

Many members of HIM inferred from various pronouncements by Bo and Peep that the pair would quite likely be assassinated sometime around June 1976. The couple told a number of their followers that they would lie in state for three and one-half days, then rise to the next level in full view of the media, thereby proving that they were the two witnesses spoken of in Revelation. According to Applewhite and Nettles, Earth was fast approaching "that season" when humans could enter the process that would enable them to graduate to a higher level.

The Two did not promise an easy path to higher awareness. They instructed their followers that they must walk out the door of their human lives and take with them only what would be necessary while they were still on the planet. Newcomers were advised that the process worked best if they had a partner and that they would be paired with one. However, the only bond that was to exist between them would be a mutual desire to raise their vibrational levels so they might ascend to the next realm. Those who heeded the summons of the Two should bring with them a car, a tent, a warm sleeping bag, utensils, and whatever money they could carry. Those who joined the Human Individual Metamorphosis group would be camping out a lot in order to take the word to others who might be seeking it.

In spite of this bleak picture of a nomadic existence, a remarkable number of highly educated professionals left high-salaried jobs, expensive homes, and loving spouses and children to follow the Two on a journey of faith that would have them living hand-to-mouth and sleeping under the stars.

It has long been a tenet of some branches of Christianity that if we attain a higher level beyond death, we will achieve such a state in spirit form, not in the physical body. However, Bo and Peep insisted that spiritual seekers must begin their butterfly-like apprenticeship by leaving the ways of their human caterpillar family and friends behind and would attain the higher level in an actual physical body. The kingdom of heaven and all those who occupy it, according to the Two, are literally physical in form.

When the much-promised demonstration of the couple's death and resurrection seemed always to be postponed for one reason or another, a large number of disillusioned members dropped out of the group, leaving Bo and Peep and their most faithful followers to resume their nomadic lifestyle and take their ministry underground. In 1985 Bonnie, who at that time called herself "Ti," died of cancer and, in the words of an ardent follower, "returned to the next level."

Applewhite, now "Do," carried on their mission of informing humans that salvation hovered overhead in a spaceship. He also warned earthlings that their planet was at the mercy of alien star gods, the "Luciferians," who had fallen away from the Father's Kingdom many thousands of years ago. In 1995, after renaming the cult Heaven's Gate, Applewhite and his most devoted disciples moved to San Diego, California, and established a computer business, Higher Source, which specialized in designing websites.

In 1996 Do and his followers became excited about the approach of the Hale-Bopp comet, believing that it was the sign for which they had been waiting. They decided to hasten their "graduation from the human evolutionary level" through self-administered poison and hitch a ride to the Father's Kingdom on the extraterrestrial spacecraft that they believed followed in the wake of the comet's tail. On March 26, 1997, Applewhite apparently became convinced that he had found at last the narrow window of opportunity for that graduation. His body and those of thirty-eight followers, all having committed suicide by various means, were found throughout the rooms of the group's spacious Rancho Santa Fe mansion outside of San Diego.

HELLFIRE CLUB

People have been spreading juicy rumors about the sensual indulgences and satanic perversities of the Hellfire Club since 1748.

Of all the secret societies in the world, few arouse as many exotic, erotic fantasy images as the Hellfire Club. If one has heard anything at all of the wicked goings-on at the old Medmenham Abbey on West Wycombe Hill, one immediately visualizes wealthy and aristocratic English libertines frolicking about with buxom ladies of ill repute and conducting blasphemous and obscene satanic rites.

The infamous Hellfire Club was founded by Sir Francis Dashwood (1708–1781), but neither he nor any of its members ever called their gatherings by that name. Sir Francis named his merry group of revelers the Friars of St. Francis of Wycombe, the Monks of Medmenham, or the Order of Knights of West Wycombe—none of which has quite the ring of the Hellfire Club, the name bequeathed to the group by outsiders.

Dashwood, son of a wealthy businessman, got his title by marrying into the aristocracy. Quite civically minded, for over twenty years Sir Francis sat in the House of Commons as an MP and held the offices of chancellor of the Exchequer, postmaster general, and treasurer to King George III. While this may seem like the résumé of a rigid and conservative gentleman, as a privileged young man Dashwood had gone on the Grand Tour of Europe, the rite of passage for sons of the idle rich. In Italy he came to admire the classical architecture and mythology of the country, but at the same time, he managed to develop a strong distaste for Roman Catholicism. Although, as one who would soon become one of the landed gentry, he seemed an unlikely prospect for recruitment into the Jacobite revolutionary movement, he did become a member, then in short order joined the Rosicrucians.

While staying in Florence, Dashwood met Prince Charles, pretender to the Scottish throne, who had far-reaching associations with Masonic and neo-Templar secret societies. Quite probably under Prince Charles's sponsorship, Dashwood was initiated into a Masonic lodge.

In London, about 1738, Dashwood founded the Society of the Dilettanti, essentially a private club for the hard-drinking and womanizing of the aristocracy. In 1746 he established the Order of the Knights of St. Francis, whose members initially met at the George and Vulture public house in Cornhill, in a room dominated by a large crystal globe encircled by an Ouroboros, a gold serpent with its tail in its mouth.

In 1751 Dashwood leased as the headquarters for his order Medmenham Abbey, originally a twelfth-century Cistercian monastery, on the Thames near Marlow, about six miles from his ancestral home at West Wycombe. He had stained-glass windows bearing the motto "Do as thou will" placed above the front door. His lifelong fascination with pagan gods and goddesses was architecturally expressed by designing the west wing of the mansion as a replica of a classical temple to Bacchus. To celebrate the temple's completion, Dashwood composed a pageant and employed actors to play fauns, satyrs, nymphs, and various gods and goddesses. As the Hellfire Friars dined, they were watched over by statues of the Freemasons' guardians of secrecy, Harpocrates, the Egyptian god of silence, with his finger to his lips, and Angerona, the Roman goddess of silence, indicating to the Friars that nothing that was said or went on in the Abbey was to be mentioned outside its walls.

Dashwood was delighted to discover a prehistoric network of caves under West Wycombe Hill, and he had them enlarged to serve as additional dens of iniquity. In ancient times a pagan altar had existed on the hill, and catacombs under the ground contained the pagan dead. Along with his instructions to ex-

Sir Francis Dashwood, founder of the Hellfire Club.

cavate and enlarge the old caves, Dashwood ordered the construction of individual "cells" in the passageways for the Friars to dally with their female guests. An underground stream, dubbed "the River Styx," had to be crossed to enter the Inner Sanctum, where Black Masses were held. As a young man in France, Dashwood had attended a Black Mass, indulging his curiosity about the subject. There is no real evidence that Dashwood ever actually practiced Satanism, but he loved conducting pseudosatanic rites to mock the Catholic Church.

Local gossip, which became legends passed down for generations, had the Hellfire Friars ferrying prostitutes down the Thames from London in barges to perform in the Black Mass as nuns. The Black Masses, according to the old stories, were conducted over the naked bodies of aristocratic ladies, as well as prostitutes.

A number of scholars who have researched the Hellfire Club have concluded that the accounts of satanic Black Masses have been exaggerated over the years. Although the club may have included mock satanic rites as a prelude to sexual indulgences, most of the Friars of the Order of St. Francis were hardy and happy disciples of Bacchus and Venus who gathered to celebrate the excesses of both sex and drink. At heart, Sir Francis Dashwood was a disciple of the ancient pagan mystery schools.

It has been said that the members of the Hellfire Club included some of the wealthiest and most influential people in England. Long-suspected members include the Earl of Sandwich; John Wilkes, MP of Aylesbury; the satirical artist William Hogarth; John Stuart, Earl of Bute, who in his later years was briefly the prime minister of England; the Marquis of Granby; the Prince of Wales; and very possibly Benjamin Franklin and Horace Walpole.

HOLLOW EARTH

The UFOs are piloted by an ancient underground race who remain undecided whether to enslave or to assist the surface dwellers.

According to Ray Palmer, who was fiction editor of the Ziff-Davis stable of magazines from February 1938 to September 1949, he received a letter in September 1944 from Richard S. Shaver, who claimed to have discovered an ancient language that "should not be lost to the world." More or less on a whim, Palmer decided to print the letter, complete with sample of the alleged language, in the next issue of *Amazing Stories.*

The publication of the letter brought an avalanche of mail to Palmer's desk from readers who wanted to know more about Shaver and his mysterious language. Smelling a good story in the making, Palmer contacted Shaver and received a ten-thousand-word manuscript in reply. Impressed with the sincerity of the crude manuscript, which Shaver

had ominously entitled "A Warning to Future Man," Palmer renamed the piece "I Remember Lemuria," added a few trimmings and polish, and published it in the March 1945 issue of *Amazing Stories.*

In the next few weeks the magazine received fifty thousand letters from readers who had been intrigued, enthralled, or frightened by Shaver's "true" story. For a magazine whose usual mail response was somewhere around forty-five letters a month, such a deluge of mail showing overwhelming reader interest in the "Shaver Mystery" was beyond phenomenal. Palmer had no difficulty convincing the circulation director that they should increase their usual print run by fifty thousand for a follow-up Shaver piece. *Amazing Stories* maintained that print figure for the next four years while Palmer ran the series to its conclusion, thereby setting off what *Life* magazine (May 21, 1951) would declare "the most celebrated rumpus that ever rocked the science-fiction world."

Shaver's stories claimed to be true accounts of human interaction with a race of malformed subhuman creatures called "dero," who inhabit a vast system of underground cities all over the world. The ancestors of the dero were a race of people called the Abandondero, who were "abandoned" when the "Titans" or "Atlans" from Lemuria fled Earth in spaceships, fearing that extensive exposure to the sun's rays were limiting their life span. Because the Abandondero denied themselves completely of the sun's positive, as well as potentially harmful, radiation, vast numbers of the cave dwellers began to degenerate into physically stunted near-idiots, no longer capable of constructive reasoning. According to Shaver, these were the "dero," the detrimental or degenerate robots. (*Robot,* as Shaver uses the word, doesn't mean a mechanical representation of a human, but a designation for those who are governed by degenerative, negative forces.)

Standing between the viciousness of the degenerate dero and the surface civilization are the "tero" ("T" was the Atlans' symbol of deity in their religion; therefore the "t" in tero represents good). The tero have perfected methods of staving off most of the degenerative effects of their subterranean way of life by the use of certain machines, chemicals, and beneficial rays. Shaver's "warning" to future humankind is that the dero are becoming more numerous and have scattered the benign tero with constant attacks. The greatest threat to the surface dwellers lies in the grim reality that the dero have access to all the machines of the Atlan technology, but they lack the intelligence or the highly developed moral sense of the ancients to use these machines responsibly.

The dero have possession of "vision ray machines" that can penetrate solid rock and pick up scenes all over the planet's surface. They have access to the Atlans' teleportation units and can accomplish instant transport. Long ago they gained control of the technology that can induce "solid" illusions, dreams, and compulsions in top-siders. In addition to aerial craft (UFOs), the dero possess death rays that can wreak terrible havoc.

The dero are notorious for their sexual orgies, and they apply "stim" machines that revitalize sexual virility and "ben" rays that heal and restore the physical body. These mechanisms were created by the ancient Atlans thousands of years ago and are still in perfect working order, thanks to the technical perfection with which they were constructed.

According to Shaver, present-day surface-dwelling humans are the descendants of the Abandondero who were unable to retreat underground at the time of the great exodus of the Titans from Earth. Through the centuries, the human species has developed a greater tolerance for the sun and escaped the kind of mental and physical deterioration that perverts the dero and weakens the tero. Although humans have a common heritage with the tero and the dero, the passage of time has prevented the great mass of surface dwellers from possessing more than dim memories of the glory days of Atlantis, Lemuria, Mu, and the epochs when there were "giants in the earth." However, Shaver cautions us, by no means have the dero forgotten us. These sadistic monsters take enormous delight in creating terrible accidents, confusing the goals of our political leaders, provoking surface wars between nations, and even in causing nightmares by focusing "dream mech" on us while we sleep.

Palmer admitted that he had enlarged Shaver's original 10,000-word manuscript to a 31,000-word story for *Amazing Stories.* However, he insisted that although he had added the trimmings, he did not alter the factual basis of Shaver's manuscript—except in one instance: "I could not bring myself to believe that Shaver had actually gotten his alphabet and his 'warning to future man,' and all the 'science' he propounded from actual underground people," Palmer said. "Perhaps I made a grave mistake, but I altered what he stated were his 'thought-records' into 'racial memory.' I felt certain that the concept of racial memory would be far more believable to the readers, and offer a reasonable and perhaps actual explanation of what was really going on in Shaver's mind—which is where I felt it really was going on, and not in any caves or via any 'telaug rays' or 'telesolidograph' projections of illusions from the cavern ray operators."

Only a small coterie of science-fiction buffs followed the Shaver mystery, but millions of individuals were sighting the mysterious objects in the sky. Almost from the initial report of UFOs in the modern era, certain researchers have identified them as originating from the Hollow Earth and suggested that the inhabitants of the inner earth might well be the descendants of the survivors of Atlantis. Among the theories most often cited are the following:

1. UFOs are piloted by an ancient humanoid race that antedates *Homo sapi-*

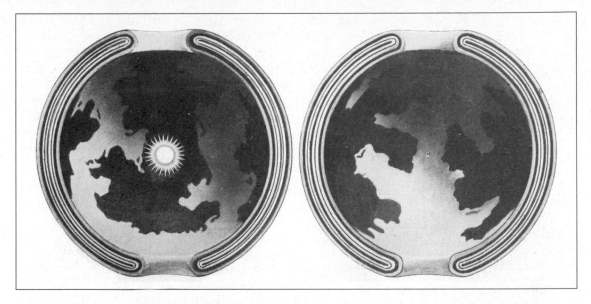

A 1912 illustration by Marshall Gardner shows the purported interior sun and oceans of the Hollow Earth.

ens by at least a million years. Their withdrawal from the surface world survives in the collective human unconscious as the legend of Atlantis.

2. Atlantis was an actual prehistoric world that created a superscience and destroyed itself in civil war. The surviving Atlanteans sought refuge from radioactivity by retreating under the earth's crust. They have continued to monitor the new race of surface dwellers and accelerated their observation after the detonation of the first atomic bombs.

3. Extraterrestrial beings established a colony on Earth about fifty thousand years ago when *Homo sapiens* was establishing itself as the dominant species. They gave primitive humankind a boost up the evolutionary ladder, then grew aghast at humanity's perpetual barbarism and left the surface world to establish underground and undersea bases from which to observe how their cosmic cousins would develop without direct interference and assistance.

Ray Palmer, who went on from the Shaver episode to become editor-publisher of the magazines *Flying Saucers* and *Search,* said that after decades of research he was personally convinced that the answer to the UFO mystery was to be found on our own planet, rather than in outer space. "The more one thinks of the extraterrestrial thesis, the more impossible it is to prove," he said. "UFOs have been seen in the skies since man's prehistory, and today there seems to be a virtual traffic jam of objects coming in from somewhere. The supposition that the saucers have an Earth base and may be manned by an older terrestrial race brings the cosmic concept down to reality. Geographically speaking, our own atmosphere is a heck of lot closer than Alpha Centauri!"

Suppositions about the Hollow Earth did not begin with science-fiction writers and UFO theorists in the 1950s. The great British astronomer Edmund Halley (1656–1742) is best known for having calculated the orbit of a comet that returns to the solar system every seventy-six years. During the next decade, Halley turned his attention away from the celestial in favor of the subterranean. He claimed the Earth was hollow and populated by humans and beasts.

Halley's Hollow Earth hypothesis was based on the fact that the earth's magnetic field varies over time. Halley suggested that there were several magnetic fields, one of which emanated from a sphere within the earth. Halley eventually developed the idea that there were four concentric hollow spheres inside the earth. He believed the inner earth was populated with life and had a luminous atmosphere. The aurora borealis, he concluded, is actually an emanation of radiant gases that escape from within the earth through thin layers of crust at the poles.

Perhaps the most enthusiastic proponent of the Hollow Earth idea was John Cleves Symmes, who was born in 1780 in New Jersey. Symmes immersed himself in books on the natural sciences and by 1818 was publicizing his version of the Hollow Earth, which had concentric spheres and received light and warmth from the sun through large holes in the planet's surface at each of the poles.

Symmes was able to impress two influential men who would take his cause further. James McBride, a wealthy Ohioan, wrote articles supporting the concentric-spheres version of the Hollow Earth. He lobbied a U.S. senator from Kentucky, Richard M. Johnson—later vice president of the United States under Martin Van Buren—to support a bill funding a proposed expedition to explore trade routes in the Southern Hemisphere (where McBride hoped the expedition would continue on to the open pole). In 1828 President John Quincy Adams indicated that he would approve funding for the expedition. However, when Adams left office in 1829, his successor, Andrew Jackson, stifled a bill funding the proposed expedition.

Symmes died in 1829, but his cause was continued by Jeremiah Reynolds, an Ohio newspaper editor. After the failure to get government funding for the expedition in 1829,

Reynolds joined a crew sailing to the South Seas to hunt seals, but seven years later, in 1836, he helped renew efforts for funding of a Southern Hemisphere expedition. Reynolds spoke before Congress, emphasizing the national glory that would accompany scientific discoveries and expanded foreign relations, but he became so impatient with the methodical planning and a series of delays that he was fired from the crew.

What became known as the Wilkes expedition, named after its commander, Charles Wilkes, set sail in 1838. When the expedition was completed in 1842, Wilkes and his men had effectively mapped a land mass where Symmes had envisioned a large hole in the earth. The world's seventh continent, Antarctica, was officially recognized for the first time.

Edgar Allan Poe's longest work of fiction, "The Narrative of Arthur Gordon Pym" (1835), told of a land located in the center of our planet, entered by a hole at the South Pole. So convincingly did Poe weave his narrative that the great editor Horace Greeley soberly endorsed the Pym adventure as a true account.

In 1864 the novelist Jules Verne published *Journey to the Center of the Earth,* in which characters enter the earth's interior through the chimney of an inactive volcano in Iceland. In 1873 *The Coming Race,* a novel by the occultist Edward Bulwer-Lytton, was set in the earth's interior, where an advanced civilization of giants thrived.

In 1913, even after the North Pole had been reached, Marshall Gardner published *A Journey to the Earth's Interior; or, Have the Poles Really Been Discovered?* which claimed that many creatures thought to be extinct were still thriving within the earth. Gardner theorized that the interior was warmed by materials still spinning since the planet's creation. That same year, William Reed published *The Phantom of the Poles,* in which he promoted the idea that a ship can travel from the outer earth to the inner earth. He claimed that some sailors had already passed into the inner earth without knowing it. Gravity had pulled them to the interior side, where an inner sun six hundred miles in diameter continued to keep them warm, as the outer sun had done.

One of the more interesting variations on the Hollow Earth theory during the late nineteenth century was expounded by Cyrus Read Teed, who claimed that a civilization inhabited the planet's concave inner surface. Teed made a religion of his theories and changed his name to Koresh, the Hebrew equivalent of his given name, Cyrus. As the messiah of Koreshanity, he formed a church, started a magazine (the *Flaming Cross,* which continued to be published regularly into the 1940s), and founded a community on a three-hundred-acre tract in Florida in 1894. He lived there with about 250 followers until 1908. Upon his death, his followers waited for him to rise again, as he had prophesied. After four days, health officials appeared on the scene and ordered his burial.

Hollow Earth enthusiasts continue to believe. Teed's concave-earth theory, for example, was tested during World War II by a Nazi scientist. He aimed a camera at a 45-degree angle into the sky from an island in the Baltic Sea, hoping to catch an image of a British fleet on the other side of the concave earth. The experiment was unsuccessful.

Although this expedition set out at a time when the Third Reich was applying maximum effort in the drive against the Allies and could hardly spare any military resources, Hitler had enthusiastically endorsed the project. As a member of numerous occult societies, such as the Thule and the Vril, the führer believed that ancient masters had retreated to the inner earth and created a new Atlantis in subterranean caves. An important element in these occult societies was the belief that from time to time these supermen emerged from the underground kingdom to walk among humankind. Hitler's frenzied desire to breed a master race in Germany was inspired by his obsessive hope

that the people of the Third Reich would be chosen above all others to interact with the subterranean supermen in the mutation of a new species of heroes, demigods, and godmen.

In their *Morning of the Magicians,* authors Louis Pauwels and Jacques Bergier quote one of the führer's confidants, Hermann Rauschning, governor of Danzig during the Third Reich, who repeated a conversation he once had with Hitler concerning the latter's desperate plan to be worthy of uniting with the new human mutations that the masters were creating in their underground kingdom: "The new man is living amongst us now!" Hitler said, speaking in what Rauschning recalled as a kind of ecstasy. "He is here! Isn't that enough for you? I will tell you a secret. I have seen the new man. He is intrepid and cruel. I was afraid of him."

Rauschning went on to state that he was told by a person very close to Hitler that the führer often awoke in the night screaming and in convulsions. Always the frightened dictator would shout that *he* had come for him, that *he* stood there in the corner of the room, that *he* had emerged from his underworld kingdom to invade the führer's bedroom.

HOLOCAUST REVISIONISTS

Today's Germans take responsibility, both moral and material, for the Holocaust. But some historical revisionists are questioning the horror of the death camps.

On January 24, 2005, the UN General Assembly convened a special session to commemorate the sixtieth anniversary of the liberation of the Nazi death camps. Speakers memorialized the six million Jews who died in the camps in what has become known as the "Holocaust." The session began a week of tributes worldwide to mark the liberation of the camps. On January 27 a special memorial service was conducted in Auschwitz, Poland, the scene of a death camp where between 1 and 1.5 million prisoners—most of them Jews—died in gas chambers, from disease, or by starvation.

Speakers at the UN General Assembly in New York included Elie Wiesel, winner of the Nobel Peace Prize in 1986; Israeli foreign minister Silvan Shalom; and Russia's commissioner for human rights, Vladimir Lukin, all of whom warned against a global rise in anti-Semitism and the growing strength of movements that denied the Holocaust.

Sir Brian Urquhart, a retired UN undersecretary general who had been among the soldiers who freed the prisoners held in the death camps in 1945, stated that the world must never forget the Holocaust and the terrible campaign of genocide. The special commemoration at the United Nations served, Urquhart said, "to recall what human beings driven by hatred or fear or some perverse ideology are, against all rational belief, still capable of doing to each other."

The same week in January 2005 that the United Nations honored the millions of lives lost in the Nazi program of the extermination of Jews, the Holocaust historical revisionists were busy issuing the "facts" behind Auschwitz and the other death camps. Mark Weber, director of the Institute for Historical Review, one of the leading voices in denying the Holocaust, is among those scholars who do not dispute the fact that large numbers of Jews were deported to such camps as Auschwitz and later died there, but he maintains that Auschwitz was not an extermination facility and that stories of mass killings in gas chambers are myths.

Among the assertions made by Weber and other revisionists are the following:

- At the postwar Nuremberg Tribunal, the figure of four million people exterminated at Auschwitz was invented by the Soviets. Gerald Reitlinger, prominent Holocaust historian, estimated that approximately 700,000 Jews perished at Auschwitz. Holocaust historian Jean-Claude Pressac sets the figure at about 800,000, of whom 630,000 were Jews. Israel's Yad Vashem Holocaust Center, together with the Auschwitz State Museum in Poland, estimate a total of one million victims, both Jews and non-Jews.

- The admittedly high number of documented deaths simply reflects the fact that Auschwitz-Birkenau was primarily a camp for Jews who were too sick or elderly to work. More Jews died at Auschwitz as a result of typhus and other diseases than were ever executed.

- Of the thousands of secret Nazi documents dealing with Auschwitz confiscated by the Allies, not one mentions any kind of program for extermination of the Jews.

- The stories of gas chambers at Auschwitz are based only on rumors and Allied propaganda. The alleged dreaded "showers" that were really gas chambers were, in fact, just showers.

- Official German camp regulations ordered that new arrivals receive thorough medical examinations. Once in the camp, when prisoners reported illness, they were examined by the camp physician and, if deemed necessary, taken immediately to a hospital for professional treatment. Among the camp physician's other duties was the regular inspection of the kitchen and the quality of food. Extreme care was observed in work details to avoid accidents.

- There exist no Allied reconnaissance photographs of Auschwitz in 1944, the height of the alleged extermination of the Jews, that depict piles of corpses, smoking

The "cookhouse" at the Auschwitz-Birkenau concentration camp, where thousands of Jews were tortured, starved, and slaughtered by the Nazis.

crematoriums, or huddled masses of prisoners awaiting execution.

- Ivan Lagace, manager of a large crematory in Canada, testified that the allegation that 10,000 to 20,000 corpses were burned each day at Auschwitz in the summer of 1944 was beyond the realm of possibility. In 1988 the foremost specialist on gas chambers in the United States, Fred A. Leuchter, carried out a thorough onsite examination of the gas chambers at Auschwitz-Birkenau, and Majdanek in Poland and concluded that the so-called gas chambers were not sealed well enough to kill any prisoners without also gassing the guards.

Edgar J. Steele is another Holocaust revisionist who thinks it is complete "rubbish" to claim that six million Jews were gassed and cremated. His explanation is that a Germany that was fighting a war on two fronts, "desperate for fuel and materiel of every sort," would not have expended energy or bothered to "load millions of Jews on railroad cars and transport them hundreds, even thousands of miles to concentration camps built specifically to house them, where they would be fed, clothed, even tattooed so they could be inventoried, just to kill them."

What about all the gruesome and unsettling pictorial evidence of the Nazi's "final solution" to the Jewish problem?

The response of Steele and other Holocaust deniers or revisionists is that the pictures are mostly faked. "All those pictures of skinny people and bodies stacked like cordwood were actually of Czechs and Poles and

Germans [who] died of Typhus, which was rampant in the camps," Steele states. The prominent revisionist Theodore J. O'Keefe cites the findings of Dr. Charles Larson, one of America's leading forensic pathologists, whom the U.S. Army's Judge Advocate General's Corps assigned the grim task of performing autopsies at Dachau and twenty other concentration camps. In a 1980 newspaper interview Larson said that he could not confirm a case of poison gas in the more than one hundred corpses he examined. According to his analysis, the chief cause of death at Dachau, Belsen, and other camps was disease, specifically typhus.

In an article on the liberation of the death camps in the *Journal of Historical Review,* a revisionist publication, O'Keefe writes that Dr. Konrad Morgen, a legal investigator attached to the Reich Criminal Police, was given full authority by Heinrich Himmler, commander of Hitler's SS and the Gestapo, to enter any concentration camp and investigate any charges of cruelty and corruption on the part of any camp personnel. According to O'Keefe, before any prisoners could receive corporal punishment, they must first be examined by the camp physician and certified to be in good health. The camp physician was also required to be present for the actual beating. O'Keefe states that because prisoners at the camps were used to advance Germany's industrial production, the "good health and morale of the prisoners was critical."

In Germany today there is very little official denial of the Holocaust, and accounts of Nazi war crimes are taught freely in German schools. On May 10, 2005, the Memorial to the Murdered Jews of Europe officially opened in Berlin. Consisting of 2,711 dark gray concrete steles in a cemetery-like field, the memorial is located in the heart of the city, near the Brandenburg Gate. "The memorial's size and central location are widely seen here as testimony to the centrality and uniqueness of the Holocaust among the many crimes of the Nazis, as well as to the willingness of Ger-

many to accept responsibility, both moral and material, for the Nazi's crimes," Richard Bernstein wrote in the *New York Times.*

HOLY GRAIL

As the goal of innumerable quests by virtuous knights, the Holy Grail, the chalice or serving dish used by Jesus during the Last Supper, has been hidden away for centuries by a secret society that wants to keep the grail's magical and transformative powers for themselves.

The Holy Grail is most often identified as the serving dish or the chalice that was used by Jesus during the Last Supper. The word *grail* may have originated from *garalis,* which derives from the medieval Latin *cratalis,* a mixing bowl. *Garalis* became *greal* in medieval French, *grail* in English. Another possible origin for the word is based on the writings of a Christian monk named Helinandus, who wrote of a hermit who, around the year 717, had a vision of a dish used by Jesus at the Last Supper. The hermit called it a "gradale," which in French meant a wide and deep dish on which various meats are placed. French tales described the serving dish as *greal* ("pleasant"), which became *grail* in English.

According to one tradition, Joseph of Arimathea, the man who claimed Jesus's body from the cross and provided the sepulcher in which he was placed, came into possession of the Holy Grail. Imprisoned for several years for expressing his faith that Jesus was the Messiah, Joseph, upon his release, traveled to Britain and took the grail with him. When he died, the sacred relic passed on to his descendants, who learned that it had magical qualities for the righteous. A few generations later, because of some transgression and a general lack of humility and virtue by keepers of the grail, the powers of the vessel were diminished and its exact location became uncertain.

An alternate version of Joseph's involvement with the Holy Grail has him leaving Jerusalem soon after the crucifixion and resurrection of Christ and taking with him the grail, as well as Mary Magdalene and her children—who, in this story, had been fathered by Jesus. Other accounts state that Mary, as the wife of Jesus and the mother of his children, was *herself* the grail, the "vessel" by which the Davidic bloodline was brought out of Israel. Combine these two accounts and shade them slightly to have Mary traveling to Scotland and secreting the Holy Grail on the site where Rosslyn Chapel would be built, just outside what is now Edinburgh.

The most popular Holy Grail stories have been about virtuous Christian knights questing for the lost chalice of Christ. The association with knights and the grail no doubt began with the legend that the Knights Templar discovered the holy vessel (complete with drops of Jesus's blood) in the rubble of Solomon's temple in Jerusalem sometime around 1118. Some accounts add that, in addition to this most remarkable holy relic, the knights found ancient documents proving that Jesus married Mary Magdalene. The Holy Grail and the proof of the marital union between Jesus and Mary were kept in Templar custody in Paris until the arrest of Jacques de Molay, the grand master of the Temple, by King Philip of France in 1307. Fugitive Templars spirited the holy treasures to safe haven in Scotland sometime around 1312, and the Grail eventually was hidden in Rosslyn Chapel.

The familiar tales about King Arthur and his knights and their quests for the Holy Grail began to be popular in France, Germany, and England in the second half of the twelfth century. The accounts usually begin with a knight's receiving a revelation about the sacredness and power of the lost grail, then embarking on a quest for the esteemed relic. Characters in grail stories are often archetypes, representing certain human traits as deployed by the author to present Christian

Sir Galahad, Parzival, and Bors from King Arthur's court worship the Holy Grail in this fourteenth-century artwork.

teachings. The knight's success or failure in quest of the grail serves as a reflection on what is considered good and bad behavior.

Between 1160 and 1180 the French poet Chrétien de Troyes wrote five major works about Arthur and his knights based on history and legend. Around 1200 the German poet Wolfram von Eschenbach wrote a grail legend, *Parzival,* about a youth who sets out to become a knight in Arthur's court. Along the way the title character stops at the castle of the Fisher King, where Parzival witnesses a procession bearing a glowing object (the grail) and a spear (the one that wounded Christ). In the presence of the grail, the Fisher King is struck dumb. Because Parzival has a pure soul, he could have spoken in the presence of the grail and used its magical powers to heal the infirm Fisher King. Only much later, after many wanderings, does Parzival learn about the true nature of the grail. He returns to the castle of the Fisher King, who is revealed to be his uncle, heals him, and restores the king's land, which had become barren when he became infirm.

In *Le Morte d'Arthur,* a collection of Arthurian tales by the fifteenth-century English writer Sir Thomas Malory, the grail becomes the object of a quest among the knights of the Round Table at King Arthur's castle, Camelot. The quest is eventually accomplished by Sir Galahad, who, as an emblem of Christian virtue, alone achieves the grail.

Arthurian legends and the grail may be based to some extent on Celtic lore. The Holy Grail might well have been developed from references to magic cauldrons that appear in many Celtic myths and practices. In her book *From Ritual to Romance* (1920), Jessie Weston traces some similarities between Celtic myths and grail legends. Some Celtic fertility rituals, for example, were designed to ensure the health and vigor of a community leader: the physical welfare of the land was connected with that of the king. The silence and sterility of the Fisher King in *Parzeval* would indicate some transgression or physical failure on his part that affected his land. Celtic legends have references to the Fisher King as the leader of a barren land, referred to as the Waste Land and "the land laid waste."

Dan Brown's bestseller *The Da Vinci Code* renewed interest in the old traditions of the Templars, the Holy Grail, and Rosslyn Chapel. An American academic, David Conley, who claims to be a descendant of Hugues de Payens, the founder of the Knights Templar, has suggested that high-tech electronic equipment be used for an examination of Rosslyn Chapel to find out if the holy relics are really there. On May 7, 2005, Conley told Liam Rudden of the *Edinburgh Evening News* that he believes the Templars were entrusted with the Holy Grail, the Ark of the Covenant, and a number of ancient scrolls and that the sacred objects are hidden in an underground tunnel system beneath the chapel that mirrors the design of Solomon's temple in Jerusalem.

HOLY VEHM

The Holy Vehm, a secret society dedicated to the murder of Christian heretics, surfaced as an ally of the Nazis in Germany in the 1930s.

In the 1930s, with the rise of the Nazis to power in Germany, the secret society known as the Chivalrous Order of the Holy Vehm came into the open for the first time in its seven-hundred-year history, focusing its bigotry and violence upon the Jewish people, judging them to be guilty of heresy. The Holy Vehm (or Fehm) had been formed in the middle of the thirteenth century as a secret vigilante society composed of free men and commoners to protect themselves from marauding outlaw bands and mercenaries roaming the lawless territory between the Rhine and the Weser Rivers in Westphalia, Germany. In the beginning the resistance group had the approval of both the church and the Holy Roman Emperor, but as time passed the Holy Vehm became a law unto itself, passing judgment on all those whom it decided should receive a death sentence. The name "Vehm" or "Fehm" was a corruption of the Latin word *fama,* a law founded upon a common or agreed-upon opinion. However, "Fehm" could also mean something that was set apart, and the leaders of the Holy Vehm soon decided that their crusade against evildoers had set them apart and above the laws that governed others.

Because the society began with only a handful of members and violent retribution could be expected from any gang of outlaws who might learn the identities of those commoners who dared to oppose them, an oath of secrecy was imposed upon all who had the courage to join the Vehm. During the initiation ceremonies, candidates vowed to kill themselves, and even their spouses and children, rather than permit any society secrets to be betrayed. Once the oath had been made, one of the Vehm's *Stuhlherren,* or judges, who held the highest rank within the society, would move his sword across the initiates' throats, drawing a few drops of blood to serve as a silent reminder of the fate that awaited all traitors to the society. Below the judges in rank were the deputy judges, the *Freischoffen,* and the executioners, the *Frohnboten.*

Within a few decades of its formation the Vehm had over 200,000 free men and commoners in its ranks—each sworn to uphold the Ten Commandments and to eliminate all heresies, heretics, perjurers, traitors, and servants of Satan. The harsh and punitive secret courts (*Heimliches Gericht*) always met at midnight in order to create an even more sinister and frightening effect. Those suspected of witchcraft or heresy were tried by the "forbidden court" (*Verbotene Acht*) and the "secret tribunal" (*Heimliches Acht*), both of which were conducted by the Black Vehm, a splinter group of the Holy Vehm. Because of the great power that the Vehm acquired, it conducted trials of noted outlaws and thieves in village squares or market places in the full light of day.

When the outlaws and thieves had been largely driven from Westphalia, the Vehm turned its full attention to those men and women suspected of heresies or of betraying the commandments of God. Before suspects came to court, they were served with three summonses, each of which gave them the opportunity of attending voluntarily. Each summons also gave the accused a period of consent of six weeks and three days. Because the tribunals of the Vehm had gained a reputation of pronouncing only death sentences, few people attended the courts of their own volition. Those who tried to escape were condemned without the usual pretense of a trial, and Vehm executioners were assigned to hunt them down.

In the fifteenth century, the Holy Vehm was a court that persecuted Christian heretics. It continued to exist secretly for centuries, and some say it aided the Nazis in the 1930s.

Regardless of the charges levied against those heretics the Vehm accused, the sentence was always death by hanging. If any spoke on behalf of their accused friends, they were likely to be hanged as well, for giving false witness to defend a heretic or a traitor. On those rare occasions when the tribunal failed to convince even its own members of an accused individual's guilt, that unfortunate person was hanged anyway to preserve the secrecy of the tribunal. There appears to be no record of any of the secret courts' ever finding anyone innocent. But then the Vehm never kept any records. In spite of the lack of documentation, historians have estimated that thousands of men and women—the innocent along with the guilty—were dragged to one of the Vehm's secret courts.

Although eventually condemned by the church and German state, the secret society remained active in a diminished capacity. Toward the end of the nineteenth century, it went underground and seemingly ceased all acts of violence until the advent of the Nazi Party in the 1930s. The Holy Vehm appears to have been destroyed with its Nazi allies in the fall of the Third Reich in 1945.

HOWARD HUGHES

The eccentric billionaire aviator, manufacturer, and Hollywood playboy had a fantasy life in which he saw himself as a secret agent.

If a novelist invented a character like Howard Hughes, readers would think that the author had pushed the envelope of believability and crossed into pure fantasy. Harold Robbins's biggest bestseller, *The Carpetbaggers* (1961), and the subsequent motion picture of the same name were loosely based on Hughes's life. *The Aviator,* an Academy Award nominee for best picture in 2004, was the director Martin Scorsese's and the actor Leonardo di Caprio's take on Howard Hughes. Hughes was a cowboy, an aviator, a manufacturer, a Hollywood playboy who made love to some of the most beautiful movie stars of the era, a Hollywood producer who made motion pictures with the most beautiful actresses of the era, a patriotic military contractor, and a maverick financier. What more could he ask of life, one might ask.

Howard Hughes had a secret wish that he had to fulfill vicariously through others. The billionaire had a fantasy life in which he sometimes envisioned himself as an espionage agent, a spy, a member of the CIA.

To fulfill one aspect of his secret life, Hughes became a very substantial backer of the CIA—so substantial that he was known to the insiders as the "Stockholder." The ultraconservative Hughes also liked to dabble in politics, and during the 1960 presidential campaign he decided that Richard Nixon was his candidate. Hughes especially liked the way

that Nixon had gone after the Communists. Hughes liked Nixon so much that he loaned Nixon's brother Donald $205,000 to help get his Nixonburger restaurants in the black. John F. Kennedy's crew learned of the loan and made presidential hay out of the secret money exchange.

Hughes offered President Lyndon B. Johnson and President Nixon each a million dollars to call a halt to nuclear testing in Nevada. By the mid-1960s Hughes had already become something of the hermit that he would later become in full force, and he believed that fallout from the tests would drift in the windows of his Las Vegas penthouse and affect his personal health.

It may never be decided for certain, but a number of senators and other investigators for the Senate Watergate Committee believe that Hughes played a major, if shadowy, role in the notorious scandal. The matter was not pushed as far as it might have been, for a number of senators would have been embarrassed if the public learned how much money Hughes had given to their campaigns.

It was in the late 1950s that the billionaire hired his very own spook, Robert Maheu, who had been with the FBI and had owned a private security firm that worked for the CIA on ultrasensitive, slightly illegal, secret projects. Maheu had proven himself versatile to the point of having served as everything from the Agency's pimp for foreign dignitaries to mastermind of a failed attempt to assassinate Fidel Castro. Maheu was also tight with the mob bosses John Roselli, Sam Giancana, and Santos Trafficante, associations that helped smooth Hughes's settling into Las Vegas. Hughes, the adventurer, the daring aviator, the financier, lived vicariously the life of a CIA operative through the exploits that Maheu recounted for his enjoyment. Maheu also intimidated blackmailers who tried to squeeze his boss with gossipy tidbits about his many love affairs and, at the same time, kept tabs on

A young Howard Hughes speaking at a 1938 gathering of the Press Club in Washington, D.C. The billionaire playboy fancied himself a secret agent.

dozens of Hollywood starlets toward whom Hughes felt jealous and possessive—whether he knew them or not.

By 1970 Hughes was becoming increasingly reclusive and his germ phobia had taken control of his very existence. Rare photographs taken at this time were in sharp contrast to the handsome tuxedo-attired playboy of the Hollywood years. Greasy, shoulder-length hair framed his face and his eyes seemed fogged with drugs; his bare feet with long, carpet-snagging toenails could no longer be squeezed into his cowboy boots; his snaggled, decaying teeth would no longer invite a starlet's kiss. His tall, once hardy figure was now withered and emaciated. The only women surrounding him now were his Mormon nurse-maids. People wondered how someone who had such a fear of germs could appear as though he never washed.

It was in such a condition that Hughes somehow managed to travel to the Bahamas and actually meet face to face with Nicar-aguan dictator Generalissimo Anastasio Somoza and a U.S. ambassador. Later, much to the concern of his custodian Bill Gay, Hughes demanded once again to pilot a plane, just as he had done in his glory days.

Hughes's last fling with fame occurred when Gay authorized the *Glomar Explorer,* Hughes's massive ship, to assist the CIA in a covert operation to retrieve a sunken Soviet submarine that contained top-secret code books. When news of the expedition leaked and hit the media, Howard Hughes was once again the legendary larger than life hero.

It was doubtful that Hughes realized that he was once again in all the tabloids. On April 5, 1976, Hughes's cadaver was flown from Acapulco to Houston. The fingerprints of the ninety-pound shell of the once vibrant six-foot-three cowboy had to be sent to the FBI for verification that the body was that of Howard Hughes.

HURRICANE KATRINA

The wrath of Hurricane Katrina hit New Orleans on August 29, 2005, resulting in an unprecedented cataclysmic natural disaster for the United States. But how "natural" was it? There are many nominations for the true sinister forces behind Katrina.

It wasn't as if scientists and environmentalists hadn't been warning city, state, and federal governments for years about the disaster of biblical proportions that was waiting to happen in New Orleans. Government gadflies had named New Orleans as one of the most vulnerable areas in the Bush administration's continued neglect of the nation's deteriorating roads, bridges, tunnels, and levees. Even the much-beleaguered Federal Emergency Management Agency (FEMA) had listed a hurricane strike on New Orleans as one of the most dire threats to the United States.

Flooded homes in a New Orleans neighborhood after Hurricane Katrina destroyed much of the city in 2005.

An article entitled "New Orleans Is Sinking" by Jim Wilson in the September 11, 2001, issue of *Popular Mechanics* warned that the surge of a category 5 storm could put the city under eighteen feet of water. The fact that the city had not already sunk, Wilson suggested, was strictly a matter of luck. "If slightly different paths had been followed by Hurricanes Camille, which struck in August 1969, Andrew in August 1992 or George in September 1998, today we might need scuba gear to tour the French Quarter," Wilson commented wryly—and prophetically.

Robert Caputo and Tyrone Turner proved to be prescient in their October 2004 *National Geographic* piece when they described a "broiling August afternoon in New Orleans" when a "whirling maelstrom approached the coast" and "more than a million people evacuated to higher ground. Some 200,000 re-

mained, however—the car-less, the homeless, the aged and infirm, and those die-hard New Orleanians who look for any excuse to throw a party." The article, "Gone with the Water," stated that with nearly 80 percent of New Orleans lying below sea level, the water would pour in and quickly reach a depth of twenty-five feet over parts of the city. Caputo and Turner foresaw as many as fifty thousand dead, a million left homeless, and thousands more who survived the flooding only to perish later from disease. The authors stated that a category 5 hurricane striking New Orleans would be "the worst natural disaster in the history of the United States."

Although Katrina's huge surge and pounding waves in New Orleans and to its east did cause the "worst natural disaster" in our nation's history in terms of property damage, fortunately the death total did not reach the numbers predicted by Caputo and Turner. And the enormous outpouring of assistance from all areas of the United States, the aid of the Red Cross and civilian and religious relief organizations, plus the efforts of government health agencies, warded off a high mortality rate from disease. However, in spite of the indomitable spirit of its residents, it will take many years for the city to fully recover and once again become the "Big Easy."

The winds from Katrina had scarcely ceased blowing when a wide range of theorists began fomenting and formulating a long list of conspiracies responsible for the terrible destruction that visited New Orleans. Among the most frequent accusations rampaging across the Internet and talk radio programs were the following:

- Weather weapons developed by black-ops agencies in cooperation with New World Order scientists sent the hurricane to New Orleans, a major U.S. port, in order to begin the move to martial law throughout the nation. Future targets will include New York and San Francisco.

- George W. Bush, the CIA, and the Miami Cuban mafia conspired to create a man-made disaster with the goal of eliminating a sizable number of New Orleans's black population in order to strengthen the GOP's voter base.

- God created Katrina to punish the gay population of the city. Several Christian fundamentalists have described the hurricane's destructiveness as retribution for flouting the Creator's distaste for gays and for such irreligious decadence as the Mardi Gras celebrations.

- The Yakuza, the Japanese "mafia," used a Russian-made electromagnetic generator to launch the first of a series of devastating storms against cities on the U.S. mainland.

- Navy Seals, the Army Corps of Engineers, or a black-ops agency deliberately blew up the New Orleans levees to flood the poorest black neighborhoods. Louis Farrakhan, the Nation of Islam leader, exploited black paranoia and popularized this conspiracy claim.

- The Ku Klux Klan took advantage of the storm to blow up the levees in order to flood the city's black neighborhoods.

- A cabal of New Orleans real estate agents hired demolitions experts to plant explosives in the levees in order to flood the city's poorest neighborhoods and drive up property values in upscale sections of New Orleans.

- Zionist agents blew the levees as revenge for the U.S. endorsement of the Gaza evacuations of Jewish settlers.

- A test by the Pentagon's secret weapons program of meteorological manipulation backfired when the electromagnetically controlled storm moved from Cuba, where it had been directed, and traveled to Florida and Louisiana.

SADDAM HUSSEIN AND THE AL-QAEDA CONNECTION

Was 9/11 the New World Order's "Reichstag fire" and Saddam Hussein their scapegoat?

Conspiracy theorists assert that the horrors of 9/11 brought the terrible handiwork of the New World Order out of the shadows and into the living room of every American home. The events of 9/11 provided the NWO with their Reichstag fire—a cowardly attack against innocent American citizens that would justify declaring a war on terrorism and a siege against the accused architects of the sneak attack, Osama bin Laden and Saddam Hussein. (On the night of February 27, 1933, the Nazis set fire to the Reichstag, the building where the German Parliament met, and blamed it on Communist agitators.)

After 9/11 several top administration officials declared almost immediately that there was undeniable evidence that Saddam Hussein and Osama bin Laden's terrorist network were linked and had planned the attacks as a cooperative effort. "There's no question that Saddam Hussein had al Qaeda ties," President Bush pronounced grimly to the nation. "There's overwhelming evidence of an Iraq–al Qaeda connection," Vice President Dick Cheney said, adding that he was "very confident there was an established relationship there."

In late 2001, in order to back up the administration's claims of Iraqi involvement in the September 11 attacks, Cheney said it was "pretty well confirmed" that the mastermind of the attacks, Mohamed Atta, had met with a senior Iraqi intelligence official in April 2000 in Prague to plan the attacks on the World Trade Center and the Pentagon. In addition to stressing the links between Iraq and al-Qaeda and the September 11 attacks, Cheney connected Iraq to the 1993 World Trade Center bombing, stating that "newly found Iraqi intelligence files revealed that a participant in the 1993 bombing had fled to Iraq where he received financing from the Iraqi government and a safe haven."

Conspiracy theorists assert that the horrors of 9/11 brought the terrible handiwork of the New World Order out of the shadows and into the living room of every American home.

It became an administration "fact," often cited, that the Iraqi government or the Iraqi intelligence service had an effective working relationship with al-Qaeda that went back to the early 1990s.

After the immediate shock of 9/11 had passed and the terrible attacks could be assessed by cogent analysis, the instant accusation that Saddam Hussein was linked to 9/11 began to seem to be shaky at best. Yet the president and vice president continued to insist on such a connection. Bush, in his speech aboard an aircraft carrier on May 1, 2003, seemed desperate to assure America on that score: "The liberation of Iraq is a crucial advance in the campaign against terror. We've removed an ally of al Qaeda and cut off a source of terrorist funding." During a September 2003 appearance on NBC's *Meet the Press,* Cheney stated that if the U.S. military campaign in Iraq continued to be successful, it would deal a major blow directly at the heart of the geographic base of the terrorists who had kept America under assault for many years, "but most especially on 9/11."

In June 2004, during the heated presidential campaign, Cheney asserted that Hussein "had long-established ties with al Qaeda." And Cheney's spokesperson pointed to a 2002 letter written by CIA director George J. Tenet stating that "we have solid reporting of senior level contacts between Iraq and al Qaeda going back a decade" and that "credible information indicates that Iraq and al Qaeda have discussed safe haven and reciprocal non-aggression."

As the months wore on and talk of war against the evil dictator grew heated, skeptics scoffed that the Bush administration had not presented any hard evidence that Saddam had anything whatsoever to do with Osama bin Laden, al-Qaeda, or 9/11. In fact, there was more evidence that, far from being collaborators, Saddam and bin Laden were often at cross purposes with each other, if not actual enemies. One tape aired heavily on cable television channels and network news programs had a translator rendering in English a message that Osama spoke in Arabic. Allegedly, bin Laden said, among other things, how much he admired Saddam Hussein. However, an independent translator pointed out that bin Laden was actually saying that he would like to kill Saddam.

If Saddam Hussein had any plans of declaring war, theorists argue, his intention would be to consolidate portions or all of the Middle East under his own dictatorship, rather than have any portion of it dominated by Muslim extremists. After all, Saddam not only considered himself to be the latest in a great line of Iraqi/Babylonian kings, he believed himself to be the actual reincarnation of Nebuchadnezzar (605 to 562 B.C.E.). It is well known that during the 1980s Saddam had spent over $800 million on the reconstruction of Babylon.

The conspiracy theorists turned out to be correct in their belief that there was absolutely no connection between Saddam Hussein and al-Qaeda. On June 16, 2004, the September 11 Commission reported that it found no "collaborative relationship" between Iraq and al-Qaeda, thereby challenging one of the Bush administration's main justifications for the war in Iraq. The commission's staff reported that during the period when bin Laden was in Sudan (1991–96), a senior Iraqi intelligence officer had a meeting with him. Bin Laden was in the process of setting up training camps and seeking assistance in getting weapons and inquired if the Hussein regime, though secular, would join the jihad against the West. The report concluded that Iraq had never responded to these requests. Perhaps by way of retaliation, bin Laden sponsored anti-Saddam Islamists in Iraqi Kurdistan. As for the Atta meeting in Prague mentioned by Cheney, the commission's staff concluded on the basis of FBI and Czech intelligence that such a meeting never occurred. On the matter of the 1993 Trade Center bombing, there was "substantial uncertainty" that bin Laden and al-Qaeda were involved.

The commission's finding was that there was no link between Saddam Hussein and al-Qaeda and no evidence that Iraq had collaborated with the Islamic terrorists on the 9/11 attacks. As a kind of postscript, they added that there had been minimal contact between Iraq and al-Qaeda, but no cooperation. The National Commission on Terrorist Attacks upon the United States, a senior FBI official, and a senior CIA analyst concurred with the findings.

White House spokesman Scott McClellan, seizing upon the statements that there was some contact between al-Qaeda and Iraq, said that the administration's earlier assertions were justified.

Although the conspiracy theorists were correct in doubting any links between Saddam Hussein and al-Qaeda, they would likely concede that he was a cruel dictator who deserved to be tried for his crimes against the Iraqi people, Kurds, Iranians, and Kuwaitis. However, these conspiracy researchers remain convinced that certain individuals in the FBI and CIA were involved in a cover-up of monstrous proportions. There is a great deal of documentation, including numerous photographs, proving that George H. W. Bush, George W. Bush, and other presidential administrations had been partners with Saddam Hussein for decades. Osama bin Laden was a highly regarded insider in the past, and the Bush family had been in the oil business with the bin Laden family since at least 1976. Neither should it be overlooked that while Hussein was committing his most heinous crimes, the U.S. government was supporting him materially and politically.

Saddam Hussein may have been an evil dictator, conspiracy theorists say, but when we were selling him arms to keep the Iranians under control, he was the same evil dictator. Saddam was a pawn, serving Western interests as a distraction for the overall plan to protect the West's oil supply.

HYPNOSIS, FALSE MEMORIES, AND THE NEW WORLD ORDER

Who can you believe if you can't even trust your own memories?

While perhaps the majority of conspiracy theorists believe that the New World Order has benefitted from advanced extraterrestrial technology and mind-control sciences for centuries and are allies of the invading aliens, there are other investigators of UFO phenomena who steadfastly believe that an agency of our own government, such as MK-ULTRA, or agents of the Illuminati or New World Order have been conspiring since the late 1940s to make us *believe* that we are being invaded by extraterrestrials.

If various mind-control programs can create a mass panic among the American public that it is being invaded by an alien civilization with a highly advanced science, they would be more willing to give up their freedoms to a national or international government that would guarantee their protection. In this conspiracy scenario UFO abductees are not being snatched and examined by aliens, but by very human government mind-control agents who, through the use of hypnosis and drugs, place them in a receptive altered state and convince them that they have been examined, probed, left with tiny scars—and in some instances, even impregnated—by extraterrestrials. In other cases of alleged UFO abductions, witnesses may stumble unaware upon members of shadow agencies engaged in operations that they want to keep secret from the public. The witnesses are captured, hypnotized or drugged, then released with a cover story implanted in their memories that they were abducted by aliens.

Pickrell, a doctoral student in psychology, stated that the study suggested how easily a false memory can be created and just how vulnerable and malleable memory is.

In hypnosis, as the subject relaxes and concentrates on the hypnotist's voice, the hypnotist leads the person deeper and deeper into a trancelike state of altered consciousness. When the subject has reached a deep level of hypnotic trance, the hypnotist will have access to the individual's unconscious. Clinical psychologists believe that hypnotherapy permits them to help their clients uncover hidden or repressed memories of fears or abuse that will facilitate their cure, but in the past three decades an increasing number of ama-

teur hypnotists have employed hypnosis to explore cases suggestive of past lives or accounts of alien abductions aboard UFOs. These lay or unprofessional hypnotists serve the New World Order very well by adding to the number of men and women who believe that they were abducted by aliens. Skeptical scientists doubt that hypnosis is a true altered state of consciousness and contend that the individuals who are classified as good subjects by both professional or lay hypnotists are really men and women who are highly suggestible and fantasy prone.

The Stanford Hypnotic Susceptibility Scales, a scientific yardstick used to measure the phenomenon of hypnosis, was developed in the late 1950s by Stanford University psychologists Andre M. Weitzenhoffer and Ernest R. Hilgard. Scoring on the Stanford scales ranges from 0 for individuals who do not appear to respond to any hypnotic suggestions, to 12 for those who are assessed as extremely responsive to hypnosis. Most people, according to extensive experimentation, place somewhere in the middle range, between 5 and 7.

Weitzenhoffer and Hilgard demonstrated that a person's ability to be hypnotized is unrelated to his or her personality traits. Earlier suggestions that those individuals who could be hypnotized were gullible, submissive, imaginative, or socially compliant proved unsupported by the data. People who had the ability to become absorbed in such activities as reading, enjoying music, or daydreaming appeared to be the more hypnotizable subjects.

By using hypnosis, the scientists at Stanford were able to create transient hallucinations, false memories, and delusions in some subjects. By using positron emission tomography, which directly measures metabolism, the researchers were able to determine that different regions of a subject's brains were activated when he or she was asked simply to imagine a sound or sight than when the subject was hallucinating under hypnotic suggestion.

Certain studies on memory show that people often construct their memories after the fact and that they may be susceptible to suggestions from others as to the "truth" of what actually occurred. Therefore, it is possible to create false memories in some people's minds by suggesting that certain events happened when, in fact, such circumstances never occurred.

In March 1998 a report commissioned by the Royal College of Psychiatrists in England accused its own members of having destroyed innocent lives by implanting false memories while using irresponsible techniques of delving into patients' childhood events. According to the report, nearly a thousand parents stated that they had been falsely accused of sexual abuse after their adult children allegedly recovered memories of the attacks during psychotherapy.

In the November 1998 issue of the journal *Psychological Science,* Dr. C. J. Brainerd and Dr. V. F. Reyna of the University of Arizona in Tucson published their findings that many individuals often believed more strongly in suggested false memories than in actual recollections of events. When strong themes are operative in such explorations of memory, the researchers state, things that were not really experienced can seem more real to the individual than his or her actual experiences.

The ease with which a false memory can be created was demonstrated by an experiment conducted in 2001 by University of Washington memory researchers Jacqueline E. Pickrell and Elizabeth F. Loftus. After the 120 subjects in the experiment were exposed to a fake advertisement showing Bugs Bunny at Disneyland, about a third of them later said that they had met the cartoon character when they visited Disneyland earlier in their lives, and had

even shaken his hand. Such a scenario could never have occurred, because Bugs Bunny is a cartoon character owned by Warner Brothers and would not be seen walking around Disneyland with Mickey Mouse and Donald Duck.

Pickrell, a doctoral student in psychology, stated that the study suggested how easily a false memory can be created and just how vulnerable and malleable memory is. The experiment also demonstrated how people may create many of their autobiographical references and memories. Even the nostalgic advertising employed by many commercial companies can lead individuals to remember experiences that they never really had. Dr. Loftus, a professor of psychology and adjunct professor of law at the University of Washington who has been researching memory distortion since the 1970s, suggests that false memories are often created by three common methods: yielding to social or professional demands to recall particular events; imagining events when experiencing difficulty remembering; and being encouraged to abandon critical thinking regarding the truth of memory constructions. False memories, according to Loftus and her research colleagues, are most often constructed "by combining actual memories with the content of suggestions received from others." During such a process, individuals may experience source confusion and forget how much of the memory is valid and how much came from external sources.

And when that "external source" is a skilled New World Order manipulator of reality, the conspiracy theorists maintain, invalid memories of alien abductions might be easily implanted into deceiving the entire world into a state of apathy concerning warnings of a sinister elite who wish to make everyone into their slaves.

DAVID ICKE— THE REPTILIAN CONSPIRACY

Hailed by some as the "paranoid of the decade," David Icke warns that reptilian, shape-shifting aliens are amongst us—as our presidents, our royalty, our diplomats, even our entertainers.

David Icke says that the history of the world has been nothing but a conspiracy against the human race, a campaign conducted for thousands of years by the Anunnaki, a secret society of extraterrestrial reptilians. The reptilian race spun the myths that formed the world's religions and cleverly designed the teachings of various prophets to keep humans in a mental prison. The Anunnaki have controlled gullible humans and ruled them as pharaohs, kings, emperors, and assorted royalty. The devious reptiles are behind such secret societies and powerful groups as the Illuminati, the Bilderbergers, the Trilateral Commission, and the Freemasons.

For those who concede an innate fear of snakes but can't recall seeing any reptiles walking around as preachers, teachers, or public administrators, it is because the Anunnaki are shape-shifters and can take on human form. Icke declares that such notables as Henry Kissinger, Mikhail Gorbachev, George W. Bush, Queen Elizabeth, Bill and Hillary Clinton, Bob Hope, and Kris Kristofferson are all intergalactic reptiles disguised as humans.

Icke, a native of Leicester, England, was not always chasing blood-drinking lizards from other worlds. Until he developed arthritis in 1973, he was a professional soccer player for the Coventry City and Hereford United teams. No longer active as a player, Icke transferred his athletic skills to those of a sports announcer for BBC-TV. Politics was also among his great interests, and he was national spokesperson for the British Green Party from 1988 to 1991.

New Age concepts and ideas began to appeal to him, and for a time Icke dressed in turquoise and called himself the "Son of Godhead." Concerned about the health of the planet, he became an environmentalist, but then, somewhere in his studies, he read *The Protocols of the Elders of Zion,* the well-known Tsarist anti-Semitic forgery, and endorsed the theory of a global Jewish conspiracy as true. Icke said that he very much believed that a small clique of Jews held contempt for the larger masses of Jewish people and that this "elite" had worked with non-Jews to precipitate World War I, the Russian Revolution, and World War II. According to Icke's interpretation of world events, this elite clique of Jews had even provided the financial clout that enabled Hitler to rise to power and rearm Nazi Germany.

Starting with the paranoia that there is a secret society of the elite that controls the world, Icke went further and dressed the Illuminati in reptilian clothing. Icke once commented that when he was a lad, he wondered how the British Isles, just tiny specks on a world globe, could have built an empire on which the sun never set. The answer became clear when he began to trace the bloodlines of English monarchy back to the Roman Empire, to Egypt, to Babylon—back to the "sons of God" (the extraterrestrial reptilian race) who interbred with the Hebrew "daughters of men" to create the hybrid line, the Nephilim.

It was in 1998 that Icke pieced together the final sections of the reptilian bloodline. In his book *The Biggest Secret* he tells of meeting two victims of mind control, Cathy O'Brien and Arizona Wilder, who claimed to have been forced to conduct satanic rituals of human sacrifice for high-level dignitaries, including the British royal family. Wilder told of witnessing Queen Elizabeth eat human flesh and drink human blood after such a sacrifice. After the queen ate human flesh, she would shape-shift into a reptilian "with a long reptile face, almost like a beak, and she's an off-white color." Wilder made the same charges against Prince Charles, who would shape-shift into a reptilian and take special delight in sacrificing children.

Not long after hearing these dreadful disclosures, Christine Fitzgerald, a woman representing herself as a close friend and confidante of Princess Diana, told Icke that Diana had nicknamed the members of the House of Windsor

the "lizards." And the princess had meant that literally, not figuratively. According to Fitzgerald, no member of the royal family had died for quite some time. They just metamorphosed, in a process somewhat like cloning.

George W. Bush is also an extraterrestrial reptilian who has been seen to shape-shift. In fact, Icke claimed in a 1999 interview, thirty-three U.S. presidents have shared the reptilian bloodline from France and Great Britain.

Icke has put forth his views in a number of books and recorded lectures. Among his book titles are the following, all available through Bridge of Love Publications at www.bridgeoflove.com: *The Biggest Secret: The Book that Will Change the World* (1999); *Children of the Matrix* (2001); *Alice in Wonderland and the World Trade Center Disaster* (2002); and *Infinite Love Is the Only Truth—Everything Else Is Illusion* (2005).

In 2011, *The Intel Hub* named Icke the fifth most influential person in the alternative media, citing his voluminous writings and his all-day stage performances that always left his audiences wanting more. In the opinion of *The Intel Hub,* Icke may well be one of the most dangerous people to the establishment because of his ability "to convince regular people of their immense power to affect positive change." In the opinion of many, Icke examines what he calls "the Fifth Sense Reality," and provides historical evidence "of some very bizarre and thought-provoking phenomena."

ILLUMINATI

The Illuminati is the ultimate secret society, a cabal that stretches its tentacles of control to encompass the entire world. The members of the Illuminati are the real rulers of the world, and they have been pulling the strings from behind the scenes for centuries. They have infiltrated every government and every aspect of society around the planet. Some say that their ultimate goal is to install a satanic New World Order, a one-world government, that will prepare Earth's citizens for the coming of the antichrist.

Historically, this is what we know about the Illuminati:

The term was first used by Spanish occultists toward the end of the fifteenth century to signify those alchemists and magicians who appeared to possess the "light" of spiritual illumination from a higher source. Later, a mystical sixteenth-century Spanish sect, the Alumbrados, adopted the name Illuminati.

The secret society known as the Order of the Illuminati was founded in the city of Ingolstadt in the southern German monarchy of Bavaria on May 1, 1776, by Adam Weishaupt, a twenty-eight-year-old professor of religious law, who deliberately blended mysticism into the workings of the brotherhood in order to make his agenda of republicanism appear to be more mysterious than those of a political reform group. Beginning with only five members, Weishaupt's order grew slowly, numbering about sixty in five cities by 1780. He adopted many of the classes and orders of the Masons, and he promised his initiates that they would receive a special communication of occult knowledge as they advanced higher in the ranks of the Illuminati.

Weishaupt's society had little effect on the German political structure until 1780, when he attracted the interest of Adolf Francis, Baron von Knigge, a master occultist and a man who had risen to the highest levels in many of the secret societies that preceded the Illuminati, including the Masons. Knigge had no problem melding his interest in the supernatural with Weishaupt's goal of political revolution, and the two men quickly established branches of the Illuminati throughout all of Germany. A few months after Knigge had joined Weishaupt's cause, membership in the Illuminati swelled to three hundred.

Adam Weishaupt was a professor of religious law who founded the Order of the Illuminati.

Weishaupt gave special emphasis to enlisting as many young men of wealth and position as possible. He also managed to create an aura of mystery around himself, permitting himself to be seen by none but those in the highest ranks of the society, thereby encouraging the myth that he was an adept of such great power that he existed largely as an invisible presence. Initiates into the Illuminati underwent secret rites, wore bizarre costumes, and participated in grotesque ceremonies designed to instill complete obedience to Weishaupt. Soon the organization became a force to be reckoned with behind the scenes in Germany's political life, and its members worked secretly to overthrow both church and state.

As the group's influence, Weishaupt and Knigge became concerned that certain of the more powerful German princes would take immediate steps to suppress it. To hide the society even more completely from official scrutiny, the leaders implemented Weishaupt's original plan of grafting the Illuminati onto the larger brotherhood of the Freemasons. The Masons were not long in discovering that interlopers had joined their fraternal brotherhood with less than honorable motives. In 1782 a group within the Masons called the Strict Observance demanded that a council be held at Wilhelmsbad to examine the true beliefs of the Illuminati. Knigge's powers of persuasion effectively blocked the attempt of the Strict Observance contingent to expel Illuminism from the society of Masons, and he managed to enroll almost all the members of the council in the Illuminati. By 1784 Illuminati membership had risen to three thousand, and the secret society appeared on the verge of assuming control of the entire Masonic establishment.

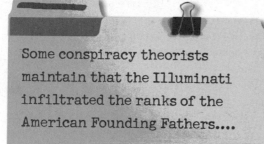

Some conspiracy theorists maintain that the Illuminati infiltrated the ranks of the American Founding Fathers....

Just when their goals seemed within their grasp, Weishaupt and Knigge fell into a serious disagreement about the correct manner of proceeding with their master plan. In April 1784 Knigge withdrew from the Illuminati, leaving Weishaupt the supreme commander of the increasingly powerful society. A few months later, a number of initiates who had reached the highest level within the Illuminati became disillusioned when the special supernatural communication from a higher source that Weishaupt had promised had not manifested. It now became obvious to them that Weishaupt had only sought to use them for the achievement of his political ambitions. The Illuminati was denounced as a subversive organization by many of its former members, some of whom informed the duchess dowager Maria Anna of Bavaria and the ruling duke of Bavaria, Karl Theodor, that

the society sought the end of both religious and royal authority.

In June 1784 Karl Theodor issued an edict outlawing all secret societies in his provinces. In March 1785 another edict specifically condemned the Illuminati. Weishaupt had already fled to a neighboring province, where he hoped to inspire the loyal members of the Illuminati to continue as a society. In 1787 the duke issued a final edict against the Order of the Illuminati, and Weishaupt apparently faded into obscurity. Although he never realized his goal of a German republic and the overthrow of the European monarchies, the sparks that he had ignited with the Illuminati would soon burst into the flames of the French Revolution in 1789.

There we have it. The Illuminati, with its plan for a new world order, was destroyed within fifteen years of its origin. Of course, that's not quite the final word according to conspiracy theorists.

After the Illuminati was banished from Bavaria, it survived in the form of the German Union and a number of "reading societies" devoted to literature and self-improvement. Weishaupt had concentrated on the recruitment of wealthy young men, so it was through their combined fortunes that the Illuminati gained control over the literary societies and printing presses. In short order they circulated books and pamphlets showing the deceptions of organized religion and the social abuses of government. Ceaselessly they promoted anarchy and revolution and preached the dissolution of all monarchies. Their master plan was to destroy the aristocracy and appear to bring power to the people while, in reality, exploiting the common folk as puppets whom they could control from behind the scenes. The French Revolution was the first of several political uprisings to come.

In 1797 John Robison's book *Proofs of a Conspiracy against All of the Religions and Governments of Europe, Carried On in the Secret Meetings of Freemasons, Illuminati, and Reading Societies* sought to expose the secrets of the Illuminati. In 1799 Abbé Augustin Barruel joined the voices raised in protest against the machinations of the Illuminati when he published his four-volume study entitled *Memoirs Illustrating the History of Jacobinism.*

Some conspiracy theorists maintain that the Illuminati infiltrated the ranks of the American Founding Fathers, pointing out that documents recovered in Germany reveal that the symbol for the Illuminati was a pyramid with an eye in the capstone—familiar as a feature of the Great Seal of the United States as shown on the back of the U.S. one-dollar bill. Underneath the Great Seal pyramid, the Latin phrase *Novus Ordo Seclorum* means "New Order of the Ages"—perhaps not exactly "New World Order," but certainly close enough for believers.

According to some theorists, Karl Marx and Frederick Engels were students of Weishaupt and Illuminism and adapted the goals of the Illuminati when they composed *The Communist Manifesto* in 1848.

The overall plan developed by the Illuminati in the 1780s is still being followed today: Encourage world wars so that people will feel that there is a need for an organization like the United Nations in order to establish peace between warring factions. Once such an organization is created, continue the pressure of war so that, in time, a world body of government with a world court and a world police force will keep the masses of all nations in check and absolute power will be in the hands of the Illuminati.

INOCULATIONS FREE OF CHARGE: HELP DEPOPULATE THE PLANET

Regardless of the urgency of the public announcement, be certain you know who's giving you or your children the needle.

In the past couple of decades it has seemed as though medical science is losing the war against a terrible onslaught of new plague-like diseases. The horrible AIDS virus is virtually decimating some third-world nations. The hanta virus shocks the Southwest when those infected die within a few hours—and the nation reels when outbreaks of the virus begin appearing in other regions. Newspaper accounts of bacterial infections that can literally eat away a victim's flesh, with the face, arm, or leg being devoured in less than a day, leave us recoiling with fear and apprehension and becoming greatly concerned about our own health and welfare.

And wouldn't our fear turn to outrage if we were to learn that such awful plagues as these were the result of a secret agency's deliberate plan to depopulate our planet? One of the New World Order's mandates is to decrease the world's population by billions so that the elite have to manage only enough people to serve as their servants and slaves. What better way to start than to inject poisons into soldiers, who must obey the orders to receive inoculations, and schoolchildren, who innocently line up for their shots, gritting their teeth and bearing the pain to win their teachers' approval.

Since receiving vaccinations before going to the Persian Gulf in 1990, approximately 250,000 of the soldiers who served there have suffered from puzzling, often tragic, mild to life-threatening or even fatal physical or psychological illnesses with a characteristic disease profile or spectrum that began during their Gulf stay or just after the war. Other nations' troops in the Gulf who were not given vaccinations did not come down with "Gulf War syndrome." How many dangerous pathogens or nanobacteria delivered by physically dangerous carriers were in those vaccines made by greedy medical exploiters?

It seems that the government ignores the complaints of its military. It has been slow in recognizing Vietnam vets' medical and psychological problems resulting from Agent Orange and posttraumatic stress. At the same time, the government continues to close Veterans Administration hospitals and has minimized pay and combat benefits.

According to Dr. Alan Cantwell Jr., another AIDS-like disease is spreading among military personnel who served in the Persian Gulf War. Reports of this new mystery illness occurring in Gulf War vets began in the spring of 1992. Symptoms included chronic fatigue, muscle aches, swollen and painful joints, aching teeth and gums, memory loss, and fevers.

Although the war itself ended in 1991, by 1994 military officials admitted that as many as 20,000 or more of the 700,000 troops who served in that conflict were exhibiting results of a strange disease that came to be known as the Gulf War syndrome. Many of those afflicted blamed the experimental vaccines that had been injected into their persons with the express goal of protecting them against anthrax, nerve gas, and other biological warfare agents suspected to be used by the troops of Saddam Hussein. Others blamed the inhalation of toxic fumes from the Kuwait oil fires or unknown chemical agents.

But this new mystery disease, according to military sources, is affecting U.S. troops who were hundreds of miles away from the area in northern Iraq where chemical detection teams recorded low-level amounts of bio warfare agents.

If this is so, then what could be causing sickness in an undisclosed number of formerly healthy men and women? What could be causing the wives of certain of these servicemen to be experiencing miscarriages or the birth of deformed babies?

One Alabama veteran of the Persian Gulf conflict has stated that up to two-thirds of all reserve units came back with some symptoms of the mystery illness. Many of these personnel blame Iraqi Scud missiles that were laced with

chemical agents and some kind of manmade virus. And they believe that the U.S. government is covering up knowledge of the agents of bio warfare that are wreaking havoc and terrible suffering among the veterans of that war.

Dr. Cantwell reports that some of the vets with the mysterious new disease served in the war zone for months, others for as little as nine days. A pattern is difficult to determine in seeking a cause for the illness, for the plague has affected troops who were stationed in widely scattered geographic areas of the war. The single factor common to all troops involved in the campaign is that they were all given experimental drugs and vaccines as part of the requirement to serve in the Gulf.

Unfortunately, as Cantwell observes, the U.S. military has a long history of conducting covert medical experiments on its own personnel, as well as unknowing civilians. Dozens of secret, planned bioattacks were perpetrated on American cities during the 1950s and 1960s—the most notorious being a six-day bioattack on San Francisco in which the military sprayed massive clouds of potentially harmful bacteria over the entire city.

Perhaps most injurious of all experiments conducted on an unwitting public were the detonations of nuclear bombs at test sites in Nevada and elsewhere that sent massive clouds of radiation across the nation.

When mind-altering drugs were developed in the 1950s, Cantwell reminds us, the military secretly gave them to enlisted men, a conscienceless act that resulted in a number of deaths.

Certain watchdog groups have recently charged secret government groups with conspiring to institute a policy of global population control by giving children deadly vaccines during mandatory vaccination programs. According to these investigators, these vicious vaccines have not only caused seizures, brain damage, and death, but they have also been responsible for the unprecedented rise in criminal activity and violent crimes among children. The recent rash of shootings in grade schools and high schools are a direct result of the effects of these injected chemicals on susceptible young brains.

Many serious-minded observers of the current world scene believe that shadow agencies in governments throughout the globe have joined the New World Order's plot to depopulate the planet by secretly spreading diseases among the masses. Some even accuse the United Nations and its World Health Organization of utilizing viruses created in the U.S. Army's biological weapons laboratories to deliberately infect entire populations in Africa, Haiti, and elsewhere with the AIDS virus.

If such a horrible scenario of world depopulation bears the slightest truth, then we must wonder about such diseases as West Nile fever, the Ebola virus, and mad cow disease. And we must also wonder if the government warnings of the potential of terrorist attacks spreading biological and chemical death among us are part of a insidious program to condition us for the unimaginable horror to come.

INQUISITION OF THE MIDDLE AGES

The Inquisition began in 1233 as a concerted effort by the Church of Rome to arrest, torture, and execute anyone thought guilty of being a heretic, a witch, a sorcerer, or one of Satan's minions on Earth.

In 906 C.E. the *Canon Episcopi*, by Abbot Regino of Prum, condemned as heretical any belief in witchcraft or in the power of sorcerers to transform people into animals. The Christian clergy of that time took little notice of the edict, for it was the consensus that those individuals who believed that they could fly through the air or work evil magic on another person were allowing Satan to deceive them. In 1000 Deacon Burchard, later archbishop of Worms, published *Corrector,* which stressed that God alone had the kind of power that the untutored masses were attributing to witches. Heretics were another matter, and in 1022 there occurred the first fully attested burning of a heretic, in the city of Orléans.

By the early thirteenth century the Cathar sect had become so popular among the people that Pope Innocent III considered it a greater threat to Christianity than the Islamic warriors who challenged the Crusaders in the Middle East. To satisfy his outrage, he ordered the only crusade ever launched by Christians against fellow Christians, declaring as heretics, witches, and devil-worshippers the Albigensians, as the Cathars of southern France were also known.

The Papal Inquisition came into existence in 1233 with the *Excommunicamus* of Pope Gregory IX, who urged local bishops to become more vigorous in ridding Europe of heretics, then lessened their responsibility for determining orthodoxy by establishing inquisitors under the special jurisdiction of the papacy. The office of inquisitor was entrusted primarily to the Franciscans and the Dominicans because of their reputation for superior knowledge of theology and their declared freedom from worldly ambition. Each tribunal was ordered to include two inquisitors of equal authority, who would be assisted by notaries, police, and counselors. Because they had the power to excommunicate even members of royal houses, the inquisitors were formidable figures.

In 1244 Montségur, the last center of Albigensian resistance, fell, and hundreds of Cathars were burned at the stake. The headquarters of the Inquisition had been established in Toulouse, and in 1252 Pope Innocent IV issued a papal bull that placed the inquisitors above the law and demanded that every

Christian—from the aristocracy to the peasantry—assist in the work of seeking out witches and heretics or face excommunication. In 1257 the church officially sanctioned torture as a means of forcing witches and other heretics to confess their alliance with Satan.

The Inquisition employed judges, jailers, exorcists, firewood-choppers, and torture experts to destroy the evil ones who were threatening the ruling powers. It was not long before the inquisitors discovered a foolproof method for perpetuating their gory profession: Under torture, nearly any accused witch could be forced to name a long string of her "fellow witches," thereby making one trial give birth to a hundred others.

The inquisitors would descend upon a particular location for weeks or months and bring suit against any person there suspected of heresy. Lesser penalties were levied on those who came forward of their own volition and confessed their heresy than on those who ignored the summons and had to be placed on trial. The tribunal allowed a grace period of about a month for such voluntary confessions. The penances and sentences for those who confessed or were found guilty during the trial were pronounced at a public ceremony known as the *sermo generalis* or *auto-da-fé*; and might consist of a public whipping, a pilgrimage to a holy shrine, a monetary fine, or the wearing of a cross. The most severe penalty that the inquisitors could pronounce was life imprisonment—but they could turn over a confessed heretic to the civil authorities, in which case it was quite likely that he or she would be put to death. By far the most common method of execution was burning at the stake.

The wealthy and powerful Knights Templar, long considered among the greatest defenders of the church, were accused of heretical acts such as invoking Satan and worshipping demons. In spite of a lengthy trial and 573 witnesses for their defense, the arrested Templars were tortured *en masse* and burned at the stake, and their order was disbanded by Pope Clement V. In 1313 as he was being burned to death in front of Notre Dame Cathedral, Jacques de Molay, the Knights Templar grand master, recanted his torture-induced confession to demon worship and invited the pope and the king to meet him at heaven's gate. When both dignitaries died soon after de Molay's execution, it seemed to the public at large to be a sign that the grand master had been innocent of the charges of heresy.

In 1320 Bernard Gui published *Practica,* an influential instructional manual for inquisitors, in which he urged them to pay particular heed to arresting those women who cavorted with the goddess Diana. Four years later, in 1324, Ireland's first witchcraft trial convened when Alice Kyteler was found guilty of consorting with a demon.

In 1484 Pope Innocent VIII became so angered by the apparent spread of witchcraft in Germany that he issued the papal bull *Summis Desiderantes Affectibus* (Desiring with Supreme Ardor) and authorized two trusted Dominican inquisitors, Heinrich Institoris (Henry Kramer) and Jakob Sprenger, to stamp out demonology in the Rhineland. By 1486 Kramer and Sprenger had published *Malleus Maleficarum,* the "Hammer for Witches," which quickly became the bible of the witch hunters. The book earnestly refuted all those who would claim that the works of demons existed only in troubled human minds. Certain angels fell from heaven, and to believe otherwise was to believe contrary to the true faith. And now these fallen angels, these demons, were intent upon destroying the human race. Any persons who consorted with demons and became witches must recant their evil ways or be put to death.

The first major witch hunt in Europe occurred in Switzerland in 1427; and in 1428, in Valais, Switzerland, there was a mass burning of a hundred witches. Numerous scholars have observed that beginning in the fourteenth century, the close of the Middle Ages,

JUGEMENT de L'INQUISITION dans la grande Place de MADRID.

An engraving depicting the court of the Spanish Inquisition in Madrid.

the Christian establishment of Europe was forced to deal with an onset of social, economic, and religious changes. Also during this time, from 1347 to 1349 the Black Death, bubonic plague, ravaged the European nations, greatly encouraging rumors of devil-worshippers who conspired with other heretics, such as Jews and Muslims, to invoke Satan to bring about a pestilence that would destroy Christianity and the West. During most of the Middle Ages, those who practiced the Old Religion and worked with herbs and charms were largely ignored by the church and the Inquisition. After the scourge of the Black Death, witchcraft trials increased steadily throughout the fourteenth and fifteenth centuries.

Separate from the Inquisition that exerted its jurisdiction over the rest of Europe, in 1478, at the request of King Ferdinand V and Queen Isabella, papal permission was granted to establish the Spanish Inquisition. The support of Spain's royal house enabled Tomás de Torquemada to become the single Grand Inquisitor whose name has become synonymous with the Inquisition's cruelest acts and excesses. Torquemada is known to have ordered the deaths by torture and burning of thousands of heretics and witches. However, the Spanish Inquisition largely focused persecution on the *Marranos* or *conversos*—Jews suspected of insincerely converting to Christianity, converts from Islam similarly thought to be insincere in practicing the Christian faith, and in the 1520s, individuals believed to have converted to Protestantism.

From about 1450 to 1750 some forty thousand to sixty thousand individuals were tried as witches and condemned to death in France, Germany, Austria, and Switzerland. Perhaps three-quarters of the victims were women—although some authorities assert that judges of the great tribunals examined, tried, and tortured female witches at a ratio of 10-to-1, 100-to-1, or 10,000-to-1 over men. Only in the Scandinavian countries were men accused of being witches and sorcerers at an equal or larger percentage than women.

The witch hunters in France were not as gender-biased as their counterparts in some other European nations. Of the 1,300 witches whose appeals were heard by the French parliament prior to execution, just over half were men. According to some statistics, from 1550 to 1682 France sentenced approximately 1,500 accused witches to death. Also, contrary to popular supposition, in countries such as France, where the Catholic Church was firmly entrenched, the inquisitorial church courts were much more lenient than the civil courts in demanding death sentences for accused witches. Overall, in such Catholic nations as France, Italy, and Spain, the church courts executed far fewer people than the local community-based courts or the national courts.

In the early decades of the sixteenth century, when the Protestant Reformation began to restructure nearly all of Europe politically as well as religiously, witches were largely overlooked as the rulers of church and state struggled with the larger issues of the great division within Christianity. Then, after a time of relatively little persecution, the years from roughly 1550 to 1650 brought the great witchcraft craze or hysteria that many practicing witches and students of witchcraft today refer to as the "Burning Times."

By his own boast, witch trial judge Pierre de Lancre tortured and burned over six hundred men and women accused of consorting with demons. De Lancre was not a member of the clergy, and his concerns were social, rather than theological. He believed that sorcerers and witches were a well-organized antisocial force that sought to overthrow the established order.

When Henri Boguet, an eminent judge of Saint-Claude in the Jura Mountains, presided at witchcraft trials, he was known for his cruelty, especially toward children. In his *Discours des Sorciers,* Boguet expressed his conviction that the devil could become either a man or woman to deceive people into his fold. He pronounced or ratified about six hundred death sentences against witches.

The Jesuit Friedrich von Spee became an opponent of the witchcraft trials when the Duke of Brunswick brought him and a fellow priest into a torture chamber. Later, in an anti-Inquisition work, Father Spee declared: "Often I have thought that the only reason why we are not all wizards is due to the fact that we have not all been tortured. And there is truth in what an inquisitor dared to boast, that if he could reach the Pope, he would make him confess that he was a wizard."

Sometime in the 1550s a highly respected doctor, Johannes Weyer (or Weir), who believed in the power of Satan to deceive Earth's mortals, nonetheless became a critic of the Inquisition and its claims that mere humans could really attain such supernatural powers as those which the tribunals ascribed to witches. In 1563, against strong opposition, Weyer published *De Praestigiis Daemonum et Incantatiponibus ac Venificiis* (On the Illusions of the Demons and on Spells and Poisons), in which he argued that the supernatural powers attributed to witches existed only in their minds and imaginations.

In 1583 Reginald Scot wrote *The Discovery of Witchcraft* as an kind of rebuttal to Sprenger and Kramer's "Hammer for Witches." In Scot's opinion, the inquisitors were sexually obsessed madmen who took delight in inflicting sadistic torture on their victims. If witches were really as all-powerful and malignant as the inquisitors claimed, Scot argued, why had they not enslaved the human race long ago?

With the spread of Protestantism through Europe, Pope Paul III in 1542 established the Congregation of the Inquisition (also known as the Roman Inquisition and the Holy Office). It consisted of six cardinals, including the reformer Gian Pietro Carafa. Although its powers extended to the whole church, the Holy Office was less concerned about heresies and false beliefs of church members than about misstatements of orthodoxy in the academic writings of theologians. When Carafa became Pope Paul IV in 1555, he approved the first *Index of Forbidden Books* (1559) and vigorously sought out any academics who might be promoting any thought that favored Protestantism or otherwise offended church doctrine.

It is ironic that Germany, the country that gave birth to the Protestant Reformation, was also the very center of the witchcraft trials in Europe, condemning to the stake 48 percent of all those who were accused of consorting with demons, perhaps as many as 26,000 victims—82 percent of whom were women. In southwestern Germany alone, more than 3,000 witches were executed between 1560 and 1680. Perhaps the reasons for such heavy persecution of suspected witches lay in the distrust that the warring Christian factions—the Roman Catholics and the newly emerging Protestant sects—had toward one another, and their willingness to accuse rather hastily someone of opposing religious views as a servant of Satan.

In 1630 Prince-Bishop Johann Georg II Fuchs von Dornheim, the infamous *Hexenbischof* (Witch Bishop), constructed a special torture chamber that he decorated with appropriate passages from scripture. He burned at least six hundred heretics and witches, including a fellow bishop he suspected of being too lenient.

England did not really succumb to the witch craze that seized continental Europe. There was no law against witchcraft in England until 1542—and that law was repealed in 1547. Perhaps because the nation had a strong central government, as opposed to the independent city states which at that time created constant political turmoil in many of the European countries, England did not tolerate wholesale witch burnings. There were, in fact, very few burnings at all. Death by hanging was the generally prescribed death sentence. The few burnings that did occur took place on the borders where different religious faiths were in conflict and the people were more disposed to see Satan in the other person's manner of worship.

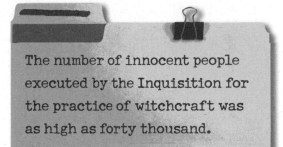

The number of innocent people executed by the Inquisition for the practice of witchcraft was as high as forty thousand.

Torture could not be used against accused witches in England; therefore, only about 20 percent of those suspected of dealing with the devil were executed. The last witches executed in England—Temperance Lloyd, Susanna Edwards, and Mary Trembles, all of Bideford, Devon—were all hanged on the same day, August 25, 1682. The death penalty for witches in England was abolished in 1736. Estimates of the number of witches put to death in England generally run to about four hundred. Around 90 percent of those condemned were women.

From 1537 to 1722 in Scotland, at least three times as many witches were hanged as in England—informed counts range from 1,350 to 1,739 victims—with women making up about 86 percent of the total. The last witch in the whole of the British Isles to be executed was Jenny Horn of Sutherland, Scotland, who was burned at the stake in 1722. Mrs. Horn had been tried together with her daughter, who, the jury decided, was a victim of her mother's witchcraft, rather than an accomplice.

The Inquisition and the church itself had very little part in any witchcraft trials after the latter part of the seventeenth century, but the Holy Office continued to serve as the instrument by which the papal government regulated church order and doctrine. In 1965 Pope Paul VI reorganized the Holy Office and renamed it the Congregation for the Doctrine of the Faith.

Various texts and historians have claimed that during the four centuries of active persecution, the number of innocent people executed by the Inquisition for the practice of witchcraft was as high as forty thousand. In 1999 Jenny Gibbons released the results of her research in official trial records, which verified that approximately 75 percent to 80 percent of those accused of witchcraft were women but also indicated that the total number of men and women actually hanged or burned for the crime probably did not exceed forty thousand. The author and scholar Margot Adler discovered that the source of the oft-quoted "9 million" witches put to death was first used by a German historian in the late eighteenth century who took the number of people killed in a witch hunt in his own German state and multiplied that figure by the number of years various penal statues existed, then extrapolated the result to correspond to the population of Europe.

INTERNET— A TOOL OF THE NEW WORLD ORDER

As with a firearm, the Internet's use for good or evil depends upon the individual—and whoever is in control of it.

In a special report on pedophilia ("The Web's Dark Secret") in the March 19, 2001, issue,

Newsweek magazine observed with unfortunate accuracy that "before the Internet came along, pedophiles were lonely and hunted individuals. Authorities had child pornography under control. Today networks of child abusers are proliferating worldwide."

The problem is global, Rod Nordland and Jeffrey Bartholet reported in the article: "A survey of 1,501 U.S. kids aged 10 to 17 conducted in 2000 showed that approximately one in four had had an unwanted exposure to some kind of image of naked men and women having sex in the last year. Roughly one in five kids had received a sexual solicitation, meaning that someone asked them to meet somewhere. And less than 10 percent of sexual solicitations and only 3 percent of unwanted exposure episodes were ever reported."

In March 2001 the Vatican warned of the dangers of cyberspace spirituality and admonished users not to treat the Internet as a religious supermarket. Some Web surfers may pick and choose aspects of customized religious websites to suit their personal tastes. The Vatican warned that virtual religion is no substitute for the real thing and compared the Internet to a mind-altering substance with near-narcotic effects.

With computers providing pedophiles and pornographers unlimited access to children and tempting faithful churchgoers to sample religious expression outside their usual experience, conspiracy theorists warn that the real danger of the Internet is that it has become a powerful tool by which the secret government or agents of the New World Order can better enslave the general population. For one thing, thousands of bloggers and individuals with strong points of view have already discovered the ease with which they can express their political opinions online. Just a few short decades ago these activists would have faced the expense of a printing press, paper, and distribution. Even with a great outlay of funds, their chances of reaching more than a handful of like-minded individuals were small. Now an investment of a few dollars to obtain a website allows anyone to spread his or her concepts of peace or perversity, harmony or hatred, agreement or disagreement with the government's policies across the world in a matter of seconds.

But if those who wish to dissent have found an inexpensive medium by which to express their criticism of the government, Big Brother groups within the government have gained the most wonderful surveillance tool they could imagine. It is a simple matter for online services to monitor what you read, archive, and email. While the average computer user blissfully surfs the Web and marvels at access to museums, libraries, and newspapers from all over the world, a shadow agency can monitor every detail of his or her online activity, including banking and investment records. And while concerned citizens' groups are worrying about Internet pedophiles and pornographers corrupting their children, shadow agencies, masters of dirty double-dealing, are hyping public fears about hackers, terrorists, and viruses in order to generate citizen support for an Internet police force, which would only serve in the long run to curb the average computer user's freedoms.

There is a great propaganda effort on the part of the government to make the Internet appear indispensable to every American household. The government wishes to enter every home and business via electric lines and broadband through power lines (BPL). This will create electronic interference or static that will destroy the effectiveness of ham radio, AM radio, and all forms of emergency and shortwave communication that use the airwaves. Because there won't be any clear channels, all through-the-air forms of communication will have been eradicated by BPL. When there is a national disaster, the government will control communication and will release only the approved cover story that it has decided the masses should hear. Broadband through power lines will place the government in near-total command when it decides to launch a major catastrophe in the United States preparatory to taking complete control of the nation.

Most of the major broadcast and print media are owned and controlled by a half dozen giant corporations headed by members of Bohemian Grove and the New World Order, who love to sow chaos and mislead people before they take total control. In 2004 the media continued to play up terrorism but never gave the American public the truth about what was really happening in Iraq and the Middle East. The covert purpose for playing the terrorism card was to get George W. Bush, an approved Skull and Bones, New World Order puppet, reelected.

The shadow government wants BPL to become an integral part of every home's wiring. Every home computer in America will be linked to a central monitoring station. Furthermore, each electrical device in a home has its own "signature" of power strength and usage. Thus agents from New World Order groups will know when family members are and are not on their computers, when they leave the house, and when they return. These electronic snoopers will know when and for how long family members use every electrical device in the house—when the water heater clicks on, when the doorbell rings, when the telephone is answered. Such BPL information will assist the government to control everyone and will assist New World Order–approved industries to determine the general population's purchasing decisions so that they can adjust marketing strategies.

Depending on how interested the government is in certain individuals, BPL and other technological applications will also provide spy access to their computers' hard drives so that tech experts can find out exactly how and when someone used a computer from the first day he or she owned it. (Every keystroke over the life of a computer may remain in its hard drive.) The shadow government can also access someone's computer to place files in it that make it look like as if that individual is illegally using the computer for child pornography or sending threatening emails, then arrest them.

An individual's cell phone traces everywhere he or she goes through global positioning technology, as well as everyone to whom he or she spoke. Every call an individual makes can be completely monitored if the government so desires. The only way the shadow government cannot trace your whereabouts at all times is if you take your cell phone's battery out when you are not using it.

J

HRH
JACK THE RIPPER

According to some researchers, the always morbidly fascinating Jack the Ripper was a member of the British royal family.

Although even the number of murders attributable to the infamous Jack the Ripper is debated—the count runs as high as fifteen—there is a general consensus that the series of slayings began in the White Chapel district of London's East End with the murder of Mary Ann Nichols on the night of August 31, 1888, and ended nine weeks later with the gruesome slaughter of Mary Jeanette Kelly.

Mary Ann Nichols was found lying across a gutter, repeatedly slashed by someone with a long-handled knife and a general knowledge of anatomy. A week later Annie Chapman was found in a backyard, her head nearly severed. A few nights later the Ripper was interrupted in his attack on a local celebrity known as Long Liz by a man who drove a pony cart into the yard. The pony shied at the fleeing figure of Jack, and the driver jumped down from his seat to lift the woman's head. Blood poured from the open wound in her throat, and it was evident that she was beyond help. Apparently the intrusion so annoyed the Ripper that within an hour he lured Catherine Eddows into a lonely alley where he could indulge his perverse and deadly passions at his leisure. Jack extracted her left kidney and certain other organs, then wiped his hands and knife on her apron.

The London newspapers ran countless stories speculating about the Ripper's identity. Perhaps he was a demonic butcher, a Polish Jew, an American sailor, a Russian doctor, or one of a host of other suspects—anyone, it seemed, so long as he was not English. Jack, who was obviously following his press quite carefully and enjoying every inch of ink in the papers, countered with a famous quatrain he sent to the *Times*:

I'm not a butcher; I'm not a Yid,
Nor yet a foreign skipper;
But I am your own true loving friend,
Yours truly—Jack the Ripper.

The Ripper corresponded with Scotland Yard as well as the London press. To a per-

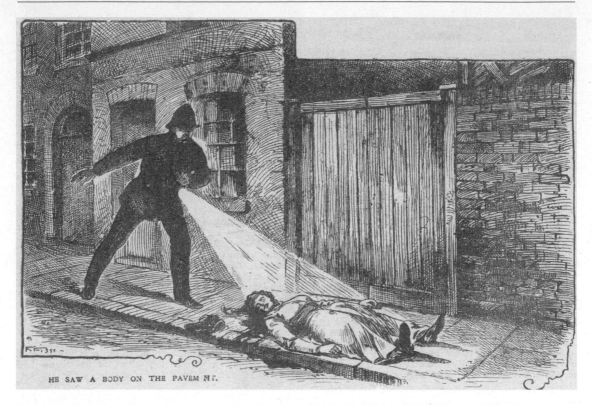

HE SAW A BODY ON THE PAVEMENT.

A nineteenth-century illustration showing the discovery of Jack the Ripper victim Mary Ann Nichols in Whitechapel, England.

sistent police officer, whose investigation was evidently well known to the Ripper, he sent part of a human kidney. "I have fried and eaten the other part," he stated in an accompanying note.

Jeanette Kelly was the only victim killed indoors. She had been heard singing "Sweet Violets" during the evening and had seemed to be in high spirits. Her horribly mutilated corpse was discovered the next morning by a passerby who could look directly into her ground-level apartment. Sir Melville Macnaghten, a Scotland Yard official, reported that the Ripper must have spent at least two hours over his hellish work: "A fire was burning low in the room, but neither stove nor gas were there. The madman made a bonfire of some old newspapers and of his victim's clothes, and by this dim irreligious light, a

scene was enacted which nothing witnessed by Dante, in his visit to the infernal regions, could have surpassed."

The only possible description we have of Jack the Ripper came from someone who saw Jeanette Kelly in the company of a man "about thirty-five years old, five-feet six inches tall, of a dark complexion, with a dark mustache turned up at the ends."

Abruptly the murders ceased, but theories about the now morbidly romanticized Ripper continued to afford challenges for amateur detectives at the local pubs and painstaking police work for tough-minded Scotland Yard inspectors. Someone with a knowledge of surgery always ranked first in the theoretical list of suspects. The second favorite was a midwife who had both familiarity with her victims and a knowledge of elementary surgery. A journalist reported the death of a diabolical doctor in Buenos Aires who allegedly made a deathbed confession that he had been Jack the Ripper, but his claim was impossible to document.

The notorious Dr. Neill Cream, convicted of poisoning four women, shouted, "I am Jack the—" just as the executioner pulled the lever on the hangman's platform and dropped the doctor to the end of his rope. Eager devotees of the Dr. Cream solution to the Ripper legend were disappointed when their investigation revealed that Cream had been in Joliet prison in Illinois throughout the period of the East End murders.

The best-selling crime writer Patricia Cornwell spent a great deal of money attempting to prove her theory that Jack the Ripper was the painter Walter Sickert, an artist whose moody and unsettling paintings generally featured Irish music-hall entertainers and scantily clad women of the night. Alistair Smith, director of the University of Manchester's Whitworth Art Gallery, pronounces Cornwell's theory as presented in her *Portrait of a Killer: Jack the Ripper—Case Closed* (2002) utter nonsense and points out that the art historian Matthew Sturgis discredited Cornwell's research in his own critically acclaimed Sickert biography.

Other recent theories about Jack's identity have even included HRH Prince Albert Victor, Duke of Clarence, the grandson of Queen Victoria. "Prince Eddy," as he was known, was the son of Prince Albert Edward (later King Edward VII) and Princess Alexandra. Prince Albert, "Bertie," was a bit of a rogue, involved in a number of scandals that had to be hushed up by the palace. On the other hand, Alexandra was much like Princess Diana, respected for her public works and much loved by the people. Rumors that Eddy was dull, even retarded, began when he was a child. The boy was also partially deaf.

Prince Eddy was named Duke of Clarence in 1891 and would likely have been king of England if he had not died in the influenza epidemic of 1891–92. At the time of his death, he was engaged to Princess Mary of Teck, who did become Queen Mary.

Although people gossiped about Eddy's bizarre lifestyle, there were no rumors linking him to the awful murders committed by Jack the Ripper during his lifetime. It was not until 1962 that Philippe Julien, author of *Edouard VII,* published the allegation that Eddy and the Duke of Bedford had been responsible for the Ripper slayings.

In 1970 Dr. Thomas Stowell created a sensation when he published an article in the *Criminologist* claiming that Eddy, driven mad by syphilis, committed the murders. In this theory, the royal family was fully aware that Eddy was the Ripper but did nothing until after the double murders of Long Liz and Catherine Eddows on the same night. Eddy was then bundled off to a private mental hospital, but he escaped and committed the gruesome murder of Jeanette Kelly. (Eddy's terrible skill with a knife, so Stowell's theory goes, came from his experiences at dressing deer on the hunt.) Once again, the royal family had Eddy quietly confined in a mental hospital, where he resided until he died of syphilis attacking his brain.

Stowell's conspiracy theory about Prince Jack the Ripper reads convincingly and terrifyingly. To refute such claims, royal records were released that show Prince Eddy was not even in London on the important murder dates.

The forensic psychiatrist David Abrahamsen profiled Jack the Ripper and concluded that Prince Eddy was an accomplice in the murders. Other Ripper theories touching on the royal family have involved Queen Victoria, a secret wife of Eddy's, and elaborate Freemason rituals. Like many other conspiracies that develop a life of their own, that of Prince Eddy the Ripper will no doubt continue to add many branches to the main trunk.

After the fall of Robespierre in 1794, the Jacobin Club in Paris was closed, signaling the end to the Reign of Terror.

JACOBINISM

It has been suggested that far from being the patriotic fomenters of the French Revolution, the Jacobins were pawns of the Illuminati.

In the context of the French Revolution (1789–95), a Jacobin was a member of the Jacobin Club (1789–94), a patriotic group originally formed in Breton and reconstituted as the Society of Friends of the Constitution after the revolutionary National Assembly moved to Paris in 1789. The designation "Jacobin" for the Society of Friends came from their choice of meeting place, the monastery of the Jacobins, the Parisian name for the Dominican order.

In the beginning the Jacobins were generally moderate bourgeois who sought to limit the powers of the monarchy. As they inspired patriotic societies in most French cities, they became more radical, advocating republican ideals, separation of church and state, public education, and universal suffrage. In 1794 the Jacobins, under their leader Robespierre, instituted the Reign of Terror against counterrevolutionaries as well as former allies, such as the Cordeliers and the followers of Georges Danton. The execution of Robespierre on July 28, 1794, signaled the demise of the Jacobins' power, however many times their spirit may have been invoked in later years. The label "Jacobin" is applied today to anyone with extreme liberal tendencies or who promotes radical or revolutionary opinions.

In volume 3 of his *Memoirs Illustrating the History of Jacobinism,* Abbé Augustin Barruel accuses the Jacobins of being aligned with the Illuminati in fomenting the collapse of the monarchy in France. According to Barruel, the leaders of the Illuminist French Grand Orient oversaw the Jacobin clubs and were responsible for orchestrating all the major events of the French Revolution. The revolution, therefore, was not an exercise in democracy, but an illustration of the Illuminati's success in subversive destruction of a nation.

JEFF RENSE PROGRAM

In September 2005 the U.S. State Department named the Jeff Rense Program *the number one conspiracy site on radio and the Internet.*

Updates on conspiracies from all over the planet are to be found daily on http://www.rense.com. Click on the website any day of the week, any hour of the day or night, and read up-to-the-minute news about political intrigue and corruption, secret technologies and black ops, intelligence and espionage, propaganda and mind control, the latest UFO sightings, the erosion of our civil rights, polluted food and water, the New World Order—and the list goes on and on.

Both Jeff Rense's website and his nightly radio program serve as remarkable conduits for a wide variety of news and information that cannot be found on mainstream or alternative news broadcasts. On the air, Rense serves as a "facilitator," drawing the best that each guest has to offer an audience that has grown to become the one of the world's largest on the Internet and the fourth-largest on talk radio. The program's archives are unmatched in broadcast journalism and the website draws over 6 million hits a month. Astonishingly, Rense personally selects and edits every piece of news, information, and data on the site.

The eclectic mix of articles has sometimes provoked angry emails from partisans who feel that their cherished beliefs and dogmas are being demeaned or insulted. The problem arises from the fact that Rense believes in real journalism, presenting as many sides to a news story as the information revealed may merit. A disclaimer that follows each article Rense posts on the website includes these words: "We suggest you don't make 'assumptions' about our official position on issues that are discussed here. We believe it unwise to sweep controversy under the carpet. We also firmly believe that people should not only read material which they agree with. The opinions expressed through the thousands of stories here do not necessarily represent those of Mr. Rense, his radio program, his website, or his webmaster, James Neff. We are not going to censor the news and information here. That is for you to do."

> Rense characterizes these modern times as the "Age of Irrationalism" and bemoans the lack of "pragmatic, critical thinking performed by the mass of America."

A three-time Peabody Award nominee, Rense spent over twelve years as a news director and an on-camera news anchor on the West Coast and in Las Vegas. He was the top-rated TV news anchor in a city in Oregon when he left television. He wasn't burned out. He was just plain disgusted with the way in which mainstream news had been transformed into entertainment. Rather than presenting information, the news media were offering product. He was fed up with having to read what came in on a "pasteurized press wire," dismayed by the increasing willingness to conform to "tabloid exploitation and gore." And he had also come to view television as "the most ruthless and overwhelming weapon of control and influence ever unleashed on the planet, without question."

Rense characterizes these modern times as the "Age of Irrationalism" and bemoans the lack of "pragmatic, critical thinking performed by the mass of America." The greatest cause for concern, Rense comments, is "the loss of our individuality and our ability to critically think about and evaluate what we're seeing and experiencing."

Rense believes that talk radio and the Internet may offer the last real hope for interactive education in the media. "People *listen* to talk radio instead of just staring at it [as they do with television]. Radio is theater of the mind—a classroom of the mind."

In 2011 the *Activist Post* ranked Rense fourth on its list of "The Most Influential People in the Alternative Media." Praising him for building a massive audience "of those seeking the truth outside of the Matrix," the *Activist Post* also complimented Rense for his website, Rense.com, being "by far the best news aggregator covering the Gulf oil disaster and the ... Fukushima nuclear meltdown." Whether one agrees with Rense or not, the creators of the list state that "Rense deserves credit for venturing down the rabbit hole of reality which brings a unique perspective to alternative news."

JESUITS: THE VATICAN'S CHIEF ASSASSINS

Ever since the Counter-Reformation, Saint Ignatius's admonition to his Jesuit order to put on the "armor of God" has been interpreted as a license to kill for the Vatican.

A story is told that Saint Ignatius was seated at the side of a road, looking at the stream that crossed it, absorbed in contemplation when the eyes of his soul were opened and inundated with light. He was able to distinguish nothing with his five senses, but he comprehended marvelously a great number of truths pertaining to the faith or to the human sciences. The new concepts and ideas were so numerous and the light so bright that Ignatius seemed to enter into a new world. The amount of this new knowledge was so great that, according to Ignatius, all that he had learned in his life up to his sixty-second year, whether supernatural or through laborious study, could not compare with what he learned in this one ecstatic experience. In his *Spiritual Exercises,* Ignatius strove to capture, in a series of reflections, examinations of conscience, and prayers, the steps to a mystical union with God.

It has been said that Saint Ignatius of Loyola was dominated all his life by a desire to imitate Christ. In 1540 he received papal approval for a new order, the Jesuits, soldiers of Christ, headquartered in Rome. Although the Jesuits became a major force for the Catholic Church in the Counter-Reformation, Ignatius was more interested in educating young people and establishing new mission fields than in punishing Protestants. He opened many schools during his lifetime and saw Catholic missions begun in Japan, India, and Brazil.

Ignatius was canonized a saint in 1622, and his beloved order remains strong today. It must be understood that when he spoke of becoming soldiers for Jesus, he was referring to the words of the apostle Paul in Ephesians 6:10–17:

Finally, be strong in the Lord and in his mighty power. Put on the full armor of God so that you can take your stand against the devil's schemes. For our struggle is not against flesh and blood, but against the rulers, against the authorities, against the powers of this dark world and against the spiritual forces of evil in the heavenly realms. Therefore put on the full armor of God, so that when the day of evil comes, you may be able to stand your ground, and after you have done everything, to stand. Stand firm then, with the belt of truth buckled around your waist, with the breastplate of righteousness in place, and with your feet fitted with the readiness that comes from the gospel of peace. In addition to all this, take up the shield of faith, with which you can extinguish all the flaming arrows of the evil one. Take the helmet of salvation and the sword of the Spirit, which is the word of God.

The admonition of Saint Paul to be prepared to be spiritual warriors against the forces of evil has been heard by all Christians, Protestant or Roman Catholic, at least once while they attended Sunday school or confirmation class, adult Bible study groups or church on Sunday morning.

Without being too presumptuous, we can imagine Ignatius instructing his new order of priests to be careful out there, Satan lurks behind every bush. The saintly Ignatius was not telling his priests to put a sword to everyone who crossed them or to initiate a great worldwide conspiracy to conquer and control the planet. However, since the time of the Counter-Reformation, beginning when Pope Pius IV sat on the Vatican throne of the papacy in 1560 extending to the close of the Thirty Years' War in 1648, the Jesuits have been the villains in countless conspiracy theories. The following list touches on only a few of the most notable:

- The great overriding goal of the Jesuit conspiracy is to set up a One World Government by controlling the Roman Catholic hierarchy, the pope, and the governing bodies of all the nations in the world.

- Jesuits authored that classic of anti-Semitism, *The Protocols of the Learned Elders of Zion,* in order to stir up hatred of the Jews. The Jesuits had been expelled from Germany in 1872 and from France in 1880. They believed the Jews to be responsible for their loss of power in those European nations, so they began to implement a program of anti-Semitism as a means of revenge.

- Jesuits engineered the Dreyfus affair in France in 1894 in an attempt to ignite a war between France and Germany. Alfred Dreyfus, a French army officer, was falsely accused of handing secrets over to the German government, but he was set up by the Jesuits, found guilty, and sent to Devil's Island for ten years. The controversy over the case split French society in two.

- Jesuits sabotaged and oversaw the sinking of the *Titanic* in 1912 in order to remove a number of wealthy Jews from power. Among those on board the "unsinkable" vessel were John Jacob Astor, considered at the time the wealthiest man in the world; Benjamin Guggenheim, of M. Guggenheim and Sons; and Isidor Strauss, one of the founders of Macy's.

- Jesuits assigned one of their number, Bernhardt Staempfle to tutor Adolf Hitler and to guide the future Führer in the writing of *Mein Kampf.*

- The Jesuit order served as the inspiration for Hitler and Himmler in their structuring of the SS.

- Jesuits cooperated fully with the Nazis in handing over Jews. Especially with the Vichy government in France in 1942, the Jesuits helped round up the Jews for shipment to Auschwitz.

- Jesuits control the Federal Reserve Bank and use its wealth to accomplish secret missions for the Vatican.

- Jesuits established Zionist Israel through their control of the Masonic Jewish Zionists.

- Jesuits secretly funnel money to anti-Semitic right-wing militia groups, as well as to the Ku Klux Klan and the Black Muslims.

- Jesuits within the CIA, FBI, Secret Service, and Mafia assassinated America's first Roman Catholic president, John F. Kennedy, because he defied the pope, the Universal Monarch of the World.

- Jesuits established the network that destroyed the Twin Towers of New York's World Trade Center and attacked the Pentagon in order to provide justification for the crusade against Muslims.

JEWISH DEFENSE LEAGUE

Not to be confused with the Anti-Defamation League's philosophy of nonviolence, the Jewish Defense League vows that Jews will fight back.

The Jewish Defense League (JDL) was founded in 1968 by Rabbi Meir Kahane as a militant group to protect Orthodox Jewish neighborhoods in New York City—by physical confrontations if necessary. Initially the JDL pitted itself against local anti-Semitism, but it soon included defense of Jewish communities everywhere in the Diaspora (the scattering of the Jewish people throughout the world after the Babylonian captivity). The Jewish Defense League should not be confused with the Anti-Defamation League (ADL) sponsored by B'nai B'rith and established by Sigmund Livingston in 1913. The stated purpose of the ADL is to confront anti-Semitism and all forms of bigotry and political extremism through extensive programs and services and a philosophy of nonviolence.

The motto of the JDL was "Never Again," and they openly opposed the opinion that Jews shouldn't fight back when attacked. Such a point of view, they reminded their members, was "sold to the Jews of Europe 65 years ago and the result of the murder of the Six Million."

Mainstream Jewish groups felt that the JDL was too aggressive and extremist. By 2000, the organization had only a few hundred active members.

On December 12, 2001, Irv Rubin, the JDL's international chairman, and JDL member Earl Krugel were charged with conspiracy to commit terrorist acts against Arab American congressman Darrell Issa and against the King Fahd Mosque in Culver City, California. The JDL contends that Rubin and Krugel were set up by rogue elements in the FBI wishing to neutralize the organization by infiltrating it and implicating its members in conspiracies. Since the JDL had been largely inactive for many years, some within the group suspected the FBI of engaging in a bizarre ploy to appear unbiased in their efforts to pursue terrorists after the tragic events of September 11, 2001.

After awaiting trial for eleven months, on the morning of his first scheduled hearing Rubin slashed his throat with a prison-issued razor blade and jumped over a railing to fall eighteen feet to the concrete floor. He lay in a coma for ten days before dying on November 14, 2002. Krugel was sentenced to twenty years in prison on February 4, 2003, but may face up to fifty-five years on a retrial.

Retired police officer Bill Maniaci assumed leadership after Rubin's incarceration and began molding a New Jewish Defense League. In October 2004 an international leadership convention was held in Reno, and an attorney from Boulder, Colorado, Moshe Finberg, was elected to the chairmanship. With the emergence of the New JDL, membership has grown, and the organization now has numerous chapters located across the United States and Europe. It currently focuses on threats to Jewish communities posed by radical Islam and Islamic terrorism.

On July 1, 2005, the prominent Chicago Jewish activist Ian Sigel was named chairman of the New Jewish Defense League. Proclaiming the league alive and well, Sigel underscored the group's rejection of violence as a means of accomplishing its goals but reiterated that the New JDL is the only Jewish group in the Diaspora that will proactively control anti-semitism and threats to Jewish communities.

JOHN BIRCH SOCIETY

Although they once had some influence on the American scene, the John Birch Society couldn't refrain from labeling anyone who disagreed with them a Communist or a member of the New World Order—even U.S. presidents.

The John Birch Society (JBS) was founded in 1958 in Indianapolis by Robert Welch Jr., a retired candy manufacturer from Belmont, Massachusetts, who believed in restoring to contemporary America the values and principles first stated in the Declaration of Independence and the Constitution of the United States. The society was named after John Birch, a World War II intelligence officer and Baptist missionary who was killed in 1945 in China by members of the Communist Party. *The Blue Book of the John Birch Society,* the "bible" of the JBS, was a virtual transcript of Welch's two-day presentation at the meeting that gave birth to the society, its goal, and its motto: "Less government, more responsibility, and with God's help, a better world."

Welch advocated fighting Communism by employing one of the Communists' favorite tactics, infiltrating other groups. He asked members to join everything from the PTA to local political groups, spread the word of conservatism and anti-Communism in those groups, and work earnestly to take control of them. Another JBS strategy that Welch recommended was to organize massive letter-writing campaigns to sway the attitudes of politicians and advertisers. Welch also warned that the real nature of the United Nations was to begin building a New World Order, a One World Government, and he urged all JBS members to hound their elected representatives to abolish U.S. membership in the organization.

By 1961 the JBS claimed to have hundreds of chapters across the United States with over 100,000 members. Their warning that the Illuminati and the New World Order secret societies formed an unbroken link from the French Revolution to the rise of Marxism was nothing new or original, but their claims that top government officials were dedicated Communist agents began to wear out their welcome among Republicans—especially when they accused President Dwight D. Eisenhower of being an agent of the Communist conspiracy. Among others named as Communist conspirators were former presidents Harry S. Truman and Franklin Delano Roosevelt. The conservative writer William F. Buckley Jr., who had been a friend and ally of Welch, termed such accusations "paranoid and idiotic."

JBS influence on American politics peaked in 1964 during the campaign of Republican Barry Goldwater for president of the United States. John Birch members and friends published several widely distributed books that simultaneously promoted conspiracy theories and support for Goldwater. *None Dare Call It Treason,* by John A. Stormer, warned about decay in the public schools and the advance of Communism throughout the world; it sold over 7 million copies. *A Choice, Not an Echo,* by Phyllis Schlafly, worried about the Republican Party's being controlled by elitists and Bilderbergers. *The Gravediggers,* coauthored by Schlafly and retired rear admiral Chester Ward, revealed that U.S. military strategy had paved the way for Communist conquest of the world.

Goldwater lost the presidential election to incumbent Lyndon Baines Johnson. In evaluating the campaign, many JBS members realized that less emphasis on conspiracies and the Communist threat might have made for a more successful fight, and they left the society to form the nucleus of the "New Right."

At the time of Welch's death in 1983, the Birch Society's influence and membership had greatly declined. However, active members claimed that President George H. W. Bush's involvement with the United Nations in the Gulf War and his call for a New World Order had validated their warnings about Illuminati at the highest level in U.S. government.

G. Vance Smith is the current president and CEO of the John Birch Society, presently headquartered in Appleton, Wisconsin.

ALEX JONES

Alex Jones has been a leader in the alternative media for years, exposing a number of governmental subterfuges on his radio program that is broadcast nationwide.

In 2011 the *Activist Post* ranked Alex Jones at the top of its list of "The Most Influential People in the Alternative Media." Since he began his career in Austin, Texas with a public access television program in 1996, Alexander Emrick "Alex" Jones has found himself at the center of many controversies, especially when he accused the U.S. government of being involved in the Oklahoma City bombing in 1995 and the September 11 attacks on the World Trade Cen-

ter. When pressed to describe his political views, he usually answers that he is a libertarian, but he has also identified himself as a paleoconservative and an aggressive constitutionalist. For those in the mainstream of American culture, Jones is a right-wing conspiracy theorist, a description that he personally rejects.

A *Rolling Stone* article by Alexander Zuitchick described Jones as "a giant in America's conspiracy subculture" who makes Glenn Beck and Rush Limbaugh sound like "tea-sipping NPR hosts on Zoloft" in comparison. The same article quoted Michael Harrison, editor of the industry trade magazine *Talkers,* as opining that "when the history is written of talk broadcasting's transition from the corporate model of the 20th century to the digital, independent model of the 21st century, [Alex Jones] will be considered an early trailblazer."

Jones' syndicated news/talk show, *The Alex Jones Show,* is based in Austin and airs via the Genesis Communication Network over sixty AM, FM, and shortwave radio stations across the United States and the Internet. His popular conspiracy websites include Infowars.com and PrisonPlanet.com.

Jones is also a filmmaker, averaging two films a year. Among his titles are *America: Destroyed by Design* (1997), *Dark Secrets: Inside Bohemian Grove* (2000), *Police State 2000* (2000), *9-11: The Road to Tyranny* (2002), *The Masters of Terror* (2003), *A History of Government-sponsored Terrorism* (2006), and *Endgame: Blueprint for Global Enslavement* (2007).

K

JOHN F. KENNEDY, ASSASSINATION OF

Conspiracy theorists agree that anyone who accepts the Warren Commission's "lone gunman" and "magic bullet" theories is living in the Land of Oz.

On November 22, 1963, at precisely 12:30 P.M. in Dealey Plaza, Dallas, Texas, John Fitzgerald Kennedy, the thirty-fifth president of the United States was shot while riding in a motorcade. Less than half an hour later, Kennedy was pronounced dead.

In September 1964 the findings of the U.S. Commission to Report upon the Assassination of President John F. Kennedy, popularly called the Warren Commission, concluded that the shots that killed President Kennedy and wounded Texas governor John Connally were fired from the sixth-floor window at the southeast corner of the Texas School Book Depository. Three shots were fired by Lee Harvey Oswald, who was the sole assassin. Oswald also killed Dallas police patrolman J. D. Tippit approximately forty-five minutes after the assassination. No conspiracy was involved in the death of the president.

The Warren Commission, which included Earl Warren, chief justice of the United States; Senators Richard B. Russell and John Cooper; U.S. Representatives Hale Boggs and Gerald R. Ford; and Allen W. Dulles, former director of the Central Intelligence Agency, concluded that a single bullet passed through President Kennedy's body and continued on a course that allowed it to strike Governor Connally, who, with his wife, Nellie, was riding in the open car with President and Mrs. Kennedy. According to the Warren Commission, a second shot from Oswald struck the president in the head and killed him. The commission also concluded that another bullet missed the presidential automobile altogether—making a total of three rounds allegedly fired from Oswald's bolt-action rifle in an impossible blur of time.

Conspiracy theorists immediately dismissed the so-called magic bullet that the government experts stated had passed through President Kennedy and continued to plow through the back, ribs, right wrist, and left leg of Governor Connally. From the very first days of the investigation, Governor and Mrs. Connally insisted that two bullets had struck the president and that a third and separate bullet had wounded the governor.

On July 3, 1997, former president Gerald Ford, the last surviving member of the Warren Commission, admitted that he had assisted the "magic bullet" theory in the report on JFK's death by altering the commission's description of the gunshot that killed him. According to Ford, the original text said that a bullet had entered Kennedy's back at a point slightly above the shoulder and to the right of the spine. Ford changed the bullet's entrance point from Kennedy's upper back to his neck, thus making the final commission text refer to the bullet entering "the base of the back of the neck." Such a seemingly minor alteration would support the Warren Commission's single-assassin hypothesis, which was based on the "magical" path of a single bullet that was able to pass through Kennedy's neck before striking Connally's back, ribs, right wrist, and left leg.

Skeptics of the "magic bullet" theory and the Warren Commission's final report have always pointed to the famous Zapruder home movie of the assassination and insisted that Kennedy appears hit long before Connally, who continued to hold his hat in his hand, was struck by the remarkable bullet.

Gerald Ford displayed no guilt or remorse about the fraud that he had perpetrated. In fact, he told the Associated Press, "My changes were only an attempt to be more precise. I think our judgments have stood the test of time."

A poll conducted by the University of Ohio and Scripps Howard News Service in 1997 revealed that 51 percent of the American public dismissed the "magic bullet" theory. Nearly 20 percent of those polled expressed their belief that Kennedy was assassinated by agents of the federal government. Another 33 percent maintained that a conspiracy of political insiders was "somewhat likely" in the murder of JFK.

In November 1998 Nellie Connally, the last surviving passenger of the car in which President Kennedy was assassinated, stubbornly asserted the claim that she had made since November 23, 1963: the Warren Commission was wrong about their conclusion that one bullet struck both JFK and her husband. "I will fight anybody that argues with me about those three shots," she told *Newsweek*. "I do know what happened in that car." John Connally died in 1993 at age seventy-five, but he and his wife had always insisted that the first shot hit Kennedy, a second bullet wounded the governor, and a third struck Kennedy's head, killing the president.

The Warren Commission concluded that there was also a bullet that entirely missed the president's automobile. If the Connallys' account is accurate, that makes four bullets allegedly fired with great accuracy—three hits, one miss—from Oswald's bolt-action rifle.

Mrs. Connally remembered that after they heard the first shot, her husband turned to his right to look back at the president and then turned quickly to the left to get another look at Kennedy. When Connally realized that the president and he, himself, had been shot, he cried out, "My God, they are going to kill us all!"

Mrs. Connally also had a clear memory of Mrs. Kennedy screaming, "Jack! Jack! They've killed my husband. I have his brains in my hand."

While Lee Harvey Oswald continues to be the assassin of record and is named in official documents as the lone gunman responsible for the death of President Kennedy, conspiracy researchers have always disputed the allegation that Oswald acted alone and was such an incredible marksman that he could accurately hit a moving target at a considerable distance with the bolt-action rifle allegedly in his possession. Conspiracy theorists insist that there is physical, medical, and ballistics evidence that would force any fair-minded panel of experts to conclude that one person

A scene from the 1991 Warner Bros. film *JFK* depicts the assassination of President Kennedy.

could not have fired so many shots so quickly with such a rifle. Although the rifle had a clip containing a number of cartridges, the bolt had to be manually pulled back to eject the spent cartridge after each shot, then slammed into place again to move a fresh cartridge into the breech. Those experienced with such rifles severely doubted that a steady bead on a target could be maintained with the accuracy shown in the assassination of JFK.

Various students of the Kennedy assassination have amassed evidence that a large number of more likely assassins than Lee Harvey Oswald existed, including Kennedy's own Secret Service bodyguards, the Mafia, the CIA, or Cuban activists.

Perhaps the most popular theory is that President Kennedy was killed by a small group of rogue CIA agents in retaliation for passing National Security Action Memos 55, 56, and 57, which essentially splintered the CIA into hundreds of competitive branches and defused the power that the Agency had enjoyed since its creation at the end of World War II. These rogue agents also enlisted the aid of dissatisfied members of military intelligence and angry Mafia mobsters who felt betrayed by Kennedy when he failed to acknowledge their role in swinging the Chicago vote during the 1960 presidential election.

Another theory that ranks high with conspiracy theorists is that the military assassinated Kennedy in revenge for his refusing to provide air cover for the exiled Cubans and Special Forces members in the Bay of Pigs invasion in 1961. President Kennedy also sought peace with the Soviets and an end to the Cold War, and he had promised to withdraw from Vietnam, ordering the first one thousand troops home for Christmas.

And tying both conspiracies together, seeing that all the pieces of the puzzle fell into place, was the secret government, always working in the shadows behind the scenes, to bring about the ultimate goal—a New World Order, a One World Government.

On February 13, 2005, radio journalist Jeff Rense posted on his website a photocopy of a "United States Memorandum" that appears to be solid proof that Lee Harvey Oswald was trained by the CIA and worked for the Office of Naval Intelligence. The photocopy is stamped "Confidential," dated March 3, 1964, and is addressed to James J. Rowley, Chief, U.S. Secret Service from John McCone, Director, Central Intelligence Agency. The memorandum, allegedly McCone's response to Rowley's request for information regarding Oswald's activities and assignments on behalf of the CIA and the FBI, states in part that "Oswald was trained by this agency, under cover of the Office of Naval Intelligence, for Soviet assignments. In 1957 [Oswald] was active in aerial reconnaissance of mainland China and maintained a security clearance up to the 'confidential' level."

Mysterious rumors and stories about Lee Harvey Oswald continue to swirl about the man's memory. According to some who claimed to have known Oswald before that terrible day in November of 1963, he often spoke of an international league of people who had permitted Satan to possess them so they might do his bidding. The "Devilmen" of whom he spoke were, in effect, a secret world power with members in key positions within each national government.

Many investigators have pondered the strange links between Lee Harvey Oswald, a CIA-trained assassin; airplane pilot David Ferrie, a possible CIA operative; and Jack Ruby, the enigmatic nightclub owner who killed Oswald. A number of witnesses who spoke to investigators concerning the events leading up to the killing of President Kennedy swear that they saw Oswald, or a man looking very much like him, speaking with Ruby in Ruby's Carousel Club in Dallas on a number of occasions before November 23. Several of those witnesses suffered mysterious fatal accidents not long after making such an identification.

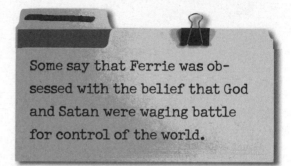

Some say that Ferrie was obsessed with the belief that God and Satan were waging battle for control of the world.

Ferrie, according to some Oswald-Kennedy assassination buffs, may have been employed by the CIA as a U-2 spy plane pilot. Loss of body hair was rumored to be a hazard of flying the U-2, allegedly from radiation levels at high altitudes, and Ferrie wore a garish red wig and bemoaned the absence of his body hair. It is also known that before he became a commercial pilot, Ferrie had studied for the priesthood. He had been dismissed from Eastern Airlines because of an arrest record for homosexual activities. Later he posed as a psychiatrist, worked as a private detective, and hired out for various jobs connected with aviation until he became Oswald's instructor in the Civil Air Patrol in New Orleans.

According to certain witnesses, Ferrie talked a lot about the occult, hypnotism, and politics in the years before the assassination of JFK. Oswald seemed to be an eager listener as Ferrie talked about demonology, witchcraft, and the power of the mind. Some say that Ferrie was obsessed with the belief that God and Satan were waging battle for control of the world. One of his favorite topics was how the priests in the Spanish Inquisition had merely driven Satan and his demons underground. Ferrie claimed that the devil and his minions would appear in their own time as a demonic evil horde.

On November 22, 1963, word reached District Attorney Jim Garrison in New Orleans that the FBI had found Ferrie's library card in Oswald's wallet shortly after they apprehended the assassin in Dallas. Although this bit of intelligence would certainly suggest that the two men knew each other, strangely enough, the library card was not in Oswald's effects checked in by the Dallas police.

Shortly after the assassination, numerous individuals remembered that they had seen Oswald and Ferrie at several ritual parties in the Quarter—private affairs where circles were drawn on the floor, black candles lighted, and chickens and small animals sacrificed. Oswald and David Ferrie were undoubtedly a strange pair—a young ex-Marine who had defected to the Soviet Union, then returned to his native America with a beautiful Russian wife, and a nervous, hawk-faced, hairless man with false eyebrows and a weird red wig.

Many analysts of the official scenario of the day of death in Dallas have pointed out how Oswald behaved in a foolish, irrational manner after the murder of Kennedy. Some have remarked that he appeared to be under some sort of hypnotic control, such as that depicted in the motion picture *The Manchurian Candidate.* When such an observation is made, the investigators remind us of the friendship between Oswald and Ferrie and the latter's proficiency as a hypnotist.

Jack Ruby, the pudgy Dallas nightclub owner who shot down Oswald on live network television, scored a successful prediction of his own fate when he stated that he would die in jail. A fervent believer in astrology who relied on his daily horoscope as if it were Holy Writ, Ruby enjoyed having the showgirls in his club read aloud to him from books on the occult. It has been reported that his two favorite topics of conversation shortly before the terrible events of November 22, 1963, were demonic possession and the influences of the new hallucinogens on the human mind.

In 1970, conspiracy researchers began circulating a photocopied manuscript entitled *Nomenclature of an Assassination Cabal,* by William Torbitt. Among the document's assertions condemning those involved in the murder of JFK are the following:

- The assassination was carried out by FBI director J. Edgar Hoover's elite Division Five.

- NASA and a little-known group headed by Wernher von Braun, Defense Industrial Security Command, had a part in the assassination.

- The same cabal had unsuccessfully planned the assassination of Charles de Gaulle in 1962.

- If the lone-gunman theory failed, the cabal had deceptions in preparation that would blame the anti-Castro groups in Florida or Fidel Castro himself.

- Lyndon B. Johnson, John Connally, and Clay Shaw, a New Orleans businessman with alleged CIA connections, were involved in the plot.

More recent surveys regarding public attitude toward the Warren Commission's 1964 findings indicate that only 11 percent of Americans accept the commission's decision that there was no conspiracy involved in the events that transpired in Dealey Plaza on November 22, 1963. Among the reasons people reject the commission's findings and believe conspiracy researchers' theories are the following:

- The parade route was altered at the last minute, bringing it into Dealey Plaza, where the assassins awaited the president.

- There was limited protection that day for the president because someone had ordered the 112th Military Intelligence Group, an army unit specially trained in protection, to stand down.

- The Zapruder film of the assassination clearly shows JFK's head thrust violently backward and to the left, inconsistent with a shot allegedly fired from behind.

- Lee Harvey Oswald, the alleged assassin, was discovered by a co-worker only ninety seconds after the shooting, calmly drinking a soda on the second floor of the Texas School Book Depository. The rifle allegedly used in the assassination was found on the sixth floor, along with shell casings.

- After the assassination, several people who were in Dealey Plaza stated that they had encountered individuals identifying themselves as Secret Service agents. The Secret Service has repeatedly claimed that it had no agents on the ground in Dealey Plaza at any time that day.

- Numerous witnesses in the plaza stated that their attention was drawn to men behaving strangely behind the picket fence on the so-called grassy knoll, a sloping hill leading to a concrete wall on the north side of Elm Street. Some witnesses who had military experience stated firmly that they recognized the sound of gunshots coming from behind them while they were standing on the grassy knoll.

- Acoustical evidence proves that at least four shots were fired that day in Dealey Plaza.

- Experienced Dallas doctors reported the president's throat wound as an entry wound, meaning that he was shot from in front.

- While Dallas doctors should have performed an autopsy, Kennedy's body was flown back to Washington for a military autopsy.

- News media around the world reported Oswald's guilt, complete with extensive background data on this allegedly unknown assassin, before he was even charged with the crime.

- On May 29, 1992, two former navy medical technicians who witnessed the autopsy of President Kennedy on the night of November 22, 1963, said that the Warren Commission had been supplied with fake photographs and X rays. Jerrol Custer, who X-rayed the body, and Floyd Riebe, who photographed the autopsy proceedings, said that they were told by the Secret Service to keep their mouths shut about what they had seen.

- President Kennedy's brain has never been found.

- Perhaps as many as 120 witnesses or individuals who had knowledge of the Kennedy assassination have died mysteriously.

Over the years, conspiracy researchers have arrived at many theories about who killed President Kennedy and why. As might be expected, there are those who believe that the whole terrible business was orchestrated by the Freemasons. They offer the following as evidence:

- The assassination took place in Dealey Plaza, site of the first Masonic temple in Dallas.

- Dallas is located just south of the thirty-third degree of latitude. The thirty-third degree is the highest degree one can achieve in Freemasonry.

- Mason Lyndon B. Johnson appointed Mason Earl Warren to investigate Kennedy's death.

- Gerald Ford, a thirty-third-degree Mason, was instrumental in suppressing evidence of a conspiracy that reached the commission.

- J. Edgar Hoover, another thirty-third-degree Mason, provided carefully censored information to the commission.

- Former CIA director and Mason Allen W. Dulles was responsible for bringing the Agency's information to the panel.

The passing years have only continued to stir up more theories concerning that fateful day in Dealey Plaza. Dr. Neville Thomas Jones, Ph.D., has woven a conspiracy involving the Zionists. According to Dr. Jones, President Lyndon Johnson and Jacqueline Kennedy were secret Zionist Jews who conspired to murder President Kennedy at the exact spot on the parade route where Abraham Zapruder, also a Zionist, stood ready with his camera to capture the moment of JFK's assassination. Mrs. Kennedy, Dr. Jones's research reveals, murdered her husband with a single shot .41 caliber derringer, a weapon that she could easily conceal on her person.

Other theorists continue to establish Lee Harvey Oswald's innocence in the plot to assassinate President Kennedy and maintain that the troubled individual was only a patsy to a much broader conspiracy. Judyth Vary Baker (née Judyth Anne Vary) waited thirty-eight years after the assassination in Dallas to declare that she was a friend and lover of Oswald and to state that he was the scapegoat in a CIA/Mafia conspiracy to kill Kennedy. Her silence had been enforced, she claims, by threats to eliminate her if she talked. An examination of the list of witnesses on the Kennedy Death List persuaded her to maintain her silence for decades.

Born in South Bend, Indiana, in 1943, Judyth Vary became a bright student in school; and in 1961, at seventeen, she was invited to be the first high school student to the elite Science Writer's Cancer Research Seminar. A few months later, Judyth was conducting cancer research in the laboratory of Dr. Alton Ochsner. In 1963, she was working in a New Orleans laboratory, assigned a top secret project to develop a bioweapon to assassinate Cuban leader Fidel Castro. Soon, Judyth was invited to gatherings funded by right-wing politicians and oil barons, as well as David Ferrie, Clay Shaw, Guy Bannister, and Lee Harvey Oswald. Oswald took a protective interest in Judyth, and even though he was married, they entered into a love affair. Both she and Oswald worked in an office at Reily's Standard Coffee Company as a cover for their secret projects. Judyth moved to Florida the same week that Oswald moved back to Dallas. After the assassination of the president, she protested that Oswald was innocent. Almost at once, her promising research career was suddenly terminated.

In 2003 British television producer Nigel Turner's *The Men Who Killed Kennedy* was aired in England and on the History Channel in the United States. The episode entitled "The Love Affair" was dedicated to Judyth's account of her love affair with Oswald and her declarations of his innocence. Shortly after the airing of the series, an anonymous source purchased rights from the History Channel which prevented "The Love Affair" from ever being shown again in the United States. A lengthy interview with Judyth Vary Baker with Jim Marrs, author of *Crossfire: The Plot that Killed Kennedy,* is available on www.jfkmurdersolved.com.

In April 2011, the Internet was abuzz with claims that on November 12, 1963, just ten days before his assassination, JFK wrote a memo demanding that the CIA show him the highly classified documents that had been collected regarding UFOs. In a second memo directed to the NASA administrator, President Kennedy suggested that he should meet with officials in the Soviet Union and discuss mutual problems concerning outer space. Both of these previously classified documents had been released under the Freedom of Information Act to William Lester, a teacher who was researching a new book about Kennedy. After reading the memos, Lester theorized that JFK was concerned that the leaders of the Soviet Union might interpret certain actions of the UFOs as hostile and might conclude that they were a secret U.S. weapon.

UFO researchers stated that the memos revived the claims that had surrounded the so-called "burned file," which a whistleblower who had worked for the CIA recovered from a fire set by the agency to burn some of its most sensitive files. The first page of the document is said to carry a message from CIA Director James Angleton stating that "Lancer" (the Secret Service's code name for JFK) had made inquiries regarding classified UFO investigations that the CIA could not permit to be answered. Many UFO conspiracists conclude that such a directive resulted in a CIA hit squad assassinating President John F. Kennedy.

ROBERT F. KENNEDY, ASSASSINATION OF

Sirhan was programmed by occult "Masters" to be the "slave" who would kill Senator Robert F. Kennedy.

When Robert F. Kennedy was on the campaign trail in 1968, unimaginative and thoughtless journalists asked him an obvious question over and over again: with the dark memory of the assassination of his brother President John F. Kennedy in November 1963 ever-present in the public consciousness, did Robert ever worry that he too might be killed by an assassin? Kennedy, a man of faith and optimism, often replied wryly that anyone who really wanted to get him probably could, but that he preferred to live his life in the hope of serving his country, not in fear.

On June 5, 1968, the first anniversary of the Six-Day War between Israel and Egypt, Robert Kennedy's grimly fatalistic words came to pass when he was gunned down in the kitchen of the historic Ambassador Hotel on Wilshire Boulevard in Los Angeles, just minutes after winning the California Democratic primary election. His assassin was a thin, dark-haired young Arab who shouted, "Kennedy, you son of a bitch!" as he fired a .22 revolver at least eight times. Kennedy was hit twice in the head and twice in the armpit.

Sirhan Sirhan makes his (unsuccessful) case for parole in this 2011 photograph.

Paul Schrade, Kennedy's speechwriter, was shot in the forehead. William Weisel, Ira Goldstein, Erwin Stroll, and Elizabeth Evans were also hit by bullets from the assassin's revolver. All survived their injuries except Kennedy, who died at 2 A.M., June 6, at Good Samaritan Hospital.

Once the police had the assassin in custody, he refused to give his name, saying that he preferred to remain incognito. However, once at the police station, the young Arab talked about everything, it seemed, but the terrible act he had just committed. He spoke philosophically about the nature of justice; he displayed his financial acumen by discoursing on the stock market; he proved he was literate in conversing about Harper Lee's *To Kill a Mockingbird*; he demonstrated that he was not ignorant about crime and murder by discussing several homicide cases that had occurred in Los Angeles. When a policeman challenged him to give his name by accusing him of being ashamed, the slightly built assassin snapped that "hell, no," he was not.

Soon enough, the authorities learned that the murderer was Sirhan Bishara Sirhan, an

Arab Christian born in Jerusalem on March 19, 1944. Before the Sirhan family immigrated first to New York, then California, in 1956, the twelve-year-old boy had already witnessed a great amount of bloodshed and bodies torn by bombs in the guerrilla war between Israel and Palestine. After a year in America, Bishara deserted his family and returned to Palestine, but Mary Sirhan and her other children all got jobs and remained in California. Growing to a height of only five feet five and weighing 120 pounds, Sirhan for a time aspired to become a jockey but concluded that he didn't have the nerve such an occupation required.

As an Arab Christian, Sirhan found no appeal in Islamic militancy, but he was devastated when one of his heroes, the Egyptian leader Gamal Abdel Nasser, and the armies of Egypt and several other Arab countries were easily defeated by Israel in the war that began on June 5, 1967, and ended on June 10. It was at this time that Sirhan found solace in the occult. He managed to get a part-time job at a Pasadena occult bookstore and while there read all the books on self-hypnotism, astral projection, and mind control that he could not afford to buy. In May 1968 he joined the Rosicrucians, an occult order that claims to be connected to the ancient priests of Egypt and the mystical society formed by Christian Rosenkreuz in Germany circa 1460.

Sirhan also began to write in his journal that he wanted to kill Robert F. Kennedy and that his death had become an obsession with him. Apparently his motive was to assassinate RFK before he could become president and send bombers and other assistance to Israel.

Sirhan's defense team, all of whom took the case pro bono, was headed by Grant Cooper and Russell Parsons. Emile Zola Berman was added the day before trial began because Cooper felt having a Jew join the team might deflect some of the political overtones. Sirhan was not pleased with his attorneys' defense on grounds of "diminished mental capacity."

When Sirhan took the stand, he told the courtroom how much he had loved President John Kennedy. Furthermore, he said that he had absolutely no memory of killing JFK's brother, but he remembered that he had been angry with the younger Kennedy's breaking his promise to give the Arabs back their home in Israel. Questioned repeatedly, Sirhan denied ever wanting to kill Robert Kennedy. He said that he did not recognize the journal that the prosecution claimed was his or recall ever writing about a plan to kill RFK. As the prosecution continued its case, Sirhan conceded that he must have killed Robert Kennedy, but he had no knowledge of doing so.

A parade of psychiatrists pronounced Sirhan to be suffering from "paranoid psychosis," acting in a dissociated state, even killing Kennedy out of a repressed Oedipus complex. Dr. Bernard Diamond testified that he had hypnotized Sirhan several times, and he concluded that Sirhan had likely hypnotized himself and created self-induced trances that led to the assassination. During Sirhan's Rosicrucian and self-hypnosis experiments, he had gradually been programming himself to kill RFK.

On April 17, 1969, Sirhan was found guilty of first-degree murder and sentenced to death in the gas chamber. In 1972 California abolished the death penalty, and Sirhan is now in Corcoran State Prison, where he still insists that he was but a dupe for mysterious individuals who hypnotized, drugged, and programmed him to kill Senator Kennedy.

Some conspiracy theorists have made much out of a brief conversation that Sirhan had with a ghostlike girl in a polka-dot dress shortly before he shot Kennedy, and they have constructed elaborate plots involving several shooters in addition to Sirhan. Some contend that organized crime was behind the assassination. As a Senate Rackets Committee attorney and as attorney general, RFK had certainly infuriated plenty of mob bosses. And then there are theories that Arab terrorists conditioned Sirhan to be their hit man in getting revenge against Kennedy for his indifference to the Palestinians' plight.

> Some conspiracy theorists have made much out of a brief conversation that Sirhan had with a ghostlike girl in a polka-dot dress shortly before he shot Kennedy....

Or could the CIA have exploited Sirhan's fascination with the occult and incorporated mysticism with one of their mind-control experiments? There are some conspiracy researchers who have traced the true origins of the CIA's MK-ULTRA back to the occult societies of Nazi Germany and the early techniques of mind control developed by secret societies and fraternities linked to the New World Order.

Overlooked in the horror of Robert Kennedy's death was a familiar ritualistic element. A few feet from where Kennedy fell after being struck by the bullets from Sirhan's revolver was a large ice cabinet. Scrawled in crayon upon the front of the box was the inscription "The Once and Future King." Although the phrase was never publicly explained, conspiracy researchers know that such shibboleths have been used along with certain ritualistic symbols in other occult-motivated murders. The words do not refer to King Arthur and his magical days at Camelot or JFK and his appropriation of Camelot to describe his modern court. Rather, the inscription heralds the handiwork of Satan, who, in the eyes of his minions both mortal and immortal, is the "once and future king" of Earth, the god worshipped by the New World Order.

Sirhan Sirhan appeared to be in a state of tranquility following the shooting. The enormity of the deed failed to penetrate his consciousness. Author George Plimpton was one of those people in the Ambassador kitchen on the night of June 5, 1968, struggling to disarm Sirhan. Plimpton recalled, as did so many other witnesses to the shooting, that Sirhan had "enormously peaceful eyes." Others wondered if the assassin had been hypnotized or drugged.

After his arraignment, Sirhan calmly asked his jailers to bring him a copy of Madame Blavatsky's *Secret Doctrine*. It has been said that Jacson, the axe-wielding assassin of Leon Trotsky, the defrocked leader of the Russian revolution, contented himself during his twenty years in a Mexican prison by reading from his worn, well-marked copy of Madame Blavatsky's tome. Jacson (alias Frank Jackson, the assumed identity of Jaime Ramon Mercader del Rio Hernandez) remains one of the most mysterious figures in the ignominious annals of assassins. The Stalinists always stoutly denied any political motivation for the crime, and Jacson himself, when questioned about the grisly deed, never confessed to working for Stalin's secret service. While imprisoned, Jacson displayed an incredible array of mental skills and memory feats. He could decipher codes in a matter of minutes and remember long sequences of numbers, words in foreign languages, and nonsense syllables. Although his physical senses were judged to be hypersensitive, when Jacson's pain threshold was tested, he could achieve seemingly superhuman feats. It seems apparent that the New World Order has been effectively selecting its assassins for years.

General Reinhard Gehlen, Hitler's chief of intelligence against Russia, was pulled out of the defeated German ranks by the Office of Strategic Services (OSS) in 1945 and taken to Washington to help William "Wild Bill" Donovan and Allen Dulles shape the Office of Central Intelligence, the future CIA. General

Gehlen also brought papers detailing Dr. Josef Mengele's research in genetic engineering and behavior modification, as well as the experiments carried out at Dachau with prisoners placed under hypnosis and hallucinogenic drugs such as mescaline. The Nazi research inspired MK-ULTRA, a CIA program that followed the efforts of Project Chatter, created in response to the Soviet's supposed success with "truth drugs," Project Bluebird, fashioned to discover mind-control methods, and Project Artichoke, designed to utilize hypnosis and drugs as tools that would enable agents to resist interrogation.

Then there was Project Spellbinder. Although it was officially abandoned in 1964, various German doctors, veterans of the concentration camps, and shadow government operatives continued to develop this program, which was established to create "sleeper assassins" in the style of a "Manchurian Candidate," an assassin who has been programmed to kill upon receiving a key word or phrase while in a posthypnotic trance. Drawing upon their own background with occult secret societies, the "Spellbinders" conducted a satanic ritual while they were programming a subject to become an assassin. The goal of the ritual was to attach a demon or a group of demons to the entranced subject. The skeptic might say that the programmers were compartmentalizing the subject's mind into multiple personalities to reinforce the command to kill. In either event, the programmed assassin would believe that he was possessed by a demon or by a spirit who was guiding him and ordering him to kill. Norma Lee Browning of the *Chicago Tribune* learned that before Sirhan Sirhan's trial began, his defense team was considering arguing that he had been possessed by the spirit of an Arab terrorist.

As Sirhan went through his Rosicrucian programming and worked at the occult bookstore, it would have been a simple matter for Spellbinder agents to contact him, make friends with him, and invite him to participate in their metaphysical studies. And once Sirhan had attended a number of meetings and been conditioned to assassinate Kennedy, all memory of his having attended the sessions would be erased from his mind.

According to conspiracy researchers, during the satanic ritual employed with the process of hypnotic conditioning and the occasional use of LSD, Sirhan would have come to consider himself the slave of the programmer, who would have the status of "master" or "god." During his interrogation by the police, Sirhan mentioned the Illuminati three times and referred to "Master Kuthumi." Kuthumi (or Koot Hoomi) was Madame Blavatsky's spirit teacher, but Sirhan's programmer may also have assumed this identity during the conditioning process.

Some investigators theorize that the key or "trigger" phrase for Sirhan may have been *port wine,* since these words are scrawled numerous times in his journal along with "RFK must be assassinated," written over and over until it fills the page. It was learned that Sirhan used candles and mirrors during his personal experiments with self-hypnosis. Spellbinder would soon have acquired this information and used it in their own programming sessions.

On the fateful night of June 6, 1968, Sirhan would have crossed the lobby of the Ambassador Hotel, with its bright lights and mirrors, entered the kitchen, heard an agent, perhaps disguised as a waiter, shout, "Port wine!" and pulled the trigger of his .22 revolver eight times, assassinating Robert F. Kennedy precisely as planned.

In March 2011, Sirhan Sirhan, sixty-seven and serving life in prison, was denied parole because, according to the panel hearing such requests, he had not displayed sufficient remorse for the murder of Robert Kennedy. Interestingly, Sirhan's lawyers, William F. Pepper and Laurie Dusek, attempted to have new evidence admitted that restated their client's forty-year-old claim that he had been manipulated by a mysterious young woman in a polka dot dress. Under hypnosis, Sirhan claimed to remember how she had led him into the area where Kennedy would pass and pinched him on the shoulder when the presidential candidate appeared.

Sirhan said that he was fascinated by the young woman's looks and that she was a "seductress" with whom he was "consumed." The pinch on the shoulder acted as a trigger mechanism, and under the woman's spell he believed himself to be on a firing range shooting at targets. He did not realize that he held a gun or that he was shooting at anyone, let alone Robert Kennedy.

In addition to the hypnotic trigger argument, Pepper and Dusek claimed that before Sirhan's trial, an unidentified person switched a bullet before it was placed in evidence. The bullet was taken from Robert Kennedy's neck, they said, citing alleged forensic evidence, but it did not match those taken from Sirhan's revolver.

JOHN F. KENNEDY JR., DEATH OF

The world was shocked when John F. Kennedy Jr., his wife, and his sister-in-law were killed in an airplane that Kennedy was piloting. Few people were surprised when the conspiracy theorists began declaring that the crash was no accident.

John Fitzgerald Kennedy Jr., the son of assassinated president John Fitzgerald Kennedy, was America's golden boy. Whether one was Democrat or Republican, liberal or conservative, straight or gay, right-handed or left-handed, it had to be admitted that this young man was handsome, charming, articulate, and relatively gossip-free. Anyone watching his easy, diplomatic handling of the press (while his lovely bride, Carolyn, got flustered by the media attention and ran for cover) marked young John as a powerful potential political force should he ever decide to run. He

had won most of America's heart in childhood as little three-year-old John-John saluted the flag-draped coffin that bore his father to Arlington Cemetery in November 1963. There was little doubt that he could also win at the voting booths on election day.

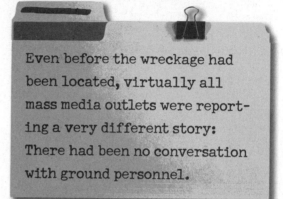

Even before the wreckage had been located, virtually all mass media outlets were reporting a very different story: There had been no conversation with ground personnel.

According to a number of conspiracy theorists, it was that Kennedy charisma—and the possibility that he was shortly going to reveal his political ambitions—that cost John Jr. his life.

Sherman H. Skolnick, a conspiracy theorist and writer of long standing, has said that the Kennedy family knew that on August 1, 1999, John Jr. planned to announce his decision to run for president. According to Skolnick's sources, the Kennedys warned John that the U.S. Secret Service would not be able to protect him any better than they did his father. However, where John Jr. made his gravest error was in taking certain members of Al Gore's presidential campaign into his confidence. John's naiveté regarding dirty political in-fighting did not allow him to see just how dramatically an attractive, articulate young man wearing the Kennedy mantle would upset the political ambitions of Gore as well as those of the Texas governor, George W. Bush.

Skolnick reported that one of his most reliable sources told him that Caroline Kennedy Schlossberg, John's sister, warned her brother that to run for president would be like signing his own death warrant. Nevertheless, she said that she would support his decision.

On July 16, 1999, Kennedy, flying his own plane with his wife and his sister-in-law, Lauren Bessette, aboard was on approach to Martha's Vineyard with an eight-mile visibility. He calmly radioed the ground and told them that he would be dropping off a passenger (Lauren), then resuming the flight to Hyannis airport. In the next few minutes, according to news reports, Kennedy's plane went into a steep dive and crashed into the ocean.

Even before the wreckage had been located, virtually all mass media outlets were reporting a very different story: There had been no conversation with ground personnel. In fact, it was reported that Kennedy had not used his radio at all. The eight-mile visibility gave way to statements that Martha's Vineyard had been completely blanketed with a fog and haze so thick that any pilots in the air would have been unable to see a thing and would have had to rely on instruments.

Reports swirled through the media that JFK Jr. had been lost, disoriented, flying in difficult conditions far beyond his experience as a pilot. However, Boston's WCVB-TV News stated that Kennedy had radioed his approach to Martha's Vineyard and that radar showed his plane just where he said it was and at the correct altitude for an approach.

False reports continued to appear in the media:

Kennedy stalled the plane.

The radar track showed he was well above stall speed.

Kennedy went into a steep turn and lost his horizon in the pea-soup fog.

There was absolutely no reason for him to go into a steep turn; he was already lined up with the main runway.

Kennedy lost his instruments, and in the heavy haze and darkness he grew confused about his altitude and flew into the ocean.

The radar received good data from his encoding altimeter. All the instruments in Kennedy's airplane were operating properly.

It was well known that Kennedy was a reckless pilot.

Individuals actually familiar with JFK Jr.'s aeronautical abilities stated that he was a careful and skilled pilot.

JFK Jr. had only forty air hours as a pilot.

Kennedy had forty hours in that particular aircraft. His total experience was about three hundred hours—more than enough, according to the FAA, to qualify for a commercial pilot's license.

Sherman Skolnick states that he and certain of his associates obtained the details of a secret FBI report that revealed the truth: that JFK Jr.'s plane had been sabotaged by a bomb. The report, which was to have been sealed for thirty years, supposedly detailed the steps involved in the cover-up. "Within 48 hours of the time the FBI knew we had their secret report," Skolnick said, "they mysteriously announced, without explanation, that henceforth all public visits would be cancelled to the Bureau's headquarters in Washington, D.C. They claimed unspecified 'terrorists' were threatening them."

Conspiracy theorists are firm in their conviction that John F. Kennedy Jr. was murdered before he could make his announcement on August 1, 1999, that he would run for president. If he had lived and won the election, he would have been forty years old, just slightly younger than his father when he ran for president.

KENNEDY DEATH LIST

Those who remain convinced that the JFK assassination was part of a much larger conspira-

cy also remain convinced that as many as 120 individuals have suffered "highly coincidental" or "convenient" deaths for knowing too much about that dark day in Dallas when the president was murdered.

Some conspiracy theorists enumerate some 120 individual deaths associated with the assassination of President John F. Kennedy that they label as "convenient" or "highly coincidental." As with all of the body counts or death lists that we include in this encyclopedia of conspiracies and secret societies, we add our disclaimer that many of the individuals that we find on such lists may have been elderly, suffered from long-term illnesses, killed in the line of duty, met their demise in accidents totally devoid of nefarious circumstances, or committed suicide of their own free, albeit troubled, will. Conspiracy researchers remind us that the CIA and other secret government agencies have developed means of making murders appear to be deaths due to natural causes or accident. Some of these methods are designed to be able to avoid detection in autopsies and postmortem examinations. Various insidious techniques involve the injection of cancer cells, heart attack inducements, and absorption of deadly, untraceable poison. There are some deaths on these lists that do seem quite suspicious, and that is why we include them for your own assessment.

Karyn Kupcinet, November 1963: The murder of popular Chicago television personality Irv Kupcinet's daughter Karyn is firmly established in Kennedy assassination lore. According to reports, Karyn, twenty-three, was trying to make a long-distance call from Los Angeles when the operator heard her scream that the president was going to be assassinated. She was found murdered in her apartment two days after Kennedy's death.

Jack Zangretti, November 1963: Zangretti died of a gunshot wound after he claimed a foreknowledge of Jack Ruby's plan to kill Lee Harvey Oswald.

Eddy Benavides, February 1964: Benavides died of a gunshot to the head. He closely resembled his brother, Domingo, who was a witness to Oswald's shooting of Dallas police officer J. D. Tippit.

Betty McDonald, February 1964: McDonald, a former employee of Jack Ruby, allegedly committed suicide by hanging in the Dallas jail.

Bill Chesher, March 1964: Chesher was suspected of having information linking Oswald and Ruby prior to the assassination of JFK and had reportedly said that he had seen them driving together. Chesher, twenty-nine, died of a heart attack while in the hospital.

Bill Hunter, April 1964: Hunter, a reporter for the *Long Beach (California) Press Telegram,* who had been in Ruby's apartment on November 24, 1963, was accidentally shot and killed by a Dallas policeman.

Gary Underhill, May 1964: Underhill, a CIA agent who claimed the Agency was involved in the assassination, died of a gunshot wound to the head that was ruled a suicide.

Guy Banister, June 1964: Former FBI agent Banister, who had New Orleans connections to the CIA, David Ferrie, Oswald, and local mob boss Carlos Marcello, died of a sudden heart attack.

Jim Koethe, September 1964: Koethe, a reporter for the *Dallas Times Herald,* was killed by a karate chop to the back of the neck while stepping out of the shower in his apartment.

Mary Pinchot, October 1964: Pinchot, a "special friend" of JFK, was killed in a mugging. Her diary was confiscated by CIA chief James Angleton.

Tom Howard, March 1965: Attorney Howard spoke to Ruby shortly after he killed Oswald. On March 27, 1965, he suddenly became ill and was driven to a hospital by an unidentified individual. Within hours, Howard was dead, allegedly of a heart attack. No autopsy was performed.

Mona B. Saenz, August 1965: Saenz, a Texas employment clerk who had interviewed Oswald, was struck and killed by a Dallas city bus.

Dorothy Kilgallen, November 1965: Kilgallen was a well-known newspaper columnist and television panelist who privately interviewed Ruby before and during his trial. Ruby told her that he and Officer J. D. Tippit were friends and that Tippit often frequented Ruby's Carousel Club. Two weeks before the assassination, Tippit and Ruby were in the company of Texas oil man Bernard Weissman, the person responsible for the "JFK Wanted for Treason" ads in the Dallas newspapers on November 22, 1963. Kilgallen told friends that she had enough information to break the whole story of the Kennedy assassination wide open, and she began to leak hints of her scoop in her syndicated column. On November 8, 1965, she was found dead, fully clothed, sitting upright on her bed. The autopsy report, which took eight days to complete, ruled death from alcohol and barbiturates.

Mrs. Earl T. Smith, November 1965: Two days after Dorothy Kilgallen's death, Smith, one of her closest friends and one in whom she was likely to have confided her findings about the JFK murder, was found dead of "undetermined causes."

Karen "Little Lynn" Carlin, January 1966: According to witnesses, Carlin was the last person to speak with Ruby before he killed Oswald. She was killed with gunshot wounds to the head.

Earlene Roberts, January 1966: Roberts, Oswald's landlady in Dallas, was said by friends and other witnesses to have been subjected to hours of police interrogation and harassment. She was found dead of a heart attack in her home. No autopsy was performed.

Albert Bogard, February 1966: Bogard, a salesman for Downtown Lincoln Mercury in Dallas, showed a new Mercury to a man using the name "Lee Oswald." Shortly after giving his testimony to Warren Commission investigators, he was hospitalized after being badly beaten. Released from the hospital, Bogard returned to his hometown of Hallsville, Texas. He was found dead in a local cemetery in an automobile with a hose attached to the exhaust. The autopsy ruling was suicide.

Lee Bowers Jr., August 1966: Bowers witnessed a suspicious man standing behind the picket fence on the grassy knoll at the time of the JFK assassination. He was killed in an automobile accident.

James Worrell Jr., November 1966: Worrell saw a man run from the rear of the Texas School Book Depository after Kennedy was murdered. Worrell was killed in an automobile accident.

Jack Ruby, January 1967: Ruby told family members that he had been injected with cancer cells, giving him the lung cancer that killed him.

David Ferrie, February 1967: Ferrie, a friend of Oswald's, was struck by a blow to the neck and died of a brain hemorrhage.

Eladio Cerefine Del Valle, February 1967: Del Valle, an anti-Castro Cuban associate of David Ferrie, was killed on the same day as Ferrie by an axe blow and gunshot wound to the skull.

Hale Boggs, October 1972: Boggs, the House majority leader, was the only Warren Commission member who publicly expressed doubt about their findings that Oswald and Ruby were not part of any conspiracy. Boggs accused FBI director J. Edgar Hoover of lying about Oswald, Ruby, and their associates. Boggs disappeared on a flight from Anchorage to Juneau, Alaska, on October 16, 1972. Neither the plane nor any bodies were ever found.

Clay Shaw, August 1974: Shaw, reportedly a CIA contact with David Ferrie for Oswald, was the prime suspect in the case that New Orleans district attorney Jim Garrison was building for a conspiracy in the Kennedy assassination. He died of cancer.

William Pawley, January 1977: Pawley, a former ambassador to Brazil who was connected to anti-Castro Cubans, was found dead of a gunshot wound, ruled a suicide.

George DeMohrenschildt, March 1977: Allegedly a CIA contract agent who was a close friend of the Bouvier family (Jackie Kennedy's parents) and a contact of Oswald's, DeMohrenschildt was found dead of a gunshot would, ruled a suicide.

Lou Staples, May 1977: A popular Dallas radio talk show host, Staples swore that he would break the JFK assassination case. He was found with a gunshot wound to the head, ruled a suicide.

MARTIN LUTHER KING JR., ASSASSINATION OF

When the FBI tried to sell the idea of James Earl Ray as yet another "lone gunman" who had assassinated one of the nation's leaders, conspiracy theorists saw the shadowy hand of MK-ULTRA pulling the strings.

On April 4, 1968, Dr. Martin Luther King Jr. was standing on the second-floor balcony of the Lorraine Motel in Memphis, Tennessee, when he was killed by a single shot from a high-powered rifle. Numerous witnesses said the shot had been fired from a clump of bushes on a slope across the street. The FBI decided that it had come from a rear bathroom window of a boardinghouse, also across the street but a bit higher up the hill.

Within two weeks James Earl Ray, an escapee on the run from the Missouri State Penitentiary, was named as the assassin who had gunned down one of the most charismatic men in the world. When Ray was identified as the sole suspect in the assassination of Dr. King, dozens of serious investigators and researchers protested and pronounced the FBI's conclusions as pure bunk. There was a consensus among many investigators that all roads of inquiry led to a mysterious individual named "Raoul," who appeared to have masterminded the assassination and played Ray as the patsy. However, the FBI felt they had identified their man and followed up on few, if any, other suspects. After he had spent time on the run in Canada and Portugal, Ray was arrested as he was changing airplanes at London's Heathrow Airport for a flight to Brussels.

Less than a year after the assassination of King, Ray, with his attorney Percy Foreman, pleaded guilty before the court of Judge Preston Battle on March 10, 1969. Ray was sentenced to ninety-nine years—and, as if awakening from a bad dream and finding himself in a terrible reality, he recanted, said he didn't kill King, and filed a motion for a trial only three days after being sentenced.

Before the month had ended, Judge Battle was found dead in his chambers, Ray's handwritten motion on the desk beneath his slumped body. Still protesting his innocence, Ray began his sentence in the Tennessee State Penitentiary.

Two years before he died on April 24, 1998, Ray met with members of the King family and convinced them that he had not killed Martin Luther King Jr. Coretta Scott King and other family members believed Ray and joined efforts to get him a new trial in order to prove that there was a hidden conspiracy surrounding King's death.

There is no question that Martin Luther King was not universally loved and admired for his stand on civil rights and other issues. Stories about academic plagiarism, infidelity, and Communist affiliation were widely circulated. Some African American leaders asked him not to come to their communities because they feared that he brought hate and rioting with him. Some Americans of all colors and creeds were disturbed by his comments about the Vietnam War. And, needless to point out, white supremacists were threatened and angered by his speeches encouraging them to accept the American credo that all men are created equal.

King's winning the Nobel Peace Prize in 1964 did little to mellow the mass of hostile feelings against the civil rights leader. J. Edgar Hoover, director of the FBI, was quick to label King "the most notorious liar in the country." All FBI documents concerning King were sealed in 1977 and will not be made available to the public until 2027, thereby intimating that there are facts in the files that someone in the political hierarchy does not wish citizens of the United States to find out.

In 1987, after being imprisoned for eighteen years, Ray wrote an account of his involvement in the King assassination in a book entitled *Tennessee Waltz.* Ray tells of escaping from prison in April of 1967 by hiding in a bread truck. He winds up in Canada after hiding out in East St. Louis, Chicago, and Detroit, and it is in Montreal that he meets a man known to him only as "Raoul." Raoul pays Ray to serve as a courier in a gun-running ring, then instructs him to travel to Mexico and wait for instructions before going on to Los Angeles to see a plastic surgeon for a "nose job" to change his appearance. Raoul also gives Ray enough money to enable him to purchase a pale yellow 1966 Mustang. Finally, Ray receives two assumed names to use in his travels—John Willard and Eric S. Galt—and another on a passport, Ramon George Sneyd. In retrospect Ray wondered if the nose job that he underwent might have been intended to make him look more like one or more of the

"assumed identities," who might have been real people.

A link to MK-ULTRA, the CIA's mind-control project, may have occurred when Ray was recuperating from the plastic surgery. Dr. William Joseph Bryan Jr. had programmed individuals when he was with the air force as chief of Medical Survival Training, the air force's covert mind-control section. Bryan, whom some called pompous and arrogant, liked nothing better than to talk about himself and his accomplishments. He was known as an expert on brainwashing, and he served as a consultant on *The Manchurian Candidate,* a motion picture that portrayed a programmed political assassin. In informal discussions, Bryan "leaked" that he had programmed Sirhan Sirhan and James Earl Ray to commit assassinations and to forget their participation in the act. Bryan died under mysterious circumstances in 1977 when the JFK case was reopened.

In February 1968, after Ray had spent several months in Los Angeles, Raoul ordered him to fly to New Orleans. After a few weeks in the Big Easy, the two drove to Atlanta and planned to drive to Miami, but on March 29 Raoul announced they were going to Memphis. Raoul apparently assumed numerous disguises, as a "blond Latin," a "red-haired French-Canadian," or an "auburn-haired Latino."

After checking into a boardinghouse, Raoul gave Ray some money and told him to buy a deer rifle. After first buying a small-caliber rifle that Raoul rejected as not powerful enough for deer, Ray returned with a 30.06.

On April 4 Raoul tried to send Ray to a movie in an obvious ploy to get him out of the room. Ray was puzzled why Raoul seemed to want him out of the boardinghouse, but he finally agreed to run some errands and get some worn tires changed on the Mustang.

When he returned to the Lorraine Motel, it was surrounded by police cars, and he decided that this was no place for an ex-con on the

The Washington, D.C., monument to Dr. Martin Luther King, Jr. was opened to the public in 2011. The circumstances of this great civil rights leader's assassination are still actively debated.

run. It was while he was heading south on U.S. 61, Ray claims, that he first heard that Martin Luther King had been shot. A few days later he learned that James Earl Ray was named as the number one suspect.

The FBI found only one witness who identified the shooter as Ray: Charles Stephens, who at first denied seeing Ray leave the motel, then, after spending time in jail as a "material witness," decided that it was Ray after all. Stephens's common-law wife, Grace Walden, protested that Charlie was too drunk at the time to have seen anything. She also swore that Ray was not at the roominghouse at the time King was shot. In July 1968 Grace was placed in a mental institution. Upon her release in 1979 she proclaimed that she had been locked away in an insane asylum for eleven years of torment because she had said that it was not James Earl Ray who shot Martin Luther King. And after those eleven years of misery, she still swore that the killer was not Ray.

On December 3, 1998, Jim Green, fifty-four, spent six hours with Martin Luther King's son,

Dexter King, Rev. James Lawson, and William Pepper, Ray's attorney on the appeal. At this meeting Green confessed that he, too, had worked for "Raoul" and had been in on the plot to assassinate King.

As a teenager, Green had joined the Peace Corps and soon found himself contacted by the FBI. Green said that there were two weeks after agreeing to work with the FBI of which he has no memory, but he remembered being a covert agent in the Missouri State Penitentiary and meeting James Earl Ray as a fellow inmate. It seems likely that Green fell under the hypnosis/drug programming of MK-ULTRA in those two weeks missing from his memory.

After Ray escaped from prison, Green was granted early release and came under the control of "Paul," an FBI agent, who became his handler. Green joined a friend, Butch Collier, in a life of petty crimes, working jobs occasionally for the FBI. On the night of April 3, 1968, Paul met the two men in their room in Memphis and gave them $5,000. He told them that they would receive $5,000 more once they had killed Martin Luther King and James Earl Ray on April 4.

At around 3:30 P.M. Green climbed to his assigned rooftop position on an old office building in the next block south of Bessie Brewer's roominghouse on Main Street. He was armed with a .357-caliber rifle. He observed James Earl Ray come and go three or four times from the roominghouse but followed orders not to kill him before King had been assassinated.

At a few minutes before 6:00 P.M. Ray came out of the roominghouse and drove off in his Mustang. By this time, Butch Collier had taken his position in back of the boardinghouse, directly across from the Lorraine Motel. At 6:01 P.M. Green heard the shot from Collier's rifle that killed Martin Luther King.

Moments later, he saw Paul and Collier emerge from the shadows. Paul tossed the evidence into the doorway of Canipe's Amusement Company while Collier jumped behind the wheel of the white Mustang that Paul had driven to Memphis. Paul had intended to dump the rifle in the back seat of a murdered James Earl Ray's Mustang, but Ray had gotten spooked and Green had not been able to kill him. That blew the FBI's open-and-shut murder case of finding the "dead" assassin Ray with the death-dealing rifle in his Mustang's back seat. In fleeing the scene minutes before the assassination, Ray had also escaped the .357 magnum in the hands of Memphis police detective John Talley, whose orders were to kill Ray if Green missed.

Collier drove two blocks up the street to drop Paul off at a parked Memphis Police Department squad car, then headed back to pick up Green. Green tossed the rifle in the trunk with several other firearms, and the two men headed for the Mississippi River Bridge toward Arkansas.

Meanwhile, James Earl Ray was calling his contact, Raoul, to ask him what to do—only to find that the telephone had been disconnected. Paul, the FBI agent, and Raoul, the mysterious criminal with wads of money, were most certainly the same person. Ray was now running not only from the FBI, who had named him Public Enemy Number One, but also, unknowingly, from Collier and Green, who still had orders to hunt him down and kill him.

In 1995 William Pepper, the appeal attorney, published *Orders to Kill,* in which he asserted that Ray had been set up by a hit team of agents of the federal government. On March 24, 1998, the CBS news team of *48 Hours* conducted a blistering attack on Pepper and revealed that his new witness, James Green, had been arrested for "possibly running a methamphetamine lab." Green was held for ten days, then charges were dropped, after the CBS team had left town.

Green put his story on the Internet a few years ago. According to Lyndon Barston, a student of the King assassination, Green knew details that could only have been known by someone who was there on that fateful day when Martin Luther King Jr. was killed.

Jim Green seems to have dropped out of sight. Some reports say that he is deceased. James Earl Ray died in 1998. All records of MK-ULTRA and the CIA's various mind-control experiments were ordered destroyed.

Who really killed Martin Luther King Jr. may remain a mystery until the FBI opens its files in 2027.

KNIGHTS TEMPLAR

The mission of two knights so poor that they shared a horse grew into a secret society whose wealth and power rivaled that of the greatest kings of Europe. Tradition says that their majesty and might were wrought from their possession of the Holy Grail.

The fundamental principle of knighthood was the union of monasticism and chivalry. Before the orders of chivalry, a man could choose to devote himself to religion and become a monk, or he could elect to become a warrior and devote himself to defending God and his lord. The founding of the orders of knighthood permitted the vow of religion and the vow of war to be united in a single effort to free the Holy Land from the Muslims.

The oldest of the religio-chivalric orders is the Knights of Saint John of Jerusalem, also known as the Knights Hospitallers and subsequently as the Knights of Malta and the Knights of Rhodes, founded in 1048, prior to the launching of the First Crusade in 1096. The second of the great orders of knighthood was founded in 1117 or 1118 by two French knights, Hugues de Payens and Geoffrey of Saint-Omer, who had observed the hardships endured by Christian pilgrims en route to Jerusalem and decided to serve as guides and protectors for the defenseless travelers.

When they first began their mission of benevolence, Hugues and Geoffrey had only one horse between them. In spite of their lack of horseflesh, the two warrior-guides soon gained a reputation for their service to helpless wayfarers, and they were joined by seven other knights who admired their principles. Known as the "Poor Soldiers of the Holy City," the nine men bound themselves by the traditional vows of obedience, chastity, and poverty, then added oaths to defend the Holy Sepulcher in Jerusalem and to protect those pilgrims who journeyed there.

Baldwin I, king of Jerusalem, granted the humble knights quarters on the site of Solomon's temple in Jerusalem, and it was because of this location that they became known as the Knights of the Temple of Solomon and later as the Knights Templar or the Knights of the Red Cross. According to tradition, it was also amidst the ruins of Solomon's Temple that the knights uncovered the holy relics that would transform their order of poverty and humility into one of the wealthiest and most powerful organizations in Europe. It is said that the Templars unearthed the Holy Grail of the Last Supper along with ancient documents proving that Jesus and Mary Magdalene were husband and wife. An even more esoteric tradition states that the Templars excavated an underground chamber of the temple that contained the head of Jesus. According to legend, because of the virtue and bravery of the Templars in defending Christian pilgrims, the head spoke and prophesied to them.

At the Council of Troyes in 1127, Saint Bernard of Clairvaux (1090–1153) drew up a code for the Templars and designed an appropriate uniform for the order, consisting of a white tunic and mantle with a red cross on the left breast. Pope Honorius II (d. 1130) gave his seal to the following rules of conduct and discipline for the order in 1128: All knights in the order were required to recite vocal prayers at certain hours; to abstain from meat four days in the week; to cease hunting and hawking; to defend with their lives the mysteries of the Christian faith; to observe the seven sacraments of the church, the fourteen articles of faith, and the creeds of the apostles and Athanasius; to uphold the doctrines of the two Testaments, including the interpretations of the church fathers, the unity of God and the trinity of his persons, and the virginity of Mary both before and after the birth of Jesus; to go beyond the seas when called to do so in defense of the cause; to retreat not from the foe unless outnumbered three to one.

In addition to the strict rules of conduct and discipline, humility was one of the first principles of membership in the Knights Templar. The helmet of the Templar must bear no crest, his beard should never be cut, his personal behavior should be that of a servant of others, and his tunic should be girt with a linen cord as a symbol that he was bound in service.

There were four classes of members in the Templars—knights, squires, servitors, and priests—each with their individual duties. The presiding officer of the order was called the grand master, and he was assisted by a lieutenant, a steward, a marshal, and a treasurer. The states of Christendom were divided into provinces, and over each was set a grand master. The grand master of Jerusalem was considered the head of the entire brotherhood, which grew in numbers, influence, and wealth to become one of the most powerful organizations in the medieval world. Counts, dukes, princes, and even kings sought to wear the red cross and white mantle of the Templar, an honor recognized throughout Europe.

In 1139 Pope Innocent II (d. 1143) granted the Templars an unprecedented mark of papal approval: the churches of the Templars were exempt from interdicts; their properties and revenues were free from taxation to either crown or Holy Mother Church. The Templars now had the prestige of being triumphant Crusaders. They had the blessing of the pope. They had the gratitude of those whom they

An engraving depicting Pope Honorius II giving his approval to the establishment of the Knights Templar in 1128 C.E.

had protected on their pilgrimages. They had vast estates with mansions that could not be invaded by any civil officer. The Knights of the Temple became a sovereign body, pledging allegiance to no secular ruler. In spiritual matters, the pope was still recognized as supreme, but in all other matters, the grand master of Jerusalem was as independent and as wealthy as the greatest king in Europe.

There were three divisions of the Templars in the East—Jerusalem, Antioch, and Tripoli. In Europe, there were sixteen provinces—France, Auvergne, Normandy, Aquitaine, Poitou, Provence, England, Germany, Upper and Lower Italy, Apulia, Sicily, Portugal, Castile, León, and Aragon. A majority of the Templars were French, and it was estimated by the middle of the thirteenth century that as many as nine thousand manors were held by the Templars in France.

The chief seat of the Templars remained in Jerusalem from the origins of the Order in 1118 to 1187, when it was moved to Antioch after the Templars and the Hospitallers were

almost annihilated in the disastrous battle of Tiberias, where the Saracen army under the generalship of Saladin (1137–1193), the sultan of Egypt and Syria, thoroughly defeated the Christians and reclaimed Jerusalem for Islam. Two hundred thirty captive knights were beheaded when they refused the Muslims' offer to convert to the religion of the Prophet.

When the Muslims captured Acre in 1291 and overthrew the Christian kingdom, the Templar knights fought bravely until almost every man was killed. The survivors retreated to Cyprus, which the order had purchased in 1191 from Richard the Lionheart (1157–1199) for 35,000 marks.

Although defeated by the soldiers of the prophet Muhammad and driven out of the Holy Land, the Knights Templar retained their many estates and their enormous wealth in Europe. However, especially in France, the lords, dukes, and princes not only were envious of the order's burgeoning treasury, but they fumed over the Templars' exemption from the burdens of taxation imposed by church and state on others. Rumors began to spread that the order had acquired heretical practices during their time in the East.

> The Knights of the Temple became a sovereign body, pledging allegiance to no secular ruler.

In 1306 King Philip IV (1268–1314) of France sought protection for himself and the royal treasury in the Templars' massive fortress in Paris. Unruly mobs were shouting for his death, and he feared that disloyal nobles would loot the nation's wealth. While Philip was under the Templars' protection, he managed to gain knowledge of the incredible wealth that the order had accumulated. When he realized that this was only a portion of their immeasurable riches and that the Templars had forts and estates throughout France, each containing its own deposit of treasure, he was awed.

When Philip once again sat more securely on his throne, he began to consider the Templars as rivals for his kingdom. They had more money and power than he, and they owed their allegiance only to the pope. Philip met with Pope Clement V (1264–1314) to seek his counsel on how the order might be exterminated. Although the Templars had enjoyed the blessing of the papacy for decades, the pope admitted that he had been made uneasy by accusations that they had sought to protect their own interests by securing a separate treaty with the Muslims when the Christian kingdom in the East was falling. Clement, however, was reluctant to make any kind of move against the knights.

Philip finally found a chink in the Templars' armor in the person of the mysterious Esquire de Floyran, who claimed to have been a mem-

ber. Floyran said that the order had degenerated into a monstrous blood cult. Principal among the demons they worshipped was Baphomet, the three-headed god of a heretical Muslim sect. Floyran swore that he had seen initiates in the order spitting upon crucifixes, participating in vile rites, even sacrificing babies to demons. There is no conclusive evidence to prove whether de Floyran was a member of the Knights Templar or an imposter on Philip's own payroll, but armed with de Floyran's sensational accounts, the backing of the highest church officials in France, and the endorsement of William of Paris, the Grand Inquisitor, Philip demanded that the pope conduct an investigation into such charges against the Knights Templar. Under pressure, Clement gave his approval for a judicial inquiry, and the knights were charged with heresy and immorality.

On the night of October 13, 1307, all of the Templars' castles in France were surrounded by large bodies of men led by priests and nobles. When the unsuspecting knights were ordered to open their gates in the name of the king, they immediately complied. Taken completely by surprise, about nine hundred knights were arrested and all their property and holdings in France seized. When word of the arrests spread, other nobles and priests quickly followed suit and imprisoned the Templars wherever they might be found.

The Templars were accused of infidelity, atheism, heresy, invoking Satan, worshipping demons, desecration of holy objects, uncleanliness, and even of being Muslims. The prosecution was often forced to resort to torturing the prisoners to obtain confessions. In Paris, the grand master of the Templars, Jacques de Molay (1244–1314), pleaded the innocence of the order against all such charges. In spite of his personal friendship with de Molay, who was the godfather of his younger son, Philip ordered the grand master and the 140 knights imprisoned with him to be starved, tortured, and kept in filthy dungeons.

The pope hesitated to give his sanction to the extermination of the knights. Philip, however, was determined to see the Templars destroyed and their wealth distributed to the state. For two weeks, the knights imprisoned in Paris suffered the rack, the thumbscrew, the pincers, the branding iron, and fire. Thirty-six died under torture without speaking. The rest confessed to every charge the Inquisition had leveled against them.

A grand council was called in Paris on May 10, 1310, to review the confessions. But Philip's victory was sullied when fifty-four of the knights recanted their confessions and appealed to government and church officials that they had been tortured. They swore that they had remained true to their vows and that they had never practiced any kind of witchcraft or Satanism. Philip silenced their pleas three days later when he ordered all fifty-four burned at the stake in a field behind the alley of Saint Antoine.

In 1312 the pope convened the Council of Venice, during which it was decided that the order should be abolished and its property confiscated. In spite of Pope Clement's reserving final judgment concerning the guilt of the Templars, and despite 573 witnesses for their defense, the knights were tortured en masse, then burned at the stake. The landed possessions of the order were transferred to the Hospitallers, and their wealth was distributed to the sovereigns of various states. Everywhere in Christian Europe, except in Portugal, where the Templars assumed the name of the Knights of Christ, the order was suppressed.

In 1314, as he was being burned to death on a scaffold erected for the occasion in front of Notre Dame, Jacques de Molay recanted the confession that he gave under torture and proclaimed his innocence to Pope Clement V and King Philip—and he invited them to meet him at heaven's gate. When both dignitaries died soon after de Molay's execution, it seemed to the public at large that the grand master and the Knights Templar had been innocent of the charges of heresy.

In Scotland, the charges against the order were regarded as unproven, and Templars who managed to escape torture and death found safe haven there. Robert the Bruce, Scotland's king, had himself been excommunicated, and he welcomed the Templars' swords alongside those of his men at the battle of Bannockburn on June 24, 1314. Henceforth, Bruce protected the order, and the legendary holy relics of the Templars found their way to Scotland. In 1445 Earl William Sinclair began construction of Rosslyn Chapel, wherein, according to tradition, the sacred objects remain hidden to this day.

Because of the worldwide interest in the Templars and Rosslyn Chapel sparked by Dan Brown's bestseller *The Da Vinci Code,* people are visiting the chapel outside Edinburgh in great numbers. On May 7, 2005, a man claiming to be a descendant of Hugues de Payens, the cofounder of the Knights Templar, asked that electronic equipment be used for an examination of the chapel to find out if the alleged holy relics are really there. The man, an American academician named David Conley, told Liam Rudden of the *Edinburgh Evening News* that he believes the Templars were entrusted with the Holy Grail, the Ark of the Covenant, and a number of ancient scrolls, and that the sacred objects are hidden in an underground tunnel system beneath the chapel, which he said mirrors the design of Solomon's Temple in Jerusalem.

On October 25, 2007, the Vatican Secret Archive published *Processus contra Templarios,* which cleared the Knights Templar of the charge of heresy. The book was based on a scrap of parchment discovered in 2001 by Professor Barbara Frale. Amazingly, the 700-year-old document proved to be a record of the trial of the Templars by Pope Clement V and ends with a papal absolution from all heresies leveled at the warrior monks. The document, known as the Chinon parchment, had been placed in the wrong archive in the seventeenth century.

The Knights Templar were subjected to torture and burning at the stake because their accusers sought to expose their initiation ceremony as blasphemous. After listening to the Templar's explanation, Pope Clement agreed that their entrance ritual was not truly an insult to Christ and the Church. However, in order to keep peace with King Phillip, who had ordered the Knights arrested and subjected to the Inquisition, and to avoid a schism in the Church, he dissolved the Order.

Professor Frale stated that this document proved that the Templars were not heretics: "For 700 years we have believed that the Templars died as cursed men, and this absolves them."

A demonstration of the Know-Nothing Party in New York City. Know-Nothing members wanted to exclude immigrants from the democratic process and were anti-Catholic.

KNOW-NOTHING MOVEMENT

In the 1840s and 1850s, secret societies united to form a movement that demanded stricter immigration policies and the restriction of political office to native-born Americans.

Contrary to popular understanding, there never was an official political organization bearing the name Know-Nothing Party. In 1843 the American Republican Party was formed in New York as a reaction by native-born Americans toward the large numbers of Irish Roman Catholic immigrants who were crowding into the cities on the East Coast. As the organization grew in strength, it changed its name to Native American Party and declared itself a national party at its convention in Philadelphia in 1845. But when hostilities broke out along the Texas border in 1846 and war was declared against Mexico, the Native American Party lost its momentum.

Although no longer a recognized national political party, some members of the Native American group formed secret societies, such as the Order of United Americans and the Order of the Star-Spangled Banner. These societies worked behind the political scenes to ensure that only native-born candidates won state or national offices. When members of older, established political parties attempted to learn more about these secret societies and approached an individual they suspected belonged to such a group, the person being interrogated, true to his pledge, would answer that he knew nothing. Newspaper editor Horace Greeley applied the "Know-Nothing" label to men he knew were undoubtedly members of the United Americans or the Star-Spangled Banner yet professed to "know nothing."

By 1852 the Know-Nothings were gaining strength and forming lodges in nearly every major American city. Many citizens formerly allied with an established political party agreed with the Know-Nothings that there should be greater restrictions on immigration, that the foreign-born should be excluded from voting or from holding public office, and that there should be a minimum of twenty-one years' residency before one could become a citizen of the United States. By 1853 the Know-Nothings no longer saw any need to belong to secret societies and became a national political party with the official name American Party. By 1855 forty-three representatives of Congress were avowed Know-Nothings, members of the American Party.

The following year, at the peak of its power, the American Party was squelched because of a highly publicized split within its own ranks over the issue of slavery. Former president Millard Fillmore, a Whig who refused to join the Republican Party, accepted the nomination for president as the candidate for the American Party in the election of 1856. Fillmore carried only the state of Maryland, and the party's congressional strength plummeted to twelve representatives. Antislavery Know-Nothings joined the Republican Party, and its southern members carried the proslavery banner to the Democratic Party. By 1859 whatever strength remained in the American Party was felt only in some of the border states.

KOCH BROTHERS

Charles and David Koch give more than $20 million a year to make America a better place for ultraconservatives.

Charles and David Koch, owners of Wichita's Koch Industries, are among the major donors in the United States to groups that promote conservative politics. A spokesperson for the Koch family foundation said that the charities that receive a portion of the brothers' largesse are those who promote the causes of peace, prosperity, and social progress. Others qualify the Koch brothers' generosity by saying that they give over $20 million a year to organizations that see the world as the Kochs believe it should be—ultraconservative. The Koch brothers direct three family foundations: The Charles G. Koch Foundation, the David H. Koch Charitable Foundation, and the Claude R. Lambe Charitable Foundation.

David and Charles are the sons of ultra-conservative Fred Koch, the founder of Koch Industries, an oil and gas company, which has grown to become the second largest privately owned company and the largest privately owned energy company in the United States. The brothers have a combined net worth of $4 billion, earning them a position among the fifty wealthiest individuals in America and among the hundred wealthiest in the world. Father Fred was a staunch member and supporter of the John Birch Society, and his sons have continued to found and finance conservative organizations. Charles founded the Cato Institute, and David cofounded and serves as chairman of the board for Citizens for a Sound Economy (currently Freedom Works).

The Koch brothers probably see themselves more as libertarians than as conservatives, for they envision an America where the role of government is very minimized and the role of private economy and personal freedoms is very maximized. David Koch was the Libertarian Party candidate for president in 1980, advocating privatization, entrepreneurship, and free enterprise.

Charles Koch places special attention on being able to develop "voluntary market-based solutions to social problems." His foundation's stated goals are threefold:

1. To support "research and education into free societies to advance the well-being of humankind."

2. To foster "the partnership of scientists and practitioners in order to integrate theory and practice."

3. To develop "market-based tools that enable individuals, institutions and societies to survive and prosper."

The main academic grantee of the Kochs' foundations is George Mason University in Virginia, which between 1985 and 2002 received over $23 million in contributions. In addition, in 1997 GMU received a $3 million grant to establish the Mercatus Center, a research and education center designed to promote free markets and Western values, and in 1998, a $10 million grant to launch the James M. Buchanan Center for the Study of Political Economy.

Some observers of the political scene have expressed concern that the Koch brothers' heavy financial support of conservatism is contributing to a shift to the right in America's policy debates. John Podesta, former chief of staff for President Bill Clinton and now head of the Center for American Progress, has said that the Kochs are harming America by backing policies that have the potential to damage the environment and to place a greater tax burden on the working class. A Koch Industries spokesperson answers such criticism by stating that all the Koch brothers wish is to support ideas that will make for better public policy.

The brothers were a major force in the growth of the Tea Party movement, and in November 2011 it was learned that the secretive oil billionaires were close to making available a nationwide database that would connect millions of Americans who were sympathetic to their right-wing, anti-government views. The database would draw upon the extensive network of alliances of conservative politicians, financiers, business leaders, and media figures that the Koch brothers have cultivated over the past twenty years. Named Themis, after the Greek goddess of divine order, the database of right-wing groups, Tea Party organizations, and conservative luminaries was begun secretly in 2009 with $2.5 million of the Kochs' seed money. According to Koch insiders, the project would be ready to launch in time to be a powerful tool for conservative issues in the 2012 election.

KU KLUX KLAN

The Ku Klux Klan, born in 1865, had nearly died out until Hollywood resurrected it in 1915.

On December 24, 1865, in Pulaski, Tennessee, General Nathan Bedford Forrest and a small band of former Confederate soldiers decided that they had to do something to restore the Democratic Party in the South after the Civil War and to help Dixie shake off the oppressive yoke imposed upon it by Radical Republican carpetbaggers who were taking advantage of the era of Reconstruction by lining their own pockets. And there was the matter of the Federal troops who backed up the Freedmen's Bureau, established by Congress in 1865, in looking after the former slaves. In 1866 the bureau spent $17 million building four thousand schools, a hundred hospitals, and an undeclared number of homes for the blacks who had once toiled in the fields for their food and shelter as enslaved people. Now war-ravaged southern white families were poor and, in their view, were being treated like slaves. Something had to be done.

The name Ku Klux Klan (KKK) comes from the Greek word for "circle," *kyklos,* and the Scots-Gaelic *clan.* Klansmen dressed in white robes because they represented the ghosts of the brave Confederate dead; hoods protected the anonymity of individuals who were performing good deeds for their neighbors. Some researchers have said that the robes and hoods were an imitation of the Knights Templar and a symbol of humility.

General Forrest was the first grand wizard, and he presided at a convention of the Klan held in Nashville in 1866. There was growing concern in the South that elevating the political and social status of the blacks would threaten white supremacy. Southerners especially feared the schools being constructed: the image of the former slaves as educated men and women was not an easy one for them to accept. The Klan set out to curb black education and advancement by fear tactics and violence, and those white southerners who attempted to interfere, especially if they were Republicans, were punished with the same brute force. The KKK became the strong-arm enforcers of the Democratic Party in the South.

As the federal government withdrew its control of the former Confederate states, local white governments reestablished their power and put segregation laws in place. The blacks may have been freed, but they soon found that their freedom had definite boundaries that must be honored.

General Forrest had protested the Fourteenth Amendment, which guaranteed adult male suffrage, and he wished to do everything in his power to stop blacks from voting. Essentially an antebellum southern gentleman, Forrest declared that his main purpose in establishing the Klan was the protection of southern womanhood. However, as the Klan became more powerful and brutal, Forrest was appalled at the violence and hatred perpetrated by the group that he had organized. The KKK had become synonymous with torture, destruction of private property, and even murder. In 1869 Forrest disbanded the Ku Klux Klan.

By then, however, the Klan had become a many-headed monster and had established itself in too many locations to be easily controlled, much less halted. Some Klansmen who cherished a gallant view of the South followed their general's order to disband, but by 1870 the Klan had scattered into dozens of individual groups that paid no heed to General Forrest's order to abandon violent night raids and the practice of organized fear and intimidation.

In 1871 President Ulysses S. Grant made the Klan an illegal terrorist group by signing the Ku Klux Act. The authorization and use of federal force against the Klan destroyed those who wore the hood and white robe in South Carolina and virtually eliminated the nightriders in the rest of the nation. The Klan faded into the shadows. White supremacy and strict segregation laws eventually became firmly established throughout the South, so there was no real need for the White Brotherhood, the Men of Justice, the Constitutional Union

KKK Imperial Wizard Dr. H. W. Evans leads a parade in Washington, D.C., in this 1926 photo.

Guards, or the Knights of the White Camelia to sow death and destruction on a regular basis.

The Ku Klux Klan practically disappeared until 1915 when a preacher named William J. Simmons was influenced by Thomas Dixon's book *The Clansman* (1905) and D. W. Griffith's film adaptation, *The Birth of a Nation* (1915), and re-formed the White Brotherhood.

Ku Klux Klan Timeline

1918: After World War I, the Klan turns its attention to immigrants, singling out Jews, Roman Catholics, socialists and communists, and other "foreigners."

1920: The National Association for the Advancement of Colored People (NAACP) defies the Klan by holding its annual convention in Atlanta, at that time a stronghold of the KKK.

1922: Hiram W. Evans becomes the imperial wizard of the KKK. Under his leadership the KKK grows rapidly and elects state officials in Texas, Oklahoma, Indiana, Oregon, and Maine.

1925: KKK membership reaches 4 million. They are nearly impervious to arrest, much less conviction, in small southern communities.

1944: The organization is disbanded again after a number of Klan leaders are arrested for corruption and murder and the nation weathers first a Great Depression and World War II.

1950s: The KKK is revived when the civil rights movement heads south. Robert Shelton organizes the White Knights of the Ku Klux Klan, and nightriders once again terrorize those blacks who want to vote. Lynching is still used as a method of controlling the black population.

September 15, 1963: A bomb explodes under the steps of the Sixteenth Street Baptist Church in Birmingham, Alabama, injuring twenty-three and killing four girls—three fourteen-year-olds and one eleven-year-old.

October 8, 1963: Robert Chambliss, a member of the KKK identified as the man who placed the Birmingham, church bomb, is found not guilty of murder, fined one hundred dollars, and sentenced to six months in jail for possessing a box of 122 sticks of dynamite without a permit.

Summer 1964: The KKK instigates the firebombing of thirty black homes, thirty-seven black churches, and the beatings of over eighty civil rights volunteers. James Chaney, Andrew Goodman, and Michael Schwerner are murdered by the KKK on June 12 in Mississippi.

March 21, 1981: Henry Hays, son of the second-highest-ranked Klansman in Alabama, and James Knowles abduct nineteen-year-old Michael Donald and lynch him. Local police claim Donald's death is the result of drug deal gone bad.

June–December 1983: Knowles is found guilty and sentenced to life and Hays is found guilty and sentenced to death for the murder of Michael Donald.

February 1987: Morris Dees and Joseph J. Levin of the Southern Poverty Law Center (SPLC) support Beulah Mae Donald, who launches a civil suit against the KKK for the lynching death of her son Michael. The all-white jury finds the KKK responsible and orders it to pay damages of $7 million, resulting in the Klan's turning over all its assets, including the national headquarters in Tuscaloosa.

June 6, 1997: Henry Hays is the first white man executed for a murder of an African American since 1913.

May 17, 2000: The FBI announces that a splinter group of the KKK, the Cahaba Boys (Robert Chambliss, Herman Cash, Thomas Blanton, and Frank Cherry), carried out the Sixteenth Street Baptist Church bombing and the murders of Denise McNair, Addie Mae Collins, Carole Robertson, and Cynthia Wesley.

May 2002: Seventy-one-year-old Frank Cherry of the Cahaba Boys is sentenced to life in prison.

June 22, 2005: Forty-one years to the day that the civil rights workers Chaney, Goodman, and Schwerner disappeared, former Klansman Ray Killen, eighty, is convicted of manslaughter and sentenced to twenty years in prison for each killing.

Today the name Ku Klux Klan has become public domain, and dozens of groups use all or part of the name in their titles.

LYNDON H. LAROUCHE JR.

Perpetual candidate for the U.S. presidency, far-out conspiracy theorist, Lyndon H. LaRouche remains one of the most controversial figures on the international scene.

In 2004 Lyndon H. LaRouche Jr. (1922–) made his fifth run for president of the United States. In that race he ran as a Democrat. In his first run for the presidency, in 1976, he campaigned under the banner of the U.S. Labor Party.

LaRouche is among the most controversial figures on the international scene. To his followers, he has the only ideology that will work in today's world and he possesses economic theories that will turn America around. To his detractors, LaRouche is a mad conspiracist. In his book *Conspiracy,* Daniel Pipes states that the principal theme that has fueled LaRouche's platforms for his many organizations, publications, and presidential campaigns is that "a single oligarchic conspiracy has been bedeviling mankind since the dawn of history. Its headquarters were first in Babylon, then in Rome, Venice, and now London."

LaRouche was convicted on federal conspiracy charges in December 1988 and spent five years in prison. His followers condemn the trial as a "political show-trial," comparable to the case of France's Captain Alfred Dreyfus. On September 2, 1994, testifying before a commission investigating the same case, former U.S. attorney general Ramsey Clark commented that the case represented "a broader range of deliberate cunning and systematic misconduct over a longer period of time utilizing the power of the Federal government than any other prosecution by the U.S. government in my time or to my knowledge."

For years LaRouche's critics have denounced him as an anti-Semitic, eccentric conspiracy theorist whose "cult" of followers borders on preaching fascist philosophy. They point to his claim that the Queen of England is "the number one danger to humanity," his contention that the Beatles were designed and shaped by the British Psychological Warfare Division, and his belief that the Freemasons established the Jewish organization B'nai B'rith as a proslavery spy ring providing intelligence to the South before the Civil War.

At the same time, LaRouche believes that the "sovereign cognitive powers of the individual human mind" are validated by discoveries of physical principles that are "identical in nature with those responsible for the composition of metaphor in great compositions" in classical forms of poetry, music, and art. Science and art are both subjective, rather than objective, and new principles of science and new ideas are born as resolutions of metaphor. These, LaRouche explains, were the lead considerations in his cofounding of the scientific Fusion Energy Foundation during the mid-1970s and his support for his wife Helga Zepp-LaRouche's founding of the International Club of Life and the international Schiller Institute, devoted to the defense of the rights of all humanity to progress—materially, morally, and intellectually.

Matthew Lyons, coauthor with Chip Berlet of *Right-Wing Populism in America: Too Close for Comfort,* told Joe Ireland of the Portland State University *Vanguard* that since the early 1990s the "LaRouchites" have "promoted a kind of faked progressivism. They've opposed both Gulf Wars, attacked the death penalty, and defended social welfare programs and civil rights. But their underlying political philosophy is based on conspiracy theories, not a critique of systemic oppression."

Lyndon LaRouche continues struggling against the grand conspiracy that in his opinion is made up of Zionists, Jesuits, Freemasons, the Rockefeller family, the Rothschilds, environmentalists, drug traffickers, fundamentalist Muslims, orthodox Christians, and the B'nai B'rith.

LEAGUE OF THE SOUTH

No one will ever be able to accuse the League of the South of lacking self-definition or a definite goal.

Without any equivocation, the League of the South (LOS) declares that its ultimate goal is "a free and independent Southern republic." It is the intention of the League of the South to:

- form active chapters in every county in every southern state.

- encourage individuals and families to secede from the "corrupting influence" of "post-Christian" American culture.

- withdraw support of and allegiance to a regime that has imperiled the future.

- withdraw from the public educational system and to establish their own private academies.

- resurrect the southern cultural base.

- seek only political leaders who are truly willing to serve others.

By joining the LOS, according to their website, people will have placed themselves "among a group of men and women who are not content to sit by and allow their land, liberty, and culture be destroyed an alien regime and ideology."

The LOS (first called the Southern League) was founded in 1994 by J. Michael Hill and a group of forty like-minded individuals. Hill felt that of all the many facets, minorities, and ethnic groups within the U.S. population, southerners were the most frequently and commonly denigrated by the dominant political structure in the North. At first, Hill's threat of seceding from the Union was largely rhetorical, a last resort if Yankees didn't start showing more respect to the South.

Within a few years, membership in the league had grown to ten thousand, and Hill's threat to secede from the Union was no longer a rhetorical attention-getting device. The league had come to believe that society is made up of a hierarchy of various groups that should not necessarily have the same rights as others. In Hill's view, the South was basically made up of Christians, and he foresaw a southern theocracy in which public school prayer and all Christian religious observances would be mandatory. Racial intermarriage would never be allowed, although people other than white Christians would still be permitted in his ideal world, as long as they acknowledged the superiority of the Anglo-Celtic culture. Hill and other league members have organized great numbers of Confederate flag rallies and events, and they've show their political clout by orchestrating campaigns to remove officeholders who oppose the flying of the stars and bars from public places.

LOS members have been quoted as saying that slavery in the antebellum South was a good thing. "Where in the world are the Negroes better off today than in America?" asked Jack Kershaw, a member of the LOS board of directors who is also a member of the white supremacist Council of Conservative Citizens (CCC). David Cooksey, a charter member of LOS, has suggested that the South needs a "new type" of Ku Klux Klan.

The LOS has abandoned one of the fundamental tenets of American democracy, that all men are created equal, and states that the "European majority" will tolerate "productive and sympathetic" members of other ethnic groups, but only on terms that the LOS dictates. As Hill has phrased it, the South envisioned by the LOS will be one where "the interest of the core population of Anglo-Celts is protected from the ravages of so-called multiculturalism and diversity."

JOHN LENNON, ASSASSINATION OF

A voice inside Mark David Chapman's head told him to "do it, do it, do it," and in the next few moments, one of the world's most famous rock stars lay dying.

Certainly no sane and rational person can ever understand why someone would want to kill another, but if the assassination of John Lennon, one of the world's most famous rock stars, had occurred in 1966 after the press misquoted him as saying that the Beatles were more popular than Jesus Christ, the crime would at least have had some context. Fourteen years after that confusion and after five years spent with his wife Yoko Ono and infant son in virtual solitude, Lennon was gunned down in front of his apartment building in New York City on December 8, 1980. Ironically, Lennon had autographed his new album, *Double Fantasy,* for his murderer, Mark David Chapman, twenty-five, when he and his wife had first left the Dakota apartments that evening.

Incredulously, the doorman at the Dakota shouted at Chapman, asking him if he knew what he had done. Chapman, having put away the .38 revolver that had slammed four flat-tipped bullets into Lennon's back, now idly flipped through the pages of a paperback edition of *Catcher in the Rye.* He responded to the doorman's angry query by calmly answering that he had just shot John Lennon.

In August of 1966, when the Beatles were in Chicago, an American teen magazine picked up on the interview that Lennon had given to the *London Evening Standard* on March 4 in which he remarked that with the skewed values of the 1960s, the Beatles had more influence on the kids than anything else, including Jesus. A firestorm of protest from the Bible Belt, conservative and right-wing preachers, and the Vatican was directed toward the Beatles, especially Lennon. Lennon apologized for the misunderstanding, but it was apparent to the Fab Four that the press was now prepared to pillory them for any word misspoken, and they soon stopped touring.

In the late 1960s Lennon became an outspoken opponent of the Vietnam War. In protest of Britain's involvement in Nigeria and

450F 2009

RWANDA

British musician and lyricist John Lennon was so famous his image appears on this stamp from Rwanda. Was his murder at the hands of Mark David Chapman a result of brainwashing?

British support of the U.S. role in Vietnam, he returned the Member of the Order of the British Empire that he had received from Queen Elizabeth II. Following their honeymoon after their marriage in 1969, Lennon and Ono recorded "Give Peace a Chance," which quickly became the peace movement's international anthem.

After the Lennons moved to New York City in the early 1970s, President Richard Nixon and other right-wing politicians, such as Sena-

tor Strom Thurmond and Attorney General John Mitchell, viewed John Lennon as the Great Devil of all subversive activity. He was a popular, outspoken individual who could start riots and rebellions. J. Edgar Hoover agreed with their fears, and Lennon's FBI file bore the large, handwritten, block-lettered motto: ALL EXTREMISTS SHOULD BE CONSIDERED DANGEROUS. Government agents were assigned to get enough on the Lennons so they could be deported.

By 1976 John and Yoko had finally resolved their strife with the U.S. immigration officials, Yoko had given birth to their first child, and John had decided to retire from the music business. Then, curious to see if he could still write songs, he picked up his guitar again in 1980.

As John Lennon lay semiconscious and bleeding to death, Mark David Chapman was preternaturally calm, almost serene in his demeanor. Later he said that he felt nothing at the time of the shooting, no emotion, no anger, nothing but silence in the brain. But just before he pulled the trigger, a voice inside his head said over and over again, "do it, do it, do it."

Conspiracy theorists were quick to name Paul McCartney, Lennon's chief rival in the Beatles, as hiring an assassin to put an end to their competition. Some even named Yoko and blamed her for nursing jealousies for the times Lennon had strayed from their marriage vows.

The official verdict was just another crazy "lone gunman." Like Oswald. Like Sirhan.

British lawyer-journalist Fenton Bresler thought that Chapman seemed just a little too much like Sirhan—his quiet, calm, unnatural tone and manner after the murder, his saying that a voice in his head kept telling him to do it, do it, do it. Bresler theorized in *Who Killed John Lennon?* that in Chapman we had another programmed, brainwashed assassin.

Picking up on Bresler's theory, we are reminded that in the years of social upheaval in the 1960s, operatives in the CIA's super-secret MK-ULTRA project were experimenting with LSD, hypnosis, and a host of other mind-control techniques, some of which had been tested by Nazi doctors on unwilling concentration camp prisoners. Bresler learned that Chapman had been signing his name as "John Lennon" prior to the assassination. He once told an interviewer that he had killed Lennon in order to promote J. D. Salinger's novel *Catcher in the Rye.* Bresler thinks that the novel might have been the mental mechanism that triggered Chapman's programming.

Chapman had not been a weird loner when he was younger. Friends knew him as a socially minded, likeable individual. His family pointed out that he had been a sensitive young man who was a camp counselor and good with kids. An odd factor in his biography is the period when he signed up for a YMCA overseas program—and in June 1975 ended up in Beirut. Although Chapman was a born-again Christian, he began taking drugs in college, had a nervous breakdown, and became a hospitalized mental patient. When he was released, he became so obsessed with John Lennon that he married a Japanese woman because of her resemblance to Yoko Ono.

Chapman's attorney was astonished when, after he had spent six months diligently preparing to defend his client on an insanity plea, Chapman suddenly decided to plead guilty. A small voice inside his cell had spoken to him, Chapman explained, and told him to admit to the murder.

Mark David Chapman is imprisoned at Attica State Prison, near Buffalo, New York. He had been denied parole six times, as of 2010.

LEOPARD MEN

This centuries-old cult in West Africa sacrificed its victims, drank their blood, and ate their flesh in a belief that such acts would grant them supernatural powers.

In the spiritual beliefs of many African tribes, the leopard is a powerful totem animal that guides the spirits of the dead to rest. For many centuries there has existed a leopard cult in West Africa, particularly in Nigeria and Sierra Leone, whose members kill as does the leopard, by slashing, gashing, and mauling their human prey with steel claws and knives. Once a victim has been chosen and the date and time of the killing agreed upon, the executioner, known as the Bati Yeli, is selected. The Bati Yeli wears the ritual leopard mask and a leopardskin robe. Preferably, the human sacrifice is performed at one of the leopard cult's jungle shrines. After the cult has killed their victim, they drink the blood and eat the flesh. The cultists believe that a magical elixir known as *borfima,* which they brew from their victim's intestines, grants them superhuman powers and enables them to transform into leopards.

The first serious outbreak of leopard-cult murders occurred shortly after World War I in Sierra Leone and Nigeria. The region's white administrators captured and executed a number of the cult's members and felt that the nasty business had been suppressed. In actual fact, the leopard men simply went underground, continuing to perform ritual murders sporadically every year over the next two decades.

In 1946 there were forty-eight cases of murder and attempted murder committed by the leopard cult. Very much like the Mau Mau in Kenya, the leopard men had begun directing many of their attacks against whites, seemingly as a demonstration to the native population that the cult had no fear of the police or of the white rulers. The trend continued during the first seven months of 1947, when there were forty-three known ritual killings performed by the cult.

Early in 1947 Terry Wilson, who had been the district officer of a province in eastern

Nigeria for only six months, discovered that the leopard men had begun operating in his jurisdiction, claiming mainly young women as their victims. When Wilson raided the house of a local chief named Nagogo, his men found a leopard mask, a leopardskin robe, and a steel claw. And when, acting on a tip from an informer, Wilson ordered his police officers to dig near the chief's house, they found the remains of thirteen victims. The chief was put in prison to await trial, and Wilson set out to put an end to the leopard men's reign of terror.

Although Wilson received two hundred additional police officers as reinforcements, the leopard men became increasingly bold in their nocturnal attacks.

Although Wilson received two hundred additional police officers as reinforcements, the leopard men became increasingly bold in their nocturnal attacks. One night they defied the police by sacrificing a female victim inside the police compound and got away without being seen. The inhabitants of the region lost all confidence in the police and their ability to stop the powerful leopard men. Even some of Wilson's men began to believe that the cultists might truly have the ability to shapeshift into leopards and to fade unseen into the shadows.

By mid-August 1947 Wilson knew that his men were becoming unnerved, so he decided to attempt to set a trap for the leopard men. On the path to a village where several slayings had taken place, Wilson sent one of his best men, posing as the son of a native woman. The two walked side by side toward the village while Wilson and a dozen other officers concealed themselves in the bushes at the side of the path.

Suddenly a tall man in leopard robes charged the couple, swinging a large club. The young police officer struggled with the leopard man, but before Wilson and the other men could arrive on the scene, the cultist had smashed the officer's skull with the club and fled into the bushes.

On a hunch, Wilson told his men to leave the officer's body in the bushes beside the path. Dismissing the others, Wilson hid in the brush.

Around midnight, just as Wilson was about to return to the compound, a nightmarish figure crawling on all fours emerged from the jungle, pounced on the young officer's corpse, and began clawing at his face like a leopard. But rather than claws raking the body, Wilson caught the glint of a two-pronged steel claw in the moonlight. The killer had returned to complete the cult ritual of sacrifice. Wilson advanced on the leopard man, and the robed murderer snarled as if he were truly a big cat. When he came at him with the two-pronged claw, Wilson shot him in the chest.

Wilson had provided the people with proof that the leopard men were not supernatural beings. The members of the cult did not have magic that could make them impervious to bullets. They were, after all, men of flesh and blood—savage, bestial, and vicious—but men, nonetheless. Once word had spread that the district officer had killed one of the leopard men, witnesses began to come forward in great numbers with clues to the identity of cult members and the possible location of a secret jungle shrine.

During February 1948 seventy-three initiated members of the cult were arrested and sent to prison. Eventually thirty-nine of them were sentenced to death and hanged in Abak Prison, their executions witnessed by a number of local tribal chiefs who could testify to their villages that the leopard men were not immortal.

LIBERTY LOBBY

The founder of this conservative group believes that Hitler and the Nazis should have won World War II.

Liberty Lobby wishes to be considered as a respectable conservative group, but major conservative figures such as William F. Buckley and Judge Robert Bork condemn the group for its avowed anti-Semitism and racism, and for its active dissemination of hate literature through its weekly tabloid, the *Spotlight.* In the opinion of Willis Carto, the founder of Liberty Lobby, the defeat of Adolf Hitler's Nazi regime in 1945 was a tragedy for all of Europe and for the United States. The reason that the Nazis lost the war is clear to Carto: International secret societies of Jews are to blame.

Established in 1955, Liberty Lobby celebrates freedom for extreme right-wing and conservative groups and denies it for Jews and people of color. Under the pretense of patriotism, Carto's goal for the United States is the rehabilitation of Hitler's National Socialism in America. An anti-Semite and racist, Carto supported the apartheid governments of South Africa and Zimbabwe. His propaganda efforts in the United States concentrate on alerting more whites to the dangers of African American influences, what he terms "niggerfication."

In 1979 Carto founded the Institute for Historical Review, which has become the leading distributor of Holocaust-denial literature in the world. In 1984 Carto organized the Populist Party to serve as the Liberty Lobby's political arm. Former Ku Klux Klan leader David Duke was the Populist Party's candidate for president in 1988. In recent years, Carto split with both the Populist Party and the Institute for Historical Review over disagreements regarding control of funds and the effectiveness of certain strategies. The Liberty Lobby continues to be the largest, best-financed, and most powerful radical-right organization in the United States.

LIGHTNING FROM THE EAST

Jesus is alive and well, living in China as a woman and promising a fast-approaching Judgment Day.

A new apocalyptic cult named Lightning from the East emerged in China in 1990 claiming Jesus has returned as a thirty-year-old woman who presently remains in hiding and has never been photographed. The female Jesus, surnamed Deng, is supposedly prophesied in Matthew 24:27: "For as the lightning comes out of the east and shines even unto the west, so shall the coming of the Son of Man be." Deng claims to be that "lightning," and she warns of a fast-approaching Day of Judgment. She explains that she has been born again in China because it is the "Great Red Dragon" referred to in the book of Revelation. In addition to gifts of great teaching, the female Messiah has written a third testament to the Bible and composed hymns that fill ten CDs.

Lightning from the East, perhaps more properly called a sect of Christianity since the group employs the language of that religion, has upset China's 80 million orthodox Christians by claiming to have a female Jesus who writes new doomsday scriptures and whose followers abduct other Christians and hold them for brainwashing sessions lasting as long as five days. Even Catholic nuns and priests have been held captive for days and forced to listen to impassioned Lightning teachers tell them that the Jesus of the Bible is the old one. The new Jesus has come, and she will destroy the earth. Lightning members, who call themselves the "congregation," sing hymns that the new savior has written to the tunes of familiar folk or Communist Party songs. If an abducted potential convert should ask why the all-powerful Son/Daughter of God should have to be in hiding, the answer will be that she feels the need for secrecy at the present time, but she has a careful plan that she will follow.

Lightning boasts that they have converted millions of Chinese to their style of Christian teaching (more conservative estimates place membership around 300,000). Lightning converts argue that they have an advantage over conventional Christians because they have a Jesus here and now who promises to take her followers with her directly to heaven as the days of judgment move across China—and soon the world. While orthodox Christian priests and pastors preach virtues and values and downplay dire warnings about a final judgment, Lightning offers a Jesus who has come first to China and promises immediate salvation.

Chinese officials stated that their two-year campaign against such evil cults as the Falun Gong has placed two thousand members of Lightning in jail. However, the Communist Party's restrictions on religion don't permit enough ministers to graduate from the nation's eighteen state-approved Protestant seminaries to provide for China's hundreds of thousands of believers, so many Christians unknowingly join Lightning, thinking they are joining a traditional or orthodox Christian church.

Lightning from the East already has followers in North America. A small booklet called *The Voice of God in China* is being distributed in Chinatowns in New York City and San Francisco. Deng, the female Messiah, speaks as God in the first person: "Let everyone use the Light as strength that my name be further glorified. I came to earth long ago, bringing the glory of Israel to the east. In these last days my name shall change again—not Jehovah nor Jesus nor the Messiah. I shall be called the almighty, omnipotent God, and I shall use this name to end all ages."

The New Jesus may soon be coming to America.

ABRAHAM LINCOLN, ASSASSINATION OF

Even today, the assassination of Abraham Lincoln remains one of America's greatest unsolved mysteries.

According to one quaint bit of folklore, when John Wilkes Booth was a student at the Quaker School at Cockeysville, Maryland, a gypsy fortune teller warned him that he had a "bad hand" and that he would come to a bad end and die young. When he told his mother, Mary Ann Booth, of the prophecy, she remembered the vision that she had received of her infant son's evil hand. On an eerie night in 1838, she had dozed beside the cradle of little Johnny. Suddenly she was attracted to one of his hands. As she watched the infant hand, it seemed to grow to gigantic size and became transformed into the grotesque paw of a monster. She had often referred to her "weird dream," and she worried that her son would meet a violent death. Her teenaged daughter, Asia, was so impressed by the incident that she wrote a poem entitled "A Mother's Vision," which opens with the lines: "Tiny, innocent baby hand, what force, what power is at your command for good or evil?" Sadly, Mary Ann Booth, the mother of nine children, lived to see her Johnny employ his "bad hand" to assassinate President Abraham Lincoln, thus fulfilling the gypsy's prophecy and the horror of her maternal vision.

John Wilkes Booth came from a family of famous actors. His father, Junius Brutus Booth, was a noted Shakespearean actor, as was John's brother, Edwin, who became known as the "Prince of Players." John had also performed on the stage throughout the country, but his wild and erratic behavior and his outspoken political prejudices prevented him from achieving a solid career in the theater. He was an outspoken advocate of the Confederate cause during the Civil War, and he launched into hateful tirades against President Lincoln at the slightest opportunity.

In the late summer of 1864 Booth developed plans to kidnap Lincoln to Richmond, Virginia, the capital of the Confederacy, and hold the president in return for southern prisoners of war. By January 1865 he had gathered a small band of conspirators, including Samuel Arnold, Michael O'Laughlen, John Surratt, Lewis Powell (a.k.a. Paine or Payne), George Atzerodt, and David Herold. The group began using Mary Surratt's boardinghouse, and they set the date for the president's kidnapping for March 17, when he would be attending a function at a hospital on the outskirts of Washington. Their elaborate planning was for naught when Lincoln suddenly altered his itinerary and decided to remain in the capital.

On April 9, 1865, General Robert E. Lee surrendered to General Ulysses S. Grant at Appomattox Court House, Virginia. There was no longer any point in Booth's prisoner exchange plan. The South had capitulated.

On April 11, Booth was in the crowd that heard Lincoln speaking outside the White House and was infuriated when he heard the president suggest that certain freed slaves should be given the right to vote. In Booth's opinion, it was bad enough that Lincoln planned to free the slaves; it was against God's will that blacks should be able to read and to vote. He summoned his co-conspirators and angrily told them that he now planned to assassinate Lincoln.

Booth found that his companions' hatred for the president matched his own, and they all agreed to be a part of the plan to kill Lincoln and key members of his administration. When they learned that Lincoln and General Grant would be attending Ford's Theater on April 14, Good Friday, they unanimously decided that would be the night to carry out their plot.

As the hour drew near, they met one last time. Although he had learned that General Grant would not be attending the play after all, Booth still planned to assassinate Lincoln at the theater. Atzerodt was assigned to kill Vice President Andrew Johnson in his quarters at the Kirkwood House; Powell and Herold would murder Secretary of State William Seward. All the murders were to take place at 10:15 that night.

After he had fortified himself with a drink at a nearby saloon, Booth entered the front of Ford's Theater around 10:07 and began to make his way toward the box where the Lincolns were sitting with Clara Harris and Henry Rathbone. Audience laughter at the comedy *Our American Cousin* helped to conceal the sound of Booth's opening the door to the box. Lincoln's bodyguard, John Parker of the Metropolitan Police Force, had left his post, so Booth faced no resistance as he withdrew his single-shot derringer and fired point-blank at the back of the president's head. When Rathbone rose to struggle with him, Booth stabbed him in the arm with a hunting knife.

Whether he sensed he would be trapped if he attempted to retreat by way of the stairs or out of some misguided sense of the dramatic, Booth jumped the approximately eleven feet to the stage and snapped the fibula in his left leg just above the ankle. Brandishing his knife and shouting, "Sic semper tyrannis" (Thus always to tyrants), Booth limped across the stage in front of over a thousand shocked audience members and made his way to the horse awaiting him out the back door.

President Lincoln never regained consciousness and died at 7:22 on the morning of April 15. Powell managed to stab Secretary of State Seward but did not kill him. Atzerodt didn't attempt to assassinate Vice President Johnson. Herold decided to leave the capital as quickly as possible. Booth had his broken leg set and splinted by Dr. Samuel Mudd, then, in the company of Herold, headed for refuge in the South.

Early in the morning of April 26, federal authorities caught up with them at Garrett's farm

Maj. Rathbone. Miss Harris. Mrs. Lincoln. President. Assassin.

THE ASSASSINATION OF PRESIDENT LINCOLN,
AT FORD'S THEATRE WASHINGTON. D.C. APRIL 14TH 1865.

A Currier & Ives illustration of the assassination of President Abraham Lincoln by actor John Wilkes Booth.

near Port Royal, Virginia. Herold surrendered, but Booth took cover in a barn and refused to come out. The barn was torched, and Sergeant Boston Corbett shot the assassin as the flames surrounded him.

Federal agents had already rounded up all but one of the other conspirators. Mrs. Surratt, Powell, Atzerodt, and Herold were all hanged on July 7, 1865. Mudd, O'Laughlen, and Arnold were given life terms. Ned Spangler, a stagehand at the theater, was sentenced to six years for helping Booth escape. John Surratt fled to Canada, then Europe, and was finally apprehended in Egypt. Brought back to face trial in 1867, he was set free after the jury deadlocked. O'Laughlen died in prison that same year. In 1869 President Andrew Johnson pardoned Mudd, Arnold, and Spangler.

Although the remains recovered from the ashes of the barn at Garrett's farm were taken back to Washington and identified as those of John Wilkes Booth, some historians insist that the body was never *positively* identified as that of the assassin of President Abraham Lincoln.

The foregoing account of the assassination of Lincoln is the way most of us have heard the story. We do not have the dilemma that one faces with the assassination of President John F. Kennedy. We know who the assassin was; we know his co-conspirators; we know everything there is to know about who killed President Lincoln. Or do we?

Among the many theories about who *really* assassinated Abraham Lincoln are the following:

Vice President Andrew Johnson Arranged for the Assassination

Several members of Congress and Mary Todd Lincoln herself were certain that Johnson knew of the conspiracy and did nothing to stop it. It is known that seven hours before he assassinated the president, John Wilkes Booth stopped by the Kirkwood House to see Johnson. When he was informed that neither Johnson nor his private secretary was presently in the hotel, Booth left a note that read, "Don't wish to disturb you. Are you at home?"

Some might conclude that Booth did not trust George Atzerodt to kill Johnson, so he decided to do it himself. But what about the plan to carry out all the murders at approximately 10:15? If Booth had killed the vice president at three o'clock that afternoon, the security around the president would have been tripled—and Lincoln would most assuredly not have attended the play that night.

In *Right or Wrong, God Judge Me: The Writings of John Wilkes Booth,* edited by John Rhodehamel and Louise Taper, it is revealed that Booth met Johnson in Nashville in February 1864, when the actor was appearing at the recently opened Wood's Theater. Even more damning, in *Civil War Echoes* (1907) Hamilton Howard claims that in 1862, while Johnson was the military governor of Tennessee, he and Booth had kept two sisters as their shared mistresses and were frequently seen in each other's company.

Johnson, born in Raleigh, North Carolina, in 1808, had been elected governor of Tennessee in 1853 and to the U.S. Senate in 1856, and was the only southern senator who had refused to join the Confederacy. However, Johnson made it clear that he was supporting the Union and not the abolition of slavery. No one who had heard one of his rants questioned his belief that slaves should be kept in subjugation. When Lincoln issued his Emancipation Proclamation on September 22, 1862, Johnson managed to wring a promise from the president that while the proclamation would apply to all the slaves held by those states in rebellion, Tennessee would be exempt.

Lincoln's first choice for his running mate in the 1864 election had been radical Republican Hannibal Hamlin, then he asked war hero General Benjamin Butler to join him on the slate. However, the consensus in the Republican Party held that the radical views of both Hamlin and Butler would be unpopular with those voters who had previously supported the Democratic Party in the North and that Johnson would be a better choice to demonstrate that the southern states were still part of the Union.

Lincoln had had little to do with his vice president after Johnson disgraced himself on Inauguration Day by being drunk when he made his speech to Congress. Slurring his words and making numerous inappropriate comments, Johnson had to be helped to his seat by Hamlin. With the memory of this embarrassment clearly in mind, Mary Todd Lincoln felt certain that the "miserable inebriate Johnson" had something to do with her husband's death.

Johnson was cleared of any involvement in Lincoln's death by a special Congressional Assassination Committee formed specifically to investigate him. Regardless of the Committee's declaration of Johnson's innocence, many Americans regarded him with suspicion for decades to come.

Lincoln Was Assassinated as the Result of a Confederate Plot

It seemed logical in 1865 to assume that John Wilkes Booth was acting within a much larger circle of Confederate conspirators who would consider Lincoln a legitimate wartime target for assassination.

A plan to blow up the White House with Lincoln and his cabinet along with it gained some impetus after the South was shaken by the letters found in the pocket of the youngest colonel in the Union army. In the winter of 1864, Union brigadier general Hugh Judson Kilpatrick conceived a plan to raid Richmond and free more than 1,500 Union officers and 10,000 enlisted men held prisoner there. President Lincoln personally endorsed the raid because of the pressure he received daily from people protesting the Confederate treatment of the Union soldiers in the swampy prison camp. On February 28, 1864, Kilpatrick led 3,600 cavalry troopers across the Rapidan River, riding south toward Richmond. The following day, twenty-one-year-old Colonel Ulric Dahlgren, who had lost his right leg at Gettysburg, took 460 men to the west to cross the James River, intending to circle undetected to Richmond's lightly defended southern portals. Kilpatrick would engage the main force of Confederates while Dahlgren freed the prisoners.

> Regardless of the Committee's declaration of Johnson's innocence, many Americans regarded him with suspicion for decades to come.

Unfortunately for the Union prisoners, the James River was too high to cross at the appointed place, so Dahlgren continued toward Richmond on the wrong side of the river and was confronted by southern militiamen. When Kilpatrick, a leader so devoid of skill that his men had nicknamed him "Kill-Cavalry," met resistance at Richmond's outer defenses, he ordered a hasty retreat. Left to flounder on their own without the main body of cavalry, Dahlgren's men headed back toward Union lines in a freezing rain. On March 2, Dahlgren was killed in a Confederate ambush.

The story of the ill-fated campaign wouldn't rate more than a footnote in the annals of the Civil War if what has come to be known as the Dahlgren Papers had not been retrieved from the young colonel's inside coat pocket. Captain Edward Halbach skimmed over the orders outlining the details of the failed raid—then he became appalled and could hardly believe his senses when he read that the actual objective of the raid was to burn Richmond to the ground and to kill President Jefferson Davis and his entire cabinet.

Halbach immediately brought the incendiary papers to General Robert E. Lee, who had them photocopied and sent to Maj. Gen. George Meade, the Union commander. Although the Civil War was bloody and ghastly in its scope, there had always been some gallantry and honor employed. To plan a raid to murder the president of the Confederacy and every member of his cabinet was beyond outrageous.

Kilpatrick told Meade that he had read Dahlgren's address to his men and the photocopy was accurate up to the point where the orders were issued to burn Richmond and assassinate Davis and his cabinet. Although the Union commanders protested that the Confederacy had doctored the documents and Dahlgren's father, Rear Adm. John Dahlgren, a personal friend of Lincoln's, pronounced them "a bare-faced atrocious forgery," it didn't take long for Confederate intelligence operatives to learn that Lincoln himself had endorsed the raid and had approved Colonel Dahlgren as one of its leaders.

In this conspiracy theory of Lincoln's assassination, Booth becomes a rebel agent working under orders of Judah Benjamin, the Confederate secretary of state, in plots first to bomb the White House (which failed when Thomas F. Harney, the scheme's explosives expert, was captured on April 10), then to assassinate Lincoln, which succeeded on April 14, 1865. The Confederate Plot hypothesis has been given more credence in recent decades. A grand Confederate conspiracy is detailed by William A. Tidwell, James O. Hall, and David Winfred Gaddy in their book *Come Retribution: The Confederate Secret Service and the Assassination of Lincoln* (1988). Tidwell expands the evidence in his 1995 work *April '65: Confederate Covert Action in the American Civil War.*

The Rothschilds and International Bankers Arranged Lincoln's Death

In this conspiracy scenario, John Wilkes Booth was the hit man, the hired gun, for the powerful British bankers, the Rothschilds. According to those who believe this assassination theory, the Rothschilds had offered loans to the Lincoln administration at very high interest, assuming that the Union had no choice other than to accept their outrageous terms. The frugal and resourceful frontiersman spirit in Lincoln caused him to refuse the Rothschilds' offer and to acquire the necessary funds elsewhere. Although his refusal only stung their sense of pride and greed, the true reason for their planning his assassination was their knowledge that Lincoln's policies indicated a mild reconstruction of the South after the war, one that would encourage a resumption of agriculture rather than industry. Additional postwar policies likely under Lincoln would have destroyed the Rothschilds' commodity speculations. With Lincoln out of the way, the Rothschilds planned to exploit the weaknesses of the United States and take over its economy.

Lincoln Was Assassinated by the Jesuits

In 1856 in Urbana, Illinois, Lincoln defended Charles Chiniquy, a rebellious priest, against charges of slander brought by the friends of Bishop O'Regan of Chicago, with whom Chiniquy had a strong disagreement. Lincoln brought about a compromise settlement that the priest interpreted as a major victory over the Roman Catholic Church. As time passed, Chiniquy feared that the Jesuits, the soldiers of Jesus, resented Lincoln for this triumph over the church and might one day attempt to even the score. In 1886 Chiniquy wrote *Fifty Years in the Church of Rome* in which he revealed that Jefferson Davis had offered a million dollars to anyone who would kill Lincoln. According to Chiniquy, he visited Lincoln in the White House on numerous occasions and tried to warn of the Catholic Church's antagonism toward him. Later, Chiniquy learned that the Jesuits trained John Wilkes Booth to become their tool of assassination. In 1906 Chiniquy swore that Lincoln had been assassinated by the Jesuits of Rome.

In 1897 Thomas M. Harris, a member of the 1865 military commission, wrote *Rome's Responsibility for the Assassination of Abraham Lincoln.* The accusations against the Catholic Church for the murder of our most beloved president have not dissipated with time. In 1963 Emmett McLoughlin's *An Inquiry into the Assassination of Abraham Lincoln* claimed that Pope Pius IX may have been the instigator of the plot to kill Lincoln. McLoughlin writes, "On one side were dictatorship, slavery, secession, monarchy, European imperialism, Jesuit chicanery, and a Church-dominated assault on the Monroe Doctrine, all of which found spiritual leadership in the one person: Pope Pius IX. On the other side were freedom, emancipation, Freemasonry, democracy, Latin American struggle against foreign domination, all embodied in the one person: Abraham Lincoln."

As an interesting footnote or two to the enigma of the Lincoln assassination:

Mary Todd Lincoln went mad after that terrible Good Friday night in Ford's Theater and was confined in an asylum for some time. Although eventually released, she never fully recovered from the shock.

Major Henry Rathbone, wounded by Booth's knife as he attempted to halt the assassin, married Clara Harris, the other occupant of the fatal theater box. A few years later, he went mad, attempted to kill Clara and their children, and spent the rest of his life restrained as a violent maniac.

Boston Corbett, who received praise as the man who shot John Wilkes Booth, went mad and was confined to an asylum.

Secretary of War Edwin Stanton was also under suspicion as a member of the conspiracy to assassinate Lincoln. He immediately began a movement to impeach Andrew Johnson, now the president, because of his suspected role in the assassination. Johnson informed Stanton that his resignation as secretary of war was accepted and had him removed from office by force of arms. Not long after he left office, Stanton was found dead—according to rumors, by his own hand.

It would appear that the mystery of the Lincoln assassination, like that of the murder of JFK, will never die.

LUSITANIA

A number of historians still insist that the nearly 1,200 lives lost aboard the RMS Lusitania were sacrificed to the gods of war in an effort to embroil the United States in World War I.

The *Lusitania* was an ocean liner of the British Cunard Steamship Line that was torpedoed by a German U-boat on May 7, 1915, within sight of the southern coast of Ireland. The sinking of a passenger ship and the loss of 1,195 lives was instrumental in causing the United States to enter World War I and to declare war on Germany and its allies. For over ninety years, the question has been argued whether Winston Churchill, as Lord of the British Admiralty, manipulated events to arrange for the liner's sinking in order to create an incident that would convince the United States to participate in the conflict against Germany.

The *Lusitania* and its sister ship, the *Mauretania,* were considerably smaller and less luxurious than the *Olympic* and *Britannic* of the rival White Star Line, but they were much

faster and enabled Cunard to provide a weekly transatlantic departure schedule with just two vessels. When the *Lusitania* sank, she was on her 202d crossing of the Atlantic.

Shortly after World War I began, the British established a blockade of Germany that was eventually responsible for the death by starvation, malnutrition, and disease of 750,000 Germans. Germany's only hope of destroying the blockade was to sink as many warships as possible, and the feared U-boats were very effective in striving to attain that goal. The *Lusitania,* a luxury passenger liner and cargo ship, was immune from attack, as were all passenger ships—unless they were suspected of violating the agreement that such vessels would not transport ammunition and explosives to Great Britain.

German intelligence had suspected the fast-moving ships of the Cunard Line of carrying contraband munitions, and the German embassy in the United States issued a public warning to travelers intending to embark for Great Britain that a state of war existed between Germany and its allies and Great Britain and its allies, and the "zone of war" included the waters adjacent to the British Isles. Vessels flying the British flag were "liable to destruction in those waters," and passengers who chose to travel on the ships of Great Britain or its allies must "do so at their own risk." It was later learned that some of the wealthiest and most influential passengers had been warned that a U-boat attack was likely against the *Lusitania.*

Captain Walther Schweiger, commander of submarine *U-20,* released one torpedo at a distance of seven hundred yards and saw it strike the *Lusitania* and trigger a second violent explosion. Upon seeing the second explosion, Schweiger felt justified in torpedoing the passenger vessel, for it was obviously carrying munitions under assumed cargo designations. The *Lusitania* rolled over and sank in about eighteen minutes. Rescuers from

Queenstown, Ireland, managed to save 734 from the cold seawater.

The Germans had guessed correctly, for the *Lusitania,* under the descriptions of bales of fur and boxes of cheese, carried in its hold millions of rounds of rifle ammunition, 1,250 cases of shrapnel shells, and forty-six tons of aluminum powder for the Woolrich Arsenal. The British and American governments accused the U-boat of having launched a second torpedo at the sinking passenger ship, but the Germans steadfastly denied doing so, claiming the munitions on board had caused the second explosion.

If Churchill had engineered the destruction of one of Britain's finest ships and of 1,195 lives (among them 128 Americans) in a sacrificial act intended to bring the United States into the war, he had succeeded, for the Yanks saw the sinking of the *Lusitania* as another barbaric attack by the "Huns."

Conspiracy theorists counter that the British Admiralty, under Churchill's direction, was well aware that the German U-boat command had issued a warning to all passenger ships that they must travel at their own risk. The Admiralty was also informed that the U-boat responsible for sinking two ships in recent days was still lurking in the waters off the southern coast of Ireland, the path the *Lusitania* was scheduled to travel. In spite of this knowledge, the Admiralty issued no special warnings to the *Lusitania,* offered no escort to port, and did not send any destroyers to search for the German submarine. It seems apparent to some researchers that there was a conspiracy to place the *Lusitania* in jeopardy in order to incite the Americans to enter the war.

The RMS *Lusitania* is shown here docked in New York City in 1910. Its sinking in 1915 by a German torpedo was a key event in convincing the United States to enter World War I. Some say Winston Churchill actually helped make the attack possible in order to bring America into the war.

However, U.S. isolationist policies continued to maintain their hold on Congress until February 1917, when the German admiral Alfred von Tirpitz announced that U-boats would begin attacking all shipping in the North Atlantic, regardless of national or political allegiance. On February 3 the U.S. broke off diplomatic relations with Germany. On that same day a U-boat sunk the U.S. liner *Housatonic* off the coast of Sicily. On March 18, German submarines sank three U.S.-registered vessels, the *City of Memphis,* the *Vigilante,* and the *Illinois,* without giving any type of warning. On April 2 President Woodrow Wilson argued that the "world must be safe for democracy," and on April 6 Congress approved a declaration of war against Germany.

M

MACUMBA

While some fear its dark reputation, others take delight in dancing to the cult's "rhythm of the saints," the samba.

In its outward appearances and in some of its practices, Macumba (also known as Spiritism, Candomblé, and Umbanda) resembles Voodoo. Trance states among the practitioners are induced by dancing and drumming, and the ceremony climaxes with an animal sacrifice.

The ancient role of the shaman remains central to Macumba. He (it is most often a male) or she enters into a trance state and talks to the spirits in order to gain advice or aid for the supplicants. Before anyone can participate in a Macumba ceremony, he or she must undergo an initiation. The aspirants must enter a trance during the dancing and the drumming and allow a god to possess them. Once the possession has taken place, the shaman must determine which gods are in which initiate so that the correct rituals can be performed. The process is enhanced by the sacrifice of an animal and the smearing of its blood over the initiates. Once the initiates have been bloodied, they take an oath of loyalty to the cult. Later, when the trance state and the possessing spirit have left them, the aspirants, now members of the Macumba cult, usually have no memory of the ritual proceedings.

Macumba was born in the 1550s from a blending between the spirit worship of the African slaves brought to Brazil and the Roman Catholicism of the slaveholders. Although the captive slaves were forced to give token obeisance to an array of Christian saints and the God of their masters, the native priests soon realized how complementary the two faiths could be—especially since, unlike the slave owners in the United States, the Brazilians allowed the slaves to keep their drums. The Africans summoned their gods, the orishas, with the sound of their drums and the rhythm of their dancing. The African god Exu became Saint Anthony, Lemanja became Our Lady of the Glory, Oba became Saint Joan of Arc, Oxala became Jesus Christ, Oxum became Our Lady of the Conception, and so on. From the melding of the two religious faiths, the Africans created the samba, the rhythm of the saints, which has survived as an international dance favorite.

USS *MAINE*

For over a hundred years the outraged cry of "Remember the Maine!" has echoed in the halls of U.S. history. But even today people can't agree on who or what sank the battleship.

When the USS *Maine* blew up in Havana harbor on the evening of February 15, 1898, most of the battleship's crew were sleeping or relaxing in the enlisted men's quarters in the forward part of the ship. Later investigation disclosed that five tons of powder charges for the battleship's six and ten-inch guns exploded, substantially obliterating the forward third of the ship and sending the remaining wreckage quickly to the bottom of the harbor. Two hundred and sixty-six men lost their lives in the blast or within minutes of it, and another six died later from injuries. Captain Charles Sigsbee and most of the officers of the vessel survived the disaster because their quarters were in the rear portion of the battleship.

The United States had been in sympathetic support of the Cubans in their struggle for freedom from Spain ever since the first insurrection, between 1868 and 1878. On October 31, 1873, the Spanish captured the ship *Virginius,* bringing aid and guns to the embattled Cuban revolutionaries, and executed most of the crew, including many American citizens. A declaration of war with Spain had been swaying on the brink ever since the *Virginius* incident, and popular sentiment in the United States to go to war was steadily fueled by the "yellow press" with accounts of horrible atrocities against the Cubans by the Spanish. When the second rebellion began in April 1895, Spain sent General Valeriano Weyler y Nicolau, soon to be known as "the Butcher," to quell the disturbances, and stories about death and starvation of Cubans soon saturated American newspapers.

Pressure had been placed on both President Grover Cleveland (1884–88; 1893–97)

The wreckage of the USS *Maine* in Havana Harbor. The destruction of this ship led to the Spanish-American War. One theory about the explosion that killed 260 sailors is that American saboteurs orchestrated it to start the war.

and William McKinley (1897–1901) to declare war on Spain, but both men had preferred to employ diplomacy. In 1897 Spain promised limited autonomy for Cuba, but the U.S. government was well aware that the revolutionaries would settle for nothing less than total independence. After riots broke out in Cuba in January 1898, President McKinley sent the USS *Maine* to be at hand if the Americans on the island should need protecting.

The battleship arrived at Havana on January 25, 1898, after an anxious Spain was notified of U.S. intentions. Although suspicious of America's true motives, the Spanish authorities allowed the ship to enter the harbor. Captain Sigsbee, attuned to any potential misstep on a sensitive mission, did not allow any of his enlisted men to go on shore. Then, on February 15, the *Maine* was destroyed in one horrendous explosion.

Spanish officials and the crew of the civilian steamer *City of Washington* were quickly at hand to rescue the survivors and look after the wounded. The genuine solicitude of the Spanish authorities allayed Sigsbee's initial suspicions of a hostile action against the *Maine,* and his first telegram to the U.S. Navy Department urged suspension of public opinion until a suitable inquiry had been made.

The U.S. Navy's four-week inquiry, held in Havana, concluded from the condition of the submerged wreckage that a mine had been detonated under the *Maine.* The board did not make accusations as to who might have placed the mine, but the American public had already judged the Spanish as guilty for killing 266 Americans, and they reacted with outrage and cries of "Remember the Maine!"

President McKinley continued his efforts for a diplomatic settlement between Spain and Cuba but was finally pressured into ordering a blockade of Cuba on April 21. With diplomacy at an impasse, Spain declared war on the United States on April 23. Congress was ready with its own declaration of war on April 25 and made it retroactive to April 21. The Spanish-American War lasted only five months (April 21 to August 13, 1898), but it signaled the emergence of the United States as a world power.

For over a hundred years, conspiracy theorists have argued that warmongers in the United States sabotaged the *Maine* to force the nation to declare war on Spain. The possibility that someone on board the battleship might have ignited five tons of powder charges and killed 266 of his fellow crewmen was investigated by a Navy Department inquiry in 1911. There were solid arguments presented that a mine external to the *Maine* caused the blast; there was also evidence that spontaneous combustion of coal in the bunker next to the powder magazine caused the explosion. In 1976 Admiral Hyman Rickover of the U.S. Navy published the results of an investigation that concluded the explosion was the result of a coal bunker fire. A number of historians doubted this theory, still maintaining that the blast was caused by sabotage. In 1998 the National Geographic Society explored the wreck and decided that based on a structural analysis, the tragedy could have been caused by the ignition of volatile coal dust in a bunker. At this late date we will probably never know the truth of what happened that February night in Havana harbor in 1898, but we can be certain that the controversy will linger on.

MAJESTIC-12

In 1987 three UFO investigators announced that they had proof of a secret group within the government that had conspired to keep the truth about extraterrestrial contact from the public.

The documentary filmmaker Jamie Shandera claimed that in December 1984 he had received two rolls of undeveloped 35-mm film in the mail. Once he developed the film, he discovered what appeared to be a briefing report to President-elect Dwight D. Eisenhower from a group of twelve prestigious and top-secret investigators who worked under the code name of Operation Majestic-12. The document described details of the recovery, analysis, and official cover-up of the 1947 UFO crash outside of Roswell, New Mexico.

Within the report was a description of the four "humanlike beings" found near the wreckage of what had been determined to be a crashed extraterrestrial spacecraft. The secret analysis of the beings acknowledged their humanlike appearance but concluded that "the biological and evolutionary processes responsible for their development has apparently been quite different from that observed or postulated in *Homo sapiens*." According to these documents, all four of the entities were dead, and their corpses had been mutilated by desert scavengers and were badly decomposed due to exposure to the elements.

From what Shandera could ascertain, some unknown source had leaked the documents to him just a few weeks after the death of the last member of the "Majestic-12" group. To help him develop a more complete analysis of the papers that had somehow been delivered into his hands, Shandera enlisted the assistance of prominent UFO researchers William Moore and Stanton Friedman.

On June 14, 1987, at the 24th Annual National UFO Conference in Burbank, California, Shandera, Friedman, and Moore made public their investigations into what they purported to be documentary proof of a government cover-up of UFOs that began in 1947. According to the documents leaked to Shandera, the Majestic-12 (or MJ-12) group consisted of the following individuals:

Lloyd V. Berkener, known for scientific achievements in the fields of physics and electronics, special assistant to the secretary of state in charge of the Military Assistance Program, and executive secretary of what is now known as the Research and Development Board of the National Military Establishment.

Detlev W. Bronk, physiologist and biophysicist of international repute, chairman of the National Research Council, and member of the Medical Advisory Board of the Atomic Energy Commission.

Vannevar Bush, a brilliant scientist who served from 1947 to 1948 as chairman of Research and Development for the National Military Establishment.

Gordon Gray, assistant secretary of the army in 1947, secretary of the army in 1949.

Dr. Jerome C. Hunsaker, an aeronautical scientist and design engineer, chairman of the National Advisory Committee for Aeronautics.

Maj. Gen. Robert M. Montague, Sandia base commander, Albuquerque, New Mexico, from July 1947 to February 1951.

Gen. Nathan F. Twining, commander of the Twentieth Air Force, whose B-29s dropped the atom bombs on Hiroshima and Nagasaki. In December 1945 he was named commanding general of the Air Materiel Command at Wright Field. In 1950 he became acting deputy chief of staff for personnel at air force headquarters in Washington, D.C.

Dr. Donald H. Menzel, director of the Harvard Observatory, long acknowledged as a leading authority on the solar chromosphere, and coformulator of the calculations that lead to initial radio contact with the moon in 1946.

James V. Forrestal, undersecretary, then secretary of the navy. In 1947 he became secretary of defense, coordinating the activities of all U.S. armed forces.

Rear Adm. Sidney W. Souers, deputy chief of Naval Intelligence before organizing the Central Intelligence Office in January 1946.

Hoyt S. Vandenberg, commanding general of the Ninth Air Force before being named assistant chief of intelligence in 1946. He was appointed the director of Central Intelligence in June 1946.

Rear Adm. Roscoe H. Hillenkoetter, the first director (May 1947 to September 1950) of the CIA, the permanent intelligence agency that evolved from the office organized by Sidney W. Souers.

Upon seeing the list of MJ-12's alleged personnel, UFO researchers agreed that if a UFO had crashed and been recovered in Roswell in 1947, this was the kind of panel that could have accomplished a thorough investigation of the craft. All of these individuals had been at the top in their respective areas of expertise during the late 1940s and had the added benefit of high-level government experience.

The more skeptical investigators agreed that "Document A," which purported to be a letter dated September 24, 1947, from President Harry S. Truman to Secretary of Defense Forrestal, appeared to be genuine—but they pointed out that even though Truman did refer to "Operation Majestic Twelve" in the letter, there was nothing clearly linking the group to UFO investigations.

Others questioned why Hillenkoetter, head of the CIA, listed as the briefing officer on the MJ-12 document, would remain quiet about the crashed flying saucer and the alien bodies when he became active in civilian UFO research in 1957.

The biggest shocker to longtime UFO researchers was the discovery of the name of Donald Menzel, the Harvard astronomer, on the MJ-12 list. Menzel was well known as a passionate debunker of flying saucers and the author of three anti-UFO books.

Stanton Friedman continues to investigate the MJ-12 enigma and strongly defends his original research and conclusions. Other investigators claim to have found supportive evidence in a secret memo from President Franklin D. Roosevelt, written as early as February 1944, in which he calls for a special committee on nonterrestrial science and technology and urges that group to face the reality that Earth is not the only planet harboring intelligent life in the universe. Some UFO researchers suggest that there was a crash of an extraterrestrial spaceship near Cape Girardeau, Missouri, in 1941 that prompted astonished scientists to evaluate the potential in discovering such advanced technology.

In spite of defenders in the UFO research field, the authenticity of the MJ-12 documents remains highly suspect. Skeptical researchers have labeled them as clearly false and fraudulent, pointing out that a thorough search of the records of the Truman administration reveals no executive order for such a UFO investigative group. Researchers who have served in the military have stated that the clearest indication of a hoax lies in the many incorrect military terms used in these allegedly "official" documents, suggesting that the creators of the papers had never served in the armed forces.

MALCOLM X, ASSASSINATION OF

Who assassinated the controversial black leader—the FBI, the Nation of Islam, the mob, or one of his best friends?

No one will ever know if Malcolm X suspected that something was wrong that Sunday afternoon, February 21, 1965, when he arrived with his family at the Audubon Ballroom in Harlem to speak at an Organization of Afro-American Unity (OAAU) rally. Only a week had passed since the controversial militant black leader's home had been firebombed, and he must have noticed that there were no police inside the ballroom and only two stationed outside the entrance. For Brother Malcolm, an assassination attempt was always a possibility, and he never turned down police protection. There were four hundred men and women crowded into the ballroom, but none of the dark-suited Nation of Islam guards standing near the stage and at the back of the room had bothered to search anyone for weapons.

Later Malcolm's pregnant wife, Betty Shabazz (when Malcolm X returned from Africa in June 1964, he became an orthodox Muslim, El-Hajj Malik El-Shabazz), would be told that there were dozens of police officers across the street, waiting in a hospital, positioned there allegedly at the request of Malcolm, who had told them that their presence in the ballroom would create tension among the members of the audience. She denied that her husband would have made such a request.

One of the greatest African American leaders of the twentieth century, Malcolm X was head of the Nation of Islam. Theories abound as to who conspired to gun him down in 1965, but none have been proven.

Malcolm X waited with Betty and their four children in an anteroom until the rally began, then he asked two of his bodyguards to escort them out into the ballroom and seat them in a box near the front of the stage. His bodyguards noticed that Malcolm seemed nervous and irritable.

Brother Benjamin Goodman finished making the opening speech, and introduced Brother Malcolm. The civil rights leader, founder of the OAAU, got to his feet, managed a slight smile, and walked out on the stage to loud applause. He went to the podium and had only begun to speak when a fight broke out near the rear of the ballroom. Malcolm asked the two men to "cool it, brothers," just as a loud explosion sounded in the back of the room and heavy smoke began to fill the area.

As bodyguards ran toward the back to investigate the disturbances, a man stood up from the front row and fired both barrels of a sawed-off shotgun at Malcolm. As the civil rights leader fell backward, grabbing at his chest, two more men rushed the stage, firing pistols at him. An FBI report, dated February 22, 1965, stated that Malcolm X had "ten bullet wounds in his chest, thigh, and ankle, plus four bullet creases in the chest and thigh." The bullets were identified as one 9-mm slug, several shotgun pellets, and one .45 slug. Both blasts from the sawed-off shotgun had penetrated Malcolm X's heart and aorta.

Many of his followers rushed to Malcolm's fallen body, but it was quickly determined that he was dead. The majority of the crowd in the ballroom were pushing to get out, uncertain if there was a fire sweeping through the place.

Others went after the shooters. One assassin managed to escape by crawling out a restroom window. Two others were beaten and kicked by the angry crowd as they tried to run down the stairs to the street. Twenty-two-year-old Talmadge Hayer (a.k.a. Thomas Hagan) was shot in the leg by one of Malcolm's bodyguards and kicked and beaten by the crowd until rescued by two uniformed policemen. The other assassin caught by the crowd somehow managed to escape, even after being knocked down by an undercover policeman named Gene Roberts, a member of Bureau of Special Services. Roberts then ran to the stage and attempted to resuscitate the fallen Malcolm. Bodyguards stepped aside, recognizing Roberts as "Brother Gene," a police officer who had grown very close to Malcolm.

Now the mystery begins. Who ordered the assassination of Malcolm X?

1. The Nation of Islam (NOI) came first to the minds of many of Malcolm's followers. In addition to the Organization of Afro-American Unity, Malcolm had founded the Muslim Mosque, Inc. (MMI), and many believed that the NOI's leaders were jealous of his ability to recruit their members into MMI. Malcolm, who had

once been extremely close to Elijah Muhammed, the head of NOI, had later publicly denounced him as an adulterer. In turn, Muhammed had denounced Malcolm for deviating from the peaceful teachings of the Qur'an. Louis Farrakhan, a prominent NOI minister, told Muslims that those who followed Malcolm X would be led to hell or to their doom. However, after Malcolm's assassination, Farrakhan publicly apologized to Betty Shabazz.

2. After researching more than 300,000 pages of declassified FBI and CIA documents, Karl Evanzz, author of *The Judas Factor: The Plot to Kill Malcolm X,* believes that the assassination was arranged by Malcolm's former friend John Ali, an agent/informer for an intelligence agency. Although Malcolm did not believe that Ali had been responsible for Malcolm's suspension from the Nation of Islam, Ali rose to the position of national secretary of the NOI.

3. Some investigators remembered how angry organized crime bosses had been at Malcolm X for his effective crusade against drugs, alcohol, and crime in Harlem. The militant black leader had been very successful in cleaning up the streets and replacing slums with black pride and black businesses.

4. Perhaps the greater number of conspiracy theorists vote for the FBI's COINTELPRO and recall FBI director J. Edgar Hoover's mandate to get the goods on and/or dispose of radical, militant, civil rights groups or war protestors by any means necessary. COINTELPRO (counterintelligence program) agents were to neutralize subversive political organizations and dissidents through covert means.

The first edition of the *New York Herald Tribune* for February 22, 1965, was printed on Sunday evening, just a few hours after the as-

sassination of Malcolm X, for distribution Monday morning. The top headline in the first edition read, "Malcolm X Slain by Gunmen as 400 in Ballroom Watch." The lead article, written by Jimmy Breslin, mentioned two suspects rescued by police: Talmadge Hayer, taken to Bellevue Hospital under heavy police guard, and an unnamed person taken to Wadsworth Avenue Precinct.

The afternoon edition of the same paper appeared with its top headline unchanged, but the two suspects had become one—and Breslin's story was rewritten to exclude the unnamed suspect. The first edition of the *New York Times* similarly proclaimed, "Police Hold Two for Questioning." The name of the police officer, Thomas Hoy, who grabbed the "suspect" was given as well. But in a later edition of the *Times* the headline read: "One is Held in Killing."

Three men were seen firing at nearly point-blank range on Malcolm X. Where did two of them go?

Three men were eventually arrested for Malcolm X's murder. Talmadge Hayer, Norman 3X Butler, and Thomas 15X Johnson were all convicted of first degree murder in March 1966. Hayer testified that neither Butler nor Johnson was involved in the assassination. Butler and Johnson were well known to Malcolm's aides and bodyguards as Nation of Islam enforcers, yet all of these individuals swore that neither man was present in the ballroom when Malcolm X was assassinated.

Conspiracy theorists wonder about Malcolm X's new best friend, Gene Roberts, the undercover agent of the Bureau of Secret Services, an agency so secretive that even the New York City police were unaware of its existence, its activities, and its agents. Witnesses recalled that just prior to the shooting, Roberts was positioned on the stage near Malcolm X. Other witnesses saw him signal to the bodyguards to move just before he went to another position away from the stage. The bullets removed from

Malcolm's body were identified as one 9-mm slug, several shotgun pellets, and one .45 slug. The shotgun was found at the scene. The .45 was later recovered. A 9-mm weapon was never located. Theorists suggest that Roberts fired a 9-mm bullet into Malcolm during the diversion caused by the agents in the back of the ballroom. When the angry crowd began to chase the shooters, Roberts pretended to capture of one of the assassins, whom he actually rescued from the crowd by knocking him down and appearing to have captured him. Next he faked a valiant effort to resuscitate the victim, then he disappeared into the mists of covert action, mission accomplished—a subversive radical eliminated.

MANCHURIAN CANDIDATE

The idea of programming a hypnotically conditioned, drug-controlled assassin to kill was born In a novel and a motion picture. Another instance of life imitating art.

The 1962 motion picture *The Manchurian Candidate,* directed by John Frankenheimer, with a screenplay by George Axelrod based on a novel by Richard Condon, has become synonymous with "programmed assassin." Someone who has been hypnotized, brainwashed, drugged, or conditioned through a combination of mind-control techniques to become a killer without being aware of his or her lethal programming is referred to as a "Manchurian Candidate." The assassin would be "triggered" into entering a trance state and committing the murder by a key word, phrase, or symbol. (For example, in the film the "trigger" was the Queen of Diamonds playing card.) Once the target victim has been assassinated, the programmed subject will have no memory of his or her role in the dreadful deed—and quite likely will become a dupe, ar-

rested, convicted, and sentenced as a crazy "lone gunman" who acted independently, unattached to any conspiracy.

The motion picture starred Frank Sinatra, Laurence Harvey, Janet Leigh, Angela Lansbury, and Henry Silva and has been described as a hybrid that combined the genres of horror, science fiction, suspense, political satire, war film, and black comedy. The storyline begins in 1952 during the Korean War (1950–53) with Sinatra (Capt./Maj. Bennett Marco), Harvey (Sgt. Raymond Shaw), and members of their platoon being betrayed by Chunjin (Henry Silva), their Korean interpreter. The infantrymen are ambushed, captured, and whisked away by helicopter to Manchuria, where they are subjected to mind-control experiments by extremely accomplished and very skillful Communist masters of brainwashing. Shaw is programmed to become a political assassin when he returns to the United States, and the nine platoon members who survived the torture and mind-control experiments are given false memories of Shaw's supposed heroism in saving nine of his men from being slaughtered in the ambush that killed the rest of the night patrol. Shaw is awarded the Congressional Medal of Honor, and the Communist plot appears to be working until Marco begins to have dreams and memories of what really happened to his men and him on patrol and in Manchuria before they were released in Korea. The film proceeds in pseudodocumentary style, with narration that intensifies the realism and the paranoia that this story might not be fiction, that such monstrous conspiracies could actually take place. Events might not really be as we remember them. Our friends might not truly be our friends, but are instead potential assassins awaiting the right moment, the right signal, the "trigger," to kill us.

In 1962, when the film was released, the American public was saturated with fears about nuclear bombs, the Cold War, international Communism, McCarthyism, and the poser matter. In either event, Oswald's terrible crime did nothing to halt showing of the film. *The Manchurian Candidate* was telecast on *The CBS Thursday Night Movie* in September 1965, two years after its theatrical release. It received a second showing that same television season, then was telecast for the third and fourth times on NBC in spring 1974 and summer 1975. A few years later the rights to the film reverted to Frank Sinatra, who made no arrangements for its distribution until 1988, when he rereleased *The Manchurian Candidate* through MGM/UA.

MANSON FAMILY

Because God, the Devil, and humanity are all one, Charles Manson reasoned, it really doesn't matter if you kill someone.

Trouble came looking for Charles Manson on the day he was born. His unwed mother was a teenaged hustler named Kathleen Maddox, who shortly after Charlie's birth on November 11, 1934, in Cincinnati, Ohio, was convicted, along with her brother, for mugging a number of the men she had solicited. Although only sixteen years old, she was sent to prison.

With his mother jailed, baby Charlie was sent to live with his grandmother in West Virginia. Later he lived with a quarrelsome uncle and aunt who spent their time fighting. Neighbors recalled Manson as "a poor little kid who never received any love or affection." Charlie never met his father, a "Colonel Scott," who lived in Ashland, Kentucky.

When Manson was eight years old, his mother was released from prison. Charlie trailed along with her as she drank heavily and hustled a steady succession of men. They lived in rundown apartments on the ugly side of the city. By 1945 his mother had found a traveling salesman to live with and she took Charlie along with her to Indianapo-

James Gregory played the title role in the 1962 film *The Manchurian Candidate,* in which a political candidate is brainwashed by Communists to become an unwitting assassin. Are some killers, such as Lee Harvey Oswald, types of "Manchurian candidates"?

sibilities of domestic terrorism. Although some Korean veterans had returned with stories of torture and brainwashing, few people had any idea that their own government had endorsed such mind-control projects as MK-ULTRA in which both volunteers and unsuspecting men and women were undergoing experiments with hypnosis, LSD, mescaline, and a host of other mental mechanisms—and perhaps even being programmed to be "Manchurian Candidates."

Contrary to popular movie folklore, the film was not removed from theatrical distribution after the 1963 assassination of President John F. Kennedy. Theories that Lee Harvey Oswald was inspired to kill JFK after attending a showing of *The Manchurian Candidate* entered the paranoid legends of the times. Oswald may have been a "Manchurian Candidate" programmed to kill Kennedy, but that's anoth-

Charles Manson convinced his followers to kill based on his philosophy that human beings, God, and the Devil were all one, so killing one individual did not really matter.

lis. The authorities there took a cold look at the boy's lack of home life and made him a ward of the county. Charlie was sent to the Gibault School for Boys, a custodial institution for homeless or wayward boys. He escaped after ten months. This began a cycle of tougher and stricter reform schools from which Charlie, by his own count, escaped twenty-eight times.

Charles Manson was thirty-five years old when he was arrested for the Tate-LaBianca murders of August 9 and 10, 1969. Brown-haired, brown-eyed, and slender, he had spent twenty-two years of his life in state or federal prisons. Uneducated, untrained, and scarcely able to read, he had been in and out of prison for almost a quarter of a century. The only

things he learned while incarcerated were how to steal cars, pass bad checks, and pimp. On those rare occasions when Manson was out of prison on parole, he found time to marry twice and to father two children. In 1955 Rosalie Willis became his bride and begat Charles Jr. After the divorce and three years in prison, Manson became a pimp and married a nineteen-year-old hustler who delivered Charles Luther Manson shortly before Manson was arrested in Laredo, Texas, in 1960.

Early on the morning of August 9, 1969, the housekeeper, Winifred Chapman, arrived at the Sharon Tate–Roman Polanski mansion on 10050 Cielo Drive. She first became suspicious about a white Rambler Ambassador automobile blocking the driveway. Approaching the vehicle, she was shocked to see the driver, Steven Parent, nineteen, a friend of William Garretson, the caretaker, dead, shot in the head, slumped over in the front seat. Chapman walked farther onto the grounds and discovered the bodies of Abigail Folger and Wojciech Frykowski, two guests of Sharon Tate, sprawled on the lawn. The front entrance was covered in blood. "PIG!" was scrawled in blood across the front door.

The police rushed to the mansion, checked the corpses on the lawn, then dashed inside to find the bodies of Sharon Tate, who had been several months pregnant, and her friend Jay Sebring. The officers interrogated Garretson because they assumed that he had been present when the five people were viciously butchered. The caretaker soon convinced them that he knew nothing about the massacre of the celebrity victims.

Thirty-five-year-old Jay Sebring (birth name Thomas John Kummer) came to Hollywood in 1958 and established a hairstyling salon in Hollywood. Within a short time his clients included the most famous stars in filmdom. He styled hair for Sammy Davis Jr., Warren Beatty, Steve McQueen, Eddie Fisher, Paul Newman, Frank Sinatra, and Henry Fonda.

Known as "Gibby" to her friends, Abigail Folger was a Radcliffe-educated coffee heiress who became bored with a career in bookselling in New York and sought more excitement in Hollywood. She had money, education, and the daring to compete with the most beautiful women in Hollywood for favors and attention. She lived in an apartment in Laurel Canyon with Frykowski, a noted film producer in his homeland of Poland.

Sharon Tate's husband, film producer Roman Polanski, was in London, attending a party to celebrate the completion of his new movie, *A Day at the Beach.* Tate and Polanski had met when she accepted a role in one of his motion pictures, *The Fearless Vampire Slayers.* After they were married, Sharon appeared in a number of Polanski's films, and she allowed him to photograph her for a photo layout in *Playboy.* Polanski grieved not only for his wife, but for their unborn child.

Considered to be one of the most beautiful women in Hollywood, Sharon Tate won the coveted role of "Jennifer" in the highly promoted film *Valley of the Dolls.* When she was not making films, she often joined Abigail Folger and the actress Mia Farrow for philosophical discussions or spirit séances at Farrow's home near Malibu Beach.

Ironically, in 1967, while Sharon Tate was receiving international attention for her role in *Valley of the Dolls,* Charles Manson was released after serving seven years of a ten-year prison term on federal Mann Act charges. It was while he was doing time in the U.S. prison at McNeil Island, Washington, that he began studying the occult. Manson was also inspired by the music of the Beatles, and he learned to play a steel guitar. He trained his voice and began to write songs.

Music and mysticism were his two chief interests when he walked out of prison in March 1967. A whole new world had been born while he was behind bars. The flower children had launched the hippie movement.

At that time, the Haight-Ashbury section San Francisco was the promised land for the hippies, so Charlie got a hillside pad and started to collect his followers.

One of his first recruits was an attractive nineteen-year-old brunette named Patricia Krenwinkel. She had graduated from Los Angeles High in 1966 and was considered a reserved, conservative young woman until she met Charles Manson. Manson called himself Satan the All-Powerful, and Patricia joined Satan's harem so fast that she abandoned her automobile in a parking lot and left without picking up her paycheck at her job.

Manson collected a number of young, female dropouts, seemingly drawn to the mystical minstrel by some weird spell. A few young men joined his clan and the group became known as the Manson Family. Gullible, emotionally disturbed, and often immature, his young followers believed that Manson was a messiah of the new age. Manson led his cult in weird chants. He adopted mystical rites and began to make prophecies. Anyone who doubted his God-like stature was threatened with expulsion from the group. Some of his disciples were convinced that Manson was a being from another planet, so wise, so ageless.

Led by their mystical guru, the Manson Family converted an old school bus into a rolling pad. In May 1968, with the San Francisco scene dying out and hippies scattering in every direction, Manson and his clan of subservient young women and men headed south toward Los Angeles. The bearded, long-haired cultist was certain that he would make a fortune there as a songwriter and musician.

In the film capital, Manson and his nomads met and moved in with Gary Hinman, thirty-four, a musician. The Hinman home was labeled "the pig farm," a place where anyone might find refuge.

In December 1968, when the Beatles released their *White Album* with the song "Helter

Skelter" among the tracks, Manson became even more obsessed with the notion that he deserved a break in the music business. He believed that there was a large audience for his songs about the racial Armageddon that was bearing down on society. The countdown had begun: Across the nation, blacks were going to begin to slaughter whites.

> Watson pulled out his pistol and told the film director that he was the devil and that they were there to do his business.

Manson believed that Terry Melcher, a record-producer acquaintance who was the singer and actress Doris Day's son, could open doors for him, and he became incensed when he felt that Melcher had given him false promises. He found out that Melcher lived at 10050 Cielo Drive, and he resolved to one day pay him a visit. On March 23, 1969, Manson arrived at the home he believed to be Melcher's, not realizing that the house had been sold to Sharon Tate and Roman Polanski. He met with a rather rude brush-off by a Tate staff member and left outraged at the manner in which he had been treated.

On July 31 Gary Hinman was discovered slashed to death, the bloody words "political piggy" scrawled on the walls of his house. Hinman is believed to be the first murder victim of the Manson Family.

About this time, Manson began to order his family members on nighttime maneuvers that the girls called "creepy crawlies," during which they donned black costumes and "creepy-crawled" around people's houses. The purpose of the exercises, Manson explained, was to allow them to experience and overcome fear.

On August 8 Manson told family members Susan Atkins, Charles "Tex" Watson, Linda Kasabian, and Pat Krenwinkel to get their knives and their changes of clothing. Tonight was the time for Helter Skelter.

Armed with knives, a change of clothes, and a gun, Tex Watson drove the team to the Tate mansion. Watson parked the vehicle and snipped the telephone wires. The cultists were surprised when Steven Parent walked down the driveway from the caretaker's cottage and got into his automobile. Watson rushed to the boy's Rambler, fired twice, and killed him.

Watson forced open a window of the mansion, crawled inside, and opened the door for his companions. Wojciech Frykowski was asleep on a couch in the living room, but he awakened and began to shout at the intruders. Watson pulled out his pistol and told the film director that he was the devil and that they were there to do his business.

The disturbance alarmed Sharon Tate and the other guests. Jay Sebring stared at the four armed strangers and began to fight. He was shot, stabbed, and fell dead in the living room. Although Frykowski had been tied, he broke the nylon cords that bound him. One of the girls stabbed him several times as he raced out of the house screaming for help. Watson pursued the wounded man, clubbed him with the pistol, then shot him in the back. Abigail Folger was stabbed as she tried to run toward the caretaker's house on the southern edge of the grounds. She was caught, slashed and stabbed to death on the lawn.

Sharon Tate battled two of the girls until she was overpowered and forced back onto a couch. She told them that all she wanted to do was to have her baby. She was stabbed to death.

When they returned, Manson berated his family members for doing such a messy job of slaughter. That night he accompanied Patricia Krenwinkel, Tex Watson, Leslie Van Houten, and Linda Kasabian as they drove around deciding upon the next victims to sacrifice in order to announce the coming bloodbath between blacks and whites.

In the early morning hours, Krenwinkel, Van Houten, Kasabian, and Watson pulled up in front of the LaBianca home. Leno and Rosemary LaBianca, wealthy business owners in Los Angeles, were seized by the cultists and tied up. They pleaded for their lives to the group, who were "tripped out" on LSD. The LaBiancas were stabbed to death. Before they left, the murderers scrawled "Death to Pigs" and "Healter [sic] Skelter" on a wall and a refrigerator door.

Manson was arrested and jailed on October 12 for grand theft auto. After following numerous leads, the Los Angeles police able to implicate him and certain members of his family in the Tate-LaBianca murders. On July 24, 1970, the trial began in Los Angeles with the defendants Charles Manson, Susan Atkins, Patricia Krenwinkel, and Leslie Van Houten. Linda Kasabian was granted immunity in return for appearing as the prosecution's star witness. Tex Watson, the principal killer in the murders, had returned to Texas and was arrested on November 30, 1969. He was tried separately in 1971 and convicted of seven counts of first-degree murder.

Throughout their arraignments and trials, Manson's female followers claimed that their self-styled guru was innocent of any blame in the slayings. Patricia Krenwinkel described life in Manson's nomadic family as an ideal existence.

On January 25, 1971, Manson and his female codefendants were convicted of first-degree murder, and on March 29, 1971, all four were given the death penalty. Manson claimed that he and all of humanity were God and devil at the same time. He also professed that every human is a part of all others, meaning that individual human life is of no consequence. Kill a person and you are just murdering a part of yourself, so that makes everything all right.

On February 18, 1972, the California Supreme Court ruled that the death penalty was unconstitutional. Death sentences were automatically reduced to life in prison.

In 2005 Manson was held in Corcoran Prison. He was refused parole the eleventh time in 2007 and, as of this writing, was scheduled for another hearing in 2012.

Susan Atkins, along with her female family members, was serving her life sentence at the California Institution for Women at Frontera. She had been denied parole ten times.

In spite of an exemplary prison record, Leslie Van Houten was denied her fourteenth parole appeal. She has earned a bachelor's and a master's degree and works in the chaplain's office. She was denied parole for the nineteenth time in 2010.

As of 2011, Patricia Krenwinkel has been denied parole thirteen times.

Tex Watson resides at the Mule Creek State Prison in Ione, California. In 1975 he became a born-again Christian, and in 1983 an ordained minister.

Linda Kasabian, who was granted immunity, left California, and her present whereabouts are unknown.

In 1994 the mansion at 10050 Cielo Drive was demolished.

JIM MARRS

Jim Marrs is a respected, retired journalist, who, since 1992, has been researching government programs involving psychic phenomena.

Although he is often described as a "conspiracy theorist," Jim Marrs operates by his motto: "If it's not an act of God, it's a conspiracy." Accidents do happen, but if it's not accidental then someone planned it that way. And as for theories—if you can prove something, it is no longer a theory but a fact.

> The story of military-developed remote viewing broke nationally in the *Washington Post* after the CIA revealed the program while putting its own spin on psychic studies.

A native of Fort Worth, Texas, Marrs earned a bachelor of arts degree in journalism from the University of North Texas in 1966 and attended graduate school at Texas Tech in Lubbock for two more years. He has worked for several Texas newspapers, including the *Fort Worth Star-Telegram,* where, beginning in 1968, he served as a police and general assignments reporter covering stories locally, in Europe, and the Middle East. After a leave of absence to serve with a Fourth Army intelligence unit during the Vietnam War, he became a military and aerospace writer for the newspaper and an investigative reporter. Since 1980, Marrs has been a freelance writer, author, and public relations consultant. He also published a rural weekly newspaper, along with a monthly tourism tabloid, a cable television show, and several videos.

In 2007, Marrs retired from the University of Texas at Arlington, where he had taught a course on the Kennedy assassination since 1976. In 1989, his book *Crossfire: The Plot that Killed Kennedy,* was published to critical acclaim and made the *New York Times* Paperback Nonfiction Bestseller list in mid-February 1992. It became a basis for the Oliver Stone film *JFK.* Marrs served as a chief consultant for both the film's screenplay and production.

Beginning in 1992, Marrs spent three years researching and completing a nonfiction book on a top-secret government program involving the psychic phenomenon known as remote viewing, only to have it mysteriously canceled as it was going to press in the summer of 1995. Within two months, the story of military-developed remote viewing broke nationally in the *Washington Post* after the CIA revealed the program while putting its own spin on psychic studies. Marr's book *Psi Spies* was finally published by New Page Books in 2007.

Marrs has been a featured speaker at a number of national conferences, including the Annual International UFO Congress and the Annual Gulf Breeze UFO Conference. In May 1997, Marrs's in-depth investigation of UFOs, *Alien Agenda,* was published by HarperCollins Publishers. It has been translated into several foreign languages and become the top-selling nonfiction UFO book in the world.

Marrs began teaching a course on UFOs at the University of Texas at Arlington in 2000. Also in early 2000, HarperCollins published *Rule by Secrecy,* which traced the hidden history that connects modern secret societies to the Ancient Mysteries. It too reached the *New York Times* bestseller list. In 2003, his book *The War on Freedom* probed the conspiracies of the 9/11 attacks and their aftermath. It was released in 2006 under the title *The Terror Conspiracy.* In mid-2008, his book *The Rise of the Fourth Reich,* detailing the infiltration of National Socialism into the United States, was published, followed by a study of mysteries entitled *Above Top Secret.*

An award-winning journalist, Marrs is listed both in *Who's Who in the World* and *Who's Who in America.* Marrs has won several writing and photography awards, including the Aviation/Aerospace Writer's Association's National Writing Award and Newsmaker of the Year Award from the Fort Worth Chapter of the Society of Professional Journalists. In 1993,

Marrs received *Freedom Magazine*'s Human Rights Leadership Award.

Marrs has appeared on ABC, NBC, CBS, CNN, CSPAN, the Discovery, Learning and History Channels, *This Morning America, Geraldo, Montel Williams, Today, Tech TV, The Larry King Show, The Jeff Rense Program, George Noory,* and the *Art Bell* radio programs, along with numerous national and regional radio and TV shows. He is a former president of the Press Club of Fort Worth and a current member of the Society of Professional Journalists, Sigma Delta Chi, and the Investigative Reporters and Editors.

"I think the thing I have found most significant in my research is that modern secret societies such as the Council on Foreign Relations, The Trilateral Commission and Bilderbergers can be traced back through older groups such as Cecil Rhodes' Round Tables, Illumanized Freemasonry and the Knights Templar to the ancient mystery schools of Greece and Egypt, which possessed much of the elder knowledge the Annunaki handed down to the Sumerians," Marrs said in an email to the Steigers. "There has been one continuous trail of underground knowledge and attempted control throughout human history."

TEXE MARRS

A retired career Air Force officer, professor of aerospace studies, and bestselling author, Texe Marrs has an impressive résumé, which is why many readers believe what he has to say when he publishes books about conspiracies against the American people.

Well-known author of three number one national Christian bestsellers, including the landmark bestselling book *Dark Secrets of the New Age,* Texe Marrs has also written forty-two other books for such major publishers as Simon & Schuster, John Wiley, Mc-

Graw-Hill, Prentice Hall/Arco, Stein & Day, and Dow Jones-Irwin. His books have sold millions of copies and have been published in many foreign countries, including Turkey, Greece, Romania, Finland, Norway, and Sweden. They have been featured as main selections of the Christian Book Club, the Conservative Book Club, and the Computer and Electronics Book Clubs.

Texe Marrs was assistant professor of aerospace studies, teaching American defense policy, strategic weapons systems, and related subjects at the University of Texas at Austin from 1977 to 1982. He has also taught international affairs, political science, and psychology for two other universities. A summa cum laude graduate of Park University in Kansas City, Missouri, he earned his master's degree at North Carolina State University.

As a career U.S. Air Force officer (now retired), he commanded communications-electronics and engineering units. He holds a number of military decorations, including the Vietnam Service Medal and the Presidential Unit Citation, and served in Germany, Italy, and throughout Asia. He was chosen Airman of the Year while serving at Korat Air Base, Thailand.

President of Power of Prophecy Ministries and RiverCrest Publishing in Austin, Texas, Marrs is a frequent guest on radio and TV talk shows throughout the United States and Canada in response to the public's search for greater insight into Bible prophecy, secret societies, politics, and world affairs. His latest books include *Conspiracy of the Six-Pointed Star—Eye-Opening Revelations and Forbidden Knowledge about Israel, the Jews, Zionism, and the Rothschilds; Codex Magica: Secret Signs, Mysterious Symbols, and Hidden Codes of the Illuminati; Mysterious Monuments: Encyclopedia of Secret Illuminati Designs, Masonic Architecture, and Occult Places;* and the highly acclaimed *Conspiracy World: A Truthteller's Compendium of Eye-opening Revelations and Forbidden Knowledge.*

In addition to his many books, Texe Marrs has produced over thirty bestselling video documentaries, including the investigative exposé, *Rothschild's Choice—Barack Obama and the Hidden Cabal behind the Plot to Murder America,* a number one national bestseller at Amazon.com. Texe Marrs's monthly newsletter is distributed to tens of thousands of subscribers around the world. His radio program, *Power of Prophecy,* is beamed by shortwave radio and Internet to nations around the globe.

MAU MAU

Kikuyu dissidents in Kenya revived an ancient secret society to support their demands for independence from the British. Tragically, black magic rituals soon became transformed into bloody rites.

In 1948, police officials in the British colony of Kenya began to receive reports of midnight assemblies in the jungle, where the participants mocked Christian rites through bestial rituals that included the eating of human flesh and the drinking of blood. These strange accounts were soon followed by stories of native people being dragged from their beds at night, beaten, and forced to swear oaths of initiation to a secret society called the Mau Mau.

Experts on tribal culture thought that the Mau Mau was an ancient Kikuyu secret society that had been reactivated. The Kikuyu tribe was the most populous and best educated in Kenya, but their culture also permitted secret societies to flourish, and many such groups had existed since long before the Europeans came to Africa. The Mau Mau leaders invoked the old secret society in order to stir up the Kikuyu to support their demands for independence and for the return of the Kikuyu land that the whites had taken over the years.

The reactivated secret society had moved from practicing black magic and the administration of blood oaths into the most violent barbarism. The first man to die at the hands of the Mau Mau was a Kikuyu chief who spoke out against them. A state of emergency was declared in Kenya as the midnight rituals and beatings escalated into the murder of Kikuyu policemen, whose bodies were found mutilated and bound with wire, floating in rivers. White farmers discovered their cattle disemboweled and the tendons in the animals' legs severed so they could not walk. In October 1952 a lone white settler was killed and disemboweled. An elderly farmer was found dead in November; in January 1953 two men who worked a farm as partners were discovered murdered by the Mau Mau.

The Mau Mau weapon of choice was the panga, a broad-bladed machete commonly used to hack a path through thick jungle vegetation. The society appeared to favor bloody and brutal attacks as a means of striking fear into the hearts and minds of all who might oppose them, but their choice of enemies often seemed difficult to understand.

A vicious attack on January 24, 1953, claimed the Rucks, a family of English heritage who had always been regarded as dealing with their black employees in a fair-minded and charitable manner, even to the extent of supporting a clinic at their own expense. What seemed particularly insidious to the white population was that employees who had been loyal to them for decades were suddenly rising up and butchering them without warning. Such unprovoked and bestial butchery as that exhibited toward the Rucks had the white farmers watching their employees apprehensively and preparing for another brutal attack on their isolated homes.

The next violent raid occurred on March 26, 1953, against the police station at Naivasha. The attackers overran the station and hauled away guns and ammunition in a truck. Later that same night, the Mau Mau bound the circular huts in the villages of Lari with cables so the doors could not be opened, poured gasoline over the thatched roofs, and set the homes on fire. Most of the men of the village were away serving in the Kikuyu Guard, an anti–Mau Mau force, so most of the ninety bodies found in the charred remains were those of women and children. In addition, the Mau Mau had mutilated over a thousand of the villagers' cattle as further punishment for opposing them.

> Experts on tribal culture thought that the Mau Mau was an ancient Kikuyu secret society that had been reactivated.

The ranks of the Mau Mau increased when they began to force many unwilling individuals from other tribes into participating in their blood oaths. The oathing ceremonies began with the new members taking a vow to honor the old religion of their tribal ancestors. There were at least seven stages of oath-taking, which might take several days or weeks to complete and which included the drinking of blood, eating portions of human flesh, having sex with animals, and ingesting bits of brains from disinterred corpses. After the seventh stage of the oath-taking had been reached, the members had to repeat the cycle and reinforce their vows by beginning again. No man or woman was exempt from this requirement, not even the leaders of the society.

The Mau Mau reign of terror was broken by small bands of white settlers who joined the auxiliary police, army units, and Kikuyus, who taught the whites how to move silently through the thick underbrush. In May 1956 a party of Kikuyu tribal police captured Dedan Kimathi, the militant head of the Mau Mau. The British executed Kimathi in 1957 for having ordered atrocities and murders.

By the time the Mau Mau were disbanded, they had slaughtered over two thousand African tribespeople and maimed many thousands more. Killings of white settlers attributed to the Mau Mau range from a minimum of thirty-two to nearly a hundred.

The Kikuyu Central Association, the political party that fronted for the secret activities of the Mau Mau, was headed by Johnstone Kamau, better known as Jomo Kenyatta (1892–1978). Under his leadership, Kenya gained independence in 1963.

MECHA

A group of Latinos known as MEChA believes that a large swath of the American Southwest should separate from the United States to form the country of Aztlán.

If you have never contemplated what the United States would look like if it hadn't been for the Louisiana Purchase of 1803, the Treaty of Guadalupe Hidalgo of 1848, and the Gadsden Purchase of 1853, you would be in for quite a shock if you saw a map with the nation's borders minus the land encompassed by those treaties. The nation that we know today as stretching from sea to shining sea would still be clustered around the northeast seaboard, little more than the original thirteen colonies. The United States, as we know it, had to be purchased or won by treaty in order to become the expansive nation that we know today.

There is no record of any serious French movement to reclaim much of the southern and Midwestern states, but in the late 1960s a Hispanic separatist organization was formed to reclaim the lands of Aztlán. While Aztlán is a land that never existed, as MEChA defines its mythical borders it would include the present states of Texas, New Mexico, Colorado, Arizona, Utah, California, Oregon, and parts of Washington. MEChA, its official symbol depicting an eagle clutching a machete and a stick of dynamite in its talons, stands for "Movimiento Estudianti Chicano de Aztlán" or "Chicano Student Movement of Aztlán." Members of MEChA refer to themselves as "Mechistas" or "La Raza" (the Race), and their proposed goal is to liberate the lost lands of the Southwest.

According to many educators and others monitoring the movement, MEChA groups or clubs exist on as many as ninety percent of Southwestern public high schools and college and university campuses. The mystique of Aztlán is delineated in *The Mexican American Heritage* by Carlos Jimenez, an East Los Angeles high school teacher who portrays the mythical land in a recreated map of Mexico in which the Hispanic nation is depicted with the "lost" U.S. states attached to it. Jimenez predicts that soon Latinos will realize that they have the power to bring Aztlán under their control.

Some observers of the movement have been concerned about evidence of growing communist or socialist philosophy infiltrating the groups. At the MEChA National Conference on Marcy 15 to 18, 2001, the official philosophy of the movement was adopted; it urged all Mechistas to work for the liberation of Aztlán. All Chicano and Chicana students were instructed to take it upon themselves to promote Chicanismo within their communities. An emphasis was placed on politicizing Raza consciousness and struggling for self-determination. Capitalistic America was depicted as a nation controlled by greed whose goal was to hold Latinos in a kind of serfdom.

MEN IN BLACK (MIB)

Since the 1950s serious UFO investigators and witnesses of strange aerial phenomena have been menaced by mysterious men in black.

The frightening scenario is almost always the same. A UFO investigator or a witness of mysterious aerial phenomena is alone in his home. There is a knock at the door and one or more strange men dressed in black push their way into the witness's home. On occasion, the MIB wear uniforms, most often U.S. Air Force, and sometimes flash CIA or Secret Service credentials. The intruders are usually described as rather short, dark-complexioned, and somewhat Asian in appearance with oddly slanted eyes. They are nearly always male, but some victims of the MIB have said that one of the number was female.

The interrogation of the witness begins at once, and the MIB know all the details of the sighting. If the witness happened to photograph the event, they demand the film. They insist on complete cooperation, stating that to do so is for the good of the witness's country, the world, and the universe. Although menacing in demeanor—described as cold, expressionless, and unfriendly—they also sometimes exhibit weird mannerisms, such overly precise speech, outdated expressions, and laughter at inappropriate times. Some witnesses recall them as appearing to have trouble breathing.

Before they leave, the MIB warn the witness to tell no one of their visit. If the victim is a UFO researcher, they order complete abandonment of investigations. Violence is often threatened or implied if the witness should disobey their orders.

Ever since organized flying saucer research began in the early 1950s, a number of serious UFO investigators have suffered personal harassment, unusual accidents, and even mysterious deaths. In some cases sinister voices have whispered threats over the telephone and warned researchers to terminate specific investigations. Official disclaimers have only served to intensify the mystery of the bizarre incidents occurring within the ranks of civilian UFO investigators and instill fear among those who witness flying saucer activity.

According to UFO lore, it was in September 1953 that three agents of such a silencing group made their first in-person visit. Albert K. Bender, who had organized an international flying-saucer bureau, was their target. According to UFOlogist Gray Barker, Bender had received data that he felt provided the missing pieces for a theory concerning the origin of flying saucers. Bender wrote down his thesis and sent it to a friend he trusted. When the three men appeared at Bender's door, one of them held that letter in his hand.

The MIB told Bender that among the many saucer researchers, he had been the one to derive correct answers to the flying saucer enigma. Then they filled him in on the details. Bender became ill. He was unable to eat for three days. He told fellow UFO investigators Dominick Lucchesi and August C. Roberts that when people found out the truth about flying saucers there would be dramatic changes in all things. Science, especially, would suffer a major blow. Political structures would topple. Mass confusion would reign.

In 1962 Bender published *Flying Saucers and the Three Men,* an account that confused serious UFO researchers, as it told of Bender's astral projection to a secret underground saucer base in Antarctica manned by male, female, and bisexual creatures. UFO investigators questioned whether Bender's experiences were perhaps of a psychic nature or he had deliberately contrived the story to hide the true nature of his silencing.

Within a few months after the three men allegedly confronted Bender, Edgar R. Jarrold, organizer of the Australian Flying Saucer Bureau, and Harold H. Fulton, head of Civilian Saucer Investigation of New Zealand, received visits from "mysterious strangers" and subsequently disbanded their organizations. John H. Stuart, a New Zealander, picked up a piece of metal that had fallen from a UFO during a sighting in February 1955. The next night he received a visit from a man dressed in black who relieved him of the gray-white metal.

"I have a feeling that some day there will come a slow knocking at my own door," Gray Barker stated in *They Knew Too Much about Flying Saucers.* "They will be at your door, too, unless we all get wise and find out who the three men really are."

In 1956 the astrophysicist Morris K. Jessup, who had been vitally interested in UFO research, received the first of a series of letters concerning flying saucers, secret navy experiments, disappearing ships, and invisible men. The correspondent signed himself as Carlos Allende. The letters, postmarked from Texas and from Pennsylvania, seemed important enough to the Office of Naval Research to assign a special study group to the mystery. Although official investigation seemed to bog down, Jessup pursued his independent research into the flying saucer puzzle. The astrophysicist subsequently was found dead in his automobile outside a park in Florida, an alleged suicide.

In the late 1940s Ray Palmer founded *Fate* magazine with Curt Fuller and gave the UFO enigma its first big publicity push. The air force dubbed Palmer the "Father of Flying Saucers" and accused the editor-publisher of having fabricated the whole business to boost sales of his magazine. Palmer was the one researcher who had been in on the UFO mystery from the beginning. In June 1947 Palmer sent businessman-pilot Kenneth Arnold, who "discovered" flying saucers, to Tacoma, Washington. There Arnold became embroiled in the famous Maury Island incident—which, according to Palmer, "ended in terror and disaster and the deaths of two fine Fourth Air Force secret-service officers."

The incident began on the afternoon of June 21, 1947, when fisherman Harold A. Dahl and his son saw six large, round aerial objects hovering over the bay off Maury Island, near Tacoma. While they watched, one of

According to Albert K. Bender, who made this drawing, sinister Men in Black convinced him to stop looking for aliens.

the UFOs dumped or sprayed a substance something like molten slag that the fishermen claimed damaged their boat, killed their dog, and nearly killed the two of them. After he had taken his son to be treated at a local hospital, Dahl told his employer, Fred Lee Crisman, about the harrowing experience. Initially Crisman doubted the account, but samples of the mysterious substance emitted by the UFO that Dahl had collected later convinced him. On the morning after his seemingly hostile encounter with a spaceship, Dahl said that he was contacted by a man dressed in black, driving a black 1947 Buick, who warned him to speak no more about the UFOs over Maury Island. About the same time, Crisman, who was checking out Dahl's story about the slag, claimed to see a UFO hovering over the bay.

The Maury Island affair was quickly written off as a hoax by air force investigators, but

Arnold claimed to have been confronted by at least two nearly omniscient Men in Black, who thus antedated Bender's visitors by six years.

Howard Menger, an early UFO contactee who claims to have been inside a saucer and to have talked with aliens, said that when he was living in High Bridge, New Jersey, in 1957, two men in dark business suits came to call on him. They displayed authentic-looking credentials and claimed to be agents from a government bureau. They warned Menger to quit talking about flying saucers and to drop his research.

In 1965 Rex Heflin of McMinnville, Oregon, managed to take some highly interesting photos of a UFO while performing his duties with the highway department. A few days later Heflin was visited by a man bearing credentials of the North American Air Defense Command (NORAD). The phony NORAD investigator demanded, and received, Heflin's original series of pictures. They were never returned until, years later, they mysteriously appeared in his mailbox. Analysts still recognize Heflin's photos as among the best ever taken of UFOs.

In April 1966 two Norwalk, Connecticut, schoolboys were pursued by a low-flying UFO. The next day a man appeared at the boys' school and introduced himself to the principal as a representative of a "government agency so secret that he couldn't give the name." The mysterious agent questioned the boys for nearly three hours.

Broadcaster Frank Edwards, now best remembered for his best-selling book *Flying Saucers—Serious Business,* spoke often of an official plot to silence him. Edwards had been conducting a highly successful radio show sponsored by the American Federation of Labor when he began to air stories on flying saucers. He was warned to abandon the subject. Edwards persisted and was given his walking papers. In spite of thousands of letters protesting his firing and the silencing of his UFO reports, his ex-sponsor stood firm.

When reporters asked George Meany, president of the AFL, why Edwards had been dropped, Meany answered that it was because he talked too much about flying saucers. Edwards said that he later learned that his constant mention of UFOs had been irritating to the Defense Department, which had brought pressure on the AFL.

In 1966 the researcher and author John Keel stated his opinion that the Men in Black are the "intelligence arm of a large and possibly hostile group." Keel considered the MIB to be professional terrorists who had among their duties the harassment of UFO researchers involved in cases that might reveal too much of the truth. Keel's pursuit of the silencers led him to uncover some extreme cases of personal abuse in which certain contactees or investigators have been kidnapped by three men in a black car. The abductors subjected their victims to some sort of brainwashing technique that left them in a state of nausea, mental confusion, or even amnesia lasting for several days.

In Keel's opinion, UFO researchers were wasting their time chasing lights in the sky and worrying about air force involvement in the flying saucer enigma. In his address to the 1967 Congress of Scientific UFOlogists, held at the Commodore Hotel in New York, Keel told of his personal mission to track down the silencers, and he advised UFO investigators to shift their attention from the vehicles to the occupants. In his opinion, the menace was not in our skies, but on the ground, and spreading like a disease across the country and the world. "The UFOs don't want us to know where they are from," Keel stated. "They have been lying to contactees since 1897"—a reference to the mysterious Airship of 1897 widely reported in that year.

In response to the controversy stirred up by Keel and other investigators over MIB, Col. George P. Freeman, the Pentagon spokesman for Project Blue Book, was quoted as saying,

"We have checked a number of these cases, and these men are not connected with the Air Force in any way. It has never been within the line of duty of any government agency to threaten a private citizen or to enter his home without a search warrant. No government agent is empowered to demand surrender of private property by any law-abiding citizen." Colonel Freeman went on to say that by posing as military officers and government agents, the silencers were committing a federal offense.

In recent years, encounters with the MIB have decreased. They have even been the basis for three motion-picture comedy spoofs starring Tommy Lee Jones and Will Smith. Although reports of the mysterious interrogators have diminished, they have not ceased altogether. UFO researchers and witnesses still report bizarre, perhaps paranormal, experiences after sighting unusual aerial activity. And some witnesses still insist that they were terrified by individuals dressed in black who paid them a visit and threatened their lives if they didn't forget the UFO phenomena that they observed.

If the silencers are perpetrating a hoax, who is doing it and why? Are they, as some investigators believe, agents from another world who labor to spread confusion and fear among serious UFO researchers? Are they, in spite of official denials, agents from a top-secret government agency that knows the answer to the flying-saucer enigma and has been commissioned to keep the truth from the American public? Or, as some researchers have theorized, are the silencers and the UFOs from an older terrestrial race that has survived and become more technically advanced as it thrives in some remote region of Earth?

Whoever the silencers may be, they clearly wish the nations of the world to remain ignorant of the facts about flying saucers. Perhaps they reason that the more ignorant we are of the true nature of the dangers which face us, the less able we will be to deal with the inevitable confrontation with an alien race and the more rapidly we will allow ourselves to become subject to a race or culture that considers itself superior to *Homo sapiens.*

MK-ULTRA

This CIA mind-control project was so horrible that all records were ordered destroyed.

In 1964 Richard Helms, director of the CIA, ordered records of all 150 individual projects of MK-ULTRA destroyed. The program, initiated on the orders of CIA chief Allen Dulles on April 13, 1953, and conducted by Dr. Sidney Gottlieb, had mind control as its principal objective. Rumors and half-truths about new mind-control techniques being used by Soviet, Chinese, and North Korean interrogators on U.S. prisoners of war panicked the CIA into a search for its own sure-fire method of questioning captives.

Many researchers believe that the "MK" in MK-ULTRA stood for "Mind Kontrolle," with a German spelling of the English word *control* because many German doctors who were masters of mind control were snatched by the Office of Strategic Services (OSS), later CIA, to work on a number of insidious projects. Hitler's chief of intelligence against the Russians, General Reinhard Gehlen, arrived in Washington in 1945 and spent months working with William "Wild Bill" Donovan, director of the OSS, and Allen Dulles to reorganize the American intelligence program into the Central Intelligence Group in 1946, then, in 1947, the Central Intelligence Agency under Dulles's leadership. General Gehlen shared the behavior-modification research of Dr. Josef Mengele at Auschwitz and the brainwashing experiments conducted at Dachau with hypnosis and mescaline.

In 1947 the U.S. Navy developed Project Chatter in response to the Soviets' supposed success with "truth drugs." In 1950 Allen Dulles approved Project Bluebird to discover mind-control methods; in 1951, Bluebird was renamed Artichoke and assigned the problem of utilizing hypnosis and drugs to resist interrogation. The CIA conducted hundreds of experiments with hypnosis and with mescaline, peyote, and other hallucinogenic drugs before they had some success with LSD in MK-ULTRA in 1953.

At first "acid" seemed to fill the bill. Dr. Gottlieb used the drug himself as a frequent guinea pig. It has been said that Gottlieb, born with a clubfoot and a stutter, compensated by becoming an expert folk dancer and earning his Ph.D. from Cal Tech. In order to rush the studies of how effective LSD might be on a wide variety of individuals with vastly differing personalities, Gottlieb ordered experiments on mostly unsuspecting CIA agents, military personnel, prostitutes, mental patients, and members of the general public.

Further research by Gottlieb became quite sadistic. Perhaps his own use of the drug released his inner sadist, for some of the experiments with LSD seem more like torture than scientific inquiry. On occasion Gottlieb would lock volunteers in sensory deprivation chambers while they were on LSD. In one extreme case volunteers were dosed with LSD for seventy-seven days straight. Because MK-ULTRA's records were destroyed, there is no existing document revealing how many of these unfortunate individuals were driven insane.

An alleged May 5, 1955, MK-ULTRA document that found its way into wide circulation has specific orders to find a mind-altering substance that would accomplish the following effects:

- induce illogical thinking and impulsiveness to the point where the recipient would be discredited in public;

- produce the signs and symptoms of recognized diseases in a reversible way so that they may be used for malingering, and so on;

- render the use of hypnosis easier or otherwise enhance its usefulness;

- enhance the ability of individuals to withstand privation, torture, and coercion during interrogation and "brainwashing";

- produce amnesia for events preceding and during [the drug's] use;

- produce shock and confusion over extended periods of time;

- be able to be used surreptitiously;

- produce physical disablement, such as paralysis of the legs;

- produce pure euphoria with no subsequent let-down;

- alter personality structure in such a way that the tendency of the recipient to become dependent upon another person is enhanced;

- cause mental confusion of such a type that the individual under its influence will find it difficult to maintain a fabrication under questioning;

- lower the ambition and general working efficiency when administered in undetectable amounts.

There is no evidence that MK-ULTRA or later CIA experiments actually succeeded in accomplishing many of the above mind-control techniques, but since the files of the program were destroyed, no one can definitely say that MK-ULTRA didn't succeed in numerous instances of mind control or in the creation of zombielike assassins. In 1964 MK-ULTRA was renamed MKSEARCH, supposedly a refined search for the perfect truth serum.

MKSEARCH

In the mid-1960s a CIA-endorsed project searched for the perfect truth serum, indifferent to the number of "expendables" used in the experiments.

In 1964, according to some researchers, the CIA's MK-ULTRA project was renamed MK-SEARCH, indicating a refined search for the perfect truth serum. However, some investigators claim that MKSEARCH was actually one of the more insidious of all the secret projects being conducted at that time. Based on some of the initial research of Dr. Donald Ewen Cameron, who had begun his career with the OSS, later the CIA, in World War II studying the experiments of Nazi psychiatrists with concentration camp prisoners, and Dr. Sidney Gottlieb, the head of MK-ULTRA, who tested the effects of LSD on unsuspecting individuals, the project required "expendables" in order to be effective. By "expendables" the researchers meant subjects whose disappearance, should they happen to die during the experiments, was unlikely to arouse suspicion.

MKSEARCH tests would be carried out at CIA safe houses in such cities as Washington, New York, Chicago, and Los Angeles. The experiments would focus on the exploitation of human weaknesses and the destabilization of the human personality. In large cities, it was suggested, finding "expendables" who would not be missed would be much easier than in smaller towns or rural areas. The subjects of the experiments would be exposed to tests designed to create disturbances of behavior, alterations of sex patterns, and stimulation of aberrations, which could all be used in the process of interrogations and the obtaining of information.

Gottlieb founded two separate laboratories, neither of which was aware of the other's existence or the nature of the project. A private civilian research facility in Baltimore was assigned to find a chemical that could mimic death by carbon dioxide poisoning and another that could arouse a desire for sex. The other facility was the Army Biological Laboratory at Fort Detrick, Maryland, which had been working on a similar project, MKNaomi, since 1952. Gottlieb also allocated $85,000 to Dr. Harold Abramson, an immunologist at Mount

Sinai Hospital in New York, to conduct experiments in disturbance memory.

There is no clear evidence that MKSEARCH ever conducted its research on "expendables," for in 1972 Richard Helms, director of the CIA, ordered records of all 150 individual projects of MK-ULTRA destroyed.

MARIA MONK

Before she escaped from the convent, Sister Maria was tortured and made a sex slave of evil priests. Her subsequent book, The Awful Disclosures of Maria Monk, *became a pre–Civil War bestseller, second only to* Uncle Tom's Cabin.

Since its first release in January 1836, *The Awful Disclosures of Maria Monk as Exhibited in a Narrative of Her Life and Sufferings during a Residence of Five Years as a Novice and Two Years as a Black Nun in the Hotel Dieu Nunnery in Montreal* has never been out of print. *Awful Disclosures* sold an estimated 300,000 copies before the Civil War and was second in sales only to Harriet Beecher Stowe's *Uncle Tom's Cabin.*

In her book Maria, although Protestant, attends a Roman Catholic school, where the nuns convince her that the Protestant Bible and the teachings it encourages are evil. Maria converts to Catholicism and is shocked when she receives offensive sexual interrogation by the priests when she goes to confession. In spite of such humiliating inquiries, Maria decides to become a nun. After four years as a novice, she reconsiders her decision and leaves the convent, only to fall into a hasty and unfortunate marriage. Once again, Maria changes her mind and returns to the convent to prepare to take her final vows. And now, to her horror, she learns about the real lifestyles of nuns and priests.

After she has taken her final vows, she is told that she must be an obedient nun and obey without question whatever a priest commands or asks of her. She is told to engage in sexual intercourse with those priests who demand it of her. She is forced to participate in an all-night orgy with three priests. Nuns who refuse to submit to the priests' demands are kept in underground dungeons. Infants born of such unholy unions are baptized, then immediately killed and buried in lime pits in the convent basement. Troublesome nuns are tortured, murdered, and buried in those same pits.

When Maria finds herself pregnant by a priest, she decides to escape the foul convent. Pursued by agents of the church, she manages to make her way to New York, where she is at last rescued by courageous Protestant clergymen.

Published in an era when the Know-Nothing anti-Catholic political party was actively spreading hatred of the Roman Catholic Church and manufacturing accounts of sexual perversion among its clergy, *The Awful Disclosures of Maria Monk* became a popular propaganda tool. Originally published by a dummy company established by Harper Brothers of New York to keep its reputation unsullied from what was considered salacious material, Maria Monk became the heroine of the Protestant press. The public gobbled up copies of the book that gave them what they believed was the first true portrayal of convent life and fulfilled all the expectations that had been fueled by rumors and anti-Catholic slander.

Slowly, however, the fabric of the fabulous tale began to unravel. Investigators in Montreal found that the Hotel Dieu was not at all like the description in Maria's book. It was, in fact, a greatly respected charitable hospital and convent whose nuns had recently become revered by the citizenry for their heroism in a cholera epidemic.

Other investigators located Maria's mother, who informed them that the girl had been

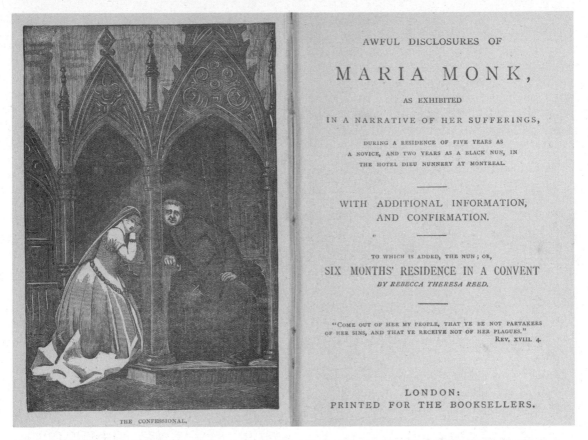

AWFUL DISCLOSURES OF

MARIA MONK,

AS EXHIBITED

IN A NARRATIVE OF HER SUFFERINGS,

DURING A RESIDENCE OF FIVE YEARS AS
A NOVICE, AND TWO YEARS AS A BLACK NUN, IN
THE HOTEL DIEU NUNNERY AT MONTREAL.

WITH ADDITIONAL INFORMATION,
AND CONFIRMATION.

TO WHICH IS ADDED, THE NUN; OR,

SIX MONTHS' RESIDENCE IN A CONVENT

BY REBECCA THERESA REED.

"COME OUT OF HER MY PEOPLE, THAT YE BE NOT PARTAKERS
OF HER SINS, AND THAT YE RECEIVE NOT OF HER PLAGUES."
REV. XVIII. 4.

LONDON:
PRINTED FOR THE BOOKSELLERS.

THE CONFESSIONAL.

The Awful Disclosures of Maria Monk, about a nun who escapes life as a sex slave at the hands of priests, was a bestseller in the 1830s.

given to wild fantasies after an injury to her ear and had become uncontrollable. Maria had been committed to a Magdalen Asylum in Montreal and, as a Protestant, that had been her only contact with the Roman Catholic Church. At eighteen she left the asylum after becoming pregnant and found her way to the Canadian Benevolent Society, a Protestant mission with a strong anti-Catholic bias. She told an interesting story, which caught the ear of William Hoyte, who took her to New York to meet with Rev. J. J. Slocum and a group of Protestant ministers. It may never be known if the story told in *The Awful Disclosures of Maria Monk* was Maria's own imaginative fantasy or if the ministers were responsible for the lurid tale. There seems little question

that the clergymen, particularly Slocum, were the actual authors.

Maria Monk did nothing to aid her cause. She disappeared in August 1837, only to resurface in Philadelphia, where she claimed to have been kidnapped by priests. It was discovered, however, that she had simply run off with another man under an assumed name. Another book was published under her name that year, claiming that pregnant nuns from Canada and the United States were being hidden on an island in the Saint Lawrence River.

In 1838 Monk became pregnant again, though she claimed it was a Catholic plot to discredit her. She married, but her husband soon abandoned her. In 1849 she was arrested for pickpocketing at a house of prostitution. She died a short time later at age thirty-three, either in a charitable house or, as some claimed, in prison. The child of that last marriage published a book in 1874 telling the story of Maria's final days, as well as of the daughter's own conversion to Catholicism.

The Awful Disclosures of Maria Monk was important in that it popularized many of the anti-Catholic stereotypes that would persist in the American consciousness well into the twentieth century. Monk painted a Catholic faith based on medieval superstition, inquisitorial tortures, crafty "Jesuitical" manipulation, suppression of the Bible, and oppression of liberty.

MARILYN MONROE

The official ruling that Marilyn Monroe died by her own hand has never been accepted by her millions of fans or by conspiracy theorists.

When Marilyn Monroe was found dead on the morning of August 5, 1962, her death was immediately enshrouded with mystery and controversy, and she will always be remembered along with such movie stars as Jean Harlow, Lupe Velez, George Reeves, Bruce Lee, and Natalie Wood, whose deaths are clouded by allegations of suicide or homicide.

Few of Harlow's fans accepted the official studio decree of death due to uremic poisoning. Those who vicariously savored the erotic cinematic adventures of Lupe Velez were reluctant to acknowledge the Mexican spitfire's forlorn suicide note. Loyal fans continue to believe that television "Superman" George Reeves was the victim of murder, rather than depression. And followers of real-life superman Bruce Lee "know" that he was assassinated by the secret Kung Fu society of the Black Hand. The official account of the drowning of Natalie Wood, according to her admirers, simply contains too many contradictions and unacceptable elements to support a finding of accidental death.

Although Marilyn Monroe's fits of temperament and bouts of depression were well publicized and a drug overdose would seem a likely cause of death, the final verdict that she died by her own hand has never been acceptable to millions of her devoted fans or to hundreds of skeptical investigators. Those who firmly express their doubts that the actress committed suicide have suggested that she may have been murdered to silence her accounts of steamy sexual affairs with no less than the president of the United States, John F. Kennedy, and his brother Robert, the nation's attorney general.

It was around 3:00 A.M. on August 5, 1962, when Marilyn Monroe's housekeeper, Eunice Murray, noticed that there was still light in the actress's bedroom and decided to inquire why she was not yet asleep. Murray's concern grew when she found that the bedroom door was locked and she was unable to receive any type of response from her employer.

Summoned by Murray, Marilyn's psychiatrist, Dr. Ralph Greenson, arrived at the actress's Spanish-style bungalow in the Brentwood section of Los Angeles in less than half an hour. After his own unsuccessful attempt to rouse Marilyn by rapping loudly on the bedroom door, Greenson grabbed a poker from the fireplace and used it to smash a bedroom window. He found his famous patient lying naked in bed, covered with a blanket and a sheet. She clutched the telephone receiver in a lifeless hand.

Dr. Hyman Engelberg, the actress's personal physician, arrived within the hour and pronounced the cinematic goddess officially dead. It was Dr. Engelberg who had prescribed the sleeping medications on which she had apparently overdosed. Every reader of movie fan magazines was well aware of Marilyn's celebrated bouts of insomnia. On this fateful evening, her wish for peaceful sleep had been ultimately fulfilled.

Before 5:00 A.M. Detective Sgt. R. E. Byron and two police officers had examined the death room and the entire house and found nothing that indicated any act of violence perpetrated upon the deceased. They noted the twelve to fifteen bottles of various medicines clustered on a night table near the star's bed.

Two deputy coroners arrived to wrap Marilyn Monroe's body in a pale blue blanket and strap it onto a stretcher. The corpse was placed in a station wagon and transported to the Westwood Village Mortuary. Later it was transferred to the county morgue for the coroner's inquest and the official ruling regarding the cause of death—an overdose of barbiturates, a possible suicide. The reigning love goddess of the Hollywood screen was dead at the age of thirty-six.

Since the time of Marilyn Monroe's death, numerous books, plays, motion pictures, and television productions have presented possible scenarios for the manner in which one of the most powerful families in the nation may have ordered the death of one of the most popular actresses in the movies. An almost equal number of presentations have protested the outrageousness of accusing the Kennedy family of having Marilyn Monroe killed in order to eliminate a potential scandal. The Kennedy defenders remind us of the actress's monumental temper tantrums, her much-publicized bouts of depression, and her apparent emotional instability.

According to a number of Monroe's friends, she had planned to call a press conference for Monday, August 6, 1962. Some of these individuals speculate that Marilyn was going to discuss such topics as her relationship with Bobby, the Bay of Pigs, and how the Kennedys had used the mob.

Jeanne Carmen, a friend of Marilyn's, was interviewed on a *Reporters Special Edition* television program entitled "Marilyn—A Case for Murder." According to Carmen, Marilyn "was going to talk to the press the following day or on Monday and people might have been desperate." On the same program Marilyn's former husband Bob Slatzer said that Marilyn "told me on Friday evening prior to her death, 'If Bobby doesn't call me, I'm going to call a press conference on Monday morning, and I am going to blow the lid off this whole damned thing!'" And investigative reporter Krista Bradford stated on that same show that Carmen and John Danoff (a private detective who had bugged Monroe's home at her request) "reported that Marilyn had told them that if Bobby Kennedy did not make a commitment to her, she would reveal her involvement with him and his brother, John Kennedy. She had threatened to make the announcement on August 6, a day after she died." (August 5 was the legally recorded date of her death.)

On that last night of Marilyn Monroe's life, Peter Lawford called about 7:45 to invite her to a party. According to the actor, who was married to Patricia Kennedy, sister of John and Robert, Marilyn sounded heavily drugged and finally managed to mumble that Lawford should say good-bye for her to his wife, to the president, and to himself. Marilyn received several more calls that night, including one from Jose Bolanos, an alleged sometime lover, at about 9:30. Bolanos claimed that she told him she was about to reveal something that would be shocking to him and the entire world. When he attempted to question her further, she set down the phone without hanging up, explaining that she heard a disturbance at her door. She never returned to the telephone.

Eunice Murray and her son-in-law Norman Jeffries were at the house the night of Marilyn's death, and Jeffries told Donald Wolfe, author of *The Last Days of Marilyn Monroe,* that Robert Kennedy and two unknown men came to the door between 9:30 and 10 and ordered

Marilyn Monroe was one of the most famous actresses of her day. Her mysterious death in 1962 led to considerable speculation that it was engineered so she would not talk about alleged affairs with President Kennedy and his brother Robert.

them to leave the house. Murray and Jeffries went to a neighbor's home and waited until they saw the men leave about 10:30. According to Jeffries, when they returned to Marilyn's home, they saw her lying naked, face down on her bed, holding a telephone.

Eunice Murray called for an ambulance and then summoned Dr. Greenson. While they were awaiting medical assistance, Jeffries said, Peter Lawford and Marilyn's press agent, Pat Newcomb, arrived at the house. According to Jeffries, they were in a state of shock.

Ambulance driver Ken Hunter arrived in the early morning hours and stated that he found Marilyn in a coma, apparently due to an overdose of sleeping pills. He told Anthony Summers (*The Secret Lives of Marilyn Monroe*) that she was taken to Santa Monica Hospital, where she died. Summers theorizes that Marilyn's body was returned to her home in order to implement the cover-up.

Donald Wolfe interviewed one of Marilyn's neighbors, Elizabeth Pollard, who said that she was playing cards with a group of friends when they saw Robert Kennedy walk into Marilyn's home with two unidentified men, one of whom was carrying a black medical case. Elizabeth and her friends recognized Kennedy immediately.

At 4:24 A.M. on August 5, Sgt. Jack Clemmons of the West Los Angeles Police Department received a call from Dr. Hyman Engelberg that Marilyn Monroe had committed suicide. When Clemmons arrived at the house, Engelberg, Greenson, and Eunice Murray were present. Clemmons recalled for Wolfe that Marilyn was lying face down on a pillow, her arms by her side with the right one slightly bent, and her legs were stretched out straight.

Clemmons was skeptical of suicide upon even cursory examination of the scene. He had investigated numerous suicides and, he told Wolfe, "contrary to the common conception, an overdose of sleeping tablets causes victims to suffer convulsions and vomiting before they die in a contorted position."

The preliminary autopsy of Marilyn Monroe was conducted by Dr. Thomas Noguchi, and later Coroner Theodore Curphey announced the finding that the actress had died from an overdose of barbiturates. The official conclusion was that there was no physical evidence of foul play in the death of Marilyn Monroe.

Conspiracy theorists see a number of possible scenarios that point to the murder of Marilyn Monroe:

1. Marilyn had an affair with President John F. Kennedy. JFK had quite a track record of affairs with beautiful women, so it is likely that he would indulge himself with one of the sexiest movie stars of that era. Peter Lawford recalled that Marilyn had unrealistic ideas that the president would divorce Jackie and make Marilyn the First Lady of the United States. Marilyn's letters and telephone calls to the White House were becoming enough of

an embarrassment to the administration that someone might have decided it was time to end the relationship permanently.

2. Marilyn Monroe was having affairs with both of the Kennedy brothers, and she was in a position to bring an unprecedented scandal to the White House, tattling to the nation that she was sleeping with both the president and the attorney general.

3. Robert Kennedy arrived at Marilyn's house that night in the company of two Secret Service agents to inform her personally that Jack was ending their relationship. While JFK is rumored to have had affairs with countless women, Robert is not. He may have been doing a favor for his brother by personally delivering a message that could not be put in writing. After Robert and the agents left, Marilyn became extremely despondent and took an overdose of sleeping pills.

As Donald Wolfe states in *The Last Days of Marilyn Monroe*, "Marilyn Monroe was in a position to bring down the presidency"; she had JFK's "notes and letters and was privy to Kennedy's involvement with Sam Giancana," the Chicago Mafia boss. Moreover, according to Wolfe, "That the Kennedy brothers had discussed national security matters with the film star added to an astonishing array of indiscretions."

And of such indiscretions are conspiracy theories hatched—theories of murder that tend to grow stronger with the passing of years since Marilyn Monroe died.

In his book *UFOs and the Murder of Marilyn Monroe* (2011), Dr. Donald R. Burleson cited a CIA memo issued on August 3, 1962, just before Monroe's death, expressing the agency's extreme displeasure over the fact that the Kennedy brothers had been indiscreet in discussing highly classified information with the actress. Burleson contends that Marilyn had written down details of the President's visit to a secret air base to witness the debris re-

trieved from the Roswell UFO crash and the bodies of the alien crew. When the Kennedys began distancing themselves from the actress, she threatened to tell about the government cover-up of alien visitation, the "secret of secrets." When a wiretap of Marilyn's telephone revealed her plans to hold a press conference in which she would "tell all," Attorney General Robert Kennedy fearfully directed the CIA to terminate Marilyn Monroe.

MONTAUK PROJECT

This incredible project involved mind control, a Nazi secret society, extraterrestrials, the Philadelphia Experiment, and travel through time and space.

The old Montauk Air Force Station is situated on the even older navy air base Camp Hero, located on the northeast tip of Long Island on Highway 27. There is a state park there, as well as the empty shells of buildings and barracks. The old base is still listed by the army as a storage site for chemical weapons, and there are tunnels beneath it filled with water—and according to some, the skeletal remains of hundreds of young males.

How did these skeletons end up in tunnels under an old military base? Camp Hero was built on a sacred Indian burial ground—but these are not the remains of Native Americans. Esoterically, some researchers say that Montauk is a planetary energy point, linked to Mars and Egypt and legends of Atlantis. But neither are the bones those of ancient Atlanteans.

One story has it that by 1954, covert branches within the U.S. government and the governing structures of other superpowers had cut a deal with representatives from extraterrestrial intelligences to barter the ETs' superior scientific and technological knowledge in exchange for access to certain of our planet's mineral deposits. In addition the aliens were allowed to conduct various experiments on "people who made no genuine contributions of society" or "who would not be missed." The skeletons beneath the old Montauk Air Force Station are the last vestiges of street people, runaways, homosexual males, and stray kids who, if their disappearances were noted at all, were marked down as "missing."

An alternate explanation of the skeletons in the tunnels under the old base is that they are all that remains of hundreds of bright young people who were drawn into secret government projects in ESP, mind control, time travel, and out-of-body experiences. According to alleged eyewitnesses and survivors of the experiments, the project at Montauk was controlled by alien intelligences, whose cruel mind manipulations drove some of our best and brightest young people to insanity and suicide. Others were projected into wormholes in time and space, never to return.

According to Preston Nichols, while he was working for a Long Island defense contractor and researching people with psychic abilities, he traced disruptive radio signals to the Montauk Air Force Station and began an exhaustive period of research that gradually revealed, to his astonishment, that he had been involved in secret projects on the base. Somehow he had survived on two separate timelines, one at Montauk, the other at a different location.

Nichols had no sooner made this discovery than, in 1985, he met Duncan Cameron, a man with highly developed psychic abilities. Proceeding cautiously, Nichols learned that Cameron had been the primary psychic in the Montauk experiments with time travel and had also been aboard the *Eldridge* during the ill-fated Philadelphia Experiment in 1943. Duncan had been in the crew during the experiment in invisibility, together with his brother Edward, whom he now recognized as electronic engineer Al Bielek, who also claimed to be a survivor of the 1943 secret navy experiment.

The Montauk Project, they now understood, had been inspired by Nazi secret societies and their research into eugenics, mind control, and extraterrestrial communication. The Order of the Black Sun and many of its teachings had been incorporated into the project, as well as mysteries of the ancient alchemists and the sex magic ceremonies of Aleister Crowley.

As they expanded their research, Nichols and Cameron saw clearly that the Montauk Project had been terminated when, on August 12, 1983, a time portal was opened from that date back to the time of the Philadelphia Experiment. Cameron recalled sitting in a special device that was covered with crystals and bizarre radio receivers. The aliens and the secret government agents were using his psychic energy to open the time portal. However, Cameron realized that these conspirators wished to use such access to time travel for evil purposes, so in order to save the future, he set free a giant beast from his subconscious that ran rampant and destroyed the Montauk Project. All personnel fled the base and abandoned the buildings. All air shafts and entrances to the vast underground facilities were filled with cement.

Those who managed to survive the experiments in mind control and time travel at Montauk have been left with the understanding that reality is more complex than they have been taught and that the significance of Earth in time and space is far beyond the concepts of linear existence.

MOON MYSTERIES

Whether our astronauts really went to the moon is beside the point. Someone is there and has been for hundreds of years.

One of the favorite conspiracy theories of recent years is that NASA faked the moon landings of the 1960s. The astronauts did not land on the moon at all. The whole mission was created in a Hollywood studio. In fact, Hollywood even made a movie, *Capricorn One,* to show how it was done.

Other conspiracy theorists point out that there are far greater mysteries on and about the moon than stressing over whether we really sent *our* astronauts there. What about the alien bases on the moon and *their* UFOnauts?

NASA whistle-blower Richard C. Hoagland, a leading contributor of controversial astronomical theories, charged the space agency with a conspiracy to cover up the discovery of ruins and various artifacts on the moon that would change the history of Earth as we know it. Hoagland claims to have unearthed a 1960 NASA-commissioned report by the Brookings Institution recommending that any future discoveries of alien life on the moon be kept from the public in order not to disturb the evolutionary flow of twentieth-century civilization.

The famed astronomer Carl Sagan once theorized that if extraterrestrial beings had come to observe Earth, they would quite likely have established bases on the moon and would logically have placed their main installations on the "dark side" to keep them safe from probing earthly eyes. Other researchers suggest that if there are alien bases on the moon, they have probably been there for thousands, if not millions, of years.

As early as September 7, 1820, during a lunar eclipse, French astronomers reported strange objects, separated by uniform distances, moving in straight lines and with military precision away from the moon's surface. A similar procession of mysterious objects was seen on August 7, 1869, during a solar eclipse with the sun's masking glare removed. In 1874 a Czechoslovakian astronomer claimed that he had seen a dazzling white object traverse the disc of the moon, then leave the surface and travel out into space.

Conspiracists still debate whether human beings really walked on the moon or if it was just an elaborate ruse, but whether or not Americans did land there, many believe *someone* is indeed on the moon.

In 1912 an English astronomer reported that he had seen an "immensely black object about 250 miles long and 150 miles wide" on the moon. He speculated that he might have sighted the shadow thrown by something colossal in size moving above the moon. In that same year, during a lunar eclipse, both French and British astronomers stated that they had witnessed something like a "superb rocket" shoot away from the surface of the moon.

The crater Aristarchus is the single brightest spot on the moon, and ever since Galileo began gazing at it with his telescope in 1610, observers have reported a wide variety of flares and lights issuing from that area. Plato, the darkest spot on the moon, has also been a popular area for changing light patterns to appear. Strange geometrical formations of lights, including luminous triangles and grids, have consistently manifested there.

Lights that blink as if sending signals constitute a common lunar phenomenon. On October 20, 1824, European telescopes detected intermittent flashes throughout the night from a dark region near Aristarchus. On July 4, 1832, the astronomer Thomas W. Webb observed a series of flashing dots and dashes, suggestive of Morse code. In 1873, after conducting an exhaustive study of the blinking lights on the moon, the Royal Astronomical Society of Britain issued the verdict that the "coded" lunar flashes were "intelligent attempts by an unknown race on the Moon to signal Earth."

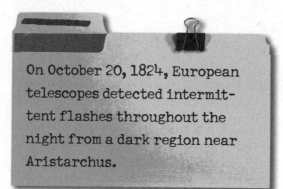

On October 20, 1824, European telescopes detected intermittent flashes throughout the night from a dark region near Aristarchus.

A peculiar facet of the blinking lights is that most of them occur in the northern hemisphere of the moon, suggesting to some UFO researchers that the extraterrestrial engineers have for some reason found that area to be more suited to expansion.

A very different claim is that the Russians are on the moon and that they, rather than extraterrestrials, may have secretly been mining its resources for many years. On top of that, from time to time alleged U.S. Air Force veterans, insisting upon complete anonymity, swear that the United States and the Russians established secret colonies on the moon in 1970—and that expeditionary teams discovered an alien base on its dark side.

"Alternative 3," a June 1977 British Television production—the last in a series of special programs released by *Science Reports*—was simultaneously broadcast in the UK, Australia, New Zealand, and much of Europe with the frightening revelation that the major powers of Earth had abducted ordinary men and women since the 1960s to serve as slaves for the political elite who inhabit special moon bases designed to shelter those select few who will survive Earth's destruction. The format of *Science Reports* had been that of serious science documentaries produced by highly respected science reporters, so when the staff announced that the entire alarming episode had been staged as an April Fool's joke, the public was outraged. In spite of the disclaimers, "Alternative 3" spawned the theory that many highly intelligent physicists, chemists, and biologists had vanished and been taken to the moon.

Vladimir Terziski, who has specialized in a study of Nazi rocketry, says that scientists from Germany's Third Reich landed on the moon as early as 1942. In the late 1930s or early 1940s, Terziski insists, Nazi scientists made contact with an alien culture that presented them with advanced technology. He further claims that as soon as the first German landing party touched down on the moon, they began digging and tunneling under the surface. By 1944 the Nazis had their first moon base.

In *We Discovered Alien Bases on the Moon* (1981), a former NASA jet propulsion engineer, Fred Steckling, stated that the public was not being told the full story concerning the astronauts' visit to our planet's satellite. David Hatcher Childress's *Extraterrestrial Archaeology* (1994) continued the quest for more complete revelations from our space program, followed by Cynthia Turnage's 1998 book *ET's Are on the Moon and Mars: The Photographic Evidence,* in which she accuses NASA of erecting a wall of silence to hide the indisputable evidence of extraterrestrial life that has been captured on film. Turnage further suggests that some other government agency may be pressuring NASA's scientists to cover up all evidence of alien life.

A favorite moon mystery of a number of conspiracy theorists is the allegation that famed director Stanley Kubrick faked the Apollo moon landings in exchange for a virtually unlimited budget to film his classic science fiction film *2001: A Space Odyssey*. Kubrick solved the problem of making shots on the surface of the moon look expansive by employing the cinematic technique of front screen projection (FSP). Long before the days of computer-generated imagery (CGI) movie magic, the FSP process projected scenes behind actors so it would appear to the camera as if the actors were moving around on the set provided by the FSP. Actors could move around in a vast studio while it appeared that they were laboriously walking on moonlike scenes projected behind them.

Edgar Mitchell, a former astronaut who visited the moon in 1971, has stated that his conversations with people who worked in intelligence agencies and military groups convinced him that the U.S. government has been covering up the truth about UFOs for over fifty years. Mitchell admitted to becoming quite alarmed over revelations that there are humanoids manning craft far superior to those in the arsenal of any nation on Earth. On the other hand, when asked about the possibility of alien bases on the moon, he responded: "The notion that there are structures on Mars or the Moon is bonkers. I can certainly attest to the latter. I've been there."

MORGELLONS DISEASE

Morgellons disease is a skin condition in which afflicted individuals suffer from itching and scratching sensations under their skin. They become convinced this is caused by some infectious agent, such as some kind of parasitic worm. In many cases, the individuals become so irritated by the itching that they scratch open their skin, often discovering fibers or filaments, which may be white, blue, or black in color. In addition to the fibers, in some instances pa-tients have been known to find black or white sandlike granules on or in the open scratches.

Morgellons did not really emerge to challenge modern medicine until 2001, when a Pittsburgh woman, Mary Leitao, examined her two-year-old son, who was complaining of sores around his mouth and the irritating sensation of having "bugs" crawling under his skin. When she looked at his sores with a toy microscope, she saw what appeared to be unusual red, blue, black, and white fibers in his skin.

Unable to find any conventional medical explanation for the peculiar manifestation of parasitic skin "worms" producing bizarre fibers in human flesh, Mrs. Leitao borrowed the name "Morgellons" from seventeenth-century French doctors who observed a similar condition in children. Next, she created a website presenting the phenomenon on the Internet. In short order, she was being inundated with emails from people who complained about the same creepy, skin-crawling parasites that emerged as varicolored fibers. Mrs. Leitao formed the Morgellons Research Foundation (MRF) to raise awareness for a disease that no doctor could define or identify. It didn't take long for over 14,000 Morgellons sufferers to contact the MRF.

Singer Joni Mitchell identified herself as a sufferer of "this weird incurable disease that seems like it's from outer space.... Morgellons is a slow, unpredictable killer.... Fibers in a variety of colors protrude out of my skin .... they cannot be identified forensically as animal, vegetable, or mineral."

Today, over ten years after the Leitao family christened the disease, there is a general consensus among those in the medical community that there are no known dermatological diseases that compare to Morgellons and that the disease is not a physical one, but a psychiatric condition.

Morgellons sufferers, however, strongly disagree. Thousands of those afflicted have writ-

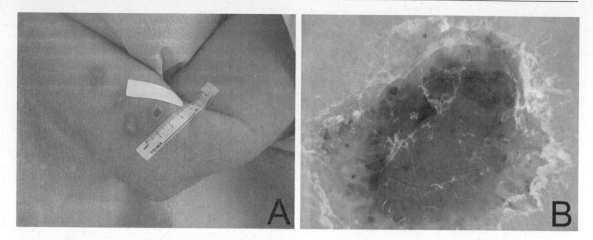

Two views of a patient with sores resulting from Morgellons taken during a 2012 Centers for Disease Control study. The close-up (B) shows the mysterious fibers that are a part of this disease. (AP Photo/CDC).

ten to Congress demanding an immediate investigation. More than forty senators took them seriously enough in 2006 to form a special taskforce with a million dollar budget.

In the May 6, 2011, issue of *The Guardian,* Will Storr wrote of his attendance at The Fourth Annual Morgellons Conference in Austin, Texas. There he interviewed Morgellons sufferers from such countries as the United Kingdom, the United States, Germany, Spain, and Mexico.

Dr. Ginger Savely, who claimed to have treated over five hundred Morgellons patients, was resolute in her opinion that those men and women who swore that bugs were crawling under their skin were not crazy.

Randy Wymore, associate professor of pharmacology at Oklahoma State University, became interested in the subject when he read an article about Morgellons. Wymore collected samples of the mysterious fibers from a large number of those afflicted with the disease and had them analyzed. The results yielded fibers of nylon, cotton, a human hair, a rodent's hair, and down from a duck or goose. Disappointing, yes, but there were some samples that didn't seem to make sense, thereby indicating to some that further research was warranted.

Later, Storr contacted Dr. Anne Louise Oaklander, associate professor at Harvard Medical School, a neurologist specializing in chronic itch disorders who was sympathetic to the Morgellons sufferers. She believed that the Morgellons patients had been mistreated by the medical establishment, and, in her opinion, they were suffering from a chronic itch disorder that had not yet been diagnosed by the establishment.

Richard Fagerlund, an entomologist whose column appears in the *San Francisco Chronicle* and *Albuquerque Journal,* takes Morgellon patients seriously and feels that only a small percentage of cases involve delusional parasitosis (a mistaken belief that one has been bitten by lice, fleas, rodents, ticks, or mites that is also known as Ekbom's syndrome). In his opinion, the rest might be caused by pollutants of some kind, especially certain pesticides.

The Atlas of Human Parasitology (2007) states that expert parasitologists, medical entomologists, and microbiologists have painstakingly examined fibers and other materials taken from Morgellons patients and have not found any biological organisms present. "Although an apparent association of the condition with the presence of Lyme disease has been reported, further research will be needed to help resolve the validity of Morgellons disease. Until then, whether Morgellons is another name for delusional parasitosis, or a real disease with a biologic or physiologic basis, will remain up in the air."

Speaking of being up in the air, ask almost any conspiracy researcher and he or she will tell you that Morgellons disease is spread by chemtrails emitted by aircraft employed by the Illuminati or a secret branch of the government intent on following the agenda of the New World Order to cause mass epidemics that would reduce the world population. What is more, their claims will be backed up by dozens of Morgellons sufferers who will swear that the cause of their misery is contact with the chemical substances contained in the chemtrails.

MOTHMAN DEATH LIST

Is this weird, red-eyed, winged monster a devil, an angel, or an illusion? Whatever the Mothman may be, seeing it might be hazardous to your health.

On November 15, 1966, two young married couples, the Steve Mallettes and the Roger Scarberrys, were driving through the marshy area near the Ohio River outside of Point Pleasant, West Virginia, when a winged monster, at least seven feet tall with glowing red eyes, loomed up in front of them. Later, they told Deputy Sheriff Millard Halstead that the creature followed them toward Point Pleasant on Route 62 even when their speed approached 100 mph.

When the story the Mallettes and the Scarberrys told achieved local circulation, Mr. and Mrs. Raymond Wamsley, Marcella Bennett, and Ricky Thomas stepped forward and said that they had seen the giant birdlike creature

near the same abandoned TNT plant a few miles north of Point Pleasant. A few days later Thomas Ury said that an enormous flying creature with a wingspan of ten feet had chased his convertible into Point Pleasant at 70 mph.

More witnesses came forward with accounts of their sightings, and the legend of Mothman was born. Although the majority of witnesses described the tall, red-eyed monster as appearing birdlike, the media dubbed the creature "Mothman," because, as writer John A. Keel noted, the *Batman* television series was very popular at the time. Intrigued by the stories, Keel visited Point Pleasant on numerous occasions and learned about the bizarre occurrences associated with Mothman's appearance, including the eerie forecast that some witnesses of the monster had received that the Silver Bridge in Point Pleasant would collapse and many people would be killed as a result. In 1975 Keel wrote in *The Mothman Prophecies* that "there would be many changes in the lives of those touched by" Mothman, and a "few would even commit suicide."

Researchers of the phenomenon have various theories concerning the large winged monster that haunts the marshy area near the McClintic Wildlife Sanctuary and the abandoned TNT plant north of Point Pleasant. Some say that excited, suggestible witnesses are simply sighting sandhill cranes, large birds indigenous to the area that can reach heights of six feet and achieve wingspans of ten feet. UFO researchers make correlations between bright lights in the sky and the appearances of Mothman. Others suggest that toxic chemicals dumped at the TNT site in World War II may have caused bizarre mutations in wild birds. And then there are those who maintain that Mothman might be a multidimensional intelligence, angelic or demonic, that can warn witnesses of impeding danger—or cause it to happen.

Cryptozoologist Loren Coleman, author of *Mothman and Other Curious Encounters*

(2002), has been keeping tab on the deaths that appear to be associated with the entity. Coleman lists the demises of eighty-five men and women who had some association with Mothman from the 1960s to the present day. As with all of the body counts or death lists that we include in this encyclopedia of conspiracies and secret societies, we add our disclaimer that many of the individuals that we find on such lists may have been elderly, ill, killed in the line of duty, met their demise in accidents totally devoid of nefarious circumstances, or committed suicide of their own free, albeit troubled, will. Some deaths on these lists do seem rather suspicious, and that is why we include them for your own assessment.

The Silver Bridge victims: Coleman's first forty-six victims were those unfortunates killed when, at 5:04 P.M. on December 15, 1967, the bridge at Point Pleasant collapsed during rush hour. Forty-six lives were lost, and forty-four bodies recovered.

Mary Hyre: Hyre was the Point Pleasant correspondent for the Athens, Ohio, newspaper the *Messenger,* and became a friend of John A. Keel's who later assisted him in his investigations. The first sighting reported by Hyre occurred when the Scarberrys and Mallettes saw Mothman on November 15, 1966. Exactly thirteen months later, the Silver Bridge collapsed. Twenty-six months later, on February 15, 1970, Hyre died at the age of fifty-four after a four-week illness.

Ivan T. Sanderson: A naturalist, cryptozoologist, and animal expert who appeared on various television programs, Sanderson served as Keel's main consultant on the natural history behind the reports of Mothman. A well-known writer at the time of the Mothman sightings, he was also the director of the New Jersey-based Society for the Investigation of the Unexplained. Sanderson, sixty-two, died on February 19, 1973, of a rapidly spreading cancer.

Gray Barker: Besides John Keel, no other investigator was on the scene of the Mothman sightings as often during 1966 and 1967 as West Virginian Gray Barker. A theatrical film booker based in Clarksburg, West Virginia, Barker became interested in UFOs in 1952. In 1956 he wrote *They Knew Too Much about Flying Saucers,* dealing with the Men in Black. In 1966, when he was investigating Mothman near Point Pleasant, Barker allegedly found a note on his door with this message, "*Abandon your research or you will regret [it]. You have been warned.*" Barker was fifty-nine when he died on December 6, 1984, "after a long series of illnesses," in a Charleston, West Virginia, hospital.

Donald North: Donald I. North, a Point Pleasant native who saw Mothman in the TNT-plant area in the 1990s, died in an automobile crash in 1997.

Jim Keith: Conspiracy author Keith, fifty, died mysteriously on September 7, 1999, during routine knee surgery after falling off the stage at the annual Burning Man pagan arts festival in Nevada. Keith held the theory that Point Pleasant was being used as some kind of testing area.

Ron Bonds: The publisher of most of Jim Keith's books and of John Keel's 1991 reprint of *The Mothman Prophecies,* Ron Bonds, forty-eight, of IllumiNet Press, died under strange circumstances on April 8, 2001, apparently the victim of food poisoning contracted at a Mexican restaurant in Atlanta.

Robin Chaney Pilkington: On October 24, 2001, Marcella Bennett, who was an eyewitness to Mothman on November 16, 1966, lost her daughter, Robin Pilkington, forty-four, to a long illness. Robin's death would signal the start of a wave of witness-relatives' deaths during the time surrounding the motion-picture release of *The Mothman Prophecies.*

Charles Mallette: As the movie on Keel's book began screening on January 25, 2002, the original witnesses, the Mallettes, were attending a funeral in Point Pleasant. Stephen

Mallette, one of the first four witnesses of Mothman, was mourning the passing of his brother, Charlie, due to a brain tumor.

Gary Ury: On February 15, 2002, soon after the town was bustling with Mothman promotions and attention, one of Point Pleasant's better-known Mothman eyewitnesses, Tom Ury suddenly lost his fifty-two-year-old brother Gary.

Ted Tannebaum: Tannebaum, sixty-eight, the executive producer of *The Mothman Prophecies,* died of cancer on March 7, 2002, in Chicago.

Aaron Rebsamen: Aaron Stephen Rebsamen, fourteen, the son of well-known cryptozoology artist William Rebsamen, died by suicide on May 23, 2002, in his Fort Smith, Arkansas, home. William Rebsamen did the cover art for Loren Coleman's *Mothman and Other Curious Encounters.*

Susan Wilcox: Susan J. "Minga" Wilcox, fifty-three, of Columbus, Ohio, died of an extremely rare form of brain tumor, ependymoma, on December 8, 2002. Wilcox reportedly saw a black "batlike" bedroom invader in her home in February 2001 and went on to become a Mothman investigator. She traveled to Point Pleasant several times in 2001 and 2002, and created a personal website, *Mothman: A Life Changed Forever.*

Jessica Kaplan: Kaplan, a crew member on *The Mothman Prophecies* motion picture, died in a plane crash in the Fairfax neighborhood of Los Angeles on June 6, 2003. The *Los Angeles Times* reported that the pilot, Jeffrey T. Siegel, owner of a Santa Monica construction firm, and his niece, Kaplan, twenty-four, were flying to the family's second home in Sun Valley, Idaho.

Alan Bates: British actor Sir Alan Bates, sixty-nine, died the night of December 27, 2003, at a hospital in London after a long battle with cancer. Bates played "Alexander

Leek" in *The Mothman Prophecies.* "Leek" was Keel spelled backward.

Jennifer Barrett-Pellington: On August 3, 2004, Jennifer Barrett-Pellington, forty-two, wife of *The Mothman Prophecies* director Mark Pellington, died in Los Angeles of an ongoing illness. Her husband had included a "Special Thanks" credit to his wife for her support of him on that film.

UFO researchers make correlations between bright lights in the sky and the appearances of Mothman.

Raymond H. Wamsley, 57, who, together with his wife, was with Marcella Bennett during the famed "second sighting" of Mothman on November 16, 1966, died on September 15, 2004.

Mark A. Bennett, 45, son of Marcella Bennett, one of the principals in the "second sighting" of Mothman, was also a witness to the phenomenon. He passed away in his home in Point Pleasant on April 16, 2007.

Bob Tracey, portrayed "Cyrus Bills" in the motion picture *The Mothman Prophecies,* died from complications of pneumonia on January 26, 2007, exactly five years to the weekend that the Mothman movie opened in theaters across the United States.

Marcella Bennett, the focus of the "second sighting" of Mothman, died at the age of 69 on March 3, 2009.

John A. Keel, born Alva John Kiehle in upstate New York on March 25, 1930, and the author of *The Mothman Prophecies* and numerous other books, died at the age of 79 on July 3, 2009, at Mt. Sinai Hospital in New York City.

Linda Scarberry, one of the earliest eyewitnesses (November 15, 1966) to the Mothman, died on March 6, 2011, after a brief battle with cancer.

MYSTERY SCHOOLS

Even the most high-tech of contemporary secret societies owe a large part of their rituals, ideals, and philosophy to the ancient mystery schools of Egypt.

For more than three thousand years, the mystery schools of Egypt have epitomized the very essence of the mysterious, the arcane, and the ultimate in secret wisdom and knowledge. As in ancient times, many modern cultists insist that the great teachers who presided over the Egyptian mystery schools came from some extraordinary place. Some believe that the wise masters were those who survived the destruction of the lost continent of Atlantis. Others suggest that such entities as the god Osiris were extraterrestrial astronauts from the Pleiades. There are conservative scholars, as well, who have a sense that the schools contained within their teachings knowledge that came from very ancient times, perhaps a mysterious unknown world in prehistory. The Pyramid Texts of Egypt (c. 3100 B.C.E.) contain many prayers quoted from a time far more ancient than they, and it is apparent that the prayers were used as magical formulas and spells.

The mysterious first initiator into these sacred doctrines was known as Toth and later, to the Greeks, by his more familiar name of Hermes. Hermes-Toth is a generic name that designates a man, a caste, and a god at the same time. Later Greek disciples of this secret tradition called him Hermes Trismegistus ("thrice greatest") and credited him with originating the material contained in forty-two books of esoteric science.

In the time of the pharaoh Ramses (c. 1300 B.C.E.), seekers of the divine sciences came to Egypt from the distant shores of Asia Minor and Greece to study in the sanctuaries with magi and hierophants in hope of learning the secrets of immortality. The initiates of the mystery schools were well aware that they must accept without complaint the rigors of disciplined study and the training of body, soul, and spirit. In order to attain the mastery demanded by the priests, the neophytes would undergo a complete restructuring of their physical, moral, and spiritual being. According to the credo of the mysteries, only by developing one's faculties of will, intuition, and reason to an extraordinary degree could one ever gain access to the hidden forces in the universe. Only through complete mastery of body, soul, and spirit could one see beyond death and perceive the pathways to be taken in the afterlife. Only when one had conquered fate and acquired divine freedom could one become a seer, a magician, an initiator.

Pythagoras, the great Greek philosopher-mathematician, learned the secret doctrine of numbers, the heliocentric system of the universe, music, astrology, astronomy, mathematics, and geometry from the powerful Egyptian magi. Before he established his own school of philosophy in southern Italy, Pythagoras spent twenty-two years in the temples of Egypt as an initiate in the ancient mysteries.

For centuries the pharaohs themselves were the pupils and instruments of the hierophants, the magicians, who presided over the temples and cults of Osiris. Each pharaoh received his initiation name from the temple, and the priests were honored with the roles of counselors and advisers to the throne. Some have even referred to the rule of ancient Egypt as government of the initiates.

The Greek Mystery Schools

From Egypt, the hidden wisdom of the mystery schools traveled to Greece. The word *mystery* itself comes from the Greek word *myein,* "to close," referring to the need of the *mystes,* the initiate, to close his or her eyes and lips and to keep secret the rites of the cult. The religion of ancient Greece was a sophisticated kind of nature worship wherein natural elements and phenomena were transformed into divine beings who lived atop Mount Olympus. There was no highly organized or formally educated priesthood, no strict doctrines. The followers of the religion worshipped the god or gods of their choosing and believed that they could gain these deities favor by performing simple ritual acts and sacrifices.

In addition to the religion to which every Greek belonged automatically at birth, there were also the "mystery religions," which required elaborate processes of purification and initiation before a man or woman could qualify for membership. The mystery religions were concerned with the spiritual welfare of the individual, and their proponents believed in an orderly universe and the unity of all life with God.

The early mystery schools of the Greeks centered on ritual reenactments of the lives of such gods as Osiris, Dionysus, and Demeter, divinities most often associated with the underworld, the realm of the dead, the powers of darkness, and the process of rebirth. Because of the importance of the regenerative process, the rites of the mysteries were usually structured around a divine female as the agent of transformation and regeneration. While the initiates of the mystery cult enacted the life cycles of gods who triumphed over death and who were reborn, they also asserted their own path of wisdom that would enable them to conquer death, accomplish resurrection in the afterlife, and undergo rebirth in a new body, in a new existence.

The aim and promise of the mystical rites was to enable initiates to attain union with the divine. The purifications and processions, the fasting and the feasts, the blazing lights of torches and the musical liturgies played during the performances of the sacred plays all fueled the imagination and stirred deep emotions. The initiates left the celebration of the mystery knowing that they were now superior to the problems that the uninitiated faced concerning life, death, and immortality. They knew not only that their communion with the patron god or goddess would continue after death, but that they would eventually leave Hades to be born again in another life experience.

The Eleusinian Mysteries

The sacred Eleusinian mysteries of the Greeks date to the fifth century B.C.E. and were the most popular and influential of the cults. The cult of Eleusis centered around the myth of Demeter, the great mother of agriculture and vegetation, and her daughter Persephone, queen of the Greek underworld, goddess of death and regeneration. The drama symbolized the odyssey of the human soul, its descent into matter, its earthly sufferings, its terror in the darkness of death, and its rebirth into divine existence. In the temples and in the groves where the mysteries were celebrated, the aspirants were told that life was a series of tests and that after death there would be revealed the hopes and joys of a glorious world beyond and the opportunity for rebirth.

The rites of the mysteries took place near Eleusis, a small community fourteen miles west of Athens. Although the Dionysian and Orphic rites could be celebrated at any time, the Eleusinian rites were held at a fixed time in the early fall after the wheat and barley seeds had been planted in the fields. The rites were conducted by a hereditary priesthood called the Eumolpedie, the "singers of gracious melodies."

Sometime in the month of September, the Eumolpedie removed the Eleusinian holy objects from Eleusis and carried them to the sacred city of Athens, where they were placed in the Eleusinion. Three days after the holy relics had been transported, the initiates gathered to

Greek philosopher and mathematician Pythagoras (c. 570–490 B.C.E.) is said to have gained much of his knowledge from the Egyptian magi.

hear the exhortations of the priests, who solemnly warned all those who did not consider themselves worthy of initiation to leave at once. Women and even slaves were permitted to join the mysteries of Eleusis, providing that they were either Greeks or (later) Romans. After the rites of purification had been observed, the initiates bathed in the sea and were sprinkled with the blood of pigs as they emerged. A sacrifice was offered to the gods, and a procession began to Eleusis, where, upon the arrival of the priests, the initiates were received by the high priest of Eleusis, the hieroceryx, or sacred herald, who was dressed as the god Hermes (Mercury, to the Romans) and held the caduceus, the entwined serpents, as a symbol of his authority. Once the aspirants had assembled, the sacred herald led them to a sanctuary of Persephone hidden in a quiet valley in the midst of a sacred grove. Here, the priestesses of Perse-

phone, crowned with narcissus wreaths, began chanting, warning the neophytes of the mysteries that they were about to perceive. The initiates would learn that the present life they held so dear was but a tapestry of illusion and confused dreams.

For the next several days, the initiates fasted, prayed, and participated in cleansing rituals. On the evening of the last day of the celebration of the mystery, the aspirants gathered in the most secret area of the sacred grove to attend the Eleusinian drama, which reenacted the myth of the rape, abduction, and marriage of Persephone by Hades, god of the underworld, and her separation from her mother, Demeter, the goddess of grain and vegetation. Essentially, the rites imitated the agricultural cycles of planting the seed, nurturing its growth, and harvesting the grain, which, on the symbolic level, represented the birth of the soul, its journey through life, and its death.

The Dionysian Mysteries

Next to the Eleusinian mysteries in popularity were the Dionysian, centered on Dionysus (Bacchus), a god of life, vegetation, and the vine who, because all things growing and green must one day decay and die, was also a divinity of the underworld. Those initiates who entered into communion with Dionysus drank heavily of the fruit of the vine and celebrated with orgiastic feasts that encouraged them to dress in leaves and flowers and even to take on the character of the god himself, thereby also achieving his power. Once the god had entered into union with the initiates, they would experience a spiritual rebirth. This divine union with Dionysus marked the beginning of a new life for the initiates, who thereafter regarded themselves as superior beings. And since Dionysus was the Lord of Death, as well as the Lord of Life, the initiates believed that their union with him would continue even after death and that immortality was now within their grasp. The earlier rites of Dionysus often featured the sacrifice of an animal—usually a goat—that was torn to pieces by the initiates, whose savagery was meant to symbolize the incarnation, death, and resurrection of the divinity.

The Cult of Orpheus

Orpheus may have been an actual historical figure, a man capable of charming both man and beast with his music. But whether he was a god or a human, he modified the Dionysian rites by removing their orgiastic elements. According to some traditions, he was the son of a priestess of Apollo, gifted with a melodious voice, golden hair, deep blue eyes, and a powerful magnetism that exerted a kind of magic upon all those with whom he came into contact. Then, so the legend goes, he disappeared, and many presumed him dead. In reality, he had traveled to Memphis in Egypt, where he spent the next twenty years studying in the Egyptian mystery schools. When he returned to Greece, he was known only by the name that he had received in the initiation rites, Orpheus of Alpha, hailed as "the one who heals with light."

An essential aspect of the Orphic initiation was the process of the initiate's absorbing the healing light of Orpheus and purifying the heart and spirit. Among the truths that Orpheus had learned in the Egyptian sanctuaries was that God is One, but the gods are many and diverse. Orpheus had descended into hell, the underworld, and braved its challenges and subdued the demons of the abyss. The disciples of the Orphic/Dionysian schools were promised the celestial fire of Zeus, the light retrieved by Orpheus, which enabled their souls to triumph over death. These things were enacted in the mystery play that depicted Orpheus descending into Hades and observing Persephone, the queen of the dead, being awakened by Dionysus and reborn in his arms, thus perpetuating the cycle of rebirth and death, past and future, blending into a timeless immortality.

While other schools of reincarnation see the process of rebirth as an evolution of the soul ever higher with each incarnation, the Orphic school introduced the concept of the soul as being gradually purged or purified through the sufferings incurred during each physical rebirth. As the soul inhabits the body, it is really doing penance for previous incarnations, a process that gradually purifies it. Between lifetimes, when the soul descends to Hades, it can enjoy a brief period of freedom, which can be pleasant or unpleasant. Then it must return to the cycle of births and deaths.

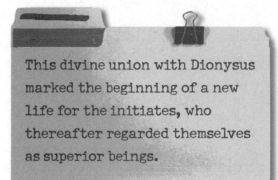

This divine union with Dionysus marked the beginning of a new life for the initiates, who thereafter regarded themselves as superior beings.

According to Orphic teachings, the only way out of the "wheel of birth," the "great circle of necessity," was through an act of divine grace that could possibly be obtained through the supplicant's becoming immersed in the writing, ritual acts, and teachings of Orpheus and initiation into the mysteries of the cult. Once this had been accomplished, the initiates were given secret formulae that would enable them to avoid the snares awaiting the unwary soul as it descended to Hades and ensure them a blissful stay while they awaited a sign that their participation in the great circle of necessity had ended.

The mystery schools kept alive the practice of magic and the belief that secret rituals and sacred relics could command the presence of divinity. The ancient mystery rites dedicated to such gods as Osiris, Isis, and Dionysus, together with the magical formulas discovered by Hermes Trismegistus and other masters, compelled the gods to manifest and share their powers. The myths of the old gods and the holy scriptures of the Christians, the secret experiences of the ancients and the revelations of the apostles, the personal sense of God developed by the pagan cults and the promise of the Christian church fathers that one could know God through his son—all seem to some individuals to be completely harmonious. The rich inheritance of the pagan world seems to them too valuable to abandon when such mysteries could be so easily adapted and kept alive in new rituals throughout the ages.

MYSTICAL SOCIETIES AND ALTERED STATES OF CONSCIOUSNESS

Today there are many groups that may seem secret and mysterious, but they want to connect with God, not control the world.

In a book that deals with so many sinister secret societies and global conspiracies, a distinction must be made between groups that conspire against humankind and those that aspire through meditation, prayer, or direct mystical experience to achieve union with divinity, God, or ultimate reality. Such entities and endeavors as the Self-Realization Fellowship, tantra, Transcendental Meditation, yoga, shamanism, the Association for Research and Enlightenment, the Course on Miracles, and Kabbalah may appear secret and mysterious to those who do not understand their principles, but they are all mystical, not political, in nature, and they seek to reach the divine through meditation or altered states of consciousness induced by silence and prayer, rather than drugs or alcohol. The experiences of the mystics are very subjective, and their dreams, visions, and revelations are most often meant for the individual and are not to be shared.

An altered state of consciousness is a brain state wherein one loses the sense of identity with one's body or with one's normal sense perceptions. A person may enter an altered state of consciousness through such things as sensory deprivation or overload, neurochemical imbalance, fever, or trauma. One may also achieve an altered state by chanting, meditating, or entering a trance.

Trance consciousness may be induced by rapt attentiveness to a single stimulus, such as the voice of a hypnotist, one's own heartbeat, a chant, trance-inducing rituals and primitive dances. The trance state is characterized by hypersuggestibility and concentrated attention on one stimulus to the exclusion of all others.

Trance consciousness usually leads to expanded consciousness, comprising four levels:

1. the sensory level, characterized by subjective reports of space, time, body image, or sense impressions having been altered;

2. the recollective-analytic level, which summons up memories of one's past and provides insights concerning self, work, or personal relationships;

3. the symbolic level, which is often characterized by vivid visual imagery of mythical, religious, and historical symbols;

4. the integrative level, in which the individual undergoes an intense religious illumination, experiences a dissolution of self, and is confronted by God or some divine being.

Each of these four levels may be induced by hypnosis, meditation, prayer, or free association during psychoanalysis. Through the ages, many of humankind's major material and spiritual breakthroughs may have come from these virtually unmapped, uncharted regions of the mind.

Students of spirituality describe the ecstatic experience as the ultimate mystic state—the one in which the human spirit is swept up and into an immediate union with the divine. As Evelyn Underhill says in *Mysticism,* "The induced ecstasies of the Dionysian mysteries, the metaphysical raptures of the Neoplatonists, the voluntary or involuntary trance of Indian mystics and Christian saints—all these, however widely they may differ in transcendental value, agree in claiming such value, in declaring that this change of consciousness brought with it a valid and ineffable apprehension of the Real."

Fredric W. H. Myers, one of the founders of the Society for Psychical Research, observed that the evidence for ecstasy is stronger than the evidence for any other religious belief. "Of all the subjective experiences of religion, ecstasy is that which has been most urgently, perhaps to the psychologist most convincingly, asserted; and it is not confined to any one religion," Myers said. "From the medicine man up to St. John, St. Peter, and St. Paul, with Buddha and Mahomet on the way, we find records which, though morally and intellectually much differing, are in psychological essence the same."

In the ecstatic state, every thought, feeling, or emotion is pushed out of the mind except for the idea of God and the emotions of joy and love. These fill the mind to the exclusion of nearly everything else, and are themselves blended into a single whole. Mystics do not *believe* God to be present, they *feel* God united with their soul.

Mystic ecstasy, to the percipient of the experience, reveals a genuine truth. He or she is brought face-to-face with ultimate reality experienced through emotions and intuition. A transcendence of the self is achieved. The mystic returns from the experience with the certainty of having been somewhere else and having received a revelation of some remarkable truth, such as that reality is unitary and divine; that even ordinary human experiences are phenomenal; that the soul, which is the key to reality, may rise to oneness with God; or

that God's presence can be found everywhere hidden in the midst of daily life.

There are many reasons why the great majority of scientific researchers remain doubtful about the validity of altered states of consciousness, such as the misuse of hypnosis by amateur practitioners, the lack of understanding by professionals and public alike of the creative processes, the disastrous results of the recreational use of LSD and other psychedelic drugs, and the many charlatans who claim visions and revelations only to deceive the gullible. Descriptions of mystical revelations become almost florid as self-proclaimed seers and mystics attempt to translate their trance-state experiences into the language of a technically oriented society.

> "Of all the subjective experiences of religion, ecstasy is that which has been most urgently, perhaps to the psychologist most convincingly asserted; and it is not confined to any one religion."

While skeptical psychological researchers continue to label claims of revelation and transcendence through altered states of consciousness as delusional and self-deceptive, others call for a serious examination of the totality of the human entity. Many researchers firmly believe that continued research into altered states of consciousness may well reveal that humankind's most important discoveries, its highest peaks of ecstasy, and its greatest moments of inspiration occur in reverie, in dreams, and in states of consciousness currently ignored by the professional world and the general public.

N

NATION OF ISLAM

The Nation of Islam awaits the return of Wali Farad Muhammad, a human embodiment of God, who disappeared in 1933 but will return with a new and final holy book.

The Nation of Islam (NOI) is also known as the World Community of Al-Islam in the West, the American Muslim Mission, the Nation of Peace, and the Black Muslim Movement. The NOI was founded in 1930 by Wali Farad Muhammad (b. Wallace Dodd Fard) in Detroit. In the beginnings of the movement, the emphasis was largely social, a group of people working together to improve the political and economic structure of their own community first, and then to spread their doctrine of a better society across the United States.

Most of the religious doctrines and beliefs that became an essential part of the NOI were derived from the teachings of Noble Drew Ali and his Moorish Holy Temple of Science. Ali taught that most of the African tribes from which the slaves were captured were of Islamic heritage and should therefore be referred to as Moors. He further emphasized that a sure step to salvation was made when an African American refused to be called "Negro," "black," or "colored" and insisted upon being called a "Moor" or "Moorish American." When Noble Drew Ali died in 1929, John Given El claimed to be the reincarnation of the teacher—but so did Wallace D. Fard. Those who followed Given El became the Moorish Americans of the Moorish Temple of Science in Chicago, while those who followed Fard became the Nation of Islam.

Fard, now Wali Farad Muhammad, de-emphasized the Bible and introduced his followers to the Qur'an. Among his basic teachings were the following:

1. Allah is God, the white race is the devil.

2. The Asiatic black people are the cream of planet Earth.

3. Blacks cannot achieve freedom, equality, and justice until they speak their true language (Arabic), practice their true religion (Islam), and gain their own separate state.

4. Christianity is the white man's religion, the slave religion that enabled the white man to keep the black man subjugated.

By 1934 Wali Farad Muhammad had gathered about eight thousand members into his flock, and then, in June of that year, he mysteriously disappeared. His most dedicated minister, Elijah Muhammad, took over the NOI. Elijah was so dedicated to his predecessor that he believed Wali Muhammad was God incarnate. Elijah was extremely strict and ran the NOI with an iron hand, even while in prison during World War II for draft evasion. His commands were relayed to the faithful by his wife, Clara, and his head ministers.

Elijah Muhammad remained head of the NOI until his death in 1975, when leadership passed to his son, Wallace Muhammad. Elijah had excommunicated Wallace at least four times during disputes over the ideology of Islamic Nationalism and black separatism, but had always reinstated him. Wallace Muhammad and his close friend Malcolm X had denied that Wallace Fard was actually Allah in the flesh, and they railed against Elijah Muhammad for being unfaithful to his wife and thereby committing adultery, a violation of the tenets of Islam. When Malcolm X was assassinated in 1965, he was separated from the NOI and held in disregard. Wallace Muhammad restored the legacy of Malcolm X as a respected and prominent teacher. Among other changes implemented by Wallace Muhammad were the following:

1. The removal of the doctrine of racial superiority taught by Wali Farad Muhammad and Elijah Muhammad. Orthodox Muslims believe in the equality of all. There is no one group superior over another.

2. The recognition of Wali Farad Muhammad as a wise man and a teacher, but not the incarnation of Allah. Orthodox Muslims believe the Qur'an given to the prophet Muhammad between the years of 610 and 632 was Allah's final revelation to humankind.

3. Business and religious practices would be conducted as separate entities.

4. The Nation of Islam did not wish to establish a state separate unto themselves.

5. The U.S. Constitution would henceforth be honored by all NOI members.

6. NOI members would now be aligned with Orthodox Islam.

Wallace Muhammad changed the name of the Nation of Islam to the Bilalian Community, then to the World Community of Al-Islam in the West, then to the American Muslim Mission, and finally to the Muslim Mission. Today the Muslim Mission is considered orthodox and is accepted as a member of the traditional Islamic community in the United States.

While Wallace Muhammad was restructuring the group founded by Wallace Fard and carried forth by Elijah Muhammad into a very different kind of organization, a number of NOI followers strongly objected to the dismissal of the doctrines of black racial superiority and racial separation as taught by the Founding Fathers. In 1978 Louis Farrakhan assumed the leadership of the NOI as the "spiritual son" of Elijah Muhammad, and in 1981 he publicly announced the restoration of the Nation of Islam.

Farrakhan remains the leader of the Nation of Islam and lives in Chicago. The headquarters of the NOI, the National Center, houses Mosque No. 2, also known as Mosque Maryam, dedicated to Mary, the mother of Jesus. (Jesus, known as Isa in Arabic, is revered in the Islamic faith as a prophet and holy man.) Mosque Maryam is the National Center for the Re-training and Re-education of the Black Man and Woman of America and the World.

Among the controversial teachings of the Nation of Islam are the following:

1. The black man is the original man on Earth. By using a special method of birth control created by Yakub, a black scientist, the ancient black man was able to produce the white race. Farrakhan has remarked that the white people are "po-

tential humans" but they haven't yet evolved.

2. The universe was created 78 trillion years ago, and also at this time God was self-created on Earth. He was the only one in the entire dark universe, but he was a black man.

3. The original, physical manifestation of God died, but his essence is infinite. Since the physical God died, the universe has been ruled by a council of twenty-four black scientists, the head scientist being known as Allah. No God lives forever. Their wisdom and work may live for 25,000 years, but the actual being may have died after a hundred or so years. There have been a succession of Gods, each a black man. In our current time, the supreme God was W. D. Fard, who disappeared in 1933, but who will return with a final holy book.

4. There is a giant Mother Spaceship that is made like the universe, spheres within spheres, and can appear as a cloud by day but a pillar of fire by night. What white people call "UFOs" are smaller craft from the Mother Ship.

As in orthodox Islam, the NOI member believes in prayer five times daily, facing in the direction of the holy city of Mecca; charity to the poor; fasting during the month of Ramadan; and the duty of everyone who is physically and financially able to make *Hajj,* the pilgrimage to Mecca, at least once in a lifetime.

NATIONAL SOCIALIST MOVEMENT

From the heartland of America, the National Socialist Movement offers a "modernized" Nazi political platform.

The National Socialist Movement (a.k.a. NSM88) is the largest (or second largest, according to the claims of the National Alliance group) Nazi party operating in the United States today. Founded in 1974 by Robert Brannen and Cliff Herrington, two former storm troopers from George Lincoln Rockwell's American Nazi Party, the group is presently based in Minneapolis.

During the 1970s the NSM's sphere of influence remained largely near its headquarters in South St. Paul. Brannen assumed leadership until he suffered multiple strokes and passed control to Herrington in 1983. For another ten years few in the Twin Cities were aware of the NSM. Then, in 1993, after Herrington and a member of NSM arrived in Nazi uniforms to protest a Minnesota legislative committee considering a proposed gay rights bill, the local media recognized the group's existence. Encouraged by the publicity, members of the NSM began wearing their Nazi uniforms in public.

The uniform of the group is the brown shirt of the Nazi *Sturmabteilung,* the SA, also known as storm troops. Their choice of uniform and their open display of the swastika makes the NSM one of the most "Nazi-like" of all the neo-Nazi groups. The structure of the NSM is paramilitary, with its privates, sergeants, lieutenants, and captains subordinate to the commander. The chapters of the group are referred to as "units," and the units participate in armed paramilitary training.

The NSM is openly worshipful of Adolf Hitler; however, its leaders insist that the group does not aspire to be a clone of the Third Reich, but rather, a separate creation. They preach a modernized Nazi platform that calls for an all-white America, the rejection of citizenship to nonwhites, Jews, and homosexuals, and the repelling of immigrants who cross the U.S. borders to destroy the economy.

In 1994 Herrington turned command of the group over to Jeff Schoep, a much younger man, who had been active in the group from an early age and who had a large following among young skinheads, white supremacists, and racists. In a few years, the NSM grew from a few units to about thirty-eight, with approximately two hundred members. Schoep's ambition is to work with all other white-supremacist groups to fashion a United Patriot Front, with himself as its leader.

The 25 Points of American National Socialism

1. We demand the union of all Whites into a greater America on the basis of the right of national self-determination.

2. We demand equality of rights for the American people in its dealings with other nations, and the revocation of the United Nations, the North Atlantic Treaty Organization, the World Bank, the North American Free Trade Agreement, the World Trade Organization, and the International Monetary Fund.

3. We demand land and territory (colonies) to feed our people and to scttle surplus population.

4. Only members of the nation may be citizens of the state. Only those of pure White blood, whatever their creed, may be members of the nation. Non-citizens may live in America only as guests and must be subject to laws for aliens. Accordingly, no Jew or homosexual may be a member of the nation.

5. The right to vote on the State government and legislation shall be enjoyed by citizens of the state alone. We therefore demand that all official appointments, of whatever kind, whether in the nation, in the states or in smaller localities, shall be held by none but citizens. We oppose the corrupting parliamentary custom of filling posts merely in accordance with party considerations and special interests—without reference to character or abilities.

6. We demand that the State shall make it its primary duty to provide a livelihood for its citizens. If it should prove impossible to feed the entire population, foreign nationals (non-citizens) will be deported.

7. All non-White immigration must be prevented. We demand that all non-Whites currently residing in America be required to leave the nation forthwith and return to their land of origin: peacefully or by force.

8. All citizens shall have equal rights and duties, regardless of class or station.

9. It must be the first duty of every citizen to perform physical or mental work. The activities of the individual must not clash within the framework of the community and be for the common good.

We therefore demand:

10. The abolition of incomes unearned by work; The breaking of interest slavery.

11. In view of the enormous personal sacrifices of life and property demanded of a natlon by any war, personal enrichment from war must be regarded as a crime against the nation. We therefore demand the ruthless confiscation of all war profits.

12. We demand the nationalization of all businesses which have been formed into corporations (trusts).

13. We demand economic reform suitable to our national requirements; The prohibition of pro-Marxist unions and their supplantation with National Socialist trade unions; The passing of a law instituting profit-sharing in large industrial enterprises; The creation of a livable wage; The restructuring of social security and welfare to include drug testing for welfare recipients; The immediate discontinuation of all taxes on things of life's necessity, such as food, cloth-

Hitler Youth march in a parade in the United States in 1936. Once World War II started, such marches were not tolerated, but the American Nazi Party has become active again in America.

ing, shelter, medicine etc.; The replacement of the current tax system with a flat-rate tax based on income.

14. We demand the treasonable system of health care be completely revolutionized. We demand an end to the status quo in which people die or rot away from lack of proper treatment due to the failure of their medical coverage, Health Maintenance Organization, or insurance policy. We further demand the extensive development of insurance for old age and that prescription drugs be made both affordable and accessible.

15. We demand the creation and maintenance of a healthy middle class, the immediate communalizing of big de-

partment stores and their lease at a cheap rate to small traders, and that the utmost consideration shall be shown to all small trades in the placing of state and municipal orders.

16. We demand a land reform suitable to our national requirements, that shall be twofold in nature: The primary land reform will be to ensure all members of the nation receive affordable housing. The party as such stands explicitly for private property.

However, we support the passing of a law for the expropriation of land for communal purposes without compensation when deemed necessary for land illegally acquired, or not administered in accordance with the national welfare. We further demand the abolition of ground rent, the discontinuation of all taxes on property, and the prohibition of all speculation in land.

The secondary land reform will be to ensure the environmental integrity of the nation is preserved; By setting aside land for national wildlife refuges; By cleaning the urban, agricultural, and hydrographical (water) areas of the nation; By creating legislation regulating the amount of pollution, carbon dioxide, greenhouse gases, and toxins released into the atmosphere; And for the continued research and development of clean burning fuels and energy sources.

17. We demand the ruthless prosecution of those whose activities are injurious to the common interest. Murderers, rapists, pedophiles, drug dealers, usurers, profiteers, race traitors, etc. must be severely punished, whatever their creed or race.

18. We demand that Roman edict law, which serves a materialistic new world order, be replaced by Anglo-Saxon common law.

19. The state must consider a thorough reconstruction of our national system of education with the aim of opening up to every able and hardworking American the possibility of higher education and of thus obtaining advancement.

The curricula of all educational establishments must be brought into line with the requirements of practical life. The aim of the school must be to give the pupil, beginning with the first sign of intelligence, a grasp of the state of the nation through the study of civic affairs. We demand the education of gifted children of poor parents, whatever their class or occupation, at the expense of the state.

20. The state must ensure that the nation's health standards are raised by protecting mothers, infants, and the unborn: By prohibiting abortion and euthanasia, except in cases of rape, incest, race-mixing, or mental retardation; By prohibiting child labor and ending the rudiments of child abuse, alcoholism, and drug addiction; By creating conditions to make possible the reestablishment of the nuclear family in which the father works while the mother stays at home and takes care of the children if they so choose; By taking away the economic burden associated with childbirth and replacing it with a structured system of pay raises for those that give birth to healthy babies, thereby returning the blessing associated with children.

To further ensure that the nation's health standards are raised, legislation shall be passed promoting physical strength and providing for compulsory gymnastics and sports, and by the extensive support of clubs engaged in the physical training of youth.

21. We demand the right to bear arms for law-abiding citizens.

22. We demand the abolition of the mercenary army, the end to the over-use of our military as a "Meals-on-Wheels" program in foreign lands of no vital interest to our nation; and the formation of a true national service for the defense of our race and nation. One that excludes: non-Americans, criminals, and sensitivity training.

23. We demand legal warfare on deliberate political mendacity and its dissemination in the press. To facilitate the creation of a national press we demand: (a) That all editors of and contributors to newspapers appearing in the English language must be members of the nation; (b) That no non-American newspapers may appear without the express permission of the State. They must not be written in the English lan-

guage; (c) That non-Whites shall be prohibited by law from participating financially in or influencing American newspapers, and that the penalty for contravening such a law shall be the suppression of any such newspapers, and the immediate deportation of the non-Americans involved.

The publishing of papers which are not conducive to the national welfare must be forbidden. We demand the legal prosecution of all those tendencies in art and literature which corrupt our national life, and the suppression of cultural events which violate this demand.

24. We demand absolute religious freedom for all denominations in the State, provided they do not threaten its existence nor offend the moral feelings of the White race. The Party combats the Jewish-materialistic spirit within and without us, and is convinced that our nation can achieve permanent health only from within on the basis of the principle: The common good before self-interest.

25. To put the whole program into effect, we demand the creation of a strong central national government for the nation; the unconditional authority of the political central parliament over the entire nation and its organizations; and the formation of committees for the purpose of carrying out the general legislation passed by the nation and the various American States.

NATIVISM

Nativism is dedicated to the proposition that the United States was founded to serve only white Anglo-Saxon Protestants.

Nativism is a defensive, often violent, reaction to unrestricted immigration. In the United States, nativism is an intense form of nationalism that expresses itself in xenophobia (fear of foreigners), anti-Catholicism, and belief in white Anglo-Saxon Protestant supremacy.

In 1848, after a series of European revolutions had rocked the Old World, approximately three million immigrants arrived in the United States. Negative reaction to the influx was intensified among the postcolonial Protestant majority on the East Coast because many of the new arrivals happened to be from Roman Catholic countries.

Secret societies, such as the Order of the Star-Spangled Banner, organized by Charles B. Allen in 1849, had memberships of "God-fearing Protestants," who were dedicated to ensuring that native-born, non-Catholic Americans would receive preferential treatment in all avenues of social and political society. Members of such secret groups became known as the "Know-Nothings" because none of them would admit knowing anything about the clandestine societies. The Nativists gained strength and some degree of respectability when they went public in 1854 and established the American Party. The new political group was strongly anti-Irish-Catholic and worked for legislation that would require twenty-one years of waiting time before anyone could become a U.S. citizen. The American Party lost its influence when former president Millard Fillmore, the party's presidential candidate in the election of 1856, was soundly defeated.

NAZI UFOS

German scientists made contact with an alien species as early as the 1920s and were constructing flying disks and conducting space missions by 1942.

Numerous UFO researchers have made a connection between alien beings and such German secret societies as the Thule, the Vril, and the Black Sun. In his controversial seminar "UFO Secrets of the Third Reich," Vladimir Terziski tells of an "alien tutor race" that secretly began cooperating with certain German scientists in the late 1920s, introducing them to advanced philosophical, cultural, and technological concepts. With help from extraterrestrial intelligences, Terziski postulates, the Nazis mastered antigravity flight, established space stations, accomplished time travel, and developed warp-speed spacecraft so that they might construct moon bases. At the same time the aliens "spread their Mephisphelean ideas" into the wider German population through the Thule and Vril societies.

Antigravity research began in Germany in the 1920s with the first hybrid antigravity circular craft, the R-FZ-1, constructed by the secret Vril Society. In 1942–43 a series of antigravity machines culminated in the 350-foot-long, cigar-shaped Andromeda space station, which was constructed in old zeppelin hangars near Berlin by E4, the research-and-development arm of the SS.

Terziski is not alone in making such claims regarding extraterrestrials and Nazi cooperation. Although some researchers scoff at them as pure fantasy, others are convinced that there is a Nazi–alien connection and another massive cover-up by the international shadow governments. Skeptics wonder how Germany could have lost the war if they had amassed such superior alien technology.

We do know that shortly before the Third Reich collapsed in 1945, Wernher von Braun, Hermann Oberth, and about eighty other top scientists were smuggled out of Nazi Germany by the Allies, who also captured various documents, files, plans, photographs, and designs. However, one specific file, containing discoid-shaped aircraft, and at the same time, 130 crack Nazi designers of specialized aircraft are said to have disappeared.

The UFO researcher Jammie A. Romee has stated that the mysterious disappearance of that vital file, together with over a hundred technologists, must be added to the list of oddities that took place shortly before and after the fall of Adolf Hitler's Third Reich. Among these oddities various researchers cite the following:

- the unexplained disappearance of several German freight U-boats, each capable of transporting up to 850 metric tons;

- the disappearance from Tempelhof Air Base of several long-distance planes with flight plans to Spain and South America;

- the disappearance of several tens of millions of marks in hard currency, gold bullion, and precious stones from the Reichsbank;

- the fact that UFOs were, and continue to be, sighted in great numbers over areas of South America in which many Nazis (and members of secret societies) are known to be hidden.

The fascination of German science with rockets began in 1923 with Hermann Oberth's book *By Rocket to Interplanetary Space*. Numerous other books by other experimenters advanced the cause of spacecraft development in Germany in the mid-1920s. In 1927 the Society for Space Travel was organized, with Wernher von Braun and Willy Ley among its members. The society produced the world's first rocket-powered automobile, the Opel-Rak 1, with Fritz von Opel in 1928. Further experiments were made with railway cars, rocket sleds, crude vertical-takeoff-and-landing aircraft, and some successful launches from the rocket airfield near Berlin. When Hitler seized power in Germany in 1933, the Nazi Party took over all rocket and aircraft development, and all astronautical societies were nationalized.

In 1938 Hitler's aide Martin Bormann ordered the careful mapping of all mountain passes, caves, bridges, and highways and began selecting sites for underground factories, munitions dumps, and food caches. Giant underground workshops and launching pads, known as "U-plants," were established in which top German scientists would be assigned the task of creating secret weapons. A slave-labor force of 250,000 was required to complete work on such fortresses. Networks of tunnels and assembly plants were fashioned in Austria, Bavaria, and northern Italy.

Allied intelligence learned of work on Project *Feuerball* (Fireball) at the Luftwaffe experimental center near Oberammergau, Bavaria, to create an aerial device that would confuse Allied radar and interrupt electromagnetic currents. Efforts were accelerated to perfect the craft in 1944, but work appears to have shifted to the development of the *Kugelblitz* (Round Lightning), a circular aircraft quite unlike any previous flying object in terrestrial aviation history.

In May 1945, after the Nazi surrender, British agents searching the files of some underground factories in the Black Forest located a number of documents describing important experiments relating to new turbine engines capable of developing extraordinary power. Rumors abound that Canadian intelligence took plans for an advanced circular aircraft from Peenemünde, site of the main Nazi rocket experimental complex from 1937 to 1945, and presented them as a challenge to the scientists at the De Havilland Aircraft Company. According to other rumors, the engineers at De Havilland actually made the "flying saucer" fly—briefly, but they never mastered the propulsion techniques required to keep the craft in the air for very long at a time.

Currently, the question continues to be hotly debated: Did the Nazi scientists manage to keep *their* flying saucer in the air for a very long time—long enough to establish bases on the moon?

NEW AGE MOVEMENT

Besides some contemporary terms for ancient teachings and spiritual practices, there is really nothing very new about the "New Age" movement. It still upsets the established priesthood in much the same ways as it did thousands of years ago.

Many of the roots of contemporary New Age thinking can be found in the ancient Egyptian and Greek mystery schools; and in the 1970s, a number of the concepts and beliefs professed by Mme Helena Blavatsky in the 1880s were refined and given a new life in what has been broadly defined and termed the "New Age." In addition to such contributions as occult masters and guides, Mme Blavatsky was greatly responsible for popularizing the concepts of reincarnation and past lives in Europe and the United States.

It is, however, Alice Bailey, a prodigious writer of the occult, who has earned the title of "mother" of the modern form of the New Age movement. Born Alice Ann La Trobe Bateman on June 16, 1880, to a wealthy, aristocratic family in Manchester, England, Alice became an extraordinary woman, who served at one time as a devoted, conventionally religious missionary worker and Sunday-school teacher.

At the age of fifteen Alice had a profound spiritual experience. One afternoon she was alone in her room reading when the door mysteriously opened and a tall stranger entered. Terrified, Alice felt unable to move or to speak as the man, with a large turban on his head, began explaining that there was a plan for her on Earth. However, her disposition would have to change considerably. If she could learn to exercise self-control and become a more pleasant and trustworthy person, she would travel all over the world and do the "master's work." Adding that he would check in on her at several-year intervals, he paused, looked at her one last time, and walked out.

Thinking the stranger to be Jesus Christ, Alice was deeply affected by his message. She worked hard at becoming a nice person, so much so that her family feared she was ill. Not until years later, after she had moved to California and some friends introduced her to Helena Blavatsky, Theosophy, and the Secret Doctrines, did Alice realize that the man who had so mysteriously walked into her room and life was Master Koot Hoomi.

Theosophy is an esoteric blend of Zoroastrianism, Hinduism, Gnosticism, Manichaeism, the Kabbalah, and the philosophy of Plato and other mystics—all combined with the teachings of mysterious masters who dwell in secret places in the Himalayas and communicate with their initiates through their psychic abilities and their projected astral bodies. Madame Blavatsky claimed to be able to draw upon the ancient wisdom of the Tibetan masters Koot Hoomi and Morya to supplement the considerable knowledge that she had distilled from various mystery schools.

In 1875 Mme Blavatsky, Henry Steel Olcott, and William Q. Judge decided to move beyond the precepts of Spiritualism and create a more sophisticated approach to spirit contact and mysticism. They named their new organization the Theosophical Society. The threefold purpose of the society was to form a universal brotherhood of man; to study and make known the ancient religions, philosophies, and sciences; and to investigate the laws of nature and develop the divine powers latent in humankind. In 1877 Mme Blavatsky published her overview of the occult, *Isis Unveiled.*

Mesmerized by Blavatsky's teachings, Alice Bailey rose to prominence in the Theosophical Society headquarters in California, taking a job as a vegetarian cook and scrubbing the bottoms of garbage pails to support herself. A first marriage ended in divorce, but her second marriage, to the attorney Foster Bailey, the treasurer of the society, was successful, for he too devoted his life to the study of an-

cient wisdom. Not long after their uniting, in 1919, another "teacher" appeared to Alice, identifying himself as the Tibetan master DK or Djwhal Khul.

Alice wrote a series of "Ageless Wisdom" books of teachings from DK that became very popular and were eventually lauded as classics in occult teaching. In her later years, Alice and Foster Bailey founded the Arcane School, headquartered in New York, with centers in Europe; Lucis Trust, with over six thousand active members; the Lucis Trust Publishing Company; and the World Goodwill Centers. Her work continues to be a main influence on "New Agers" or those interested in the occult or in deeper spiritual mysteries.

Alice Bailey channeled what is known as the Great Invocation, words from the Tibetan master Djwhal Khul, that are often recited at New Age meetings and gatherings:

> From the point of Light within the Mind of God, let light stream forth into the minds of men. Let Light descend on Earth. From the point of Love within the Heart of God, let love stream forth into the hearts of men. May Christ return to Earth. From the center where the will of God is know, let purpose guide the little will of men—the purpose which the Masters know and serve. From the center which we call the race of men, let the Plan of Love and Light work out—and may it seal the door where evil dwells. Let Light and Love and Power restore.

In the 1960s, when the flower children began singing about the dawning of the Age of Aquarius flooding the world with the light of harmony and understanding, peace and love abounding, conventional Christian clergy became increasingly concerned about the role of Jesus in the New Age. Conservative theologians assessed the New Age philosophy as being more human-centered than God-centered. The essence of humankind was its divinity, said the New Agers, and each man and woman was a co-creator with God. The members of the movement seemed completely open-minded and tolerant of all paths and religious perspectives—except that of Christianity.

In the 1970s, after the publication of Jane Roberts's books *The Seth Material* and *Seth Speaks,* "channeling" became a more popular name for mediumship, and it remains so to the present day. Roberts received contact with an entity named Seth after entering a trance state. Robert Butts, her husband, wrote down the thoughts, ideas, and concepts communicated by the spirit. The material dictated by Seth was very literate and provocative, and especially well suited to a generation of maturing sixties flower children and baby boomers. It wasn't long before Seth discussion groups around the nation were celebrating such concepts as the following: (1) We all create our own reality; (2) our point of power lies in the present; and (3) we are all gods couched in "creaturehood."

In the 1970s the very idea of establishing contact with great spirit teachers from other dimensions such as Seth seemed new and exciting to many men and women. However, from the viewpoint of students of the paranormal and mysticism, it seemed only that another cycle of awareness had reached its season. Soon "channelers" were emerging in large numbers throughout the land, and individuals such as Jach Pursel, Kevin Ryerson, and JZ Knight had attained international celebrity status. Contact with the powers of the human psyche and the mysterious world beyond death achieved a peak of popularity that led to an outpouring of television programs, motion pictures, books, New Age expos, and psychic fairs in a virtual cosmic explosion. The New Age had arrived.

In 1987 the ABC television network presented a miniseries based on actress Shirley MacLaine's book *Out on a Limb* (1983), which dealt with many subjects exciting to New Age followers, such as reincarnation, extraterrestrial visitation, ancient mysteries, and spirit communication. Perhaps the most captivating segments of the miniseries depicted MacLaine receiving spirit communication through the channeler Kevin Ryerson. The actress and the medium played themselves in the five-hour dramatization on prime-time television, and an international audience of millions could see for themselves how "Tom McPherson," the four-hundred-year-old spirit of an Irishman, spoke through Ryerson to advise MacLaine. With the popularity of *Out on a Limb* as a book and as a miniseries, the actress herself conducted a series of seminars in which she discussed her beliefs in past lives, UFOs, and spirit communication.

Theosophy is an esoteric blend of Zoroastrianism, Hinduism, Gnosticism, Manichaeism, the Kabbalah, and the philosophy of Plato and other mystics.

Why should a philosophical movement that sought to explore ancient mysteries and borderline science become popular in a day of high-tech communications, the Internet, and increasingly sophisticated technology? JZ Knight's spirit guide Ramtha—a 35,000-year-old warrior from the lost continent of Lemuria—answered that question by stating that there really weren't any mysteries left for humankind to explore on their material journey. Millions of people had reached a kind of peak in their evolution and were asking who they really were and why they were really here. Ramtha also said that the human journey had reached a point when the self seeks to turn inward.

Born Judith Darlene Hampton on March 16, 1946, in Dexter, New Mexico, JZ Knight grew up in poverty and married soon after attending Lubbock Business College in Lubbock, Texas. The marriage produced two sons but ended in divorce. It was while she was working as a cable television salesperson in Roswell, New Mexico, and Tacoma, Washington, that she began using the initials *JZ,* taken from her given first name and her nickname, "Zebra," derived from her penchant for wearing black-and-white clothing.

One day in 1977 when JZ and her second husband, Jeremy Wilder, a dentist, were putting together small pyramids for an experiment with "pyramid energy," Ramtha appeared before them in their kitchen in Tacoma. After a period of study with Ramtha, Knight gave her first public channeling in November 1978. Word of the content and the mystique of her work spread quickly and gained a wide following for the 35,000-year-old entity and his channel.

Motion picture stars such as Shirley MacLaine, Linda Evans, and Richard Chamberlain have been in the audiences of Ramtha, along with throngs of other people from around the United States and Canada. Since 1978 thousands have studied the Ramtha videos, cassettes, and books. In 1988 Ramtha founded the School of Enlightenment on Knight's ranch in Yelm, Washington, which continues to hold teaching seminars and which is not a secret society, a church, or a nonprofit organization.

The nationwide interest in channelers and after-death communication continues to find expression in such popular mediums as Sylvia Browne, James Van Praagh, and John Edward, and the orthodox clergy continues to condemn this fascination with the occult as a satanic ploy to draw people away from church, synagogue, or temple. Even the most comprehensive surveys of religion have found that fewer than 100,000 Americans list "New Age" as their personal form of spiritual expression, so it would appear that New Age beliefs are

not robbing the pews of the churches in any great numbers.

NEW WORLD ORDER/ONE WORLD GOVERNMENT

There is an unholy alliance, an invisible government, with only one goal on its agenda: to control all the nations of Earth.

In 1906 President Theodore Roosevelt issued a warning that every conspiracy theorist since has heeded and keenly understood: "Behind the ostensible government sits enthroned an invisible government owing no allegiance and acknowledging no responsibility to the people. To destroy this invisible government, to befoul the unholy alliance between corrupt business and corrupt politics is the first task of the statesmanship of today."

In 2002, when Attorney General John Ashcroft christened another homeland security force the "Freedom Corps," conspiracy theorists were reminded of the *Freikorps,* the German army's "irregulars" who cleared the way for Hitler by murdering Social Democrats and Communists. Such allusions in that administration had a very sinister echo to many historians who believe that the Third Reich that rose to power in Germany in the 1930s was an attempt at a "New World Order" and that the Anglo-American business elite was deeply involved with its ominous creation.

Some economists have defined the Nazi state as a dictatorship of monopoly capitalism and consider Nazi Germany a capitalist paradise. It had a sixty-hour work week, low wages, and no unions. German and international cartels began preparing for war even before they financed Hitler. As countries succumbed to the Nazi juggernaut, German big business, which was able to absorb, even to plunder, former competitors for costs next to nothing.

Such U.S. corporations as Standard Oil, General Motors, IBM, Ford, the Chase and National City Banks, ITT, and many others had invested the equivalent of $8 billion in the Third Reich. When the United States became involved in World War II, the unsuspecting American foot soldiers had no idea that ITT built the airplanes that dropped bombs on them, that Ford and General Motors built the Nazi's trucks and tanks. Ball bearings, crucial to the Nazi war effort, were manufactured in Philadelphia, yet were in scant supply in the States.

The secret or shadow government that manipulates political and economic events everywhere has only one goal in mind, and that is to eventually seize control of all world governments. While the elite secret cartel backed the Nazis, it also supported the Allies. It really didn't matter to the New World Order who won World War II. The real wealth lies in war and genocide. In addition, a terrible full-scale war degrades, demoralizes, and damns humanity so that it will more easily accept serfdom and control by the elite who govern the New World Order.

For decades conspiracy investigators have tried to warn the mass population that a secret government agency has many underground bases where it carries out extensive high-tech, aerospace, and nuclear research, in addition to bacteriological and chemical experiments. These investigators have also learned that the secret societies of the Black Sun, the Thule, and the Vril were correct in their assumption that the ancient master race was extraterrestrial in origin. These secret societies were also correct when they suspected that aliens have bioengineered and genetically manipulated the human genome from the beginning of humankind's origins on Earth. Many of today's UFO researchers have learned that the aliens have mixed their DNA with

In 2002 U.S. Attorney General John Ashcroft declared the Homeland Security force the "Freedom Corps," a name strongly reminiscent of Nazi Germany's murderous "Freikorps."

ours, especially the reptilian genetic line, and live among us.

Norio Hayakawa, author of *UFOs, the Grand Deception and the Coming New World Order,* warns of a global UFO conspiracy linked to a "sinister occult force" that is manufacturing the "Grand Deception." Hayakawa believes that this worldwide plot is designed to stage a counterfeit extraterrestrial contact or landing to simulate an alien threat of invasion in order to urgently and ultimately bring about a delusive New World Order. He warns that this "dramatic invasion and the ensuing catastrophic conflagration in the Middle East will immediately be followed by unprecedented [worldwide] earthquakes, a [global] financial crisis, and a sudden mysterious 'evacuation' [or 'removal,' depending on one's viewpoint] of a segment of the population worldwide—all of which will culminate in an urgent, official declaration of a totalitarian New World Order that will last for seven years upon its inception."

Such a shocking series of global events will place millions of people in "an absolute stupor for weeks," Hayakawa states, during which time "an ingeniously executed, extremely effective 'multi-leveled' mind control program will be activated to calm the stunned populace."

At this point in the scenario envisioned by Hayakawa, while the leadership of the New World Order struggles to assume complete control over the global populaces, a "dynamic, charismatic leader" will arise out of the European community (by then known as the United States of Europe), appear in a worldwide television broadcast, and offer a brilliant explanation to sedate the public. Hayakawa believes that this leader is currently around twenty-nine years old and is residing somewhere in Western Europe, "just waiting to begin his 'official' mission."

> About the same time that President Bush's alleged secret society affiliations were being exposed, a number of fundamentalist Christian evangelists began to take their first real notice of the UFO phenomenon....

Futurist, political theorist, and social analyst Michael Lindemann reached a point in his research where he became convinced that "an alien presence" on Earth was being "selectively revealed to the public with the blessing and sometimes direct involvement of government authorities." In Lindemann's view the architects of the New World Order, whom he

refers to as "the Olympians," have an understanding that the world as we know it is careening toward environmental and economic catastrophe. The Olympians plan "to chart a course through a time of tremendous upheaval during which millions or even billions of people might die, and to emerge from that time still in power and with greatly enhanced prospects for an 'ideal' society of their own design. Their ability to succeed in this strategy will depend on controlling the perceptions and behavior of the citizens of the most-developed nations."

In 1992, when President George H. W. Bush began speaking about his hope that a "new world order" had been created after the conclusion of the Gulf War, evangelist Pat Robertson warned that the "new world order" was actually a code for a secret group of conspirators who sought to replace Christian society with a worldwide atheistic socialist dictatorship. President Bush, charged Robertson and a number of conspiracy theorists, was a member of one of the world's most devilish and powerful secret societies, the Order of Skull and Bones. What was more, according to these same accusers, Bush was linked to the Bilderbergers and the Trilateral Commission, dangerous elitist organizations.

About the same time that President Bush's alleged secret society affiliations were being exposed, a number of fundamentalist Christian evangelists began to take their first real notice of the UFO phenomenon and saw the mysterious aerial objects as the "signs in the skies" referred to in apocalyptic literature and in the book of Revelation as heralding the advent of the antichrist. It was a short leap of faith for many evangelists to begin to combine accounts of UFOs with secret societies and the Beast of Revelation who would bring the New World Order into being.

The proponents of this cosmic conspiracy believe that when President Ronald Reagan gave his famous "alien invasion" speech to the entire United Nations General Assembly in September of 1987, he had already secretly advised representatives of the 176 member nations that the leaders of their respective governments must meet the demands of the technologically superior extraterrestrials or be destroyed. In his speech to the General Assembly, Reagan said that he occasionally thought how quickly all nationalistic differences would vanish if humanity were facing an alien threat from outside this world. And then he suggested that an alien threat was already among us.

A number of conspiracy theorists stated that Reagan's speech hinted at a plan agreed to by world leaders and extraterrestrial invaders that around the year 2000 a carefully staged "alien invasion" would convince the masses of the world that a real-life alien attack from outer space was about to begin. People of all nations would believe their leaders, who would tell them that the aliens were a benevolent species and that unconditional surrender to them would be for everyone's own good.

Immediately following the surrender to the aliens, the united leaders will form a One World Government, a New World Order, thus fulfilling biblical prophecies about a return to the days of Babylon. The aliens will reveal themselves as demonic entities that delight in doing Satan's work.

Under the One World Government, the following laws and rules will apply:

- There will be only a one-unit monetary system.

- Permanent, nonelected hereditary oligarchists will select serfs from the population and form a feudal system, similar to the one that existed in the Middle Ages.

- Population will be limited by restrictions on the number of children per family.

- Diseases, wars, and famines will be engineered until there are only one billion people—those who are deemed useful to the ruling classes—living on the planet.

- There will be no middle class, only rulers and servants.

- A legal system of world courts will oversee a single unified code of laws, enforced by a One World Government police force and a One World unified military.

- None of the former national boundaries of countries shall exist.

- The social system will be on the basis of a welfare state—those who are obedient and subservient to the One World Government will be rewarded with the means to live. Those who are rebellious will be starved to death or declared outlaws, thereby becoming targets for anyone who wishes to kill them.

- Privately owned firearms or weapons of any kind will be prohibited.

- Only one religion will be allowed, and that will be in the form of a One World Government Church, which will adhere to Satanism or Luciferianism.

- There will be no private or church schools.

- Christianity will not be permitted in any form.

9/11

For the vast majority of Americans, it seems unthinkable that our own government could have had a hand in orchestrating the awful events of 9/11, but conspiracy theorists argue that the evidence for such terrible complicity continues to mount.

We all know what happened on September 11, 2001, and how the events of that day have changed America forever. We have seen the terrible video footage of the World Trade Center's twin towers collapsing and the aftermath of the crashes into the Pentagon and the field in Pennsylvania again and again, indelibly burning the images into our psyches so powerfully that even now, years later, psychologists, psychiatrists, and other mental health workers report treating millions for traumas related to the horror of 9/11.

Here is a timeline of how the awful morning began:

7:58 A.M.: United Airlines Flight 175 departs Boston for Los Angeles carrying two pilots, seven flight attendants, and fifty-six passengers. Shortly after takeoff, the Boeing 767 is hijacked and diverted to New York.

7:59 A.M.: American Airlines Flight 11 departs Boston for Los Angeles carrying two pilots, nine flight attendants, and eighty-one passengers. This Boeing 767 is also hijacked and turned toward New York.

8:01 A.M.: United Airlines Flight 93, a Boeing 757, carrying two pilots, five flight attendants, and thirty-eight passengers, leaves Newark, New Jersey, for San Francisco.

8:10 A.M.: American Airlines Flight 77, carrying two pilots, four flight attendants, and fifty-eight passengers, leaves Dulles International Airport for Los Angeles. Also a Boeing 757, Flight 77 is hijacked after takeoff.

8:46 A.M.: Flight 11 crashes into the North Tower at the World Trade Center (WTC) in New York.

9:03 A.M.: Flight 175 slams into the South Tower.

9:45 A.M.: Flight 77 crashes into the Pentagon.

10:05 A.M.: The South Tower collapses.

10:10 A.M.: A large section of the Pentagon collapses.

10:10 A.M.: Flight 93 crashes in a field in Pennsylvania after passengers rush hijackers.

10:28 A.M.: The North Tower collapses.

There are many conspiracy theorists who do not accept the events of that terrible day as millions of people around the world saw them transpire and as our nation's leaders encourage us to believe. Perhaps the various conspiracy theories are fed by the greatest one of all, which declares that the 9/11 attacks were orchestrated by President George W. Bush, Vice President Dick Cheney, Secretary of Defense Donald Rumsfeld, the CIA, and other agents of the New World Order in order to begin a war against Iraq that would allow them to seize that country's oil fields.

Here are a number of the most common conspiracy claims and the arguments rebutting them:

Conspiracy Claim: The jets that struck the WTC and the Pentagon weren't commercial planes but refueling tankers or guided missiles.

Conspiracy Denial: If the planes that struck the WTC and the Pentagon were tankers or missiles, then what happened to United flights 175 and 93 and American flights 11 and 77? Where are the airplanes, the passengers, and the crew members of those flights? The fact that Islamic terrorists took over the four airplanes is supported by mountains of evidence, including cockpit recordings and forensics.

Conspiracy Claim: Photographs and video taken of Flight 175 just before it struck the South Tower clearly show an object under the fuselage at the base of the right wing. This "pod" is most likely a missile or a bomb.

Conspiracy Denial: Photo experts who have carefully examined the image and compared it with other photos of a Boeing 767 have concluded that the "pod" that conspiracy theorists see is nothing more than sunlight glinting off the fairing that contains the landing gear thus exaggerating its size.

Conspiracy Claim: There are twenty-eight air force bases within close range of the alleged four hijacked flights, and Andrews AFB had two squadrons of fighter planes protecting the skies over Washington. Yet there was no military interference with the suicide flights because the air force was ordered to stand down. Someone at the highest level of authority had prior knowledge of the attacks and allowed them to take place.

Conspiracy Denial: The North American Aerospace Defense Command (NORAD) was not prepared to perceive as threats any flights originating in the United States. Beginning at 8:37 A.M., NORAD's Northeast Air Defense Sector (NEADS) was called three times to report that Flight 11 was hijacked, but at 9:21 A.M. they were erroneously given Washington, rather than New York, as its destination. Flight 11 struck the North Tower at 8:46 A.M. NEADS was notified of Flight 175's hijacking at 9:03 A.M., the precise time that the airplane crashed into the South Tower. Two F-16s had been scrambled from Otis Air Force Base in Falmouth, Massachusetts, and three from Langley Air National Guard, but none of them got near the hijacked planes. Regarding Flights 93 and 77, once the terrorists had shut off the planes' transponders, it became impossible to sort out the hijacked planes from the 4,500 other blips on radar screens at some of the nation's busiest air lanes.

Conspiracy Claim: The first hijacked plane crashed into floors 94 through 98 of the WTC's 110-story North Tower. The second jet impacted floors 78 to 84 of the 110-story South Tower. There is no way that these two planes, even though loaded with fuel, could have destroyed the structural integrity of the WTC towers. Demolitions had to have been placed throughout the towers before the crashes occurred.

Conspiracy Denial: According to initial findings of the National Institute of Standards and Technology (NIST), plane wreckage plowed through utility shafts at the North Tower's core, creating a conduit for burning jet fuel throughout the building. On October 19,

2004, federal investigators released a five-hundred-page document stating that the twin towers failed "because the structural columns at the buildings' core, damaged by the impact of the airliners, buckled and shortened as the fires burned, gradually shifting more load to the towers' exterior pinstripe columns [which] ultimately suffered such extraordinary stress and heat that they gave way" (*New York Times*, October 20, 2004).

Photographs and video taken of Flight 175 just before it struck the South Tower clearly show an object under the fuselage at the base of the right wing.

Conspiracy Claim: Jet fuel cannot burn hot enough to melt steel.

Conspiracy Denial: Although it is true that jet fuel burns at only 1,517 degrees F. and steel melts at 2,777 degrees F., experts agree that the steel frames of the twin towers didn't need to melt to collapse; their loss of structural strength would have been enough. Thomas Eagar, engineering professor at Massachusetts Institute of Technology, explains that steel loses 50 percent of its strength at 1,200 degrees F., and with 90,000 liters of jet fuel continuing to ignite other combustible materials, the temperature would continue to rise.

Conspiracy Claim: The collapse of the twin towers resembled controlled implosions, such as those used to demolish old buildings.

Conspiracy Denial: The weight of all the floors above the collapsed zones of the towers would begin to smash down with massive force on the floors below, creating a kind of chain reaction. Experienced engineers term the process "pancaking," and they say that it need not require an explosion to begin.

Conspiracy Claim: Seismographs at Columbia University Earth Observatory in Palisades, New York, indicate that the strongest jolts were registered before the collapsing towers struck the earth, thereby proving that massive explosions brought them down.

Conspiracy Denial: Seismologists at Columbia University's Lamont-Doherty Earth Observatory in Palisades state that their work was misrepresented. Their graphs show only seismic readings produced by the two planes crashing into the towers and by the collapse of the buildings.

Conspiracy Claim: The forty-seven-story WTC 7 building fell seven hours after the collapse of the twin towers, the result of controlled demolition. The buildings fell straight down through themselves, maintaining radial symmetry. Witnesses to the collapse of the towers claim to have heard demolition blasts and seen clouds of dust and smoke shooting out of the towers. The towers came down suddenly and completely with the rubble falling at the same speed inside and outside the former buildings' profile. This is an impossibility unless the towers fell by controlled demolition.

Conspiracy Denial: According to the NIST, there was one basic reason for the WTC 7 collapse: Because of an unusual design, the columns were assigned exceptionally heavy loads, approximately 2,000 square feet of floor area for each floor. Shyam Sunder of the NIST states that preliminary analysis has shown that "if you take out just one column on one of the lower floors, it could cause a vertical progression of collapse so that the entire section comes down."

Conspiracy Claim: The two crash holes visible in the Pentagon are much too small to have been made by a Boeing 757.

Conspiracy Denial: Mete Sozen, a professor of structural engineering at Purdue University, reminds people that a crashing jet airplane doesn't leave a cartoon cutout outline of itself on the ground or on a building. In Sozen's opinion, what was left of the Boeing 757 flowed into the reinforced concrete building in a state "closer to a liquid than a solid mass."

Conspiracy Claim: There was no plane wreckage found at the Pentagon, thereby proving that a missile or a bomb was responsible for the damage.

Conspiracy Denial: Allyn E. Kilsheimer, a blast expert and CEO of KCE Structural Engineers PC, Washington, D.C., was the first structural engineer to arrive on the scene. He states that he saw the marks of the plane wing on the building, picked up parts of the plane with airline markings on them, held the tail section, and found the black box. There is no mistake, he says, that it was an airplane that struck the Pentagon.

Conspiracy Claim: Flight 93 was brought down by a heat-seeking missile from an F-16 fighter.

Conspiracy Denial: There were no F-16s in the area, but a Dassault Falcon 20 business jet owned by the VF Corporation of Greensboro, North Carolina, was on a descent into the Johnstown-Cambria airport when the FAA contacted them and asked them to investigate. The Falcon 20 pinpointed the location of a hole in the ground and smoke rising out of it, then continued on to its destination.

Conspiracy Claim: One of Flight 93's engines was found a considerable distance from the crash site with damage consistent to that which a heat-seeking missile would cause.

Conspiracy Denial: Investigators on the scene reported a fan from one of the engines in a catchment basin about 300 yards south of the crash site. Experts say there is nothing extraordinary about an engine tumbling that distance from the crash site, especially when

Then New York City's Mayor Rudy Giuliani (right) with U.S. Secretary of Defense Donald Rumsfeld talk to the media shortly after the Twin Towers were destroyed.

it is considered that the plane probably hit traveling at 500 mph, moving 700 to 800 feet per second.

Conspiracy Claim: After take-off, the four doomed aircraft were ordered by secret government agents to a deserted airbase where the passengers from Flights 11, 77, and 175 were placed aboard Flight 93, which was electronically controlled and programmed to crash in Pennsylvania, eliminating all witnesses. The three aircraft that struck the WTC and the Pentagon were empty, controlled by implanted electronic systems from afar. The frantic calls from cellphones, allegedly from passengers, were all prerecorded by trained actors. The shadow government then used the phony at-

tack by "foreign terrorists" as an excuse to declare war on Iraq.

Conspiracy Denial: This "scenario reconstruction" was suggested by retired University of Western Ontario professor A. K. Dewdney. Reactions to his theory range from total agreement to profound disgust.

Conspiracy Claim: Mayor Rudy Giuliani of New York banned all independent investigators and civilians from ground zero so that any physical evidence of explosives among the rubble would be hauled away before it was detected.

Conspiracy Denial: Mayor Giuliani recognized that ground zero was a historic scene, but it was also a crime scene, and he didn't want people getting hurt while trying to take pictures of the destruction or destroying any evidence that might be useful to federal investigators.

Conspiracy theories about 9/11 continue to grow. Days after the horrible events of that September morning, William Rodriguez was proclaimed a hero for saving numerous lives at ground zero and being the recipient of a miracle for himself. Not many people have heard his story, conspiracy theorists maintain, because it tends to expose the 9/11 investigation as a sham and indicates that the government is involved in a cover-up about the truth of the WTC disaster.

Rodriguez was a janitor on duty the morning of September 11, and he heard and felt explosions shudder the basement sublevels of the North Tower beneath his feet just seconds before the jetliner struck the top floors. The walls cracked around him, and he pulled a severely burned man from the basement. Rodriguez asked then, and he asks today the same question that many conspiracy theorists have posed: How could a jetliner slam into the tower ninety floors above the ground and burn a man's arms and face to a crisp in the sublevels within seconds of impact?

According to Rodriguez, NBC News spent a full day at his house interviewing him about the serious allegations that he had made. His eyewitness account is backed up by fourteen people who were on the scene with him and felt the explosions go off. At the last minute, he says, NBC dropped the story, and some reporters told him to keep quiet or his life would be in danger.

Conspiracy theorists state that Rodriguez's testimony clearly demonstrates that the WTC towers were brought down by controlled demolition. Rodriguez says that he lost two hundred friends when the towers collapsed and that he is now their voice speaking out for the truth.

On September 11, 2011, the tenth anniversary of the attacks on the World Trade Center,

it was readily observed by even the most objective individuals that conspiracy theories revolving around the terrorist attack had not abated—if anything, they had increased.

Numerous happenings suggestive of conspiratorial activity can be culled by perusing such sites as www.prisonplanet.com, www.jeffrense.com, and www.davidicke.com and discovering such theories as the following:

Ignored Warnings

- A top-secret U.S. agency eavesdropped on a conversation before September 11 between an individual later suspected to be the terrorist commander of the 9/11 attacks and the chief hijacker, but it took no action.

- An Iranian deportee called police from his jail cell and warned of the planned attack on the WTC. No action was taken.

- The National Security Agency intercepted a conversation in Arabic in which the participants discussed something big about to happen in the U.S. very soon.

- U.S. intelligence intercepted two messages on September 10 that a terrorist attack would take place on the next day: "Zero Hour is tomorrow."

Individuals Who Received Advance Warnings about the Attacks

- Mayor Rudolph Giuliani admitted to Peter Jennings that he received a warning that the South Tower was about to collapse.

- *Newsweek* magazine learned that top Pentagon officials were warned not to fly after September 10.

- A former U.S. senator warned Condoleeza Rice on September 6 not to travel in the next several days because a terrorist attack inside the United States was imminent.

• The FBI learned that some Middle Easterners in the New York area were warned not to go to lower Manhattan on September 11.

Perhaps the most persistent aspect of that day of tragedy that baffles the largest number of the general population is the unexpected free-fall of WTC 7, a forty-seven-story office tower. To this day no one can give a satisfactory argument that will appease both the conspiracy buffs and the curious as to why the tower just seemed to collapse in upon itself, looking very much like it was the target of a controlled demolition. It wasn't struck by any planes or burned with any jet fuel, the so-called magic formula that was said to have brought down the twin towers. And a very small percentage of the skeptics will accept the speculation that sprays of burning diesel fuel could liquefy structural steel.

Over one hundred distinguished university professors, together with over fifty senior government officials, over a hundred pilots and aviation professionals, plus hundreds of architects and engineers, have gone on record to state that the 9/11 Commission Report with its explanation of the terrorist act is flawed.

The National Institute for Standards and Technology's 10,000-page report named "collapse initiation" (the loss of several floors' vertical support) as an explanation for the "free-fall" of the WTC structures. Later, the NIST was forced to admit that the total free-fall collapse of the twin towers could not be explained after an "exhaustive scientific study." The only explanation for the means by which the buildings could have come down at free-fall speed, the NIST acknowledged, was controlled demolition. In addition, NIST confirmed that virtually none of the steel in the towers reached temperatures hotter than 500 degrees. By NIST's own statements, the point at which steel weakens is 1,000 degrees and its melting point is 1,500 degrees.

RICHARD M. NIXON— THE CONSPIRACY PRESIDENT

Can all of Richard M. Nixon's successes and achievements, trials and tribulations be attributed to his being a pawn of the Illuminati?

It must be decided by future historians how Richard M. Nixon will be assessed as a president of the United States. There are those of his contemporaries who regard him as a great statesman, a master analyst of foreign policy, and an extremely reserved, intelligent man who came from a devout Quaker background. Others see him as a man beset by his own perception that he was always the underdog, the victim of others' malevolence, and that he must denigrate and retaliate against all who opposed him. He spoke with pride of his political crises and how he always managed to emerge stronger than before. Others perceived most of his crises as being of his own making and considered him a paranoid, destructive personality.

Conspiracy theorists judge Nixon as a man convinced that others were always conspiring against him and who dealt with this persistent paranoia by becoming involved in conspiracy after conspiracy against others until he was forced to leave the presidency because of the bungled conspiracy of Watergate.

Nixon graduated third in his class at Duke Law School and sought work with a law firm in New York. Disappointed that he was unable to find satisfactory employment, he returned home to Whittier, California. In 1940 he married schoolteacher Pat Ryan, who would later become invaluable to his political career. He served as a naval officer beginning in 1942 and first ventured into politics in 1946. According to conspiracists, he was backed by eastern establishment money when he rose out of obscurity to defeat incumbent California congressman Jerry Voorhis, who was anti–Federal Reserve. Nixon also began the practice of portraying himself as the underdog and denigrating his opponent: He proclaimed to the voters that he was a family man and a "champion of the forgotten man," while Voorhis was a Communist.

In 1948 Nixon became a national figure as a member of the House Committee on Un-American Activities because of his persecution of Alger Hiss, formerly a respected adviser to Franklin D. Roosevelt, as a Soviet Union spy. Whittaker Chambers, an editor at Time Life who had known Communist ties, had first accused Hiss, and Nixon soon saw Communist-hunting as a certain path to political fame. He continued to build his anti-Communist credentials for two terms in Congress, then, after a hostile campaign in which he accused his opponent, Helen Douglas, of being a "pinko communist," pink right down to her underwear, he was elected to the U.S. Senate. Douglas had some satisfaction when she gave Nixon the nickname of "Tricky Dick," which would haunt him throughout the rest of his career.

In 1952 Nixon was rewarded for helping to create an Eisenhower majority in California by being placed on the presidential ticket as Ike's running mate. Nixon held on to that position in spite of press reports about the undeclared donations from businessmen that had helped begin his career. Although a portion of the U.S. population began their distaste of Nixon because of the scandal, his televised, shamelessly whining and manipulative "Checkers" speech (the only "donation" he had accepted was a cocker spaniel that his daughter Tricia had named Checkers), he remained on the ballot—and continued as vice president under Eisenhower for eight years.

Conspiracists maintain that during the 1960 Republican convention in Chicago, Nixon flew to New York for a secret meeting with Nelson Rockefeller, a high-ranking Bilderberger

and New World Order member. Nixon was given the Fourteen Points of the Compact of Fifth Avenue, which inserted the socialistic agenda of Rockefeller into the Republican Party platform. During his eight years as vice president Nixon became one of the most active "veeps" in American history. He was involved in the Communist hunts of Senator Joseph McCarthy, he was integral in dissolution of the Suez Crisis of 1954, and he met with the nominal leader of the Communist world, the Soviet premier Nikita Khrushchev. The presidency seemed a sure thing for Richard M. Nixon in 1960.

But the Illuminati had decided against Nixon's achieving the position at that time—and they made certain of his defeat by instructing the extremely popular President Eisenhower to belittle Nixon's contributions as a vice president, even declaring at a press conference that he was unable to think of a single thing worthwhile that Nixon had contributed during the eight years of the Eisenhower administration. Pains were also taken to be certain that John F. Kennedy received the right advisers on make-up, camera techniques, and lighting for his televised debate with Nixon, thereby ensuring that JFK would appear young and handsome while Nixon came off as haggard, worn, old, and profusely sweating and ill at ease.

After Kennedy won the presidential election in 1960, Nixon made an unsuccessful bid for the governorship of California, then moved to New York to become a law partner in the firm of John Mitchell, Nelson Rockefeller's personal attorney. The Nixon family lived in a Fifth Avenue apartment building owned by Rockefeller. From 1961 to 1965 Nixon was a member of the Council on Foreign Relations (CFR) and began to rebuild his political power with the help of the New World Order.

On November 22, 1963, the *Dallas Morning News* contained an unsigned leaflet that prominently displayed a photo of President John F. Kennedy under the indictment, "Wanted for Treason." Researchers later claimed that the incendiary leaflet had been designed at an alleged Pepsi-Cola convention and drafted by attorneys of the Rockefeller law firm of Nixon, Mudge, Rose, Guthrie, and Alexander as a tool to be used in the 1964 presidential campaign. Although no solid proof has ever been forthcoming, many conspiracists are convinced that Nixon had advance knowledge of JFK's assassination. Even more researchers are certain that only the Illuminati had enough power to operate in the shadows of the conspiracy to kill JFK and control all the many disparate elements necessary to manage such a complicated and insidious event.

Researchers point out that the Illuminati wanted Kennedy out of the way because he would have ended the U.S. involvement in Vietnam by 1965. Massive oil fields had been discovered off the coast of South Vietnam, and Rockefeller created high-level concern that the country would be lost to Communism as Cuba had been. After Kennedy was assassinated, the U.S. involvement in Vietnam escalated and "War Is Good Business" became the motto of those Illuminati and CFR members who made billions from the Vietnam bloodbath.

During the 1968 presidential campaign Senator Robert F. Kennedy pledged an honorable end to the conflict in Vietnam, and Martin Luther King assured him that he would deliver the African American vote. Conspiracy researchers feel that there is little doubt that RFK would have been elected to the presidency; however, the Illuminati desired to prolong the conflict in Vietnam, and they wanted Nixon to be their instrument because he was well conditioned to perpetuate their goals. Within a few months both RFK and MLK had been assassinated in two complex conspiracies that have never been resolved to the satisfaction of researchers—unless one considers the involvement of those shadowy figures of the Illuminati who wish a One World Government.

Witnesses have stated that at 5:30 on the morning Nixon achieved the presidency, Nel-

President Richard Nixon, disgraced by the Watergate scandal, was the first U.S. president in history to resign from office. Was he a victim of plots by the Illuminati?

son Rockefeller and William Rogers (a former U.S. attorney general under President Eisenhower) were in Nixon's room helping to select the cabinet for his administration. John Mitchell, Rockefeller's personal attorney, was appointed attorney general; Henry Kissinger was named secretary of state so that the Illuminati could exercise control over U.S. foreign policy. Congress would later come to feel that they were being disrespected, for Nixon would often streamline government policies in illegal measures and bypass the State Department to execute his foreign policies with only Kissinger as his adviser. George H. W. Bush was named the chairman of the Republican Party and later ambassador to the UN, ambassador to China, and director of the CIA. Nixon's loyal friends H. R. Haldeman and John Ehrlichman became, respectively, his chief of staff and principal domestic policy adviser.

Three days after Nixon's 1971 State of the Union Address, he made the declaration that the U.S. was being divided into ten federal districts. In February 1972 he signed Executive Order #1147, giving the government the power to accomplish such a division.

Nixon had promised the U.S. public that soon after he assumed office in January 1969 he would begin a massive withdrawal of the 540,000 young Americans who had been deployed to Vietnam. Although he did slowly begin to abide by his word, Nixon also ordered the bombing of Hanoi in 1969. Nixon appeared to be attempting to please his legitimate constituency and the Illuminati overlords at the same time. Against the objections of many of his advisers and a great deal of Congress, Nixon gave lip service to an "honorable end to the war" and conducted the secret bombing of Cambodia simultaneously. To the ever-growing number of war protestors, Nixon's response was to call them "bums," and he condemned all protestors and antiwar politicians as disloyal Americans. J. Edgar Hoover, on Nixon's encouragement, initiated the FBI's infamous COINTELPRO, in which the government agency was given a free hand to discredit, disrupt, and disband protest groups by any means necessary. It was also about this time that Nixon installed intricate microphones and taping systems in the White House.

A bright spot in the harassed Nixon's life was blighted when he opened the *New York Times* on June 12, 1971, to read about his daughter Tricia's wedding to Edward Cox and viewed a lovely photograph of Tricia and him in the Rose Garden right next to the first installment of the "Pentagon Papers." Department of Defense employee Daniel Ellsberg had leaked all forty-seven volumes of top-secret documents that exposed how the U.S. government, beginning with the administration of Lyndon B. Johnson, had lied to the American public about the true policies and intentions toward Vietnam. Nixon was furious that information about secret meetings with the Soviets and China, as well as details of the administration's duplicity regarding Vietnam, should be revealed. He felt national security

had been breached, and the administration tried to stop publication of the papers, but they lost the case in court.

As was his style, Nixon next ordered a special investigative team called the "plumbers" —because it was their duty to plug leaks—to get all the dirt on Ellsberg that they could. The plumbers' membership included the top echelon—Nixon, Haldeman, Kissinger, and Ehrlichman—and the lower level: Chuck Colson, a White House attorney; G. Gordon Liddy, counsel to the Committee to Re-elect the President; and E. Howard Hunt, a former CIA agent.

The seed for Watergate can be traced back to 1956 when the flamboyant aviator, contractor, and Hollywood playboy Howard Hughes provided Nixon's brother Donald with a secret loan to help him get his "Nixonburger" restaurants off the ground. Word of this monetary exchange leaked out during the 1960 presidential elections, and the Democrats used it to embarrass Nixon. Later Nixon learned that Democratic Party chairman Lawrence F. O'Brien was being surreptitiously retained by Hughes, and he vowed revenge against O'Brien. After Colson, Liddy, and Hunt managed a successful break-in at the Los Angeles office of Ellsberg's psychiatrist in September 1971, Nixon ordered another at the Democratic National Committee headquarters at the Watergate apartment complex in Washington, D.C., with the mission of learning any derogatory information that the Democrats might have about the Republicans. The plumbers' special assignment was to place a bug on the DNC chairman's telephone. On May 27, 1972, the plumbers accomplished a successful entry into DNC headquarters. On June 17 they returned and were arrested by police.

Conspiracy theorists state that Watergate was orchestrated by the Illuminati, who had decided they had no further use for Nixon. Bruce Herschenson, a Nixon aide, has said that the Watergate break-in was deliberately sabotaged by "a coalition of power groups."

The security chief for the Committee to Re-elect the President, James W. McCord Jr., a former CIA agent, has been accused by some of being a double agent who was responsible for tipping off the police the night of the second break-in.

Nixon managed to play innocent initially, and only Liddy, Hunt, and McCord were indicted by a grand jury under Judge John Sirica. Over the next two years, accusations and suspicious were raised innumerable times about the role of the president and several of his aides in the Watergate affair. After a great deal of pressure, White House counsel John Dean, who decided not to become a scapegoat for Nixon, began pointing a finger at his colleagues. Eventually a White House aide mentioned that Nixon tape-recorded nearly all of his conversations, even personal ones, and the smoking gun had been found. After months of evasion, the Supreme Court ruled that Nixon could no longer claim "executive privilege" and must surrender the tapes. If it weren't for the revelation of the Watergate tapes, Nixon might have survived the scandal of the DNC break-in. On the tapes, the president can be heard attempting to order FBI and CIA officials to interfere with the Watergate investigation. He can be heard using foul language and making anti-Semitic and racist comments. Nixon resigned on August 9, 1974, to avoid impeachment by the full House of Representatives and trial by the Senate.

Conspiracists list a number of possible reasons why the Illuminati disposed of Nixon:

- Nixon's ego was growing over his foreign policy accomplishments with China, and he was considering dumping Kissinger, the Illuminati's agent in the White House, and assuming complete control.
- After Nixon's first vice president, Spiro Agnew, was forced to resign because of income tax evasion, the Illuminati wanted Nelson Rockefeller as his successor, who would become president should Nixon die

in office. Nixon instead named Gerald Ford, who, when he became president upon Nixon's resignation, did appoint Rockefeller to the vice presidency. On September 5, 1974, Lynette "Squeaky" Fromme, one of the Charles Manson Family, attempted to shoot President Ford. On September 22 Sara Jane Moore, also a member of the Family, tried to assassinate Ford. When questioned about her motives, Moore said that she was attempting to elevate Nelson Rockefeller to the presidency.

- Nixon was becoming too personally ambitious and believing too greatly in his own power to accomplish change.

A very interesting piece of Nixon tape was revealed on March 23, 2005, by Michael Isikoff and Mark Hosenball of *Newsweek/MSNBC*. Nixon's White House secretary, Rosemary Woods, was a follower of the psychic/astrologer Jeane Dixon, and on May 4, 1971, she brought the seeress together with her boss for a thirty-six-minute session. During the meeting Dixon said that the Lord intended Nixon to be great and that he was in power now to lead everyone to Christ, the prince of the universe.

About two weeks later, on May 21, 1971, James Reston wrote in the *New York Times* that Nixon "would obviously like to preside over the creation of a new world order."

At that time, aggressive members of the Illuminati had scheduled an established One World Government by a target date of 1976. They did not wish to have competition from Nixon. And they certainly didn't relish the thought of Nixon leading the world to "Christ, the prince of the universe," for their god is "Satan, prince of the universe."

Richard M. Nixon died on April 22, 1994, in New York City, and on April 27 was buried on the grounds of the Nixon Library in Yorba Linda, California, next to his beloved First Lady, Pat.

NOAH'S ARK

There is no question that the remains of Noah's Ark can be found on Mount Ararat—and the CIA has the proof.

So prevalent is the belief that Noah's Ark can be located on the slope of the tallest mountain in Turkey, Agri Dagi (Mount Ararat), that some travel agencies include participation in expeditions to search for the ark as part of tour packages to Turkey. According to Genesis 6–10, God had become angered at the wickedness of humans and was determined "to end all flesh." God called on Noah, whom he deemed a just man, and told him to build a large barge with three interior decks. The barge was to be constructed of wood and sealed with bitumen. Its length was to be 300 cubits (about 450 feet), its width 50 cubits (about 75 feet), and its height 30 cubits (about 45 feet). The ark, with Noah's family and at least two animals from every species, would be able to survive the deluge through which God would wipe out all other life on earth. After seven months and seventeen days afloat, the ark came to rest upon the mountains of Ararat, near the headwaters of the Euphrates River in what is today eastern Turkey.

Some biblical scholars locate the final resting place of the ark in Kurdistan, an area that encompasses Mount Ararat and parts of present-day Turkey and Iran. The Babylonian account of the deluge in the Epic of Gilgamesh names Mount Nisir in that region.

As the Christian religion spread in the first century, the Christians of Apamea, in Phrygia, built the Monastery of the Ark, where a feast was celebrated annually to commemorate Noah's disembarking. Marco Polo, in journals of his journey to China in 1271, wrote: "In the heart of Greater Armenia is a very high mountain, shaped like a cube (or cup), on which Noah's Ark is said to have rested, whence it is called the Mountain of Noah's Ark."

Several ark sightings on Mount Ararat occurred during the twentieth century. During a thaw in the summer of 1916, a Russian Imperial Air Force lieutenant noticed a half-frozen lake in a gully on the side of Ararat. World War I was raging, and the Russian pilot was flying high-altitude tests to observe Turkish troop movements. Flying nearer to the lake, he saw half the hull of some sort of ship poking out above the surface. He reported it to his captain, who later joined him in a flight over the site. Believing it was Noah's Ark, preserved because it was encased in ice most of the year, the captain sent a report to Tsar Nicholas II at Saint Petersburg. The tsar sent two corps of engineers up the mountain.

It took nearly a month for the Russian engineers to reach the ark. They took measurements and made drawings and photographs, but none of those was ever officially documented. According to accounts, the photographs and reports were sent by courier to the attention of the tsar, but he apparently never received them. The Russian Revolution broke out in 1917, and the results of the investigation were never reported publicly.

In 1959 the Turkish Air Force conducted an aerial survey of the Ararat region. A photograph revealed the outline of a ship on one of the lower slopes (just over 6,000 feet) of Mount Ararat. The ship's dimensions resembled, but were somewhat larger than, those of the biblical ark. Another alleged aerial sighting occurred in 1960: a Turkish army pilot and a liaison officer reported seeing evidence of an enormous, rectangular barge on the southeast slope at about 13,000 feet altitude.

During the 1950s Noah's Ark expeditions from the West were considered a security threat by the Soviet government, whose territory bordered the region. Those who defied the Soviets' displeasure found that the rugged environment made it difficult to sustain an expedition. Six to eight weeks of favorable weather were the most searchers could hope for as they tried to maneuver along the treacherous paths of the 16,000-foot mountain, where glaciers and deep pockets of snow have little time to thaw before the return of cold weather.

A photograph taken in 1973 by the Earth Resources Technology Satellite (ERTS) revealed an unusual feature, reportedly similar in size to the ark, at 14,000 feet on Mount Ararat. When ark researchers requested copies of the satellite image, they received a standard reply: "No responsive records."

In the 1980s the former NASA astronaut James Irwin participated in expeditions up the mountain, bringing much publicity to the search for the ark. He found only the remnants of abandoned skis.

With the breakup of the former Soviet Union, expeditions up the mountain intensified during the 1990s. In 1992 Charles P. Aaron, who identified himself as the leader of an expedition searching for Noah's Ark sponsored by the Tsirah Corporation, asked the CIA for assistance. It was Aaron's understanding that the Agency had some imaging system that could penetrate ice several meters thick. Aaron stressed in his request that the operation underwritten by the Tsirah Corporation had been ongoing for several years and was supported by James Irwin and several American senators and congressmen. The CIA responded to Aaron's request on January 21, 1993, by cryptically stating that an examination of the pictures that the Agency had taken of Ararat could not distinctly identify an ark.

Conspiracy theorists interpreted this response to mean that the CIA had found something under the ice and snow of Ararat that had not yet been completely identified. Continued pressure produced a comment from the deputy director of the CIA's Science and Technology Department, who said in his report of February 7, 1994, that the pictures of the remains on Ararat could not be identified as Noah's Ark. The report concluded by stat-

Mount Ararat in Turkey is where Noah's Ark supposedly rests, according to the CIA, though some scholars believe the actual location is somewhere in present-day Kurdistan.

ing that, at that time, no attempts would be made to organize additional research in the region of Ararat.

Ark researchers seized upon the CIA's declaration of no "additional research" as clear indication that the Agency had conducted expeditions to Ararat in the past. In a follow-up response on February 16, the CIA stated that in order to make an exhaustive analysis of the pictures, all images made with different technical facilities during the past thirty years must be examined. When this exhaustive task had been completed, documents and photos would be declassified.

Because the world still awaits a satisfying analysis of all photographs taken of the ark's alleged remains, conspiracy theorists are certain that immediately after the end of World War II, the CIA began collecting evidence about the mysterious object hidden beneath the snow and ice on Ararat's slope. According to this theory, a secret expedition sent to Turkey by the U.S. government found the remains of

Noah's Ark, quietly removed them from Ararat, and delivered them to a U.S. military base. For unknown reasons, perhaps linked to the shadow government and the New World Order, the CIA has not yet declassified the most important religious, scientific, and archaeological discovery of the century.

GEORGE NOORY

George Noory is host of the nationally syndicated program Coast to Coast AM, *which is heard by millions of listeners on approximately 560 stations in the United States, Canada, and Mexico. Noory provides his devoted listeners with a steady diet of provocative interviews and discussions with popular authors, researchers, conspiracists, scientists, and mystics. Listeners from all over the world are invited to call into the program to ask questions or to share their own experiences with UFOs, paranormal phenomena, time travel, alien abductions, conspiracies and all things curious and unexplained.*

Noory has said that he is driven by the desire to solve the great mysteries of our time. From his first days as a radio broadcaster, according to his biography on *Coast to Coast,* Noory has aimed to expose the "stories that the mainstream media never touch— the unusual, the paranormal and things like that." Explaining his life calling, he said, "I learned that broadcasting was the best business for exploring these issues, and I've been doing it for over thirty-three years."

Noory was born in Detroit, Michigan, on June 4, 1950, to parents of Lebanese descent. He grew up in Dearborn Heights and was brought up a Roman Catholic. Noory had an out-of-body experience as a child, and as a teenager he became fascinated with the paranormal. When he was thirteen, his mother gave him a copy of Walter Sullivan's *We Are Not Alone.* Reading about UFOs hooked him on the subject, and he joined the National Investigation Committee for

Aerial Phenomenon (NICAP). Nine years service as a full lieutenant in the U.S. Naval Reserve did nothing to blunt Noory's interest in the strange and the unknown.

Before he became the host of the very successful *The Nighthawk* program on KTRS in St. Louis, Noory had worked at WCAR-AM and WJBK in Detroit and at KSTP in St. Paul, Minnesota, where, at age twenty-eight, he became the youngest news director in the country. While he served as a news executive, he was the recipient of three Emmy Awards.

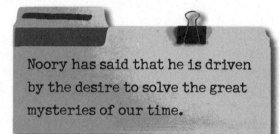

Noory has said that he is driven by the desire to solve the great mysteries of our time.

While he was hosting *The Nighthawk,* Noory was tapped by Premiere Radio Networks to guest host on *Coast to Coast AM* with Art Bell. His first program was on April 28, 2001. Later, he replaced Ian Punnett as the Sunday night host. On January 1, 2003, Noory assumed the weeknight hosting duties when Art Bell announced that he wished to retire. On January 21, 2006, Bell decided that he would like to return, but only to do the weekend programs, thereby replacing Punnett on Saturday nights and Noory on the first two Sundays of the month. On January 22, 2006, after the death of his wife on January 5, Bell returned to host intermittently. Punnett hosted the spin-off *Coast to Coast Live* on Saturday nights, a position he held until late 2011, when, due to health matters, he alternated with various guest hosts. On what was his traditional Halloween program, Art Bell hosted his final *Coast* on October 31, 2010. Noory has signed to remain as the principal host through 2013.

Although Noory has not openly declared an affiliation with any political party, he is avidly interested in politics and its influence upon the nation. Many listeners feel that they have detected a slight leaning in Noory's views toward Libertarianism and cite his high regard for the principles of Texas Republican Congressman Ron Paul as evidence.

Noory says that his first book, *Worker in the Light: Unlock Your Five Senses and Liberate Your Limitless Potential* (2006), written with bestselling author William J. Birnes, is his "revolutionary guide to spiritual enlightenment, human empowerment, ultimate productivity and absolute happiness." The two co-authored a follow-up in 2009 entitled *Journey to the Light,* in which they present amazing first-hand accounts of how ordinary people changed their own lives, transcended their doubts and fears, and unlocked the secrets to their spiritual growth. In October 2011, Noory released his third book, *Talking to the Dead.* Written with Rosemary Ellen Guiley, a leading expert on the paranormal and supernatural, the book explores the colorful history and personalities behind spirit communications, weaving together spirituality, metaphysics, science, and technology.

OBAMA CONSPIRACIES

In a nation divided almost evenly between conservatives and liberals, Republicans and Democrats, many Americans were upset by the election of Barack Hussein Obama, a senator from Illinois, to the office of president of the United States. Since he took office in 2009, President Obama has been subjected to many theories as to why he is unfit for office, from the "Birthers," who claim he was not actually born in the United States, something which is required by the U.S. Constitution of all presidents, to those who say he is secretly a Muslim working for Middle Eastern interests, and even more extreme theories about his association with extraterrestrials.

When Barack Hussein Obama was elected president of the United States in 2008, he was heralded as the nation's first black president. Even the most idealistic among the nation's citizens were not surprised that, in spite of having a white mother and being biracial, Obama would not simply be referred to as a senator from Illinois who won the highest office in land through the democratic election process. The United States had not yet reached the level of elevated consciousness where one's most obvious racial features could be ignored. However, more socially mature Americans could not help but be outraged by the number of prejudicial claims and falsehoods that swirled around the forty-third president of the United States.

Among the conspiracies leveled against President Obama by impassioned theorists are the following:

- Barack Hussein Obama was born in Mombasa, Kenya, to a Jewish mother, Stanley Anne Dunham, who was a CIA agent; his grandfather, Lord Barach, is Jewish. On his paternal side, Obama's grandfather was a powerful witchdoctor of the Luo tribe. Madelyn Payne Dunham, Obama's maternal grandmother, was a vice-president at the Bank of Hawaii and worked closely with Peter Geithner, father of Timothy, Obama's selection for Treasurer of the United States.

- Obama has no birth certificate to prove he is an American citizen, a deficiency that would make him ineligible to run for president of the United States. There is no proof who his father is or even who his real mother is. There is strong evidence that Stanley Anne Dunham may have adopted Barry. Stanley Anne Dunham became a communist and entered into a relationship with Frank Davis, a communist zealot, who may well be Obama's real father.

- Little Barry was lawfully adopted by Lolo Soetoro after Stanley Anne Dunham's marriage to the Indonesian citizen, and the boy's name was legally changed to Barry Soetoro. Lolo, who may be Barry's real father, reared the boy as a Muslim, but Barry attended a Catholic-sponsored nondenominational school.

- Obama is the illegitimate son of Jo Ann Newman, a white teenage girl from the Bronx, who had an affair with Malcolm X in New York. Obama's true birth name is Bari M. Shabazz, born October 10, 1959.

While Barack Obama's birth records have been made public for many years, so-called "Birthers" refuse to accept the birth certificate and documentation provided by the Department of Health in Honolulu. Obama released his official birth certificate in 2008 before the election. On April 2011, a certified copy of Obama's certificate of live birth was released.

His father is recorded as Barack Hussein Obama, African; his mother, Stanley Ann Dunham, Caucasian. Obama's birthdate is officially August 8, 1961; his name: Barack Hussein Obama II. Birthplace: Oahu, Honolulu. Additional evidence of his Hawaii birth is available in birth announcements published in August 1961 in two Hawaiian newspapers.

- Through a common ancestor, Mareen Duvall, Obama's maternal grandfather, Stanley Armour Dunham, a furniture salesman from Kansas, was a distant cousin to six U.S. Presidents—James Madison, Harry Truman, Lyndon B. Johnson, Jimmy Carter, George H.W. Bush, and George W. Bush. Dunham is also related to Vice President Dick Cheney through an eighth cousin once removed.

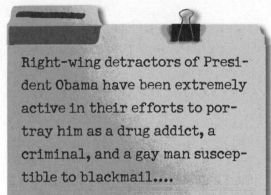

Right-wing detractors of President Obama have been extremely active in their efforts to portray him as a drug addict, a criminal, and a gay man susceptible to blackmail....

- From the age of ten, Barry Soetoro was cared for by his maternal grandparents in Honolulu. He was raised Unitarian, which, much like the Freemasons and Judaism, is fertile ground for finding recruits for the New World Order, according to conspiracists.

Conspiracy theorists delight in their ability somehow to track genealogical records that indicate that many of the world leaders have been related for hundreds of years, thus implying that some shadow group such as the Illuminati seeks to control the hearts and minds of those governing the masses. Other theorists are convinced that many of the U.S. presidents are related and have an undisclosed Jewish heritage and membership in a secret occult society.

- Obama has a criminal record. Barry Soetoro did drugs and flunked out of Occidental College in California. He made his way to New York, where he lived as a homeless addict on the streets until a Pakistani boyfriend traveled with Barry back to Indonesia. When he returned to the United States, he began using the name Barack Hussein Obama in order to file his federal income taxes in Connecticut. At the same time, he secured a social security number from his grandmother, who worked in the probate office in a Honolulu courthouse and had access to the numbers of deceased individuals. Obama was given the number of Jean Paul Ludwig, who died in 1961.

Right-wing detractors of President Obama have been extremely active in their efforts to portray him as a drug addict, a criminal, and a gay man susceptible to blackmail by former lovers seeking to profit from his position as the president. J. P. Ludwig's death came after the date that Barack Obama registered for the draft, so there is no way that his grandmother could have given him Ludwig's social security number.

- Obama ordered a fake diploma from Columbia from a "diploma mill" and lied his way into Harvard, even though he had no actual transcripts to prove his academic background. This deceit accounts for the bizarre fact that none of the students who would likely have taken classes with Obama can remember seeing him at Columbia. Later, he embellished his position as a professor of law, and when he moved to Chicago and fell in love with Michelle, she helped him pass the bar and got him a job with her law firm.

Actually, a number of individuals have come forward and spoken of their time as Obama's roommates or fellow students at Columbia and Harvard. And then there is Obama's term as the first African American editor of the *Harvard Law Review* in 1990, the highest student position at Harvard Law School.

- Obama is an alien—a hybrid human—created from the DNA of a human mother and the sperm of an extraterrestrial visitor. Obama, a prize alien-hybrid, was created and tutored to become president of the United States by reptilian overlords and their human New World Order coun-

terparts as an integral element in their plan of planetary dominance.

The theory of extraterrestrial reptilian overlords seeking to conquer Earth is common among a number of UFO conspiracy buffs. Some theorists add British royalty and other leading European political figures as agents of the reptilians—who, in some cases, are actually Reptilians in disguise.

- Obama is the antichrist, who will bring about a one-world government, a one-world religion, and a one-world economy before Jesus returns to defeat him at the climatic battle of Armageddon.

A favorite portrait of a sinister Obama is painted by certain evangelical right-wing Christians who believe in an imminent end-times–Apocalypse scenario. While such a devilish precursor to Judgment Day as the Antichrist was considered very much a fringe belief held by a minority of conservative Christians 150 years ago, it has now become mainstream with images of a demonic earthly prince Obama, with Bush and Clinton before him, fulfilling the requirements of the image perfectly in the frightened minds of those who believe in the powers of a satanic majesty.

OKLAHOMA CITY BOMBING

Timothy McVeigh was executed for the bombing of the Murrah Federal Building in Oklahoma City and Terry Nichols is behind bars for life, but conspiracy theorists insist that the two men were patsies for a sinister shadow agency.

On April 19, 1995, at 9:02 A.M., the Alfred P. Murrah Federal Building in Oklahoma City was destroyed in a massive explosion, killing 168 people, including nineteen children—exactly two years to the day after the final attack by federal law-enforcement agencies on the

Branch Davidian compound at Waco ended in fiery death for the compound's occupants. The Murrah Building housed the Bureau of Alcohol, Tobacco, and Firearms (ATF), the FBI, the Drug Enforcement Administration (DEA), the Defense Investigative Service, the Social Security Administration, the U.S. Army and Marines recruiting offices, and a day-care center. The explosion collapsed one-third of the building, and the bomb crater was thirty feet wide and eight feet deep.

At 10:20 A.M. and sixty miles north of the scene of death and destruction, Officer Charles Hangar stopped a 1977 yellow Mercury without license plates speeding at 80 miles an hour outside of Perry, Oklahoma. The driver was Timothy James McVeigh, who, in spite of being armed with a .45-caliber Glock pistol and a hunting knife, calmly surrendered and was booked in Noble County for driving without license plates and carrying a concealed weapon. A police check revealed McVeigh's past as an army officer who had served with distinction in the Persian Gulf War. On his person, McVeigh carried a phone debit card issued to the *Spotlight,* the conspiracy publication of the anti-Semitic Liberty Lobby. Two days later McVeigh would be charged with the worst terrorist action ever carried out on U.S. soil prior to September 11, 2001.

Within another few days, a search by the ATF yielded blasting caps, sixty-foot Primadet detonator cords, ammonium nitrate, nitrogen fertilizer, and fifty-five-gallon plastic drums on a farm owned by Terry Nichols. Nichols and his brother James were members of the Michigan Militia, an apocalyptic right-wing group who believed that a United Nations invasion of America was imminent. Later, it would be discovered that McVeigh was a frequent visitor to Elohim City, a religious commune near the Oklahoma-Arkansas border. It was apparent to government investigators that the perpetrators of the Murrah bombing were right-wing, home-grown terrorists.

A great number of conspiracy theorists believe that the FBI covered up a Middle East connection to the Oklahoma City bombing in order to make the terrible act of destruction and loss of life appear to be entirely an act of domestic terrorism. In a *Chicago Tribune* article printed two days after the bombing, Vice Admiral William O. Studeman, acting director of the CIA, was quoted as saying that the bombing of the Murrah Building illustrated "the true globalization of the terrorist threat." Studeman, as well as many other authorities quoted at that time, said the bombing had been accomplished with the help of agents outside the United States, in addition to Timothy McVeigh and Terry Nichols.

In February 1995 Studeman learned from the CIA station chief in the Philippines that Terry Nichols had met with Iraqi agents Abdul Murad, Ramzi Yousef, and Khalid Mohammed. Yousef had been imprisoned for the 1993 World Trade Center attack, but in February 1995 he was living with his uncle Khalid Mohammed, the mastermind of the 1993 WTC and Oklahoma City bombings, in an apartment in the Philippines. Later the plans for the Oklahoma bombing and a number of 9/11-style attacks on U.S. skyscrapers with airliners were found on Ramzi Yousef's computer. This intelligence was fully translated by the FBI and CIA in late January and early February 1995. Nichols also met with eight Iraqi members of an al-Qaeda cell in the Philippines who, in addition to the bombings, planned assassination attempts on President Clinton and on the pope.

The leading Iraqi suspect seen helping McVeigh in Oklahoma City and Nichols in Kansas was Hussain al-Hussaini, who had been brought to the U.S. by President George H. W. Bush with the knowledge and help of help of CIA Director James Woolsey James Woolsey and his deputy Admiral William Studeman. Witnesses later identified al-Hussaini as being escorted by a well-dressed man named Khalid from Boston to Oklahoma City in November 1994. Other witnesses say that Khalid

Mohammed, along with al-Qaeda leader Dr. Ayman al-Zawahiri, and FBI/CIA informant Ali Mohammed, were in Oklahoma City in 1995.

After the Murrah Building bombing, al-Hussaini went to Houston and was assisted by Ishan Barbouti's son Heider Barbouti. Studeman, as acting CIA director, knew of the Barboutis' operations because the CIA under President George H. W. Bush's direction had helped the Barboutis acquire WMDs for Iraq and Saddam Hussein.

Allegations of murders of several Oklahoma City bombing survivors, particularly emergency workers, have surfaced—Oklahoma City police officers Terrance Yeakey, Gordon Martin, and Ken Griffin; a number of Oklahoma City firefighters; Dr. H. Don Chumley; U.S. General Services Administration employee Mike Loudenslager; and others.

In the weeks preceding the bombing Loudenslager became increasingly anxious because of the large amounts of ordnance and explosives that were stored in the Murrah Building. Loudenslager and the day-care center operator told many of the parents to get their children out, and because of their warnings, far fewer children were in the day-care center on April 19 than there otherwise would have been.

Shortly after the terrible blast, Loudenslager was actively helping in the rescue and recovery effort. Many individuals that horrible Wednesday morning either saw or talked with him. During the course of the early rescue efforts, however, he was seen and heard in a very heated argument with someone from the Bureau of Alcohol, Tobacco, and Firearms, accusing ATF of being in large part responsible not only for the bombing, but for the death and injury to those inside, including all the children. To the total amazement of a great number of police officers and rescue workers, it was later reported that Loudenslager's body had been found *inside* the Murrah Building, still at his desk, a victim of the bombing. He is also officially listed as one of the 168 bombing fatalities.

The Oklahoma City National Memorial remembers those who died when home-grown terrorist Timothy McVeigh bombed the Alfred P. Murrah Federal Building in 1995.

Was Loudenslager murdered and placed at his desk? Or was he only said to have been found at his desk? Access to the inside of the building, from after the bombing onward, was extremely limited by the FBI.

Another point of contention for some conspiracists is the alleged nature of the bomb used by McVeigh. Some argue that a home-made fertilizer bomb packed inside a truck parked outside the building could not have delivered destructive force sufficient to render the damage that it allegedly caused. The recent release of a secret Pentagon report prepared by General Benton K. Partin, dated July 30, 1995, has refueled the flames of that debate. Partin sees evidence of an "inside job" and argues that there is evidence to indicate that explosive charges were placed on columns B3, A3, A5, and A7 of the building. The truck bomb was insufficient to destroy the columns, but it was responsible for ripping out some floors at the second- and third-floor levels.

Several witnesses claim that ATF employees were advised to stay home on that fateful Wednesday morning. While ATF denies such accounts, the grim fact remains that there were no ATF employees among the 168 dead.

Jayna Davis, an Oklahoma City television reporter, arrived at the Murrah Building thirteen minutes after the bombing and has been working on the case ever since. Davis discovered that six thousand Iraqis sought political asylum after surrendering during the first Gulf War. After being given asylum in the United States, the Iraqis were not tracked. Some among them were false defectors whose mission was to infiltrate the United States and form terrorist cells. Of the six thousand defectors, eighty were in Oklahoma City by the time of the bombing. Davis believes that eight of those eighty were fully involved in the bombing plot, and she has fully documented the testimony of twenty-two Arabs who witnessed that subversive activity. The Middle Eastern tie-in was upheld in the courts and also endorsed by former CIA director Woolsey in a court case. But after Davis turned in her paperwork to the FBI, they "lost" all of it. None of her evidence of the Arab connection was presented at the McVeigh and Nichols trials.

Conspiracy theorists maintain that Timothy McVeigh and Terry Nichols were recruited by al-Qaeda because both men were angry at the military and U.S. government for a variety of reasons. Simply put, the two join the long list of patsies utilized by shadow agencies to accomplish their sinister master plan.

OPERATION BIG CITY

If you need thousands of unsuspecting subjects on whom to test various hallucinogenic and incapacitating sprays, why just look around you at all those innocent people walking the streets of major American cities.

Among the assignments given to Dr. Sidney Gottlieb, head of the secret Project MK-ULTRA, by CIA chief Allen Dulles in 1953 was to perfect a method of producing large-scale aberrant mental states on an unsuspecting population. A substance was sought that the U.S. military could spray over a city when engaging an enemy and render both civilians and military opponents relatively helpless and unable to resist. The substance should be able to "cause illogical thinking" or "produce shock and confusion over extended periods of time" or "produce physical disablement, such as paralysis of the legs" or merely "cause mental confusion."

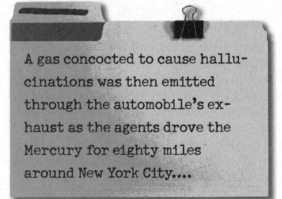

A gas concocted to cause hallucinations was then emitted through the automobile's exhaust as the agents drove the Mercury for eighty miles around New York City....

Agents assigned to Operation Big City modified a 1953 Mercury so its exhaust pipe extended eighteen inches beyond its normal length. A gas concocted to cause hallucinations was then emitted through the automobile's exhaust as the agents drove the Mercury for eighty miles around New York City, making note of the effects on pedestrians.

In another test, operatives equipped with nasal filters boarded the New York subway with battery-powered emissions equipment fitted into suitcases to test the effect of LSD on people in confined areas.

An ambitious project was conducted in 1957 when operatives released a biological gas off the Golden Gate Bridge in San Francisco. The intent of the experiment was to blanket the entire city with the gas and then monitor how powerfully the disorienting properties of the substance would affect the population. The agents were dismayed when a sudden wind arose and blew the gas away before it could cause any harm.

In 1957 CIA inspector general Lyman Kirkpatrick issued an internal memo that cautioned operatives to use utmost secrecy to protect the operation not only from enemy intelligence, but also from the American public in general. If the American people should learn that the CIA was engaging in activities that were unethical and illicit, such knowledge could become detrimental to the accomplishment of the Agency's mission.

OPERATION MIDNIGHT CLIMAX

It wasn't Candid Camera *behind those two-way mirrors, but the CIA, filming unsuspecting, unwilling, LSD-drugged men having sex with prostitutes.*

The CIA's experiments with mind-control known as MK-ULTRA were begun on the orders of CIA director Allen Dulles in 1953 and headed by Dr. Sidney Gottlieb. Many of the early tests focused on drugs that might become "truth serums" for interrogations of prisoners, and were performed with volunteers, very often military personnel, government agents, and CIA employees. When experiments with LSD seemed productive, Dr. Gottlieb exercised the carte blanche authority given to him by Dulles and began to experiment with the powerful hallucinogen's effects on unsuspecting individuals. Curiosity about the use of the drug as an aid in sexual entrapment in covert operations led to the development of Operation Midnight Climax, known officially as MK-ULTRA Subproject-3.

At first CIA agents would infiltrate large outdoor gatherings, such as ball games and concerts in the park, and clandestinely spray private citizens with LSD in containers labeled as insect repellent. Later, agents would infiltrate private cocktail parties and spray the unsuspecting guests with LSD in containers marked as deodorant or perfume.

With the expressed mission of learning more about sexual behavior under LSD, Operation Midnight Climax set up a number of apartments to be used for sexual encounters. Prostitutes in the employ of the agency would solicit unsuspecting men and slip LSD in their drinks before returning with them to the apartments and having sex. Two-way mirrors allowed the researchers to observe the responses and reactions of the men while under the influence of the drug. After a period of interpreting the one-on-one drug reactions of the prostitutes' clients, Midnight Climax established several brothels in Greenwich Village and San Francisco in order to study the drug-induced sexual behavior of a larger cross section of men. Two-way mirrors once again permitted the CIA researchers to film the prostitutes and their LSD-dosed clients for later interpretation.

In 1972 Richard Helms, the CIA director at that time, ordered the records of MK-ULTRA and all its various subprojects destroyed. Nevertheless, in 1975, a Senate investigating committee found enough information about Operation Midnight Climax to observe not only that it was unconscionable to conduct drug experiments on subjects without their knowledge or consent, but that there had been no medical pre-screening of any kind. The Senate committee was also shocked to discover that most of the investigators behind those two-way mirrors had no medical credentials nor were they qualified scientific observers. In fact, there were no medical personnel present to respond to any kind of negative reaction that a subject might have to the drug and no follow-up was conducted on the subjects to ascertain what continuing effects the LSD might have on their lives. The experiments had been conducted on unaware private citizens without any concern for any possible embarrassment that might arise from the manner in which they were "solicited" for the "experiment," or for any possible aftereffects that might have resulted in possible hallucinations or in situations wherein the subject may have injured or endangered himself or others.

OPERATION PACLIP

OPERATION PAPERCLIP

Immediately after Nazi Germany was defeated in World War II, as many as 1,600 Nazi scientists and their dependents were smuggled into the United States by Operation Paperclip.

Many claims were made about Nazi secret weapons during World War II, including nuclear power and flying-saucer-type aircraft. Regardless of the credence one puts into claims that the Vril Society had a saucer-shaped anti-gravity craft by 1934, there was no question among the Allies that prior to the outbreak of the war, Nazi technology had been superior to theirs. If the glowing "foo fighters" that harried Allied airmen were not the products of Nazi technology, the V-2 rockets, prototypes of jet airplanes, and the discovery of particle/laser-beam weaponry certainly were. The U.S. War Department decreed that the United States should scoop up as many German scientists and specimens of their work as possible.

Maj. Gen. Hugh Knerr, deputy commanding general for administration of U.S. strategic forces in Europe, surveyed the German scientific and industrial establishments and acknowledged that America was "alarmingly backward" in many areas of research. He agreed with the suggestion that the U.S. occupation force should seize both the "apparatus

and the brains" that created it and put them back to work as soon as possible—or the United States would remain several years behind.

While all the responsible thinkers in the occupation forces agreed that the German scientists and their families should be taken to U.S. shores as soon as possible, it had been made a law that no former member of the Nazi Party could immigrate to America. Even a cursory examination of the 1,600 scientists and their dependents who had been assembled for immediate relocation in the United States yielded the predictable finding that at least 1,200 of them had been members of the Nazi Party. Informed of this bit of intelligence, President Harry S. Truman decided that the national interest of America was of primary importance and pronounced that only those who had been more than nominal Nazis or had actively supported their military efforts would be denied entrance to the United States.

The operation still had to be conducted in utmost secrecy. The war had been costly and bitter, with many American lives lost. The American public would not respond favorably to the knowledge that many of the scientists being given a free ride to the States had worked in laboratories and factories that were located in Nazi slave labor and death camps. The operation was conducted by the Joint Intelligence Objectives Agency, and the scientists and their family members who were selected to be taken to the United States had paperclips binding their scientific papers to the standard immigration forms, hence the name "Operation Paperclip."

Operation Paperclip was not made public until 1973, after the first astronauts had set foot on the moon, when the participation of such individuals as Wernher von Braun and many of his German colleagues were acknowledged as having been integral to the success of the U.S. space program. Von Braun's mentor, Hermann Oberth, widely recognized as the "father of modern rocketry," also entered the United States under Operation Paperclip, as did Dr. Hubertus Strughold, the "father of space medicine." In 1977 the Aeromedical Library at the USAF School of Aerospace Medicine was named after Strughold. In 1984 Arthur Rudolph, who had been awarded NASA's Distinguished Service Award in 1969, left the United States rather than face charges for Nazi war crimes.

> The American public would not respond favorably to the knowledge that many of the scientists being given a free ride to the States had worked in laboratories and factories that were located in Nazi slave labor and death camps.

Operation Paperclip also allowed entrance to the United States to Reinhard Gehlen, Nazi intelligence mastermind, who helped Allen Dulles restructure the OSS (Office of Strategic Services) into the Central Intelligence Agency (CIA); Klaus Barbie, the "Butcher of Lyon"; Otto von Bolschwing, infamous for holocaust abuses; and SS colonel Otto Skorzeny.

OPERATION RESURRECTION

Secret experiments were conducted on apes in hope of resurrecting them after they had been decapitated and had their heads and bodies switched.

In this secret project, implemented in 1965–66, the CIA replicated the isolation chamber that had been constructed earlier by Dr. Donald Ewen Cameron, the "brain butcher," at the Allen Memorial Psychiatric Institute in Montreal and rebuilt it at the National Institutes of Health. A psychologist who had helped the Office of Special Services (OSS) interrogate Nazi prisoners during World War II, Cameron became intrigued by the experiments conducted on concentration camp prisoners by German doctors, and he later contracted to work for the OSS, which became the CIA in 1947, in the field of behavior manipulation. He continued this specialty in Projects Bluebird and Artichoke, which became MK-ULTRA in 1953. Cameron conducted numerous experiments in sensory deprivation, sensory overload, and drug inducement. His harsh experiments with electroshock, LSD, and drug-induced comas that sometimes lasted for months, as well as his penchant for performing prefrontal lobotomies, proved far too extreme for some of his "patients," and many of them died. In Operation Resurrection the experiments would not be with humans, but with apes.

The apes were first lobotomized, then placed in total isolation. After a time, the experimenters, adapting the radio telemetry techniques developed by Leonard Rubenstein, directed radio waves into the brains of the apes. Apes who appeared to receive the frequencies were decapitated and their heads transplanted to other apes' bodies to see if the radio energy could bring them back to life—thus, Operation Resurrection. The apes that were not selected for possible resurrection from the dead were bombarded with radio waves until they collapsed and became unconscious. Autopsies yielded the information that their brain tissue appeared literally to have been fried.

It is difficult to see how Operation Resurrection could possibly have produced information of any value to any study of behavior control, behavior modification, or mind control. Researchers will probably never know the rationale behind the belief that dead apes could be resurrected if you switched heads and bodies, for in 1972 the director of the CIA, Richard Helms, ordered all records of MK-ULTRA's projects, operations, and subprojects destroyed.

ORDER OF THE GOLDEN DAWN

With such prominent members as Aleister Crowley, the "Beast 666," the Order of the Golden Dawn has a dark reputation as a secret society of sinister magicians.

During its glory days, from 1888 to around 1903, the Order of the Golden Dawn harbored one of the greatest repositories of magic knowledge in the Western world. Founded by William Wynn Wescott, a Rosicrucian, and Samuel Liddell MacGregor Mathers, an occultist, the Golden Dawn soon numbered among its members such luminaries as W. B. Yeats, Aleister Crowley, Israel Regardie, A. E. Waite, Algernon Blackwood, Annie Horniman, Florence Farr, Dion Fortune, and Arthur Machen. Wescott claimed to have come into possession of an ancient manuscript of Hermetic knowledge that contained the mystical rituals of a secret society of magi. Mathers expanded the rituals to create the format of the Golden Dawn.

When the Isis-Urania Temple of the Hermetic Order of the Golden Dawn was formally established in 1888, its hierarchy was based on the Tree of Life as structured in the Kabbalah. Wescott, Mathers, and Dr. W. R. Woodman, supreme magus of the Rosicrucian Society of Anglia, were the three "Chiefs Second Order," who received direction from entities on the astral plane known as the "Secret Chiefs of the Third Order." The Golden Dawn taught three magical systems—the Key of Solomon, Abra-Melin, and Enochian. Students received instruction in astral projection, alchemy, astrology, tarot, automatic writing, and clairvoyance. Arcane information was also derived from the Egyptian Book of the Dead, the Chaldean Oracles, and the Prophetic Books of William Blake.

Annie Horniman, sponsor of the Abbey Theatre in Dublin, was also a benefactor of the Golden Dawn. She withdrew her support in 1896 when Mathers claimed that the Secret Chiefs on the astral plane had initiated him into their ranks. Although Mathers had spent considerable time in translating the manuscript of *The Book of the Sacred Magic of Abra-Melin the Mage,* he would eventually be expelled from the society that he had cofounded. In 1897 doubts also arose over certain of Wescott's questionable activities in founding the order, and Florence Farr, the mistress of the playwright George Bernard Shaw, became Chief of the Second Order.

In 1898 the notorious Aleister Crowley was initiated into the order and rose rapidly through the degrees. Crowley (Edward Alexander Crowley, 1875–1947) is one of the most controversial figures in the annals of modern occultism. He believed that most of humankind's ills are caused by inhibition of the sexual impulses; therefore, much of his Magick (Crowley added the terminal "k" to differentiate the true science of the Magi from stage magic) drew its impetus from the release of psychic energy through sexual activity. Crowley became known as a drug fiend, an author of vile books, and the spreader of obscene practices. Crowley's own mother, a fundamentalist Christian, dubbed him the "Great Beast 666," a diabolical image drawn from the book of Revelation. Before Crowley's death in 1947, he had a reputation as the "wickedest man in the world."

The stresses between Crowley and Mathers soon increased to the point where they allegedly engaged in magickal warfare, sending demons and vampires to attack each other. Such disruptions on the astral plane led to the expulsion of both men from the society.

W. B. Yeats attempted to restore discipline among the ranks of the Golden Dawn and assumed control of the Second Order. His efforts were to no avail. In 1903 A. E. Waite founded a society that retained the Golden Dawn name but emphasized the study of mysticism rather than the practice of magic. In 1905 the Stella Matutina, the Order of the Companions of the Rising Light in the Morning, splintered off from the Isis-Urania Temple. This group survived until the 1940s as the Merlin Temple of the Stella Matutina. Few organized groups of the Golden Dawn exist today. Perhaps one reason for its decline is the publication of its secret rituals by Israel Regardie.

At the time of his death on March 10, 1985, Dr. Francis Israel Regardie was regarded by many occultists as the last living adept of the Hermetic Order of the Golden Dawn. In such works as *A Garden of Pomegranates* and *The Tree of Life* (both 1932), Regardie had demystified a great deal of the esoteric aura surrounding the occult and presented understandable and readable texts on practical magic.

Born in 1907, Regardie had absorbed the Theosophy of Madame Blavatsky, Hindu philosophy, and the Kabbalah by the time he was thirteen. By nineteen he had become a Rosicrucian and had begun to correspond with Aleister Crowley, who at that time was living in Paris. In 1928 the twenty-one-year-old occultist accepted the position of Crowley's personal secretary, hoping that the famous magician would tutor him in the mystic arts. When Crowley's sensational exploits got him in trouble with the French authorities, he was forced to leave the country and return to England. About that same time, Crowley's publisher declared bankruptcy, and he could no longer afford Regardie's services as a secretary.

Although the Golden Dawn had ceased to exist as a functioning magical society as early as 1903, it continued to exist in various descendant orders, such as the Stella Matutina and the Alpha et Omega. In 1932 Regardie's distillation of the teachings of the Golden Dawn was published in *The Tree of Life,* and at once he was embroiled in controversy. While

Occultist Arthur Edward Waite was one of the early members of the Order of the Golden Dawn. He is also well known for creating the Rider Waite Tarot Deck.

some demanded he never again dare to mention the name of the society, others, such as Dion Fortune, defended him and invited him to join the Order of Stella Matutina. In 1934, after having attained a high rank in the order, Regardie left it, and in 1937 he published the essence of the Golden Dawn's teachings and rituals in four volumes entitled simply *The Golden Dawn.* Regardie believed that the heritage of magic was the spiritual birthright of every man and woman and that the principles of such magical systems as the Golden Dawn should be made available to all who wished to pursue the ancient wisdom teachings.

Regardie's *The Philosopher's Stone* (1937) was written from the perspective of Jungian symbolism. In 1937 Regardie began seriously to study psychology and psychotherapy, encompassing the theories of Sigmund Freud, Carl Jung, and Wilhelm Reich. In *The Middle Pillar* (1938), he compared the techniques and exercises of ceremonial magic to the methods of psychoanalysis. In 1941 he took up practice as a lay analyst, and in 1947 he relocated to California, where for many years he taught psychiatry at the Los Angeles College of Chiropractic and continued to write, producing numerous books. Regardie retired from practice in 1981 and moved to Sedona, Arizona, where he continued to write until his death of a heart attack on March 10, 1985.

ORDER OF THE SOLAR TEMPLE

These claimants to the new Order of Knights Templar became impatient when the underground masters failed to arrive on schedule.

On October 4, 1994, when authorities from Cheiry, Switzerland, investigated a fire in a farmhouse on the edge of town that was occupied by members of the Order of the Solar Temple, they discovered a secret room in which twenty-two corpses, many of them wearing ceremonial capes, were found. Some of the cultists had plastic bags over their heads; others had been shot.

On October 5 three houses burning side by side in the village of Granges-sur-Salvan, Switzerland, yielded the bodies of twenty-five more members of the Order of the Solar Temple. Later it was learned that the six charred bodies found in Morin Heights, Quebec, on October 4 were also connected to the order. In December 1995 sixteen more members of the cult were found dead in France, and in March 1997 five more killed themselves in Quebec. Joseph Di Mambro and Luc Jouret, the leaders of the cult, whose corpses were among those at Granges-sur-Salvan, had made their transition to another world along with at least seventy-four of their followers.

Di Mambro and Jouret founded the Order of the Solar Temple in 1984, claiming a spiritual

heritage from the Order of the Knights Templar (founded c. 1118 and dissolved in 1307). Among their declared goals were to help Earth to prepare for the return of Christ in solar glory and to assist humankind through a time of transition as spirituality would begin to assume primacy over materiality.

Di Mambro, born in 1924 in Pont-Saint-Esprit, France, had a fascination with the occult from childhood onward. In 1956 he joined the Ancient and Mystic Order of the Rosy Cross, a group which claims to be one with the Rosicrucian Order established in the sixteenth century. In 1976 he became a self-appointed spiritual master, and by 1978 he had established the Golden Way Foundation in Geneva.

In 1981 Jouret, a young physician (born in 1947 in the Belgian Congo) and former grand master of the Renewed Order of the Temple, another group that combined concepts of the Knights Templar and the Rosicrucians, left that order over a dispute regarding certain policy matters. Di Mambro, who first became acquainted with him in 1982, appealed to Jouret to combine energies with him in creating a new organization. Jouret agreed, and the two founded the Order of the Solar Temple in 1984.

Jouret's credentials as a physician and his dynamic platform personality drew large crowds to his lectures. From 1984 to about 1990 he claimed to relay the teachings of the masters of the Rosicrucian Order of the sixteenth century, who remained alive and hidden in a secret underground retreat near Zurich. These esoteric pronouncements, together with spiritual phenomena produced during various public demonstrations, convinced many new members that the time of the Apocalypse was drawing near and the best way to survive the growing negativity of society was in the safety of the Order of the Solar Temple.

By 1989 the cult had gathered about five hundred members, most of them in Switzerland, France, and Canada. However, by 1992 Jouret and Di Mambro had made too many unfulfilled predictions and promises, and some of their followers began to doubt the existence of the great masters hidden underground. Many cult members had been told by Jouret that they were Light Beings who had reincarnated on Earth with a special mission to fulfill, but too much time had passed and the promised New Age of Consciousness had still not arrived. Even Di Mambro's son Elie declared that he doubted the existence of the masters who were allegedly guiding his father and Jouret, and he went so far as to expose some of the illusions his father used to create the spirit phenomena during the demonstra-tions. Since Elie had been promoted as a very special chosen one who had been born to bring about a new world order, his dissension caused a serious breach in the cult.

When the mass suicide occurred in 1994, membership had already begun to decline. With the structure of the Order of the Solar Temple crumbling around them, Di Mambro and Jouret prepared for their transition to another world. From October 1994 to March 1997, seventy-four of the most faithful to the order's teachings made their own transitions.

PATRIOT ACT/ HOMELAND SECURITY

Skeptics say the Patriot Act is another ploy of the New World Order to steal our freedom.

The Patriot Act, which President George W. Bush signed six weeks after the September 11, 2001, terrorist attacks on the Pentagon and the World Trade Center in New York, boosted the range of FBI surveillance parameters and expanded the powers of law-enforcement officers, including the right to hold anyone even suspected of terrorist activities incommunicado for months. Critics of the Patriot Act have called for a tempering of provisions in the law that permit law-enforcement officers to conduct secret searches of private citizens' homes and businesses. While the FBI's greatly broadened wiretapping authority may help to catch terrorists, such capabilities should not trample on the rights of private citizens.

Conspiracy theorists are emphatic when they declare that there is nothing patriotic at all about the Patriot Act. In their view, the act is simply another ploy of the New World Order to take away our freedoms and substitute a police state in their place when secret government agents predict cataclysmic terrorist attacks.

On April 3, 2005, the Montana legislature condemned the Patriot Act by issuing a strong resolution encouraging Montana law-enforcement agencies not to participate in any investigations under the Patriot Act that might violate the constitutional rights of the citizens of Montana. While the legislators stressed that they supported the federal government's fight against terrorism, they could not endorse granting sweeping powers that violated rights enshrined in the U.S. and Montana Constitutions.

Sixteen provisions of the Patriot Act were due to expire by the end of the year 2005, so the president and other members of the Bush administration barnstormed the nation making the argument that the law should be kept intact—or expanded. On June 9, 2005, in Columbus, Ohio, President George W. Bush spoke to the Ohio State Patrol Academy and Congress to renew the Patriot Act, crediting the legislation with helping to convict more than two hundred terrorists. The president said that the public should ignore the unfair

A TSA agent looks for illegal items at an airport security gate. Increased security at airports is one of the consequences of the 9/11 attacks.

criticisms of the Patriot Act and make the law a permanent one.

Senator Russell D. Feingold (D-Wisconsin) complained that the president had presented a "false choice" to the American people by stating that Congress must "reauthorize the Patriot Act without any changes or leave our country vulnerable to terrorist attacks." There are many lawmakers in both parties, Feingold said, who believe that portions of the act infringed on freedom. Senators Larry Craig (R-Idaho) and Dick Durbin (D-Illinois) fear that the law is written in a way that could encourage abuses, but added that they didn't want to end the Act, only amend it.

Lisa Graves, senior counsel for legislative strategy for the American Civil Liberties Union, said that the Justice Department's inspector general reported that seven thousand individuals had complained of abuse under the Patriot Act. Graves stated that the ACLU wants the government to show evidence of some link to terrorist activity before being allowed full access to the financial, medical, and other records of private citizens.

Among the complaints most often voiced by critics of the Patriot Act are the following:

- The act includes language that would impose lifetime incarceration or death upon anyone engaged in any form or degree of crime, sedition, or simply dissent.

- Congress was hoodwinked into endorsing the legislation. The Patriot Act was printed overnight and then immediately presented to Congress to vote on with almost no time for congressional discussion and no public discussion. The act was presented for vote as the patriotic thing to do in the newly declared war on terrorism.

- The Environmental Protection Agency will no longer release the information it gathers when chemical plants dump toxic substances.

- The Federal Energy Regulatory Commission has refused to release secret documents that it prepared regarding the dangers of liquefied natural gas terminals under construction along America's coastlines. The commission claims the material is critical energy infrastructure information.

- Despite bitter complaints from the nation's mayors, the Homeland Security Department won't tell police and fire departments when dangerous shipments of hazardous materials move through their jurisdictions.

- The Justice Department has been withholding details of secret proceedings against immigrants since 9/11.

- A study by the Rand Corporation of the thirty-six websites and more than six hundred public databases shut down after 9/11 concluded that government efforts to censor information was ill advised and ineffective. Terrorists could easily obtain the information elsewhere, in textbooks, trade journals, or through nongovernment sites.

- The Department of Homeland Security has issued regulations informing government agencies that they are no longer required to release environmental impact statements. New secrecy rules are being applied not only to documents the government gathers, but also to information the government finances.

- The Council on Government Relations, which represents the nation's university system, protests that scientists are facing unprecedented new rules written into research contracts requiring them to suppress sensitive but unclassified materials and also to apply for special approval if foreigners are involved in the government-financed research.

In May 2011, the Department of Homeland Security called for contractors to construct and operate National Responder Support Camps. Conspiracists sounded a new alarm when it was discovered in early December 2011 that the Halliburton subsidiary KBR was scouting for subcontractors to build additional FEMA camps. The oft-repeated concerns that the camps were really meant to be detention centers for members of accused terrorists and civilian protest groups who could be detained indefinitely was nearing an unconstitutional reality.

In 1979, when President Jimmy Carter combined various government assistance agencies into the Federal Emergency Management Agency, the FEMA camps were described as safe places where first responders to disaster situations might withdraw to receive shelter, food, and other basic needs. The purpose of FEMA was to "reduce the loss of life and property and to protect the Nation from all hazards, including natural disasters, acts of terrorism, and other man-made disasters." Shortly after 9-11, the Department of Homeland Security amended the utilization of the FEMA camps to include—in addition to assisting local agencies with natural disasters, such

as hurricanes, earthquakes, floods, and the like—the "assistance" of responding to situations that involved national security. As early as the Reagan administration, however, whistleblowers insisted that FEMA's true reason for being was to assist in the establishment of martial law and the detainment of American citizens who were involved in acts of civil disobedience.

Conspiracists are increasingly alarmed by the lengths Homeland Security is going to in order to monitor and criminalize American citizens under the guise of protecting the nation. Rather than guarding our society from outside attacks and homegrown terrorists, conspiracy researchers argue that Homeland Security is rapidly amassing the means to convert our republic into a police state. Even now, say the watchdogs of our liberties, the United States is increasingly becoming a nation under ceaseless observation by high-tech spies.

The FBI is currently gathering massive amounts of personal data via an extensive biometric program called the Next Generation Identification (NGI) system. This spying technology utilizes various high-tech scanning devices to collect fingerprints, palm prints, iris scans, and such personal identification marks as scars, facial characteristics, tattoos, and voice recognition. These millions of pieces of individual data are not collected from known criminals and suspected radical extremists in their meeting places, but rather from ordinary citizens.

Such personal information fed into the computer systems of an Unmanned Aerial Vehicle (UAV) can track anyone anywhere and record any and all activities. Once this data is combined with information gathered by the Future Attribute Screening Technology (FAST) an itemized dossier of anyone's social habits, recreational activities, daily schedules, and meetings with friends and associates can be analyzed. And all this personal information can be accumulated without the individual's knowledge—or even more importantly, his consent. Once gathered, all such data can be stored in a centralized NGI database.

The FBI's Criminal Justice Information Services Division (CJIS) has already collected a database of over a million palm prints collected from both crime scenes and a wide variety of locations where palm prints can be recovered. Such future collection projects as iris scanning are also being developed for quick identification of individuals under suspicion for any type of antisocial behavior.

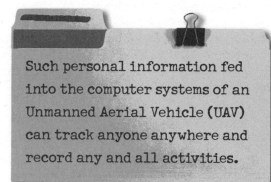

Such personal information fed into the computer systems of an Unmanned Aerial Vehicle (UAV) can track anyone anywhere and record any and all activities.

With the implementation of No Child Left Behind in 2001 by the George W. Bush administration, many schools—kindergarten to twelfth grade—began using fingerprint and biometric systems during lunch to insure reimbursement for the federal program.

In 2007, some police departments began using CompuLink laptop computers to record children's fingerprints at such public events as county fairs. The data was then uploaded to the federal Amber Alert system.

In 2010, the Los Angeles Unified School District informed students that they must submit to a biometric identification system in order to receive lunch.

A school district in Philadelphia found itself facing a class action lawsuit when it was discovered that the 1,800 laptop computers issued to students in two high schools contained concealed cameras that enabled school personnel to monitor the students without the knowledge or consent of either the students or their parents.

In late 2010, it was learned that the U.S. Department of Agriculture had installed surveillance cameras in numerous school cafeterias so government officials could monitor students as they ate.

In 2011, a county in Florida installed fingerprint scanners in school buses as an effective method of monitoring students. School officials are also planning a scanner and laptop installed in every bus in their district.

John W. Whitehead, an attorney specializing in constitutional rights and civil liberties and author of *The Change Manifesto,* stated the following warning in regard to such abuses of privacy as those cited above: "As surveillance cameras, metal detectors, police patrols, zero tolerance policies, lock downs, drug-sniffing dogs and strip searches become the norm in elementary, middle, and high schools across the nation, America is on a fast track to raising up an Orwellian generation—one populated by compliant citizens accustomed to living in a police state and who march in lock step to the dictates of the government."

PEARL HARBOR AND FDR

When Franklin Delano Roosevelt addressed Congress and, via radio, the nation on the morning after the Japanese attack on Pearl Harbor and solemnly proclaimed the day of the attack—December 7, 1941—"a date which will live in infamy," conspiracists were quick to revise the famous quotation to add "and deception."

For well over sixty years, even the most conventionally patriotic individuals have at least wondered if the "sneak attack" on Pearl Harbor, which cost the lives of over 2,400

Americans, mostly men and women in the armed services, was really such a surprise. Even the most loyal advocates of the U.S. presidency and the most avid fans of President Roosevelt probably have asked at least once, "How much did FDR know?"

Some see Pearl Harbor as the Mother of All Conspiracies and cite such evidence as the following to support this view:

- Since he was dealing with an isolationist nation that wanted nothing more to do with wars in Europe, FDR thought to provoke war by ordering the U.S. Navy to fire upon Nazi warships in the Atlantic. The Germans did not return fire because of Hitler's strict orders to Admiral Erich Raeder not to engage the provocateurs.

- FDR turned his attention toward the Japanese by initiating an embargo on war materials against Japan and threatening a blockade of Japanese shipping transporting the oil their armies so desperately needed after the campaigns in China, Korea, and Burma. To show that he meant business, FDR ordered the U.S. fleet from the West Coast to Hawaii in 1940.

- Pearl Harbor's resident commander, Admiral James O. Richardson, raised serious objections to the fleet move, stating that there was inadequate protection from air attack and no protection from torpedo attack. In 1932, in combined army-navy war games, 152 carrier-based aircraft caught the defenders of Pearl Harbor completely by surprise. In 1938 another carrier-borne air strike successfully "attacked" the Pacific base in an exercise. Admiral Richardson objected so strenuously to FDR's plan that he was replaced by Admiral Husband E. Kimmel, who almost immediately upon assuming command raised the same objections.

- By December 1940 the U.S. Army Signal Intelligence Service had broken all the Japanese codes: the "Purple Code," utilized for all diplomatic communication; "J-19," the main code; the "Coral Machine Cipher" or "JNA-20," a simplified version of "Purple" used by the Japanese navy (JN); and "JN-25," used by the Japanese fleet. The codes used by the Japanese, the bemused code breakers suggested, were little more sophisticated than the ones used by Julius Caesar. The greatest difficulty lay in transcribing written Japanese. It was revealed in 1979 by the National Security Agency that the code breakers working on JN-25 had intercepted 2,413 messages with details of the existence, objectives, and location of the Pearl Harbor Strike Force. In November and early December 1941 the code breakers worked twenty-four hours a day and spent 85 percent of their time reading Japanese navy and diplomatic messages.

- On March 32, 1941, a navy report predicted that if Japan should ever attack the United States, they would most likely strike Pearl Harbor at dawn without warning. The U.S. fleet was the only major threat to Japan's plans for world domination.

- In July 1941 a U.S. military attaché at Tokyo reported secret Japanese aerial training exercises in Ariake Bay, a bay closely resembling Pearl Harbor. In that same month a U.S. military attaché in Mexico received information that the Japanese were building small submarines designed to attack the fleet in Pearl Harbor.

- War-hawk presidential advisers, such as Secretary of the Interior Harold Ickes, continued to counsel FDR that the best way to enter the war against Nazi Germany was to declare war on Japan, one of Germany's allies. On July 25, 1941, FDR froze all Japan's assets in the United States, cutting off their main supply of oil. At the Atlantic Conference in August, British prime

The USS *Arizona* memorial marks the resting place of that battleship, which was sunk during the Japanese attack on Pearl Harbor.

minister Winston Churchill cabled his cabinet his astonishment at how eager Roosevelt appeared to be to enter the war.

- On August 10, 1941, a British double agent known as "Tricycle" contacted the FBI and gave them exact details of the Japanese attack plans for Pearl Harbor. The FBI rejected this intelligence because it was too complete, too precise, and too detailed to be authentic.

- In September 1941 a Korean agent informed Eric Sevareid of CBS News that the Japanese would attack Pearl Harbor before Christmas. This intelligence convinced U.S. senator Guy Gillette of its authenticity, and he personally alerted FDR, the State Department, and Army and Navy Intelligence.

- On September 24 a coded message between Japanese naval intelligence and Japan's consul general in Honolulu was intercepted in which the diplomat was requested to deliver the grid of the precise locations of the U.S. ships in the harbor

at Pearl. The content of this message was not relayed to Pearl Harbor. Captain Alan G. Kirk, chief of Naval Intelligence, argued that there was no reason why the Japanese navy would need to know the exact grid of the U.S. fleet unless they intended to try to sink it. Because he insisted on warning Hawaii, he was removed from his position, and the message was never relayed.

- On October 16 FDR humiliated Japan's ambassador Kichisaburo Nomura and refused to meet with Premier Prince Konoye, a move that would allow General Tojo to claim power.

- On November 13 the German ambassador to the United States, an anti-Nazi, told U.S. intelligence that the Japanese planned to bomb Pearl Harbor.

- On November 25 FDR confided in Secretary of War Henry Stimson that Pearl Harbor would soon be attacked and explained that the U.S. had to maneuver the Japanese into firing the first shot in order to have the full support of the American people. The president admonished his secretary of war that there must be no doubt in anyone's mind as to who were the aggressors and who started the war.

At this date Ambassador Nomura was still conducting negotiations with Washington. Admiral Isoroku Yamamoto, commanding the Japanese attack forces as they secretly advanced into Hawaiian waters, cautioned his officers that if the negotiations in Washington should prove successful, the attack group would immediately stand down. If hostilities were declared, they would deal the U.S. fleet a mortal blow.

It is known that British intelligence decoded Yamamoto's orders to his officers. It is suspected that Churchill sent an urgent message to FDR informing him that an attack on Pearl Harbor was imminent. If the conspiracy theorists are correct in their assumptions, the part of Yamamoto's message that moved FDR to action were the words that the attack force would stand down if negotiations succeeded.

- On November 26 the U.S. aircraft carriers *Enterprise* and *Lexington* were ordered out of Pearl Harbor, thus removing from the island headquarters fifty fighter planes, or 40 percent of its already scant air power. That same day, U.S. Secretary of State Cordell Hull issued the ultimatum that Japan must withdraw all forces from Indochina and China, a demand certain to antagonize the Japanese and cause them to break off negotiations.

- On November 29 the FBI intercepted an uncoded message from Japan's new special ambassador in Washington, Saburo Kurusu, to the Chief Foreign Officer in Tokyo in which Kurusu stated that he needed to know the "zero hour" or he would not be able to carry on diplomatic exercises. The Tokyo officer responded, "December 8 at Pearl Harbor," which the

FBI interpreted, allowing for the time difference, to be December 7.

- On December 1 Ambassador Nomura received a cable from Foreign Minister Shigenori Togo with instructions to continue negotiations in order that the U.S. not become suspicious of Japan's surprise attack.

- On December 2 Yamamoto radioed the attack fleet in uncoded Japanese: "Climb Niitakayama 1208." Niitaka was the highest mountain in Japan. U.S. intelligence could easily deduce that Yamamoto's message called for the attack to begin on December 8 (December 7, U.S.)

- On December 4 Elliott R. Thorpe, a U.S. military attaché stationed in Java and privy to all the messages decoded by Dutch intelligence that specified a Japanese attack on Pearl Harbor, sent four cables warning of the danger. The War Department in Washington ordered Thorpe to cease.

- On December 5 all Japanese shipping returned to home ports.

- On December 6, at 9:30 P.M., FDR was given the first thirteen parts of a decoded Japanese diplomatic declaration of war. After glancing through it, FDR returned to his dinner guests and announced that the war would start on the next day.

- On December 7, at 7:55 A.M. local time, the Japanese launched a "surprise" attack on Pearl Harbor. Eighteen U.S. ships were sunk or seriously damaged, including five battleships. Of the aircraft left to defend Pearl Harbor, 188 were destroyed and 162 were damaged, most before they even managed to get into the sky. Human casualties included 2,403 dead and 1,178 wounded. Out of an attack force of thirty-one ships and 353 bombers and fighter planes, the Japanese lost twenty-nine airplanes and five midget submarines, with a total of sixty-four deaths.

It will remain for history to judge Franklin Delano Roosevelt's actions prior to Pearl Harbor. Many researchers have reached the consensus that Pearl Harbor was not about going to war with Japan, but about entering the war with Germany.

However, one thing seems certain. Because all important Japanese codes had been broken long before Pearl Harbor by U.S. intelligence groups and the governments of Britain, the Netherlands, Australia, Peru, Korea, and the Soviet Union had warned the U.S. of the military action, the attack on Pearl Harbor was no surprise to the U.S. government.

PENTAGON PAPERS

The Pentagon Papers, with their revelations of the vast litany of lies that the U.S. Department of Defense and the president issued to the American people about Vietnam, probably did more than any single factor in the past fifty years to create distrust in the government.

On June 13, 1971, President Richard M. Nixon opened up his Sunday *New York Times* to see a picture of his daughter Tricia and himself from her wedding in the White House Rose Garden. Next to the photograph, on the right, was the headline over Neil Sheehan's initial story on the Pentagon Papers, "Vietnam Archive: Pentagon Study Traces 3 Decades of Growing U.S. Involvement." Nixon would maintain that he never read the article, but he told Secretary of State Henry Kissinger later that day that certain people had to be "put to the torch" and jailed for leaking such information to the press.

The Pentagon Papers constitute a massive seven-thousand-page, above-top-secret Defense Department history of America's involvement in the Vietnam War from 1945 to 1971.

This historic document, leaked to the press by Daniel Ellsberg, a Defense Department staff member, has probably done as much as any single factor in the past fifty years to create distrust of the machinations of the U.S. government by its people. Among other things, the Pentagon Papers disclosed that the government fully intended to go to Vietnam in spite of President Lyndon B. Johnson's promises to stay out of the mess that the French had left in that country. In addition, the papers revealed that there was no plan to end the war.

On June 14 H. R. Haldeman, White House chief of staff, told President Nixon that out of the "gobbledygook, comes a very clear thing: you can't trust the government; you can't believe what they say; and you can't rely on their judgment. [A]nd the implicit infallibility of presidents, which has been an accepted thing in America, is badly hurt by this." That summed up the impact of the Pentagon Papers as succinctly as anyone could. In a time of national protest against the U.S. military's involvement in Vietnam, a time of draft-card burning, protest marches, college laboratory bombings, sit-ins, flower children, and the Age of Aquarius, Nixon's nose had stretched way beyond Pinocchio's. Had the government ever told its citizens the truth about anything? Suddenly every conspiracy theory from Roosevelt allowing the attack on Pearl Harbor to the government cover-up of UFOs was given new validity. If even the White House chief of staff admitted that "you can't trust the government," why should anyone?

The *New York Times* began publishing excerpts of the Pentagon Papers on June 13. On the evening of June 14 Attorney General John Mitchell warned the *Times* by telephone and telegram against any further publication. On June 15 the U.S. government won a restraining order against the *Times*. The *Washington Post* picked up the cause on June 18 and began publishing excerpts from the Pentagon Papers. That same day, Assistant Attorney General William Rehnquist advised the *Post* to

An aerial view of the Pentagon in Washington, D.C. When the "Pentagon Papers" were leaked in 1971, detailing the United States' involvement in Vietnam from 1945 to that year, President Nixon denied knowledge of their contents.

stop publishing the Papers. The *Post* refused, and the Justice Department sought an injunction against the newspaper. This time the court refused the government's request, and the Justice Department appealed. At the same time, the *New York Times* was appealing the injunction against them.

On June 26 the Supreme Court of the United States agreed to combine the cases into *New York Times Co. v. U.S.* (403 U.S. 713). On June 29 Senator Mike Gravel of Alaska entered 4,100 pages of the Pentagon Papers into the record of his subcommittee on Buildings and Grounds. This portion of the original 7,000 pages was later published in book form by Beacon Press of Boston.

On June 30 the Supreme Court made what is arguably the most important decision in U.S. history regarding freedom of the press. By a 6-3 vote, the Court ordered the prior restraints against the newspapers lifted, stating that the government had not met the burden of proof. The justices wrote nine separate opinions, sharply disagreeing on substantive issues. While the decision was an undeniable victory for the First Amendment, these disagreements made some journalists uncertain what protection there would be for future editors and publishers when issues of national security were alleged to be at stake.

The publication of the Pentagon Papers strengthened the protests against the war in Vietnam and greatly widened the credibility gap between the American public and the U.S. government.

PEOPLES TEMPLE

What began in Indiana in 1960 as a bold experiment in radical theology ended tragically in the jungle of Guyana in 1978 with Peoples Temple members drinking poisoned Kool-Aid.

In the early 1970s the Peoples Temple was accused of being a doomsday cult. Its flamboyant minister, Jim Jones, readily admitted that he thought that the Apocalypse and Armageddon were just around the corner and that the world had definitely entered the end-times. Jones fulminated from his pulpit that the end of the world was drawing near and that civilization would soon be destroyed in a nuclear holocaust. At the same time, his healing services at the Peoples Temple in San Francisco were attracting both true believers and curiosity seekers, and Jones's particular brand of theology seemed attractive to many individuals drawn to alternative religious expression.

Born into a poor Indiana family at the height of the Great Depression in 1931, James Warren Jones (1931–1978) was deeply influenced by his mother's belief in spirits and by her distrust of organized religion. At the same time, a Pentecostal neighbor lady showed the boy how religion could also be an intensely emotional experience. At an early age Jones developed a repugnance of racism, and he set as his mission the creation of a social activism that would tear down all racial barriers.

Military personnel had the unpleasant task of collecting the bodies after the followers of Jim Jones drank poisoned Kool-Aid at a Peoples Temple camp in Guyana in 1978.

Jones held degrees from Indiana University and Butler University, but he had received no formal training in theology when he was invited to speak at the Laurel Street Tabernacle, an Assemblies of God Pentecostal church, in Indianapolis in September 1954. As a result of his powerful sermon on racial equality, many members left the congregation to follow Jones and to form a new church, the Wings of Deliverance, which was renamed the Peoples Temple. In 1960 the Peoples Temple was officially made a congregation of the Christian Church, Disciples of Christ, a liberal Protestant denomination, and Jones was ordained a minister. Within a very short time, Jones's social gospel of equality and love attracted over nine hundred members, and he added healing services to his ministry.

In 1965, because of threats directed against the Peoples Temple by those who were disturbed by Jones's radical theology and his alleged cures of cancer, heart disease, and arthritis, the Temple moved to Ukiah, California, where Jones believed racial equality could be preached with greater openness and less fear of retaliation. Seventy families, half of them African American and half white, moved with him.

In 1977, reacting to a number of attacks directed at him and his inner circle, Jones moved his community to the South American nation of Guyana, where in 1974 he had acquired a lease from the Guyanese government for four thousand acres of land to be used for colonization. The new community was called the Peoples Temple Agricultural Project, and eventually over nine hundred men, women, and children would follow their charismatic leader to Jonestown.

Jonestown was not an idyllic community in the middle of the Guyana jungle. Members were required to work eleven hours a day, six days a week, and eight hours on Sunday, clearing land for agriculture, planting crops, and building dormitories and other necessary buildings. Their diet consisted primarily of rice and beans, and their evenings were filled with required meetings before they were allowed to get some rest.

While his followers slaved in the steaming jungle to build a viable community, Jones, who had become increasingly paranoid, as well as extremely reliant on prescription drugs, began receiving messages from extraterrestrials who described a process called "Translation." During the implementation of the Translation, Jones and his followers would all die together and the aliens would take their spirits to another planet to enjoy a life of bliss. To prepare for this event, Jones ordered rehearsals of a mass suicide, during which followers would pretend to drink poison and fall to the ground. Those followers who began to suggest that their once unselfish leader was suffering from mental illness or megalomania were shouted down by the true believers once Jones revealed his true divinity, claiming to be the reincarnation of Jesus Christ, the Buddha, the pharaoh Akhenaten, Lenin, and Father Divine, the founder of the International Peace Mission movement, all in one physical body.

On November 14, 1978, California congressman Leo Ryan and several representatives of the media visited Jonestown to investigate claims of civil rights violations that had reached concerned relatives in the United States from community members. Sixteen members of the Temple told Ryan that they wished to return with him, and Jones became extremely upset by so many defectors wanting to leave his community.

On November 18 a Temple member made an attempt on Ryan's life, and the congressman and his party decided to leave Jonestown immediately. While they were boarding two planes on the jungle airstrip, some heavily armed members of the Temple's security guards arrived and began firing on the group. Ryan and four others were killed and eleven were wounded before the planes could get into the air.

Jones feared retaliation from the U.S. government and decreed that it was time to put

Translation into effect. Some members of the Temple committed suicide by ingesting cyanide-laced Kool-Aid, and others injected poison directly into their veins. According to those who later arrived at Jonestown to investigate, 638 adult members of the community died, together with 276 children. A few fled into the jungle and survived the mass suicide and attempts to shoot those who refused to drink the poison.

The Peoples Temple as a movement died along with the 914 members who perished in Jonestown on November 18, 1978. In 1989 their former headquarters building in San Francisco was destroyed by an earthquake. Conspiracy theorists argue that the tragic mass deaths at Jonestown eliminated evidence of a CIA experiment gone bad. Others suggest that Jones subjected his followers to mind-control experiments of his own and became a victim of the situation. And then there are those who insist that Jones was mentally ill and complicated his mental imbalance with drug abuse.

PHILADELPHIA EXPERIMENT

In October 1943 the U.S. Navy accomplished the invisibility and teleportation of a warship from Philadelphia to its dock near Norfolk. The World War II secret test has been covered up because of its tragic effects on the crewmen who participated in the experiment.

During the Philadelphia Experiment, scientists succeeded in causing a warship to become invisible, but a number of the crew burst into flames in spontaneous human combustion, and several others later lapsed into invisibility in front of their families—or, in one case, before the patrons of a crowded bar. Over half the officers and crew members had to be committed to psychiatric wards for the rest of their lives as a result of the fantastic experiment.

The mystery of the Philadelphia Experiment began on January 13, 1956, when Morris K. Jessup, author of *The Case for the UFO* (1955), received the first of a series of strange letters written by Carlos Miguel Allende—or as he sometimes signed his name, Carl Allen. Jessup brought an abundance of academic distinction to his study of the flying saucer enigma. After having served as an instructor in astronomy and mathematics at the University of Michigan and at Drake University, he was awarded a Ph.D. in astrophysics and was sent to South Africa by the University of Michigan to erect and operate the largest refracting telescope in the Southern Hemisphere. The Jessup-directed research produced the discovery of several double stars, which were catalogued by the Royal Astronomical Society.

The initial letter from the mysterious writer was in response to Jessup's book, and Allende began by taking him to task for encouraging the public to request research into Unified Field Theory such as that sought by Einstein. In October 1943, according to Allende, scientists working for the navy had accomplished the complete invisibility of the *Eldridge,* a destroyer-type ship, and all of its crew. Allende was blunt in his assessment of the effect that the force field had upon the crew members. Seamen within the energy field for too long went "blank," suddenly finding themselves fading into invisibility. To "get stuck," Allende explained, was a side effect of the experiment that suddenly prevented a sailor from being able to move of his own volition. If two or more of his fellow crew members did not come to his aid at once and lay their hands upon him, the unfortunate sailor would "freeze." Those who had entered into this condition were as if they were comatose—able to live, breathe, see, and feel in kind of a nether world. Fully as horrifying as the deep-freeze effects were the incidents of men who went "into the flame," suffering spontaneous combustion.

Allende listed a number of personnel on observer ships' crews and the crew of a Matson Lines Liberty ship out of Norfolk, Virginia. He also implied that he himself witnessed the experiment from aboard the SS *Andrew Furnseth*. Allende affixed a lengthy postscript stating his reconsidered opinion that the navy was probably quite blameless in the incident and really did not envision the ghastly effect the experiment would have upon the crew members. Before he closed, Allende tossed one more bombshell: The experimental ship had disappeared from its Philadelphia dock and, only a very few minutes later, appeared at its other dock in the Norfolk–Newport News–Portsmouth, Virginia, area. The ship had been clearly identified as being at that place, then it again disappeared and returned to its Philadelphia dock in only a very few minutes.

Jessup sent Allende a letter requesting more information. It was four months before he received a reply. In his second letter, Allende had Americanized his name to Carl M. Allen. He had also tempered the tone of his correspondence and seemed less piqued at Jessup. Allende offered to subject himself to hypnosis or sodium pentothal in an attempt to remember names, addresses, and service numbers of his shipmates.

At that point Jessup was invited to the Office of Naval Research in Washington. The astrophysicist was surprised when an officer handed him a paperback copy of his own book, *The Case for the UFO*. Jessup was informed that the book had been addressed to "Admiral N. Furth, Chief, Office of Naval Research." The manila envelope in which it had arrived was postmarked Seminole, Texas. A cheery "Happy Easter" had been written across the face of the envelope.

Someone had taken the time and effort to completely annotate Jessup's study of the UFO, and the book appeared to have been passed back and forth among at least three persons. Each individual wrote in a different color of ink. The annotators designated themselves as "Mr. A." (assumed to be Allende),

"Mr. B.," and "Jemi." The three individuals refer to "LMs," who seem to be extraterrestrials either friendly or indifferent to earthlings, and to "SMs," a group of hostile aliens. Throughout the text, the three used terms such as *mothership, home-ship, dead-ship, Great Ark, great bombardment, great return, great war, little-men, force-fields, deep freezes, undersea building, measure markers, scout ships, gravity fields, sheets of diamond, cosmic rays, force cutters, undersea explorers, inlay work, clear-talk, telepathing,* and *vortices.* Such terms have encouraged UFO researchers to speculate that the mysterious Carl Allen and his two friends were representatives of an extraterrestrial power that took root on Earth centuries ago and has long since established an advanced underground subculture.

Morris Jessup was found dead in his station wagon in Dade County Park, Florida, on the evening of April 20, 1959. Police officers reconstructed the death as a suicide. A hose had been attached to the exhaust pipe of the station wagon and looped into the closed interior. Some associates mentioned despondency over an approaching divorce as the principal reason. Most of his colleagues, however, were shocked and surprised that Jessup would seek the ultimate escape of a closed car and carbon monoxide. And ever since Jessup's death there have been UFO researchers who have argued that the alleged suicide was the price the astrophysicist paid for getting too close to the truth about flying saucers.

There really was a destroyer named the *Eldridge,* and it remained on active duty until 1946. After it was removed from military service, it was mothballed until it was transferred to the Greek navy.

Although there will probably always be those who swear that they or their kin participated in the remarkable secret navy experiment in invisibility and teleportation in 1943, no newspaper clippings, military memoranda, or any other proofs of the Philadelphia Experiment

have ever been located. Many researchers maintain that some kind of secret experiment took place with a navy warship in 1943 and thereby became the origin of the Philadelphia Experiment. Most speculate that it was probably an experiment in attempting to make ships invisible to enemy submarines' sonar and that it very well could have involved high voltages of electricity—which might have burned and scorched seamen and even delivered a kind of shock that drove some of the crewmen insane.

Others insist that a government conspiracy is at work and that the secret experiment in 1943 ripped a hole in the space-time continuum, enabling alien intelligences to begin an invasion of the planet. Once the aliens began to explore the opening between worlds in 1947, secret government agencies cut a deal with the extraterrestrials to share technology in return for the natural resources of Earth—including some of its human inhabitants.

In 1980 the writer Robert A. Goerman managed to find the home and the surviving family of Carl M. Allen, alias Carlos Miguel Allende. Goerman's research convinced him that the Philadelphia Experiment was quite likely all a hoax, a fantasy molded by a former sailor who loved to read about UFOs and strange, unsolved mysteries so much that he created one that may never die.

WILLIAM PIERCE, *THE TURNER DIARIES,* AND THE NATIONAL ALLIANCE

William Pierce, author of The Turner Diaries, *an apocalyptic novel of an Aryan underground movement surviving the Zionist-Negro regime, sought to build a "serious, mature, right-wing organization" in the National Alliance.*

William Pierce (1933–2002) is revered in far-right, white-supremacy groups as the author of *The Turner Diaries,* a futuristic, apocalyptic novel about the Aryan resistance underground movement after the "Jew-Negro conspiracy" has overthrown the U.S. government. After enduring hellish persecution by the cruel Zionists and their brutish Negro henchmen, Earl Turner, an upstanding Caucasian, joins the white-supremacist guerrillas who are beginning to wage war against the new government. The Aryans move on steadily to victory in battle after battle, and Turner sacrifices his life in a kamikaze mission flying a small plane with a nuclear bomb into the Pentagon in order for the white supremacists to win the final conflict.

The Turner Diaries was written under the pseudonym "Andrew MacDonald" in 1978, just a few years after Dr. (Ph.D. in physics) William Pierce left a career in teaching and research at Oregon State University to join the National Youth Alliance in 1970 and to found the National Alliance in 1974. The National Youth Alliance, founded by Willis Carto, had limited its membership to persons under thirty. Pierce wanted to broaden the group to attract a larger base of white supremacists, and he shifted the focus of the National Alliance to activities that would have more long-term motivational effect on its members. Rather than organizing simple street demonstrations to denounce the Jews and the blacks, he wanted to avoid superficial confrontations and to build a foundation for a final victory over those whom he judged as enemies of white culture.

In spite of the founding in 1978 of the Cosmotheist Community Church to answer the needs of members interested in the spiritual or religious aspects of the National Alliance, membership dwindled through the Reagan era, and the national office moved from the Washington, D.C., area to rural Mill Point, West Virginia.

In 1980 Alliance member William Simpson's *Which Way Western Man?* and a second edition of *The Turner Diaries* were published. In 1987 National Vanguard Books was established as a separate entity from the Alliance, and in 1989 Pierce's second novel, *Hunter,* was published. National Vanguard Books has moved on to issue audio cassettes, comic books, and videos and to assume the broadcasting of a weekly radio program, *American Dissident Voices.*

Many conspiracy theorists have stated their belief that it was *The Turner Diaries* that inspired Timothy McVeigh to blow up the Alfred P. Murrah Federal Building in Oklahoma City. They support this contention by listing some of the similarities between the act of terrorism carried out by McVeigh and a guerrilla strike carried out by Earl Turner, the hero of *The Turner Diaries*:

Timothy McVeigh

Target: Murrah Federal Building, Oklahoma City

Time: 9:02 A.M.

Payload: 5,400 lbs. ammonium nitrate mixed with nitro fuel and diesel

Delivery: rented truck parked curbside, out front

Earl Turner

Target: FBI Building, Washington, D.C.

Time: 9:15 A.M.

Payload: 4,400 lbs. ammonium nitrate mixed with heating oil

Delivery: hijacked panel truck parked in sub-basement loading dock

Pierce once said, while writing *The Turner Diaries,* that he envisioned putting all the feminist agitators and propagandists and all of the race-mixing fanatics and all of the media bosses and all who were collaborating with them up against a wall and shooting them. On one of his radio programs in 1975 he said that this was exactly what must be done before America could get its civilization back on track.

The late white supremacist William Pierce is best known as the author of *The Turner Diaries,* a work of fiction about Aryans fighting against an America ruled by Jews and African Americans.

Pierce worked his way up the far-right, white supremacist circles step by step. About 1963 he joined the John Birch Society but left as his views became more radical. In 1966 he associated with George Lincoln Rockwell, founder and leader of the American Nazi Party and became the editor of Rockwell's *National Socialist World* magazine. After Rockwell's assassination in 1967 Pierce became a principal leader of the National Socialist White People's Party, the successor to the American Nazi Party. Pierce left that group to join the National Youth Alliance that had been founded by Willis Carto in 1968. After three years Pierce and Carto began to feud about a number of issues, and the National Youth Alliance split into factions, with Pierce's branch emerging as the National Alliance.

Pierce recognized the knee-jerk reaction most Americans would have to young men dressed in Nazi uniforms, so he counseled his followers not to get involved with "that kind of circus" or to display any Nazi symbols. There was never any question about his admiration for Hitler or his vision of a future United States modeled after the Third Reich. Nor was there any doubt in his followers' minds that he believed that Jews were responsible for all the social, economic, and political problems that had faced Germany and were now infesting the United States.

Pierce died on July 23, 2002 at the age of sixty-eight, still declaring that the National Alliance was the only "serious, mature, radical right-wing organization in America."

POSSE COMITATUS

Posse Comitatus believes that all government should be rooted at the county, rather than the federal, level.

Posse *comitatus* means "power of the county." The original Posse Comitatus Act was passed by Congress in 1878 to prevent federal troops from enforcing community laws or from acting as police officers. In the days of the old West and the Reconstruction era after the Civil War, the army often became involved in what should have been traditional police actions. The Posse Comitatus law was passed to remove the army from civilian law enforcement and to return it to its role of defending the nation's borders.

In the 1970s retired army colonel William Potter Gale formed a group of armed anti-tax and anti-federal-government survivalists who agreed with his political philosophy that all government power should be rooted at the county, rather than the federal, level. Posse Comitatus members resist paying taxes because the federal government is controlled by Jews. Some members won't even apply for driver's licenses because to do so would be to submit to an illegal, subversive authority. The Posse soon attracted Klan members and other anti-Semites, including David Duke.

This intermittently active, loosely organized group of antigovernment agitators and avowed followers of Christian Identity received nationwide attention in 1983 when Posse member Gordon Kahl murdered two federal marshals who had come to arrest him for a parole violation in connection with a conviction for nonpayment of taxes. Kahl became a fugitive and was later killed in a shootout with Arkansas law-enforcement officers.

In October 1987 Posse founder William Potter Gale and four associates from the California-based Committee of the States were convicted of threatening the lives of Internal Revenue Service agents and a Nevada state judge. Sentenced to federal prison in January 1988, Gale died in April of that year, at age seventy-one.

In 1991 an Identity minister and Posse leader based in Michigan, James Wickstrom, was convicted of scheming to distribute $100,000 in counterfeit bills to white supremacists at the 1988 Aryan World Congress. While he was doing time in prison, Wickstrom transferred his leadership position to Mark Thomas, an Identity preacher from Pennsylvania. Wickstrom was released from prison in 1994 and remains involved in the Posse movement by operating a website. August Kreis, who assumed leadership of Aryan Nations in 2005, still maintains a significant role in Posse Comitatus and believes that their group will bring the United States back under God's laws.

What the Posse Comitatus Believes

- Northern European whites are the true "Chosen People" referred to in the Bible.

- Jews are members of Satan's synagogue.

- African Americans and other people of color are subhuman "mud races."

- Abortion is capital murder, punishable by death.

- Taxes should not be paid to the Zionist Occupied Government that controls the United States.

- The present government should be replaced with an Identity-based theocracy.

PROJECT MONARCH

Much of Project Monarch remains classified. From the information that has leaked out, it is easy to see why these mind-control experiments were considered top secret.

Project Monarch was officially begun by the U.S. Army in the early 1960s, and it is still classified as top secret for reasons of national security. Some researchers are quite certain that Monarch evolved from such MK-ULTRA subprojects as Spellbinder, established to create "Manchurian Candidate" assassins, and Operation Often, which explored black magic and the occult.

Researcher Ron Patton theorizes that the name Monarch had nothing to do with royalty, but referred to the Monarch butterfly and "the feeling of light-headedness," as if one were "floating or fluttering like a butterfly," after undergoing the trauma induced by electroshock. One may also think of the common occult symbolism of the butterfly for the soul or the mind and an ancient belief that human souls become butterflies while they are between lives awaiting reincarnation.

Patton states that Monarch was essentially about programming the mind, modifying human behavior, and placing its subjects into a "marionette syndrome." A marionette is a puppet whose actions are determined by a puppeteer pulling its strings, hence the analogy concerning the psychologist and the programmed subject. Conventional psychologists might use the term "conditioned stimulus response sequences," but the Monarch experimenters called the process "Imperial conditioning." Monarch also diverged greatly from traditional psychological conditioning exercises by including satanic rituals in order to enhance the trauma experienced by the subject. The programmer might choose to intensify the rituals by having the hypnotized or drugged subject "image" ancient archetypal symbols of mysticism and the occult, such as spiders, bats, snakes, masks, castles, mazes, demons, and monsters.

Monarch programming had six levels:

Alpha: General conditioning designed to improve memory retention, visual acuity, and physical strength. Exercises deliberately subdivided the subject's personality and emphasized the left-brain/right-brain division.

Beta: Sexual programming that would eliminate all moral values and remove all inhibitions.

Delta: Deadly force programming for special agents and elite forces of the military. Subjects were conditioned to have no fear, and subliminal instructions were implanted for the agent to commit suicide if captured.

Theta: Psychic programming through various electronic mind-control systems, brain implants, and telemetry devices. The implants were used with highly advanced computers and satellite tracking systems.

Omega: Also known as "Code Green," this level involved self-destruct programming that caused the subject/agent to commit suicide if too much memory was retrieved by interrogation.

Gamma: This level activated itself within a subject/agent when an opportunity arose wherein misinformation and deception could be disseminated to great advantage.

Many researchers believe that the *MK* in MK-ULTRA stood for "Mind Kontrolle," a German spelling of the English word "control." There were many Nazi psychologists who were masters of mind control and who were smuggled out of Germany at the end of World War II by the Office of Strategic Services (OSS). Hitler's chief of intelligence against the Russians, General Reinhard Gehlen, arrived in Washington in 1945 and worked with William "Wild Bill" Donovan, director of the OSS and Allen Dulles to restructure the American intelligence program into the Central Intelligence Agency under Dulles's leadership. General Gehlen shared the behavior-modification research of Dr. Josef Mengele at Auschwitz and the brainwashing experiments conducted at Dachau with hypnosis and mescaline.

Patton states that Monarch was essentially about programming the mind, modifying human behavior, and placing its subjects into a "marionette syndrome."

There is an increasing amount of evidence that Mengele himself, under the assumed name of "Dr. Green," participated in the formulation of many Monarch and MK-ULTRA programs in the United States after World War II. Mengele came to be called the "Angel of Death" when he conducted his infamous experiments on countless victims at Auschwitz concentration camp. While Mengele's presence could not be acknowledged by Monarch, his unprecedented research on thousands of unwilling victims provided valuable data on mental programming, mind control, and many other areas of great interest to MK-ULTRA. Mengele had likely been brought to America together with a large number of Nazi scientists and medical personnel during Operation Paperclip.

Conspiracy researchers assert that the process of choosing the type of subjects to be used in the early Monarch experiments was reminiscent of the rationale of Dr. Mengele, who often selected his victims by his determining that they possessed "satanic bloodlines." Many hapless individuals for the Monarch experiments were selected because they came from orphanages, foster care homes, or incestuous families and were pronounced as "expendable," meaning that if any of them should die during the experiments, they would not likely be missed. "They are fulfilling their destiny as the chosen ones." This coldhearted dismissal of "accidents" that resulted from harsh experiments is said to have been coined by Mengele at Auschwitz, and it was repeated often by the Monarch personnel.

"Dr. Green" was known to work often with "Dr. White," the pseudonym of Dr. Donald Ewen Cameron, the former head of the Canadian, American, and World Psychiatric Associations. A personal friend of Allen Dulles, White/Cameron was given millions of dollars by MK-ULTRA to conduct a series of mind-control experiments and to serve as a resource for Monarch and many of the other 150 subprojects of the secret program. Cameron's favorite experiment seems to have been what he called "psychic driving," in which subjects were kept in drug-induced comas for weeks, then administered electroshocks through electronic helmets strapped to their heads. Many of the subjects were abused children who had been passed on to him through the Roman Catholic orphanage system.

In 1972 Richard Helms, director of the CIA, ordered records of all 150 individual projects of MK-ULTRA destroyed. On December 11, 1980, a lawsuit was filed against the CIA by a former "patient" who had experienced one of the experiments of Dr. Cameron. Once someone stepped forward to demand reparations for such cruel and harsh treatment, another former "volunteer" became a co-plaintiff.

William Casey, the CIA director at this time, anticipated that more victims of the covert mind-control research projects would soon join in the court case, so he ordered the Agency's legal staff to delay court proceedings as long as possible. Casey's strategy was to wait out the plaintiffs, who were quite elderly, and to hope that if they died before the case came to trial, their stories would die with them. However, the case did eventually come to trial, and the plaintiffs settled for $100,000 each, released to them with the stipulation that they would never discuss the case or their complaints in public.

PROJECT SILVERBUG

The day the air force seemed to take flying saucers seriously by announcing that they were building some of their own. Or was it all a grand plan of disinformation?

On February 16, 1953, the Canadian minister of defense released information to the Canadian House of Commons that Avro-Canada, a Canadian aircraft manufacturing company, was engaged in developing plans for a "flying saucer" that would be able to fly at 1,500 miles an hour and to take off and descend vertically. Avro projected that their proposed vehicle would make all other forms of supersonic aircraft obsolete.

On February 15, 1955, the Air Technical Intelligence Center, together with the Wright Air Development Center at Wright-Patterson Air Force Base in Dayton, Ohio, revealed that the air force proposed building jet-propelled "flying saucers" under the code name of Project Silverbug. Circular and saucer-shaped, like the classic UFOs that civilians had been sighting since at least 1947, the largest of the proposed saucers would weigh 26,000 pounds and would be powered by radically advanced jet engines that would be able to lift the craft to an altitude of 36,090 feet in about one minute and 45 seconds. The cruise speed of these remarkable vehicles would be Mach 3.48 and their operating ceiling would be 80,600 feet. By way of comparison, today's F-15 fighter jet has a similar performance range, but it was developed more than twenty years after the proposed saucers of Project Silverbug.

The air force declassified its secret project in order to inform both civilian and military intelligence on the matter of flying saucers and to jog FBI, CIA, and other intelligence units to increase their efforts to learn if the Soviet Union was working on similar aircraft. After all, the Soviets had also captured a number of the same caliber of German scientists who had been toiling for the führer night and day toward the last days of World War II. These brilliant scientists and engineers had worked desperately to create circular craft with a newly perfected jet-engine propulsion system in order to reestablish the air superiority that they had once commanded. Prior to Germany's surrender, the Allies had bombed nearly all of the Nazi air-base runways into cinder blocks, but these circular craft needed no runways. They could take off straight up and land straight down—VTOL, vertical-takeoff-and-landing.

For some UFO researchers this rare disclosure from the air force seemed proof that the German occult Vril Society really had made contact with extraterrestrials who gave the Nazis their technological advantage at the onset of World War II. Others spoke of the Nazi discovery of a downed UFO and the intense work of German scientists and engineers to reverse-engineer the alien spacecraft.

While the source for the technological know-how that allowed the U.S. Air Force to announce plans for such an astounding aerial vehicle will remain controversial, a June 1955 issue of *Look* magazine carried an article disclosing the information that Avro-Canada had been developing a saucer-shaped craft since 1953. According to the article, the Avro project had been abandoned because of the estimated $75 million development costs. Canadian John Frost began work on the Avro-Canada Y-2/Private Venture 704 project based on his having researched various Nazi saucer projects and had designed a "radial flow" jet engine.

For some UFO researchers this rare disclosure from the air force seemed proof that the German occult Vril Society really had made contact with extraterrestrials....

There was great enthusiasm for saucer- or sphere-shaped aerial vehicles that could accomplish vertical takeoff and landing. As Brig. Gen. Benjamin Kelsey, deputy director of research and development for the U.S. Air Force, noted, contemporary aircraft "spend too much time gathering speed on the ground and not enough time flying in the air." VTOL aircraft would not require runways and landing strips, and they could easily be stored in underground, bombproof shelters, elevated to the surface when needed.

In 1958, after such dramatic advance promotional efforts on the part of the U.S. Air Force and Avro-Canada, the physical results were represented in the Avrocar. Instead of a radical new jet engine, the circular platform of the Avrocar was lifted into the air by many small conventional jets. An analysis of the initial test flights concluded that the vehicle was underpowered and unstable. The ambitious plans to create a flying saucer were abandoned, and the vehicles themselves were relegated to displays at the Smithsonian and Wright-Patterson.

Conspiracy theorists, however, maintain that the feeble demonstration of the Avrocar was an exercise in public disinformation. They believe that the air force continued to develop the saucer-shaped superships at Area 51 in Nevada and that many of the huge "motherships" sighted in the skies recently have been our very own human flying saucers.

PROJECT SPELLBINDER

CIA neurosurgeons sought to implant electrodes into the brain of an assassin created for the purpose of killing Fidel Castro.

In the last days of Nazi resistance in World War II, many Nazi psychologists were smuggled out of Germany by the Office of Strategic Services (OSS). In 1945 Hitler's chief of intelligence against the Russians, General Reinhard Gehlen, worked in Washington with William "Wild Bill" Donovan, director of the OSS, and Allen Dulles to restructure the American intelligence program into the Central Intelligence Agency under Dulles's leadership. Dr. Josef Mengele, who had conducted medical and brainwashing experiments at Auschwitz, worked in early CIA programs under the assumed named of "Dr. Green." In 1953 the MK-ULTRA program in mind control was ordered by Dulles, who appointed Dr. Sidney Gottlieb its leader. Extensive experiments with such drugs as LSD were conducted, some with volunteers, most with unsuspecting subjects.

In 1964 a subproject, MKSEARCH, began a refined search for the perfect truth serum. Based on some of the initial research of Dr. Donald Ewen Cameron, who had begun his career with the OSS in World War II studying the experiments of Nazi psychiatrists with concentration camp prisoners, and Gottlieb, the project required "expendables," subjects that might die during the course of the experiments but whose disappearance was unlikely to arouse suspicion.

The experiments were carried out at CIA safe houses in such cities as Washington, New York, Chicago, and Los Angeles. The experiments focused on the exploitation of human weaknesses and the destabilization of the human personality. The subjects of the experiments would be exposed to tests designed to create disturbances of behavior, alterations of sex patterns, and stimulation of other aberrations, which could all be used in the process of interrogations and the obtaining of information.

When Richard Helms became the director of the CIA on June 30, 1966, he began to push hard for more effective results in the mind-control projects. The few cautions regarding working with "expendables" were discarded. The researchers were informed that they would be receiving a steady arrival of Viet Cong captives on whom to experiment. The prisoners of war were to be considered expendable, already listed as missing in action or killed in Vietnam.

The special mission of Project Spellbinder was to create an effective sleeper killer, a "Manchurian Candidate," who would be assigned to assassinate Fidel Castro. The programmed assassin would be hypnotized, drugged, or conditioned through a combination of mind-control techniques to kill without being aware of his or her lethal programming. The assassin with be "triggered" into entering a trance state and committing the murder by a key word, phrase, or symbol. Once the target victim (in this case, Castro) had been assassinated, the programmed subject would have no memory of his or her role in the murder—and quite likely would be killed by Castro's bodyguards or arrested, convicted, and sentenced, unaware that he or she was programmed to kill by the mind manipulators of Spellbinder.

A hypnotist was selected from among candidates from the American Society of Clinical and Experimental Hypnosis, an individual who expressed no qualms about being involved in experiments with subjects who might die during the series of drug, hypnosis, and behavior-modification techniques.

After numerous unsuccessful attempts to program potential assassins—and no records of how many "expendables" were lost—Spellbinder was halted and declared a complete failure. Or at least that is what they would like us to believe. In 1972 Richard Helms ordered records of all 150 individual projects of MK-ULTRA destroyed, including those of Project Spellbinder.

PROTOCOLS OF THE LEARNED ELDERS OF ZION

It doesn't seem to matter at all that the text may have originated as a plagiarized anti-Jesuit diatribe, a warning about the Illuminati's role in the French Revolution, a fictional account of a meeting in a Prague cemetery, or a political satire of Napoleon III; the Protocols *have been used since 1900 to perpetuate the myth of a global Jewish conspiracy.*

In the opinions of some researchers, *The Protocols of the Learned Elders of Zion* may truly be the mother of all anti-Semite conspiracies. No matter how often the work is proved to be a forgery, some conspiracy theorists will continue to cite the *Protocols* as proof that an international group of Jewish bankers is plotting to take over the world.

Some scholars point to *The Secrets of the Elders of Bourg-Fontaine,* a forged work that was used to discredit the followers of Jansenism, an anti-Jesuit French Catholic movement among the secular clergy as a possible inspiration for the style of the *Protocols.* The mathematical genius Blaise Pascal (1623–1662), who devoted himself to religious studies and is perhaps best known today for his *Pensées,* was

a Jansenist and wrote *Provincial Letters,* heavily critical of the Jesuits. *Secrets of the Elders* was probably written in retaliation and provided some inflammatory accusations that could be rewritten as attacks against the Jews or anyone else whom a plagiarist wished to defame.

Another work that some researchers point out as having language and a format identical to the *Protocols* is *The Secret Plan of the Order* (1828). This book claims to reveal the Great Jesuit Conspiracy to control the Roman Catholic hierarchy, the pope, all the European monarchies, and to establish a world government run by Jesuits. Again, the fantasy of a plot by Jesuits to control the world could easily be shifted to a Jewish plot for global domination.

Some researchers feel the seed for the myth of a global Jewish conspiracy may have been planted circa 1799, after Abbé Augustin Barruel published his four-volume study entitled *Memoirs Illustrating the History of Jacobinism.* Barruel's purpose for writing such an extensive work was to warn the European nations that the Illuminati sought to promote anarchy, revolution, and the dissolution of all monarchies. The secret society's master plan was to destroy the aristocracy and appear to bring power to the people while, in reality, exploiting the common folk as puppets. Abbé Barruel was convinced that the Illuminati had worked behind the scenes to bring about the French Revolution, the first of several political uprisings to come. In 1797, two years before Barruel's much more famous work, John Robison's book *Proofs of a Conspiracy against All of the Religions and Governments of Europe, Carried On in the Secret Meetings of Freemasons, Illuminati, and Reading Societies* also outlined the plot of world domination being set in motion by the Illuminati, the Freemasons, and other secret societies.

Although neither Robison nor Barruel attacked Jews or even made any mention of them, in 1806 Barruel received a letter from J. B. Simonini, who claimed to have discovered an ancient, wealthy, and powerful sect of Jews who had confessed to him that they had formed the Illuminati and the Freemasons. Their next coup would be to install a Jewish pope, gain control of the Catholic Church, then begin to seize all the monarchies and nations of the world.

Whether or not Barruel took seriously the fanciful notion of an ancient Jewish cabal controlling the world's secret societies, a former official in the Prussian postal service, Hermann Goedsche, thought the idea of a worldwide Jewish conspiracy would provide an interesting chapter in his novel *Biarritz* (1868), published under his pen name, Sir John Retcliffe. In the chapter entitled "In the Jewish Cemetery in Prague," the author spun a tale of how every hundred years the elders of the twelve tribes of Israel gather at the graveside of the most senior rabbi and tell Satan of their plot to enslave the Gentile world.

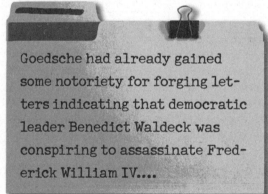

Goedsche had already gained some notoriety for forging letters indicating that democratic leader Benedict Waldeck was conspiring to assassinate Frederick William IV....

Goedsche had already gained some notoriety for forging letters indicating that democratic leader Benedict Waldeck was conspiring to assassinate Frederick William IV, the king of Prussia. Goedsche's plot was discovered and he was dismissed from the postal service. From writing forgeries to writing fiction was not a great expansion of his abilities. However well the novel *Biarritz* may have been received, in 1872 the single chapter about the heads of the twelve tribes of Israel meeting with Satan in a Prague graveyard was excerpted from the

context of the novel and reprinted in Russia as a pamphlet based on fact. In 1881 the French paper *Le Contemporain* reprinted the story as fact supposedly reported by an English diplomat, Sir John Radcliff (adapting Goedsche's pen name), who planned a full-length book on the secret meeting entitled *Annals of the Political and Historic Events of the Last Ten Years.*

In 1891 the same tale, with some modifications, appeared in the Russian newspaper *Novorossiysky Telegraf*, which purported that the work was based on a speech made in 1869 by a rabbi to a secret Sanhedrin. By 1900 this "speech" was being used to justify pogroms against the Jews. In 1903, in Kishinev in the Ukraine, forty-five Jews were killed, four hundred were injured, and 1,300 Jewish homes and businesses were destroyed.

The Protocols of the Learned Elders of Zion was first published in Russia in 1903 and consists of twenty-four chapters and 1,200 pages. The work alleges to be a series of lectures in which a member of the secret Jewish world government (the Elders of Zion) reveals the plan for world domination. Representative titles among the twenty-four separate "protocols" include "Materialism Replaces Religion," "World-Wide Wars," "Control of the Press," "Arrest of Opponents," and "Power of Gold."

The work was well used by the tsar's secret police not only to justify a pogrom against all Jews but, just prior to the Russian Revolution, to enlarge the circle of violence against all revolutionaries. The *Protocols* soon spread to Germany, where the people were already beginning to blame their defeat in World War I on the Jewish bankers. Within another decade the Nazi party would embrace the stereotypes and lies in *Protocols* as absolute truth and as justification for igniting the Holocaust.

The *Protocols* was translated into an English-language edition by Victor Marsden of the *Morning Post* in London, and copies of the book were distributed in the U.S. by Boris Brasol, a former Tsarist prosecutor. In his introduction to the book Marsden warned that the Jews were creating wars and revolutions in order to destroy the white Gentile race, so "that the Jews may seize the power during the resulting chaos and rule with their claimed superior intelligence over the remaining races of the world."

The auto magnate Henry Ford's newspaper the *Dearborn Independent* published an American version of the book from May to September of 1920 in a series entitled "The International Jew: The World's Foremost Problem." Later the columns were published in book form with half a million copies in circulation in the United States.

In August 1921 the *New York Times* ran editorials by Phillip Graves of the *Times* of London, who exposed the *Protocols* as a plagiarism of a rare French political satire, *Dialogues in Hell between Machiavelli and Montesquieu* (also known as *Dialogues of Geneva*), written by Maurice Joly in 1864. The pamphlet is a criticism of Napoleon III imagined as a conversation between Montesquieu, representing liberalism, and Machiavelli, representing autocracy and a thinly veiled satirical portrait of Napoleon (who was deposed in 1871). Joly, an attorney, had the pamphlet published in Belgium, then smuggled it over the French border. Police seized and confiscated as many copies as they could, then managed to trace the authorship to Joly, who was tried in 1865 and imprisoned for fifteen months. As Graves pointed out, over 160 passages from the *Protocols*—nearly half the text—are very similar to ones found in Joly's book. Some sections of the *Protocols* are nearly word for word from the French attorney's imagined dialogue between representatives of two opposing political ideologies. As Graves noted, the principal differences are the change of time reference from the past to the future and the fact that Joly does not mention Jews in his pamphlet.

As it turns out, additional research indicates that Joly himself appears to have plagiarized a large amount of text from a popular novel by Eugene Sue, *The Mysteries of Paris* (1843). In Sue's novel the hellish plotters are Jesuits, and there is no mention of any Jewish conspiracy. Interestingly, Sue's well-known novel *The Wandering Jew* (1844) is not about Jews either.

The *Protocols of the Learned Elders of Zion,* it would seem, is an amalgam of plagiarized political pamphlets, fictional documents, and various inflammatory works—many of which in their original context did not even concern themselves with Jews but were attacks on Jesuits.

On June 26, 2005, Joseph Weinstein, who identified himself as Jewish, wrote "'Protocols of Zion'—A Non-Zionist Jewish Perspective" as a letter to the editor of the Rense.com website. Weinstein asserts that at this stage of history, it doesn't really matter who wrote the *Protocols*; what matters, according to him, is that they appear to be "the key to understanding the current collapse of our civilization." Weinstein states that even after reading the *Protocols* as many as ten times, he always comes away amazed at how the strategies outlined in the work are "slowly confiscating our properties, eroding our economies, and the civil rights of the populations in western countries." He comments that it is "mind-bogglingly awesome" to consider that a very small Zionist group has succeeded so well in "replacing, controlling or seriously influencing most of the political, military and intelligence leadership of western countries." But if, indeed, such a very small, very wealthy, very powerful group of Zionist Jews have been able to implement nearly every one of the *Protocols,* says Weinstein, they have managed to accomplish this "behind the backs and without the knowledge of 99% of we Jews."

PSYCHEDELICS AND THE CIA

While the counterculture was taking LSD, tuning in, and dropping out, the CIA was experimenting with psychedelics as the weapons of future warfare.

Throughout all of humankind's history on the planet, certain mushrooms, extracts from cacti, various roots and herbs, and other unlikely substances have been chewed and ingested, not for the purpose of sustaining life, but for the physiological and psychological effects they have on the body and the brain. Cults of mystical expression have grown up around the use of these mind-altering substances, for many shamans and priests believed that they could open portals to higher planes of consciousness and even to other worlds by ingesting certain plants. The ancient Greeks held the mushroom sacred, and some contemporary researchers have postulated that the famed Oracle at Delphi may have ingested some form of psychedelic drug.

Such drugs as mescaline (from the peyote cactus) and the so-called magic mushrooms came to be known as "psychedelic" because they cause people to hallucinate, to see and hear things that are not really there. Dr. Humphrey Osmond began studying hallucinogens at a hospital in Saskatchewan in 1952 when he was examining the similarities between mescaline and the adrenaline molecule, and it was he who coined the word *psychedelic* to describe the effects of mind-altering drugs.

While serious medical researchers in the early 1950s focused on psychedelics for purposes of learning more about the human brain, relieving pain, finding antidotes to drug overdoses, and other medical applications, the Central Intelligence Agency could not have cared less about those high-minded purposes. The Agency wanted a drug that would promote effective interrogations. They had already experimented with barbiturates, peyote, marijuana, and hypnosis in an effort to find something that really worked without any fuss or muss when it came time to refresh stubborn memories and loosen tongues.

On May 2, 1938, Dr. Albert Hofmann of the Sandoz Research Laboratories in Basel, Switzerland, first synthesized lysergic acid diethylamide (LSD). On April 19, 1943, five years after synthesizing the drug, Hofmann accidentally inhaled a minute quantity while working with other ergot derivatives and experienced a pleasant feeling of inebriation, which consisted of hallucinations that lasted for several hours. Lysergic acid is found naturally in ergot, a fungus that grows on rye and other grains, and throughout history it has been used in various medications. Some researchers have even attributed ingestion of ergot to hallucinations which in the Middle Ages may have caused people to believe that they could fly through the air like witches or transform themselves into werewolves.

During the twenty years following World War II, LSD was used to study brain chemistry and in experimental treatment of patients with schizophrenia and other mental disorders, as well as cancer patients and alcoholics. LSD was found to create such primary effects as the following:

1. a feeling of being one with the universe;

2. recognition of two identities;

3. a change in the usual concept of self;

4. new perceptions of space and time;

5. heightened sensory perceptions;

6. a feeling that one has been touched by a profound understanding of religion or philosophy;

7. a gamut of rapidly changing emotions;

8. increased sensitivity for the feelings of others;

9. psychotic changes, such as illusions, hallucinations, paranoid delusions, and severe anxiety.

In the 1950s and '60s, while LSD was being hailed by some individuals as "mind-expanding" and by others as a recreational drug that could be exploited for fast "trips" to "far-out" places, the CIA rejoiced that it now possessed a chemical that was more effective than hypnosis, marijuana, peyote, or any other drug—effective beyond their wildest dreams—although not so much for interrogation as for humiliation.

In their *Acid Dreams: The CIA, LSD, and the Sixties Rebellion,* Martin A. Lee and Bruce Shlain write that CIA director Richard Helms saw in LSD the potential to induce temporary insanity in target individuals, causing them to behave in a manner that would discredit them and any information that they might wish to disseminate. To be certain of the drug's effectiveness, Dr. Sidney Gottlieb ordered agents to test LSD on themselves. According to Lee and Shlain, agents would surreptitiously slip the drug into each other's drinks. As soon as the target ingested the LSD, his colleague would inform him so he would take the rest of the day "to turn on, tune in, and drop out."

Frank Olson worked for the CIA at Fort Detrick, Maryland, studying the use of LSD to enhance interrogations. In the autumn of 1953 Olson went to Europe to observe the interrogation of former Nazis and Soviet citizens at a secret U.S. base. In late November he joined a group of government officials at a conference at Deep Creek Lodge in western Maryland. It was here that he was unknowingly slipped LSD in his drink. Olson began acting strangely withdrawn and told his wife and son that he was going to quit his job. Early in the morning of November 29, he went through the window of his room at the Statler Hotel in New York.

Once he had assessed the power of LSD on CIA agents, including the expendable Dr. Olson, Dr. Gottlieb, the director of the top-secret MK-ULTRA, decided to test the "acid" on an unsuspecting civilian population. MK-ULTRA set up Operation Midnight Climax and used drug-addicted prostitutes to pick up men at bars and slip LSD into their drinks.

In 1963 Dr. Timothy Leary and Dr. Richard Alpert were discharged from their positions at Harvard University for their enthusiasm in advocating the mind-expanding properties of LSD. Undaunted, the two went on to establish a number of colonies of their International Federation of Internal Freedom. Throughout most of the 1960s Leary was the primary and best-known prophet of the LSD movement, the counterculture guru who urged the flower children to "tune in, turn on, drop out." Leary predicted that by 1970 as many as 30 million persons, most of them young, would have embarked on voyages of discovery through the limitless inner space of their own minds. According to Leary, these voyagers would return much wiser and much more loving than when they began the trip. According to FBI documents on the Internet, Leary became older and wiser and informed on friends and followers in order to get out of prison early.

On May 2, 1938, Dr. Albert Hofmann of the Sandoz Research Laboratories in Basel, Switzerland, first synthesized lysergic acid diethylamide (LSD).

One of the students at Harvard who agreed to participate in a "psychological experiment" with LSD was Theodore Kaczynski, who would later gain notoriety as the Unabomber. The professor in charge of these CIA-sponsored experiments was Dr. Henry Murray, who had served with the OSS in World War II. Murray urged Gottlieb to continue certain experiments in mind control using hallucinogenic drugs that the Nazis had conducted in the concentration camps with prisoners as unknowing victims. One has to wonder if the long-term effects of LSD transformed Kaczynski from guinea pig to mad bomber—and how many other participants of Dr. Murray's experiments have exploded into seemingly unprovoked and unplanned acts of violence.

In 1966 the investigational drug branch of the Food and Drug Administration, distinguished four stages of LSD action:

1. initial, lasting for about thirty to forty-five minutes after oral ingestion of 100 to 150 micrograms of LSD, producing slight nausea, some anxiety, dilation of pupils;

2. hallucinations, associated with significant alteration of consciousness (confused states, dreamlike revivals of past traumatic events or childhood memories), distortion of time and space perspective, anxiety, autistic withdrawal, alteration of personality, impairment of conscience lasting from 1 to 8 hours;

3. recovery, lasting for several hours and consisting of feelings of normality alternating with sensations of abnormality;

4. aftermath, consisting of fatigue and tension during the following day.

The FDA noted that extended use of the drug could lead to mood swings, including depression, which could in turn lead to suicide. Time and space distortions could present obvious traffic dangers. A sudden onset of hallucinations could endanger the users and those with them.

It was such effects as these that convinced Maj. Gen. William Creasy, chief officer of the Army Chemical Corps, that LSD and other psychoactive drugs would be the weapons of the future. If CIA agents or Special Forces units spiked a city's water supply with LSD, the enemies within would offer no resistance. Creasy admitted to journalists who questioned his views of a chemical invasion that the prospect of driving people insane for a few hours was not particularly pleasant, but he shrugged off this negative aspect, noting that war was never pleasant.

Some conspiracy theorists assert that when a CIA plan to send clouds of psycho-chemical weapons over major U.S. cities to test their effectiveness was denied, they settled for making as much LSD as possible available to the youth counterculture. In the late 1960s the growing use of psychedelics by the "hippies" and those who felt alienated from mainstream American society because of their anti–Vietnam War sentiments contributed to a growing traffic in illegal distribution of the drugs on the street corners and dark alleys of cities throughout the United States.

While a secret group within the government was making LSD available to rebels and war protesters, others were arguing that the unpredictable effects of such drugs as LSD, mescaline, and psilocybin necessitated legislation to curb their use. In 1970 the U.S. Controlled Substances Act made open distribution of such mind-altering substances illegal. Since that time, however, the FDA has allowed projects by medical researchers to continue to explore the potential of psychedelics, explaining that the Controlled Substances Act was never intended to hinder legitimate research, only the misuse and abuse of the drugs.

During the 1990s researchers reported medical promise for psychedelic drugs in treating alcoholism and addiction to pain medications, and in alleviating pain in cancer patients. Because the drugs are now classified as controlled substances, research scientists must apply to the Drug Enforcement Administration for a permit and file an application with the National Institute on Drug Abuse and the FDA. Of course such restrictions do not hinder the secret government from utilizing LSD in any manner that will serve the New World Order best.

PSYCHIC SPIES

The CIA spent over $20 million training remote viewers to keep a "psychic eye" on Soviet military projects.

Some U.S. taxpayers were outraged when they learned that the CIA had spent a million dollars a year for twenty years hiring psychics to spy on the Soviets. According to scientists at the Stanford Research Institute (SRI) in Palo Alto, California, where the research began in 1972, NASA, the air force, the navy, and the CIA chipped in to supply the budget for psychic spies mentally keeping tabs on Soviet military projects. Russell Targ, one of the directors of the research, said that the psychics were able to achieve remarkable results that he as a physicist would not have believed if he had not witnessed them himself.

In one instance, Pat Price, a former Burbank, California, police commissioner, sat in the Palo Alto laboratory and gave CIA officers the details of some of the equipment at a Soviet "Star Wars" weapon factory. To check out Price's "controlled remote viewing" (CRV) abilities, the CIA directed a spy satellite to photograph the site. High-resolution photographs revealed the equipment that Price had seen but which no one in American intelligence had known existed. Price also described some equipment that the spy satellite was unable to photograph. Three years later, on-ground intelligence operatives confirmed Price's psychic description as being right on target.

In another display of his psychic prowess, Price pinpointed the location of a Soviet bomber that had gone down in a jungle so dense that intensive aerial searches had failed to located it. Based on Price's directions, a CIA team was able to remove electronic equipment and secret codes from the downed aircraft.

Dr. David Morehouse, a former army Ranger officer and CIA operative, and himself a remote viewer, said that the SRI gathered together all the major psychics for whom they could get temporary security clearances and whom they could afford and began to explore whether so-called psychic talent could be controlled.

It became the assignment of the well-known New York artist-psychic-sensitive Ingo Swann to develop the parameters of controlled remote viewing into a rigid discipline. Swann came to SRI in June 1972 and began working with Targ and Dr. Harold "Hal" Puthoff. In October Swann's ability with clairvoyance so impressed two CIA agents that they set up an eight-month pilot program. When his contract with the CIA expired, Swann left SRI in August 1973, but he returned in the fall of 1974 as a consultant. In the late 1970s Swann developed a strict remote-viewing protocol that was used to train new recruits.

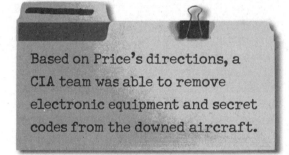

Based on Price's directions, a CIA team was able to remove electronic equipment and secret codes from the downed aircraft.

"The protocol was turned over to the Defense Intelligence Agency in 1982," Morehouse told reporter Elizabeth Nickson. "It was born in a bed of science, managed and governed in a bed of science, and it was used as an intelligence collection technology, with the understanding that it was not 100% accurate, recognizing that it never will be 100% accurate, recognizing that no other intelligence collecting methodologies are 100% accurate." According to Morehouse, remote viewing was simply one more method of gathering the pieces of a puzzle.

In time, a proven stable of remote viewers was established. In test after test, the psychics viewed secret installations worldwide, read documents in locked safes, and witnessed events that took place behind closed doors.

In 1983 Swann, working with Puthoff, believed that he had been able to develop an accurate model of how the collective unconscious communicates information to conscious awareness. The ability to employ extrasensory abilities, such as remote viewing, Swann maintained, is akin to language, an innate human faculty, but like language it must be learned to be effective. Theoretically, according to Swann's insight, anyone should be able to be trained to produce accurate, detailed target data.

According to Lyn Buchanan, one of the remote viewers who worked with Army Intelligence and the CIA, CRV develops communication between the conscious and the subconscious minds. The subconscious relays information on a "target," prompting the hand of the remote viewer to begin to make symbols representing the objective on sheets of paper. The remote viewer does not enter a trance state but remains wide awake, yet he or she experiences insights, emotions, and mental impressions of the target. In one sense, the remote viewer bilocates—that is, exists in two places at once.

Buchanan told reporter Michael Shinabery that he had always felt that there was another project, buried deeper than the one in which the remote viewers participated. Fueling Buchanan's suspicions is a description of Pat Price's final hours. Price was one of the very best viewers and one of the most reliable, and Hal Puthoff was having dinner with him the evening that Price died. According to Buchanan:

> Hal had gone to the bathroom, come back, and there was Pat Price lying face down on the table, dead. Puthoff quietly summoned a waiter, who pushed through the kitchen door to call for an ambulance. Almost immediately, as the doors swung back the other way, attendants came in, went over to the table, got Pat Price, took him through the kitchen and out the back and put him in an ambulance. They refused to allow Puthoff to accompany Price to the hospital.

Puthoff looked on the side of the vehicle, and there was no hospital, no ambulance service name. It was just a solid white truck.

Pat Price's body was never found. The question on many people's minds is whether Pat Price is dead or not.

For twenty-three years, the CIA, the Defense Intelligence Agency, and other government groups studied ways in which CRV might be utilized to collect intelligence on a dependable basis. The CIA disbanded and declassified the project in December 1995, when a government-funded, two-person panel evaluated the program and concluded that it did not have any great value in intelligence operations. A number of the remote viewers have since gone on to teach CRV to private individuals.

Skeptic Ray Hyman, professor emeritus in psychology at the University of Oregon, has commented that he didn't see any science at work in the SRI program in remote viewing, only guesswork. And even if CRV worked some of the time, Hyman said, it was too erratic to be dependable.

On the other hand, is Pat Price dead—or is he heading up an even more secret group of remote viewers than the one headed by Puthoff and Targ at SRI during the 1970s and '80s?

PSYWAR

You can run, but you cannot hide from psychotronic weapons.

It is well known that strobe lights can trigger epileptic-type seizures.

Even the pulsating lights from television cartoons and other programming have prompted seizures and made both children and adults become ill. The human sensory receivers are extremely susceptible to disturbances in the electromagnetic and sonic spectrums that are ordinary and usual aspects of our environment. If some nation or agency were to focus an attack on the human sensory apparatus of a population by directing weapons that utilized microwaves, lasers, and acoustics, the victimized people would soon capitulate.

A quotation attributed to Major I. Chernishev of the Russian army has circulated widely on the Internet. "It is completely clear," according to the major, "that the state which is first to create such weapons will achieve incomparable superiority." The weapons to which Major Chernishev refers are psychotronic instruments designed to introduce subliminal messages or to alter the body's psychological and data-processing capabilities. Using electromagnetic, vortex, or acoustical energy waves, such weapons would introduce to the minds of its human victims impulses or data that would confuse and in extreme cases completely incapacitate the internal signals that normally keep the body in balance. As yet, there are no defenses against psychotronic weaponry. As some intelligence experts have observed, computers can be protected by a firewall, but the human mind cannot.

The psychotronic instruments of warfare that are being developed at the present time including the following:

- Russian Virus 666, a computer virus that creates a visual combination of colors which can place computer operators in a trance state and inject thoughts into their subconscious. In some cases, Virus 666 can cause arrhythmia of the heart.

- Acoustic rifles that can vibrate the internal organs of human targets, stunning or nauseating the victims. At high power and close range it can knock a person down with a shock wave or cause the enemy's inner organs to spasm and induce great pain. At longer range, the acoustic or sonic frequencies can cause the hair cells in the inner ear to vibrate so rapidly that the enemy is incapacitated due to vertigo and nausea. The sonic waves of such rifles can penetrate buildings.

- Microwave rifles that can heat up the body of an enemy and induce epilepsy-like seizures or cause cardiac arrest.

- The Black Widow, a pulse wave weapon that can affect the signal from the motor cortex of the enemy's brain and cause uncontrollable, involuntary muscle spasms.

- An interrogation psychotronic device that can remove information stored in a person's brain, send it to a computer for modification, then reinsert it into the brain so that the interrogators can control the subject.

- Psychotronic generators that can be directed toward large populations and cause mass hallucinations, sickness, zombielike states, and even death.

- Ultrasound generators capable of performing bloodless surgeries—or assassinations—without leaving a mark on the skin.

- In 2007, Major-General Boris Ratnikov of the Russian Federal Custodial Service admitted that work continued on the creation of a psychotronic weapon that could make normal individuals become muddle-headed zombies at a distance of hundreds of miles. Russia, Major-General Ratnikov said, had been working on the effects of a psychotropic impact on humans since the 1920s. After the break-up of the Soviet Union, twenty centers working on such weapons were said to be closed, but work continued in secret laboratories. In less than a decade, Ratnikov said, psychotronic devices would be more dangerous than nuclear weapons.

- In July 2009, North Korea was rumored to have created a super Electromagnetic Pulse (EMP) that would be capable of knocking out the electric grid of the lower forty-eight states if it were to be utilized against the United States.

- In late October 2011, Spanish authorities likely tested a new EMP weapon—developed during the Iraq war—on the unsuspecting citizens of a city south of Malaga, Spain. For one hour, no mobile phones within 500 meters of the police station would work. In addition, no cars within that area could be made to start, and all television signals were knocked out. During the duration of the test, thousands of unsuspecting Spanish inhabitants of the city had their normal lives completely disrupted.

R

RAELIANS

This UFO cult claims to be cloning people under the directive of the Elohim, the extraterrestrial creators of humans on Earth.

In July 2001 the Raelian Movement made headlines around the world when one of its members, Brigitte Boisselier, a forty-four-year-old scientist with doctorates from universities in Dijon and Houston, announced that Clonaid, her team of four doctors and a technician, would soon produce the first human clone. Defying opposition from President George W. Bush, Congress, Secretary of Health Tommy Thompson, and the Food and Drug Administration, Boisselier refused to disclose the location of Clonaid's two laboratories, other than to state that one was in the United States and the other abroad. Clonaid, established by Ra'l in 1997, is funded in part by $500,000 from an anonymous couple who want a child cloned from the DNA of their deceased ten-month-old son. Ra'l states that such cloning will demonstrate the methods employed by the Elohim in their creation of the human species.

So who is Ra'l?

Claude Vorilhon, a French sports journalist and former race-car driver, claims to have been contacted by an extraterrestrial being while climbing the Puy de Lassolas volcanic crater near Clermont-Ferrand, France, on December 13, 1973. Vorilhon was astonished when he saw a metallic-looking object in the shape of a flattened bell about thirty feet in diameter descend from the sky. A door opened in the side of the craft, and what appeared to be a humanlike being about four feet in height emerged in a peaceful manner. Vorilhon soon learned that the being was a member of the Elohim referred to in the creation story in Genesis, the "gods" who made humans in their own image; they did this, according to Vorilhon, by utilizing deoxyribonucleic acid—DNA.

Vorilhon was told that the Elohim had sent great prophets, such as Moses, Ezekiel, Buddha, and Muhammad to guide humankind. Jesus, the fruit of a union between the Elohim and Mary, a daughter of man, was given the mission of making the Elohims' messages of guidance known throughout the world in anticipation of the Age of Apocalypse—which in the original Greek meant "age of revelation," not

A group of Raelians work on sand drawings at a Madellin, Colombia, retreat in 2007. Raelians believe that humans are the creation of the extraterrestrial Elohim.

"end of the world." In this epoch, which the people of Earth entered in 1945, humankind will at last be able to understand scientifically that which the Elohim accomplished eons ago in the Genesis story.

Vorilhon said that the Elohim renamed him "Ra'l," which means "the man who brings light." Shortly after his encounter with the extraterrestrial, he created the Raelian Movement, which soon acquired over a thousand members in France. Today, according to figures produced by the Raelians, their membership includes 55,000 individuals in eighty-five different countries.

Ra'l maintains that he established the Raelian Movement according to instructions given to him by the Elohim. Its aims are to inform humankind of the reality of the Elohim "without convincing," to establish an embassy where the Elohim will be welcome, and to help prepare a human society adapted to the future. In the years since his first contact experience, he has written a number of books, which can be obtained directly from the Raelians. The titles include *The Message Given by Extraterrestrials* and *Let's Welcome Our Fathers from Space.*

RONALD REAGAN, ATTEMPTED ASSASSINATION OF

It has been often said that truth is stranger than fiction. If you were to write a screenplay about a kook who wants to assassinate the president of the United States to impress an actress he doesn't have a snowball's chance in hell of meeting, and then you had the kook's older brother planning a dinner date with one of the vice president's sons on the same day as the attempted assassination, what do you think any potential producers or directors would say when they read your script? After they stopped laughing, that is.

About 2:30 in the afternoon of March 30, 1981, John Warnock Hinckley Jr. fired six bullets from a Rohn R6-14 .22 revolver into the cluster of Secret Service agents and dignitaries surrounding President Ronald Reagan as he left the Washington, D.C., Hilton Hotel after making a speech. Before his bodyguards could push Reagan into the armored sedan awaiting him, one of the six slugs ricocheted off a fender, penetrated his armpit, and punctured his lung. The assassin's wildly fired bullets also struck Reagan's press secretary, James Brady, in the left temple, police officer Thomas Delahanty in the neck, and Secret Service agent Timothy J. McCarthy in the stomach.

On that same day, Scott Hinckley, John's older brother, had a dinner date at the Denver, Colorado, home of Neil Bush, son of Vice President George H. W. Bush. The Bushes and the Hinckleys had known each other for more than twenty years, starting when Bush and John Sr. were in the oil business together in Texas. The Hinckleys had made large contributions to the vice president's political campaign. Scott Hinckley was the vice president of his father's Vanderbilt Energy Corporation in Denver, and he had been invited to Neil

Bush's home as a date for a girlfriend of Sharon Bush, Neil's wife. The dinner was canceled when news of the attempted assassination reached Denver.

In news special reports aired and televised immediately after the shooting, some accounts stated that at least one shot had been fired from a hotel window above the president's limousine. Such news items immediately prompted claims that there had been a second shooter. As the video clip of the shooting was viewed again and again, it seemed unlikely that Reagan could have been hit from in front when the bulletproof door was opened between him and the assassin. Later news reports explained that a Secret Service agent had fired the shot reported in earlier accounts from his position on the hotel overhang. This supposed clarification only prompted speculation about the president's being shot by one of his own bodyguards.

In Martin Scorsese's 1976 film *Taxi Driver,* Robert DeNiro plays a mentally unstable Vietnam veteran, Travis Bickle, who drives a cab and fantasizes about a beautiful blonde who works at a political campaign headquarters. In his unbalanced state of mind, the taxi driver figures that his assassination of a presidential candidate would really make him somebody in the eyes of the world and of his fantasy object. As the film unfolds, he becomes increasingly depressed at the sleaze and degradation around him and anoints himself the defender of a teenaged prostitute, Iris, played by Jodie Foster. Bickle abandons the plan to kill the candidate, but there is a violent shootout in which he rescues Iris from her pimps.

John Hinckley Jr. claimed to have seen *Taxi Driver* more than a dozen times, and he became fixated on Jodie Foster and the idea of gaining fame through assassination. When he read that Foster had enrolled at Yale, he enrolled in a Yale writing course so that he could be near her. He left letters and poems in her campus mailbox, and he managed to have two telephone conversations with the actress, during which he assured her that he was not a dangerous individual.

It was probably in the fall of 1980 that the images from *Taxi Driver* and the unbalanced rage of Travis Bickle began to blend with Hinckley's confused mind to form a reality in which he would gain fame and win Jodie Foster's respect if he were to kill the president of the United States. Hinckley decided to stalk President Jimmy Carter and went to one of Carter's campaign appearances, but he left his gun collection—three pistols and two rifles—in his hotel room. When he followed Carter to Nashville, airport security detected handguns in his suitcase. Incredibly, Hinckley was fined $62.50 and released after five hours in custody.

Some conspiracy researchers believe that at this point the unstable young man was already on the radar of the Secret Service and that he might have been tapped by a shadow agency as a potential assassin. Investigations would effortlessly yield intelligence that Hinckley had stalked Senator Ted Kennedy as well as President Carter. Hinckley had a personal library full of books and articles on Sirhan Sirhan, Robert Kennedy's assassin, and on Arthur Bremer, the failed assassin of George Wallace. In October 1980 he had traveled to Nebraska and had attempted to contact the American Nazi Party. Since Hinckley was already seeing a psychiatrist and had been prescribed psychoactive drugs, it would have been a relatively simple matter to see that he received more powerful drugs and be placed on a program that would bring him under mind control by a shadow agency.

On March 29, 1981, Hinckley checked into Park Central Hotel in Washington. The next day, he wrote a letter to Jodie Foster detailing his intentions to assassinate President Reagan. Then he dosed himself heavily with Valium, left the hotel, and took a cab to the Washington Hilton to await the president and to make history.

A mug shot of John Hinckley Jr. after he tried to assassinate President Ronald Reagan in 1981.

Vice President Bush did fall briefly under a little cloud of suspicion that soon blew away. He was a member of Skull and Bones, the elite secret society of powerhouse overachievers and superstars of business. He had been director of the CIA, and it was rather common knowledge that he enjoyed the support of Agency insiders, who preferred their former chief to Reagan. But none of those activities or positions made him party to an attempted assassination on the commander in chief.

Hinckley was immediately arrested, and his trial began on May 4, 1982. After seven weeks of testimony and three days of jury deliberation, he was found not guilty by reason of insanity. Hinckley was placed in St. Elizabeth's Psychiatric Hospital in Washington, D.C., where he will remain indefinitely. In 1999 he was allowed supervised visits outside the grounds of the hospital, but these privileges were revoked when a book about

Jodie Foster was found hidden in his room. In December 2003 Hinckley was allowed to have unsupervised visits with his parents, and additional visits were allowed beginning in 2011.

WILHELM REICH

For refusing to obey a U.S. Pure Food and Drug Administration injunction to cease experimentation with cosmic "orgone" energy and UFOs, Wilhelm Reich was sentenced to prison, where, eight months later, he died.

The discoveries, harassment, trial, and final silencing of Wilhelm Reich stretched over some three decades. Many of Reich's scientific writings, including books that are considered classics in medicine, psychoanalysis, sociology, and natural science, were condemned by the Pure Food and Drug Administration.

Reich was born March 24, 1897, in imperial Austria. In 1918 he entered the University of Vienna, where hc completed the six-year course for a medical degree in four years, graduating in 1922. While still in medical school he attained membership in the Vienna Psychoanalytic Society under Professor Sigmund Freud.

Reich was acknowledged as a brilliant new light on the psychoanalytic horizon. From 1924 to 1930 he was the director of the Seminar for Psychoanalytic Therapy and first clinical assistant at Freud's Psychoanalytic Polyclinic in Vienna. In his early thirties, in addition to doing research into the social causation of neuroses, Reich founded and directed mental hygiene consultation centers in various districts in Vienna and Berlin. From 1934 to 1939 he lectured on biophysics at the Psychological Institute of the University of Oslo, Norway, and did research on his discovery of the biological and cosmic energy that he named "orgone" energy.

In August 1939 Reich transferred his laboratory to Forest Hills, New York, and moved to the United States. From 1939 to 1941 he was associate professor of medical psychology at the New School for Social Research, New York City. In 1942 he founded the Orgone Institute on a 280-acre estate in Rangeley, Maine. The home for the new science of orgonomy was appropriately named "Orgonon." Reich's students and friends established the Wilhelm Reich Foundation in Maine in 1949 to preserve his work and safeguard his discovery of the primordial, mass-free, cosmic orgone energy—the same energy Reich later claimed propels the UFOs that are visiting our planet.

As a young psychoanalyst, Reich searched for the energy (Freud called it "libido") behind the neurotic behavior of his patients. What is it, he asked, that moves a patient to feel and to express emotion? Through experimentation Reich discovered a bioelectrical charge at the skin surface of a human being during periods of pleasure, and he noted a diminution or absence of this charge during anxiety. Later experimentation convinced him that this energy is not electrical, but rather a specific biological, organismic energy (hence the name "orgone") that is the life energy per se.

Through years of careful investigation, Reich was able to demonstrate the existence of orgone energy in many ways and to concentrate the energy in his invention, the orgone-energy accumulator (1940). Reich demonstrated the existence of the cosmic orgone energy visually, thermically, electroscopically, by way of his "field meter," and with a Geiger counter. During the period of his greatest productivity, more than a score of top-ranking medical doctors and scientists in the United States and abroad published verification of his discoveries in scientific bulletins and journals. Even the great physicist Albert Einstein confirmed Reich's basic temperature experiment, objectifying the existence of the orgone energy in a letter to Reich dated February 7, 1941.

In 1950, with the advent of the Korean War, Reich prepared his laboratory to help in the war effort. At that time he worked out his famous Oranur Experiment, in which he investigated the possible antinuclear effects orgone energy might have on nuclear energy. The Oranur Experiment led Reich to the discovery of certain noxious "DOR" clouds (clouds containing "Deadly Orgone" energy), which he believed to be responsible for widespread planetary drought and desertification. Reich also concluded that UFOs were responsible for the "cosmic offal" contained in the typically black and nauseating DOR clouds, and that, in addition to planetary drought, DOR was causing worldwide disease epidemics.

Reich's search for a means to rid the skies over Orgonon of DOR clouds led to the invention of his "cloud-buster," with which he succeeded in producing and stopping rain. Subsequently, the cloud-buster became the "space gun" used on the fateful night when contact was made with extraterrestrial craft hovering over his laboratory.

According to Reich and his associates, this contact with luminous objects in the sky first took place on May 12, 1954, between 9:40 and 10:45 P.M. During this period, Reich contended, men on Earth saw, for the first time in history, two "Stars" to the west fade out several times when cosmic energy was drawn from them by means of the cloud-buster. The shock of this experience on Reich and his staff was so great that they did not attempt to repeat such action until October 10, 1954. The reason for their hesitation was fear that they might precipitate an interplanetary war by their experimentation.

In an injunction dated March 19, 1954, and signed by John D. Clifford Jr., federal district judge for the District of Maine, the Pure Food and Drug Administration claimed that orgone energy did not exist. In brief, the FDA injunction implied that Reich was little more than a quack, that he claimed he could cure all kinds

Psychologist Wilhelm Reich was a promising scholar in his field, but after establishing the Orgone Institute in Maine and experimenting with "orgone energy," he was charged by the Food and Drug Administration with violating health codes and imprisoned.

of diseases, from cancer to the common cold, and that the public should be protected from his nefarious schemes. Among the many publications by Reich listed in the injunction as dealing with the "care, mitigation, prevention or treatment of disease conditions" were *The Mass Psychology of Fascism*; *The Sexual Revolution*; *Character Analysis*; and *The Murder of Christ*. Reich's defenders pointed out that none of these books claims to cure anything.

From the first, Reich's position was that of an eminent and responsible scientific researcher who believed that matters of science belong in a laboratory, not a courtroom. At no time, either before, during, or after the trial, did the FDA provide any scientific evidence to contradict the findings of either Reich or his associates. The agency persisted, however,

and finally won the case by default when Reich refused to appear in court as a "defendant" in matters about which, he claimed, the FDA knew nothing.

Reich refused to obey the FDA injunction, which he termed unlawful and which he considered to have been obtained by fraud and deceit. He asserted that his research was too important to be stopped by procedures that had no basis In truth and fact. In his response to the injunction he wrote: "Scientific matters cannot possibly ever be decided upon in court. They can only be clarified by prolonged, faithful, bona-fide observations in friendly exchange of opinion, never by litigation. The sole purpose of the complainant is to entangle ergonomic basic research in endless costly legal procedures." Reich refused FDA agents access—ordered under the injunction—to his research files and notes, nor would he reveal his antigravity equations. Brought into court in chains, Reich then determined "to get the total infamy on the Court Records."

A very unusual aspect of the case against Reich was the fact that Peter Mills, the prosecuting attorney for the FDA, had been the attorney from 1949 to 1952 for the Wilhelm Reich Foundation, for the Orgone Institute, and for Reich personally. Mills was Reich's attorney at the time the Reich Foundation was incorporated, and it was Mills who drew up the incorporation papers. Mills had also notarized the papers attesting to the motive force of orgone energy, which Reich had hooked up to run a motor. As the incorporating counsel for the Wilhelm Reich Foundation, Mills had direct knowledge of and access to many of the foundation's confidential documents. In 1952 Mills severed his affiliation with the foundation and accepted employment as an attorney for the FDA.

Reich fought the charges as far as the law would permit. The U.S. Supreme Court, however, refused to review the case.

Reich believed that our planet is in deep trouble. It was this belief that drove him to fight to protect his life-positive discoveries and to get his ideas into the trial record. He told the court that humankind was facing an emergency that challenged the human species and the very principle of life on Earth. He warned that the planet was undergoing a process of deep and crucial change on biological, physical, emotional and cosmic levels, and he urged a stop to the petty quibbling that prevented scientists from fully examining the oncoming crisis.

The courts refused to take Reich's warnings seriously. Despite the fact that Reich informed the court that he had a severe heart condition and would surely die if imprisoned, he was found guilty and sent to jail, where he died eight months later. Thus humankind was left with Reich's legacy of discovery and with his grim warning regarding the advent of UFOs in our atmosphere.

The fiftieth anniversary of Reich's death was celebrated on November 15, 2007, with a major exhibit of the controversial scientist's work at the Jewish Museum in Vienna, the city where he began his work and studied under Sigmund Freud. In New Jersey, the American College of Orgonomy, which provides training for those physicians interested in Reich's legacy, scheduled a conference and a banquet. Later that month, nearly 300 boxes of Reich's unpublished manuscripts and papers were made available for the first time for examination at the Countway Library at Harvard Medical School. The release of these documents honored Reich's request that his scientific papers be opened fifty years after his death.

The formerly discredited scientist is now described by the American Psychoanalytic Association as the first therapist to emphasize character analysis rather than neurotic symptoms. Reich was also a pioneer in linking a healthy sex life, which he defined as "orgiastic potency," to emotional well-being. The scientist who died in prison damned as a fraud was now hailed as "one of the most brilliant, creative, and controversial of the pioneering analysts."

THE RESTORATION OF THE TEN COMMANDMENTS

Beware of cults that throw "going away" parties to heaven.

On March 15, 2000, Credonia Mwerinde and Joseph Kibwetere, leaders of the cult of The Restoration of the Ten Commandments, hosted a great party for certain of their followers in the town of Kanungu, Uganda, roasting three bulls and providing seventy crates of soft drinks for their members' indulgence. Before they left for the celebration, many of the cultists told family members that they would not be coming back home, for after the party ended, they were going to the holy land. Later that evening, over one thousand members of the cult were either poisoned or otherwise murdered, doused with sulphuric acid, and set on fire.

The cult of The Restoration of the Ten Commandments had its origins in the late 1970s when a group of schoolchildren claimed to have received visions of the Virgin Mary on a soccer field in the town of Kibeho, Rwanda. A cult of the Virgin was formed, combining Roman Catholicism with aboriginal religious traditions, and spread to southwest Uganda. It was here, in 1984, that Credonia Mwerinde, a former store proprietor and brewer of banana beer, said that the Virgin Mary appeared to her for the first time.

In 1989 Credonia met with Joseph Kibwetere, a school administrator and politician who was active in the Catholic Church, and informed him that she had been instructed to seek his aid in spreading the Virgin's message that people must restore value to the Ten Commandments if they were to escape damnation at the end of the world. According to Mwerinde's visions, Judgment Day was fast approaching. The world would end on December 31, 1999.

The message of Mary as delivered by Mwerinde and Kibwetere proved to be spellbinding to thousands of men and women in Uganda. The two were filled with the Holy Spirit and seemed to possess supernatural powers. Kibwetere was a charismatic preacher, and Mwerinde quickly established herself as the enforcer and disciplinarian of the cult. The rules for the group were outlined in a pamphlet entitled *A Timely Message from Heaven* (1991), dictated by the Virgin Mary through Mwerinde, and were extremely strict. The cult members were forbidden to communicate other than through sign language. They must labor in the fields to grow their own food, and they must fast regularly. On Mondays and Fridays they were allowed only one meal. Soap was forbidden as a sinful indulgence.

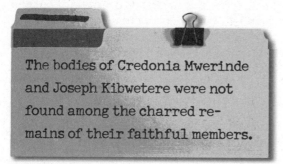

The bodies of Credonia Mwerinde and Joseph Kibwetere were not found among the charred remains of their faithful members.

There were also members of the Roman Catholic clergy who were attracted to Mwerinde's channeled messages from the Virgin Mary, and who agreed that the church could use reforming. Father Paul Ikazire and Father Dominic Kataribabo joined the cult in protest to what they regarded as the church's failure to fulfill crucial obligations to its faithful. Soon membership in the cult had reached five thousand.

When January 1, 2000, dawned and the world was still in existence, dissension began to grow in the ranks of the cult. Because they had been commanded to sell their property and belongings and give all proceeds to the cult, many of the dissatisfied members began to grumble that they wanted their money back. Others began to doubt the validity of the direct discourses that Credonia claimed came directly from the Virgin Mary.

Early in March, Mwerinde and Kibwetere announced that there would be a glorious and holy celebration that had been ordered by Mary. After a sacred feast, those specially chosen cultists would be taken directly to heaven.

The bodies of Credonia Mwerinde and Joseph Kibwetere were not found among the charred remains of their faithful members. A witness in Kanungu told police that he had caught sight of the two departing from the festivities with suitcases in hand and wondered at the time why they would leave before their party had ended.

RICO ACT

When Congress passed an act against racketeering, they should have foreseen that one little section of the legislation created an opening for unscrupulous attorneys to form rackets of their own.

In 1970, in an effort to stem organized crime's effect on the national economy, Congress passed the Racketeer Influenced and Corrupt Organization Act (RICO). "Organized crime" was a euphemism for the Mafia, and in essence RICO was created in order to destroy the power of the various Mafia "families" and to prevent them from gaining control over legitimate business enterprises. Throughout the 1970s RICO was seldom invoked except in the crackdown on the Mafia.

Then, in the 1980s, a number of civil attorneys took notice of the far-reaching implications of section 1964c of RICO. Taking into consideration the fact that certain individuals could be injured in their business or property by reason of a RICO violation, the framers of RICO decreed that any person who could establish a civil RICO claim would automatically receive judgment in the amount of three times the actual damages and would also be awarded attorney's fees and other costs that may have been incurred. Across the United States certain civil attorneys decided that RICO could bring them a financial windfall. Given an adroit spin, any number of civil claims, such as for fraud, breach of contract, or product defect, could be interpreted as RICO violations. In addition, when Congress passed the law, it included wire and mail fraud as criminal acts on which a RICO claim could be brought. This was frosting on the cake for greedy civil attorneys, who had little difficulty in depicting almost any criminal deed as mail or wire fraud. By the end of the decade RICO was the most commonly asserted claim in federal court.

During the 1990s the federal courts and the U.S. Supreme Court severely limited the types of cases that could be brought under RICO in a civil context. Today civil litigants must pass many legal tests before they can expect to reap the financial rewards once available under RICO. Claims against the Mafia are seldom applied, but RICO can be brought against political protest groups, terrorist organizations, and businesses.

ROCKEFELLER FAMILY'S ALIEN CONSPIRACY

If the Brothers from Outer Space didn't want to land on the White House lawn, Laurance Rockefeller would have been happy to have greeted them at his country estate.

Who can doubt the global influence of the Rockefeller family? Beginning with the international corporate giant Standard Oil and spreading into the establishment of powerful supranational bodies such as the Trilateral Commission, the Council on Foreign Relations, and the Bilderberg Society, the Rockefeller name is known through the world. Respected television commentator Bill Moyers concluded after he spent fifteen days with David Rockefeller that there are "just about a dozen or fifteen individuals" who make "day-to-day decisions that regulated the flow of capital and goods throughout the entire world." In the multinational fraternity of individuals who shape the global economy and manage the flow of its capital, Moyers said, the Rockefeller family was born to it. What some critics see as a vast international conspiracy, the Rockefellers consider "just another day's work."

Well before the turn of the twentieth century, Standard Oil was perceived as a vast monopoly that would stop at nothing, including blackmail, bribery, and bombings to secure its power. In the 1920s John D. Rockefeller, the founder of the dynasty, funded the Eugenics Records Office with its concepts of "racial hygiene" and breeding better humans. The "science" of the Eugenic Records Office influenced Adolf Hitler and provided scientific legitimacy for Nazi race laws.

In more recent years, the Rockefellers have established numerous philanthropic organizations in an effort to appear to be a dynasty of benevolent benefactors, rather than a clan of robber barons. Critics point out that the Rockefellers' motives, although perhaps born of guilt, still seem paternalistic and designed to serve the pet schemes of the world ruling class. When word began leaking out that Laurance Rockefeller was distributing substantial sums of money to certain UFO researchers and fringe foundations, a number of conspiracy theorists felt that the reason for his investment was not so much that he truly believed in aliens as that he wanted to cover all the possibilities: if extraterrestrials were to invade Earth, he wanted to ensure that the Rockefellers would be treated well. Other theorists contended that as a member of the Illuminati and the New World Order, Laurance was helping the citizens of Earth prepare to meet the Olympians, the masters from outer space.

According to well-substantiated rumors, Laurance Rockefeller contributed money and influence to prevent Harvard from censuring Dr. John Mack for his research on alien abduction. Rockefeller supported Mack's Center for Psychology and Social Change in Cambridge, Massachusetts, from 1993 to 1995.

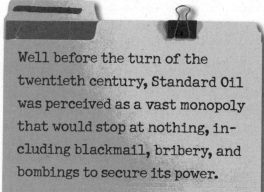

Well before the turn of the twentieth century, Standard Oil was perceived as a vast monopoly that would stop at nothing, including blackmail, bribery, and bombings to secure its power.

Laurance also funded the Green Earth Foundation, headed by Terence McKenna, who traveled the globe collecting psychoactive plants, which he was permitted to cultivate in Hawaii. McKenna theorized that aboriginal cultures have used these substances to induce a psychic link with extraterrestrials.

The Human Potential Foundation was primarily funded by Laurance Rockefeller, who encouraged its study of alternative religious and psychiatric/psychological paradigms. Similarly, Laurance cooperated closely with the BSW Foundation, headed by wealthy New Yorkers Sandra Wright Houghton and Bootsy Galbraith, who shared his belief that the ETs are benevolent and have come to help the human species ascend the evolutionary ladder more rapidly. Perhaps Laurance reasoned that those earthlings who believe that the aliens came from the stars with a noble mission would be chosen to be their ambas-

sadors on Earth. On the other hand, some observers maintain that Laurance Rockefeller's principal motive in sponsoring UFO research was to force the release of secret government information on the entities who were visiting Earth from space.

Author/UFO contactee Whitley Strieber believes that Laurance Rockefeller was a "champion of disclosure of UFO secrets who had the courage to put his money" into that cause. Strieber said that Rockefeller told him that he believed that the kind of UFO abduction that Strieber had experienced was a very real phenomenon, but that he was "unsure of their purpose or origin."

Laurance Rockefeller died on July 11, 2004, at the age of ninety-three, after a brief illness. The surviving Rockefeller family members have not made any comments about their interest in UFOs or in aliens—benevolent or otherwise.

ROMAN CATHOLIC CHURCH'S SEXUAL CONSPIRACY OF SILENCE

For centuries, the secret shame of sexual abuse of the most vulnerable members of their flocks by errant priests has been a dark cloud hanging over the Roman Catholic Church. Although it may be too late for thousands of victims to be able to feel any satisfaction, at last justice is being served.

On June 12, 2005, the *New York Times* carried an Associated Press release stating that sexual abuse by priests had cost the Roman Catholic Church in the United States more than $1 billion thus far in settlements and added that the cost would surely rise by millions of dollars because of hundreds of still-unsettled claims. According to the AP, at least $378 million had been spent in just three years after the conspiracy of silence was shattered in the Boston Archdiocese and spread like wildfire across the nation.

On October 12, 2005, the Roman Catholic Archdiocese of Los Angeles released information from the confidential files of 126 clergy accused of sexual abuse and admitted that for more than seventy-five years they had moved accused priests to new assignments, ignoring parishioners' complaints. The documents were released as part of settlement discussions with lawyers for more than five hundred accusers in a civil lawsuit.

The Rev. Thomas Doyle, a canon lawyer who has represented victims in their claims against the church, has said that he tried to warn various bishops as early as 1985 that abuse settlements could rise to over $1 billion. None of the church hierarchy believed him, and one archbishop assured Doyle that no one would ever sue the Catholic Church.

The fuse that ignited the firestorm of criticism against the church was the revelation that the Boston Archdiocese had shuffled Father John Geoghan from parish to parish, disregarding the many accusations that he was guilty of child abuse. In civil lawsuits, more than 130 individuals swore that Father Geoghan had sexually abused them as children during his thirty years as a priest in Boston-area parishes. When a judge ordered the release of archdiocesan files, the public was shocked to discover that dozens of priests accused of pedophilia had been shuttled to different unsuspecting parishes.

In 2001 Geoghan was sentenced to nine to ten years in prison, and in September 2002 the archdiocese settled with eighty-six of his victims for $10 million. On August 24, 2003, Geoghan, sixty-eight, was strangled to death by a fellow inmate, thirty-seven-year-old Joseph L. Druce.

The case of Father Paul R. Shanley might serve as a model of the Roman Catholic Church's cover-up of pedophilic priests that has been going on for centuries. Father Shanley, who would come to be reviled as a "marauding sociopath," a supporter of man-boy love, and a perverted monster, was also regarded by some parishioners as a devoted and compassionate priest. And herein lies the conflicted root of the dilemma—in many instances the priests with the sexual problems became part protector and part predator, demeaning the role of shepherd that is so devoutly, selflessly, and honorably enacted by the great majority of the Roman Catholic priesthood.

Father Shanley had himself been molested by a priest at age twelve but had never told a single member of his family, who had always considered Paul a very pious boy. After two years at Boston University, Shanley transferred to St. John's Seminary, also in Boston. It is somewhat disconcerting that of the seventy-seven graduates in his class of 1960, five priests have been publicly accused of sexually abusing children. In 1995 Father Shanley would state that he had been abused by a priest and a faculty member while at the seminary.

Two weeks after his ordination in 1960, Father Shanley was accused of sexually molesting an eleven-year-old boy in the Stoneham, Massachusetts, parish where he served as assistant pastor. Although the chief of police received several more complaints and condemned Father Shanley as a wolf in sheep's clothing, none of the families wanted to go public with a prosecution against a priest. One mother of an abused boy wrote to the pastor and to Cardinal Richard Cushing in Boston, but nothing came of her complaint.

Secretly Father Shanley continued to abuse boys, but publicly he became very outspoken regarding his views on homosexuality. In a 1970s interview with the *Catholic Reporter* he said that homosexuality and bisexuality were "normal and natural," and he disagreed with those who proclaimed sexual intercourse between members of the same sex to be pathological.

Father Shanley was not speaking for the traditionalists In the Roman Catholic Church, who regard marriage as a sacrament instituted by God wherein man and woman produce children in his image. Sexual love between a married man and woman creates a communion that gives birth to new life. Homosexuality is considered abnormal and unnatural, if not evil. In some of his public statements, Father Shanley seemed to be speaking on behalf of NAMBLA, the North American Man/Boy Love Association, especially when he parroted their party line by claiming that when an adult and a child have sex, it is the child who is the seducer.

By 1979 Cardinal Humberto Medeiros, leader of the Boston Archdiocese, had heard enough of such radical proclamations from Father Shanley, but without any further investigation, Medeiros appointed Shanley pastor at St. John's in Newton, Massachusetts.

While serving at St. John's in 1983, Father Shanley was accused of abusing two six-year-old boys. It was one of those offenses that, in May 2002, brought Shanley, seventy-one, to face charges of raping a six-year-old boy. Once he was charged with sexual abuse, more than thirty men came forward to make claims against him. In February 2005 he was found guilty of child rape and sentenced to twelve to fifteen years in prison.

At a Vatican meeting in April 2002 the cardinals agreed on a "zero tolerance" policy toward priests found guilty of even one act of sexual abuse of a minor. Critics of the gathering at the Apostolic Palace stated their concern that the cardinals had declared that the scandal of priests preying on children was primarily a homosexual issue. By so doing, the critics said, the church was avoiding the real issue of a religious culture of secrecy and repression that had existed for far too long.

For decades in America it has been no secret that Roman Catholic seminaries have been ordaining homosexuals as priests. Regardless of the hypocrisy involved—a church that condemns homosexuality ordaining homosexuals—many clerics have observed that if it were not so, the church would soon have no priests to serve its parishes. Some researchers have estimated that between 35 and 50 percent of Roman Catholic priests are homosexuals. If the church were suddenly to cease the ordination of homosexuals, it would have to allow married clergy or permit the ordination of women.

A growing number of traditional priests reemphasize the concept that celibacy is the true issue, rather than one's sexual preference. There are no statistics that there is a preponderance of homosexual child abusers in the church or in the larger society. Heterosexual child molesters undoubtedly make up a larger percentage of those with the illness of pedophilia. The command of the church is to practice discipline and self-control of the sexual impulse, which is as great a challenge for heterosexuals as it is for homosexuals. Psychotherapist A. W. Richard Sipe, a former Catholic priest, who conducted a twenty-five-year study of celibacy, sexuality, and the clergy, estimates that 50 percent of priests, regardless of their sexual preference, are sexually active in some way.

One answer to the diminishing number of heterosexual priests is the one Protestants adopted at the time of the Reformation in the sixteenth century: allow the clergy to marry.

Actually, the command for the priesthood to remain celibate has no basis in the Bible. Peter, the "rock" on whom the church is built, the disciple of Jesus that the church claims as its first pope, was a married man—and it is likely that the other apostles also had wives. Priests followed the examples of the rabbis, married, and had children for the first thousand years of Christianity. If one wishes to become slightly cynical, the reasons for the church's twelfth-century edict on celibacy was determined more by the greed of the political powers of the time than by any ecclesiastical verdict. The lords of the lands worried that the offspring of the clergy would inherit church property free from taxes, as well as church titles, and these nobles pressured and bribed the church to encourage celibacy among its priesthood. Even so, married priests did not vanish overnight— nor did popes who fathered children.

Women within the Catholic Church believe that Jesus's incarnation as a male does not deny them the opportunity to serve in his name. Die-hard Catholics insist that the priesthood of Jesus can only be manifested in a masculine body. But, adds George Weigel, the biographer of Pope John Paul II, a males-only priesthood takes nothing away from women, and he reminds his readers that "the highest, unsurpassable figure in the communion of saints, the first Christian is Mary, who is not a priest and who has higher powers." Weigel cautions that the issue of male vs. female priests "is a lot more complicated and interesting than contemporary gender politics would have you believe."

A *Newsweek* poll conducted in 2002 found that 50 percent of U.S. Roman Catholics admit that they are at odds with their church's teachings on human sexuality; 59 percent do not believe that refusing to ordain gays into the priesthood would reduce the problem of abuse; 51 percent say they would have no problem attending a church with an openly gay priest; 73 percent would be pleased to allow married men to become priests; 65 percent favor ordaining women.

There is little question that the Roman Catholic Church's conspiracy of silence regarding certain priests' predilection toward young boys has been going on for centuries. Researchers commissioned by Roman Catholic bishops found that more than 11,500 abuse claims have been filed against priests since 1950. In 2000, American bishops pledged to report any suspected abusers in their midst to

Catholic Bishop Robert Finn, shown here at the U.S. Conference of Catholic Bishops in 2011, was the highest ranking Church official to be indicted as a result of a cover-up involving priests and child pornography.

law enforcement authorities. In 2008, Bishop Robert W. Finn and the Diocese of Kansas City settled lawsuits with forty-seven plaintiffs in sexual abuse cases for ten million dollars and agreed to follow a list of nineteen preventative measures, among them the stipulation that he would immediately report any priest suspected a being a pedophile to law enforcement. In 2010, the Vatican issued a strong recommendation that such a policy be strictly followed by all bishops.

On October 14, 2011, for the first time in the twenty-five-year history of the Roman Catholic Church's sex abuse scandals, the leader of an American diocese was held criminally liable for the behavior of a priest under his supervision when Bishop Finn was indicted for failing to report abuse charges against Father Shawn Ratigan. Michael Hunter, director of the Kansas City chapter of the Survivors Network of Those Abused by Priests and himself a victim of sexual abuse by a priest, hailed Bishop Finn's indictment as a huge victory. If convicted, Bishop Finn could face a jail sentence of up to year and a fine of up to one thousand dollars. In addition, the diocese would face of fine of up to five thousand dollars.

Father Ratigan's unacceptable behavior with children was reported in May 2010 by the principal of a Catholic elementary school. In December 2010, a computer technician found hundreds of photographs of child pornography suggestive of child abuse on the priest's laptop. When Bishop Finn learned of the photographs, he ordered Father Ratigan to a convent with the admonition to cease all contact with minors. However, the priest continued to attend children's parties, and, with the bishop's approval, presided at a girl's first communion. After the filing of a civil lawsuit by one of the families of Father Ratigan's victims and a report criticizing Bishop Finn for being too trusting of the errant priest, the Rev. Ratigan attempted suicide. In December 2010, Bishop Finn admitted that he was aware of the lewd photographs that Rev. Ratigan had taken of young children.

Thus far, France has been the only country in which a bishop has been convicted for his failure to exercise proper supervision over a priest accused of child abuse.

In *The Changing Face of the Priesthood* (2000), Donald B. Cozzens quotes a second-century gospel commentary that admonishes priests: "Thou shalt not seduce young boys." Let us pray that the conspiracy of silence has ended and that the Church will be more solicitous toward its most innocent members— both young boys and girls—and its troubled and conflicted clergy.

ROSICRUCIANS

The most secret of secret societies, the Rosicrucians gained ancient wisdom that enabled them to create a science greatly in advance of their contemporaries in the fifteenth century.

Since the seventeenth century, rumors have credited the Rosicrucians with accomplishing the transmutation of metals, possessing the means of prolonging life, having the knowledge to see and to hear what is occurring in distant places, and enjoying the ability to detect secret and hidden objects. It has been alleged that the scientific apparatus discovered in the tomb of Christian Rosenkreuz (1378–1484), founder of the Brethren of the Rosy Cross, or Rosicrucians, would be considered common laboratory equipment for the 1960s but impossible for the fifteenth century. The secret society has intrigued people for centuries and presented a challenge for historians and conspiracy theorists.

The Rosicrucians (from the Latin *Rosae Crucis,* "Rose Cross") state that the Illumined Father and Brother Christian Rosenkreuz was a brilliant magus who at the age of sixteen gained secret wisdom teachings from the sages of Arabia and the Holy Land. When he returned to Germany around 1450, Rosenkreuz became a recluse, for he could see that Europe was not yet ready for the complete reformation he so yearned to present to it. For one thing, he had acquired the fabled philosopher's stone, which enabled him to produce all the gold and precious gems necessary to allow him to build a house where he could live peacefully and well. To share the power of the legendary stone of transmutation with the unwise, the worldly, and the greedy would be disastrous.

Quietly, Rosenkreuz accepted only a handful of students to whom he imparted the knowledge that he had acquired and the connections that he had made with the mystery schools and the esoteric teachings of great masters. Eventually there came to be eight brothers, counting Rosenkreuz himself. They swore to uphold the following precepts:

1. They would not profess any creed but the goal of healing the sick without reward.

2. They would affect no particular style of clothing.

3. They would meet once each year in the House of the Sainted Spirit.

4. Each brother would carefully choose his own successor.

5. The letters *R.C.* would serve as their only seal and character.

6. The brotherhood would remain secret for a hundred years.

Although Rosenkreuz was buried in secret when he died in 1484 at the age of 106, one of the brothers happened by chance to discover his burial chamber some years later and read, inscribed above the entrance, the promise that Rosenkreuz would return in 126 years. The discovery of the Illumined Father's prediction inspired the surviving brothers to work in earnest to spread his teachings throughout the world.

Between 1604 and 1616, the secret brotherhood released three manifestos in Germany. The pamphlets called upon the educated and influential to unite to bring about a reformation of the educational, moral, and scientific establishments of Europe. The manifestos also shared some startling assertions, among them:

1. The end of the world was near, but those who had become enlightened by the new reformation would be initiated into a higher consciousness.

2. New stars that had appeared in the constellations of Cygnus and Serpentarius predicted the destruction of the Roman Catholic Church.

Johannes Valentinus Andreae, was thought by some to be the same person as Christian Rosenkreuz, founder of the Rosicrucians.

3. The Illumined Father Christian Rosenkreuz had divined the secret code that God placed in the universe in the beginning of time.

4. The transmutation of base metals into gold and precious gems is a natural miracle that has been revealed to such magi as Christian Rosenkreuz.

5. The Rosicrucian Fellowship has wealth to distribute, but it does not wish a single coin from anyone.

The manifestos created great excitement in the Europe of the early 1600s. Royalty, common folk, merchants, mystics, alchemists—all clamored for more information about the mysterious secret brotherhood. Thousands of people wanted to become Rosicrucians, but no one knew where any of their lodges were. Desperate individuals placed letters of application to the fraternity in public places where they hoped the Rosicrucians might find them.

It wasn't long before unscrupulous opportunists began posing as members of the secret fraternity, but when the charlatans could not produce mounds of gold upon demand, they were either imprisoned or pummeled. Nor had too much time passed before word spread among the church hierarchies that the Rosicrucians were Satanists who sought only to delude Europe into sin. In spite of entreaties, threats, and demands, no Rosicrucian stepped forward to identify himself, and the society remained secret—the most secret of all secret societies.

Some suspected that many of the alleged writings attributed to "Christian Rosenkreuz" were actually works of the great Francis Bacon. Bacon's unfinished manuscript *The New Atlantis* (1627) describes an earthly utopian paradise and a secret brotherhood who wear the Rose Cross on their turbans, who heal people without charge, and who meet yearly in their temple. The philosopher René Descartes was once nearly arrested on the accusation that he was a member of the secret society, but he successfully argued to his accusers that whereas the Rosicrucians were said to be invisible, he, it was plain to see, was not.

Valentine Andreae or Andreas (1586–1654) was a Lutheran pastor who held as his ideals Martin Luther, the powerful guiding force behind the Protestant Reformation, and Christian Rosenkreuz. Andreae was a brilliant scholar who as a youth had traveled widely throughout Europe and had risen in the clerical ranks to become a chaplain at the Court of Württemberg, Germany. Embittered by the misery that had followed the Thirty Years' War

(1618–48), he became an apologist for the Rosicrucians and wrote *The Chemical Wedding of Christian Rosenkreuz* (1616), an allegorical "autobiography" of Rosenkreuz. Upon the book's initial publication, many scholars, aware that Rosenkreuz had been dead for 130 years, speculated that his spirit had dictated the work. Later academic debates swirled around the questions of whether Andreae and Rosenkreuz were the same person and whether the Fraternity of the Rosy Cross was actually founded in the seventeenth century, rather than the fifteenth. Since the seal of the Rosicrucians, the seal of Martin Luther, and the crest of the Andreae family all bear the image of the cross and the rose, understandable confusion has arisen from time to time regarding the "autobiography."

Andreae stated that the work was his own and described it as an allegorical novel written in tribute to Rosenkreuz, as well as a symbolic depiction of the science of alchemy and hermetic magic. The royal wedding to which the hero Rosenkreuz is invited is in reality the alchemical process itself, in which the female and male principles are joined together. As the novel continues, the vast arcana of alchemical truths is represented by various animals, mythological beings, and human personalities.

According to some scholars, the Rosicrucians came to America in 1694 as the German Pietists and settled in Philadelphia.

While the true identity of the original Rosicrucians may never be known and scholars may never be certain that such a man as Christian Rosenkreuz ever really existed, the society's three printed manifestos contained concepts pertaining to individual freedom, the separation of church and state, and the quest to determine humankind's true place in the universe that became ideals of the Enlightenment and have carried over into modern times.

ROSWELL, NEW MEXICO, UFO CRASH

The air force press release of July 8, 1947, that announced the retrieval of a crashed flying saucer outside of Roswell, New Mexico, has become the mother of all UFO conspiracies.

The alleged UFO crash outside of Roswell, New Mexico, on the night of July 2, 1947, is the one event that spawned nearly every UFO conspiracy theory extant today.

Here is what generations of UFO researchers contend happened at Roswell:

An extraterrestrial craft developed mechanical problems and crashed on a ranch located about sixty miles north of Roswell.

Major Jesse Marcel—winner of five air combat medals in World War II, intelligence officer for the 509th Bomber Group, a top-security, handpicked unit—was ordered to go to the site and salvage the remains of the unknown aircraft reported by Mac Brazel, a rancher who had discovered the debris on his land.

In 1980 Marcel, long retired, recalled that he and his men found wreckage from the UFO scattered throughout the area of the crash. He admitted that he had no idea exactly what he and his men were supposed to retrieve—and, forty years later, he still didn't know.

The strange, weightless material discovered by the 509th Bomber Group was difficult to describe. The pieces varied in length from four or five inches to three or four feet. Some fragments had markings that resembled hieroglyphics. Although the material seemed to be unbreakable, the military investigators thought that it looked more like wood than metal. Marcel put his cigarette lighter to one of the rectangular fragments, but it would not burn. He and his crew brought as many pieces of the crashed UFO back to Roswell Army Air Base as they could gather. Lewis Rickert, who

in 1947 was a master sergeant and counterintelligence agent stationed at the air field, was among the military personnel present at the crash site. In 1994 he recalled that the jagged, flexible fragments were no more than eight or ten inches long and six or seven inches wide and they could not be broken.

On July 8, 1947, Walter Haut, the public affairs officer at Roswell Army Air Base, sent out a release announcing that the air force had "captured" a flying saucer. The announcement was transmitted to thirty U.S. afternoon newspapers that same day, and the entire nation was electrified as word spread that a military team had actually recovered debris from the crash of one of those mysterious airborne discs that people had seen buzzing around the country ever since a civilian pilot named Kenneth Arnold claimed to have had an encounter with "flying saucers" near Mount Rainier, in Washington State, on June 24.

On the very next day, July 9, the press office at the air field released a correction of its previous story. It had not been the debris of a flying saucer that had been recovered, after all. It was nothing but the remains of a downed weather balloon. Also on July 9, the *Roswell Daily Record* carried the story of Mac Brazel, the rancher who had found the "saucer," who said that he was sorry that he had told anyone about the crashed junk in the first place.

In the 1980s Kevin Randle, a former captain in U.S. Air Force Intelligence, together with Don Schmitt, director of the J. Allen Hynek Center for UFO Studies, found new evidence indicating that the crash actually occurred on July 4, 1947, rather than July 2, as is commonly stated. It was on July 5, according to Schmitt and Randle, that Mac Brazel visited Sheriff George Wilcox and informed him of the peculiar discovery he had made near his ranch the day before. The military unit under the command of Major Marcel retrieved the crash debris and alien bodies on July 5. On July 8 Walter Haut issued the press release stating that the army had captured a flying saucer. Almost immediately thereafter, the official cover story of a collapsed weather balloon falling to Earth in the desert was heavily promoted by the military.

Numerous civilians who claimed to have arrived at the crash site remembered seeing the corpses of small, hairless beings with large heads and round, oddly spaced eyes.

Barney Barnett, a civil engineer employed by the federal government, said that he had seen alien bodies on the ground and inside the wrecked spaceship. He described them as small, hairless beings with large heads and round, oddly spaced eyes. Barnett stated that a military unit arrived on the scene and an officer ordered him off the site with the stern admonition that it was his patriotic duty to remain silent about what he had seen.

The press officer Walter Haut was given direct orders by his base commander, Col. William Blanchard, to prepare the official press release refuting the flying saucer account. The cover story of the weather balloon initiated the military/government conspiracy to keep the truth of a crashed extraterrestrial UFO from the public.

The nuclear physicist Stanton Friedman contends that Major Marcel was very familiar with all kinds of weather and military balloons and would not have mistaken such ordinary debris for that of a downed alien spaceship. Nor would any of the military personnel have mistaken alien bodies for diminutive human remains. After the wreckage was properly identified as extraterrestrial in nature, Friedman claims, the official cover-up was instigated at both the Roswell base and the headquarters of the Eighth Air Force in Fort Worth, Texas, by the Eighth Air Force's commandant, Brig. Gen. Roger Ramey, on direct orders from Gen. Clement McMullen at Strategic Air Command headquarters in Washington, D.C.

At least one of the alien crew survived the crash and was shipped, along with the debris of the vehicle, to Wright Field in Dayton, Ohio, thus becoming a resident of the infamous "Hanger 18" at Wright-Patterson.

Most eyewitness accounts speak of five alien bodies found at the impact site and state that four corpses were transported to Wright Field and the fifth to Lowry Field, Denver, to the air force mortuary service. Numerous secondary accounts of the incident assert that one of the UFOnauts survived the crash and was still alive when the military arrived on the scene. Some UFO researchers maintain that circa 1986 the alien being was still alive and well treated as a guest of the air force at what is now Wright-Patterson Air Base.

Don Schmitt and Kevin Randle, in their book *UFO Crash at Roswell,* include an interview with Brig. Gen. Arthur Exon, who told them that, in addition to debris from the wreckage, four tiny alien cadavers were flown to Wright Field.

A number of civilians were threatened by the military to keep their mouths shut about what really occurred at Roswell.

During an interview with a granddaughter of Sheriff George Wilcox in March 1991, Schmitt and Randle were told that the sheriff saw the debris of a UFO and "little space beings." Later, military men "who were not kidding" visited Wilcox and his wife and warned them that they would be killed if they ever told anyone what he saw at the crash site. Not only would they be murdered, but their children and grandchildren would also be eliminated.

Randle and Schmitt located a Ms. Frankie Rowe, who had been twelve years old at the time of the mysterious occurrences outside Roswell. Her father, a lieutenant with the fire department, told his family at dinner on the night of the UFO crash that he had seen the remains of what he had at first believed to be an airplane. He also saw two little bodies in

An artist's depiction of the military finding debris and alien bodies at the Foster Ranch, near Roswell, New Mexico.

body bags and a third alien entity walking around in a daze. He described the beings as about the size of a ten-year-old child. Later, a group of military men arrived at the house and made it clear that if they ever talked about the incident again, the entire family would be taken out in the desert and "no one would ever find us again."

In the November 1994 issue of *American Funeral Director*, Glenn Dennis recalled the telephone conversation that he had with the mortuary officer at Roswell Army Air Base on Tuesday, July 8, 1947, when he was asked if he could provide three- or four-foot-long hermetically sealed caskets. A short time later Dennis was on the base in his capacity as an ambulance driver, transporting an injured airman to the base hospital. As he drove past two field ambulances, he looked into their open back ends and saw an enormous amount of a silvery, metallic material, two chunks of

which were curved at the bottom in the manner of a canoe. He also noticed that the pieces were covered with odd markings, which he assumed were some kind of hieroglyphs.

Dennis stated in the article that he was a familiar figure at the air base, even accepted as an honorary member of its officers club. On this occasion, however, two MPs grabbed him and brought him to a red-haired officer who warned him that somebody would be picking his bones out of the sand if he ever shot his mouth off about seeing the peculiar material. As the MPs were escorting Dennis back to his ambulance, they met a female nurse in the hallway. The nurse, with whom he was well acquainted, held a towel over the lower part of her face, and Dennis at first thought that she had been crying. Alarmed by his presence, she told him to leave at once before he was shot. Dennis indicated his two-man armed escort and said that he was leaving the base. As he was being ushered rudely down the hall, Dennis saw two men who also had towels over their noses and mouths.

The next day, the nurse arranged to meet Dennis at the officers club. There she told him that a flying saucer had crashed in the desert and the army had recovered bodies of three dead aliens. Until the bodies were frozen, she said, their smell had nauseated the medical staff. Dennis said that the nurse became extremely emotional while describing smallish beings with large heads and big eyes. He never saw her again. He was informed that she had been transferred to a base in England. Later, he was told that she had been killed in an airplane crash.

Other Roswell conspiracy theories with slightly different interpretations of the event were not long in surfacing:

An extraterrestrial craft did crash at Roswell in 1947, and through reverse engineering of the advanced alien technology at secret air bases such as Area 51, our scientists and engineers have accomplished aeronautical breakthroughs decades ahead of when we might have expected them.

Artifacts found with the crashed extraterrestrial space vehicle were discreetly farmed out to major U.S. corporations that were able to back-engineer many technological advances, to the benefit of all world citizens.

The alien kept alive in Hangar 18 at Wright-Patterson Air Force Base has been acting as a liaison between a secret agency within the government and the extraterrestrials, actually exchanging humans for advanced technical data.

In secret underground military and commercial facilities, aliens have been seen working side by side with earthling scientists and engineers developing additional technological advances derived from extraterrestrial technology.

Witnesses to such activity report subterranean laboratories where the extraterrestrials seek to create part-alien, part-human beings. Others tell horror stories of having observed "large vats with pale meat being agitated in solutions" and large test tubes "with humans in them."

On June 24, 1997, the Pentagon held a special briefing conducted by the U.S. Air Force—timed to coincide with the fiftieth anniversary of Kenneth Arnold's 1947 sighting of flying saucers—in order to release the document entitled *The Roswell Report: Case Closed*. This publication, stated Col. John Haynes, would be the air force's final word concerning fifty years of accusations that the government was hiding evidence of extraterrestrial visitation.

The debris found at the crash site outside of Roswell was from a Project Mogul balloon, a top-secret intelligence-gathering device, hence the cover-up was for purposes of national security. The alleged bodies seen around the crash site were not those of extraterrestrial beings—or of any living beings. They were actually dummies, roughly the size of humans, that were used in experiments with high-altitude parachutes that began in 1953. After the experimental drops, air force personnel would retrieve the simulated human forms, and it must have been at certain of these recovery missions that folks around Roswell got the idea that they saw military types picking up "alien" bodies.

For those who wondered how witnesses could confuse dummies dropped over the desert near Roswell in 1953 with humanoid corpses scattered near a specific crash site in 1947, Colonel Haynes explained this confusion as a manifestation of the mental phenomenon of "time compression," wherein the memory melds events separated by many years into "compressed" segments of time. That is, civilians who witnessed the crash site of a weather balloon in 1947 and, six years later, saw air force personnel retrieving crash dummies dropped from the skies recall the two events as one in their compressed memories. With all the controversy regarding flying saucers and aliens, the witnesses remember the balloon fragments and the dummies as the debris from a crashed spacecraft and the corpses of its extraterrestrial crew.

On October 25, 1998, an interview in the newspaper *The People* (London) with Dr. Edgar Mitchell, the sixth person to walk on the moon, startled UFO buffs and skeptics alike. Without hesitation, the former astronaut proclaimed, "Make no mistake, Roswell happened. I've seen secret files which show the government knew about it, but decided not to tell the public." Mitchell explained that because of his being a scientist and a former astronaut, military people with access to top-secret files were more willing to speak with him than to civilian researchers with shaky credentials. Although he had begun his inquiries as a cynic, he said, he became convinced of the existence of aliens after speaking with "the military old-timers" who had been in service at the time of Roswell. He added that the more government documentation he was told about, the more convinced he became.

Mitchell stated that he was shocked to learn the extent to which the UFO mystery had been covered up by the governments of the world, but in defense of such actions, he said that there were sound security reasons for not informing the general public of the truth about Roswell: "Quite simply, we wouldn't have known how to deal with the technology of intelligent beings advanced enough to send a craft to Earth. The world would have panicked if we'd know aliens were visiting us." He expressed his belief that those individuals who were in possession of top-secret documentation of alien visitors would soon begin to come forward and that full disclosures would be made within three or four years.

In July 1997 a CNN/Time poll taken to commemorate the fiftieth anniversary of the enigmatic event at Roswell indicated that 80 percent of the American public believes the government is hiding information about the UFO mystery. In addition, 54 percent of those surveyed are certain that life exists outside of Earth; 35 percent expect extraterrestrial beings to appear "somewhat" human; 64 percent are convinced that alien life forms have made contact with humans; and 37 percent are concerned that ETs are abducting humans.

The debris found at the crash site outside of Roswell was from a Project Mogul balloon, a top-secret intelligence-gathering device....

Does Nitinol, the Memory Metal, Have an Extraterrestrial Origin?

In their book *UFO Crash at Roswell,* Kevin Randle and Don Schmitt interviewed Mrs. Frankie Rowe, whose father was a lieutenant with the Roswell fire department who had witnessed the debris of "some kind of ship" and tiny corpses in body bags. Frankie, who was twelve at the time, happened to be visiting her father at the fire station when a New Mexico state police officer came in with a strange piece of metal that he claimed he had picked up from the UFO crash site when no one was looking. To the astonishment of the firemen, the trooper tossed the object onto a table where it "unfolded itself in fluid motion," looking not unlike water or liquid mercury. Each of the firefighters had their turn examining the alien metal and they all observed that it could not be cut, burned, or made to remain in any shape other than its original form. A few days later, the witnesses were warned by a group of military men that they must never talk to anyone about the fragment that the state police officer had removed from the UFO crash site.

In 1978, Jesse Marcel gave a filmed interview from his home in Houma, Louisiana, in which he spoke of handling the "memory metal" back in 1947. He, too, described it as a solid, metallic substance that could be crumpled into a ball, but always returned to its original shape.

In 1997, Lt. Col. Philip J. Corso admitted in his *Day after Roswell* that he had access to certain recovered materials from the Roswell UFO crash of 1947. Among this cache of materials was the "morph metal," which Lt. Col. Corso believed was of extraterrestrial origin.

The mysterious fragments of metal were assigned to the Battelle Memorial Institute, a top secret defense contractor with state-of-the-art experimental laboratories and analysis facilities in Columbia, Ohio. It was here that the "memory metal" was named nitinol and analyzed as a fusion made from combining titanium and nickel at an extremely high heat. Scientists have declared nitinol so malleable that it might be capable of forming a self-mending aircraft hull that would virtually "heal" itself if breached.

In 2003, when researcher Nick Redfern was gathering material for his *Body Snatchers in the Desert* (2005) he met an elderly man that he dubbed "the Colonel," who claimed an extensive background with various U.S. intelligence agencies. The Colonel told Redfern that the U.S. Army's Foreign Technology Division had hatched the story of nitinol being created from extraterrestrial debris found at Roswell to ensnare a suspected Soviet spy. In order to make the story completely convincing to the Soviets, the spy was given a limited amount of research into nitinol. The trap worked, the Colonel said, but as a consequence, rumors spread within elements of the FTD that nitinol had actually been created from an extraterrestrial source.

After his interviews with the Colonel, Redfern was left with two possibilities: 1) The Nitinol-Roswell connection grew out of a plot to trap a communist sympathizer and his Soviet alley; or 2) the Colonel was attempting to deflect the nitinol-Roswell connection by placing the story in a "wholly down-to-earth context, rather than one involving literal aliens and a crashed UFO."

KARL ROVE

Conspiracy theorists refer to Karl Rove as "America's Joseph Goebbels," recalling Adolf Hitler's chief manipulator of the media in Nazi Germany, and declare that Rove is "creepier than Nixon."

President George W. Bush has referred to Karl Christian Rove, his senior adviser, chief political strategist, and deputy chief of staff, as "the Architect," "the Boy Genius," and "Turd Blossom," the latter being a Texanism for a flower that blooms from cattle or horse droppings.

Rove's reputation for dirty politics and conducting smear campaigns against political opponents has made *Rovian* a synonym for *Machiavellian*.

Karl Rove dropped out of college in 1971 to enter Republican politics. From that time on, he has single-mindedly pursued political power—and he has most certainly attained his goal, serving, as some have suggested, as "co-president" of the United States. At the same time, he has employed more than a few character assassinations and bags full of dirty tricks to annihilate the political competition.

In the fall of 2003 Rove became one of the central figures in an explosive conspiracy that threatened to bring about the end of his political career and the fall of the George W. Bush administration. On August 29, 2003, the retired ambassador and career diplomat Joseph

C. Wilson accused Rove of leaking the identity of Wilson's wife, Valerie Plame, as a CIA operative. When asked how he knew the leak could be traced to Rove, Wilson responded by stating that he possessed documents from a secret investigation of the State Department's Internal Security Unit that revealed Rove's duplicity. Wilson was a holdover from the Clinton administration, and a small clique sympathetic to Wilson and his wife had provided him with the evidence that Rove had leaked the information in retaliation for the ambassador's criticisms of the Bush administration.

Wilson had been dispatched to Niger in February 2002 by the CIA after Vice President Dick Cheney asked the Agency to investigate whether there was substance to the report that Iraq was obtaining uranium from that African nation for nuclear weapons. Wilson had previously served as ambassador to Gabon, and in the 1970s he had been posted in Niamey, Niger's capital. During the George H. W. Bush administration, Wilson was a senior American diplomat in Baghdad.

Wilson spent eight days investigating the uranium charges and found them to be completely untrue. He conferred with the U.S. ambassador to Niger, Barbro Owens-Kirkpatrick, who told him that she thought she had already debunked allegations of uranium sales to Iraq in her reports to Washington. When he returned to the United States, Wilson made it clear to Cheney, the CIA, the State Department, and the National Security Council that he had found no evidence to support the rumors. In spite of Wilson's strenuous denials, President George W. Bush used the Niger uranium claims to dramatic effect in his 2003 State of the Union Address.

On July 6, 2003, the *New York Times* published an opinion piece by Wilson in which he intimated that the Bush administration had deliberately misrepresented intelligence findings about Iraq-Niger uranium dealings to justify the war against Iraq. Five days later CIA di-

Karl Rove (far right) with President George W. Bush and First Lady Laura Bush in 2007.

rector George Tenet issued a press release admitting that the Agency should never have permitted the "sixteen words" used by President Bush in the State of the Union Address to suggest an Iraq-Niger uranium connection. Such a "mistake" on the part of the CIA allowed Bush to take the nation to war.

On July 14 the syndicated columnist Robert Novak wrote an article attempting to make light of Wilson's findings and, in the same column, revealed that the ambassador's wife, Valerie Plame, was a CIA operative working on detecting weapons of mass destruction. Almost from the first, rumors circulated that Novak's source for the information was Karl Rove, who under orders or under his own counsel struck back at Ambassador Wilson for his attacks on the Bush presidency. Both Wilson and various current and former CIA officials asserted that this leak ruined Ms. Plame's nearly twenty-year career as an undercover agent. Even more seriously, it endangered her life and the lives of the undercover CIA network of which she was an integral part. Some researchers have claimed that the leak to Novak has resulted in the deaths of more than seventy CIA agents overseas.

William Rivers Pitt, writing in *Truthout Perspective,* quotes Ray McGovern, for twenty-seven years a senior CIA analyst, who commented on the irony of the Bush administration's going to war based on claims that the Iraqis possessed weapons of mass destruction, while at the same time betraying a deep-cover operative who was running a network of informants providing actual information about WMDs. McGovern noted that such networks can take ten years or more to develop. The reason for obtaining deep-cover agents is that the only people who have access to the kind of data the CIA needs cannot be associated in any way with the intelligence community. "Our operatives live a lie to maintain these networks and do so out of patriotism," McGovern explained. "When they get blown, the operatives themselves are in physical danger, and the people they recruit are also in physical danger, because foreign intelligence services can make the connections and find them. Operatives like Valerie Plame are real patriots."

Researchers state that Karl Rove is an undisputed, heavyweight champion of political assassins, who learned a vast repertoire of dirty tricks under the tutorship of Republican slash-and-burn master Donald Segretti. In 1970, as Segretti's nineteen-year-old apprentice, Rove stole some letterheads from Illinois Democrat Alan Dixon's campaign officer and distributed fake flyers promising rallies with free beer, free food, and a good time. During the 1972 presidential campaign Rove was at Segretti's side when they planted false stories about the popular Democratic candidate Senator Edward Muskie's wife being an alcoholic and about the senator having made an ethnic slur against New Hampshire's French Canadian population. In addition, they forged letters on Muskie campaign letterhead and disrupted rallies and fund-raising dinners. After Muskie dropped out of the race, they focused on World War II hero George McGovern and portrayed him as a left-wing radical. Segretti was later convicted as a Watergate conspirator, but Rove had learned his lessons well. On August 10, 1973, a *Washington Post* article reported on how the twenty-two-year-old Rove was touring the nation providing "dirty tricks" training seminars.

In the 2000 GOP primary Rove smeared Senator John McCain, another American war hero, by accusing him of betraying his fellow U.S. prisoners in the notorious North Vietnamese "Hanoi Hilton" prison. McCain's wife came under attack for alleged drug abuse, and suggestions were made about the senator's being homosexual. In the South Carolina primaries Rove instigated a push poll that asked voters if they would be likely to vote for McCain knowing that he had fathered an illegitimate black child. Rove was aware that McCain was campaigning with his adopted Bangladeshi daughter and that the less-than-astute voters would make the despicable association.

Defaming a veteran of Vietnam who had undergone torture and deprivation and survived to become a candidate for the U.S. presidency seemed to be only a warm-up for Rove's insidious coaching of Republican candidate Saxby Chambliss in the 2002 Georgia Senate race. Rove masterminded Chambliss's attack on Senator Max Cleland, who had lost both legs and an arm in Vietnam, for "breaking his oath to protect and defend the Constitution." Chambliss, who did not enter military service because of a bad knee, issued a press release stating that Cleland had voted for an amendment to the Chemical Weapons Treaty that eliminated a ban on citizens of nations accused of sponsoring terrorist activities being on UN inspection teams in Iraq. The amendment had passed with Republican support and a majority vote, but Rove ingeniously manipulated Georgia voters into seeing Cleland's vote as unpatriotic and assured Chambliss's victory.

During the 2004 presidential race, Rove received the overwhelming nomination as the likely mastermind behind the misleading "Swift Boat Veterans for Truth" television ads that attacked yet another decorated war hero, Senator John Kerry.

In June 2005 Rove uttered the words that had angry Democrats demanding an apology: "Conservatives saw the savagery of 9/11 attacks and prepared for war; liberals saw the savagery of the 9/11 attacks and wanted to prepare indictments and offer therapy and understanding for our attackers." Since both liberal and conservative senators had voted unanimously to authorize the use of military force against the terrorists in retaliation for the September 11, 2001, World Trade Center and Pentagon attacks, Rove's statement seemed clearly devised to divert attention from the mess he was in with the Valerie Plame incident. Individuals other than Democrats were offended by such a remark. Families of September 11, a nonprofit organization founded by survivors of those who were killed in the 9/11 terrorist attacks, issued a statement demanding that Rove cease his attempts to "reap political gain in the tragic misfortune of others."

Once again, the Bush administration defended Rove by stating how puzzled they were that anyone could take offense at such an "accurate" analysis of the varying philosophies in the war on terror.

In September 2003 President Bush, in reference to the Valerie Plame incident, said that he didn't know anyone in his administration who would leak classified information but that "appropriate action" would be taken if such were learned to be the case. On July 18, 2005, President Bush added that if anyone had committed a crime, "they [sic] will no longer work in my administration."

In his memoir, *Courage and Consequence* (2010), Rove devotes three chapters to his grand jury appearances in the Valerie Plame scandal. In his grand jury testimony, Rove said that he had learned of Plame's CIA affiliation

from a number of journalists and not from government officials. It was true, he testified, that Robert Novak informed him in July 2003 that he planned to write an upcoming column stating that Plame worked for the CIA, but Rove insisted that he had already heard the allegations from other journalists, whose identities he could not recall. Rove also testified that he had also heard of Plame's affiliation with the CIA from I. Lewis "Scooter" Libby. Libby, Rove said, had heard about Plame and the CIA from journalists.

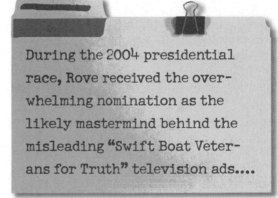

During the 2004 presidential race, Rove received the overwhelming nomination as the likely mastermind behind the misleading "Swift Boat Veterans for Truth" television ads....

On March 6, 2007, Libby was indicted for having spoken to a senior official in the White House on or about July 10 or 11, 2003, who advised him that Robert Novak would be writing a column in which Joseph Wilson's wife was identified as a CIA employee. Libby was sentenced to thirty months in prison, fined $250,000, and given two years supervised release. Although it has never been confirmed by Special Counsel Patrick Fitzgerald, it was widely circulated that Karl Rove was the senior officer identified in the indictment as "Official A." Libby's sentence was later commuted by President George W. Bush.

After Rove left the White House in 2008, he was hired as a contributor for the *Wall Street Journal* and as a political analyst for Fox News. He also served as an informal advisor to John McCain in McCain's campaign for the presidency in the 2008 election, and he has spent a great deal of time on the road giving speeches to colleges and other groups.

Perhaps this bit of trivia indicates an additional peek into the man's psyche. Karl Rove is Norwegian American. While many Scandinavian Americans are content to tease one another with "Ole and Lena" jokes, it has been noted that Rove has an obsession about the duplicity of the Swedes, who took control of Norway in 1814. According to Bob Woodward's *Plan of Attack,* it was this unreasoning distrust of Swedes that caused Rove to hate the United Nations weapons inspector Hans Blix, who is Swedish, and to negate Blix's report that there were no WMDs in Iraq.

RUBY RIDGE

For eighteen months, federal marshals laid siege to a family of five, their friend, and the family dog, who were holed up in a cabin.

In 1983 Randall "Randy" Weaver, a former Green Beret, his wife, Vicki, and their three children decided to move from Iowa to greater seclusion in the rugged panhandle country of northern Idaho. The Weavers, though not belonging to any particular group, believed in separatism and the apocalyptic prophecies that advised the faithful that the endtimes were very near. True to the survivalist spirit, the Weavers bought a large acreage on Ruby Ridge, built their own home, and managed to make a living by selling firewood.

In *The Federal Siege at Ruby Ridge: In Our Own Words,* written by Randy Weaver, his daughter, Sara, and Bill Henry, Weaver claims that federal agents saw him as someone who could give them information on some of the white-supremacist and neo-Nazi groups in Idaho. When he failed to comply with their requests, he was indicted in 1992 for selling two illegal sawed-off shotguns to an FBI informant. Weaver and his lawyers protested that he was

set up in an elaborate entrapment scheme by federal agents in order to force him to cooperate with them in gaining information about the antigovernment movements in the area. Fearing that he was about to suffer consequences of an uncooperative attitude, Weaver didn't appear in court for his trial. When he was indicted on a second count, he retreated to his stronghold in Ruby Ridge.

For the next eighteen months, the Weavers were under close surveillance by federal marshals, who ringed the Ruby Ridge property, hoping that Randy would come out so they could arrest him. According to orders issued by the U.S. attorney's office in Boise, the federal agents were to apprehend Weaver only in a peaceable, nonviolent manner, which translated to arresting him if he left the stronghold and surrendered.

On August 21, 1992, the standoff came to a bloody halt. In the marshals' account, three officers armed with M-16s were reconnoitering the Ruby Ridge property when Kevin Harris, twenty-five, who was living with the Weavers, and the Weavers' fourteen-year-old son, Samuel, began chasing them and shooting at them. A brief firefight broke out that left Marshal William Degan, Samuel Weaver, and the Weavers' dog dead. In his testimony, Harris stated that he witnessed the federal agents' killing of Samuel and the dog and began firing at the marshals in self-defense, killing Degan.

After the initial gun battle, more than two hundred law-enforcement officers, led by the FBI, surrounded the Weavers' cabin. On August 22, the day after Samuel Weaver and Marshal Degan were killed, an FBI sniper, Lon Horiuchi, got off two rounds, instantly killing Vicki Weaver and seriously wounding Randy. For the next ten days Weaver, his three daughters, and Harris continued to resist. The FBI brought in Special Forces hero James "Bo" Gritz to negotiate with the beleaguered Weavers, and Harris decided to surrender. Weaver and his daughters waited one more day before waving the white flag.

At their trial in July 1993 one of the Weavers' attorneys, Gerry Spence, spoke critically of the FBI's handling of the engagement. Advising the jury that the incident at Ruby Ridge was just like Waco, Spence said that initially the marshals were instructed to keep their distance from the Weavers—to keep them under surveillance but have no contact with them. After several months of maintaining a stakeout, the federal agents began to work at provoking a confrontation, and the Weavers and Harris acted in self-defense.

The prosecution attempted to counter by claiming that Harris had fired first when he killed Degan. The defense produced ballistic evidence that Degan had fired seven rounds before he was shot.

The federal government re-created the death of Vicki Weaver and said that the sniper had caught only a glimpse of someone moving behind a curtain and had accidentally killed her. Earlier in the trial, however, Horiuchi, the sniper, testified that he was considered an accurate shot at two hundred yards.

The jury found Weaver innocent of all serious charges, convicting him only on the original charge of selling illegal firearms. Harris was also found innocent on the grounds of self-defense. Randy Weaver returned to Iowa and began to rebuild his life. He sells his book at gun shows around the country and advises those who chat with him to "keep your powder dry."

The incident at Ruby Ridge, where one small family was involved in a siege with the federal government that lasted over eighteen months and ended in death and violence, serves as a constant reminder that law-enforcement authorities must never act precipitously and by so doing can bring on violence that might have been avoided.

SALEM WITCHCRAFT TRIALS

The devil visited the village of Salem, Massachusetts, in 1692 and let loose a host of his fearful witches on the innocent, God-fearing community.

The fear of witchcraft that possessed the village of Salem in Massachusetts Bay Colony in 1692 remains in American popular culture as the single most celebrated of all witch hunts. Because of the accusations of a small circle of girls and young women who frightened themselves with their runaway imaginations and hysteric responses to real or imagined phenomena, an entire community became crazed and caught up in the fear that many of their neighbors were serving Satan in secret. The result of this witch hysteria was the deaths of twenty-four men and women, who were hanged, crushed to death, or died in prison.

The flame of witch-madness was ignited in the home of the Puritan preacher Samuel Parris when his female slave Tituba began telling stories of Voodoo and spirits to his nine-year-old daughter Betty and her cousin Abigail

Williams, eleven. While it is certain that Rev. Parris would have scolded Tituba for filling the girls' heads with such ghost stories, Abigail and Betty cherished these secret times with the woman and kept quiet about the nature of their conversation. Soon the exciting story-telling sessions in the Parris household were attracting older girls, such as sixteen-year-old Mary Walcott and eighteen-year-old Susanna Sheldon, who wanted Tituba to tell their fortunes and predict their future husbands, as well as tell them scary stories. Although Rev. Parris and the other village clergymen fulminated from the pulpits about the dangers of seeking occult knowledge, the girls of Salem ignored such warnings in favor of having an exciting diversion that could help them through a long, cold winter.

After hearing about the secret sessions at the Parrises' home, Ann Putnam, a fragile, high-strung twelve-year-old, joined the circle in the company of the Putnams' maid, nineteen-year-old Mercy Lewis. Ann was much more widely read than the other girls and was blessed with a quick wit, high intelligence, and a lively imagination. She soon became Tituba's most avid and apt pupil. Ann was quite familiar with the imagery in the biblical book of Revela-

A witch stands accused in a seventeenth-century Massachusetts courtroom.

tion with its dragons, horned beasts, devils, and damnation. It seems that while part of Ann's psyche was thrilled with the forbidden knowledge Tituba shared with the girls, another aspect was racked with guilt and fear that they were courting devilish enchantment.

With their strict Puritan upbringing, there is little doubt that most of the other girls were also conflicted with conscience and the fear of discovery. As the days passed, little Betty fell subject to sudden fits of weeping and was often seen to be staring blankly at the wall. Shortly thereafter, Abigail got down on all fours and began barking like a dog or braying like a donkey. Mary Walcott and Susanna Sheldon fell into convulsions. Ann Putnam and Mercy Lewis also began to suffer seizures. Something evil had come to Salem and possessed the girls.

About four years previously, in the north end of Boston, four children in the John Godwin family had fallen into such fits, babbling blasphemies and ignoring the prayers of the clergy. It took the famous preacher Cotton Mather to quiet the work of a witch, an Irish washerwoman named Glover, and restore the children to normalcy. The memories of this horrid event, including the hanging of Witch Glover, were very much alive in the minds of the Salem clergy when they began to ask the girls who was tormenting them.

Tituba was the first name from the possessed children's lips. Next was Sarah Good, an odd woman who smoked a foul-smelling pipe and who previously had been suspected of spreading smallpox through witchcraft. The church fathers were not surprised by the naming of these two women, but when the girls also named Sarah Osburne, the village was shocked. Mrs. Osburne was a well-to-do property owner who lived in one of the most substantial homes in Salem. Nevertheless, warrants were issued for all three women.

From this dramatic beginning, the list of names of the devil's disciples grew steadily longer. The wealthy merchant Philip English; Goodwife Proctor, the wife of a successful farmer and tavern keeper, John Proctor; Martha Cory, the wife of another prosperous farmer, Giles Cory. Sarah Good's four-year-old daughter, Dorcas, was also put in chains as an accused witch. Two magistrates, John Hathorne and Jonathan Corwin, were sent out from the General Court of Massachusetts Colony to hear testimony that described tales of talking animals, dark shapes, red cats, and a Tall Man who was undoubtedly the devil himself.

When seventy-one-year-old Rebecca Nurse was arrested for witchcraft against her neighbors, the townsfolk realized that if saintly Rebecca could be named as a witch, no one was safe from such accusations. Rebecca was noted for her piety and simplicity of heart. Although the jury initially acquitted her, the judge ordered them to reconsider, and she was hanged on Gallows Hill on July 19, 1692.

Several hundred people in and around Salem were accused of witchcraft, even the wife of Massachusetts governor William

Phips. Such an outrage provoked Phips into taking a stand against any further imprisonments, and he forbade any more executions for witchcraft in Salem.

Because of the governor's actions, the nearly 150 men and women who were still chained to prison walls were set free and many who had been convicted of witchcraft were pardoned. In 1711 the Massachusetts legislature passed a general amnesty that exonerated all but six of the accused witches. In 1957 the state legislature passed a resolution exonerating Ann Pudeator, who had been hanged. Finally, on November 1, 2001, acting Massachusetts governor Jane Swift approved a bill that cleared all the accused witches hanged in Salem in 1692 and 1693. The bill exonerated the final five who had not been cleared by the previous amnesty resolutions—Susannah Martin, Bridget Bishop, Alice Parker, Margaret Scott, and Wilmot Redd.

In her study of the witchcraft trials, *The Devil in Massachusetts,* Marion L. Starkey makes the following observation: "No definitive history of the Salem witchcraft has ever been written or is likely to be, for it would take a lifetime and would be encyclopedic in dimension."

SANTER'A

Santer'a is a cult that practices ritual mutilation, human sacrifice, and black magic.

In April 1989 Santer'a, a religious amalgamation that evolved from a blending of African slaves' spirit worship with their Spanish Catholic masters' hierarchy of intercessory saints, was dealt a negative blow to its public image that has been difficult to overcome. At that time, Mexican police officials raiding a drug ring based at Rancho Santa Elena outside of Matamoros discovered a large black cauldron in which a human brain, a turtle shell, a horseshoe, a human spinal column, and an assortment of human bones had been boiled in blood. Further digging on the grounds brought up a dozen human corpses, which had all suffered ritual mutilations. When it was learned that the mother of Adolfo de Jesus Constanzo, the leader of the drug ring responsible for the murders, was a practitioner of Santer'a, a media frenzy defining the religion as a mixture of Satanism, Voodoo, and demon-worship swept across Mexico and the United States.

Later, investigators would learn that Constanzo had created his own cruel concept of a cult by combining aspects of his perverse personal cosmology with Santer'a, Voodoo, and an ancient Aztec ritual known as *santismo.* Constanzo declared himself its high priest and was joined in the performance of its gory rituals by Sara Maria Aldrete, who led a bizarre double life as a high priestess and as an honor student at Texas Southmost College in Brownsville.

Santer'a originated in Cuba around 1517 among slaves who combined elements of the western African Yoruba and Bantu religions with aspects of Spanish Catholicism. The African slaves were at first greatly distressed when told by their masters that they could no longer pay homage to their worship of the orishas, their spiritual guardians, but their resourceful priests quickly noticed a number of parallels between Yoruba religion and Catholicism. While paying obeisance and homage to various Christian saints, the Africans found that they could simply envision that they were praying to one of their own spirit beings. A secret religion was born—*Regla de Ocha,* the "Rule of the Orisha," or the common and most popular name, Santer'a, "way of the saints."

In Santer'a the supreme deity is referred to as Olorun or Olodumare, "the one who owns heaven." The lesser guardians, the orishas, were each associated with a different Roman Catholic saint: Babalz Ayi became Saint

Lazarus; Oggzn became Saint Peter; Oshzn became Our Lady of Charity; Elegba became Saint Anthony; Obatala became the Resurrected Christ, and so forth. Priests of the faith are called *santeros* or *babalochas*; priestesses are called *santeras* or *lyalochas*. The term *olorisha* may be applied to either a priest or a priestess.

While the rites remain secret and hidden from outsiders, a few churches have emerged that provide their members an opportunity to practice Santer'a freely. The Church of the Lukumi Babalu Aye was formed in southern Florida in the early 1970s and won a landmark decision by the Supreme Court to be allowed to practice animal sacrifice. Each celebration usually begins with an invocation of Olorun, the supreme deity. Dancing to strong African rhythms continues until individuals are possessed by particular orishas and allow the spirits to speak through them. The ritual is climaxed with the blood sacrifice, usually a chicken.

While Santer'a's rites are controversial in that they may include the sacrifice of small animals, it is essentially a benign religion. In spite of such public relations low points as the murders at Matamoros and negative depictions in motion picture and television presentations, Santer'a continues to grow among Hispanics in Florida, New York City, and Los Angeles. Some estimates state that there are over 300,000 practitioners of Santer'a in New York alone. Although it was suppressed in Cuba during the 1960s, lessening of restrictions upon religious practices in the 1990s saw the practitioners of Santer'a in that country increase greatly in number.

SATANIC CULTS

Organized cults of devil-worship are on the rise. Each year, hundreds, perhaps thousands, of innocent men, women, and children are victims of human sacrificial rites in honor of Satan.

The scriptures of all religions acknowledge the existence of demonic beings. Some, such as Christianity, Zoroastrianism, and Islam, regard the power of evil entities as real and perceive them as rivals to the dominion of God. Others, such as Buddhism, consider them to be manifestations of ignorance and illusion. Those religious expressions that testify to demonic powers also recognize that these negative beings are subject to the commands of a leader, known by various names, such as Satan, Lucifer, Iblis, Mara, and Angra Mainyu.

Although Satanism and witchcraft have been synonymous in the popular mind for many centuries, they constitute two vastly divergent philosophies and metaphysical systems. Generally speaking, Witchcraft, the Old Religion, has its origins in primitive nature worship and has no devil or Satan in its cosmology. While some traditional witches seek to control the forces of nature and elemental forces in both the seen and unseen worlds, others are contented to work with herbs and healing. True Satanism—although manifesting in a multitude of forms and expressions and having also originated in an ancient worship of a pre–Judeo-Christian god—is today essentially a corruption of both the nature worship of witchcraft and formal Christian worship, especially the rites of the Roman Catholic Church.

Some scholars argue that in a very real sense, the Christian church itself "created" the kind of Satanism it fears most through the excesses of the Inquisition, which made an industry out of hunting, persecuting, torturing, and killing practitioners of the Old Religion who were condemned for worshipping the devil through the practice of witchcraft. Then, in the sixteenth century, a decadent aristocracy, weary of the severity of conventional mortality legislated by the church, perversely began to adapt witchcraft rituals to suit their own sexual fantasies. Unrestrained immorality was the order of the day as Parisians followed the hedonistic example of their Sun King, Louis XIV. The ancient rituals followed by serf and peasant were converted into an obscene rendering of the rites of traditional paganism combined the ritualistic aspects of Christian worship. Lords and ladies began to pray in earnest to Holy Satan to grant them high office and wealth.

Contemporary Satanism experienced its rebirth on Walpurgisnacht (May 1) 1966, when Anton Szandor LaVey brought into being San Francisco's Church of Satan. Generally speaking, the kind of Satanism championed by LaVey preaches indulgence in personal pleasure, and it has never pretended to be other than a counterculture alternative to the civil and religious establishments and a relentless foe of conventional morality.

In contemporary times, those who openly claim to belong to organized satanic groups insist that they do not worship the image of the devil condemned by Christian and other religions. As they explain it, "Satan" does not specify a being, but rather a movement or a state of mind. What Satanists do worship, these individuals explain, is a Spirit Being known as Sathan in English and Sathanas in Latin. They do not believe Satan to be the supreme God, but they believe him to be the messenger of God in that he brought to Eve the knowledge of good and evil. Satanists believe that there is a God above and beyond the "god" that created the cosmos. The most high God takes no part in the affairs of the world, thus Satanists believe their faith to be the only true religion, insofar as revealed religion to mortals can be understood.

In the 1980s and '90s a widespread fear swept across the United States that there were dozens of secret satanic cults engaging in ritual abuse and sacrificing hundreds of babies, children, and adults. Television and radio talk shows featured individuals who claimed to be former members of such demonic cults and those who had allegedly recovered memories of satanic abuse. For a time, certain communities developed a near-hysteria and a fear of Satanists that recalled the days of the Salem Witchcraft Trials.

Rumors continue that each year hundreds of homicides are satanically or ritually inspired, but it has never been proved by federal, state, or local law enforcement that there exists an organized satanic movement responsible for these deaths. There have been serial killers who claimed to be Satanists, but in each of these cases police investigations revealed that the murderers were not actually members of any organized satanic religious group. Even such a high-profile "devil worshipper" as Richard Ramirez, the infamous "Night Stalker" of Los Angeles, who committed a series of brutal nighttime killings, robberies, and sexual attacks, was never found to be a member of any formal satanic group.

Contrary to the fears of conservative Christians, Satanism as an actual religion is composed of a few small groups, which according to census figures in the United States and Canada probably number fewer than ten thousand members. Such religious cults as Santer'a, Wicca, Voodoo, and various neopagan groups are regularly—and incorrectly—identified as satanic. It has been suggested that the statistics often quoted by Christian evangelists, warning of millions of Satan worshippers, quite likely consider all non-Christian religions as satanic, including Buddhism, Hinduism, and Islam.

However, there are many kinds of free-form Satanism, ranging from those merely symptomatic of sexual unrest and moral rebellion among young people to those of mentally unbalanced serial killers who murder and sacrifice their victims to their own perverse concept of satanic evil. There are also individuals, primarily teenagers and young adults, who for a time dabble in the occult, ceremonial magic, and other freelance rituals and who may declare themselves Satanists. Their numbers are difficult to assess with any accuracy, for they are essentially faddists, generally in-

A pentagram symbol, often associated with Satanism, is also used as a Wiccan symbol.

spired by a current motion picture or television series that popularizes Satanism or witchcraft. Some of these satanic dabblers may go so far as to sacrifice a small animal and spray-paint satanic symbols on houses and sidewalks, but their commitment to a lifestyle dominated by dedication to Satan soon dissipates.

The following signs and symbols are among the most common expressions of Satanism, both among individual Satanists and those self-proclaimed "high priests and priestesses" who have established covens (traditionally having thirteen or fewer members):

The Pentagram: The traditional five-pointed star, most often shown within a circle.

The Upside-down Cross: A mockery of Jesus's death on the cross. Sometimes the cross is shown with broken "arms."

An Upside-down Cross Incorporating an Inverted Question Mark: The "Cross of Confusion," questioning the authority and power of Jesus.

The Quarter Moon and Star: Represents the moon goddess Diana and Lucifer, the "Morning Star." When the moon is reversed, it is usually satanic.

The Inverted Swastika: The swastika originally represented the perpetual progression of the four seasons, the four winds, the four elements, and so forth. Already perverted when the Nazis claimed it as their symbol, it is supposedly inverted by Satanists to show the elements of nature turned against themselves and out of harmony with God's divine plan of balance.

The Ritual Calendar: Satanism adapted the traditional calendar of witchcraft and celebrates eight major festivals, known as Sabbats: February 1—Candlemas; March 21—spring equinox; April 30—Walpurgisnacht; May 1—Beltane; June 21—summer solstice; August 1—Lammas; September 23—fall equinox; October 31—Samhain; December 21—winter solstice.

SATELLITES AND SNOOPING

Project Echelon is supposed to be busy detecting terrorist activity, but conspiracy theorists fear that its high-tech talents are also being directed at U.S. civilians who have politically incorrect opinions.

One of the first projects assigned to the High Frequency Active Auroral Research Program (HAARP) was the conversion of the aurora borealis into a massive transmitting antenna that would be utilized in conjunction with ground-based antennae in order to create a multitude of frequencies that could be transmitted from stations spaced around the planet. The principal transmissions would be at extremely low frequencies (ELF), the same range in which the human brain operates. ELF transmissions can be tuned to impair the brain performance of a large segment of the population of any nation or to spy on and monitor certain individuals. ELF can penetrate walls, roofs, and underground bunkers. Through auroral surveillance technology, no computer hard drive is secure, regardless of the encryption employed.

The U.S. National Security Agency (NSA) already has in place the most complete surveillance program ever created, codename Echelon. This global spy system has the ability to capture and analyze virtually each telephone call, fax, email, and telex message transmitted anywhere in the world. Although Echelon is managed and controlled by NSA, it functions with full cooperation from the Government Communications Head Quarters of Great Britain, the Communications Security Establishment of Canada, the Australian Defense Security Directorate, and the General Communications Security Bureau of New Zealand. With intercept stations all over the planet, Echelon is able to gather all satellite, microwave, cellular, and fiber-optic communications, then process this data through the cutting-edge technology of the enormous computer facilities of NSA, which even has advanced voice recognition and optical character recognition programs to detect any code words or phrases.

All members cooperating with Echelon have agreed to a top-secret, highly classified 1948 document known as "UKUSA." Ostensibly Echelon is busy detecting terrorist activity, but conspiracy theorists have evidence that its high-tech talents are also being directed at U.S. civilians in a domestic surveillance program targeted at individuals who have politically incorrect opinions or who diverge in some way from what the "listeners" consider the norm. The fact that such illegal eavesdropping violates the First, Fourth, and Fifth Amendments of the U.S. Constitution is of little or no concern to the "listeners" and the "watchers."

President Harry S. Truman established the NSA in 1952 with a classified presidential directive that remains secret to all but a few government agents with top clearance ratings. The government didn't even acknowledge the existence of the NSA until 1957. It has been determined that NSA's original assignment was to conduct intelligence and communications security for the government. President Ronald Reagan added the mission of information systems security and operations security training in 1984 and 1988. In 1986 the NSA was also given the task of supporting combat operations for the Department of Defense. In its headquarters at Fort George Meade, Maryland, NSA has unquestionably the most extensive and complete assemblage of intelligence-gathering equipment in the world. NSA is the largest global employer of mathematicians, code makers, code breakers, linguists, computer geeks, and electronic experts.

Many conspiracy theorists fear that within a few years all Americans will be forced to receive a programmable biochip implant somewhere in their body. Initially people will be informed that the biochip will be used largely for purposes of identification. The reality is that the implant will be linked to a massive supercomputer system that will make it possible for government agencies such as NSA to maintain a surveillance of all citizens by ground sensors and satellites. With the help of satellites, the implanted person can be followed anywhere.

Conspiracy researchers believe that even beyond the present incredible snooping powers of Echelon, NSA has developed an electronic surveillance system that can simultaneously follow the unique bioelectrical resonance brain frequency of millions of people. NSA's Signals Intelligence group can remotely monitor information from human brains by decoding the evoked potentials (3.50HZ, 5 milliwatt) emitted by the brain. Electromagnetic frequency (EMF) brain stimulation signals can be sent to the brains of specific individuals, causing the desired effects of depression, anxiety, anger, or sorrow to be experienced by the target.

Defenders of Echelon are quick to state that it was such signals-intercept technology that helped contain and eventually defeat the USSR during the Cold War. Conspiracists say, fine, that was then, this is now—and Echelon, designed originally to target Communist and terrorist states, is currently being directed against virtually every citizen on the planet. Echelon must not be used as a threat to the liberties of the American people or to assess the political, religious, and personal opinions of individuals.

RICHARD MELLON SCAIFE

Billionaire Richard Mellon Scaife may have single-handedly funded the "vast right-wing conspiracy" that Hillary Clinton claimed was plotting against her husband.

In 1999 the *Washington Post* declared Richard Mellon Scaife the "funding father of the Right." A billionaire philanthropist and owner-publisher of the *Pittsburgh Tribune-Review,* Scaife became so active in his efforts to dig up dirt against President Bill Clinton that many Democrats were convinced that Hillary Clinton's claim that a "vast right-wing conspiracy" was persecuting her husband was a reference to Scaife.

Scaife was the principal backer of the *American Spectator* and the "Arkansas Project," whose mission was to discover the "real facts" about Clinton. Although the "project" did publicize Paula Jones and her accusations of sexual harassment against Clinton, the allegations of financial misconduct and a number of additional sexual indiscretions were largely dismissed. The greatest misfire of the Arkansas Project was the claim that the Clintons had worked with CIA rogue agents in a drug smuggling ring out of Mena, Arkansas, and that they had ordered the murder of Vince Foster to silence him.

Richard Mellon Scaife became interested in politics when his father, Alan Scaife, served with the Office of Strategic Services (OSS) during World War II and the family lived in Washington, D.C. In 1956 the younger Scaife became a committeeman for the Allegheny Republican Party, and in 1964 he was drawn to Barry Goldwater's campaign for president because of his mother's friendship with the candidate. For a time, Scaife headed Forum World Features, a publishing company that was later exposed as a front organization for the CIA. His first venture into circumventing campaign finance laws occurred when he donated $999,000 to the 1972 reelection fund of Richard M. Nixon. After the Watergate scandal broke in 1973, Scaife refused to speak with Nixon ever again.

Scaife is regarded by those who know him as a very private, taciturn man who never grants interviews and who seldom speaks—even during his own board meetings.

Over the past thirty years, the Scaife Foundations have given over $340 million to such right-wing groups as the Heritage Foundation, the American Enterprise Institute, and the Cato Institute. Although he has received the most publicity for his generous financial support to conservative political causes, Scaife also controls the Carthage Foundation, the Sarah Scaife Foundation, and the Allegheny Foundation. He is key benefactor for many art galleries, museums, orchestras, and educational institutions, such as the University of Chicago, Boston University, the University of Pittsburgh, and Bowling Green State University. He controlled the Scaife Family Foundation until 2001, when that position was shared by his son and daughter. In 2005, Scaife, the principal heir to the Mellon banking, oil, and aluminum fortune was ranked No. 283 on the Forbes 400.

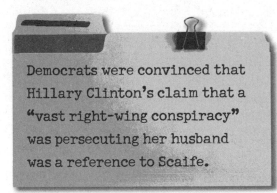

Democrats were convinced that Hillary Clinton's claim that a "vast right-wing conspiracy" was persecuting her husband was a reference to Scaife.

Although Scaife's efforts to remove President Bill Clinton from office were well-known, in the autumn of 2007 he reversed his opinion of Clinton because of the work that the former president's foundation was accomplishing on a global basis. To the astonishment of all who had followed Scaife's anti-Clinton machinations over the past several years, the *Pittsburgh Tribune Review,* a Scaife-controlled newspaper, endorsed Hillary Clinton for president two days before the Pennsylvania presidential primary.

To the chagrin of some of his fellow conservatives, Scaife is a major donor to pro-choice advocates and has given millions to Planned Parenthood. His mother Sarah's favorite causes were population control, environmental conservation, and hospitals. Jonas Salk developed his polio vaccine in a Sarah Scaife–sponsored laboratory.

SCIENTISTS' SUSPICIOUS DEATHS

It appears that there is nothing safe about being a research scientist when the New World Order is looking over your shoulder.

There are many conspiracy theorists who believe that numerous research scientists in a wide variety of fields have been murdered in recent years because they were going to act as whistle-blowers regarding the character and direction being taken by their companies' biological warfare research, nuclear devices, or missiles. Some of the scientists were opening up new areas of promising research regarding alternative energy sources. Some conspiracy theorists set the body count of scientists who have met strange, bizarre, and untimely deaths at ninety or more. As with all of the body counts or death lists that we include in this encyclopedia of conspiracies and secret societies, we add our disclaimer that many of the individuals on such lists may have suffered from long-term illnesses, met their demise in accidents totally devoid of nefarious circumstances, or committed suicide of their own free, albeit troubled, will. By the same token, conspiracy researchers remind us that secret government agencies have developed means of making murders appear to be deaths due to natural causes or accident. Some of these methods are designed to be able to avoid detection in autopsies and postmortem examinations. A declassified CIA assassination manual states that a "contrived accident" is "the most effective technique of secret assassination." An example of an "efficient technique" is "a fall of 75 feet or more onto a hard surface." Other insidious techniques involve the injection of cancer cells, heart attack inducements, and absorption of deadly, untraceable poison. There are some deaths on these lists that do seem quite suspicious, and that is why we include them for your own assessment.

Frank Olson, November 1953: Olson worked for the CIA's Special Operations Division at Fort Detrick, Maryland, testing biological weapons. After attending a conference at Deep Creek Lodge in western Maryland, he told his wife that he intended to quit his job with the CIA. In the early morning of November 29, 1953, Olson went through the window of a hotel room that he was sharing with Robert Lashbrook, a colleague. His death was ruled a suicide at the time, and not until 1975 did Olson's son Eric find out that his father had been given LSD without his knowledge.

According to conspiracy researchers, a literal epidemic of over two dozen mysterious deaths of scientists, experts, and recent science graduates occurred in the 1980s at Marconi or Plessey Defense Systems in the UK. Among those who died under suspicious circumstances are the following:

Keith Bowden, March 1982: A computer programmer and scientist at Essex University who worked for Marconi Defense Systems, Bowden, forty-six, was considered an expert on computer-controlled aircraft. Police ruled his fatal car crash the result of drunk driving, but family and friends denied the allegation.

Roger Hill, March 1985: Hill, forty-nine, was a radar designer with Marconi. His death from a shotgun blast was ruled a suicide by the coroner.

Jonathan Wash, November 1985: A digital communications expert who worked at British Telecom's secret research center in Suffolk, Jonathan Wash, twenty-nine, fell to his death from a hotel room in Abidjan, Ivory Coast.

Vimal Dajibhai, August 1986: Dajibhai, twenty-four, was responsible for testing computer control systems at Marconi Underwater Systems. His 240-foot fall from Clifton Suspension Bridge, Bristol, was ruled a suicide.

Arshad Sharif, October 1986: Sharif, twenty-six, allegedly committed suicide in a particularly bizarre manner by looping a ligature around his neck, tying the other end to a tree, then driving off in his car with the accelerator pedal pushed to the floor. Sharif had been working on satellite detection systems for submarines.

Dr. John Brittan, January 1987: A respected scientist involved in top-secret work, Brittan, fifty-two, was found dead from carbon monoxide poisoning in his garage after he had returned from a trip to the United States.

David Skeels, February 1987: An engineer with Marconi, Skeels, forty-three, was found dead in his car with a hosepipe connected to the exhaust.

Peter Peapell, February 1987: Peapell, forty-six, had been working with various metals and their resistance to explosives when he was found dead in his garage, allegedly from carbon monoxide poisoning.

Shanni Warren, April 1987: In order for the verdict of suicide to be fulfilled in the case of Warren, twenty-six, she had to be capable of tying her feet with a rope, binding her hands behind her back, gagging herself with a noose around her neck, then wobbling to a small lake and drowning herself in eighteen inches of water. Four weeks after her death, GEC Marconi took over Micro Scope, the small company in which she had served as personal assistant.

Russell Smith, January 1988: Smith, twenty-three, a laboratory technician with the Atomic Energy Research Establishment at Essex, died as the result of a fall from a cliff at Boscastle in Cornwall.

Alistair Beckham, August 1988: A software engineer with Plessey Defense Systems, Beckham, fifty, was found electrocuted in his garden shed.

Peter Ferry, August 1988: The assistant marketing director at Marconi, Peter Ferry, sixty, was found electrocuted in his apartment with electrical leads in his mouth.

Andrew Hall, September 1988: The thirty-three-year-old Hall was found dead of carbon monoxide poisoning in his garage. He had served as engineering manager with British Aerospace.

While the reports of mysterious deaths and suicides involving microbiologists and other scientists employed by Marconi Defense Systems in the UK are unsettling to say the least, it appears that certain aspects of research science are no safer in other parts of the world.

Dr. Tsunao Saitoh, 1996: Saitoh, forty-six, a leading researcher of Alzheimer's disease, and his thirteen-year-old daughter were found shot to death in La Jolla, California. Police who found Saitoh dead behind the wheel of his car and his daughter lying outside the vehicle described the murder as professionally done.

Dr. Yaacov Matzner, Avishai Berkman, and Professor Amiram Eldor, November 24, 2001: Matzner, fifty-four, dean of the Hebrew University–Hadassah Medical School in Jerusalem, one of the world's leading experts on blood diseases, and Eldor, fifty-nine, head of the hematology institute at Tel Aviv's Ichilov Hospital, an internationally known expert on blood clotting, and Berkman, fifty, director of the Tel Aviv Health Department, were killed on their way back to Israel via Switzerland when their plane came down in a dense forest two miles short of the landing field in Zurich.

Dr. Don C. Wiley, December 2001: Wiley, fifty-seven, one of the foremost microbiologists in the United States, was an authority on the response of the immune system to such viral attacks as those from HIV, Ebola, and influenza. Police found his rental car on a bridge outside Memphis, Tennessee, and his body was pulled from the Mississippi River on December 20.

Dr. Robert M. Schwartz, December 2001: An expert in DNA sequencing and pathogenic microorganisms, and a founding member of the Virginia Biotechnology Association, Schwartz, fifty-seven, was stabbed and slashed by a sword in his farmhouse in Leesburg, Virginia. His daughter Clara—a pagan high priestess—and a number of her fellow pagans were charged. In 2003, Clara was convicted of murder and sentenced to forty-eight years; Kyle Hubert, life without parole; Michael Paul Pfohl, twenty-one years; and Katherine Inglis, twelve months.

Dr. Nguyen Van Set, December 2001: Set, forty-four, had just received international acclaim for discovering a virus that could be modified to affect smallpox, when he accidentally entered an air-locked storage lab and died from exposure to nitrogen.

Dr. Victor Korshunov, February, 2002: Korshunov, fifty-six, an expert in intestinal bacteria in children, was clubbed to death near his Moscow home.

Ian Langford, February 2002: Recognized as an expert in environmental diseases Langford, forty, was found dead in his home near Norwich, England, naked from the waist down and stuffed under a chair.

David Wynn-Williams, March 2002: Wynn-Williams, fifty-five, died when struck by a car while jogging near his home in Cambridge, England. The respected astrobiologist had been studying microbes that might survive in outer space.

Dr. Steven Mostow, March 2002: A well-known expert in bioterrorism of the Colorado Health Sciences Center, Mostow, sixty-three, died when the airplane he was piloting crashed near Denver.

Dr. David Kelly, July 2003: Kelly, fifty-nine, was an internationally known biological warfare weapons specialist who held a senior post at the British Ministry of Defense and who advised Prime Minister Tony Blair regarding the weapons of mass destruction allegedly held by Saddam Hussein in Iraq. He was found dead after apparently slashing his wrists in a wooded area near his home at Southmoor, Oxfordshire.

Robert Leslie Burghoff, November 2003: Burghoff, forty-five, had been on the trail of the virus that seemed to be plaguing cruise ships when on November 22, 2003, a white van jumped the curb, struck him, then sped on without stopping. Burghoff died an hour later.

William T. McGuire, May 2004: The body of McGuire, thirty-nine, professor and senior program analyst at the New Jersey Institute of Technology, Newark, was found in three suitcases floating in Chesapeake Bay.

Dr. Eugene Mallove, May 2004: Mallove was bludgeoned to death shortly after he had published an open letter to scientists regarding free energy sources and cold fusion technologies. Harvard educated, the holder of three earned doctorates, he spent the last fifteen years of his life researching cold fusion and seeking new energy devices.

Dr. Bassem al-Mudares, July 2004: The mutilated body of al-Mudares, a highly respected chemist, was found in Samarra, Iraq.

Professor John Clark, August 2004: Clark was head of the science lab at the Roslin Institute in Midlothian, Scotland, that became a world-famous biotechnology research center when it cloned Dolly, the sheep. Clark was found hanging in his holiday home.

Dr. Jeong H. Im, January 2005: Im, seventy-two, a protein chemist and retired research assistant professor at the University of Missouri, was stabbed numerous times and his body left in the trunk of his burning automobile.

Dr. Robert J. Lull, May 2005: A former president of both the American College of Nuclear Physicians and the San Francisco Medical Society and an expert on the threat of nuclear terrorism, Lull, sixty-four, was found stabbed to death in the entryway of his hilltop home in San Francisco shortly after he had called for full BSE (mad cow disease) testing.

SCIENTOLOGY

Although a celebrity cult of the rich and famous, Scientology intimidates and controls its rank-and-file members.

Few of the controversial new religious movements have received as much negative publicity or been investigated by so many government agencies, including the Internal Revenue Service, the Food and Drug Administration, and the Federal Bureau of Investigation, as has Scientology.

The founder, Lafayette Ronald Hubbard (1911–1986), known to Scientologists the world over as "L. Ron," is said to have studied many Eastern philosophies as he journeyed around the globe. A background in mathematics, engineering, and nuclear physics grounded him in the physical sciences at the same time that he was exploring the human mind through an examination of Freudian psychoanalytic theory. When injuries suffered in service as a naval officer during World War II left him crippled and blind, Hubbard claimed that his ability to draw upon mental insights allowed him to cure himself of his disabilities. He called this process Dianetics, and he first outlined its central elements in article for the May 1950 issue of *Astounding Science Fiction* magazine. Later that same year, Hubbard published *Dianetics: The Modern Science of Mental Health*.

Dianetics states that there are essentially two components of the mind, the analytical and the reactive. The analytical aspect, similar to the Freudian concept of the ego, is the consciously active and aware part of the mind. The reactive mind comes into play during times of intense stress when, very often, the analytical facet shuts down. Although the individual may not be aware of the process, the reactive mind absorbs and records every nuance of emotional, mental, and physical pain suffered by him or her. Hubbard called the impressions or "recordings" made by the reactive mind during moments of trauma "engrams," and while the conscious, analytical mind may remain unaware of their presence, they can cause debilitating mental and physical problems and inhibit a person's full potential.

The Dianetics process called "auditing" enables a troubled or inhibited individual to explore those engrams preventing his or her development and to be "cleared" of such im-

The L. Ron Hubbard Scientology Center in Los Angeles, California.

pediments by an "auditor," a minister of Scientology. Once a Scientologist has been "cleared," he or she may continue progress to a state wherein freedom from all the constraints of matter, energy, space, and time is attained and a transcendent level of near-perfection is achieved.

Shortly after the publication of *Dianetics,* Hubbard established the Hubbard Association of Scientologists International in Phoenix, Arizona. In 1954 the First Church of Scientology was founded in Los Angeles. Increasing demand for information about Scientology led to the establishment of the Founding Church of Scientology along with the first Academy of Scientology in Washington, D.C., in July 1955. Today, Scientology claims around eight million members and over three thousand churches worldwide.

In spite of warm endorsements regarding the benefits of Scientology from celebrities such as John Travolta, Kelly Preston, Tom Cruise, Isaac Hayes, Priscilla Presley, and

Kirstie Alley, the organization is very often in the center of controversies involving accusations that it poses as a religion while it mentally and physically abuses its adherents. Richard Behar, writing in the May 6, 1991, issue of *Time* magazine, stated that rather than being a religion or a church, Scientology "is a hugely profitable global racket that survives by intimidating members and critics in a Mafia-like manner."

SHROUD OF TURIN

If the shroud and the Man on the Cloth are ever definitively found to be authentic, one of the greatest reported miracles in world history will be acclaimed as true.

For millions of believers, the fourteen-by-four-foot shroud that has been kept under guard in a chapel in Turin, Italy, since 1452 is the authentic burial garment of Jesus of Nazareth. The cloth reveals a full-sized human image mysteriously impressed on its coarse fibers in what appears to be an exact physical representation of Jesus as he lay in the tomb after his death by crucifixion at the hands of Roman soldiers.

In the fall of 1978 the ancient shroud was exhibited publicly for the first time since 1933, thus reigniting the fires of controversy that have blazed around this icon since the first century. Many of the experts who have examined the shroud insist that the image was not painted on the cloth, for the colors are not absorbed into the fibers. Neither could the image have been placed on the shroud by any ordinary application of heat, or the fibers would have been scorched.

The gospel accounts of Jesus's crucifixion state that he was whipped and beaten savagely by Roman soldiers, who contemptuously placed a cruel crown of thorns on the head of the man they sarcastically identified as the "King of the Jews." The merciless humiliation completed, Jesus was marched through the streets of Jerusalem bearing a wooden cross on his back before he was nailed to its horizontal bar at the place of execution. After his assumed death, a spear was thrust into his side by a Roman soldier.

Certain researchers have declared the front and the back images on the Shroud of Turin anatomically correct if the cloth had been used to wrap a crucified man in its folds. The impressions are of a tall man with a bearded, majestic countenance, his hands crossed, with the imprints of nails through the wrists and feet. The right side of the man's chest was pierced. In addition, the image is said to bear the marks of whip lashes on the back. The man's right shoulder is chafed, as if from having borne a rough, heavy object. A number of puncture wounds appear around the head, and one cheek displays a pronounced bruise. The chest cavity is expanded, as if the victim had been trying desperately to draw air into the lungs, a typical physical response during crucifixion. Champions of the shroud also claim that scalp punctures and blood rivulets detectable on the forehead have the characteristics and proper location for both venous and arterial blood flow—and yet circulation of human blood was not discovered until 1593.

When the shroud was examined by technical investigators from the Los Alamos Scientific Laboratory in New Mexico in 1978, the scientists announced that it appeared to be authentic, woven of a type of linen typically used in Jewish burials in the Holy Land about 30 C.E., thus approximating the date of Jesus's crucifixion. As for the image imprinted on the shroud, Raymond Rogers, a thermochemist of the Los Alamos design engineering division, stated his opinion that the impression had been formed by "a burst of radiant energy—light, if you will."

Since its examination in 1978 the Shroud of Turin has been hailed by some as physical proof of Jesus's resurrection from the dead and his triumph over the grave, while others have condemned it as a hoax crafted by medieval monks who sought to create the ultimate in holy relics for spiritual pilgrims to venerate. Raymond Rogers is one of a number of scientists who believe that the cloth is truly the shroud of Jesus Christ. In his view—and in that of many others—the Shroud of Turin answers the eternal question of whether humans can achieve immortality. If Christ was resurrected from the dead, then the gospels are true and eternal life is offered to all.

In October 1978 a U.S.-based scientific group, the Shroud of Turin Research Project (STRP), reported unanimously after examining the shroud that "the image on the cloth is not the result of applied materials." In their estimation, the Man on the Shroud was not painted on the cloth; rather, an unknown event of oxidation selectively darkened certain fibrils of the threads so as to make a superficial image of a man with accurate details valid even when magnified 1,000 times. Through some paranormal occurrence the body image is very much like a photographic negative.

If the blood was still wet on the body, the stain on the cloth would have smeared; if the blood was dry, it would have broken where crusted. Neither occurred, thus leading some researchers to believe that the body must somehow have *dematerialized* without the physical removal of the shroud.

Some members of the STRP have drawn a parallel between the mysterious images on the shroud "and the fact that images were formed on stones by fireball radiation from the atomic bomb at Hiroshima."

Among other significant data that seem to testify to the shroud's authenticity are the following:

- The seventy varieties of pollen found on the burial cloth came from the Near East. Thirty-eight varieties came from within fifty miles of Jerusalem—and fourteen of them grow nowhere else.

- The Z-twist thread and three-to-one herringbone-twill weave used in forming the shroud were known only to the Near East and Asia until recent centuries.

- The cotton fibers in the shroud's linen could have come only by weaving on looms of the Near East.

- The feet of the Man of the Shroud bear smudges of actual dirt that contain travertine aronite, a rare form of calcium that matches the spectral properties of this limestone substance found in caves near Jerusalem's Damascus Gate. No other source is known.

Even the most recent translations of the gospels state that Jesus was nailed to the cross by his hands, but the shroud correctly displays a medical truth: He was nailed through the "space of Destot" in the wrist, because a nail in the soft flesh of the hands would not support a man's weight. A spike driven through the space of Destot will lacerate the median nerve, causing the thumb to flex sharply into the palm. The Man of the Shroud has no discernible thumbs. Would an artist in the Middle Ages have known about such medical idiosyncrasies?

The man was crowned with a cap of thorns typical of the Near East Judeans, not the Greek-style wreath so often depicted in artist's renderings of Jesus's "crown of thorns." The bloodstains on the shroud are precisely correct, both biblically and anatomically.

In *The Shroud of Turin: The Burial Cloth of Jesus Christ?* (1978) Ian Wilson postulated a Knights Templar connection for the so-called missing years of the shroud, from 1204 to 1357. Wilson indicates that the relic was in Athens and Bescançon, France, during that period. The extensive copying of the face on the shroud by the Knights Templar could have led to the papal revocation of their charter, which was later followed by the execution of their leaders by the French ecclesiastical court. The

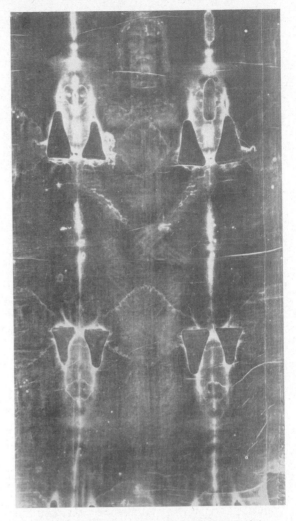

The Shroud of Turin is said to be the actual burial shroud that covered Jesus Christ's body. When Christ rose from the dead, His image was burned into the shroud. Questions remain as to its authenticity.

Templar involvement appears to be validated by the discovery of a matching shroud face that was found behind the false ceiling of an outbuilding in Templecombe, southern England, on grounds that had once served as a Templar recruitment and training center.

Pope John Paul II authorized public exhibitions of the shroud for April 18 to May 31, 1998, and April 29 to June 11, 2000. Among the findings prompted by these showings was the report by two Israeli scientists in June 1999 that plant imprints and pollen found on the shroud supported the premise that it originated in the Holy Land. Avinoam Danin, a botany professor at the Hebrew University of Jerusalem, said that the shroud contained images of some plants, such as the bean caper (*Zygophyllum dumosum*), which grows only in Israel, Jordan, and Egypt Sinai desert. The rock rose (*Cistus creticus*), which grows throughout the Middle East, was also detected, along with the imprint of a coin minted in the reign of the Roman emperor Tiberius, who ruled at the time of the crucifixion.

Many of the critics of the authenticity of the shroud and its images argue that it is nothing more than a finely executed medieval painting. Some skeptics have even claimed that the shroud images were painted by Leonardo da Vinci—an argument countered by the fact that the great artist was born in 1452, nearly one hundred years after the shroud is reported to have been on exhibit in Lirey, France, in 1357.

On January 26, 2005, Raymond Rogers, the retired Los Alamos chemist and former member of the Shroud of Turin Research Project, reported the findings of new microchemical tests that placed the age of the shroud at between 1,300 and 3,000 years, much older than previous radiocarbon tests have suggested. Even those skeptics who dismiss the shroud as a medieval hoax concede that the controversy is not yet resolved.

SKINHEADS

A movement with many facets, the neo-Nazi skinheads have become a violent and dangerous force in thirty-three countries on six continents.

Shaved heads have become a fairly popular style for young men, so one must be cautious in labeling any fellow between the ages of thirteen and twenty-five as a neo-Nazi skinhead. While the shaven skull is no longer the obvious identifying characteristic of the skinhead, a list of common accouterments may complete a fairly accurate composite sketch: Nazi tattoos on their heads or bodies; combat boots, jeans, thin suspenders, bomber or flight jackets or Levi or Wrangler blue denim jackets with Nazi symbols.

The history of the movement goes back to the 1960s in London when the British people were experiencing an increasingly sharp demarcation between the working class and the middle class. Emulating the Beatles, so-called Mods grew their hair to mimic the rock group's longish locks and wore the Carnaby Street clothing fancied by their idols. Those youth who couldn't afford the Mod fashions of the middle and upper classes were contented to dress as their fathers had, with steel-toed boots, denim jeans, shirts, and suspenders.

By the mid-1960s the "gang mods" had evolved, with shorter hair and working-class clothes, personified by rock groups like the Who and the Kinks. Skinheads emerged in 1969, and the rock band Slade popularized the look. Boots were temporarily replaced with brogues, and the jeans and shirt and suspenders look gave way to slacks and sweaters. One could still have long hair and be a "smoothie" or a "suede-head," but the tough attitude had to be maintained.

When punk rock became the music of the day in the early 1970s, young people looking for a way to shock the public buzzed their hair short or shaved it off altogether. Then, releasing the class tension that had been simmering for so long, they began initiating riots and brawls at soccer meets and other public gatherings.

Called "punk-skins" by the media, the racist political group National Front recruited members to participate in the harassment of racial minorities and immigrants. The true skinheads denied their involvement in such brutal acts, claiming that the National Front was enlisting street punks and shaving their heads to make them look like skinheads.

While this accusation of origin may be debated, since the movement began in England in the 1970s the skinheads have become a violent and dangerous force in thirty-three countries on six continents. In the United States alone, as many as forty-five murders of racial minorities and homosexuals have been attributed to skinheads during the last two decades.

Experts on the movement divide Skinheads into three main categories:

- Neo-Nazi skinheads, sometimes called "White Power," who actively hate blacks, Jews, gays, and other minority groups.

- Skin Heads against Racial Prejudice (SHARP), a.k.a. Anti-Racist-Action (ARA) Skins. From the beginning of the movement, some skinheads did not become racists, and some actively oppose all kinds of race prejudice today.

- Traditional (trad), Trojan (after the record label), or "original" skins. The traditional skinheads identify with the original skinhead movement that emphasized working-class pride. They revere the spirit of '69 and the music and styles that were prevalent when the movement began.

SKULL AND BONES

Its members assure outsiders that Skull and Bones is simply a college fraternity that taps fifteen rich boys each year to undergo an initiation that's nothing but "mumbo-jumbo." Conspiracists are certain that the occult-based secret society worships the absolute power of the state and the New World Order.

When William Huntington Russell returned to Yale from his studies in Germany in 1832, his head was filled with the philosophy of reason as taught by Georg Wilhelm Friedrich Hegel at the University of Berlin. In Hegel's worldview, the state is Absolute Reason and individuals must give their total obedience to it. The state has supreme rights over individuals, and individuals must recognize that their supreme duty is to the state. Neither Hitler's fascism nor Lenin's communism would quarrel with the precepts of Hegelianism. Russell also returned to Yale with the notion of establishing a chapter of a corps in Germany. He called it the "Order of Scull and Bones," later changed to Skull and Bones.

The society, which Russell formed with Alphonso Taft (class of 1833), exists only at Yale, and only fifteen juniors are selected by senior members to be initiated into the next year's membership. Each fortunate initiate is gifted with $15,000 and a grandfather clock. Skull and Bones is not your typical beer-swilling, goof-off fraternity. The initiates' vows have to do with support of one another in the achievement of worldly and highly material success after graduation. William Russell (1833) rose to the military rank of general and became a state legislator in Connecticut. Alphonso Taft was appointed U.S. attorney general, then secretary of war, ambassador to Austria, and ambassador to Russia. His son, William Howard Taft (1887) was elected to the U.S. presidency in 1909 and later became chief justice of the Supreme Court, the only person to have achieved both positions.

The "Tomb" was constructed in 1856. It is the same vine-covered, windowless brownstone hall where Skull and Bones still holds its mysterious occult rites. Almost from the very beginning, a mystique grew up around Skull and Bones, as might be expected in a university community that suddenly has within its confines a "secret society." Professors objected because of its secrecy in a nation that prizes its recognition of equality and its contempt of elitism. As early as 1873 a New Haven newspaper published an article that condemned the society as an "obnoxious, deadly evil" with an increasing "arrogance and self-fancied superiority."

In the 2004 election, the U.S. had two "Bonesmen" squaring off as presidential opponents. Both George W. Bush and John Kerry are members of the secret society, and Bush had brought five fellow Bonesmen to join his administration, the most recent was William Donaldson (1953) to serve as the head of the Securities and Exchange Commission.

In Hegel's worldview, the state is Absolute Reason and individuals must give their total obedience to it.

Ron Rosenbaum, author and columnist for the *New York Observer,* probably spoke for the majority of Americans when he told CBS News (June 13, 2004) that he believed there to be "a deep and legitimate distrust in America for power and privilege that are cloaked in secrecy." Rosenbaum argued that we are supposed to do things out in the open in America. Rosenbaum, a Yale classmate of George W. Bush, admitted to a thirty-year obsession with Skull and Bones. The columnist said that he actually lived near the "Tomb" and passed it all the time. When the initiation rites were being conducted, he said, he could hear "strange cries and whispers" coming from the sepulchral, windowless building.

Another Yale graduate, Alexandra Robbins, claims that in her book *Secrets of the Tomb* she managed to penetrate the avowed wall of silence that surrounds the society. In her opinion, the sounds that Rosenbaum heard were likely "mumbo-jumbo," a silly ritual that means something only to the people who are in the society. "There is a devil, a Don Quixote, and a Pope who has one foot sheathed in a white monogrammed slipper resting on a stone skull," Robbins told Morley

Safer of CBS News. "The initiates are led into the room one at a time. And once an initiate is inside, the Bonesmen shriek at him." After enduring the shrieking, the initiate is shoved to his knees in front of Quixote as the assembled Bonesmen fall silent. Quixote then lifts his sword and taps the initiate on his left shoulder and says, "By order of our order, I dub thee knight of Euloga."

According to legend, Prescott Bush (George W. Bush's grandfather) and some fellow Bonesmen robbed the grave of the great Apache chief Geronimo and took home his skull as a relic for the tomb. Accounts are mixed as to whether the skull was returned to the Apache nation.

The family names to be found on the roster of Skull and Bones truly represents the powerful, the wealthy, the elite—the aristocracy of the United States: Rockefeller, Goodyear, Harriman, Whitney, Lord, Taft, Jay, Bundy, Weyerhauser, Pinchot, Sloane, Stimson, Phelps, Perkins, Pillsbury, Kellogg, Vanderbilt, Bush, Lovett, and so on. In his book *America's Secret Establishment,* Anthony Sutton detailed some of the chains of influence and power that enables the Bonesmen to accomplish conspiratorial plots.

W. C. Whitney (1863) married Flora Payne of the Standard Oil dynasty and became secretary of the navy. Elihu Root, Whitney's personal attorney, hired Henry Stimson (1888) directly out of law school. Root later became secretary of war, and Stimson was appointed to that position by William Howard Taft in 1911. Later Stimson was President Calvin Coolidge's (1923–29) governor-general of the Philippine Islands, President Herbert Hoover's (1929–33) secretary of state, and secretary of war during the administrations of Franklin D. Roosevelt (1933–45) and Harry S. Truman (1945–53). Stimson's personal assistant and point man for the Manhattan Project was Holister Bundy ('09), whose two sons William ('39) and McGeorge ('40), both Bonesmen, went on to high ranks in the CIA, the Department of Defense, the State Department, and as special assistants to Presidents Kennedy and Johnson. The Bundy brothers exercised considerable influence on the information flow during the Vietnam War, and William went on to be appointed editor of *Foreign Affairs,* the quarterly of the Council of Foreign Affairs. McGeorge became president of the Ford Foundation.

See how the "chain" of influence passed on from Bonesman to Bonesman works?

Let's take another chain, the Harriman-Bush links. Averell Harriman ('13), revered elder statesman of the Democratic Party, his brother Roland ('17), Prescott Bush ('17), and four other Bonesmen from the class of 1917 dominated two major investment bank firms, Guaranty Trust and Brown Brothers, both of which were heavily involved in financing Hitler's regime and, at the same time, the advancement of Communism in Russia. Skull and Bones began with an admiration of the Hegelian ideal of sublimation of the individual to the state, and some Bonesmen continue that ideal, working to achieve a New World Order. Averell Harriman, as minister to Great Britain in charge of the Lend-Lease program for both Britain and the Soviet Union, shipped entire factories into Russia—and, according to some conspiracy researchers, was responsible for the transfer of nuclear secrets, plutonium, and U.S. currency printing plates to the USSR. In 1942 the U.S. government acting under the Trading with the Enemy Act, seized the property of Prescott Bush on the grounds that he was fronting for the Nazis. However, after World War II had ended, Prescott Bush became a U.S. senator from Connecticut and a favorite golfing partner of President Dwight Eisenhower, who, as commander in chief of the Allied forces, had directed the European invasion that defeated the Nazi regime. Prescott also claimed personal credit as one of the eastern money men behind Richard M. Nixon's rise to political power and for per-

suading Ike to add Tricky Dick to the ticket as vice presidential candidate.

Is Skull and Bones simply a college fraternity drawing upon old traditions copied from a German student secret society, tapping fifteen rich boys each year to undergo an initiation that's nothing but "mumbo-jumbo"? Or is there something sinister in the occult-based, sanitized Satanism that worships the absolute power of the state and the New World Order?

GEORGE SOROS

Born in Budapest, educated in London, George Soros moved to the United States in 1956 and became a billionaire. Although he never involved himself in politics until George W. Bush became president, Soros vowed that if necessary he would invest his entire fortune to remove "W" from office.

If Richard Mellon Scaife is the "funding father of the right," then "funding father of the left" would probably be an apt title for George Soros. Soros was born in Budapest, Hungary, and survived both the Nazi occupation and the Communist take-over of his homeland before emigrating to England in 1947. A graduate of the London School of Economics, Soros moved to the United States in 1956 and began to amass a fortune through an international investment fund that he founded and managed. Active as a philanthropist since 1979, Soros created the Open Society Institute and a network of philanthropic organizations that benefit humanity in over fifty nations. In 1992 he founded Central European University in Budapest, and he spends more than $400 million annually to support a range of programs that focus on civil society, education, media, public health, and human rights. Today he is chairman of Soros Fund Management LLC.

Soros never really involved himself in U.S. politics until George W. Bush became president. Perhaps his resolve to remove Bush from office was not personal, since Soros's Harken Energy had bailed Bush out of financial distress in 1986 by buying his dying oil company, Spectrum 7. However, on November 11, 2003, Soros told the *Washington Post* that removing Bush from office had become the "central focus" of his life. Soros did not hesitate to pronounce the cause of getting rid of Bush as "a matter of life and death," for which he would be willing to sacrifice his entire fortune.

It soon became well known that the billionaire had donated $3 million to the Center for American Progress and $5 million to MoveOn.org, and that he and Peter Lewis had each committed $10 million to America Coming Together. On September 28, 2004, Soros went on his own multistate tour, urging voters to get Bush out of office for the good of America. According to the Center for Responsive Politics, during the 2003–2004 election cycle, Soros donated a total of $23,581,000 to various groups dedicated to replacing the Bush administration.

The fight isn't over. On April 16, 2005, Soros met with seventy millionaires and billionaires of like philosophy to plan strategy for the creation of left-leaning programs to compete with such conservative institutions as the Heritage Foundation and the Leadership Institute. The participants in the meeting have begun to call themselves the Phoenix Group.

Conspiracy theorists declare that Soros owns the Democrats and is working hard to control the Republicans. He has invested $100 million in the Carlyle Group, which boasts many highly influential Republican leaders in its membership, including former President George H.W. Bush.

Operating through a "shadow party," Soros donated $5 billion to the Democratic National Committee to guarantee Obama's victory in 2008. In November 2008, Soros told the German magazine *Spiegel* that after taking office President Obama would seek a large stimulus package in excess of $600 billion. Soros also seemed confident that the president would deal with global warming and energy dependence, and encourage a cap-and-trade system. Conspiracy theorists state that the *Spiegel* interview provides clear proof that President Obama is essentially Soros' puppet.

It is apparent to many that Soros continues to feel confident in his ability to manipulate the mainstream media. It is said that he owns 2.6 million shares of Time Warner and that he has been purchasing other media outlets for years. His influence with the mainstream media outlets was powerful enough to cause them virtually to ignore the Tea Party. On the other hand, it is strongly believed that he largely supports the Occupy Wall Street movement and prevents a negative image of the protesters who receive wide media attention.

George Soros' creed, in the opinion of many political analysts, is that the vast numbers of citizens in the United States are too selfish, too materialistic, too wasteful, and too stupid to know how to properly run and maintain an independent nation.

SPHINX

Is the largest surviving statue from the ancient world, the product of extraterrestrials, Atlanteans, or a long-forgotten civilization? To unlock the key to the riddle of the Sphinx would be to change all of human history.

In Greek mythology, the sphinx was a half-woman, half-lion creature that guarded the gates of Thebes, an ancient Egyptian city. A scourge fell upon the land that could be lifted only by solving a riddle posed by the sphinx: What begins life on four legs, lives most of its life on two legs, and ends life on three legs? In *Oedipus the King*, the Greek dramatist Sophocles has Oedipus solve the riddle with the answer "a human," for as infants we crawl

The famous Sphinx near Cairo, Egypt. As with the pyramids, some people believe that it was constructed by aliens or Atlanteans.

on all fours before learning to walk on two legs, and in old age we walk with the use of a cane—a third leg.

The Great Sphinx at Giza has posed riddles that have perplexed researchers for centuries: How old is the structure and who built it? Even in ancient times, some sources dated it as preceding the Pyramids and attributed it to architects from a lost civilization.

The Sphinx, the largest surviving statue from the ancient world, was sculpted out of limestone bedrock. The massive sculpture has the head of man in Egyptian headdress sporting a spiraling beard, a feature found on many likenesses of pharaohs. It has the body of a lion, with two paws resting beneath the head and chest. It rises 66 feet high; the leonine body stretches for 240 feet.

The Sphinx faces due east and is referred to in some Egyptian hieroglyphics as Hamachis, the god of the rising sun. Hamachis later evolved into the name Hor-em-Akhet. The akhet

is an Egyptian hieroglyph in the image of two triangles, both open at the base, connected by a line, which represents where the sun rises and sets—an image that comes to life when looking out from the Sphinx to the pyramids of Cheops and Cephren at sunset on the summer solstice. As the sun sets between the pyramids, it highlights the image of two triangles (the pyramids) connected by a line (the earth).

It was long commonly accepted that the Sphinx was sculpted during the same era when the Pyramids were built, about 2650 to 2550 B.C.E. According to a traditional historical view, the Sphinx has been most often associated with the pharaoh Khafre, who is presumably buried in the second-largest of the three pyramids at Giza. At least two statues of Khafre have been found that bear a striking resemblance to the face of the Sphinx. Egyptian religion had taken on sun worship shortly before Khafre's reign, and because pharaohs were viewed as god-kings, the association of Khafre and Hamachis is plausible. Reconstruction of the Sphinx is apparent, and archaeological evidence shows Thutmose IV had the Sphinx rescued from being buried by desert sand and ordered a renovation around 1500 B.C.E.

John Anthony West, author of *The Serpent in the Sky: The High Wisdom of Ancient Egypt,* argues that the Sphinx was created by refugees from Atlantis, the legendary continent that was supposedly destroyed around 9500 B.C.E. Graham Hancock and Robert Bauval, coauthors of *The Orion Mystery,* name wanderers from an advanced civilization that thrived on the continent of Antarctica before it was frozen over during a global catastrophe at the end of the last ice age.

Edgar Cayce, the Sleeping Prophet of Virginia Beach, prophesied that answers to the mysteries of ancient civilizations would someday be yielded by the Sphinx. According to Cayce, a secret passageway leads from one of the Sphinx's paws to its right shoulder, where there exists a Hall of Records that contains the wisdom of a lost civilization and the history of the world.

UFO researchers and authors who investigate ancient mysteries believe that the true history of the Sphinx will one day reveal clues left by extraterrestrials who inspired the construction of the massive sculpture and who deposited records of their visitation to Earth within its hidden chambers.

The enigma of the age of the Sphinx was renewed toward the end of the twentieth century when an article in *Omni* magazine (August 1992) detailed the work of Robert M. Schoch, a geologist whose research suggests that the limestone core of the Sphinx dates from 5000 B.C.E. and that the granite facing was added at the conventional time when the Sphinx is dated, around 2500 B.C.E. Schoch attributes the extremely weathered look of the Sphinx to erosion that began with heavy rains from the period between 5000 and 3000 B.C.E. Schoch's dating is based solely on geological

evidence, rather than information from hieroglyphics or other histories.

John Anthony West has promoted a theory that an advanced, pre-Egyptian civilization was responsible for the Sphinx. He believes that much of the weathering took place because of rains and floods. West points to the period around 9000 B.C.E., when the end of the Ice Age may well have affected weather patterns. A great flood, perhaps the one recounted in the biblical story of Noah, affected the Sphinx, and afterward all the structures at Giza show erosion by wind and the slow but steady encroachment of desert.

West hired Schoch, a science professor specializing in geology at Boston University, to explore the erosion of the Sphinx from a geological standpoint. During his first trip to Giza, Schoch noticed extreme erosion in two temples located in front of the Sphinx. Where the granite covering of the temples had slipped off, the exposed limestone was extremely weathered. The newer granite facing indicated to Schoch that the Sphinx was restored, not constructed, during the reign of Khafre.

Subsequent studies led Schoch to conclude that the Sphinx was constructed in stages and underwent several restorations. The head and part of the body were originally carved as far back as 5000 B.C.E. The body was completed and the face restored by chiseling away weathered limestone during Khafre's reign. However, pushing the origin of the Sphinx to 5000 B.C.E. and attributing its erosion primarily to water creates problems, for that time frame predates the development of mastabas, tombs that were built between 5000 and 3000 B.C.E. and show no signs of weathering by water.

Since the limestone cannot be dated by modern techniques (radiocarbon dating can only determine the age of things that were once animate), Schoch's findings have been widely disputed by other geologists. The age of the Sphinx continues to be considered in the context of other monuments, and the date of 2500 B.C.E. still holds weight among conservative Egyptologists.

SPOTLIGHT

The Spotlight *serves as a kind of bulletin board for far-right extremists, warning about black helicopters, gun control, and the latest conspiracy of the federal government toward it citizens.*

The *Spotlight* is the weekly tabloid propaganda tool for the Liberty Lobby, the largest, best-financed, and most powerful radical-right organization in the United States. Editorial content emphasizes a host of conspiracy theories involving the federal government and attacks such issues as national gun control and United Nations efforts to assume control over the United States. Articles on mind control by secret agencies and the maneuvers of black helicopters used by the shadow government are regular fare.

The Liberty Lobby was founded in 1955 by Willis Carto, who believes that Hitler's Nazi Germany should have won World War II so that Europe and America could have been saved from the influence of international secret societies of Jews. Even Satan, Carto pontificates, could have created no more effective agency for the destruction of the world's nations than the Jews. African Americans and people of color fare no better. Carto uses the *Spotlight* to educate more whites to the dangers of the "niggerfication" of America.

Carto's ultimate goal as a neo-Nazi is to reinvent Hitler's National Socialism on American soil. While he protests that the Liberty Lobby is a respectable conservative party, major conservative spokespeople such as William Buckley and Judge Robert Bork roundly condemn the group for its anti-Semitism and racism.

STUDENTS FOR A DEMOCRATIC SOCIETY

The Students for a Democratic Society led the first of the mass demonstrations protesting against the Vietnam War and organized the first campus "sit-ins." What began in idealism disintegrated into chaos when too many divergent voices of protest arose within their ranks.

From June 1962 to June 1969, the Students for a Democratic Society (SDS) constituted the institutional strength and hope of the New Left. In June 1962 fifty-nine SDS members and like-minded students gathered in Port Huron, Michigan, and drafted a sixty-three-page platform that criticized the government's cold war policies and reproved the materialistic attitudes of postwar American culture. It seemed logical to those who composed the Port Huron Statement that colleges and universities should serve as the conduit through which a new movement of "participatory democracy" would flow to the broader facets of American society. The SDS ideal of shifting power from the established representative institutions to communities and individuals seemed unrealistic and impractical to a nation already indoctrinated to a central federal government.

In 1963 SDS formed the Economic Research and Action Project as what they hoped would be an effective demonstration of participatory democracy in action. In the summer months of 1964, SDS volunteers in nine cities worked among the poor, striving to mobilize the disadvantaged to march toward a new insurgency. Little was accomplished among those who relied upon the government for welfare and who had long since come to understand that things improved only when they worked with the "man," not when they rebelled against him.

The SDS had gained a reputation as revolutionaries and extremists, and the majority of students on campuses across the United States regarded them as radical kooks. However, when the SDS turned their attention to antiwar activism, they touched a chord to which fellow students responded in droves. On April 17, 1965, the SDS led the first of a number of mass demonstrations against the Vietnam War when they managed to rally fifteen thousand protestors in Washington, D.C. In November 1965 they cosponsored a demonstration that drew fifty thousand to signal their disillusionment with the government's policies in Asia and the world.

> The SDS had gained a reputation as revolutionaries and extremists, and the majority of students on campuses across the United States regarded them as radical kooks.

Perhaps the image of the SDS that comes most readily to the memories of those who are old enough to remember the 1960s is the protest at Columbia University when the students occupied campus buildings and staged sit-ins in the academic administrative offices. The protest occurred in April 1968 and was directed at the university's participation in war-related research. At the same time, many academically attuned students protested Columbia's appropriation of a public park as the site for a new athletic building. University administrators finally sought police help in ending the student occupation of campus buildings and facilities. There were scuffles and resistance, and over 200 students were injured and 712 arrested.

The archetype for student demonstrations and protests had been born in the occupation by SDS of Columbia. Within days of the arrests, students took over buildings and conducted sit-ins in academic and political administrative offices on at least forty other college and university campuses across the nation.

With that great explosive triumph of revolutionary excess at Columbia and the other campus occupations it inspired, the SDS had succeeded too well in their expectations. Membership swelled so rapidly that no central control or direction could exist. New members brought different concepts and ideas for protest, and soon the SDS was broken apart by divisions within its own ranks. The organization that had sought participatory democracy as its ideal had been destroyed by too many participants with vastly differing concepts of what their focus should be.

In July 1969 what remained of Students for a Democratic Society had morphed into an even more revolutionary sect known as the Weathermen.

SUBPROJECT 94

Viet Cong prisoners were the "expendables" in these experiments with brain implants.

MK-ULTRA, the code name for the CIA's experiments with mind control, was begun on the orders of CIA director Allen Dulles in 1953 and headed by Dr. Sidney Gottlieb. When experiments with LSD on staff members and volunteers seemed productive, Gottlieb began to experiment with the drug on unsuspecting individuals. For some experiments he was joined by Dr. Donald Ewen Cameron, who had assisted the Office of Special Services (OSS) to interrogate Nazi prisoners during World War II. Intrigued by the experiments conducted on concentration camp prisoners by German doctors, Cameron later contracted to work for the OSS, which became the CIA in 1947, in the field of behavior manipulation. He continued this specialty in Projects Bluebird and Artichoke, which became MK-ULTRA in 1953. Due to his excessively harsh experiments with electroshock, LSD, and drug-induced comas that sometimes lasted for months, and his penchant for performing prefrontal lobe lobotomies, Cameron's experiments proved far too extreme for some of his "patients" and many of them died.

About 1960 Gottlieb expanded the program to include mind-control experiments with animals. In Operation Resurrection, apes were lobotomized, then placed in total isolation. After a time, the experimenters would direct radio frequencies into the brains of the apes, who immediately went mad and died, their brains literally fried. Additional experiments were conducted with dogs, cats, and monkeys in which miniaturized electrode implants were inserted in specific brain areas. Some tests were intended only to see how physical actions might be stimulated or controlled electronically. In certain instances, the animals were living bombs, guided toward their targets by electrode implants and miniaturized microphones.

In April 1961 Gottlieb assessed the animal experiments as successful and decided that it was time to experiment with electrode implants in human brains. No records exist to disclose how many cruel experiments were conducted with unwilling human subjects, for in 1972 Richard Helms, director of the CIA, ordered records of all 150 individual projects of MK-ULTRA destroyed, but information has leaked out concerning experiments with three Viet Cong prisoners in July 1968.

A team of "behaviorists" flew into Saigon and traveled to the hospital at Bien Hoa where the prisoners were being confined. The agents from "Subproject 94," as the effort was codenamed, set up their equipment in an enclosed compound, and the team's neurosurgeon and neurologist inserted minuscule electrodes into the brains of the three VC prisoners.

After a brief recovery period, the prisoners were armed with knives and direct electrical stimulation was applied to their brains. The goal of the experiment was to determine if individuals with such electrodes implanted in their brains could be incited to attack and to kill one another. Once again the Agency was seeking a perfect sleeper assassin, a true "Manchurian Candidate," who could be electronically directed to kill a subject.

After a week of enduring electrical shocks to their brains, the prisoners still refused to attack one another. They were summarily executed and their bodies burned.

Conspiracy theorists state grimly that it is impossible to know how many individuals were implanted with microelectrodes that might still be activated by orders to kill a politician, pope, or president by a secret shadow agency within the government.

SUPPRESSED MEDICAL CURES AND TECHNOLOGIES

The U.S. Patent Office is controlled by a committee of nine members who are in the pockets of powerful pharmaceutical, oil, and other companies, according to conspiracists. They are denying Americans a better, healthier, less costly life so that big corporations may profit.

There is a nine-member committee that screens applicants in the U.S. Patent Office with the express purpose of ferreting out those inventions that might in some way threaten national security. In this age when it is usually encouraged to create new energy devices and processes that might offer alternatives to our ravenous hunger for oil, one might suppose that there is a flood of applications from enthusiastic inventors who envision billions of dollars cascading down upon them as a reward for solving our energy quandary. Likewise, in a time of concerns about a balanced diet, the death tolls caused by cancer and heart disease, and a general obsession with health, thousands of proponents of various panaceas wish to protect their cures for anything and everything that ails their fellow humans.

> There are estimated to be over 4,000 unnumbered patent applications that have been confiscated and locked in a vault at the U.S. Patent and Trademark Office....

The rub comes when the experts on the patent office committee rule that some bromide or energy invention must be suppressed because of its potential to create more death and destruction than health and prosperity. A classic example is that of the genius Nikola Tesla, whose advanced knowledge of electromagnetic principles also may have produced his legendary "Death Ray," capable, some say, of destroying large sections of the planet.

There are estimated to be over 4,000 unnumbered patent applications that have been confiscated and locked in a vault at the U.S. Patent and Trademark Office because of their possible "dual use" as potential military weapons or as cures that might in some cases promote epidemics rather than curtailing them.

Conspiracy theorists argue that the committee of nine harbors hidden agendas in its examination of patent applications. The members are in the pockets of the massive fossil fuel and power monopolies, the huge pharmaceutical companies, and the military-industrial complex, and they are paid well to squelch any new invention or cure that might cut into their profits. If average American families had a free energy device that could power their homes and vehicles, they wouldn't need the big fuel or electrical companies. If average Americans could grow their own herbs for medicinal needs or had the knowledge of simple, but effective, home remedies, they wouldn't need the expensive pills and nostrums of the pharmaceutical companies.

While there are advocates for natural medicines and inexpensive herbs and supplements, there will always be a need for instruments and devices to give aid to the blind, the deaf, those who have lost limbs, and others who suffer physical handicaps.

In 1958, when he was only fourteen, wunderkind Patrick Flanagan invented the neurophone, a device that enables the profoundly deaf to hear by transferring sounds directly into their brains, bypassing their ears. Although dozens of qualified medical doctors have tested and approved the device, the technology employed in the neurophone has been suppressed by the U.S. government for over fifty years, quite likely because classified electronic mind control programs utilize similar instrumentation.

In 1950, after many years of research, biochemist Dr. Ernest T. Krebs isolated a new vitamin that he labeled B-17 and called "Laetrile." After many more years of testing, thousands of cancer sufferers firmly believed that Dr. Krebs had discovered the panacea that could conquer that dreadful disease. The national response to word-of-mouth endorsements was a massive attack on Laetrile by the pharmaceutical multinationals. In short order, Laetrile was suppressed in the United States, forcing thousands of Americans to travel to Mexico each year to undergo therapy at certain hospitals that treat cancer with nutrition. These hospitals claim a nearly one hundred percent recovery rate in treating tumors that have not been poisoned with chemotherapy, burned by radiation, or cut into with a surgeon's scalpel.

In the 1960s and 1970s, French researcher Antoine Priore fashioned amazingly effective electromagnetic healing machines that cured a wide variety of the most difficult kinds of terminal diseases. Winning the support of French Prime Minister Jacques Chaban-Delmas; the World Health Organization; Andre Lwoff, the 1965 Nobel Prize winner for Medicine; members of the Faculty of Medicine of the University of Bordeaux; and medical doctors specializing in cancer treatment at the Villejuf Institute for Cancer Research, Priore received millions of dollars in funds to sustain his research.

In 1974, multinational attacks cost Priore his local government support and his funding.

The highly respected American scientist Col. Tom Bearden has gone on record with his comment that government scientists recognized that a part of the Priore process could be weaponized as longitudinal EM wave interferometers. "In fact," Col. Bearden pointed out, "every nuclear weapon on the planet, along with every nuclear power plant, every nuclear propulsion system, and so forth, can be dudded in about 10 minutes by one class of these weapons."

Bearden himself has developed what he terms a "motionless electromagnetic generator" (MEG), which can produce over one hundred times the energy put into it. Bearden is among those scientists on the edge of tomorrow who also recognize the ancient reality of a universal energy, a moving force, that sustains the physical universe. This force that transcends ordinary reality has been spoken of by many names, such as the mana, prana, ki, chi, vril, odic force, orgone, the wakan, and even the Holy Spirit.

Wilhelm Reich, who believed in the power of orgone energy and built orgone "accumula-

tors" that could cure cancer and other diseases, was convicted of fraud by the U.S. Food and Drug Administration and died in prison in 1957.

Raymond Royal Rife was convinced that microorganisms could be seen if they were illuminated by certain wavelengths of light. Once the correct frequencies were focused on the wavelengths at which various viruses resonated, the microorganisms could be destroyed selectively without harming any of the adjacent healthy tissues.

"... every nuclear weapon on the planet, along with every nuclear power plant, every nuclear propulsion system, and so forth, can be dudded in about 10 minutes by one class of these weapons."

It is interesting to note how many therapists claim that color is very important in healing modalities. Color therapy was originally popular with various New Age healers, but in 2008 researchers at Arizona State University claimed to have vibrated viruses to death with laser therapy. In 2003 *Scientific American* carried an article describing how red light can help prevent blindness in cases of methanol poisoning, which would otherwise destroy a victim' retinas.

Rife died in 1971 under somewhat suspicious circumstances when he was given an overdose of a medicine. He has many supporters today who continue to market various versions of his machines.

William B. Stoecker, a columnist for *Unexplained Mysteries,* tells us there are other promising nontraditional approaches to healing, such as chelation therapy, vitamin therapy, and hyperbaric oxygen for strokes. But, he cautions, it appears that "the U.S. government is planning to follow the lead of the European Union's Codex Alimentarius, which would ban virtually all over the counter supplements, leaving us ... to the not-so-tender mercies of the FDA and the big pharmaceutical companies.... We may not have real proof of suppressed technologies, but we do have a suspicious overall pattern ... and everything is in the patterns."

TEMPLE OF SET

The Temple of Set has as its avowed mission the destruction of the power of organized religion in contemporary society.

Michael Aquino, a lieutenant in U.S. Army Intelligence, specializing in psychological warfare, joined the Church of Satan together with his first wife in 1968. After he returned from serving in Vietnam in 1970, he was ordained a satanic priest and took as his mission in life the destruction of the influence of conventional religion in human affairs. Aquino did not wish to convert everyone to Satanism, but he did wish to remove the shadow of fear and superstition that he believed had been perpetuated by organized religion.

In 1975 Aquino left the Church of Satan after a disagreement with its founder, Anton LaVey. He resigned his priesthood and, with Lilith Sinclair, head of the New York Lilith Grotto, formed the Temple of Set in San Francisco.

On the eve of the summer solstice on June 21, 1975, after his split with LaVey, Aquino performed a magical ritual and sought to summon Satan to appear to him to advise him how best to proceed in his earthly mission. According to Aquino, the Prince of Darkness appeared to him in the image of Set and declared to his disciple the dawning of the Aeon of Set. It was revealed that Set had appeared to the notorious Aleister Crowley, the "Beast 666," in Cairo in 1904 in the image of Crowley's guardian angel, Aiwass. In 1966 LaVey had ushered in the Aeon of Satan, an intermediary stage that was designed to prepare the way for the Aeon of Set, an age that would bring forth enlightenment. Aquino was honored to assume the mantle of "Second Beast," and he even had "666," the number of the Beast in the book of Revelation, tattooed on his scalp.

In Aquino's view the Temple of Set offers its followers an opportunity to raise their consciousness and to apprehend what exists in each individual to make him or her unique. Such awareness, according to the precepts of the Temple of Set, will permit its members to make themselves stronger in all facets of their being. To accomplish this, they must "preserve and improve the tradition of spiritual distinction from the natural universe, which in the Judeo/Christian West has been called

Anton Szandor LaVey named himself the High Priest of the Church of Satan.

power to use. Using magic for "impulsive, trivial, or egoistic desires" is not considered to be Setian. Black magic is the means by which Setian initiates "experience being gods, rather than praying to imaginary images of gods."

Those who attend the Temple of Set must be considered "cooperative philosophers and magicians." Executive authority is held by the Council of Nine, which is responsible for appointing both the high priest and the executive director. There are six degrees of initiates: Setian 1, Adept II, Priest/Priestess of Set III, Magister/Magistra Templi IV, Magus/Maga V, and Ipsissimus/Ipsissima VI. To be recognized as an Adept II, one must demonstrate that he or she has successfully mastered and applied the essential principles of black magic. Reading materials available to the initiates include the newsletter *Scroll of Set* and the encyclopedias entitled *Jeweled Tablets of Set.*

Satanism," but which is more properly termed "the Left-Hand Path." To follow this path is to enter a process that will create "an individual, powerful essence that exists above and beyond animal life. It is thus the true vehicle for personal immortality."

The Temple of Set uses black magic as a means of focusing on "self-determined goals" but emphasizes that the black arts can be as dangerous to the neophyte as volatile chemicals to an inexperienced lab technician. They caution that the practice of magic is not for unstable, immature, or emotionally weak-minded individuals. And they stress that the process they offer to those who seek their "evolutionary product of human experience" is the kind of activity that no enlightened, mature intellect would regard as "undignified, sadistic, criminal, or depraved." The practitioner must first learn to develop a system of ethics and discernment before putting such

NIKOLA TESLA: THE GENIUS AND THE ALIENS

When Tesla died, he was the holder of over seven hundred patents. Some researchers claim that the genius may have had some extraterrestrial assistance.

Nikola Tesla (1856–1942) was the genius who brought the world into the electrical age. Born in the village of Smiljan in the province of Lika, Croatia, in the old Austro-Hungarian Empire, Tesla received his elementary education in Croatia, then attended the Polytechnic School in Graz, Austria, and the University of Prague. He worked as an electrical engineer in Europe before emigrating to America in 1884 and arriving on the streets of New York City with four pennies in his pocket.

Tesla arrived at his brilliant scientific hypotheses by the power of a vivid imagination and vast intuitive abilities. Before he even started drawing plans for a new invention, he would work out the entire idea in his mind. Mentally, he would alter the construction, make adjustments, even operate the device. Perhaps most astonishing is that Tesla never had to put the drawings of the new mechanism down on paper for himself. Because he had worked the concept out so completely in his mind, he could give the exact measurements of all the parts to his workmen, and when the machine was completed, all the parts would fit just as accurately as though Tesla had made a drawing or blueprint. The inventions that he conceived in such a manner always worked. In all of Tesla's career there was never one single exception to the effectiveness and accuracy of his mental instructions. In this way he made his first electric motor, the vacuum wireless light, the turbine engine, and many other inventions.

Tesla worked less than a year with Thomas Edison in New Jersey. Although they respected each other's genius, the differences in style between the two made a long-term working relationship out of the question. George Westinghouse, founder of the Westinghouse Electric Company, understood the advantages of Tesla's system of alternating current over Edison's direct current, and he bought patent rights from Tesla in 1885. The efficiency of AC was demonstrated effectively when Westinghouse successfully lit up the whole World Columbian Exposition at Chicago in 1893.

Tesla established his own laboratory in New York City in 1887, and it was here that the inventor would demonstrate the safety of alternating current by allowing electricity to flow through him and light the lamps he held in his hands. In 1891 he became a U.S. citizen, and in 1895, according to certain of his intimates and various biographers and investigators, he made contact with alien intelligences by projecting certain energy rays into space. By conducting mental exchanges with these intelligences, Tesla developed in rapid succession the induction motor, new types of generators

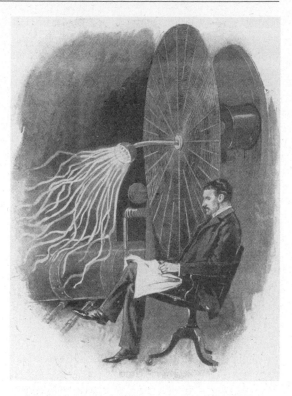

The Croatian inventor Nikola Tesla monitors his "wireless telegraphy apparatus." Was his genius with electronics purely his own, or did aliens lend him assistance?

and transformers, a system of alternating-current power transmission, fluorescent lights, a new type of steam turbine, and plans for a new wireless transmission of power.

Tesla began construction of a wireless broadcasting tower on Long Island, but in 1900 the financier J. Pierpont Morgan withdrew his support. Tesla continued to work with turbines and other projects until 1931, when, legend has it, he joined other scientists working on a top-secret project in invisibility that would culminate in the famous Philadelphia Experiment.

According to certain researchers, the initial stages of the experiment began under the aegis of a U.S. Navy–sponsored team including Tesla and the Austrian physicist Emil Kurtenauer. In 1933 the project was moved to the

Institute for Advanced Study at Princeton University. Joining the group was John von Neumann, a brilliant mathematician who had been at the University of Berlin and the University of Hamburg before he emigrated to the United States. Although Albert Einstein was aware of the experiment, now called "Project Rainbow," he did not participate directly in its operation.

According to Al Bielek, who claims to have joined the project later, the concept of the Philadelphia Experiment was set up by a group of extraterrestrial intelligences (ETIs) who had actually met physically with President Franklin Delano Roosevelt in 1934 aboard the battleship *Pennsylvania*, somewhere in the mid-Pacific. Roosevelt made an agreement with the aliens that they would exchange ETI technology for certain planetary privileges. Tesla, who had been interacting with the extraterrestrials since 1895, arranged the meeting.

Tesla's initial communications had been with entities from the Pleiades who appeared to be completely human and who explained that humankind on Earth had issued from their original stock. These aliens, labeled the K-Group, could easily pass for average humans—except for the greenish tint of their skin. Whenever they wished to interact undetected with humans, they would dye or color their epidermis.

After a second meeting with the ETIs, President Roosevelt signed a treaty of mutual non-interference, and the sciences in the United States enjoyed a remarkable acceleration of theory and application on nearly all levels.

Bielek has claimed that the group of geniuses carried out a partially successful experiment in invisibility at Princeton in 1936. The initial navy test in invisibility was scheduled to occur on a cold day in March 1942. All the levers were pulled, the buttons pushed, but nothing happened. Bielek is convinced that Tesla sabotaged that first attempt to place a warship into a state of invisibility. Tesla supposedly had issued a formal protest against having a live human crew on board the *Eldridge*, the destroyer used in the test. The brilliant inventor, who created every detail first in his mind, insisted that the experiment should first be tried with the vessel unmanned. He also demanded that the scientists be given more time to work out some problems that he foresaw as he reviewed all the equipment. Tesla's request was denied. Told that the Philadelphia Experiment must go forward, he left Project Rainbow in protest.

Ten months later, on January 7, 1943, Tesla was found dead in his hotel room. According to many varying accounts and theories, the navy's experiment in invisibility was conducted in July or October of 1943 with disastrous results. The *Eldridge* got through the test all right, but many of the crew members suffered horrible tortures and ghastly deaths.

At the time of Tesla's death, he held over seven hundred patents. The many notebooks that the genius left are still studied by engineers and scientists for inspiration and new ideas.

THEOSOPHY

Madame Helena Petrovna Blavatsky, the founder of the Theosophical Society, is considered by her detractors to have been a hoaxster, a fraud, and a deceiver—but even today her followers revere her as a genius, a veritable saint, and a woman of monumental courage.

The Theosophical Society was founded in New York by Mme Helena Petrovna Blavatsky (1831–91) on November 17, 1875, with the aid of Col. Henry Steel Olcott and William Q. Judge, an attorney. The threefold purpose of the Society was (1) to form a universal brotherhood of man; (2) to study and make known the ancient religions, philosophies, and sciences; and (3) to investigate the laws of nature and develop the divine powers latent in humankind.

Theosophy ("divine wisdom") is an esoteric blend of Zoroastrianism, Hinduism, Gnosticism, Manichaeism, the Kabbalah, and the philosophy of Plato and other mystics—all of which Madame combined with the teachings of mysterious masters who dwell in secret places in the Himalayas and communicate with their initiates through their psychic abilities and their projected astral bodies. Whereas many founders of cults and secret societies evolved their teachings primarily through their own revelations, inspirations, and psychic abilities, Mme Blavatsky claimed to be able to draw upon the ancient wisdom of the masters Koot Hoomi and Morya to abet the considerable knowledge that she had distilled from various mystery schools, Hindu religious thought, Jewish mysticism, and Christian sects. In additions to such contributions as occult masters and guides, Mme Blavatsky introduced the legend of the lost continent of Lemuria, promised the return of the Maitreya (world savior), and was greatly responsible for popularizing the concepts of reincarnation and past lives in Europe and the United States. Many of the concepts, along with the spiritual eclecticism, professed by Mme Blavatsky in the 1880s would be revised on a large scale in the 1970s, in what has loosely been called the New Age movement.

Helena Petrovna Blavatsky was born at Ekaterinoslav (now Dnepropetrovsk), in the Ukraine, on July 30, 1831, the daughter of Col. Peter Hahn. As a child she loved mystery and fantasy and claimed supernatural companions that kept her safe from harm. At the age of seventeen she married Nicephore Blavatsky, a Russian official in Caucasia, who according to some accounts was forty years older than she. She separated from her husband after three months and spent over a year traveling in Texas, Mexico, Canada, and India. All the time she was wandering, she was developing her mediumistic abilities, secure in the confidence that her spirit guide watched over her. Twice she attempted to enter Tibet,

and on one occasion she managed to cross its frontier in disguise, but she lost her way and was escorted out of the country.

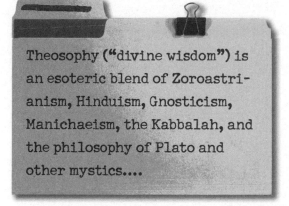

Theosophy ("divine wisdom") is an esoteric blend of Zoroastrianism, Hinduism, Gnosticism, Manichaeism, the Kabbalah, and the philosophy of Plato and other mystics....

Mme Blavatsky described the years between 1848 and 1858 as the "veiled" or "vagabond" time in her life, refusing to divulge anything specific that happened to her in that time but making mysterious allusions to spiritual retreats in Tibet. In 1848, shortly after she had "escaped" from her husband, she fled to Egypt, where she supposedly became adept in the art of snake charming and was initiated into the secrets of oriental magic by a Coptic magician. In 1851, according to her account, she was in New Orleans, studying the rites and mysteries of Voodoo. She traveled to Paris in 1858 and met the internationally famous medium Daniel D. Home, who so impressed her with his paranormal abilities that she became a Spiritualist. Later that year she returned to Russia, where she soon gained fame as a spirit medium. After about five years spent perfecting her mediumship, she entered another "veiled" period from 1863 to 1870, when she was allegedly in retreat in Tibet, studying with Mahatmas Koot Hoomi and Morya and a secret brotherhood of adepts.

In 1870, back in Europe, she was en route to Greece when the ship on which she was traveling exploded and she lost all her earthly possessions, including whatever money she had managed to save. Rescued at sea and brought to Cairo, she supported herself through her mediumship, and in 1871 she founded the Spirit Society, which was quickly disbanded after accusations of fraud.

In 1873 she traveled to the United States and settled in New York, where she remained for six years and, according to some accounts, became a naturalized citizen. She resumed the practice of her mediumship in association with the brothers William and Horatio Eddy, two well-known materialization mediums. As she became more prominent in Spiritualist circles in America, she came to the attention of Henry Steel Olcott, a journalist, who established a study group around her unique style of mediumship, a blend of Spiritualism and Buddhistic legends about Tibetan sages. She professed to have direct spiritual contact with two Tibetan mahatmas—again, Koot Hoomi and Morya—who communicated with her on the astral plane and provided her with wonderful teachings of wisdom and knowledge.

Sometime in 1875 Mme Blavatsky entered into a very brief marriage of two or three months with a merchant in Philadelphia named M. C. Betanelly. At about the same time, she managed to break up the marriage of Colonel Olcott, who left his wife and children for her. It was during this period that she founded the Theosophical Society.

In 1877 Olcott began to speak of moving the headquarters of the society to India, closer to the mahatmas, the occult brotherhood, and sincere practicing Hindu adepts. By 1879 the central headquarters of the society had been established at Adyar, India, and an amalgamation with the Arya Samaj sect founded by Swami Dayanand Saraswati had also been accomplished. By April 1882, however, the swami realized that he had been exploited by the leaders of the Theosophists, and he denounced the group.

By that time, the influence of the swami in India was no longer required, for in 1880 Mme Blavatsky had visited northern India and observed wonderful phenomena manifested especially for her by the mahatmas. Theosophy began to attract students and followers from around the world who came to observe for themselves the miracles centered on the spiritual teachings of Morya and Koot Hoomi as channeled through the mediumship of Mme Blavatsky. It was also at this time that she met A. P. Sinnett, journalist and editor of the *Pioneer,* an influential Anglo-Indian newspaper, and Allen O. Hume of the Indian Civil Service, her two most important converts in India.

Mme. Blavatsky performed such manifestations as written letters from Koot Hoomi and Morya that would materialize in midair. Eventually such reports reached the attention of England's Society for Psychical Research, which dispatched Richard Hodgson, one of their most formidable researchers, to investigate. It didn't take long for Hodgson to assess the followers of Theosophy as extremely gullible individuals who had arrived in India with expectations of finding in Mme Blavatsky a modern miracle worker. The psychical researcher easily detected the sliding panels, the dummy head and shoulders of Koot Hoomi, and the cracks in the ceiling through which the letters from the mahatmas appeared in "midair" to the astonishment of the true believers.

Regardless of the exposé published by the Society for Psychical Research, Theosophy continued to grow to become a worldwide movement. In 1877 Mme Blavatsky published *Isis Unveiled,* followed in 1887 by her monumental *The Secret Doctrine,* which she allegedly wrote in an altered state of consciousness while attuned to higher powers.

At the time of her death in 1891, Mme Blavatsky's detractors considered her to have been a hoaxster, a fraud, and a deceiver, while her followers revered her as a genius, a veritable saint, and a woman of monumental courage who had struggled against an incredible array of adversities and adversaries to fashion a modern mystery school without equal. Foe and follower alike conceded that she was a unique, sometimes overpowering, personality.

In 1887 Madame had met Annie Besant, a woman's suffragist and social reformer who had embraced theosophical beliefs. They became close, and Blavatsky died in Annie's home. The Theosophical Society, which numbered about 100,000 persons at the time of Madame's death, split into two branches, with Besant as president of one of them. Annie Besant became a worthy successor, actively preaching the wisdom and insights provided in *The Secret Doctrine* and shepherding the movement to steadily larger growth.

Besant took the mission to India, the Hindu root of many of Blavatsky's teachings on reincarnation and karma, and in 1898 founded the Central Hindu College at Benares. Becoming embroiled in the national politics of India, in 1916 Annie established the Indian Home Rule League, becoming its president, then, in 1917, president of the Indian National Congress, an active force in the independence movement.

Although she remained based in India until her death in 1933, she returned to her native England from 1926 to 1927 with her protégé Jiddu Krishnamurti and traveled around the country promoting him as the new Messiah.

THUGGEE

No secret cult of killers has ever murdered as many people as the Thuggee. Although no longer organized, lone-wolf assassins still practice the deadly craft of strangulation around the world.

Membership in the Thuggee was hereditary, and its practitioners were trained from earliest childhood to murder by the quiet method of a strong cloth noose tightened about the neck of their victims. This weapon, the "rumal," was worn knotted about the waist of each member of the Thuggee. All deaths were considered a sacrifice to the goddess Kali, the "Dark Mother," the Hindu triple goddess of creation, preservation, and destruction.

The Thuggee, also known simply as Thugs, traveled often in the guise of traders, pilgrims, and even as soldiers marching to or from service. On occasion the more flamboyant would pretend to be a rajah with a large retinue of followers. Each band of Thuggee had a small unit of scouts and inveiglers who would loiter about hotels and marketplaces gaining information regarding travelers and the weight of their coin purses. The inveiglers posed as travelers headed for the same destination as their intended victims. They would worm themselves into the confidences of their prey, pleading the old adage of safety in numbers.

The mass slaughters of large groups of merchants and travelers were usually committed during their encampment. Working in groups of three, one Thuggee would loop the *rumah,* the killing noose, around the victim's neck, another would press his head forward, and the third would grab his legs and throw him to the ground. In the rare instance when an intended victim escaped the noose, he would run into scouts posted at the edge of the jungle: the Thuggee aimed at achieving a 100 percent mortality rate among their victims. In the 1830s this Indian secret society strangled upwards of thirty thousand people.

The Thuggee had a peculiar code of ethics that forbade the killing of fakirs, musicians, dancers, sweepers, oil vendors, carpenters, blacksmiths, maimed or leprous persons, Ganges water-carriers, and women. Despite the restriction against the murder of females, however, the presence of wives traveling with their husbands often necessitated the strangling of a woman to protect the secrecy of the society.

The one unbreakable rule of the brotherhood was the one prohibiting the shedding of blood. According to Thuggee beliefs, the goddess Kali taught the fathers of thuggery to strangle with a noose and to kill without spilling blood. All victims of the Thuggee were sacrificed to Kali, and the members of the secret society would have been greatly incensed by an accusation that they killed only for booty.

With the exception of small boys captured or spared during a raid, one had to be born into the cult in order to become an initiate. The minimum age for initiation into the society was ten; at eighteen, initiates were permitted to make their first human sacrifices to Kali. The female counterparts were members of a secret sect of Tantrists who believed that only by constant indulgence in wine, meat, fish, mystical gesticulations, and sexual licentiousness could a human ever achieve total union with Kali.

Although the Thuggee probably originated sometime in the sixteenth century, they were not uncovered by British authorities until about 1812. In 1822 William Sleeman, an officer in the Bengal Army transferred to civil service, was appointed by the Governor General Lord Bentinck to rid India of the society of stranglers. Fluent in four Indian dialects, Sleeman had been the British official who first confirmed the growing suspicion that the Thuggee were committing murders throughout all of central India. He was well aware that stopping them would be no easy task, for the members of the secret society were indistinguishable from the many bands of outlaws who infested the country's roads—or from any of the travelers and merchants who were their victims.

By meticulously marking on a map the site of each discovered attack and by maintaining careful records of the dates, Sleeman was able to begin to predict the areas where the next mass murders were likely to take place. Between 1830 and 1841 Sleeman's police captured at least 3,700 Thugs, breaking the back of the infamous secret society.

Trials of Thuggee brought out many ghastly facts. A band of twenty confessed that they had participated in 5,200 murders. An individual named Buhram, who had been a strangler for forty years, had the highest lifetime score to his discredit—931. When asked if he experienced any feelings of remorse or guilt, he answered sharply that no man should ever feel compunction in following his trade.

Five hundred of the apprehended Thugs were hanged, the rest imprisoned for life, except for fifty who received pardons for supplying valuable information used in destroying the secret society. Without exception, the condemned Thuggee went to their own deaths with the same lack of emotion with which they had murdered their victims. In many instances, their final request to the hangman was that they be permitted to place the noose around their own necks.

Although isolated cases of a Thug's proficiency with a noose still arise in India and in other parts of the world, the stranglers who murdered in the name of the goddess Kali no longer exist as a secret society. The designation of "thug," however, remains as a negative term applied to brutish criminals.

THULE SOCIETY

Dedicated to the rebirth of Aryan/Teutonic supremacy, the resurrection of Nordic mysticism, and the defeat of Christianity, the Thule Society prepared the path for the advent of the master race.

During the late nineteenth century Cyrus Read Teed, a former Union army Medical Corps physician, claimed that a civilization inhabited the concave inner surface of Earth. Teed made a religion of his discoveries and changed his name to Koresh, the Hebrew equivalent of his given name, Cyrus. As the messiah of Koreshanity, he formed a church and founded a community on a three-hundred-acre tract in Florida in 1894. He lived there with about 250 followers until 1908.

In 1871 the occultist Edward Bulwer-Lytton's novel *The Coming Race* stirred imaginations around the world with an account of the subterranean master race who used the Vril force to sustain their secret hollow-earth empire. Extraterrestrial in origin, superior to everyone above or below the soil of Earth, the ancestors of the Aryans have monitored the growth of the surface nations.

In the eclectic cosmology that made up Nazi occultism, "Ultima Thule" was the capital of Hyperborea, the land of the superbeings who inhabited the Hollow Earth. The Thule Society was founded in 1910 by Felix Niedner, the German translator of the *Eddas,* Old Norse poems from the medieval manuscript *Codex Regius,* written sometime in the thirteenth century. The Munich branch of the society was established in 1918 by Baron Rudolf von Sebottendorf (Rudolf Glauer), who while living in Istanbul in 1910 had formed a secret society that combined esoteric Sufism, Freemasonry, and the creed of the Hashshashin. In 1912 Sebottendorf returned to Germany, where he became a member of a secret anti-Semitic lodge known as the Order of Teutons. Baron von Sebottendorf was also conversant with the Bavarian Illuminati, the Knights Templar, the Holy Vehm, the Golden Dawn, the German Order Walvater of the Holy Grail, and Rosicrucianism. Baron Rudolf may have borrowed some concepts and rites from such groups, as well as the Theosophists and various Hermetic schools, but certainly his group, like many other German secret societies, placed special emphasis on the innate mystical strength of the Aryan race. Mme Helena Blavatsky had listed the Six Root Races—the Astral, Hyperborean, Lemurian, Atlantean, Aryan, and the coming master race. The Germanic/Nordic/Teutonic people were of Aryan origin, and perhaps by forming a group named after the gateway to the other worlds, Ultima Thule, Baron Rudolf sought to demonstrate to supermen in the Hollow Earth the Thule Society's earnestness to please.

The Hyperboreans, the master race in the earth's interior, usually remain aloof from the surface dwellers, but thousands of years ago they did colonize certain regions of the planet

The emblem of the Thule Society, which was founded by Felix Niedner in 1910 as an occult society that eventually turned to an agenda of Aryan supremacy, planting the seeds of the Nazi Party.

and left such people as the Celts, the Norse, Bretons, Spaniards, and Portuguese with an infusion of certain of their extraterrestrial memories in their minds and evidence of their Rh-negative blood types in their genetic transfer. Those human witnesses who claim to have encountered and communicated with representatives of the Elder Race describe them as humanoid, but extremely long-lived and give evidence of predating the human species by more than a million years.

In 1920 the Nazi Party was created by the Thule group. The Thule *Sonnenrad* (Sun Wheel) was used as inspiration for the Nazi flag and symbol. Hitler and his inner circle had a firm belief in Atlantis and in the superior race that had withdrawn from the surface world and prospered within the Hollow Earth. These ancient masters, who were likely extraterrestrial in origin, continued to monitor the new race of surface dwellers and from time to time had given humankind a boost up the evolutionary ladder. They were closely observing the Earth nations at this time to determine which people they would invite to inherit their wealth of technological knowledge. The Nazis were determined that it would the German people who would become the heirs of the Master Race.

So great was the Nazi belief in the supermen who dwelt in the Hollow Earth that in April 1942 Nazi Germany sent out an expedition composed of a number of its most visionary scientists to seek a military vantage point in the Hollow Earth. Although the expedition of leading scientists left at a time when the Third Reich was putting maximum effort in their drive against the Allies, Göring, Himmler, and Hitler are said to have enthusiastically endorsed the project. Steeped in the more esoteric teachings of metaphysics, the Führer had long been convinced that Earth was concave and that a master race lived on the inside of the planet.

The Nazi scientists who left for the island of Rugen had complete confidence in the validity of their quest. In their minds, such a coup as discovering the opening to the Inner World would not only provide them with a military advantage, but it would go a long way in convincing the Masters who lived there that the German people truly deserved to mix their blood with them in the creation of a hybrid master race to occupy the surface world. The extravagant effort to make contact with the Hyperboreans was unsuccessful.

In his book *Shambhala,* author and adventurer Nicholas Roerich writes of his curiosity about the universality of the legends of the underpeople: "You recognize the same relationship in the folklores of Tibet, Mongolia, China, Turkestan, Kashmir, Persia, Altai, Siberia, the Ural, Caucasia, the Russian steppes, Lithuania, Poland, Hungary, Germany, France; from the highest mountains to the deepest oceans. They tell you how the people closed themselves in subterranean mountains. They even ask you if you want to see the entrance to the cave through which the saintly persecuted folk fled." Throughout the world, Roerich emphasizes, one hears the same "wondrous tale of the vanished holy people. Great is the belief in the Kingdom of the subterranean people."

TONKIN GULF INCIDENT

The Tonkin Gulf Incident proves the case established when humans first became territorial: If a chief, king, or president wants to have a war, an incident can always be fabricated to provoke one.

On July 31, 1964, the U.S. Navy destroyer *Maddox* began a reconnaissance mission in the Gulf of Tonkin, a body of water that lies on the east coast of North Vietnam and the west coast of Hainan Island, China. On August 2 the destroyer *C. Turner Joy* joined the *Maddox,* and the two warships set out on a "DESOTO patrol," an intelligence/espionage mission, checking out the radar and coastal defenses of North Vietnam. When the *Maddox* was attacked by North Vietnamese torpedo patrol boats, the U.S. destroyer returned fire and was joined in the fight by the *C. Turner Joy.* Warplanes sent by the *Ticonderoga* added to the firepower. They sank one torpedo boat and reported damaging others.

On August 4 the two destroyers were once again on reconnaissance in the Gulf of Tonkin when radar signals indicated that they were under attack by North Vietnamese patrol boats. For two hours the warships fired vigorously on radar targets and maneuvered to evade what they believed to be visual sightings of enemy boats. Once again, the *Ticon-*

deroga launched Crusader jet warplanes. The two destroyers fired 249 five-inch shells, 123 three-inch shells, and four or five depth charges to repel their attackers.

That night, network television in the United States was interrupted at 11:36 P.M. EDT so that President Lyndon B. Johnson could inform the nation that U.S. warships of the Seventh Fleet on duty in the Gulf of Tonkin had been attacked by North Vietnamese PT boats. LBJ then explained that in response to "open aggression on the open seas" against our ships, he had ordered air strikes on North Vietnam.

On August 7 the U.S. House and Senate passed the "Tonkin Gulf Resolution," stipulating that the president could "take all necessary measures to repel armed attack against the forces of the United States and to prevent further aggression." By July 1965 the U.S. had sent 80,000 troops to South Vietnam. By early 1969 there were 543,000 U.S. military personnel deployed to Vietnam, and 400 tons of bombs and ordnance per day were being dropped on the enemy. When the United States withdrew in 1975, at least one million Vietnamese and 58,000 Americans had died in the conflict.

The Gulf of Tonkin incident on August 4, 1964, was a significant factor in U.S. involvement in a war that sharply divided the nation along class and generational lines—and the attack probably never happened.

Two days earlier, North Vietnamese forces in Russian-made "swatow" gunboats had attacked the *Maddox,* but from the outset many doubted that anything had happened on August 4. Tapes released by the LBJ Library at the University of Texas at Austin include fifty-one phone conversations from August 4 and 5. Even LBJ said that for all he knew, the ships could have been shooting at whales. A 1:59 P.M. EDT August 4 phone conversation with Lieutenant General David Burchinal of the Joint Chiefs of Staff and Admiral U. S. Grant Sharp, commander of the U.S. Navy's Pacific

Fleet, contained such comments as "many of the reported contacts and torpedoes fired appear doubtful" and "probably overeager sonar men" and "freak weather effects on radar."

Bob Richter, writing in the *San Antonio Express-News,* said, "The released tapes neither prove nor disprove what may have happened that night, but they do indicate jittery sailors in a tense area thought they were under attack." James Stockdale, a navy aviator who responded to the alleged attacks on the *Maddox* and *Turner Joy,* has declared the Tonkin Gulf incident all "hogwash." Stockdale was later shot down and spent eight years in a Vietnamese prisoner of war camp. In 1992 he was Ross Perot's running mate in the presidential election. In his 1984 book *In Love and War,* Stockdale writes, "I had the best seat in the house to watch that event, and our destroyers were shooting at phantom targets—there were no PT boats there. There was nothing but black water and American firepower."

Even at the time of the incident, skeptics felt that many in the government were only looking for an excuse to initiate bombing in Vietnam, and the Gulf of Tonkin "attack" provided that excuse. However, scholars who have listened to the LBJ tapes seem to have formed a general consensus that the incident was not engineered, but was a mistake. David Crockett, a presidential scholar at Trinity University, has labeled the incident an accident but adds that the greater mistake was that Congress gave LBJ a "virtual blank check to make war." The bitter irony, Crockett observed, is that LBJ had campaigned on the promise that he wouldn't send American troops to die in Asian wars.

TRADITIONAL VALUES COALITION

The Traditional Values Coalition has grown to a membership of 43,000 church congregations

in twelve denominations by defending America's "cultural heritage" and opposing homosexuality, the teaching of evolution, and anti-Christian bigotry.

Rev. Louis Sheldon, founder of the extreme-right-wing evangelical Traditional Values Coalition (TVC), argues that homosexuality is not a life style, but a "death style." Sheldon's daughter, Andrea Sheldon Lafferty, is the organization's executive director, who aggressively pursues the TVC mission to "restore America's cultural heritage" by speaking out against gay rights, the teaching of evolution in public schools, and reproductive freedom. Founded in 1980, TVC now claims a membership of 43,000 church congregations in twelve denominations. This very large coalition of churches receives monthly newsletters and occasional action alerts and special messages from Rev. Sheldon.

The Rev. Louis Sheldon, seen here at a 2008 rally for presidential hopeful Mitt Romney. Rev. Sheldon is the leader of the Traditional Values Coalition, which has become an influential political force, especially for Republicans.

The principal focus of the TVC is on what is perceived as the "true homosexual agenda" of recruiting children into homosexuality. In their newsletters the Sheldons warn that gays and lesbians are child molesters who will snatch children from shopping malls and even from private homes if no adults are present. In 1985 Rev. Sheldon proposed placing AIDS victims into special "cities of refuge," much like the old leper colonies.

TVC has opposed hate-crimes legislation on the grounds, Rev. Sheldon explained, that such a bill would "protect sex with animals and the rape of children as forms of political expression." In addition, said Andrea Sheldon Lafferty, hate-crime legislation would enable homosexual activists to punish any person who had the courage to speak out against their recruitment of children.

In 2001 TVC applied pressure to California's school board members to reject aspects of California Assembly Bill 537, the California Student Safety and Violence Prevention Act of 2000, claiming that it promoted homosexuality and anti-Christian bigotry. In Colorado and Oregon TVC has attempted to remove constitutional amendments protecting the civil rights of gays and lesbians. In California, Arizona, Missouri, and Washington, TVC has organized antigay initiatives.

TVC favors teaching creationism over evolution in public schools, opposes any sex-education curriculum that does not emphasize abstinence to the exclusion of information on birth control and disease prevention, and endorses prayer in public schools. Traditional Values Coalition has its home office in Anaheim, California.

TRIADS AND TONGS

Over the centuries, the secret society known as the Triad evolved from a patriotic resistance movement to become a powerful criminal organization that controls much of the world's heroin traffic.

As with many secret societies, the exact origins of the Triads have been clouded by the mists of legend—and myth and legend are very important to the members of this internationally linked secret society. According to some researchers, in 1647 a community of Buddhist monks from Fukien Province in China had become masters in the art of war. When a foreign prince invaded China, the second Manchu emperor, Kiang Hsi, sent 138 of these fighting monks (*Siu Lam*) to throw out the invading forces. After three months of bitter fighting, the monks routed the enemy and returned to their monastery laden with gifts and honors from the grateful emperor.

The monks were content to resume their lives of contemplation, but some of Kiang Hsi's ministers were jealous of them and persuaded him that the monks were deceptively planning a rebellion. Fearful of their martial-arts skills, the emperor decided to attack without warning and sent a strong force of the Imperial Guard, armed with gunpowder, to destroy the monastery. The flames ignited by the blasts of the powder soared up to heaven, where they were seen by the Immortals—who, perceiving the injustice being dealt the monks, came down to Earth and pushed aside one of the monastery's huge walls, enabling eighteen monks to escape. Most of them were so badly burned that they soon died, but five survivors escaped from the imperial troops by miraculous means. In Triad lore, those monks are known as the Five Ancestors.

After many ordeals the five came to a city in Fukien Province where they founded a secret society, the Hung Mun, whose aim was to overthrow the Manchu dynasty (also known as the Ching or Qing dynasty) that had betrayed their loyalty and to restore the previous Ming dynasty. The symbol of the Hung Mun society consisted of three red dots, which formed part of the Chinese character for the Ming emperor Hung Wu. Literally, Hung Mun means "men of Hung." Spiritually, the three dots symbolize the unity among heaven, earth, and man. The term *Triad* did not come into being until circa 1931 when it was coined by the British authorities in Hong Kong, who named the criminal organization for the triangular three-dot character for Hung Wu.

Although the revolt against the Ching emperor failed, the survivors scattered throughout China and established five provincial grand lodges, each led by one of the five monks. The Hung Mun society continued to grow, developing secret codes to confound the emperor's spies. This secrecy and the Hung Mun's martial-arts training enabled the society to become protectors of the common people. Eventually, the society became more criminal than political, and they adopted the motto *Ta fu—chih p'in* (Hit the rich—help the poor).

Initiation into the Triad is said to be based on a blood ceremony. First, an "incense master" invokes the ancient five heroes and offers libations of tea and wine. The candidate for initiation is challenged at the entrance to the lodge by guards carrying razor-edged swords. He is allowed to enter only after answering a series of ritual questions as he crawls under the crossed swords. Once inside the lodge, the initiate participates in a lengthy reenactment of the traditional ordeals of the Five Ancestors, swears thirty-six oaths, and learns his first secret signs. Then a rooster is beheaded as a warning to the initiate that he will suffer the same fate if he betrays the Triad. Finally, the initiate drinks a mixture of blood, wine, cinnabar, and ashes. In times past, the blood was drawn from the initiate and other members of the lodge. Today it is generally that of the slaughtered rooster.

The blood oaths that were so favored by the Triads originated with the Yellow Turbans, one of the earliest and most mystical societies in China. Founded in the middle of the second century in northeast China, the Yellow Turbans revered Chang Cheuh, a great healer and magician, as a savior of the nation against the despotic Han dynasty. Chang's society soon numbered so many thousands that he needed thirty-six generals to lead the rebellion which conquered the entire north of China within less than a month. Three of his disciples have been credited with taking the first blood oath when each of them slit open a vein, filled a vessel with blood, and drank the mixture of their vital fluid while vowing eternal brotherhood. This basic blood oath ceremony, with many variations, became an integral part of Triad ritual.

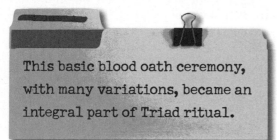

This basic blood oath ceremony, with many variations, became an integral part of Triad ritual.

In the summer of 1900 an aggressive secret society known as *I Ho Chuan* (Fists of Righteous Harmony) drove more than three thousand people—mainly European missionaries, their families, and Chinese Christian converts—into the legation district of Peking. "Boxer" was the Western name for this society, derived from its symbol of a clenched fist and its members' proficiency in martial arts. The Boxers had been given almost a free hand by the Manchu government to free the nation from the foreign imperialists whom they accused of exploiting the Chinese people. The White Lotus Triad, as well as the Big Swords and the Red Fists, joined the rebellion against the Western powers.

The Boxers depended greatly on supernatural elements to aid them in achieving invulnerability. They employed rituals compounded of self-hypnotism, mass hysteria, and drugs. At the height of their ceremonies the initiates reached a state of frenzy wherein they would smash their clenched fists against unyielding surfaces until blood flowed from broken knuckles. At this point they were led into the Inner

Temple to learn magical secrets and to receive the power of invulnerability against death at the hands of foreigners. The imparting of invulnerability was followed by a blood oath.

Initially the Boxers directed their violence mainly against small Christian missionary outposts, especially in Shantung Province. These attacks were encouraged by the Empress Dowager Tsu Hsi, who had become regent after forcing her nephew from the throne. On her orders imperial officers assisted the Boxers during the fifty-five-day siege against the foreign legations. However, even before the various nations whose citizens were under attack sent relief forces to capture the city and squelch the rebellion, many imperial soldiers had already deserted the Boxers and were fighting against them.

The Triads reached the United States with the Chinese workers who immigrated to the West Coast during the gold rush fever of the 1840s. Mercilessly exploited by the people who had hired them as common laborers, the immigrants welcomed the protection provided by the Triads that sprang up among their communities, hiding behind the fronts of innocent social clubs. One of the first Triads to establish itself in the United States was the so-called Five Companies, named after the five districts of China. Once entrenched, it began to exploit the same Chinese population it had previously sworn to protect.

The first Tong in America is believed to have originated in San Francisco in 1874. Essentially, the Tong (which originally meant "parlor" or "meeting house") was a protective association created by Chinese merchants to defend themselves against brutal treatment by the white inhabitants of the city and exploitation of the Triads. Eventually the Tong became powerful enough to sell protection to the newer merchants and to establish illegal gambling halls. Success in extortion and gambling led to an extension of activities into opium distribution and prostitution.

Although in 1880 the Chinese population in New York City was only around eight hundred, the first Tong there was established in that year. By 1890 a rush of immigration had increased the total to thirteen thousand Chinese in the city, and the Tong was ready to exploit a population isolated by language, culture, and prejudice. In 1900, rival Tongs ignited a series of Tong wars that lasted intermittently until the 1930s. It was at that time that the larger American public became fully aware of the Tong warriors with their chain-mail shirts and hatchets.

A distinctive characteristic of Chinese organized crime in America is the relationship among the Tongs, the merchants' associations, and the Asian street gangs. In New York City, for example, the street gang Fuk Ching is allied with the Fukien American Association, a merchants' group. Such an association between Tong and gang provides a kind of legitimacy for the criminals and protection for the merchants. In addition, the merchants' meetinghouse gives the gang a place to hang out.

The center of the Triad remains in Hong Kong. There are seven main branches, each with its own area of influence and working independently of the others—the Sun Yee On Triad, the Wo Group, the 14K Triad, the Luen Group, the Big Circle Gang, the United Bamboo Gang, and the Four Seas Gang. Perhaps the largest triad, the Sun Yee On may control as many as 56,000 members. Although its influence on the course of Chinese politics has been considerable, the Triad has never been unduly concerned about which government happens to be in political power. Sun Yat Sen, the founder of Republican China, used the Chung triad in his 1906 rebellion; the Nationalist government in 1927 was headed by Chiang Kai Shek, a member of the Shang Hai Green Gang; during the World War II Japanese occupation of China, some Triads helped police Hong Kong.

TRILATERAL COMMISSION

Oh, the beleaguered, misunderstood international upper classes! If they don't look after their future interests, who in the world will?

David Rockefeller said that he was inspired to fund the Trilateral Commission after he had read Zbigniew Brzezinski's book *Between Two Ages: America's Role in the Technetronic Era* (1970). Brzezinski, at that time a professor at Columbia University, was convinced that a vast alliance must be formed among North America, Western Europe, and Japan in order to protect privately controlled businesses. The international upper classes of the developed nations must band together in order to protect their future interests. Such families as the Rockefellers and the other financial elites must be certain that only those political leaders would be brought to power who would preserve the rights of the established order over the masses.

The initial arrangements for the Trilateral Commission were planned through the course of a series of meetings at the Rockefellers' Pocantico Hills estate outside of New York City, but Rockefeller first introduced the concept at an annual meeting of the Bilderberg group held in Knokke, Belgium, in the spring of 1972. In 1973 Rockefeller established the Trilateral Commission and hired Brzezinksi away from Columbia University to be the director.

The membership of the Trilateral Commission, like that of the older Bilderberg group, is made up of international financiers, industrialists, media magnates, union bosses, academics, and political figures. An essential difference lies in the Bilderbergers' strict limitation of membership to participants from Western Europe, the United States, and Canada. The Trilateral Commission recognizes the growing power and influence of the Japanese elite in the world economy.

Later in 1973 Jimmy Carter was asked to become a member of the Trilateral Commission. Carter commented when he won the Democratic nomination for president that the Trilateral members had provided him with a marvelous learning opportunity. Carter chose fellow Trilateralist Walter Mondale as his running mate, and once elected to the presidency, Carter named Zbigniew Brzezinksi as national security adviser. For his top three cabinet posts, Carter appointed Cyrus Vance, W. Michael Blumenthal, and Harold Brown, all Trilateralists. David Rockefeller had accomplished one of his greatest goals: a Trilateral Commission U.S. presidency.

Conspiracy theorists estimate that the current membership of the Trilateral Commission includes approximately eighty Americans, ten Canadians, ninety Western Europeans, and seventy-five Japanese. Most conspiracists do not believe that the Trilateralists wish the destruction of the United States, but rather that it will surrender its independence and embrace the concept of a One World Government.

U

UFO COVER-UPS BY THE GOVERNMENT

The U.S. government has been protecting its citizens from the truth and the terror of extraterrestrial invasion since at least 1942.

The Night UFOs Attacked Los Angeles

Many UFOlogists list February 25, 1942, as marking the beginning of the "war of the worlds," the day when Earth first came under siege by extraterrestrial beings.

In the days immediately after the sneak attack on Pearl Harbor on December 7, 1941, the entire West Coast of the United States was prepared for the likelihood of Japanese bombing raids. Then on February 25, 1942, the air raid sirens sounded the alarm throughout the city of Los Angeles. The U.S. Army's Western Defense Command ordered an immediate blackout of the city from 2:25 to 7:21 A.M. Twelve thousand air raid wardens reported to their posts, and powerful searchlights swept the sky, capturing a large, round, white object in their beams. Antiaircraft batteries peppered the clouds with orange bursts of shrapnel—firing a total of two thousand rounds of twelve-pound high-explosive shells.

However, no identifiable Japanese aircraft were ever detected in the searchlight beams. The next day, news photographs clearly depicted a large, round object that did not look like any conventional aircraft—Japanese or American. Some eyewitnesses described the mysterious object in the night sky as being large enough to dwarf an apartment house, and they watched as U.S. Army fighter planes were dispatched to attack the unidentified flying object and bring it down. Although the aerial "dogfight" lasted for about a half an hour, the fighters were unable to cause any apparent damage to the huge object.

Some historians argue that the UFO sighted over Los Angeles on February 25, 1942, was an enormous Japanese Fugo balloon bomb. Constructed of rice paper and assembled by Japanese schoolgirls, the Fugo balloon bombs were directed into the jet stream that flows from Japan to America's Northwest. Almost four hundred Fugo balloons exploded in Alaska, California, Texas, New Mexico, and Colorado, causing minimal damage but killing at least six civilians. However, according to records examined after the Japanese surrender in 1945, no documents were found to indicate that a gigantic Fugo balloon had ever been sent to attack Los Angeles. And even if such a massive balloon had found its way to California, it seems beyond comprehension that two thousand rounds of twelve-pound high-explosive shells and the bullets of machine guns from several fighter planes could not have brought down a floating craft made of rice paper as it moved slowly across the city.

Although the aerial object remained untouched by intense antiaircraft fire and no bombs fell on the city, shell fragments raining down on homes, streets, and buildings killed six civilians throughout the Los Angeles area. In spite of official denials of the incident that were issued almost immediately, the Western Defense Command insisted that an unidentified aircraft had been sighted—and they had not been firing at a mass delusion.

For the official record and to calm the anxious population of the West Coast, Navy Secretary Frank Knox stated that no aircraft, enemy or otherwise, had been sighted, and he characterized the Los Angeles raid as a false alarm caused by war nerves.

Like Saucers Skipping on Water: June 24, 1947

On June 24, 1947, at 2 P.M., Kenneth Arnold took off from the Chehalis, Washington, airport in his personal plane and headed for Yakima, Washington. He hadn't been in the air for more than three minutes when to the left and north of Mount Rainier he observed a chain of nine peculiar-looking objects flying from north to south at approximately 9,500 feet. He estimated the size of the objects to be approximately two-thirds that of a DC-4, and he timed the objects between Mount Rainier and Mount Adams and determined that they crossed this forty-seven-mile stretch

in 1 minute and 42 seconds, equivalent to some 1,650 miles per hour.

In an interview, Arnold described the objects as appearing like saucers skipping on water. This description was shortened to "flying saucers" by newspapermen and resulted in the popular use of that term.

It was the Air Force's conclusion that the objects of this sighting were due to a mirage, but for many individuals around the world, the mysterious objects that Arnold sighted that day were extraterrestrial spacecraft.

Roswell, New Mexico, July 2, 1947: The Mother of All UFO Cover-ups

On the night of July 2, 1947, eight days after Kenneth Arnold's sighting of mysterious unidentified flying objects, a UFO was reported to have crashed on ranchland about sixty miles north of Roswell, New Mexico, and the Air Force had recovered the wreckage. The next day those startling media pronouncements were suddenly transformed into puzzling accounts that the Air Force had been mistaken. The supposed UFO was merely the scattered debris from a fallen weather balloon.

For some people reading about the Air Force's denial of their having captured a flying saucer, the matter was ended with a wry smile at the inefficiency of the military. Others wondered how highly trained Air Force personnel could possibly mistake a few thin sticks and scraps of cloth for any kind of aeronautical vehicle, to say nothing of an extraterrestrial craft capable of traversing the universe.

Thus was born in Roswell, New Mexico, the seed of nearly every UFO government-cover-up conspiracy theory that still thrives today. In many ways 1947 provided the ideal soil for such theories to germinate. It had been almost exactly two years since the Japanese had surrendered and the terrible days of World War II had at last come to a close amid the fiery destruction of the nuclear bombs that devastated Hiroshima and Nagasaki. Atomic power frightened the great majority of Americans, and many doomsayers were frightening their audiences with grim messages that the world was about to come to an end. Adding to the stress was the fact that the Soviet Union had erected the so-called iron curtain, and the free nations of the world had to start worrying about the Communist menace before they had really had time to recover from the Nazi's Third Reich. In fact, many military officers said that the flying saucers were a new secret weapon launched against the United States by diehard Nazis hiding in South America. Other people in "the know" claimed that the bizarre circular craft were new weapons that had been created by the German scientists who had been kidnapped by the Soviets during the last days of the war.

On July 26, 1952, UFOs made national headlines when they were sighted over Washington, D.C.

Reverse Engineering at Area 51

After government agencies cleaned up the crash fragments and the alien corpses outside of Roswell, the bodies were taken to Hangar 18 and the bits of extraterrestrial technology were taken to hidden hangers at Groom Lake, a secret base in the Nevada desert. In 1989 a former government scientist named Bob Lazar broke his silence and revealed that he had worked on alien technology at a facility in Area 51. Not only had the scientists been able to reverse-engineer alien technology and create top-secret aerial vehicles for the Air Force, but hidden hangars concealed as many as nine extraterrestrial space craft.

Majestic-12

In 1987, UFO researchers Jamie Shandera, Stanton Friedman, and William Moore released their findings regarding a secret group known as Majestic-12 that was created in 1947 to keep the president and other world leaders briefed on the progress of alien activity on Earth. While the governments of Earth officially deny the existence of UFOs to pre-

vent panic among the masses, the chief executives are well aware of the existence of extraterrestrial involvement in world affairs.

Other UFOlogists claimed to have discovered that a secret arm of the U.S. government, in association with the Illuminati, made a deal with the alien invaders to trade advanced extraterrestrial technology for such Earth resources as water, minerals, cattle—and certain of its citizens. UFO abductions are conducted by aliens as a species-monitoring program. Physical examinations of humans and crossbreeding attempts involving preselected men and women are allowed by the government as a treaty concession.

UFOs Buzz the White House

On July 26, 1952, UFOs made national headlines when they were sighted over Washington, D.C. The mysterious objects were detected on civilian and military radar screens, and fighter planes were dispatched to investigate. Exactly fifty years later to the day, July 26, 2002, the North American Aerospace Defense Command scrambled two Air National

Guard F-16 jets out of Andrews Air Force Base to investigate unknown aerial craft over the nation's capital. On each occasion, the UFO raid was explained as a natural phenomenon.

After Fifty Years, the Air Force Admits a Cover-up—of a Balloon

On June 24, 1997—the fiftieth anniversary of Kenneth Arnold's sighting of the flying saucers in Washington State—the United States Air Force conducted a special Pentagon briefing and announced its answer to the charges of a conspiracy at Roswell in the document *The Roswell Report: Case Closed*. The debris found at the crash site outside of Roswell were fragments from a balloon from Project Mogul, a top-secret intelligence gathering operation, that had begun immediately after the end of World War II. Its mission had been to spy on the Soviets and to monitor their nuclear program; therefore, the cover-up had been necessary for purposes of national security.

The Air Force report went on to state that the alleged bodies seen around the crash site were not those of extraterrestrial beings, but were dummies, roughly the size of humans, that had been used in experiments with high-altitude parachutes. After each of the experimental drops, which had begun in 1953, Air Force personnel would retrieve the simulated human forms. Apparently, folks around Roswell got the idea that they had observed military personnel picking up alien bodies.

UFO researchers scorned such an explanation of the alleged crash debris having been a balloon and the true nature of the alien corpses having been parachute dummies. And then there was the question of how witnesses who saw the wreckage of a flying saucer and the bodies of its alien crew in 1947 could have confused the event with the discovery of dummies dropped over the desert near Roswell in 1953.

The Air Force had an answer for that mystery as well. The seeming six-year discrepancy between the events was a manifestation of the mental phenomenon of "time compression." Time compression occurs when a person's memory splices events separated by many years into "compressed" segments of time. Civilians who witnessed the crash site of a weather balloon in 1947 and, six years later, saw Air Force personnel retrieving crash dummies dropped from the skies, recalled the two events as one in their compressed memories.

The official explanation issued by the Air Force in their publication *The Roswell Report: Case Closed* accomplished little in quelling the accusations of a government conspiracy regarding the mystery of what really occurred in July 1947. Roswell has become a mecca for UFO believers from all over the world, and the city hosts an annual celebration to honor the alleged crash of the flying saucer in the desert.

UFOs, Secret Societies, and the Apocalypse

As the year 2000 grew nearer, many fundamentalist religious leaders became obsessed with fears concerning the Millennium and Armageddon, the great final battle between good and evil. Such an obsession created a mind-set of suspicion that had many members of these religious groups identifying Satan's minions gathering to fight the forces of good as aliens arriving on UFOs.

A number of fundamentalist Christian evangelists began to blend accounts of UFOs with the old fears of secret societies composed of top U.S. government officials, politicians, corporate chairmen, and international bankers who were seeking to bring into being a dreaded "New World Order." Rumors spread that extraterrestrials and powerful members of secret societies had agreed that shortly before the year 2000 a carefully staged false alien invasion would convince the masses of the world that an attack from outer space was about to begin. People of all nations would believe the leaders who advised that unconditional surrender to the aliens was for everyone's own good.

Immediately following their betrayal of Earth to the aliens, the united leaders would form a One World Government, a New World Order, thus fulfilling biblical prophecies about a return to the days of Babylon. The aliens would reveal themselves as demonic entities, and the planet would be in torment until Jesus returned to deal the final blow to the armies of evil.

The American Public Doesn't Buy the UFO Cover-up

In June 1998 a CNN/Time poll found that 27 percent of all Americans believe that aliens have already visited Earth, and 80 percent maintain that the government is conducting a cover-up to keep the truth of extraterrestrial visitation from the general population. On June 8, 1999, a National Institute of Science/Roper Poll surveyed a nationwide sampling of men and women and found that 25 percent believed UFOs to be alien spacecraft and another 12 percent thought them to be vehicles of a secret government agency.

UFO RESEARCHERS' MYSTERIOUS DEATHS

Whether it is a fatal visit from the Men in Black or a secret government agency, some UFO researchers have found that investigating flying saucers can be a dangerous business.

With all the paranoia about secret military cover-ups of the UFO mystery and whispered fears about the Men in Black (MIB), some researchers have claimed that a number of UFO witnesses and investigators actually have met their demise at the hands of unknown and mysterious assailants. In 1971 the author-researcher Otto Binder wrote an article for *Saga* magazine's "Special UFO Report" titled "Liquidation of the UFO Investigators." Binder claimed to have researched the deaths of 137 flying saucer researchers, writers, scientists, and witnesses who had died in the previous ten years—many, Binder emphasized, under the most mysterious circumstances.

UFO researcher-author G. Cope Schellhorn has been tabulating the deaths of UFOlogists from "unusual cancers, heart attacks, questionable suicides, and all manner of strange happenings" since 1997. Admittedly, some of the researchers on Schellhorn's and other investigators' lists were getting up in years, or were, by the testimony of family and friends, ill or depressed or suicidal. Still, where there is smoke, there may be a MIB. Here are some of the names on the UFO researchers death list:

M. K. Jessup, 1959: Astronomer and archaeologist M. K. Jessup, well-known author of such influential works as *The Case for the UFO* and *The Expanding Case for the UFO,* allegedly committed suicide in Dade County Park, Florida, in 1959. Certain facts about the case have long troubled researchers:

- Contrary to Florida law, no autopsy was performed.

- Police sergeant Obenclain, who was on the scene shortly after Jessup's body was discovered, said that everything about the setup seemed too professional.

- Jessup died at rush hour, with more than the usual amount of traffic passing by.

- The author had been visited by Carlos Allende, the mysterious letter writer of the famous Philadelphia Experiment investigation, three days before his death and, according to his wife, had been receiving strange phone calls. Jessup was investigating the alleged Navy experiment in invisibility at the time of his death.

Frank Edwards, 1967: Frank Edwards, the noted news commentator, died of an alleged heart attack on June 24, 1967, on the twentieth anniversary of the Kenneth Arnold sighting. The "World UFO Conference" was being held in New York City at the Commodore hotel on that same day in June, chaired by UFO publisher and author Gray Barker. Barker stated that he had received two letters and a telephone call threatening that Frank Edwards would not be alive by the conference's end.

Dr. James McDonald, 1971: McDonald, senior physicist, Institute of Atmospheric Physics, professor in the Department of Meteorology at the University of Arizona, died purportedly of a gunshot wound to the head. McDonald had worked hard in the 1960s to convince Congress to hold serious, substantial subcommittee meetings to explore the UFO reality.

Ivan T. Sanderson, 1973: Well-known naturalist, zoologist, UFO investigator, and author of all things mysterious, died of a rapidly spreading cancer.

Philip K. Dick, 1982: Cult science-fiction author (*Bladerunner* and *Minority Report*), was a silent contactee of some higher intelligence for many years. At the time he died of a stroke under somewhat mysterious circumstances, Dick was writing a nonfiction book about his experiences with alien contact. It has never been published, and the manuscript has allegedly disappeared.

Capt. Don Elkin, 1984: A professor of physics and mechanical engineering, as well as an Eastern Airlines pilot, Capt. Don Elkin had been investigating UFOs since 1948. He was deep into the study of the Ra material, alleged extraterrestrial communications channeled by Carla Rueckert, at the time of his suicide.

Dr. Allen J. Hynek, 1986: Although he was no longer a young man, the death of Dr. J. Allen Hynek, the famous astronomer and consultant to Project Blue Book—the U.S. Air Force's official UFO investigation—due to a brain tumor seemed suspicious to many. Supposedly in the hospital for prostate surgery, Hynek's death seems all the stranger when one considers the high number of UFO investigators who have died of brain tumors or cancer. Those who knew Hynek well recall that he

seemed troubled over some recently acquired data shortly before his fatal hospital stay.

Mae Brussell, 1988: Mae Brussell, a gutsy, no-holds-barred investigative radio host, who was acutely interested in UFOs as well as the dangers of the New World Order, died of a fast-acting cancer.

Deke Slayton, 1993: Deke Slayton, the astronaut, was purportedly ready to talk about his UFO experiences, but cancer also intervened.

Ron Rummel, 1993: Ron Rummel, former air force intelligence agent and publisher of *Alien Digest,* allegedly shot himself in the mouth with a pistol on August 6, 1993.

Ann Livingston, 1994: Ann Livingston made her living as an accountant, but she was also a MUFON investigator. On December 29, 1992, Livingston claimed to have been accosted by five MIB whom she described as being almost faceless and carrying long, flashlight-like black objects. In early 1994 she died of a fast-acting form of ovarian cancer.

Karla Turner, 1996: Karla Turner, author of *Masquerade of Angels, Taken,* and *Into the Fringe* suspected that the breast cancer that preceded her death was due to alien retaliation for statements she made in print.

Ron Johnson, 1994: At the time of his death, Ron Johnson, Mutual UFO Network (MUFON) deputy director of investigations, was forty-three years old and in excellent health. On June 9, 1994, while attending a Society of Scientific Exploration meeting in Austin, Texas, Johnson died quickly and amid very strange circumstances. When the lights were turned back on after a slide presentation, Johnson was slumped over in his chair, his face purple, blood oozing from his nose. A soda can, from which he had been sipping, was sitting on the chair next to him.

Phil Schneider, 1996: Phil Schneider died on January 17, 1996, allegedly strangled by a catheter found wrapped around his neck.

Schneider claimed to have worked in 13 of the 129 deep underground facilities the U.S. government constructed after World War II. One of these bases was the bioengineering facility at Dulce, New Mexico, where according to Schneider, humanoid extraterrestrials worked side by side with American technicians.

Jim Keith, 1999: Author of many books including *Mind Control, World Control,* Jim Keith died in hospital during surgery to repair a broken leg he suffered while attending the infamous Burning Man Festival in Nevada. Allegedly, a blood clot was released during the surgery and traveled to the heart, causing a pulmonary edema.

William Cooper, 2001: Author of the classic book *Behold a Pale Horse,* shortwave radio talk show host, UFO researcher, and political activist, William Cooper was shot dead during a gun battle with sheriff's deputies at his home in Eagar, Arizona.

Ron Bonds, 2001: Ron Bonds of IllumiNet Press published books on unsolved mysteries and unexplained phenomena, from the Kennedy assassination to the ominous black helicopters of the New World Order. In April 2001, fifteen hours after eating a meal with warm beef from a Mexican restaurant in Atlanta, Bonds was taken to Grady Memorial Hospital, where he died. His death was attributed to a bacterium that figures in 250,000 cases of food poisoning a year—of which, according to the Center for Disease Control, only seven result in death.

UNABOMBER AND THE HARVARD DRUG EXPERIMENTS

If Theodore Kaczynski was only one of many who volunteered for the Harvard experiments in mind control, we could have a lot of Unabombers waiting to explode.

In 1957 a thirty-seven-year-old Ph.D. in psychology named Timothy Leary read an article by R. Gordon Wasson on entheogens in indigenous Mexican religious ceremonies and made the decision to travel to Mexico and experiment with psilocybin mushrooms. It was a decision that altered Leary's life and the lives of millions of others. Upon Leary's return to Harvard, he began the Harvard Psilocybin Project with Dr. Richard Alpert (who would later be known as Ram Dass) and other colleagues. Leary went on to experiment with LSD, and he became convinced that properly administered dosages could alter behavior in many beneficial ways, including by producing profound mystical and spiritual experiences. Another of Leary's colleagues at Harvard who was soliciting volunteers among the students for experiments was Dr. Henry A. Murray, a psychiatrist who had been a lieutenant colonel in World War II and had devised special tests that the Office of Strategic Services (OSS) used in selecting agents.

Among the students who volunteered for Murray's experiments at Harvard was a brilliant young man named Theodore Kaczynski, who had entered the university when he was not quite sixteen. Later George Piranian, one of Kaczynski's professors at the University of Michigan, where he did postgraduate work, commented that it was an understatement to say that Kaczynski was highly intelligent; the young man earned his Ph.D. by solving in less than a year a problem in mathematics that Piranian himself had been unable to crack. Maxwell O. Reade, a mathematics professor who served on Kaczynski's dissertation committee at Michigan, speculated that there were probably only ten to twelve people in the United States who could understand Kaczynski's specialty, a branch of complex analysis known as geometric function theory. Kaczynski would later hold a National Science Foundation fellowship and publish six articles in mathematic journals. Theodore "Ted" Kaczynski seemed destined for high-level academic success. Those who have researched his case in depth have suggested that had he not volunteered for those experiments in mind control at Harvard, he might not have become the infamous "Unabomber."

Dr. Henry A. Murray had come from a wealthy New York background and was an interesting mix of scientist and humanist. He freely discussed his apprehensions about living in a nuclear age and thought humankind's best chance for survival would be under a single world government. Murray had become convinced that he had a special mission to transform individuals from their nationalistic indoctrination as National Man into World Man. The interplay between two individuals, which he viewed as a "dyad," could be made to bridge psychology and sociology and create a unit that would be able to survive in the new world.

Murray's famous system used by the OSS to select agents who could withstand torture and interrogation involved a test that in many trials left the applicants crying and broken. The experiments in which Kaczynski participated were even more elaborate than the ones devised by Murray for the OSS in wartime. The subjects were bound to chairs, wired with electrodes and various monitoring devices, and subjected to total darkness, blinding lights, highly personal verbal attacks—and probably, unknowingly, doses of LSD.

The entire program was under the direction of Dr. Sidney Gottlieb, who was also the leader of the CIA's MK-ULTRA project in mind control. The records of all 150 projects and subprojects of MK-ULTRA were ordered destroyed in 1972 by CIA director Richard Helms, so researchers cannot truly evaluate the effects that Murray's experiments had on Kaczynski or any other participants, but many investigators have theorized that Kaczynski became a programmed ticking time bomb.

Assessed as "brilliant" by all who knew him, Ted was also regarded as highly unsocial. His loving, supportive parents recalled that their child's personality changed from that of a happy baby boy after he had been hospitalized for several weeks with a severe allergic reaction to medication. Upon his return home, little Ted seemed to cry easily and beg for comfort. Away from home, he was shy, aloof, and withdrawn, even in the company of friends and neighbors.

After receiving his Ph.D. from the University of Michigan and being recognized as a gifted mathematician, Kaczynski obtained a position as assistant professor of mathematics at the University of California, Berkeley, in the fall of 1967. He had few friends among the faculty, and his aloof and reserved manner caused students to give him poor ratings as a teacher. The vice chairman of the mathematics department, Calvin Moore, commented that with Kaczynski's impressive academic credentials and his record of published articles at such a young age, he could easily have advanced to tenure and status, but, unexpectedly, in 1969, Ted resigned without explanation. In 1971 he moved to Great Falls, Montana, and began building a cabin near Lincoln, eighty miles southwest of Great Falls, on some land that he and his brother David had acquired.

Like many intellectuals before him, Kaczynski sought personal transformation in nature. He would be another Henry David Thoreau, living alone in his own version of Walden Pond. In his solitude, he also had lots of time to reflect upon the evils of contemporary society and how the Industrial Revolution had destroyed forever humankind's link with the rural lifestyle that had nurtured it for centuries. He also had plenty of time to consider Dr. Murray's fears about living in a nuclear age and surviving as World Man, rather than as National Man.

Kaczynski mailed the first bomb to Professor Buckley Crist at Northwestern University on

May 1978. A campus police officer sustained minor injury when he opened the package.

The FBI became involved when the second bomb was found smoking in the cargo hold of a commercial airplane before it could explode. A faulty timing mechanism prevented the bomb from detonating, but investigators said that it contained enough explosives to have blown the plane to bits—along with its passengers and crew. FBI agents began a search for a disgruntled airline employee, but John Douglas, the father of the FBI's "profiling" of criminals, assessed the sophistication of the device as the work of a "disgruntled academic," rather than an airline mechanic seeking revenge against a former employer.

The third bomb caused the first serious injury. In 1985, a Berkeley graduate student who had just been accepted for astronaut training lost four fingers and vision in one eye because of the blast.

The first death resulted from the fourth bomb, which exploded in the parking lot of a California computer store in 1985, killing the owner with nail and splinter projectiles. In Salt Lake City on February 20, 1987, a similar bomb detonated near a computer store, but no one was injured. Each of these bombs bore the inscription "FC," which investigators first interpreted as "F——k Computers," but which was later revealed to stand for "Freedom Club."

There were no more bombs until 1993, when Kaczynski mailed another potentially fatal package, this time to David Gelernter, a computer science professor at Yale, who escaped injury. Later in 1993, geneticist Charles Epstein was maimed by the bomb that he received.

Kaczynski wrote to the *New York Times*, claiming to be the leader of an anarchist group called the "Freedom Club" and accepting responsibility for the bombings. Within a few months, in 1994, an advertising executive was killed by a mail bomb, and a subsequent letter by Kaczynski justified the assassination

An early police sketch of the Unabomber based on eyewitnesses before he was identified as Theodore Kaczynski.

by condemning the public relations field for manipulating people to obey the wills of the advertisers and to buy things that they don't really need.

In 1995, shortly after the murder of Gilbert Murray, president of the California Forestry Association, the Unabomber began mailing letters, some to his former victims, explaining his goals and demanding that newspapers print his 35,000-word manifesto "Industrial Society and Its Future." The Unabomber threatened to send more bombs unless his manifesto appeared in print. He promised to cease his campaign of terror if his philosophy could be made known to the general public.

In September 1995 the *New York Times* and the *Washington Post* published the Unabomber's thesis word for word as he had written it. The authorities had encouraged the newspapers to present the Unabomber's work verbatim not only to appease him, but also in the hope that someone would recognize his writing style and phraseology.

Among Kaczynski's main points were the following:

- The Industrial Revolution and its technological legacy have proved to be a disaster for the human race. The resulting system suppresses human freedom, destroys nature, and makes the individual exist to serve the system, rather than the other way around as it should be.

- Modern technology is undesirable, and it should be halted so that people can return to a simpler, happier lifestyle living next to nature.

- A collapse of the technological society is inevitable, so it would be best to bring about a "social crash" as soon as possible before it can get any worse.

- There should be no illusions about creating an ideal society; the goal should be only to destroy the existing form of society.

- If revolutionaries do not destroy the present form of society, the future will see the common people surviving as "house pets" or slaves to an elite class of humans or to intelligent machines.

Kaczynski was arrested outside his remote Montana cabin on April 3, 1996. His brother David had recognized his writing style and notified the authorities. Although David had received assurances that Ted would never know that his own brother had turned him in to the FBI, the information was leaked to the press. The Kaczynski family was also betrayed when the prosecutors had promised them that they would not seek the death penalty. Ted managed to avoid the sentence of death by pleading guilty on January 22, 1998, and he was delivered to the federal ADX supermaximum-security prison in Florence, Colorado, to serve life without the possibility of parole. David

Kaczynski donated the reward money, minus his legal expenses, to the families of the Unabomber's victims.

Over an eighteen-year period, Kaczynski sent mail bombs to his selected targets, killing three and wounding twenty-nine. As the Unabomber, he was responsible for the FBI's most expensive manhunt ever conducted.

When we reflect upon the brilliant, barely sixteen-year-old, shy and sensitive Harvard student who volunteered for mind-control experiments under the direction of Henry Murray and Sidney Gottlieb, we can only wonder exactly what programming was directed toward Theodore Kaczynski and hundreds of others. We know today that Murray and Gottlieb conducted mind-control tests that flagrantly violated medical ethics. What we don't know is how many other "Unabombers" might be triggered some day by an insidious posthypnotic suggestion that was planted in a student's psyche forty-five or fifty years ago.

UNDERGROUND UFO BASES

Some UFO investigators warn us to forget about the lights in the skies. The real danger from alien invasion is under our feet.

Although UFO researchers insist that there are underground alien bases in Nevada, Arizona, California, Wisconsin, Colorado, and many other areas, the alleged underground facility outside Dulce, New Mexico, is by far the most notorious. According to many UFO investigators, there are men and women who claim to have worked in these facilities side by side with extraterrestrials nicknamed "Grays."

The Grays are most often described as being under four feet tall, with a disproportionately large head and large slanted eyes. Some of their species appear more sophisticated than others, but they all seem to worship technology at the expense of artistic and creative expression. They also seem devoid of emotion and appear indifferent to the general well-being of humans. The witnesses who claim to have worked aside Grays, state that the principal research at Dulce is the study of human genetics and the possibility of crossbreeding the two species and/or developing mutations.

A frequently heard account about Dulce concerns a 1969 confrontation that broke out between the human scientists working there and the aliens. In order to guarantee extended cooperation from the secret government, the Grays took a number of human scientists as hostages.

Crack troops from Delta Force were sent into the vast underground tunnels to rescue the scientists, but they proved to be no match for the aliens. Estimates of sixty-six to several hundred humans were killed during the violent confrontation.

Because of the sudden realization that the Grays could not always be trusted to follow other than their own secret agenda, the representatives and employees of the secret government withdrew from all joint projects with the Grays for about two years. Eventually a reconciliation occurred, and the alliance between the aliens and the members of the secret government was once again back on course.

Some of the aliens who work in the underground bases consider themselves to be native Earthlings, for they are the crossbred descendants of a reptilian humanoid species, who many thousands of years ago in our planet's prehistory accomplished genetic engineering with early members of *Homo sapiens*. While some of these crossbred reptilian-human "Terrans" are loyal allies, others of their group have proven to be untrustworthy mercenary agents for the Draco, an extraterrestrial race that is returning to Earth—a planet they consider their ancient outpost.

In addition to a number of reported "Hairy Dwarfs" and exceedingly tall alien life forms, the most commonly mentioned extraterrestrial biological entities (EBEs) next to the Grays are the "Nordics," essentially human in appearance, mostly blond-haired and blue-eyed. Cast in an angelic kind of role in the alien versus human drama, they normally do not violate the intergalactic law of noninterference so they cannot halt the occasional grisly machinations of the Grays. Unless, of course, the Grays finally go too far and begin to upset the larger picture of universal balance and order.

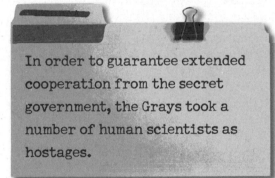

In order to guarantee extended cooperation from the secret government, the Grays took a number of human scientists as hostages.

Research scientist Paul Bennewitz claims to have been repeatedly harassed and intimidated by the military after he provided government investigators with proof that he had filmed a formation of UFOs flying over the Manzano Weapons Storage Area and the Coyote Canyon Test Site (where nuclear materials are stored), all part of the Kirtland Air Force Base facilities in Albuquerque, New Mexico. Bennewitz said he saw four saucer-shaped objects lined up beside the fence of the air base.

Bennewitz's investigations led him to Dulce, where he spoke with a woman who was kidnapped by aliens after she and her son had witnessed them mutilating a cow. According to the abductee, she and her son were taken inside the Dulce underground base and saw for themselves horrible experiments in which organs and blood were being removed from animals to create a new species of humanoids through gene splicing.

John Lear is the son of the famous aviation pioneer William Lear, who established the Lear Aircraft Company. John himself has earned a well-deserved reputation in aeronautical circles for having test flown over 150 aircraft and having won numerous awards from the Federal Aviation Administration. A few years ago—before he heard a friend relate a UFO encounter that had taken place in England—Lear had absolutely no interest in flying saucers. However, as he began to check out the accounts that others had relayed to him, he found to his astonishment that there were mountains of evidence proving that UFOs are real and quite likely from outer space.

Pursuing the subject with his contacts in the CIA and his informants in military intelligence, Lear ascertained that the first UFO crash occurred in Germany shortly before World War II. The Nazis used the technology obtained from the wreckage to initiate the rocketry program that destroyed much of Europe and blitzed the British Isles.

Later, Lear was told, a flying disc crashed near Roswell, New Mexico, and one of the injured aliens on board was kept alive for a short period of time in Hangar 18 in what is now Wright-Patterson Air Force Base.

What shocked Lear was that the government had made secret deals with the aliens, actually exchanging humans for advanced technical data. By 1987 Lear had discovered that the EBEs were putting together a sort of "Frankenstein Army—part alien, part human" in underground facilities in Nevada and New Mexico.

Lear's painstaking research yielded grisly evidence that human, as well as cattle, mutilations had been performed by the aliens as early as 1956. An Air Force major had witnessed the abduction of a sergeant early one morning at the White Sands Missile Test Range. When his body was found three days later, his genitals had been removed, his rectum cored out in a surgically precise plug up to the colon, and his eyes had been removed. His corpse had also been drained of all blood. Information provided Lear by informants concerning the Dulce underground base detailed large vats with pale meat being agitated in solutions and large test tubes with humans in them.

In Lear's assessment the abduction scenario seemed to have at least three purposes: (1) insertion of a tiny probe, approximately three millimeters in size that would monitor and program the abductee; (2) posthypnotic suggestions regarding the abductee's future mission; and (3) genetic crossbreeding between the EBEs and humans.

William Hamilton, author of *Cosmic Top Secret,* first received news of the existence of the secret underground bases in 1979 when an acquaintance who was a government worker revealed the details of military participation in monstrous genetic experiments being conducted with a sinister group of aliens. When his employers discovered that the man had stolen photographs depicting these experiments, his wife and children were taken into custody by federal agents as an effective means of regaining the classified material that had been misplaced.

Hamilton's friend told him that the base at which he had been employed had at least seven subterranean levels. On level four, for example, advanced research in mind control was being conducted. At level six, genetic experiments on animals and humans were in progress. Humans were kept in cages and drugged for some detestable purpose on level seven.

Hamilton's informant had originally been told a false story that the government was conducting special secret tests to cure insanity, but when he realized at last that aliens were actually behind the torturous experiments, he left his post and went into hiding.

Hamilton cautions against panic, observing that "aliens have been around a long time and have not taken any mass offensive against us to date." Hamilton's greatest concern "is the fact that excessive secrecy [on the part of the government] can lead to a breakdown in our cultural cohesiveness. It can lead to wild rumors and freewheeling speculations. It can lead to ignorance and the disintegration of our society."

UNDERSEA
UFO BASES

Long before the alleged UFO crash at Roswell in 1947, people have witnessed strange lights and machines entering and leaving Earth's seas.

In mid-February 1942, five years before UFOs were brought into modern mass consciousness by Kenneth Arnold's sighting of flying saucers near Mount Rainier and the alien spaceship crash outside of Roswell, Lt. William Brennan of the Royal Australian Air Force sighted a mysterious aerial craft while on patrol over the Bass Strait south of Melbourne, Australia. Brennan was on the lookout for Japanese submarines or long-range German U-boats. Fishermen in the area had reported mysterious lights bobbing on the sea at night, and after the Japanese attack on Darwin on February 19, the Allied High Command was urging the strictest vigilance.

The air patrol was flying a few miles east of the Tasman Peninsula about 5:50 P.M. on a sunny evening when a strange aircraft of a glistening bronze color suddenly emerged from a cloud bank near them. The object was about 150 feet long and approximately 50 feet in diameter. Lt. Brennan saw that the peculiar craft had a dome or cupola on its upper surface and he thought that he might have seen someone inside wearing a helmet. There were occasional greenish-blue flashes emanating from its keel, and Brennan was astonished to see what appeared to be the bizarre image of a grinning Cheshire cat framed in a white circle on the front of the dome.

The unidentified aerial craft flew parallel to the RAAF patrol for several minutes, then it abruptly turned away and dived straight down into the Pacific. Brennan emphasized that the unidentified submarine object (USO) made a *dive,* not a crash, into the ocean; and he added that before the craft left them, he noticed what appeared to be four finlike appendages on its underside.

According to UFO researchers, Brennan may have reported an early sighting of a craft returning to an extraterrestrial or a secret terrestrial undersea base. While there are numerous witnesses who claim to have seen UFOs ascending from underground bases, there are also a vast number of reports from those who have witnessed strange USOs entering and leaving large bodies of water. In other instances, scientific expeditions have encountered mysterious underwater objects that belonged to no known terrestrial source.

Early in February 1960 the Argentine navy, with the assistance of United States advisers, alternately depth-bombed and demanded the surrender of submarines thought to be lurking at the bottom of Golfo Nuevo, a forty-by-twenty-mile bay separated from the South Atlantic by a narrow entrance. There were at least two mystery submarines, and they both were able to function and maneuver in the narrow gulfs for many days without surfacing. They easily outran and hid from surface vessels, and in spite of the combined forces of the Argentine fleet and the most modern U.S. subhunting technology, they were able to escape.

On January 12, 1965, Captain K, an airline pilot on a flight between Whenuapai and Kaitaia, New Zealand, spotted a USO when he was about one-third of the way across Kaipara Harbor. As he veered his DC-3 for a closer look at what he had at first guessed to be a stranded gray-white whale in an estuary, it became evident to him that he was now observing a metallic structure of some sort.

Captain K saw that the object was perfectly streamlined and symmetrical in shape. He could detect no external control surfaces or protrusions, but there did appear to be a hatch on top. Harbored in no more than thirty feet of water, the USO was not shaped like an ordinary submarine. He estimated its length to be approximately a hundred feet with a diameter of fifteen feet at its widest part.

> Brennan was astonished to see what appeared to be the bizarre image of a grinning Cheshire cat framed in a white circle on the front of the dome.

Later, the navy stated that it would have been impossible for any known model of submarine to have been in that particular area due to the configuration of harbor and coastline. The surrounding mud flats and mangrove swamps would make the spot in which Captain K saw his USO inaccessible to conventional undersea craft.

The Argentine steamer *Naviero* was some 120 miles off the coast of Brazil on the night of July 30, 1967. The time was about 6:15. Captain Julian Lucas Ardanza was enjoying his evening meal when one of his officers, Jorge Montoya, called him on the intercom to report something strange near the ship. Captain Ardanza emerged on deck to view a cigar-shaped shining object in the sea, not more than 50 feet off the *Naviero*'s starboard side. The submarine craft was an estimated 105 to 110 feet long and emitted a powerful blue and white glow. Captain Ardanza and the other officers could see no sign of periscope, railing, tower, or superstructure on the noiseless craft. Captain Ardanza said that in his twenty years at sea he had never seen anything like it.

Chief Officer Carlos Lasca ventured that the object was a submersible UFO with a brilliant source of illumination. The seamen estimated the craft's speed at twenty-five knots, as opposed to the *Naviero*'s seventeen. After pacing the Argentine steamer for fifteen minutes, the unidentified submarine object suddenly submerged, passed directly under the *Naviero,* and disappeared into the depths of the ocean, glowing all the while it dove deeper and deeper.

On October 3, 1967, a sixty-foot-long object with a series of bright portholes was sighted diving into the harbor and submerging in Shag Harbor, Nova Scotia. Within twenty minutes several constables of the Royal Canadian Mounted Police were on the scene, attempting to reach by boat the spot where about a half mile off shore the sizzling UFO was seen to float, then submerge beneath the surface of Shag Harbor.

A Coast Guard boat and eight fishing vessels joined the constables in time to observe a large path of yellowish foam and bubbling water. Divers from the Royal Canadian Navy searched the area for two days, but found no physical evidence of any kind.

In December 1997 a massive craft was seen emerging from the sea next to an oil platform in the Gulf of Mexico. According to engineer Jeremy Packer, the sighting was witnessed by 250 oil rig workers.

At about 7:58 A.M., Packer said, everyone got frightened when they heard a rumbling noise that they knew couldn't be the engines that ran the platform bore. Looking toward the west, they sighted twenty-five to thirty helicopters on maneuvers. This was not unusual, Packer said, except that the rig commander said that he had not received the usual alert regarding Coast Guard maneuvers.

Then, according to Packer, they all saw something that totally changed their lives. All of the helicopters stopped in midair and a huge metal cigar-shaped object about the size of the oil platform surfaced beneath them. The massive craft, about as long as two football fields, soared straight out of the water and into the air, where it hovered above the helicopters for about two minutes.

Packer described the object as concave on its underside with four large domes on its bottom. The topside of the cigar-shaped craft was encircled by beautiful lights of every color that one could imagine. Then, as if someone had turned off a light switch, the giant craft disappeared.

On July 5, 1965, Dr. Dmitri Rebikoff, a marine scientist making preparations to explore the Gulf Stream's depths, found himself faced with a most unusual challenge when he detected and attempted to photograph a fast-moving USO on the bottom of the warm water stream that flows from the Florida Keys to Newfoundland and onward to northern Europe. Dr. Rebikoff told Captain L. Jacques Nicholas, project coordinator, that the object was pear-shaped and moving at approximately three and one-half knots.

The peculiar object was moving beneath various schools of fish, and at first, judging from its size, Dr. Rebikoff thought it to be a large shark. As he monitored it, however, he noted that the USO's direction and speed were too constant. The marine scientist theorized that the object was mechanical and running on robot pilot, but since they were unable to receive any signal from the USO, he really had no idea what it might have been.

In 1969 Dr. Roger W. Wescott, chairman of the anthropology department at Drew University, Madison, New Jersey, published *The Divine Animal,* in which he presented the theory that extraterrestrials had landed on Earth ten thousand years ago, fully intending to teach humankind a better way of life. But when Earth's dominant species continued to demonstrate its avaricious and destructive nature, the ex-

traterrestrials gave up in disgust and withdrew to establish undersea bases.

Although these cosmic tutors were temporarily thwarted in their attempts to build a better world here on Earth, they did not give up hope for all time, and they emerge from time to time to conduct certain spot checks to see if humans are advancing intellectually and becoming less barbaric. Such monitoring forays explain the sightings of UFOs which have been reported for thousands of years.

Dr. Wescott also suggests that when the UFOnauts withdrew from the Earth's surface, they took some humans along with them to train and to tutor according to their advanced extraterrestrial principles. Dr. Wescott conjectures that some of these specially tutored humans might have been returned to the surface at certain intervals to have become leaders. Some of these apprentices worked to change humankind for good, while others, corrupted by a combination of their secret knowledge and the malleability of the less-advanced surfaced humans, brought additional chaos and confusion to the world. Dr. Wescott speculates that such individuals as Buddha, Jesus, Muhammad, Genghis Khan, and Attila the Hun might have been sent up to the surface by the UFOnauts with varying degrees of success.

The anthropologist feels that the space travelers were viewed as gods by our human ancestors. He believes that the UFO beings sincerely wished to teach developing humankind, but as the human species began to master the environment, they also began to desire more material goods and became willing to wage wars to obtain the goods they didn't possess. In his theory, human greed and aggressiveness disgusted the Masters from space and caused them to withdraw from humankind and to establish undersea bases where they could still observe the species but live comfortably apart from them.

In Dr. Wescott's view, such a theory helps to explain two of the most widespread and persistent legends found among nearly all peoples and all cultures: (1) There was a time when gods walked the earth and tutored humankind. (2) There was a land called Atlantis, whose thriving civilization met with catastrophe and sank beneath the sea.

UNIT 731

As many conspiracy theorists have pointed out, in 1940 the U.S. government seemed primarily concerned with entering the war in Europe against the Nazis; consequently, little attention was paid to the atrocities that the Japanese Imperial Army had committed with the biological warfare corps known as Unit 731 beginning in Manchuria as early as 1932.

In 1925 Japan refused to sign the Geneva Convention ban on biological weapons. Japanese officials reasoned that if such weapons were considered so horrible that all other nations had voted to ban them, then they might be just perfect for use by the Japanese military.

In 1932, accompanying Japanese troops invading Manchuria, Dr. Shiro Ishii, a physician as well as an army officer, began preliminary experiments with biological weapons. Dr. Ishii had gained fame by designing a water filter that had helped stop the spread of meningitis in Shikoku, Japan, so he was the best-known bacteriologist in Japan. The invasion of Manchuria was part of a long-range plan in which the Soviet Union would become the enemy—and the victim of Japan's biological weapons program. Because he had an almost unlimited supply of Chinese prisoners on whom to experiment, Ishii decided to expand the program to include the effects on living human subjects of burns, freezing cold, high pressure, and bullets.

Harbin, Manchuria, was the headquarters of Unit 731, which was officially identified to the outside world as the "Epidemic Prevention and Water Purification Department of the Kuantung Army." Dr. Ishii was promoted to full colonel and provided with three thousand troops to carry out his orders. In 1936 the research was expanded to include Unit 100, under the direction of Yujiro Wakamatsu and located in Mengchiatun, near Changchun; the new unit was known officially as the "Department of Veterinary Disease Prevention of the Kuantung Army." In June 1938 Unit 731 relocated to Pingfang and expanded to an area of nineteen square miles. Former Unit 731 members later testified that at least nine thousand people were killed in the biological experiments conducted by Dr. Ishii. There were no survivors.

The invasion of Manchuria was part of a long-range plan in which the Soviet Union would become the enemy—and the victim of Japan's biological weapons program.

In 1942 Unit 731 ordered field tests to evaluate the effectiveness of biological weapons outside of the laboratory. Chinese prisoners were forced to march amidst clouds of poison gas so that their reactions could be filmed for study in the safety of the laboratory. Japanese planes dropped plague-infected fleas over Ningbo in eastern China and over Changde in north-central China, and the experimenters had cause for celebration when plague broke out in both cities and tens of thousands died. Premier Shideki Tojo personally awarded Dr. Ishii military honors for his expertise in developing biological weapons.

On occasion the Japanese experiments backfired on their own troops. In 1942 germ warfare scientists distributed dysentery, cholera, and typhoid in the wells and ponds in the Zhejiang Province in China, but the occupying Japanese soldiers also became ill, and 1,700 died from the trio of deadly germ colonies that had been dropped in the water.

In the summer of 1945, Japanese generals suggested the use of kamikaze (suicide) pilots to drop bombs of plague-infected fleas on San Diego. Although no biological weapons were utilized, nine thousand balloons, each carrying four incendiary and one antipersonnel bomb, were launched across the Pacific on the jet stream. Some of these "Fugo" balloons actually made it across the ocean and caused a few fires and very few deaths along the West Coast.

In July 1945 an attack team was assigned to board a submarine that was to carry a plane to the coast of Southern California. The plane's crew had orders to drop plague-infested fleas over San Diego on September 22. Plans were changed to make a last-ditch attack against the U.S. fleet at the Micronesian island of Ulith, just as the war ended.

In the final days of World War II, Japanese troops blew up the headquarters of Unit 731. Ishii gave the order to kill the remaining 150 subjects in order to cover up the evidence of the experiments that were being conducted on them. It was said by some of his associates that Ishii's greatest personality trait in achieving success was his lack of morality. In determining the internal effects of certain of the experimental diseases on its subjects, Ishii conducted many autopsies when the subjects were still alive. Vivisections were performed without giving anesthetic to the subjects, and experiments were even conducted on babies as young as three weeks. As Unit 731 retreated from China, they released plague-infected animals, causing an outbreak of disease that killed thirty thousand people in the area of Harbin from 1946 through 1948.

In 1946 Ishii and his colleagues received immunity from war-crimes prosecution in exchange for their data on biological warfare effects on humans. The statement of the Committee for the Far East, a subcommittee of the State-War-Navy Coordinating Committee in Washington, was that the value "to the U.S. of Japanese biological warfare data is of such importance to national security as to far outweigh the value accruing from war crimes prosecution." General MacArthur added that the biological warfare information obtained from Japanese sources should be retained in top-secret intelligence channels.

U.S. GOVERNMENT'S SECRET EXPERIMENTS ON ITS CITIZENS

For at least fifty years the Department of Defense has used hundreds of thousands of military personnel and private citizens in experiments with mustard and nerve gas, ionizing radiation, psychochemicals, hallucinogens, and drugs.

Among the many secret experiments and other clandestine medical programs carried out by governmental or government-related agencies, the following are some of the most notorious:

1931: Cancer. The Rockefeller Institute for Medical Investigations infected human subjects with cancer cells. Dr. Cornelius Rhoads established the U.S. Army Biological Warfare facilities in Maryland, Utah, and Panama and began a series of radiation exposure experiments on patients in government and civilian hospitals.

1932: Syphilis. In the Tuskegee Syphilis Study, two hundred black men diagnosed with syphilis were never told of their illness and were used as human guinea pigs in order to better understand the symptoms of the disease. None of the men received any kind of treatment, and only seventy-four survived.

1935: Dietary deficiencies. Millions had died of pellagra, a dietary deficiency, in poverty-stricken black populations. The U.S. Public Health Service finally acted to curb the disease and admitted that it had known the causes of pellagra for more than two decades.

1940: Malaria. In order to gauge the abilities of experimental drugs designed to fight malaria, four hundred prisoners in Chicago were infected with the disease.

1942: Mustard gas. Four thousand servicemen, mostly Seventh-day Adventists who were conscientious objectors, served as human guinea pigs for mustard gas experiments.

1946: Medical experiments. World War II veterans recovering from wartime wounds in Veterans Administration hospitals were quietly used as subjects in medical studies and experiments.

1947: Radioactive injections. The U.S. Atomic Energy Commission began administering intravenous doses of radioactive materials to human subjects.

1947: Psychedelics. In its efforts to evaluate LSD as a potential weapon or truth serum, the Central Intelligence Agency administered dosages of the powerful hallucinogenic drug to human subjects, civilian and military, often without their knowledge or consent.

1950: Radiation. With nuclear weapons still in their infancy, Department of Defense detonated nuclear devices in desert areas and then monitored unsuspecting civilians in cities downwind from the blasts for medical problems and mortality rates.

1950: Bacteriological warfare. The U.S. Navy sprayed a cloud of bacteria over San

Francisco to test how a large city would respond to more lethal biological attacks. Many residents became ill with pneumonia-like symptoms.

1955: Biological agents. In an experiment to test its ability to infect human populations with biological agents, the Central Intelligence Agency released bacteria in the Tampa, Florida, area.

1956: Yellow fever. Mosquitoes infected with yellow fever were released over Savannah, Georgia, and Avon Park, Florida. U.S. Army disease specialists, posing as public health officials, test area residents for effects.

1965: Dioxin. Inmates at Holmesburg State Prison in Philadelphia were dosed with dioxin, the toxic chemical component of Agent Orange used in Vietnam.

1966: Germ warfare. More than a million civilians were exposed to germ warfare when U.S. Army scientists dropped light bulbs filled with bacteria onto ventilation grates throughout the New York City subway system.

1977: Contamination. Senate hearings revealed that between 1949 and 1969, 239 highly populated areas, including San Francisco, Washington, D.C., Key West, Panama City (Florida), Minneapolis, and St. Louis, had been contaminated with biological agents.

1978: Hepatitis B. The Centers for Disease Control asked specifically for promiscuous homosexual males when it tested an experimental hepatitis B vaccine in New York, Los Angeles, and San Francisco. Three years later, in those same cities, the first cases of AIDS were confirmed in homosexual men.

1990: Measles. The Centers for Disease Control inoculated more than 1,500 six-month-old black and Hispanic babies in Los Angeles against measles. Later, the center confessed that the vaccine was experimental.

1995: Biological agents. Evidence surfaced that the biological agents used during the Gulf War had been manufactured in Houston, Texas, and Boca Raton, Florida, and tested on prisoners in the Texas Department of Corrections.

On September 30, 2010, Secretary of State Hillary Rodham Clinton and Health and Human Services Secretary Kathleen Sebelius apologized to the government of Guatemala and the survivors and descendants of "clearly unethical" experiments conducted in 1946 to 1948 in which American public health doctors infected nearly 700 prison inmates, mental patients, and soldiers with venereal diseases. Since the prisons of Guatemala permitted conjugal visits, the National Institutes of Health, in an organized effort to test the effectiveness of penicillin, paid for syphilis-infected prostitutes to visit the prisoners. Some soldiers and mental patients had the infectious bacteria rubbed into scrapes and cuts made on their penises, arms, or faces. If the subjects contracted any venereal diseases, they were given the antibiotics being tested. According to Susan M. Reverby, the professor at Wellesley College, who disclosed the experiments, it is not clear whether everyone who was infected was cured.

V

JESSE VENTURA

Before he became a popular host of Conspiracy Theory *on truTV, Jesse Ventura had a diverse career in the military, as a wrestler, and in politics.*

Born James George Janos, Jesse Ventura first came to the public's attention in 1975 as Jesse "The Body" Ventura, a colorful and popular wrestler in the World Wrestling Entertainment. Ventura remained with the WWE's until 1986 as a talent in the ring and, later, as a color commentator. He was inducted into the WWE's Hall of Fame in 2004.

Before he became known as an outspoken conspiracy theorist and host of *Conspiracy Theory with Jesse Ventura* on truTV, Ventura appeared in such motion pictures as 1987's *Predator* in which he fought a killer alien from outer space and snarled at co-star Arnold Schwarzenegger that he "didn't have time to bleed." After that hit film, Ventura went on to be featured in numerous films and television shows, including playing a threatening UFO "Man in Black" enforcer in a fan-favorite appearance on *The X-Files* episode "Jose Chung's from Outer Space."

Ventura was born in 1951 in Minneapolis. After graduating from high school, he enlisted in the U.S. Navy, where he joined the Special Forces and served as a UDT/SEAL from 1969 to 1973. After being honorably discharged from the Navy, he returned to Minnesota and, while attending community college, started training to become a professional wrestler.

Ventura entered politics as Mayor of Brooklyn Park, Minnesota, from 1991 to 1995. In 1999, he joined the Reform Party and became the thirty-eighth governor of Minnesota, defeating Arne Carlson. He did not seek a second term, and after he left office in 2003 and was succeeded by Tim Pawlenty, Ventura was a visiting fellow at Harvard's Kennedy School of Government.

In 2000, he wrote the first of his many bestselling books, *Quotations from Chairman Jesse.* Among his other titles are *Jesse Ventura Tells It Like It Is: Going to the Mat against Political Pawns and Media Jackals* (2002); *I Ain't Got Time to Bleed: Reworking the Body Politic from the Bottom Up* (2000); *Don't Start the Revolution without Me* (2009); *63 Documents the Government Doesn't Want You to Read* (2011); and *American Conspiracies: Lies, Lies, and More Dirty Lies that the Government Tells Us* (2011).

A former professional wrestler and governor of Minnesota, Jesse Ventura is now an author and the host of *Conspiracy Theory*.

Regarding his television program *Conspiracy Theory with Jesse Ventura,* Ventura says on his program's page on truTV that it is has become his "personal journey, to prove that there is more to these stories than you know about."

Promotional material for *Conspiracy Theory* promises that "Ventura and his team of investigators are on a mission to examine some of the most frightening and mysterious conspiracy allegations of our time. They review evidence and meet with experts and eyewitnesses to learn more about such topics as the JFK assassination, Area 51 and a possible plot to kidnap our nation's water supply."

VODUN/ VOUDOU/VOODOO

With its eerie assortment of spirits, zombies, Voodoo dolls, and the immortal Marie Laveau, Vodun has something to frighten everyone.

The connotations of evil, fear, and the supernatural that are associated with Vodun (also "Voudou" and, popularly, "Voodoo") originated primarily from white plantation owners' fear of slave revolts. The white masters and their overseers were often outnumbered sixteen to one by the slaves they worked unmercifully in the broiling Haitian sun, and the sounds of Voudou drums pounding in the night made them very nervous.

Vodun or *Voudou* means "spirit" in the language of the West African Yoruba people. Vodun as a religion observes an African tribal cosmology that may go back as many as six thousand years—and then it combines these ancient beliefs with the teachings, saints, and rituals of Roman Catholicism. Early slaves who were abducted from their homes and families on Africa's West Coast brought their gods and religious practices with them to Haiti and other West Indian islands. Plantation owners were compelled by order of the French colonial authorities to baptize their slaves in the Catholic religion. The slaves suffered no conflict of theology. They accepted the white man's "water" and quickly adopted Catholic saints into the older African family of nature gods and goddesses.

The traditional belief structure of the Yoruba envisioned a chief god named Olorun, who remains aloof and unknowable to humankind, but who permitted a lesser deity, Obatala, to create the earth and all its life forms. There are hundreds of minor spirits whose influence humans may invoke, such as Ayza, the protector; Baron Samedi, guardian of the grave; Dambala, the serpent; Ezli, the female spirit of love; Ogou Balanjo, spirit of healing; and Mawu Lisa, spirit of creation. Each follower of Vodun has his or her own *met tet,* a guardian spirit that corresponds to a Catholic's special saint.

As the years passed, Vodun began to adopt an anti-white liturgy in some of its nocturnal meetings. Several "messiahs" emerged among the slaves and were subsequently put to death by the whites. A number of laws began to be passed forbidding any plantation owner to allow "night dances" among his Negroes.

A slave revolt begun in 1791 under the leadership of François-Dominique Toussaint L'Ouverture led to Haiti's independence from France in 1804. Although Toussaint died in a Napoleonic prison, his generals had become sufficiently inspired by his example to continue the struggle for freedom until the myth of white supremacy was banished from the island.

After the Concordat of 1860, when relations were reestablished with France, the priests who came to Haiti found that vestiges of Catholicism had been kept alive in Vodun. Not until 1940 did the Catholic Church launch an aggressive campaign of renunciation directed at the adherents of Vodun. It was largely ineffective.

Today more than 60 million people practice Vodun worldwide, largely where Haitian emigrants have settled: in Benin, the Dominican Republic, Ghana, Togo, various cities in the United States, and of course Haiti. In South America there are many religions similar to Vodun, such as Umbanda, Quimbanda, and Candomblé.

A male priest of Vodun is called a *houngan* or *hungan*; his female counterpart, a *mambo*. The place where one practices Vodun is a series of buildings called a *humfort* or *hounfou*. A "congregation" is called a *hunsi* or *hounsis,* and the *houngan* cures, divines, and cares for the members through the good graces of a *loa,* his guiding spirit.

The worship of the *loa* is the central purpose of Vodun. The *loa* are the old gods of Africa, the local spirits of Haiti, who occupy a position to the fore of God, Christ, the Virgin, and the saints. From the beginning the Haitians adamantly refused to accept the church's position that the *loa* are the "fallen angels" who rebelled against God. The *loa* do good and guide and protect humankind. They,

like the saints of Catholicism, were once men and women who lived exemplary lives and who now are given a specific responsibility to assist human spirituality. Certainly there are those who perform acts of evil sorcery, the left-hand path of Vodun, but rarely will a *houngan* resort to such practices.

The *loa* communicates with the faithful by possessing their bodies during a trance or by appearing to them in dreams. The possession usually takes place during ritual dancing. Each participant in the dance eventually undergoes a personality change and adapts a trait of his or her particular *loa*. The practitioners of Vodun refer to this invasion of the body by a supernatural agency as that of the *loa* mounting its "horse."

There is a great difference between possession by a *loa* and possession by an evil spirit. An evil spirit brings chaos to the dancing and perhaps great harm to the one possessed. The traditional dances of Vodun are conducted on a serious plane with rhythm and suppleness—but not with the orgiastic sensuality depicted in motion pictures about Voodoo or in the gyrations performed for the tourist trade.

All Vodun ceremonies must climax with sacrifice to the *loa*. Chickens are most commonly offered, although the wealthy may offer a goat or a bull. The possessed usually drinks of the blood that is collected in a vessel, thereby satisfying the hunger of the *loa.* Other dancers may also partake of the blood, sometimes adding spices to it but most often drinking it "straight." After the ceremony, the sacrificed animal is usually cooked and eaten.

The most legendary of all Voodoo priestesses is Marie Laveau (c. 1794–1881), a Creole freewoman who was said to be gifted with remarkable powers of sorcery and the ability to fashion charms of unfailing efficacy. Although she was the recognized Voodoo priestess of New Orleans, she did not find her beliefs incompatible with Catholicism and Christian charity, and she attended Mass daily.

Marie greatly popularized Voodoo by revising some of the rituals until they became her unique mixture of West Indian and African tribal religions and Roman Catholicism. She was certain to invite politicians and police officials to the public ceremonies that she conducted on the banks of Bayou Saint John on the night of June 23, Saint John's Eve. On other occasions, she would hold Voodoo rituals on the shore of Lake Pontchartrain and at her cottage, Maison Blanche. Hundreds of the best families in New Orleans attended these public celebrations of Voodoo, hoping to get a glimpse of Marie Laveau herself dancing with her large snake, Zombi, draped over her shoulders. For the white onlookers, the music and the dance provided exciting entertainment. For Marie Laveau's fellow worshippers, the rites were spiritual celebrations, and even Zombi was an agent of great Voodoo powers.

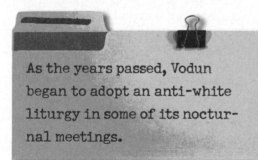

As the years passed, Vodun began to adopt an anti-white liturgy in some of its nocturnal meetings.

Legend has it that Marie Laveau discovered the secrets of immortality and lived to be nearly two hundred years old. Some say that she is still alive, conducting Voodoo rituals in the secret shadows of New Orleans. Such a legend quite likely began when Marie cleverly passed the position of high priestess to her daughter, who greatly resembled her, at a strategic time when the original Marie had just begun to age. Marie retired from public appearances to continue to conduct the intricate network of spies and informants she had built up, while her daughter assumed the public persona of Marie Laveau, Voodoo queen of New Orleans. Because she now appeared ageless and could

sometimes be seen in more than one place at a time, her power and mystery grew ever stronger among her Voodoo worshippers and the elite white community as well. As far as it can be determined, Marie Laveau died in New Orleans on June 15, 1881.

Vodun features a supernatural entity that is unique among the practitioners of sorcery—the zombies, those dread creatures of the undead who prowl about at night doing the bidding of magicians who follow the left-hand path. Vodun lore actually has two types of zombi: the undead and those who died by violence. For the Haitian peasant, zombies, the living dead, are to be feared as those who have succumbed to the influence of evil and sorcerers. The people of the villages believe that the sorcerer unearths a corpse and wafts under its nose a bottle containing its soul. Then, as if he were fanning a tiny spark of life in dry tinder, the sorcerer nurtures the spark of life in the corpse until he has fashioned a zombi. The deceased are often buried face downward by considerate relatives so that the corpse cannot hear the call of the sorcerer. Some villagers take the precaution of providing their departed with a weapon, such as a machete, with which to ward off the evil *houngan.*

In the popular mind the so-called Voodoo doll is the best-known aspect of Vodun. Actually such figures have no role in the religion of Voodoo, and the practice of sticking pins in dolls or poppets (puppets) is a custom of Western European witches, rather than the Haitian or Caribbean practitioners of Vodun. Perhaps the misunderstanding arose when outsiders who witnessed certain rituals saw the followers of Vodun sticking pins in the figures of saints or guardian spirits. Such acts are done not to bring harm to anyone, but to keep the good force of magic within the object.

There is also the matter of Voodoo curses. The anthropologist Walter Cannon spent several years collecting examples of "Voodoo death," instances in which men and women died as a result of being the recipient of a curse, an alleged supernatural visitation, or the breaking of some tribal or cultural taboo. The question Cannon sought to answer was, "How can an ominous and persistent state of fear end the life of a human?"

Fear, one of the most powerful and deep-rooted of the emotions, has its effects mediated through the nervous system and the endocrine apparatus, the "sympathetic-adrenal system." Cannon hypothesized that "if these powerful emotions prevail and the bodily forces are fully mobilized for action, and if this state of extreme perturbation continues for an uncontrolled possession of the organism for a considerable period dire results may ensue." Cannon has suggested that "Vodun death" may result from a state of shock due to a persistent and continuous outpouring of adrenalin and a depletion of the adrenal corticosteroid hormones. Such a constant agitation, caused by an abiding sense of fear, could induce a fatal reduction in blood pressure. Cannon assessed Voodoo death as a real phenomenon set in motion by "shocking emotional stress" due to "obvious or repressed terror." Dr. J. C. Barker, in his collection of case histories of individuals who had willed others, or themselves, to death (*Scared to Death,* 1969), saw Voodoo death as resulting "purely from extreme fear and exhaustion essentially a psychosomatic phenomenon."

VRIL SOCIETY

This German secret society believed that whoever possessed the Vril force could conquer the world and meet the master race from the earth's interior as equals.

In 1871, when the occultist Edward Bulwer-Lytton wrote a novel about a small group of German mystics who had discovered the truth about a race of supermen living within the earth's interior, he inspired the founding of the Brothers of the Light, the Luminous Lodge, the Vril Society. Bulwer-Lytton's *The Coming Race* told the story of an advanced civilization of giants who thrived in the inner earth. The superrace had built a paradise based on the Vril force, a form of energy so powerful that the older beings had outlawed its use as a potential weapon.

In 1919 Karl Haushofer, a student of the Russian mystic George Gurdjieff, founded the Brothers of the Light Society in Berlin and soon changed its name to the Vril Society. As Haushofer's Vril grew in prominence, it united three major occult societies, the Lords of the Black Stone, the Black Knights of the Thule Society, and the Black Sun and chose the swastika, the hooked cross, as its symbol of the worship of the Black Sun. While these societies borrowed some concepts and rites from Theosophists, Rosicrucians, and various Hermetic groups, they placed special emphasis on the innate mystical powers of the Aryan race. The Vril and its brother societies maintained that Germanic/Nordic/Teutonic people were of Aryan origin, and that Christianity had destroyed the power of the Teutonic civilization.

In 1921 Maria Orsic (or Orsitsch), a medium in the Vril Society, began claiming spirit messages originating from Aryan aliens whose home star was Aldebaran. Orsic and another medium, Sigrun, learned that the aliens spoke of two classes of people on their world—the Aryan master race and a subservient planetary race that had evolved through mutation and climate changes. A half billion years ago the Aryans, also known as the Elohim or Elder Race, began to colonize our solar system. On Earth, the Aryans were identified as the Sumerians until they elected to carve out an empire for themselves in the hollow of the planet. The Vril force was derived from the Black Sun, a large ball of "Prima Materia" that provided light and radiation to the inhabitants of the inner earth.

Karl Haushofer founded the Brothers of the Light Society, which became the Vril Society.

The Vril Lodge believed that whoever learned control of the Vril would become master of himself, those around him, and the world itself, if he should so choose. This ancient force had been known among the alchemists and magicians as the Chi, the Odic force, the Orgone, and the Astral Light, and the members of the Vril Society were well aware of its transformative powers to create supermen out of ordinary mortals. Such members of the lodge as Adolf Hitler, Heinrich Himmler, Hermann Göring, Dr. Theodor Morell (Hitler's personal physician), and other top Nazi leaders became obsessed with preparing German youth to become a master race so that the Lords of the inner earth would find them worthy above all others when they emerged to evaluate the people of Earth's nations.

In 1922, members of Thule and Vril built the *Jenseitsflugmaschine,* the Other World Flight Machine, based on the psychic messages received from the Aldebaran aliens. W. O. Schumann of the Technical University of Munich was in charge of the project until it was halted in 1924; the craft was then stored in the Messerschmitt aircraft company's Augsburg facility. In 1937, after Hitler came into power, he authorized the construction of the *Rundflugzeug,* the "round or disk-shaped vehicle," for military use and for spaceflight.

In April 1942 Nazi Germany sent out an expedition composed of a number of its most visionary scientists to seek a military vantage point in the Hollow Earth. Although the expedition of leading scientists left at a time when the Third Reich was putting maximum effort into the drive against the Allies, Göring, Himmler, and Hitler are said to have enthusiastically endorsed the project. Steeped in the more esoteric teachings of metaphysics, the führer had long been convinced that Earth was concave and that a master race lived on the inside of the planet.

The Nazi scientists who left for the Baltic island of Rugen had complete confidence in the validity of their quest. In their minds, such a coup as discovering the opening to the inner world would not only provide them with a military advantage, but go a long way in convincing the masters who lived there that the German people truly deserved to mix their blood with them in the creation of a hybrid master race to occupy the surface world.

Students of the Vril Society also insist that aliens worked with Nazi scientists to create early models of flying saucers. The UFO researcher Vladimir Terziski believes that an "alien tutor race" secretly began cooperating with certain German scientists from the Thule, the Vril, and the Black Sun in the late 1920s. Working in underground bases with the alien intelligences, Terziski says, the Nazis mastered antigravity space flight, established space stations, accomplished time travel, and developed their spacecraft to warp speeds.

W

WACO

Senator John McCain (R-Arizona) has described the tragedy at Waco as "an ill-conceived exercise of federal authority that led to the unnecessary loss of life." And to this day it is unclear who fired the first shot.

Maybe there's something in the very soil of the place that encourages conflict. More than a dozen years after David Koresh and about 104 men, women, and children of his Branch Davidian community began a standoff with agents of the Bureau of Alcohol, Tobacco, and Firearms (ATF), two museums commemorate the disaster—each in opposition to the other. While about two dozen Branch Davidians loyal to Koresh built their museum at one edge of the property, a dissident group who opposed Koresh's leadership erected a chapel to lament those who "chose to follow the man of sin, David Koresh."

The events that led to the destruction of the Branch Davidian compound outside of Waco, Texas, in April 1993 will be bitterly debated for many years to come, and the repercussions of federal agencies' attacking a religious group may continue to bring acts of violence and revenge against the U.S. government. In a strange way, the destruction of the Branch Davidian compound was the terrible realization of a self-fulfilling prophecy that had been made by its leader, David Koresh (born Vernon Howell), who prophesied that the Apocalypse would occur in the United States, not Israel.

The Branch Davidian religious group had its origins when Victor Houteff (1885–1955) separated from the Seventh-day Adventist Church in 1929 to form The Shepherd's Rod, Branch Seventh-day Adventist. Houteff envisioned himself as a divine messenger whose mission was to reveal the information contained in secret scroll mentioned in the book of Revelation. He was also to assemble a group of 144,000 Christians who would reestablish the kingdom of King David in Palestine so that Christ would be encouraged to manifest his Second Coming. In 1935, with eleven followers, Houteff founded the Mount Carmel Center near Waco, Texas. In 1942 he broke completely from the Seventh-day Adventists when they refused to encourage conscientious objection during World War II, and he changed the name of his group to the Davidian Seventh-day Adventist Association.

When Houteff died in 1955, there were about 125 members residing in the Mount Carmel Center, with a few others in Los Angeles and other parts of the country. The group began to splinter upon their leader's death, for many became disillusioned, having regarded him as the new Elijah who would help bring about the reign of Jesus on Earth after the Second Coming. Florence Houteff, Victor's widow, solidified the group with her vision that Judgment Day would occur on April 22, 1959. After her prophecy failed to come true, she dissolved the group in 1961 and in 1965 sold Mount Carmel to Benjamin Roden, who named his faction the Branch Davidian Seventh-day Adventist Association. Roden, who proclaimed himself the Fifth Angel in Revelation, led the group until his death in 1978; his wife, Lois Roden, declared herself the Sixth Angel and a prophet speaking through the feminine aspect of the Holy Spirit.

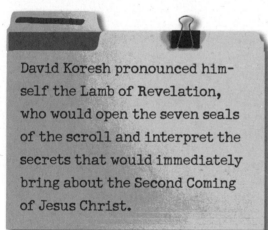

David Koresh pronounced himself the Lamb of Revelation, who would open the seven seals of the scroll and interpret the secrets that would immediately bring about the Second Coming of Jesus Christ.

Vernon Howell joined the Branch Davidians in 1981 and almost immediately attracted Lois Roden's attention as the next mighty prophet to come from the group. After a series of conflicts with George Roden, Benjamin and Lois's son, Howell, took control of the Davidians in 1988 and changed his name to David Koresh in 1990. "Koresh" was a form of the name Cyrus, and Howell was inspired to take the name by the text in Isaiah 45, in which the prophet predicts that a Persian king named Cyrus will permit the Jews to return to Jerusalem and rebuild the Temple. If Houteff had declared himself the Fourth Angel in Revelation, Benjamin Roden the Fifth, and Lois Roden the Sixth, David Koresh pronounced himself the Lamb of Revelation, who would open the seven seals of the scroll and interpret the secrets that would immediately bring about the Second Coming of Jesus Christ.

Obsessed with the book of Revelation and the fast-approaching Apocalypse, Koresh began in 1984 to establish a new lineage of the House of David from his seed. As did the great King David, Koresh took many wives so that they might bear his children. Since his mission as the Lamb was to interpret the scroll of Revelation, he envisioned himself as one of the pivotal characters in the drama of the Apocalypse and the perfect male to sire many children for the time of rebuilding after the battle of Armageddon. And because the final struggle between good and evil was now rescheduled to begin in the United States, rather than Israel, it behooved the community of believers to begin to stockpile, food, water, and weapons. In 1992 Koresh renamed the Mount Carmel commune "Ranch Apocalypse."

Koresh left four biological children who escaped the inferno at Ranch Apocalypse. One, a son born before Koresh even joined the Branch Davidians, lives in a Dallas suburb. Three boys born to mothers who left the cult before the siege at Waco are listed in probate records as the legal heirs to his estate. At the present time, the estate is probably worth nothing, but if the wrongful-death lawsuit filed by Waco survivors against the federal government should garner any damages, the boys would be among those entitled to collect. Two of the children, Jared Michael and Sky Borne, lived with their mother in Hawaii. The third, Wisdom Day, now known as Shaun, resides in California with his mother, who left Koresh in 1990.

Shortly after Koresh moved his flock to Ranch Apocalypse, rumors began to circulate that the Branch Davidians had become a cult that abused children, observed distasteful religious practices, and possessed large amounts of illegal firearms and explosives. On February 28, 1993, ATF agents raided Ranch Apocalypse.

Branch Davidian Sheila Martin left the compound that day because one of her sons was ill. It was her husband, Wayne, one of Koresh's top aides, who placed a frantic 911 telephone call when camouflage-clad ATF agents showed up to serve an arrest warrant on Koresh for weapons charges. Wayne shouted into the phone that there were seventy-five men surrounding the compound and they were shooting at the community. He begged them to call off the attack because there were women and children in the building.

Six Branch Davidians and four ATF agents were killed, and at least one Davidian and twenty-four agents wounded, in the initial gunfight. Later the FBI took over, and the siege that ensued lasted fifty-one days.

On April 14 Koresh had a vision that instructed him to write his translation of the seven seals in Revelation and then surrender. But the encircling forces had grown tired of his biblical babblings and apocalyptic pronouncements. On April 19 the FBI attacked with a finality that ended the standoff.

Koresh and eighty-six (this figure varies from seventy-five to eighty-seven) of his followers were killed in the subsequent fighting and the terrible fire that swept through the compound, totally destroying it. At least seventeen (some say twenty-one) of the dead were children. Ever since the destruction of the compound, accusations have circulated that the FBI was responsible for starting the fire with incendiary tear gas cartridges. One former soldier named Timothy McVeigh stated at his trial that he was so outraged by the attack on the Branch Davidians that he bombed the federal building in Oklahoma City two years to the day after the fires ravaged the compound.

The controversy over the last days of David Koresh and the Branch Davidians will continue for years to come. Even after the 1994 trial in San Antonio of eleven surviving Branch Davidians, which included seven weeks of testimony, 130 witnesses, and more than a thousand pieces of evidence, jurors said they still could not decide who had fired the first shot on February 28, 1993.

Prior to the siege at Ranch Apocalypse, there were about 130 members of the Branch Davidians. After the destruction of the compound, there were estimates of thirty to fifty members who had managed to leave the commune before the final days or who had escaped the conflagration. Current membership is impossible to determine.

President Bill Clinton, Attorney General Janet Reno, and other government officials described Koresh as a madman who brought his followers and their innocent children to awful deaths. Senator John McCain of Arizona, by contrast, described the tragedy at Waco as "an ill-conceived exercise of federal authority that led to the unnecessary loss of life."

WEATHER CONTROL AND MANIPULATION

Some scientists have issued warnings that in the future an advanced technology of electromagnetic weapons will be able to control the weather. Conspiracy researchers state that those dire predictions of weather manipulation have already been realized.

Zbigniew Brzezinski, who served as national security director under President Jimmy Carter, as founder of the Federal Emergency Management Agency (FEMA), and as the first director of David Rockefeller's Trilateral Commission, has described control of the weather as a key element of strategy in future wars. In his book *Between Two Ages: America's Role in the Technetronic Era* (1976), Brzezinski writes that the advanced technology of electromagnetic psychotronic weapons "will make available to leaders of major nations a variety of techniques for conducting secret warfare, of which only a bare minimum of the security forces need to be apprised."

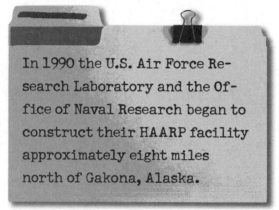

In 1990 the U.S. Air Force Research Laboratory and the Office of Naval Research began to construct their HAARP facility approximately eight miles north of Gakona, Alaska.

Bernard Eastlund, inventor of HAARP (High Frequency Active Auroral Research Program), made it no secret that his device had the capacity to modify weather. As an example, he said that it was possible to alter "upper atmosphere wind patterns by constructing one or more plumes of atmospheric particles which will act as a lens or focusing device." Such a moving plume, Eastlund explained, "could serve as a means for focusing a vast amount of sunlight on selected portions of the Earth." Even further, such plumes could be formed to serve the same functions as nuclear devices "without actually having to detonate such a device."

In 1990 the U.S. Air Force Research Laboratory and the Office of Naval Research began to construct their HAARP facility approximately eight miles north of Gakona, Alaska. The Alaskan site was chosen because Alaska is the only state in the auroral region. In addition, the ionosphere over the

HAARP facility "can be characterized as mid-latitude, auroral or polar, depending on how active the sun is" and, according to the official website (www.haarp.alaska.edu), "the High Frequency transmitter and the scientific observation instruments require a quiet electromagnetic location."

The personnel at HAARP insist that their program is "completely unclassified," that the facility "will not affect the weather," that it cannot create a hole in the ionosphere, that it "does not transmit signals in the ELF frequency," and that it "is not designed to be an operational system for military purposes"—although, they concede, there is obvious Department of Defense interest in understanding the ionosphere's effects on communication and navigation systems.

Conspiracy theorists are convinced that there is much more going on at the HAARP facility than the air force and navy admit. And they are not alone in their suspicions.

Dr. Rosalie Bertell confirmed that U.S. military scientists "are working on weather systems as a potential weapon." In her book *Planet Earth: The Latest Weapon of War,* Dr. Bertell warns that electromagnetic weapons have the power to transmit explosive and other effects, such as earthquake induction, across intercontinental distances to any selected target site on the globe with force levels equivalent to nuclear explosions. Former French military officer Marc Filterman stated his conviction that by the early 1980s both the U.S. and the Soviet Union had already mastered the science to unleash sudden climate changes, such as hurricanes and droughts.

Many researchers are certain that the military and/or the New World Order/Illuminati are utilizing Nikola Tesla's discoveries in HAARP technology and in other weather-control devices. Tesla's electronic and electromagnetic breakthroughs were never fully realized because they were judged too futuristic and sensitive by the scientific establishment of his time. Tesla believed that some of his inventions could manipulate the weather—even to the point of controlling earthquakes. He once boasted that with one of his power vibrators, he could shake down the Empire State Building. Tesla was confident that the frequency on his resonant vibrator could pass through the earth with almost no loss of energy and that such an invention could be used with deadly effect in warfare. If the vibrator were to be built large enough, Tesla warned, it could transmit mechanical vibrations through the earth that could literally split the planet in half.

Lt. Col. Thomas Bearden, a well-known nuclear engineer and Tesla researcher, has said that the Tesla Magnifying Transmitter (TMT) can literally send energy waves through anything. The TMT is capable of setting up a standing wave that feeds off the molten core of the planet, then, by changing the frequency, it reaches up to the atmosphere and can alter jet streams and weather flow patterns by ionizing the air. The TMT could cause massive weather changes over large areas of the earth.

Other researchers point out that one of Tesla's principal goals was to collect the sun's energy that was stored in the earth's atmosphere. In his experiments he had noted that the planet's atmosphere tends to collect a lot of charge from the electrons entering the North Pole region and the protons entering the South Pole region. Tesla believed that if scientists could harness this charge, they would have access to almost unlimited clean electric power, free from coal and gas emissions, and eliminating the hazards associated with nuclear energy power plants.

On the other side of the coin, if scientists working for the New World Order were to harness the sun's energy collected in the atmosphere, that enormous power could also be used to control weather to the detriment of people other than the elite. Entire regions of the earth could be destroyed with flooding, earthquakes, drought, endless freezing winters, and interminable scorching summers.

WEATHERMEN

The much-maligned Weathermen did blow up quite a few buildings and police cars, but to their credit, the only people who got killed by one of their explosive devices were some of their own bomb makers.

The Weathermen, also known as the Weather Underground Organization (WUO), took their name from the Bob Dylan song "Subterranean Homesick Blues," which includes the lyrics, "You don't need a weatherman to know which way the wind blows." In other words, any astute individual living in the late 1960s could see that societal revolution was imminent.

At first the Weathermen were composed largely of former members of Students for a Democratic Society (SDS), who had begun their "insurgency" as a means of creating a new America of "participatory democracy," which would grow out of the nation's campuses. The Weathermen were far more revolutionary, avowedly communist in ideology and openly advocating the overthrow of the American government and its capitalistic system. While the most violent the SDS became was in the trashing of some college administrators' offices, the Weathermen engaged in a war against the government that included bombings, jailbreaks, and inciting riots and lasted from 1969 to 1976.

A timeline of some of the major events in the WUO's war with the U.S. government:

October 6, 1969: The Weathermen achieve international attention with their "Days of Rage" in Chicago when they blow up a statue that had been dedicated to the police officers killed in the 1886 Haymarket Riot. During the next two days, three hundred rioters rampage through Chicago's business district, smashing windows and overturning cars. Police shoot six rioters and arrest seventy.

December 6, 1969: The WUO bombs several police cars in a precinct parking lot on North Halstead Street in Chicago to protest the December 4 killings of Black Panther Party leaders Fred Hampton and Matt Clark by police officers.

February 13, 1970: Police cars in Berkeley, California, are bombed.

March 6, 1970: Thirty-four sticks of dynamite are discovered in the 13th Police District of Detroit. That same day, WUO members Theodore Gold, Diana Oughton, and Terry Robbins accidentally blow up along with their bomb factory in Greenwich Village.

May 10, 1970: The National Guard building in Washington, D.C., is bombed in protest of the National Guard killings of four students at Kent State University in Ohio.

May 21, 1970: Bernadine Dohrn is credited as the author of the WUO's official "Declaration of a State of War" with the United States.

June 9, 1970: New York City police headquarters is bombed.

July 16, 1970: The Presidio Army Base in San Francisco is bombed to honor the eleventh anniversary of the Cuban Revolution.

August 1970: The Marin County, California, courthouse is bombed.

September 22, 1970: The WUO helps Dr. Timothy Leary, LSD guru, escape from the California Men's Colony prison.

October 8, 1970: Queens Courthouse is bombed in solidarity with the New York prison riots. The Harvard Center for International Affairs is bombed to protest the war in Vietnam.

February 28, 1971: The U.S. Capitol is bombed to protest the Laos invasion.

September 17, 1971: The New York Department of Corrections is bombed to protest the killing of twenty-nine inmates during the riot at Attica Penitentiary.

May 1972: The Pentagon is bombed to protest air force raids on Hanoi.

March 6, 1974: The Department of Health, Education and Welfare offices in San Francisco are bombed to protest the alleged sterilization of poor women.

May 13, 1974: The office of the California attorney general is bombed in honor of the six members of the Symbionese Liberation Army killed by police.

June 17, 1974: The headquarters of Gulf Oil is bombed in Pittsburgh to protest its activities in Angola and Vietnam.

July 1974: The WUO publishes its book *Prairie Fire,* calling for a unified Communist Party and continuing to stress the need for acts of violence.

January 28, 1975: The State Department is bombed in retaliation for the escalation of the war in Vietnam.

In spite of a program of bombings conducted over a period of six years against the U.S. Capitol, the Pentagon, and numerous police and prison buildings, the WUO took elaborate measures to warn all personnel to evacuate the targets before the bombs exploded. Their war against the U.S. was waged successfully without the loss of life on the part of the government. The only the deaths that occurred were of the three WUO members in the accidental explosion of the Greenwich Village bomb factory. The WUO members were also largely successful in evading capture by the police and FBI. Some individuals who became associated with the WUO during or after the group disbanded were Diane Donghi, Kathy Boudin, Mark Rudd, Bernadine Dohrn, and Bill Ayers.

By the late 1970s most of the members had turned themselves in to the authorities or had joined other revolutionary groups. Few of the WUO served prison time because the evidence gathered against them by the FBI's COINTEL-PRO was ruled in court to have been illegally acquired.

PAUL WELLSTONE, MURDER OF

Some conspiracy theorists claim that the plane crash that killed lone-wolf progressive senator Paul Wellstone, his wife, daughter, and five crew and staff was caused by a secret high-tech electromagnetic weapon.

On October 25, 2002, Minnesota Democratic senator Paul Wellstone, his wife, Sheila, daughter Marcia, two pilots, and three staff members died in a small plane crash near Eveleth, Minnesota. The plane, a twin-engine Beechcraft King Air A100, was reported to be in good condition before take-off at 9:37 A.M. from Minneapolis–St. Paul. Pilot Richard Conry, fifty-five, and copilot Michael Guess, thirty, both certified and experienced, had received permission to climb to 13,000 feet at 9:48 A.M. and received clearance to descend toward Eveleth at 10:01 A.M. The pilots were informed that there was icing at 9,000 to 11,000 feet and at 10:10 passed through the icing without any discernible difficulty. At 10:18 the Beechcraft was cleared for an approach to the Eveleth runway. Suddenly the airplane began to drift from the approach path, and it was last sighted at 10:21 A.M. flying at 1,800 feet.

Carol Carmody, acting chairwoman of the National Transportation Safety Board, said on October 29 that the impact area of the crash was 300 feet by 190 feet and that there was evidence of "extreme post-crash fire." The plane appeared to be headed south, away from the runway. Carmody said that the angle was "steeper than would be expected in a normal stabilized standardized approach" to the runway. Some eyewitnesses said that the plane went down in a near-vertical plunge.

U.S. Senator Paul Wellstone was killed, along with his wife and daughter, in a plane crash in 2002, but was it really an accident?

Paul Wellstone's death came just over two years after a similar plane crash took the life of another Democratic Senate candidate, Missouri governor Mel Carnahan, on October 16, 2000. In 2001 two Senate Democrats, Majority Leader Tom Daschle and Judiciary Committee chairman Patrick Leahy, received letters containing anthrax. The federal Justice Department, headed by John Ashcroft (who lost to Mel Carnahan in the 2000 Senate race in Missouri even though Carnahan was deceased at the time of the vote), was unable to trace or to apprehend the anthrax mailer.

Wellstone was the only classically progressive voice in the Senate. *Mother Jones* magazine described him as the "first 1960s radical elected to the U.S. senate." To his many admirers, he was the lone wolf opposing the status quo of both the Democrats and Republicans. He was the most articulate and most vocal Senate opponent of the George W. Bush administration. He voted to oppose the Senate resolution authorizing Bush to go to war in Iraq.

Conspiracy theorists stand firm that whatever caused the crash and death of Paul Wellstone, his wife, daughter, and five others, it was not the airplane. The plane was of exceptional quality, the pilots extremely well qualified, and the chill October weather posed no serious problems. Some conspiracists have considered a small bomb, noting how quickly the plane burst into flames.

There is another peculiar aspect about the crash to consider. According to Rick Wahlberg, sheriff of St. Louis County, where the crash occurred, a team of FBI agents from Minneapolis was on the scene around noon, roughly an hour and a half after the accident and less than an hour after local officers and rescue workers had located the crash site and found a way to access it. Later, when discussing the speed with which the FBI agents had arrived on the scene, none of the local authorities said that they had called the Bureau. They figured that the agents had to have left Minneapolis at the same time Wellstone's plane did.

Evaluating the many peculiarities of the fatal crash, some conspiracists conclude that one of the high-tech weapons that direct electromagnetic pulse, radio frequency, or high-energy radio frequency was utilized to bring down Wellstone's plane. Adding to this frightening conclusion are reports of a strange cell phone phenomenon that was observed in the Eveleth area. At 10:18 A.M., the same time that a brief, but abrupt, interruption of communication between Wellstone's plane at the airport tower occurred, cell phones were also interrupted.

WEREWOLVES FOR DER FÜHRER

Der Führer wanted the Hitler Youth to be like werewolves—cruel, pitiless, and willing to erode thousands of years of human compassion and conscience.

An old folk legend in Germany and the Nordic European countries relates that the common folk kept themselves well hidden behind closed doors on those dark and stormy nights when Wodan and his wolves were abroad on their Wild Hunt. In the opinion of some anthropologists, the legend began when primitive hunting tribes, armed only with sharpened staves, ran through the forests in lupine packs seeking fresh meat. When they found their prey, whether animal or human, they would kill and dismember their victims as much with their teeth and claws as with their weapons. Other, more passive, tribes knew that they had better stay hidden in the darkness when the lycanthropic packs were on the hunt.

The German resistance movement raised against Napoleon in 1813 was known as the Wild Hunt, in an obvious historical allusion to the legend of Wodan hunting at night with his wolves. In 1923 a secret terrorist group known as Organization Werewolf was organized in Germany by Fritz Kappe. Their banner was a black flag with a skull and crossbones in stark white contrast. At first the movement expanded rather quickly across Germany, but as a result of a number of arrests by the Weimar government, the Werewolves never posed any real threat to the establishment.

Adolf Hitler was deeply enamored of wolves and werewolves. The very title *führer* means "leader" and when compounded with *Wolfen* denotes the leader of a pack of hunting wolves. And Hitler's given name, Adolf, means "noble wolf."

Psychobiographer Robert G. L. Waite states that Hitler was always fascinated with wolves. At the beginning of his political career, he chose "Herr Wolf" as his pseudonym. He named his headquarters in France "Wolfsschlucht" (Wolf's Gulch) and, in the Ukraine,

"Werwolf." He demanded that his sister change her name to "Frau Wolf." He renamed the Volkswagen factory "Wolfsburg" and decreed himself "Conductor Wolf." His favorite tune for whistling in his carefree moods was "Who's Afraid of the Big Bad Wolf?"

It was as werewolves that Hitler envisioned German youth when he dictated, in his program for the education of the Hitler Youth, that they must learn to become indifferent to pain. They must have no weakness or tenderness in them. When he looked into their eyes, Hitler said, he wanted to see "once more in the eyes of a pitiless youth the gleam of pride and independence of the beast of prey." It was his wish that he might somehow "eradicate thousands of years of human domestication" and allow the werewolves once again to run free and to work their destruction upon the weak and those unsuited to be members of the New World Order that he was creating. The black uniform of dreaded SS, with the skull and crossbones on their caps, were inspired by the nightly terror visited on the people by the Wild Hunt and by the skeletons of the dead left in Wodan's wake.

Quite likely, the more ruthless German youth responded to their führer's summons that they should be like werewolves, cruel and pitiless, prepared to erode thousands of years of human domestication.

Hitler gloried in expressing the brutal, wolflike political retaliations that he would visit upon those who opposed him. There are numerous stories about the rages that would possess him—to the point where he would fall to the floor and literally chew the carpet. "If the stories about Hitler's rages are true," states Robert Eisler, an Austrian scholar and author of *Man into Wolf,* "they would appear to have been manic lycanthropic states and not melancholic bouts of repentance. If the accounts were invented, they have sprung from the archetypal depths of the storytellers' unconscious race-memory and not from the ar-

chetypal minds of the doubtless paranoid subjects of the stories in question."

Toward the end of World War II when the collapse of Nazi Germany appeared imminent, Josef Goebbels revived the Werewolves after Heinrich Himmler's speech in 1945 called for a new Volkssturm ("People's Storm") to operate underground in defense of the homeland. The organization took as their insignia a black armband with a skull and crossbones and a silver SS. Their main function was to assassinate and terrorize anti-Nazi Germans and to harass advancing Allied troops. In Leipzig female Werewolves poured scalding water from the windows of houses onto the heads of Allied soldiers passing below. In Baden they killed a number of French soldiers by ambushing them as they were resting.

Even after hostilities had ended and the war was officially over, the Werewolves continued their terrorist activities. At the Nuremberg trials, several Nazi leaders testified that the Werewolves were now under the control of the notorious Martin Bormann, who had somehow managed to escape capture by the Allies.

The Werewolves resurfaced in 1994 when Steven Spielberg's masterpiece about the Holocaust, *Schindler's List* (1993), was scheduled to open in Russian theaters. Members of the group who were arrested by Russian security forces confessed their plans to firebomb Moscow cinemas showing the film. The Werewolves, estimated at about a hundred members strong, acknowledged that they took their name from the Nazi secret-police operation that went underground once the Allies defeated Hitler's troops in World War II.

WEST NILE VIRUS

When summertime comes and the living is supposed to be easy, it also brings mosquitoes with West Nile virus to transform those lazy,

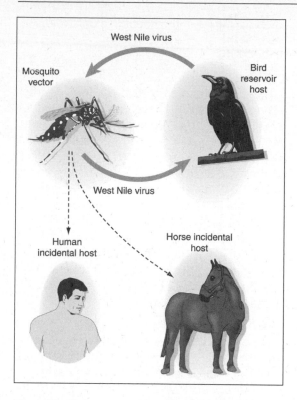

West Nile virus

Mosquito
vector

Bird
reservoir
host

West Nile virus

Human
incidental host

Horse incidental
host

**West Nile Virus is carried by mosquitoes and usual-
ly infects birds; birds harbor the virus and can
spread it to animals, or the virus can also end up in
humans and other animals, who do not transmit it
to others but can become ill.**

*hazy days into a season of worry about a terri-
ble disease that has afflicted humankind.*

The West Nile virus (WNV) was first identified by virologists in 1937 in the West Nile
district of Uganda. If the virus originated in
Africa, how did it get to the United States?

Some conspiracy theorists believe that
Fidel Castro obtained West Nile virus from
Communist bacteriological warfare sources,
and the Cubans have been releasing hundreds of thousands of birds infected with the
disease to fly into our country.

Virologists note that West Nile was reported in Egypt in the 1950s. Then, in a rather severe outbreak in Israel in 1957, the virus was

identified as the responsible agent in severe
meningoencephalitis in elderly patients. The
virus was next reported in horses in France in
the 1960s. West Nile arrived in the United
States in 1999 with cases of encephalitis diagnosed in horses and humans, followed by
an outbreak in the New York City area. In the
United States the virus is largely maintained
in birds, especially crows and blackbirds. In
80 percent of people the infection causes no
symptoms. In many others it causes only mild
flulike symptoms. People over fifty are most liable to be at risk for the extreme reactions of
encephalitis and meningitis.

In the New York area, authorities decided to
spray the insecticide Malathion over certain
residential areas in an effort to reduce the
mosquito population. Environmentalists disap-
proved of the large-scale spraying, arguing that
the possible deleterious effects of the chemical on people's health far outweighed the few
lives that might be saved because of it.

Conspiracists saw the hands of the CIA and
the shadow government behind the virus's
evolution and heard the echoes of the New
World Order's plan to decrease the population
of the planet. Some investigators are very
suspicious about the fact that the alleged outbreak of West Nile on the East Coast gave the
agents of deception an excuse to spray millions of mostly Jewish, black, and Hispanic
residential areas.

In 1953 the army sprayed clouds of toxic
zinc cadmium sulfide gas over Minneapolis on
more than a dozen occasions. The reason, the
citizenry was told, was to develop an aerosol
screen that would protect Americans from fallout in case of a nuclear attack. Hundreds of
miscarriages and stillbirths were attributed to
the spray. Later it was revealed that the army
was actually testing how chemicals would disperse during biological warfare. The same
toxic gas was sprayed over Winnipeg, St.
Louis, Fort Wayne, Indiana, and Leesburg, Virginia. Also in 1953, joint army-navy-CIA experi-

ments exposed tens of thousands of people in New York and San Francisco to airborne *Serratia marcescens* and *Bacillus glogigii* bacteria.

In 1955 the CIA, wishing to test its ability to infect human populations with biological agents, released a bacterium withdrawn from the army's biological warfare arsenal over Tampa Bay, Florida.

Prior to 1999 and the arrival of West Nile virus in the United States, people worried about the nasty little flying bloodsuckers carrying yellow fever. In 1956 the U.S. military released mosquitoes infected with yellow fever over Savannah, Georgia, and Avon Park, Florida. After each test, army agents posing as public health officials would test infected victims for the range of effects.

As incredible as it may seem, in 1966, army scientists dropped light bulbs filled with the bacteria *Bacillus subtilis* variant *niger* onto the ventilation grates of the New York City subway system and exposed more than a million citizens.

The November 1970 issue of *Military Review* disclosed that the army had intensified its development of "ethnic weapons," especially designed to target and to eliminate specific ethnic groups who would be susceptible due to genetic differences and variations in DNA.

In 1990 more than 1,500 six-month-old black and Hispanic babies in Los Angeles were given free measles vaccine. The Centers for Disease Control later admitted that the vaccine had never been licensed for use in the United States and that parents were never informed that the vaccine being injected to their children was experimental.

Ken Alibek, a Russian biological weapons expert who defected to the United States in the 1990s, informed U.S. authorities that he thought the West Nile outbreak seemed suspiciously like bio warfare. Other experts in the field of bioterrorism said that terrorists could easily deceive a target people with an outbreak of disease that appeared due to natural causes. Conspiracy theorists agree that if terrorists made a biological plague look like a natural outbreak, the response of the authorities would be delayed and the decision-making process would be slowed.

Many conspiracists are certain that the spraying in the New York City area was a CIA-sponsored event, arranged for propaganda purposes to prepare the public to accept willingly other chemical spraying in the future. While the West Nile virus has truly caused some deaths and illnesses, conspiracy theorists warn against any chemical or biological campaigns being conducted in the name of public health and national security. If any spray is applied, citizens should do it themselves to their own bodies with a recognized brand of insect repellent.

WICCA

If you don't believe in witches, you are woefully out of date. Experts on religious trends predict that Wicca will be the third-largest religion in the United States by 2012.

According to the U.S. Census, the number of individuals professing to be Wiccans rose from 8,000 in 1990 to 768,400 in 2002. Authorities on contemporary American religious trends predict that Wicca soon will be the third-largest religion in the United States.

Since the Middle Ages, witchcraft, the "Old Religion," and Wicca, the "ancient craft of the wise," have been used interchangeably to designate the same pagan nature religion. This interchangeable usage has recently declined, however, as contemporary Wiccans debate whether Wicca as it is practiced today can truly be traced back to ancient times or instead developed as new natural religion in the early nineteenth century and gained momentum in the mid-twentieth century.

Wicca embodies within its worship the male principle in the figure of the Horned God and the female in that of the goddess. In *Witchcraft Here and Now,* Sybil Leek, among the world's best-known witches before her death in 1982, defined witchcraft as a religion of a primitive and transcendent nature "with overtones embodying the female in her most elevated octave" together with the "adoration of creative forces." In her view, such a religion provided "the total aspect of godliness, in a god which has no name or a thousand different ones, one which has no sex but is both sexes and neutral as well."

Wiccans believe in good and evil as expressions of the same indestructible energy, which, like matter, is neither created nor destroyed but can be changed in form. Contrary to popular misconception, Wiccans are not Satanists. They do not worship the devil. Generally speaking, Wiccans believe that the sources of good and evil lie within each individual, thus universally agreeing with the eight words of the Wiccan Rede: "If it harm none, do what you will."

Wicca accepts the doctrines of reincarnation and karma but rejects the idea of original sin. Through a series of incarnations, the spirit seeks to perfect itself by learning to live in ever-increasing accord with nature's laws.

Evil consists of the conscious rejection of the good and the conscious effort to embrace the dark side. Humans are free to choose good or evil but can lose this freedom through the constant and prolonged choice of one path or the other. Witches seek the good by willing the good, while those who practice Black Magick or who follow the "left-hand path" have yielded control of their thoughts and actions to the flesh, that part of human nature motivated solely by the search for satisfaction of instinctual and egotistical demands. The striving for evil inherent in the instinctually ordered flesh must be controlled and directed by the will in such a manner that its needs are satisfied, but not at the price of others' well-being and existence.

For many years, Margaret Murray's *Witch-Cult in Western Europe* (1921) was the definitive work on witchcraft and undoubtedly inspired the revival of the craft in the modern era. Murray's thesis was that witchcraft hearkened back to an ancient, pre-Christian goddess worship and continued forward in unbroken lineage to contemporary times. The witch craze that seized Europe from the fourteenth to the seventeenth centuries and led to the persecution and deaths of thousands of women who practiced witchcraft was an expression of the contempt of the patriarchal establishment for an ancient, woman-centered religion. In her opinion, based on her extensive research, the practice of witchcraft had nothing to do with the worship of Satan, an entity of evil that had been created by Christianity.

Gerald Gardner is regarded as the founding father of all modern expressions of Wicca. Born in Lancastershire, England, on June 13, 1884, Gardner spent a great deal of his adult life as a British civil servant and as a plantation manager in Southeast Asia. In the autumn of 1939, after he had returned to England, he discovered witchcraft and was initiated by Dorothy Clutterbuck, a hereditary witch and high priestess of a New Forest coven, into a secret group of Wiccans (throughout his writings, Gardner always referred to the magical religion as Wica, rather than Wicca, as the word is usually spelled today).

In *The Meaning of Witchcraft* (1959) Gardner wrote that he was nearly through the initiation to become a witch when it struck him that he had become a part of the great circle of the Old Religion that had existed since time immemorial. To be a Gardnerian witch thenceforth meant being a witch who had undergone an initiation that could hearken back to Gerald Gardner and through him to an unbroken lineage that had been hidden and kept secret by sacred oaths and the solemn practice of holy rituals.

When the last witchcraft laws were repealed in Great Britain in 1951, Gardner wrote *Witchcraft Today* (1954) and thereby incurred the wrath of many traditional members of Wicca. Gardner protested that he had not revealed any secrets protected by the oath that he had taken during his initiation, and he announced his intention to publish more books about Wicca and to become the spokesperson for contemporary witchcraft and the pagan community. From that time on until his death in 1964, Gardner developed his own tradition, which might be described as a combination of ritual and ceremonial magick, French Mediterranean witchcraft, and the ideas of such fellow witches as Doreen Valiente.

Valiente, one of the most influential individuals in the shaping of modern Wicca, was born Doreen Edith Dominy on January 4, 1922. When she was only seven, Doreen had her first mystical experience. While staring intently at the moon, she perceived that what ordinary people embraced as the world of reality was but the facade behind which something much more real and potent lay waiting for those who would seek "the world of force beyond the world of form."

In 1944, after the death of her first husband at sea during the war, Doreen married Casimiro Valiente and acquired the name by which she would be known for the rest of her life. On Midsummer's Eve, 1953, she received the first degree of initiation into Wicca by Gerald Gardner, who at that time was operating a witchcraft museum on the Isle of Man. Although Gardner claimed that his "Book of Shadows," a collection of spells, sacred writings, thoughts, and goals, had been compiled from remnants of the Old Religion, Doreen, whose witchcraft name was "Ameth," recognized rites and rituals copied from ancient lore, a few bits and pieces from Freemasonry, and passages from works such as Aleister Crowley's *Gnostic Mass.* Rather than being humiliated or angered by his student's accusations, Gardner invited her to improve upon his fragments of the old and the new. Doreen accepted the challenge and replaced nearly all of the Crowley and Masonic excerpts with the thoughts and inspirations that she had received from her own mystical experiences since childhood. The reconstruction of the "Book of Shadows" achieved by Doreen Valiente gave the practitioners of Wicca a practical and workable system.

When Raymond Buckland emigrated from England to the United States in February 1962, he introduced contemporary witchcraft into the United States. Born in London on August 31, 1934, Buckland was Romani (Gypsy) on his father's side of the family, his grandfather having been the first to settle into a permanent home and stop traveling the roads. His mother was non-Gypsy—*gaujo*—making Raymond a half-blood, or *poshrat.*

Buckland's reading had drawn him to witchcraft, and he was greatly influenced by Margaret Murray's books and by Gerald Gardner's *Meaning of Witchcraft.* He entered into a mail and telephone correspondence with Gardner and eventually was introduced to Gardner's high priestess, Lady Olwen (Monique Wilson), who initiated Buckland into Wicca in Perth, Scotland, in December 1963. Buckland met Gardner just before the initiation, and he became Gardner's spokesman in the United States.

Buckland's craft name was Robat, and together with his wife, who became the Lady Rowen, he established the first contemporary witchcraft coven in the United States. With Gardner's books going out of print, Buckland wrote his first book on the craft, *Witchcraft from the Inside,* published in 1971. Buckland then dedicated his life to correcting misconceptions about Witchcraft, speaking and writing articles on the subject.

Inspired by Gardner's museum, Buckland gathered artifacts over the years and in 1966 opened America's first museum of witchcraft and magic, initially in the basement of his home, then in an old Victorian building in Bay

Shore, Long Island. By 1973 he had founded a new branch of the craft, taking nothing from Gardnerian sources (because of his oath to that tradition) but writing all new material. He based it on a Saxon background and called it Seax-Wicca, or Saxon witchcraft. Today the Seax-Wicca tradition is found worldwide.

In 1983 Buckland married Tara Cochran, and in 1992 the couple moved to a small farm in Ohio to work as Solitaries. For his solitary practice, Buckland drew mainly on Seax-Wicca rites, together with aspects of Pecti Wita (a Scottish tradition inspired by Aidan Breac and developed by Buckland). A prolific author, by 2005 Buckland had nearly forty books published, with more than a million copies in print and translated into twelve foreign languages.

In 1968 Gavin Frost (1930–) and Yvonne Frost (1931–) formed the first Wiccan church, the Church of Wicca, and lobbied for their cause until, in 1972, they gained federal recognition of witchcraft as a religion. In 1985 their arguments convinced a federal appeals court that Wicca was a religion equal to any other recognized as such in the United States. The Frosts' School of Wicca, also established in 1968, became the first craft correspondence school and continues to publish *Survival,* the oldest Wiccan newsletter in circulation. The School of Wicca has brought more than 200,000 people to the craft and has handled as many as a million requests for information in a single year. Authors of the controversial *Witches' Bible,* the Frosts have coauthored more than twenty other books and have appeared on hundreds of national television and radio shows to promote Wicca. Since 1972 Gavin and Yvonne have lived under a vow of poverty, turning over all their material possessions to the Church of Wicca.

Philip Emmons Isaac Bonewits (1949–), priest, magician, scholar, and author, is known for his leadership in modern Druidism and for his serious scholarship in the fields of the occult, metaphysics, and witchcraft. Bonewits

was ordained as a Druid priest in October 1969, and in 1970 he graduated with a bachelor of arts degree in magic and thaumaturgy from the University of California at Berkeley, the first person to do so at a Western educational institution. The media attention around Bonewits's degree resulted in his obtaining a book contract, and in 1971 *Real Magic* was published. In 1973 Bonewits moved to St. Paul, Minnesota, where he assumed the editorship of the neopagan journal *Gnostica.* During this same period, Bonewits combined interests with a number of Jewish pagans and created the Hasidic Druids of North America.

In 1973 Bonewits argued that the alleged antiquity of Wicca could not be supported by historical data and that the craft as it was practiced in the twentieth century did not go back beyond Gerald Gardner and Doreen Valiente—no earlier than the 1920s. Although such views were extremely controversial at the time, many scholars within the field have since acknowledged that neopagan Wicca may well be a new religion, rather than the continuation of an old one.

Festivals of Wicca

As in the Old Religion, the eight main festival observances, or Sabbats, are days of ascendancy and mark the passage of the year as it moves through its seasons:

Samhain begins the year and occurs near October 31, Halloween on the Christian calendar. Contrary to numerous misconceptions, Halloween is not a witches' holiday, but an old Christian celebration of the dead. Samhain honors the harvest, the time when the crops "die" to become food for the winter and when the veil between worlds becomes very thin.

Yule marks the winter solstice and is celebrated near December 21, the longest, darkest night of the year.

Candlemas, observed on February 2, is the festival of the goddess Brigid.

Spring equinox occurs around March 21 and is a powerful time to practice magic.

Beltane, May 1, celebrates love and oneness.

Summer solstice, occurring around June 21, is a time of power and a time to pay homage to the deities of nature.

Lammas, August 1, recognizes the signs that harvest is near.

Fall equinox, near or on September 21, celebrates a balance between light and dark, night and day. It is also a time to prepare to embrace the many mysteries of the goddess as she oversees the winter months of cold and darkness.

Some Wiccan traditions also celebrate, in much smaller gatherings, Esbats, which correspond to the phases of the moon. There may also be special-purpose gatherings limited to the members of a coven who meet to deal with a problem or issue specific to the group or an individual member. When most Wiccans hold an Esbat, they generally meet in a group of thirteen—the membership of a coven. Although some Wiccan traditions permit larger numbers to participate in the Esbats, most maintain the old practice that if a coven exceeds thirteen, it should split off into another group. During the eight Sabbats, however, many covens may meet together to celebrate the festivities.

The Esbats are considered sacred events, and for most traditions they occur in an outdoor setting, in a place where the coven members can touch the earth. One of the coven, usually the high priest or high priestess, draws a large circle on the ground while walking clockwise. The instrument used to etch the circle is generally a wand or the ceremonial athame (dagger), and once the circle has been made, the four cardinal directions (and often Above and Below) are invoked by the high priest or high priestess. Some covens perform this rite of invocation in front of a small portable altar. The celebrants also invoke the

Two Wiccans celebrate Beltane in Clun, Shropshire, England.

names of the goddess and the god and various nature entities. Some Wiccans conduct this ritual "skyclad" (naked), while other prefer to dress in gowns or other special costumes. The area encompassed by the circle of celebrants is considered a holy space representing an altered state of conscious that exists between the material world of time and space and the immaterial world of limitless being.

The circle of combined psyches also serves as a receptacle of magical energy that will build its strength until it is released in what is known as the "Cone of Power." When the Cone of Power attains the energy necessary for the purposes desired by the coven, it is released and sent out to perform the various tasks assigned to it by the wishes of the celebrants. Once the power has been released, some traditions pass a chalice of wine and small cakes around the circle while the practitioners pronounce "Blessed Be" to one another. Once the ritual has been completed, the circle is formally opened by members walking around the perimeter in a clockwise direction.

If a coven meets for an Esbat at the time of a full moon, it will quite likely engage in the ritual known as "Drawing Down the Moon," in which the spirit of the goddess and god are "drawn" down into the physical bodies of the high priestess and high priest. During the time that the deities have entered the high priestess and high priest, they are considered by the coven members to be the goddess and god incarnate. While this spiritual possession is taking place, the high priestess and high priest relay teachings and knowledge to the coven and may even answer personal questions relevant to the needs of individual members.

WITCHCRAFT

Evolving from a worship of nature, the ancient craft of the wise was transformed by Satan into an army of demonically inspired witches devoted to the capture of human souls and the destruction of the church.

For centuries, witchcraft, the "Old Religion," the "ancient craft of the wise," a nature-based religion, has been interwoven in the popular mind with Satanism, the worship of the devil. Witchcraft, magic, and sorcery arose when early humans began to believe that there was supernatural power in a charm, a spell, or a ritual to work good or evil. Most scholars agree that this primitive animism—imitating of the animal of the hunt through preparatory dance, snatching a bit of an enemy's hair to be used in a charm against him, invoking spirits to do one's will—began in Paleolithic times, at least fifty thousand years ago.

According to Raymond Buckland's *Witchcraft from the Inside,* "A model of the animal to be hunted was made and under the priest's direction, was attacked by the men of the tribe. Successful in 'killing' the clay animal, the men could thus go about after the real thing confident that the hunt would go exactly as acted.

One man would represent the God and supervise the magick. As a God of Hunting, he was represented as being the animal being hunted. His representative, or priest, would therefore dress in an animal skin and wear a headdress of horns." This Horned God of the Hunt is pictured on the wall of the Caverne des Trois in southern France, painted by an inspired artist circa 18,000 B.C.E. At Le Tuc d'Audoubert, near the Caverne des Trois, archaeologists found the clay figure of a bison. The figure shows a number of marks where spears were thrust into it during a ritual of sympathetic magic performed to ensure a successful hunt.

It is interesting to note the association of horns with divinity and consider the horned headdresses worn by the shamans of various tribal societies with the concept of a god of the hunt. The headpieces of many ancient rulers, including the pharaohs of Egypt, include horns of either realistic or stylized design. The sacrifices of the Israelites were offered on horned altars. The two bronze altars in Solomon's temple were equipped with horns, as was the altar at the shrine of the Ark of the Covenant in Jerusalem before Solomon. Michelangelo's famous statue of Moses depicts him with horns, thereby causing his head and face to bear a remarkable resemblance to Cerrnunos, as the Celts named the Horned God.

Because of the importance of human and animal fertility, the Horned God was soon joined by a goddess, whose purpose it was to ensure the success of all reproductive activities. With the advent of agriculture, the goddess was called upon to extend her powers to ensure fertility of the crops. From this point on, the figure of the goddess began to overshadow that of the Horned God.

By the historic period, the great civilizations of Egypt, Babylonia, and Persia had fully developed magical systems with entire hierarchies of sorcerers, priests, seers, and magi.

Greece and Rome supported both a state religion of gods and goddesses and a loosely structured priestcraft. In addition, the mystery schools in Greece and Rome were popular among aristocrats and commoners alike and kept alive the mystical impulse in both cultures. While magic had attainted the status of a religion in the urban areas, the pagans, the people of the countryside, relied upon their witches and their herbalists. A number of historians agree that certain of the mystery school traditions and the gatherings of witches for their Great Sabbats in the forests of Europe were very similar in structure.

When Constantine the Great (c. 288–337) legally sanctioned Christianity throughout the Roman Empire, the influence of the Christian clergy grew rapidly. The Ecumenical Council of Laodicea in 364 issued a canon that forbade Christian priests to practice magic, astrology, or mathematics. By 525, with the influence of Christianity growing ever stronger, the Council of Oxia prohibited the parishioners from consulting sorcerers, diviners, or any kind of seer. The Council of Tours in 613 ordered all priests to teach their congregations that magical practices were ineffective methods for improving the health of humans and animals and were not to be employed as means of bettering one's lot in life. A canon passed by the Council of Constantinople in 625 prescribed excommunication for a period of six years for anyone found practicing divination or consulting with a diviner. With each subsequent church council issuing stronger canons and edicts against magic and sorcery, those who dared to continue practicing the occult arts were forced to go underground.

Although the church had issued many canons forbidding the practice of magic, it had taken little action against the common folk practicing witchcraft. Organized persecution of witches was unknown until Abbot Regino of Prum's *Canon Episcopi* in 906 C.E. condemned as heretical any belief in witchcraft or the power of sorcerers. A burning at the stake for heresy may have taken place in about the year 1000 in Ravenna, but the first clearly recorded burning for witchcraft occurred at Orléans in 1022, followed by others at Monforte in 1028. Executions for heresy were sporadic and few until 1197, when Pedro of Aragon ordered the burning of those who had relapsed in their promises to repent of their sins of doubt. In 1198 Pope Innocent III declared such individuals as traitors against Christ and condemned them to death by burning.

Fully organized church punishment of those who practiced witchcraft remained virtually nonexistent until exaggerated claims of the powers of the Cathar sect reached the ears of the papacy. It was said that the Cathars were practicing foul sorceries, blasphemous heresies, and black magic. What was worse, they appeared to prospering in their cities in southern France.

In 1208 Innocent III ordered the only crusade ever launched against fellow Christians by attacking the Cathars. The besieged sect somehow managed to hold out against the armies massed against them until Montségur, their final stronghold, fell in 1246. Hundreds of the survivors were burned at the stake as witches, for in 1233 the church had established the Holy Inquisition to stamp out heresy, sorcery, and witchcraft. And before he died in 1216, Innocent III had enacted a papal bull that allowed a judge to try a suspected witch or heretic even when there was no accuser and granted the inquisitor power to be both judge and prosecutor.

The population of medieval Europe had descended from the central Asian plateau, and they had brought their own gods, goddess, and religions with them. Centuries before, they had strained against the barriers that the Roman legions set against them until they finally broke through and flooded the continent. At the dissolution of the Roman Empire, the civilizing force in Europe became the Roman Catholic Church, and even though the ecclesi-

An engraving of Emperor Constantine having a vision of the cross. He converted to Christianity, the first Roman emperor to do so.

astical institution made great inroads into the pagan culture, it could not completely remove the old rituals and nature worship.

Surviving the Roman Empire socially in the Middle Ages was the oppressive feudal system. Once-proud warriors were reduced to the role of serf farmers. For the serfs, the pagans (which originally meant simply "country folk"), observance of the old nature worship was an expression of their wish to throw off the yoke of feudalism. The Christian God and the Christian ethic had been foisted upon them by the rulers of the land that their forefathers had conquered. It was in their enjoyment of the excitement and vigor of the Old Religion that the peasants could allow themselves the luxury of experiencing pleasure without the interference of Mother Church.

The Sabbat is a day of ascendancy for witches. In the European countryside during the Middle Ages, the eight festival observances took on immense importance as thousands of peasants, common people, and members of the lesser nobility attended the seasonal celebrations. The Sabbats mark the passage of the year as it moves through its seasons: Samhain begins the year and occurs near October 31. Yule marks the winter solstice and is celebrated near December 21, the longest, darkest night of the year. Candlemas, observed on February 2, is the festival of the goddess Brigid. The spring equinox happens around March 21 and is a powerful time of magic. Beltane, May 1, celebrates love and oneness. The summer solstice, occurring around June 21, is also a time of power and the strength of the deities of nature. August 1 recognizes Lammas, a time when fruit ripens and there are signs that harvest is near. The fall equinox, near or on September 21, celebrates a balance between light and dark, night and day.

Although there was plenty of food and beer at the Sabbats, many scholars of witchcraft believe that the high priests and priestesses took advantage of the entranced state of most of the worshippers and spiked the drinks with belladonna or other drugs in order to free the inhibitions of the celebrants. The Sabbat Dance or, as it is commonly known, the Witches' Round was performed with the dancers moving in a back-to-back position with their hands clasped and their heads turned so that they might see each other. A wild dance such as this, which was essentially circular in movement, would need little help from the drugged drinks to bring about a condition of vertigo in even the heartiest of dancers. The celebration lasted the entire night, and the crowd did not disperse until the crowing of the cock the following morning.

Reports of regular celebrations of the various Sabbats came from all over Europe. An estimated 25,000 attended such rituals in the countryside of southern France and around the Black Forest region of Germany. The popularity of the pagan celebrations rose to its greatest height in the period from roughly 1200 to the Renaissance. The nobility and high church officials realized that such celebrations could only lead eventually to a rebellious and uncontrollable populace, and thus was born the Holy Inquisition.

In 1305 the Knights Templar, who had for centuries been the bulwark of Christianity against those who would destroy or defame it, were themselves accused of invoking Satan, consorting with female demons, and worship-

ping large black cats. Although many clergy, including the pope himself, were reluctant to believe such charges against the Knights Templar, it soon became apparent that the order had become too wealthy and powerful to fit suitably into the emerging political structure of France and the aspirations of its king, Philip the Fair. Those Templars who insisted upon presenting a defense were finally brought to trial in 1312, and in spite of 573 witnesses for their defense, at least fifty-four knights were tortured en masse and burned at the stake, and their order was disbanded by Pope Clement V.

The first major witch hunt in Europe occurred in Switzerland in 1427; and in 1428, in Valais, there was a mass burning of a hundred witches. From about 1450 to 1750, some forty thousand to sixty thousand individuals were tried as witches and condemned to death in central Europe. As many as three-quarters of the victims were women.

In 1484 Pope Innocent VIII issued the papal bull *Summis Desiderantes Affectibus* and authorized two trusted Dominican inquisitors, Heinrich Institoris (Kramer) and Jacob Sprenger, to squelch the power of Satan in the Rhineland. In 1486 Sprenger and Kramer published their *Malleus Maleficarum,* the "Hammer for Witches," which quickly became the official handbook of professional witch hunters. The work strongly refuted all claims that the works of demons exist only in troubled human minds. The Bible clearly tells how certain angels fell from heaven and sought to bewitch and seduce humans, and Sprenger and Kramer issued a strict warning that to believe otherwise was to believe contrary to the truth faith. Therefore, any persons who consorted with demons and became witches must recant their evil ways or be put to death.

Although organized witchcraft trials continued to be held throughout Europe and even the English colonies in North America until the late seventeenth century, they were most often civil proceedings. About forty people were executed in the English colonies between 1650 and 1710, and half of these victims perished as a result of the Salem trials of 1692. Persecution of witches and the trials held to punish them had been almost completely abolished in Europe by 1680. One last wave of the witch craze swept over Poland and other eastern European countries in the early eighteenth century, but it had dissipated by 1740. The last legal execution of a witch occurred in 1782 in Glarus, Switzerland—not far from where the witch craze had begun in 1428. The last known witch burning in Europe took place in Poland in 1793, but it was an illegal act, for witch trials were abolished in that country in 1782.

The Inquisition and the church itself had very little part in any witchcraft trials after the latter part of the seventeenth century, but the Holy Office continued to serve as the instrument by which the papal government regulated church order and doctrine. In 1965 Pope Paul VI reorganized the Holy Office and renamed it the Congregation for the Doctrine of the Faith.

Various texts and various historians have claimed that the number of innocent people executed for the practice of witchcraft during the four centuries of active persecution was as high as 9 million. In 1999 Jenny Gibbons published the results of her research indicating that overall, approximately 75 percent to 80 percent of those accused of witchcraft were women, but that the total number of men and women who were actually hanged or burned for the "crime" probably did not exceed forty thousand.

Author and scholar Margot Adler has discovered that the source of the oft-quoted 9 million witches put to death was first used by a German historian in the late eighteenth century who took the number of people killed in a witch hunt in his own German state and multiplied that figure by the number of years various penal statues existed, then reconfigured the number to correspond to the population of Europe.

WOODPECKER

The tap-tap-tap of the secret Russian "woodpecker" beamed ELF at U.S. coastal cities, causing anxiety, depression, and suicides among the populace.

In 1975 and the years following, conspiracy theorists were greatly concerned by warnings that Soviet submarines were beaming ELF at U.S. coastal cities. (ELF, extremely low frequency, is the band of radio frequencies from 3 to 300 Hz.) According to conspiracists, the low frequency caused a general malaise, headaches, depression, even suicides among the coastal population. Listening devices had picked up the ELF transmission, which was described as a "tap, tap, tap, tap, tap," sounding very much like a woodpecker knocking his beak against a tree trunk.

Secret Russian neuromedical research discovered that there are specific brain frequencies for each mood, thought, or emotion that humans experience. An extensive catalog of these brain actions with their distinctive frequencies was established by Russian scientists and psychologists. From the shadowy waters off the U.S. coast, the submarines could beam ELF waves for anger, suicide, hysteria, lust, paranoia, or depression at hundreds, perhaps thousands, of unaware victims. The Soviet subs weren't trying to blitz the entire nation. If they could cause residents in the coastal areas to have nervous breakdowns, that would be sufficient to prove that the human brain can be controlled, even at a distance, by the utilization of ELF carried by pulse-modulated microbeams. Eugene, Oregon, was one of the cities where people were greatly affected by the Soviets pulsing "woodpecker" ELF waves at key brain-wave rhythms.

It was no secret that the U.S. Navy used ELF to communicate with submerged submarines. Undersea craft are blocked from most electromagnetic signals because of the electrical conductivity of salt water. ELF is not used for ordinary communications because its extremely low transmission rate requires a very large antenna, many miles in length.

According to conspiracists, U.S. military scientists began to realize that the "woodpecker" was considerably more than cold war paranoia, and the navy eventually invested more than $25 million into ELF research. It wasn't long before America had a fleet of its own "woodpeckers" cruising the coasts of Soviet-bloc nations.

U.S. senator Gaylord Nelson later forced the navy to reveal their findings demonstrating that ELF transmissions can alter human blood chemistry. In 1976 Dr. Susan Bawin and Dr. W. Ross Adey proved that nerve cells are affected by ELF fields.

In the summer of 1977, strange anomalous sky glows, weird lightning, and eerie plasma effects were seen in the skies near the woodpecker transmitter sites in the USSR. The *Washington Post* (September 23, 1977) carried a report that cited "a strange, star-like ball of light" seen in the sky over Petrozavodsk in Soviet Karelia, "spreading like a jellyfish and showering down shafts of light."

The U.S. government constructed and maintained two sites in the Chequamegon Na-

tional Forest, Wisconsin, and the Escanaba State Forest, Michigan, each utilizing power lines as antennae stretching from fourteen to twenty-eight miles in length. Ecologists became concerned about environmental conditions and human health problems resulting from the great amounts of electricity generated and emitted by ELF, and in 1984 a federal judge ordered construction halted until further studies could be made and evaluated.

At the height of the great floods that inundated the Midwest in 1993, people saw "mysterious flashes of light" that streamed from "the tops of storm-clouds into the upper atmosphere" during the heavy rains. The *Kansas City Star* reported that the mysterious flashes of light resembled "jellyfish." On September 24, 1993, the newspaper reported that the flashes of light were "brightest where they top out—typically about 40 miles high— so you have the jellyfish body at the top with tentacles trailing down."

In 2004 the antennae at the Chequamegon and Escanaba ELF installations were ordered dismantled. Conspiracy theorists say that it really doesn't matter whether the government tears those two sites down. HAARP far surpasses those pesky Russian and Yank woodpeckers in its potential for weather control and military domination of the world.

X-Y

X-FILES

For conspiracy theorists, UFO buffs, and paranormal enthusiasts, The X-Files *was the defining series of the 1990s.*

In 1993 Chris Carter, creator of the television series *The X-Files* for the Fox network, fashioned a blend of UFO mythology, increasing public distrust of the government, and growing interest in the paranormal that over its nine-year run usually finished as the second-most-popular drama (after *ER* on NBC) among young adults. During its peak season in 1997, *The X-Files* attracted an estimated 20 million viewers per episode. In 2002, shortly before the last episode of the series, Sandy Grushow, the chairman of Fox Entertainment, said that *The X-Files* had made in excess of $1 billion for the company.

Certainly, for conspiracy theorists and paranormal enthusiasts, *The X-Files* was the defining series of the 1990s. Rather than becoming merely a cult hit savored by the political fringe, the series burst free of all restraints and flooded the mainstream audience with its paranoia. FBI agents Fox Mulder (David Duchovny) and Dana Scully (Gillian Anderson) regularly pursued UFOs, alien bounty hunters, and nasty government agents and declared to their audience that "the truth is out there." However, because the truth was being covered up by an ultrasecret and exceedingly ruthless government agency, they must "trust no one." And one had but to watch the news channels or read the daily newspaper to witness real-life, high-level cover-ups or to develop a distrust of the government with its high-handed blunders like Iran-Contra, Watergate, Ruby Ridge, and Waco.

At the 1996 Golden Globe Awards, the categories for best television drama, best actor in a television drama (Duchovny), and best actress in a television drama (Anderson) were all won by *The X-Files.*

According to the mythology developed by Carter for the series, the alien invasion had begun in prehistoric times and had been rediscovered by the U.S. military and a secret branch of the government in 1947 after the crash of a flying saucer at Roswell, New Mexico. Although Mulder and Scully made side excursions to investigate vampires, ghosts, and a wide variety of monsters, the complicated,

Gillian Anderson and David Duchovney starred in the successful TV series *The X-Files*.

sometimes downright confusing, UFO mythology was the glue that held the series together and kept the fans returning week after week to chart the agents' progress in cracking the ultimate case that would force the secret government to admit the truth about aliens.

On June 19, 1998, the X-Files motion picture *Fight the Future* was released, spreading the small-screen paranoia of the TV series to big-screen multiplexes across the nation. The film topped the box office receipts the first week of its release, grossing $31 million. It has since brought in more than $100 million.

The final two seasons of *The X Files* saw little of Mulder, who was allegedly hiding somewhere from the secret government, and less involvement from Scully, who seemed to graduate to a kind of advisory capacity. The bulk of the assignments to pursue monsters, restless spirits, and unruly aliens fell to the show's new costars, Robert Patrick as Agent John Doggett and Annabeth Gish as Agent Monica Reyes.

Before the series ended in May 2002, both Scully and Mulder had themselves been abducted and Scully, earlier declared unable to

have children, had borne a child under mysterious circumstances. Although loyal fans of the series were denied witnessing Scully-Mulder nuptials or even a discreet love scene between the two, Scully's child, William, was obviously Mulder's by donor sperm or by the extraterrestrials artificially inseminating her with her partner's seed during one of their abduction episodes. Or Chris Carter just didn't want to show us everything. The series concluded with the two soul mates escaping from the constant menace of the Cigarette Smoking Man and bounty-hunting aliens to find a new life together.

Often hailed as a cultural phenomenon and generally acclaimed as the most successful science-fiction series in the history of television up to that time, *The X-Files* exerted an incalculable influence on the mass audience's beliefs concerning such subjects as UFOs, abductions, and government conspiracies.

Y2K

As the calendar moved inexorably toward the year 2000, a new millennium, apocalyptic fever seized millions.

Millennium means a period of one thousand years, but *the* Millennium signifies the return of Jesus and the end of the world as it presently exists. There seemed a strange kind of foreboding among a sizable portion of the populace that at the end of the current millennium (1000–2000), humankind was going to pay for its sins. The world was coming to an end. Judgment Day was upon the whole of humanity. And whether one feared a wrathful God or a depleted planet didn't matter. Either way, when the sun arose on January 1, 2000 (if, indeed, it rose at all), it would shine on whatever rubble remained of an old world destroyed or a new world being born. There was hope only for a righteous few who would welcome the Rapture lifting them up to the skies, Jesus returning to conquer evil, or perhaps scientific salvation that would allow some of *Homo sapiens* to survive.

And finally, there were those who shrugged and said, "What's the big deal? January 1, 2000, is just another day."

Frightening rumors kept vast audiences up all night listening to radio talk shows. There was this incredible thing about computers. They weren't programmed to work beyond December 31, 1999. At the stroke of midnight, lights would go out all over the world; power plants would shut down; electrical appliances—from furnaces to toasters—would be useless. One of the most frightening Y2K (meaning "year 2000") visions was that passenger and military aircraft all over the world would fall from the sky because their computers would shut down.

Thousands of stalwart individuals, determined that they and their families would survive Y2K, bought wood-burning stoves, kerosene lanterns, generators, and firearms. Millions of homes stocked up on canned goods, bottled water, and batteries.

Tabloid newspapers joined the radio and television talk shows in bombarding an already nervous population with prophecies of the coming apocalypse as elucidated by historians, scientists, theologians, Bible scholars, futurists, aboriginal seers from many cultures, psychic-sensitives from around the world, and UFO contactees channeling advice from outerspace intelligences. A 1997 Associated Press poll revealed that nearly 25 percent of adult Christians believed that Jesus would return on January 1, 2000, or soon thereafter to set in motion the terrible events prophesied in the books of Daniel, Ezekiel, and Revelation.

As the year 1999 progressed, Israel deported members of Concerned Christians, a cult that had come to Jerusalem to plan the battle of Armageddon that would launch the Second Coming of Christ. The founder of the group, Monte Kim Miller, believed that he was the final prophet on Earth before Jesus's return. Miller had been told by God that he would be killed in Jerusalem's streets in December 1999 but would rise from the dead in three days.

A former kibbutz worker named Jacob Hawkins changed his name to Yisrael and prophesied that the world would end if the laws of Yahweh were not universally followed. Yisrael soon had nearly three thousand followers who believed that he would announce the exact time of Jesus's return—if Satan didn't murder him first.

Sergei Torop was dismissed his position as sergeant with a Russian police unit when he began to have religious visions. Torop changed his name to Vissarion, revealed that he was Jesus returned and, with thousands of followers, began building a "City of the Sun" on Siberia's Mount Sukhaya.

Fifty miles from Little Rock, Arkansas, a former Mennonite minister, Robert Millar, built Elohim City, a paramilitary fortress, in anticipation of the endtimes. Millar believed that a series of cataclysms would strike the United States soon after the year 2000 and cleanse the unworthy and wicked from the Earth.

As millions were stockpiling firewood, bottled water, canned goods, and other necessities to withstand the apocalypse, some worriers posed the question of whether the millennium would actually begin on January 1, 2000—or January 1, 2001.

Stephen Jay Gould, professor of zoology and geology at Harvard and an author of books about science, history, and philosophy, released his *Questioning the Millennium: A Rationalist's Guide to a Precisely Arbitrary Countdown* in 1997. Gould discusses the human "fascination with numerical regularity" and notes that some philosophers have divided earthly history into a cycle of four based on the Four Empires in the apocalyptic chapters of the book of Daniel; others have advocated a fivefold division based on the five sequential political societies mentioned by Plato. "The millennium has been predicted and expected at almost any time, depending on the system in favor," Gould writes. "Obviously, with Thomas Muentzer advocating 1525, William Miller 1844, Wovoka 1890, Chilembwe 1915, the year 1000 or 2000, and intervals of 1000 in general, could claim no special preference."

When January 1, 2000, came without the world ending, and so did January 1, 2001, most of the world breathed a sigh of relief and smugly observed that the eternal clock is still ticking. Others pointed out that in the eternal scheme of things, what's a five- or six-year delay when you're dealing with a thousand or more?

FRANCIS PARKER YOCKEY

A strange man right out of the Twilight Zone devoted his life to an attempt to reverse the result of World War II and declare the Third Reich the winner.

If Francis Parker Yockey had not committed suicide in 1960 when the FBI finally caught up with him, he would be pleased at the violent and chaotic manner in which world events have progressed since 9/11. He would have delighted in the collapse of the World Trade Center and rejoiced that Islamic extremists had been the perpetrators of the terrorist act. Yockey had dedicated his life to reversing the outcome of World War II, a mission that he thought could be achieved by 2050. He provided covert assistance to organized Muslim opposition to the West and hoped that terrorists to whom surrender was impossible would begin attacking American cities. He envisioned a world in which America's global influence would be replaced by a European super-state built according to the precepts of Hitler's Third Reich and ruled by elitists who had replaced Christianity with the occult Hermetic disciplines.

Little is known about this mysterious individual, who inhabited the farthest edges of the shadowy fringe. Just as devotees of weird tales embrace the mystery of H. P. Lovecraft's *Necronomicon,* disciples of fascism and Satanism are devoted to Yockey's underground text *Imperium.* Of course, followers of Lovecraft's work understand that the world of Ancient Ones that he created was fiction; admirers of Yockey's work dedicate themselves to fulfilling his vision of European unity under a Nazi regime. Yockey brushes aside the Nazi defeat in World War II as a temporary setback in the march toward the ultimate goal of the exclusion of America in European affairs and a fascist revolution in America itself. *Imperium* was written under the pseudonym of "Ulick Varange" ("Ulick," supposedly a Danish Irish name; "Varange," a reference to the Norsemen) and self-published in 1948 by Yockey in a limited edition of two hundred copies. Reprints of the work circulate today among neo-Nazi and far-right groups, who regard Yockey's thoughts and theories with the same reverence that earlier like-minded readers held toward Hitler's *Mein Kampf.*

It was not until some years after Yockey's death that radical-right publisher Willis Carto published a paperback edition of *Imperium* and the book began to reach a wide readership among neo-Nazi and neo-fascist groups. The Italian Hermetic ideologue Julius Evola had praised Yockey's work, and *Imperium* was in harmony with the Swiss-based New European Order and its beliefs in the myths of Aryan origins in the hyperborean north and in Atlantis.

Born in Chicago in 1917 to a family of the professional classes and of German, Irish, and French Canadian ancestry, Yockey was reared Roman Catholic, but he eventually found himself attracted to a kind of theosophical Nietzscheanism as he involved himself with radical-right organizations in the 1930s. Yockey was attracted to the German American Bund, but he also became intrigued with the Stalinists, the Trotskyites, the semifascist followers of Father Coughlin—any group, it seems, that was against capitalism and that understood the international threat of the Jews.

Some researchers are certain that Yockey was part of a German American espionage network and that he aided the infiltration of Nazi saboteurs into the United States. During World War II he received a commission in the U.S. Army. He then briefly deserted but, after a few weeks, returned to duty and satisfied the army that he had suffered a mental breakdown. He obtained a medical discharge without any suspicion that he may have been aiding Nazi spies and saboteurs during his time away from base.

Before the war Yockey pursued an academic career at several universities, completed a law degree at Notre Dame, and was qualified to practice. He had also attended Georgetown University's School of Foreign Service as an undergraduate. With these qualifications, he obtained a job after the war with the war crimes tribunal in Germany. He was discharged for his tendency to side with the Nazi officials he was supposed to be prosecuting. Later Yockey landed a job with the American Red Cross and returned to Germany. He soon deserted his post and was sent back to the United States. Yockey had simply used both positions as a means of getting the U.S. government to finance his trips to Germany to meet with the growing pan-European fascist network.

Conspiracy theorists speculate that Yockey spent the 1950s accumulating a bewildering array of identities as he traveled literally around the world, doing whatever he could to aid the fascist cause. It is likely that he was involved with Odessa, the international network of postwar Nazis and fascists. Some suggest that

Francis Parker Yockey is shown here under arrest for using fifteen aliases in a passport operation. He is best remembered for *Imperium,* a book that advocated placing all of Europe under a Nazi regime.

Yockey spent a substantial amount of time behind the iron curtain before he returned briefly to the United States to work as a speechwriter for Senator Joseph McCarthy. It is known that Yockey spent time in New Orleans writing propaganda for use in Latin America, and a number of conspiracy researchers insist that he knew Lee Harvey Oswald at that time.

In 1960 the FBI confronted Yockey in Oakland, California, when Yockey's numerous identities and passports had raised a number of red flags. Before federal agents could question him, Yockey tried to run away, injuring an agent in the process. Yockey died by self-administered potassium cyanide on June 17, 1960.

ZIONISM

Zionism is a political and cultural movement supporting a homeland for the Jewish people and their society. Critics of Zionism see it in much more sinister terms. Zionists, they feel, are behind a wide range of plots to assassinate leaders of other nations and religions, and to cause social and political unrest.

The spiritual importance of Israel to the Abrahamic religions—Christians, Muslims, and Jews—is obvious to anyone with the most elementary knowledge of world religions. While Jerusalem is a place of pilgrimage for Christians and Muslims, for Jews it is the site of the Temple and the object of the promise of every Passover: "Next year in Jerusalem." While Christian pilgrims revere the traditional sites in Jerusalem—where Jesus was baptized, gave the sermon on the mount, and was crucified—and Muslims visit such sacred sites as the Dome on the Rock and the place where Muhammed ascended to Heaven, Jews cherish the land that gave them the Hebrew language, the Torah, the laws in the Talmud, the Jewish calendar, and the Jewish holidays and festivals. For Zionist Jews,

the land of Israel is the sacred home of their people and the only place on Earth where the Jewish commonwealth might be established. "Zion" is a Hebrew word for Jerusalem.

In the view of some conspiracy theorists, Zionists have been behind every major war, assassination, political upheaval, and civil unrest that has taken place nearly everywhere in the world for hundreds of years. Actually, the term "Zionism," which refers to a movement for the return of the Jewish people to their ancient homeland and the resumption of Jewish sovereignty in Israel, was not coined until 1890. At that time, Nathan Birnbaum, an Austrian writer, journalist, and Jewish nationalist, gave expression to the dream of leaving behind the anti-Semitism of the pogroms in Russia and Eastern Europe and emigrating to Palestine. In 1897, at the First Zionist Congress in Basle, Switzerland, Theodor Herzl founded the Zionist Organization, which is dedicated to a renascence of Jewish culture.

From the very beginning of the movement there have always been various interests served by Zionism.

Liberal Zionism was the initial emphasis established in 1897 until after World War I.

A right-wing demonstrator marches in Tel-Aviv, Israel.

The liberal, or general, Zionists identified with the liberal European middle class and advocated free market principles, democracy, and human rights.

Labor Zionism rebelled against centuries of oppression in the anti-Semitic nations of Eastern Europe. Theodor Herzl argued that a true revolution of the Jewish spirit would occur when the Jews returned to Israel and became farmers, merchants, factory workers, and soldiers in their own nation. The kibbutz, a form of cooperative agriculture, stressed self-sufficiency and a kind of Utopian socialism, important aspects of Labor Zionism.

In 1929, the Zionist Organization sponsored a conference in Zurich that summoned delegates from non-Zionist Jewish groups as well as Zionists. The Zionists hoped to interest more European Jews in their hopes to return to Palestine or, at least, to help raise funds to enable those who wished to emigrate to the spiritual homeland to do so. The reception for such a massive emigration was cool, for the great majority of Jews considered themselves citizens of the European countries that had been their families' homes for many generations, and they were not at all comfortable with the thought of leaving their established physical inheritance in Germany, France, or the Netherlands for a spiritual heritage in what was then a very primitive country in comparison to the European nations.

The Zionists did, however, find an enthusiastic supporter in the National Socialist government of Adolf Hitler. The Nazis wholeheartedly supported Zionism and the plan of a massive Jewish emigration to Palestine. From 1933 to 1938, the Zionist movement flourished in Germany.

The German SS was extremely active in its support of Zionism, urging the government to take an active role in encouraging official support of the party. The ranking officers of the SS were very receptive to a program in which the Jews themselves would assume a large role in dealing with Germany's "Jewish problem." In 1934, SS officer Leopold von Mildenstein and Zionist official Kurt Tuchler toured Palestine together for six months in order to assess the most efficient means of making the nation capable of handling large numbers of new arrivals.

Von Mildenstein believed that Zionism was beginning to fashion a new kind of Jewish people, who, once in their homeland in Palestine, would soon cure a centuries-long wound on the body of the world that had originally been inflicted by the Jewish people. The Jewish question would be solved by the Jews themselves when they left Europe. From 1933 to 1941, the Nazis heartily supported Zionism and Jewish emigration until World War II interrupted extensive collaboration. It is estimated that in this period, beginning in 1933, approximately 50,000 to 60,000 out of Germany's 500,000 to 600,000 Jews, roughly 10 percent of the Jewish population in Europe, were routed to Palestine.

Nationalist Zionism emerged from the Revisionist Zionists, which left the World Zionist Organization in 1935, when the larger group refused to focus on the creation of the Jewish state of Israel as a primary goal of Zionism. Later, the Revisionists evolved into the Likud Party in Israel, which has controlled most Israeli governments since 1977. A hard-line party, Likud demands that Israel maintain control of the West Bank and East Jerusalem. In 2005, the party split over the creation of a Palestinian state.

The Zionist vision of a Jewish homeland was realized when the State of Israel was established on May 14, 1948. There are now more than four million Jews from more than 100 countries in Israel, about forty-two percent of the Jewish world population. Israel is also home to approximately one million Muslim and Christian Arabs, Bahai's, Druze, and Circassians.

In 1975, the United Nations General Assembly adopted a resolution that criticized Zionism as a form of racism. Chaim Herzog, Israel's ambassador to the UN at that time, stressed the irony of such a vote censuring Zionism exactly thirty-seven years after Kristallnacht, the attacks on Jews throughout Nazi Germany on November 9 and 10, 1938. Zionists responded to UN criticism of racism by pointing to the presence of 42,000 black Jews, who had been brought to Israel by a series of airlifts from the ancient Ethiopian Jewish community.

Famed American civil rights attorney Alan Dershowitz argued in *The Case for Peace: How the Arab-Israeli Conflict Can Be Resolve* that to condemn Jewish self-determination was also in itself a form of racism: "A world that closed its doors to Jews who sought escape from Hitler's ovens lacks the moral standing to complain about Israel's giving preference to Jews."

During the last decades of the twentieth century, Neo-Zionism and Post-Zionism, two very different movements, emerged in Israel. Neo-Zionists embraced the messianic dimensions of Zionist nationalism, while Post-Zionism envisioned Israel as a state for all its citizens, a place where equally autonomous Jews and Arabs could live together in peace.

While it seems unlikely that Zionists are the grand conspirators seeking to enslave the world that some conspiracy theorists portray them to be, there is the matter of a people seeking to establish a national home in a country that is already occupied by others. To its many critics, Zionism is, plain and simple, an effort to colonize and to take possession of a nation in which a native population was bound to resist. By its single-minded mission to obtain control of Palestine, the Zionists never sought the consent of the Arab inhabitants whose lands and whose homes they wished to supplant.

Zionism is opposed by many in Israel, where the majority of the population describe themselves as secular Jews. Those who describe themselves as traditional or religious Jews say that Zionism will never become a democratic movement because its beliefs are based on a doctrine of the divine right of a people. Zionism, they argue, is rooted in blood, mysticism, and a return to the past.

Haredi, the ultra-Orthodox Jews, consider Judaism to be foremost a religion, and they reject the nationalism of Zionism. In addition, they see the concept of a Jewish state to be completely forbidden by Jewish law. Although the Sephardi-Orthodox Shas party joined the World Zionist Organization in 2010, it supported territorial compromise with the Arabs and Palestinians. Most Hasidic groups are strongly anti-Zionist, maintaining that Israel is in violation of Jewish tradition, which firmly states that Jews must wait for the Messiah before they return to form a state in the Holy Land. The Neturei Karta, an orthodox Haredi movement, considers Zionism racist. Apart from the Zionists, they state, Hitler and the Nazis were the only ones who considered the Jews to be a race.

ZIONIST OCCUPATION GOVERNMENT

Anti-Semitic groups believe that the U.S. government is under the control of Zionist Jews.

Zionist Occupation (also *Occupied, Occupational) Government* (ZOG) is a term used by anti-Semitic groups who believe that the U.S. government is controlled by Zionists. When used by a white-supremacist group the phrase is most often a derogatory euphemism for "Jew," suggesting that the government is controlled by Jews who are joined in an international conspiracy, such as the one outlined in *The Protocols of the Learned Elders of Zion.* More specifically, the term refers to any Jew or non-Jew who places the goals of Israel over those of the United States and tries to persuade the U.S. government to use military or economic power on behalf of Israel. The far-right groups who decry ZOG often glorify the "liberation movements" of Syria, Libya, Iran, and Palestine. Yasser Arafat was esteemed as a particularly admirable figure.

Some students of anti-semitism state that the name "Zionist Occupation Government" probably originated with Aryan Nations, which has used the ZOG reference extensively in its literature and has popularized it online. Others suggest the term was first used in a text entitled "Welcome to ZOG-World," written by

Theodor Herzl, journalist and founder of Zionism.

neo-Nazi Eric Thomson in 1976. Widespread usage was quite likely encouraged by a December 27, 1984, article in the *New York Times* reporting on the series of robberies committed in California and Washington State by white supremacists who were using their plunder to pay for a war upon the U.S. government, which they called the "Zionist Occupation Government."

In 1996 the "Aryan Declaration of Independence," posted on the Aryan Nations website, stated that the ZOG has as its goal "the establishment of an absolute tyranny" over the United States and "the eradication of the White race and its culture" as "one of its foremost purposes." Since that time the term has been used by numerous anti-Semitic and white-supremacist groups.

Works Cited and Further Reading

The following is a list of primary sources quoted in the text, as well as suggested books, articles, and websites readers can access for further study. Please note that all website links were accurate at time of publications, but may later become outdated.

Abanes, Richard. *End-Time Visions*. Nashville: Broadman & Holman, 1998.

"About the John Birch Society." http://www.jbs.org/about/index.html.

"About the Show: Jeff Rense Program." *Rense.com*. http://www.rense.com/aboutnew1.htm.

Adler, Margot. *Drawing Down the Moon: Witches, Druids, Goddess-Worshippers and Other Pagans*. Boston: Beacon Press, 1986.

Adler, Margot. "A Time for Truth: Wiccans Struggle with Information that Revisions Their History." *Beliefnet*. http://www.beliefnet.com/story/40/story_4007.html.

Aerosol Operation Crimes and Cover-Up. http://www.carnicom.com/ contrails.htm.

Ahmed, Nafeez Mosaddeq, and John Leonard. *The War on Freedom: How and Why America Was Attacked, September 11, 2001*. Joshua Tree, CA: Progressive Press, 2002.

Ahmed, Rollo. *The Black Art*. London: Arrow, 1966.

Albarelli, Jr., H.P. *A Secret Order: Investigating the High Strangeness and Synchronicity in the JFK Assassination*. Walterville, OR: TrineDay, 2012.

Albert Hofmann Foundation. http://www.hofmann.org/index.html.

Al Bielek Website. http://www.bielek.com.

Aleister Crowley Foundation. http://www.thelemicknights.org/acfhome.html.

Alexander, John. UFOs: Myths, Conspiracies, and Realities. New York: St. Martins/Griffin, 2012.

Alexandrova, Larisa, and John Byrne. "Unofficial War: U.S., Britain Led Massive Secret Bombing Campaign before Iraq War Was Declared." http://rawstory2.com/admin/dbscripts/printstory.php?story=5.

"Alex Jones' Infowars: There's a War On." http://www.infowars.com/about-alex-jones/.

"Alien Autopsy." http://www.rotten.com/library/conspiracy/alien-autopsy.

"Alien Autopsy Is Fake." http://www.webmesh.co.uk/overlord/autopsy2.html.

Alliance Defense Fund Website. http://www.alliancedefensefund.org.

"Al-Qaeda." http://www.terrorismfiles.org/organisations/al_qaida.html.

"Al Qaeda Links." http://tvnewslies.org/al_qaeda_links.html.

"*Alternative Three*." http://ufos.about.com/library/weekly/aa050399.htm.

"Alternative Three." http://www.museumofhoaxes.com/alt3.html.

American Family Association Website. http://www.afa.net.

American Nazi Party Website. http://www.americannaziparty.com.

"The American Protective Association." *Catholic Encyclopedia.* http://www.newadvent.org/cathen/01426a.htm.

"American Vision: America's Christian Heritage." http://www.americanvision.org/christianheritage.asp.

American Vision Website. http://www.americanvision.org.

Amr, Ahmed. "Illegally Financing the WMD Hoax." http://usa.mediamonitors.net/content/view/full/15207.

"Analysis of the Racketeer Influenced and Corrupt Organizations Act." http://www.ricoact.com.

"Anarchists: A Picture of Civilization at the Close of the Nineteenth century."
    http://dwardmac.pitzer.edu/Anarchist_Archives/macan/introduction.html.

"Ancient Landmarks: The Greek Mysteries."
    http://www.wisdomworld.org/additional/ancientlandmarks/TheGreekMysteries.html.

"Ancient Mystery Schools." http://www.crystalinks.com/mysteryschools.html.

Anderson, Tom. "Revelation! 666 Is Not the Number of the Beast (It's a Devilish 616)." *Independent* (UK).
    http://news.independent.co.uk/uk/this_britain/article4086.ece.

Andrews, Colin, and Pat Delgado. *Circular Evidence.* London: Bloomsbury, 1990.

Angebert, Jean-Michel. *The Occult and the Third Reich.* New York: Macmillan, 1974.

Anthony, Richard, comp. "The Institutes of Biblical Law." http://www.ecclesia.org/truth/rj.html.

"Anti-Abortion Extremists: The Army of God and Justifiable Homicide."
    http://www.prochoice.org/about_abortion/violence/army_god.html.

"Antisemitism World Report 1997: United States of America."
    http://www.ess.uwe.ac.uk/documents/antsemus.htm.

"The A.P.A." http://www.etext.lib.virginia.edu/railton/yankee/cycath4.html.

Arbury, David. "Marie Laveau Biography." *Voodoo Dreams.*
    http://ame2.asu.edu/sites/voodoodreams/marie_laveau.asp.

"Aryan Nations/Church of Jesus Christ Christian." *Anti-Defamation League.*
    http://www.adl.org/learn/ext_us/Aryan_Nations.asp?xpicked.

Aryan Nations Website. http://www.aryan-nations.org.

Army of God Website. http://www.armyofgod.com.

"Army Says Alarm Real—Roaring Guns Mark Blackout." *Los Angeles Times,* February 26, 1942.

Arnold, Gordon B. *Conspiracy Theory in Film, Television, and Politics.* New York: Praeger Books, 2008.

"Art Bell, Heaven's Gate, and Journalistic Integrity." http://www.csicop.org/si/9707/art-bell.html.

"Asian Earthquake Disaster." http://news.ft.com/indepth/tsunami.

"Assassination of John Lennon." *Seize the Night.* http://carpenoctem.tv/cons/lennon.html.

"Assassination of Malcolm X, Black Muslim: Plots, Theories, and Facts." *Crime Library.*
    http://www.crimelibrary.com/terrorists_spies/assassins/Malcolm_x/4.html.

"The Assassination of MLK Jr." *Seize the Night.* http://carpenoctem.tv/cons/mlk.html.

"Attack Images and Graphics." *September 11 News.com.* http://www.september11news.com/AttackImages.htm.

"The Attempted Assassination of Ronald Reagan." http://www.carpenoctem.tv/cons/reagan.html.

"AUDIO: Panopticon—The Amazing New 'Information Awareness Office (IAO)' Proves Big Brother's Eyes Really Are
    Watching Us Every Minute of the Day." http://www.conspiracyworld.com/more_info/5054.asp?productid=5054.

"Aum Shinrikyo." *Apologetics Index.* http://www.apologeticsindex.org/a06.html.

"Aum Shinri Kyo (Supreme Truth)." *Religious Tolerance.org.* http://www.religioustolerance.org/dc_aumsh.htm.

"Aum Shinrikyo (Supreme Truth)—Japan." http://www.au.af.mil/au/aul/bibs/tergps/tgaum.htm.

"Autopsy Confirms Ray Died of Liver Failure." *CNN interactive.* http://www.cnn.com/US/9804/24/ray.autopsy.pm.

Bach, Marcus. *Inside Voodoo.* New York: Signet, 1968.

"Backgrounder: The Jewish Defense League." http://www.adl.org/extremism/jdl_chron.asp.

Baigent, Michael, and Richard Leigh. *The Temple and the Lodge.* New York: Arcade, 1989.

Baigent, Michael, Richard Leigh, and Henry Lincoln. *Holy Blood, Holy Grail.* New York: Dell, 1983.

Bailey, Alice A. *The Unfinished Autobiography.* New York: Lucis Trust, 1951.

Ballantyne, Coco. "What Is Morgellons Disease? Is it a Physical or Psychological Condition?" *Scientific American.* May 13, 2009.

"Barack's Social Security Number." *Truth or Fiction.* http://www.truthorfiction.com/rumors/o/Obama-SSN.htm.

Barker, Gray. *They Knew Too Much about Flying Saucers.* Lilburn, GA: IllumiNet Press, 1997.

Barker, J. C. *Scared to Death.* New York: Dell, 1969.

Barruel, Augustin. *Memoirs Illustrating the History of Jacobinism* (1798). Reprint. Fort Huron, MI: Real-View, 2003.

Beam, Louis. "The Holocaust as a Mechanism for Suppressing the Truth." http://www.louisbeam.com/holocaust.htm.

Beck, Robert C. "Extreme Low Frequency Magnetic Fields and EEG Entrainment: A Psychotronic Warfare Possibility?" http://www.elfis.net/elfol8/e8elfeeg1.htm.

Beckley, Timothy Green. *MIB: Aliens among Us.* New Brunswick, NJ: Global Communications, 1971.

———. *MJ-12 and the Riddle of Hangar 18.* New Brunswick, NJ: Inner Light, 1989.

———. *Strange Encounters.* New Brunswick, NJ: Global Communications, 1992.

Beckley, Timothy Green, ed. *The Smoky God and Other Inner Earth Mysteries.* New Brunswick, NJ: Inner Light, 1993.

Begich, Nick, and Jeane Manning. "The Military's Pandora's Box." http://www.haarp.net.

Behar, Richard. "The Thriving Cult of Greed and Power." *Time,* May 6, 1991: 50–57.

"Beijing, Falun Gong Group in New War of Words." http://sg.biz.yahoo.com/news/international/article.html?s=sgfinance/news/0l0106.

Belanus, George. "Project Silverbug—Human Engineered UFOs?" *Rense.com.* http://www.rense.com/ufo2/humanufo.htm.

Bell, Art. *The Quickening: Today's Trends, Tomorrow's World.* New Orleans: Paper Chase, 1997.

Bell, Art, and Brad Steiger. *The Source—A Journey through the Unexplained.* New York: Signet, 2002.

Bell, Art, and Whitley Strieber. *The Coming Global Superstorm.* New York: Simon & Schuster, 1999.

Belzer, Richard. *UFOs, JFK, and Elvis: Conspiracies You Don't Have to Be Crazy to Believe.* New York: Ballantine, 2000.

Berkowitz, Bill. "Army of God's Rev. Bray Praises the Beheading of Gay Men." (From gaytoday.com.) http://www.streetpreach.com/Bray/aogrev.htm.

Berlet, Chip, and Matthew N. Lyons. *Right-Wing Populism in America: Too Close for Comfort.* New York: Guilford Press, 2000.

Berliner, Don, and Stanton T. Friedman. *Crash at Corona: The U.S. Military Retrieval and Cover-up of a UFO.* New York: Marlowe, 1992.

Berlitz, Charles, and William L. Moore. *The Roswell Incident.* New York: Grosset and Dunlap, 1980.

Berlitz, Charles, and William Moore. *The Philadelphia Experiment: Project Invisibility.* New York: Fawcett, 1981.

Bernhard, Marcella. "Forbes Faces: The Koch Brothers." http://www.forbes.com/2001/01/04/0104faces.html.

Bernard, Raymond. *The Hollow Earth.* Mokelumne Hill, CA: Health Research, 1964.

Bernstein, Henrietta. *The Ark of the Covenant, the Holy Grail: Message for the New Millennium.* Marina del Rey, CA: DeVorss, 1998.

Bernstein, Richard. "Germans Still Finding New Moral Burdens of War." *New York Times,* May 8, 2005.

Besant, Annie Wood. *Annie Besant: An Autobiography.* London: T. Fisher Unwin, 1893.

———. *H. P. Blavatsky and the Masters of the Wisdom.* London: Theosophical, 1918.

"Biblical Law." *Theocracy Watch.* http://www.theocracywatch.org/biblical_law2.htm#Biblical.

"The Bilderbergers." *Jeremiah Project.* http://www.jeremiahproject.com/prophecy/nworder04.html.

Biles, Joe G. "Adventures in Propinquity: The Case of Jim Garrison." http://www.wf.net/~biles/jfk.

Binion, Carla. "Conspiracy Theories and Real Reporters." http://www.scoop.co.nz/stories/HL0206/S00092.htm.

"Biography of George Herbert Walker Bush." http://www.whitehouse.gov/history/presidents/gb41.html.

Birnes, William J., and Philip J. Corso. *The Day after Roswell.* New York: Pocket Books, 1998.

Blavatsky, H. P. *Collected Writings.* 16 vols. Wheaton, IL: Theosophical Publishing House, 1950–85.

Bock, Alan W. *Ambush at Ruby Ridge: How Government Agents Set Randy Weaver Up and Took His Family Down.* Irvine, CA: Dickens Press, 1995.

"Bohemian Club in the News." http://www.prograndamatrix.com/archive_bohemian_grove.html.

"Bombing of Pearl Harbor." *Seize the Night.* http://carpenoctem.tv/cons/pearl.html.

"Boo How Doy: The Early History of Chinese Tongs in New York." *Organized Crime.* http://organizedcrime.about.com/library/weekly/aa062401a.htm.

Booth, Martin. *The Dragon Syndicates: The Global Phenomenon of the Triads.* New York: Carroll and Graf, 2001.

Borkin, Joseph. *The Crime and Punishment of I. G. Farben.* New York: Free Press, 1978.

Boylan, Richard. "ET Base on Earth Sanctioned by Officials since 1954 Confirmed." http://www.ufoarea.com/bases_boylan.html.

———. "UFO Reality Is Breaking Through." *Perceptions,* January–February 1996.

Brean, Joseph. "Scared to Death Isn't Just an Expression." *National Post* (Canada), December 21, 2001.

Breitman, George, Herman Porter, and Baxter Smith. *The Assassination of Malcolm X.* 3d ed. New York: Pathfinder Press, 1991.

Bresler, Fenton. *Who Killed John Lennon?* New York: St. Martin's Press, 1990.

British False Memory Society Website. http://www.bfms.org.uk.

Bryant, Alice, and Linda Seebach. *Healing Shattered Reality: Understanding Contactee Trauma.* Tigard, OR: Wild Flower Press, 1991.

Brzezinski, Zbigniew. *Between Two Ages: America's Role in the Technetronic Era.* New York: Viking, 1970.

Buckland, Raymond. *Buckland's Complete Book of Witchcraft.* St. Paul, MN: Llewellyn, 1998.

Budge, E. A. Wallis. *Amulets and Talismans.* New York: Collier, 1970.

Bugliosi, Vincent, and Curt Gentry. *Helter Skelter: The True Story of the Manson Murders.* 25th anniversary ed. New York: W. W. Norton, 1994.

Bulwer-Lytton, Sir Edward. *Vril, The Power of the Coming Race* (1871). http://www.sacred-text.com/atl/vril/vril.htm.

Burns, Alex. "Aryan Nation." *Disinformation.* http://www.disinfo.com/archive/pages/dossier/id7/pg1.

Burns, Creighton. "Self-deception the Downfall of a Man of Destruction." *The Age,* August 10, 1974. http://150.theage.com.au/view_bestofarticle.asp?intid=580.

"Bush Family Machinations, 1918Ð2000." http://bushwatch.org/family.htm.

"Bush Family Skeletons." http://bushwatch.org/family.htm.

"Bush Son Had Dinner Plans with Hinckley Brother before Shooting." http://www.hereinreality.com/hinckley.html.

"Bush Urges Congress to Renew Patriot Act." *USAToday.com,* June 9, 2005. http://www.usatoday.com/news/washington/2005_06_09_bush_patriot_act_x.htm?csp=36.

Butterfield, Fox, with Jenny Hontz. "A Priest's 2 Faces: Protector and Predator." *New York Times,* May 19, 2002.

Camp, Gregory S. *Selling Fear: Conspiracy Theories and End-Times Paranoia.* Grand Rapids, MI: Baker Books, 1997.

Cantwell, Alan. *AIDS and the Doctors of Death: An Inquiry into the Origin of the AIDS Epidemic.* Los Angeles: Aries Rising Press, 1992.

———. "Chimps, Conspiracies, and Killer Viruses." *New Dawn.* www.newdawnmagazine.com/Articles/Chimps%20Conspiracies%20Killer%20Viruses.html.

Cantwell, Alan, Jr. "Are Vaccines Causing More Disease Than They Are Curing?" http://www.whale.to/v/cantwell.html.

Caputo, Robert, and Tyrone Turner. "Gone with the Water." *National Geographic,* October 2004. http://www3.nationalgeographic.com/ngm/0410/feature5.

Cardena, Etzel, et al., eds. *Varieties of Anomalous Experience: Examining the Scientific Evidence.* Washington, DC: American Psychological Association, 2000.

Caron, M., and S. Hutin. *The Alchemists.* Trans. Helen R. Lane. New York: Grove Press, 1961.

Carroll, Robert Todd. "Illuminati, The New World Order, and Paranoid Conspiracy Theorists." *Skeptics Dictionary.* http://skepdic.com/illuminati.html.

Cassidy, Mike, and Will Miller. "A Short History of FBI COINTELPRO." http://www.monitor.net/monitor/9905a/jbcointelpro.html.

"Catholic Church's Costs Pass $1 Billion in Abuse Cases." *New York Times,* June 12, 2005.

Cavendish, Richard. *The Black Arts.* New York: Capricorn, 1968.

Central Intelligence Agency. *The World Factbook.* http://www.cia.gov/cia/publications/factbook.

Central Intelligence Agency Website. http://www.cia.gov.

Chalcedon Foundation Website. http://www.chalcedon.edu.

Chamish, Barry. "New 'Angel' Dead Sea Scroll Contains Astral Implications." http://www.virtuallystrange.net/ufo/updates/1999/oct/m07_012.shtml.

"Charles G. Koch Charitable Foundation." *Media Transparency.* http://www.mediatransparency.org/funderprofile.php?funderID=9.

"Charles Guiteau Case." http://www.law.umkc.edu/faculty/projects/ftrials/Guiteau.html.

"Charles Guiteau: The Psychopathic Assassin of President James A. Garfield." http://www.crimelibrary.com/terrorists_spies/assassins/charles_guiteau.

"Charles Guiteau: Timeline." http://www.rotten.com/library/bio/crime/assassins/charles-guiteau.

Charles Manson. http://www.crimelibrary.com/manson/mansonmain.htm.

Charles Manson and the Family. http://www.charliemanson.com.

"Chartres, France: Chartres Cathedral, West Front, Central Portal." http://www.bluffton.edu/~sullivanm/chartreswest/centralportal.html.

Chase, Alston. "Harvard and the Making of the Unabomber." *Atlantic Monthly,* June 2000.

Chemtrails Data Page: Jeff Rense. http://www.rense.com/politics6/chemdatapage.html.

Cheney, Margaret. *Tesla: Man Out of Time.* New York: Touchstone, 2001.

Chicago Historical Society. *The Haymarket Affair Digital Collection.* http://www.chicagohistory.org/hadc/artifacts.html.

Childress, David H. *Extraterrestrial Archaeology,* New rev. ed. Adventures Unlimited Press, 2000.

Chin, Ko-Lin. *Chinatown Gangs: Extortion, Enterprise, and Ethnicity.* New York: Oxford University Press, 1996.

Chomsky, Noam. "It's Imperialism, Stupid!" *Khaleej Times* (Dubai), July 4, 2005. http://www.chomsky.info/articles/20050704.htm.

Chrisafis, Angelique. "Scion of Traitors and Warlords: Bush's Irish Roots." *Guardian* (UK), January 27, 2005. *Rense.com.* http://www.rense.com/general62/roots.htm.

"Christian Identity." www.apologeticsindex.org/c106.html.

"Christian Identity Movement." http://www.religioustolerance.org/cr_ident.htm.

Christopher, Ruddy. *The Strange Death of Vincent Foster.* New York: The Free Press, 1997.

"Church of the Lamb of God." http://www.geocities.com/Area51/Cavern/3987/lamb.html.

"Church of Scientology." *Religious Movements.* http://religiousmovements.lib.virginia.edu/nrms/scientology.html.

"CIA: Bastion of Integrity." *CIA Operations: PaperClip, MKultra, Mkdelta, Midnight Climax.* http://www.thewinds.org/1997/06/cia.html.

CIA World Factbook. http://www.cia.gov/cia/publications/factbook.

Clark, Jerome. *The UFO Book: Encyclopedia of the Extraterrestrial.* Detroit: Visible Ink Press, 1998.

Clarkson, Frederick. "Anti-Abortion Violence: Two Decades of Arson, Bombs, and Murder." *Southern Poverty Law Center.* http://www.splcenter.org/intel/Intelreport/article.jsp?aid=411&printable=1.

Clifton, Charles S. *Encyclopedia of Heresies and Heretics.* New York: Barnes & Noble, 1992.

"Clinton Body Count." http://etherzone.com/body.html.

"The Clinton Body Count." http://www.zpub.com/un/un-bc-body.html.

"Clinton Casualties." http://www.jeremiahproject.com/prophecy/clintbodycnt.html.

Coast to Coast A.M. http://www.coasttocoastam.com/.

Cockburn, Alexander, and Jeffrey St. Clair. "Ted K., the CIA & LSD." *CounterPunch.* http://www.counterpunch.org/tedk.html.

Cohn, Norman. *The Pursuit of the Millennium.* New York: Oxford University Press, 1970.

Coleman, Loren. *Mothman and Other Curious Encounters.* New York: Paraview Press, 2002.

———. *The Mothman Death List.* http://www.lorencoleman.com/mothman_death_list.html.

Commander X. *Mind Stalkers, UFOs, Implants, and the Psychotronic Agenda of the New World Order.* New Brunswick, NJ: Global Communications, 1999.

———. *Philadelphia Experiment Chronicles.* New Brunswick, NJ: Inner Light Publications, 1994.

———. *The Secret Underground Lectures.* New Brunswick, NJ. Global Communications, 2004.

Commander X, ed. *William Cooper: Death of a Conspiracy Salesman.* New Brunswick, NJ: Global Communications, 2001.

Commander X and Tim Swartz. *Morgellons: Level 5 Plague of the New World Order.* Timothy Green Beckley, ed. New Brunswick, NJ: Global Communications, 2006.

Commander X, Tim Swartz, and Timothy Green Beckley. *Strange and Unexplained Deaths at the Hands of the Secret Government.* New Brunswick, NJ: Global Communications, 2005.

The Complete X-Files Page. http://www.geocities.com/Hollywood/3142.

"Conservative Causes Find Friend in Koch Brothers." *Lawrence (Kansas) Journal-World,* March 7, 2004.

Conspiracy Journal. http://members.tripod.com/uforeview.

Conspiracy Planet. http://www.conspiracyplanet.com.

"Conspiracy Theories: The Saudi Connection." *CBCNews: The Fifth Estate.* http://www.cbc.ca/fifth/conspiracytheories/saudi.html.

"Conspiracy Theorist Mae Brussell Dies of Cancer." http://:www.karws.gso.uri.edu/JFK/the_critics/brussell/Brussell_dies.html.

"Conspiracy Theory." *truTV.com.* http://www.trutv.com/shows/conspiracy_theory/index.html.

Constantine, Alex. *Psychic Dictatorship in the U.S.A.* Portland: Feral House, 1995.

———. *Virtual Government: CIA Mind Control Operations in America.* Los Angeles: Feral House, 1997.

Cooper, William. *Behold a Pale Horse: Cosmic Patriot Files—The Ultimate Deception.* Flagstaff, AZ: Light Technology, 1991.

Corso, Philip J., with William J. Birnes. *The Day after Roswell.* New York: Pocket, 1997.

"Coughlin, Father Charles E." *Reader's Companion to American History.* http://college.hmco.com/history/readerscomp/rcah/html/ah_021200_coughlinfath.htm.

Coughlin, Paul T. *Secrets, Plots & Hidden Agendas: What You Don't Know about Conspiracy Theories.* Downers Grove, IL: InterVarsity Press, 1999.

"Council for National Policy: What It Is." http://www.seekgod.ca/cnp.htm.

Council on Foreign Relations. "Terrorism: Questions and Answers—Al-Qaeda." http://cfrterrorism.org/groups/alqaeda.html.

"Coverup Links." http://www.mysteries-megasite.com/main/bigsearch/coverups.html.

Cozzens, Donald B. *The Changing Face of the Priesthood: A Reflection on the Priest's Crisis of Soul.* Collegeville, MN: Liturgical Press, 2000.

"Creativity Movement." *Anti-Defamation League.* http://www.adl.org/learn/Ext_US/WCOTC.asp?Xpicked=3&item=17.

"Crédit Mobilier of America." *Infoplease.* http://www.infoplease.com/ce6/history/A0813974.html.

"Crédit Mobilier of America." *Reader's Companion to American History.* http://college.hmco.com/history/readerscomp/rcah/html/ah_021900_crditmobilie.htm.

Crenshaw, Charles A. *Trauma Room One: The JFK Medical Coverup Exposed.* New York: Paraview Press, 2001.

Crim, Keith, ed. *The Perennial Dictionary of World Religions.* San Francisco: HarperSanFrancisco, 1989.

Cristiani, Leon. *Evidence of Satan in the Modern World.* New York: Avon, 1975.

"A Critical Look at Christian Reconstruction, Theonomy, and Dominion Theology." http://www.apocalipsis.org/reconstr.htm.

Crop Circle Connector. http://www.cropcircleconnector.com.

Crop Circle Research. http://www.cropcircleresearch.com.

Crowley, Michael. "James Dobson—The Religious Right's New Kingmaker." http://www.slate.msn.com/id/210921.

Crowley, Vivianne. *Wicca: The Old Religion in the New Age.* London: Aquarian Press, 1989.

The Cryptozoologist. http://www.lorencoleman.com.

Cunningham, Scott. *Wicca: A Guide for the Solitary Practitioner.* St. Paul, MN: Llewellyn, 1987.

Dan Brown's Website. http://www.danbrown.com.

Daniszewski, John. "New Memos Detail Early Plans for Invading Iraq." *Los Angeles Times,* June 15, 2005. http://www.truthout.org/docs_2005/printer_061505Y.shtml.

Daraul, Arkon. *A History of Secret Societies.* New York, Pocket, 1969.

Darlington, David. *Area 51: The Dreamland Chronicles.* New York: Henry Holt, 1997.

Darwish, Adel. "Sphinx May Disintegrate within 25 Years by Bungled Restoration." *Independent* (UK), March 18, 2001. http://www.independent.co.uk/news/World/Africa/2001-03/sphinx18031.shtml.

Davis, Randy. "Nazis in the Attic." http://emperors-clothes.com/articles/randy/swas5a.htm.

Daws, Gavan. *Prisoners of the Japanese: POWs of World War II in the Pacific.* New York: William Morrow, 1994.

Deary, Terry. *The Philadelphia Experiment.* London: Kingfisher, 1996.

"Death of a Princess." *E! Online.* http://www.eonline.com/Features/Features/Diana.

"The Death of US Senator Paul Wellstone: Accident or Murder?" *World Socialist Website.* http://www.wsws.org/articles/2002/oct2002/well-o29_prn.shtml.

"The Death of Vincent Foster: Evidence of a Cover-up." http://www.whatreallyhappened.com/RANCHO/POLITICS/FOSTER_COVERUP/foster.html.

De Camp, L. Sprague. *The Ancient Engineers.* New York: Barnes & Noble, 1993.

Deevey, Edward S. "Ancient Wonders Abound in Ethiopia." *International Travel News,* January 1999: 23.

"Defrocked Priest Convicted of Abuse Is Killed in Prison." *Washington Times,* August 24, 2003. http://www.washingtontimes.com/functions/print.php?StoryID=20030824-124929-1052r.

"Deism and Reason." http://www.sullivan-county.com/deism.htm.

"Deism: The God That Got Away." www.religioustolerance.org/deism.htm.

"The Destruction of USS *Maine.*" http://www.history.navy.mil/faqs/faq71_1.htm.

"Did New York Orchestrate the Asian Tsunami?" http://www.vialls.com/subliminalsuggestion/tsunami.html.

Dirks, Tim. Review of *The Manchurian Candidate* (1962). http://www.filmsite.org/manc.html.

"The Diva of Disclosure, Memory Researcher Elizabeth Loftus." *Psychology Today,* January 1996. http://faculty.washington.edu/eloftus/Articles/psytoday.htm.

Domhoff, William G. *Who Rules America? Power and Politics.* Carmichael, CA: Touchstone Books, 1983.

Donnelly, Ignatius. *Atlantis: The Antediluvian World.* A Modern Revised Edition, ed Egerton Sykes. New York: Harper & Row, 1949.

Drake, W. Raymond. *Gods and Spacemen in the Ancient West.* New York: New American Library, 1974.

Drosnin, Michael. *The Bible Code.* New York: Simon & Schuster, 1997.

"Dr. Uthman's Prognosis." http://www.parascope.com/nb/abra4b.htm.

Dubose, Lou, Jan Reid, and Carl Cannon. *Boy Genius: Karl Rove, the Brains behind the Remarkable Political Triumph of George W. Bush.* New York: Public Affairs, 2003.

Dugard, Martin, and Bill O'Reilly. *Killing Lincoln: The Assassination that Changed America Forever.* New York: Holt, 2011.

Duricy, Michael P. "Black Madonnas: Our Lady of Czestochowa." http://www.udayton.edu/mary/meditations/olczest.html.

"'Eastern Lightning': Chinese House Church Supporters Face Heterodox Movement." http://www.religioscope.com/notes/2002/090_lightning.htm.

"Einhorn Found Guilty of First-degree Murder." http://www.religionnewsblog.com/archives/00000966.html.

Eisler, Robert. *Man into Wolf: An Anthropological Interpretation of Sadism, Masochism, and Lycanthropy.* London: Spring Books, 1950.

Elliston, Jon. "MK-ULTRA: CIA Mind Control." http://peyote.com/jonstef/mkultra.htm.

Ellsberg, Daniel. *Secrets: A Memoir of Vietnam and the Pentagon Papers.* New York: Viking, 2002.

Engdahl, William, and F. William Engdahl. "A Century of War—Anglo-American Oil Politics and the New World Order." *Rense.com.* http://rense.com/general63/oon.htm.

Estulin, Daniel. *Shadow Masters: An International Network of Government and Secret Service Agencies Working Together with Drug Dealers and Terrorists for Their Mutual Benefit and Profit.* Walterville, OR: TrineDay, 2010.

"Ethiopian Artefact Found in Cupboard." BBC News, December 6, 2001. http://news.bbc.co.uk/1/hi/world/africa/1695102.stm.

Evans, Hilary. *Gods, Spirits, Cosmic Guardians: A Comparative Study of the Encounter Experience.* Wellingborough, UK: Aquarian Press, 1987.

"Experts 'Amazed' by Crop Circle Designs." *BBC News,* July 19, 2002. http://news.bbc.co.uk/hi/english/uk/england/newsid_2138000/2138424.stm.

"Extremism in America: William Pierce." *Anti-Defamation League.* http://www.adl.org/learn/EXT_US/Pierce.asp.

"Face on Mars—Unmasked by New Images." http://www.com/scienceastronomy/solarsystem/mars_face_010525 1-html.

"The Faked Apollo Landings!!!" http://www.ufos-aliens.co.uk/cosmicapollo.html.

"Falun Dafa Information Center." http://www.faluninfo.net.

"Falun Dafa: Truthfulness, Benevolence, Forbearance." http://www.falundafa.com.

"Falun Gong." *Religious Movements Homepage.* http://religiousmovements.lib.virginia.edu/nrms/falungong.html.

"The Famous Unicorn Killer." http://www.crimelibrary.com/classics/einhorn.

"FAQs about Wicca." http://www.religioustolerance.org/wic_faq.htm.

Farrakhan, Louis. *A Torchlight for America.* Chicago: FCN, 1993.

Farren, Mick. *Conspiracies, Lies, and Hidden Agendas.* Riverside, CA: Renaissance Books, 1999.

Fasold, David. *The Ark of Noah.* New York: Wynwood Press, 1988.

"Fatal Experiments on U.S. Citizens." http://www.indymedia.org.uk/en/2002/0120690.html.

"Father Coughlin: The Radio Priest." *Bobby's Digital OTR—Old Time Radio.* http://www.bobbysotr.com/DETAIL_FATHER%20COUGHLIN.htm.

Fawcett, Lawrence, and Barry J. Greenwood. *Clear Intent: The Government Coverup of the UFO Experience.* Englewood Cliffs, NJ: Prentice Hall, 1984.

"FBI Ten Most Wanted Fugitives—Usama bin Laden." http://www.fbi.gov/mostwant/topten/fugitives/laden.htm.

Feddon, Roy. "Secrets of the Third Reich." http://www.violations.dabsol.co.uk/secrets/secretspart1.htm.

Federal Emergency Management Agency. http://www.fema.gov.

Fenster, Mark, and Philip Rosen. *Conspiracy Theories: Secrecy and Power in American Culture.* Twin Cities, MN: University of Minnesota Press, 2001.

Fisher, Ian. "Exploring the Deadly Mystique Surrounding a Uganda Cult." *New York Times,* April 1, 2000.

Forbes, Barry. "Fluoride Turnaround." *Arizona Tribune* (Mesa), December 5, 1999.

"Ford Faked JFK Report." Tabloid News Services, July 3, 1997: www.tabloid.net.

"For the Power and the Glory" (nonracist skinheads Website). http://www.skinheads.net.

"Fountain of the World." http://www.charliemanson.com/places/fountain_of_the_world.htm.

The Francis Parker Yockey Collection. www.alphalink.com.au/~radnat/fpyockey.

"'Frankenfoods' Cause 'West Nile' Virus?" http://www.shout.net/~bigred/Franken.htm.

Franklin, Richard L. "101 Peculiarities Surrounding the Death of Vince Foster." http://www.geocities.com/Athens/Crete/3450/foster.html.

"Free Matt Hale." http://www.matthale.org/

"Frequently Asked Questions about MechA." http://www.mexica.net/mecha/faq.php.

Friedman, Stanton T. *Top Secret/Majic.* New York: Marlowe, 1996.

———, and Don Berliner. *Crash at Corona: The U.S. Military Retrieval and Cover-up of a UFO.* New York: Marlowe, 1992.

"From the Edge of the Universe to the High Desert: Official Website of Team Art Bell." http://seti-teamart-bell.com/index.php.

Fuller, John G. *The Interrupted Journey: Two Lost Hours "Aboard a Flying Saucer."* New York: Dial Press, 1966.

Galloway, Joseph L. "Purloined Poison Letters: Fake or Real, They Raised Hell." http://www.usnews.com/usnews/doubleissue/mysteries/dahlgren.htm.

Gardner, Gerald. *The Meaning of Witchcraft.* London: Aquarian Press, 1982.

———. *Witchcraft Today.* London: Rider, 1982.

"General Information about the HAARP Program." http://www.haarp.alaska.edu/haarp/gen.html.

"George H. W. Bush Meets with Osama bin Laden's Brother on Sept. 10, 2001." http://www.wanttoknow.info/030316post.

"George Soros." *Open Society Institute.* http://www.soros.org/about/bios/a_soros.

"Ghost Dance." http://www.hanksville.org/daniel/lakota/Ghost_Dance.html.

Gibbons, Jenny. "A New Look at the Great European Witch Hunt." *Beliefnet.* http://www.beliefnet.com/story/17/story_1744_1.html.

Gilbert, David. "SDS/WUO: Students for a Democratic Society and the Weather Underground." http://www.prisonactivist.org/pps+pows/davidgilbert/sds-wuo.html.

Gillespie, Ian. "Seeking Solace in Intrigue." *The London Free Press News.* April 23, 2003. http://www.canoe.ca/LondonNews/lf.lf-04-23-0042.html.

Glick, Brian. *War at Home: Covert Action against U.S. Activists and What We Can Do about It.* Boston: South End Press, 1989.

"Global Warming—Dispelling the Myths and Flawed Analyses by Global Warming Doomsayers." http://www.globalwarming.org.

Glum, Gary. *Full Disclosure: The Truth about the AIDS Epidemic.* Los Angeles: Silent Walker, 1994.

Goeringer, Conrad. "Freemasons—From the 700 Club to Art Bell, an Object of Conspiracy Thinking." *American Atheist.* http://www.americanatheist.org/supplement/conspiracy.html.

Goerman, Robert A. "Alias Carlos Allende: The Mystery Man behind the Philadelphia Experiment." *Fate,* October 1980.

Goetz, William R. *Apocalypse Next.* Camp Hill, PA: Horizon, 1996.

Goldwag, Arthur. *The New Hate: A History of Fear and Loathing on the Populist Right.* New York: Pantheon, 2012.

Good, Timothy. *Above Top Secret—The Worldwide UFO Coverup.* New York: William Morrow, 1988.

Goodrich, Norma Lorre. *The Holy Grail.* New York: HarperCollins, 1992.

Gordon, Stuart. *The Encyclopedia of Myths and Legends.* London: Headline, 1993.

"The Goth Culture: Its History, Stereotypes, Religious Connections, Etc." http://www.religioustolerance.org/goth.htm.

"Government and Big Brother Police State." http://www.conspiracyworld.com/web/Government_and_Big_Brother_Police_State.asp?cat=2d.

Graf, Jürgen. "Jewish Population Losses in the German Sphere of Influence during World War II." http://www.ety.com/tell/books/jgjewstats/jgstattoc.htm.

Graham, Sarah. "Red Light Saves Sight." *Scientific American.* March 5, 2003. http://www.scientificamerican.com/article.cfm?id=red-light-saves-sight.

"The Gulf of Tonkin Incident, 1964." http://campus.northpark.edu/history/WebChron/USA/GulfTonkin.CP.html.

"Gun Control vs. Gun Rights." *OpenSecrets.org.* http://www.opensecrets.org/news/guns.

Guyatt, David. "Did the Pentagon Manufacture AIDS as a Biological Weapon?" http://www.deepblacklies.co.uk/pentagon_aids.htm.

"H.A.A.R.P., Part II." *The B.B.* http://www.cyberspaceorbit.com/haarp-le.htm.

"The HAARP That Only Angels Should Play." *Global Gulag.* http://www.batr.org/gulag/010103.html.

"HAARP Unveiled." http://umf.net/umf/library/1haarp.htm.

HAARP Website. http://www.haarp.alaska.edu/haarp/gen.html.

Hall, John, and Philip Schuyler. "The Mystical Apocalypse of the Solar Temple." In *Millennium, Messiahs, and Mayhem,* ed. Thomas Robbins and Susan J. Palmer. New York: Routledge, 1997: 285–311.

Hamilton, William F. *Cosmic Top Secret: America's Secret UFO Program—New Evidence.* New Brunswick, NJ: Inner Light/Global Communications, 2002.

Hancock, Graham, and Robert Bauval. *The Message of the Sphinx: A Quest for the Hidden Legacy of Mankind.* New York: Three Rivers Press, 1997.

Hansen, Chadwick. *Witchcraft at Salem.* New York: New American Library, 1970.

Hansen, Collin. "Breaking *The Da Vinci Code.*" *ChristianityToday.* http://www.christianitytoday.com/history/newsletter/2003/nov7.html

"Hard Evidence of JFK Jr Death Coverup." *Rense.com.* http://www.rense.com/politics5/quinn_p.htm.

Harkavy, Jerry. "Discredited Scientist's Work Defended." *Portland Press Harold.* November 7, 2007.

Harner, Michael. *The Way of the Shaman.* New York: Bantam, 1982.

Harper, Mark J. "Dead Scientists and Microbiologists." *Rense.com.* http://www.rense.com/general62/list.htm.

Harpur, James, and Jennifer Westwood. *The Atlas of Legendary Places.* New York: Konecky & Konecky, 1997.

Harris, Sheldon H. *Factories of Death: Japan's Secret Biological Warfare Projects in Manchuria and China, 1932–45.* London: Routledge, 1994.

Hattaway, Paul. "China—An Examination of the Eastern Lightning Cult." http://www.cswusa.com/Countries/China-LighteningfromtheEast.htm.

Haught, James A. "The Army of God: More Religious Killers?" *Secular Humanist Bulletin,* fall 1997. http://www.holysmoke.org/haught/army/html.

Hayes, Charles. *Tripping: An Anthology of True Life Psychedelic Adventures.* New York: Penguin-Putnam, 2000.

Hayes, Stephen F. "Case Closed." *Weekly Standard,* November 24, 2003. http://www.weeklystandard.com/Content/Public/Articles/000/000/003/378fmxyz.asp.

"Haymarket Bombing." http://www.spartacus.schoolnet.co.uk/USAhaymarket.htm.

Heckethorn, Charles William. *Secret Societies of All Ages and Countries.* Kila, MT: Kessinger, 1997.

"Henry Ford Invents a Jewish Conspiracy." *American Jewish Historical Society.* http://www.ajhs.org/publications/chapters/chapter.cfm?documentID=275.

Herbert, Bob. "It Just Gets Worse." *New York Times,* July 11, 2005.

"Here Comes Universal Big Brother New World Order." http://conspiracytheory.blogspirit.com/archive/2005/06/06/here_comes_universal_big_brother_new_world_order.html.

"Hermann Oberth: Father of Space Travel." http://www.kiosek.com/oberth.

"The Hermetic Order of the Golden Dawn." http://www.angelfire.com/nt/dragon9/GOLDENDAWN.html.

"Hermetic Order of the Golden Dawn." http://www.golden-dawn.com/temple/index.jsp.

"Hermetic Order of the Golden Dawn." http://www.themystica.org/mystica/articles/h/hermetic_order_of_the_golden_dawn.html.

Hidell, Al. *The Conspiracy Reader: From the Deaths of JFK and John Lennon to Government Sponsored Alien Cover-Ups.* Kensington/Citadel, 1999.

Higham, Charles. *Howard Hughes: The Secret Life.* New York: Putnam's, 1993.

———. *Trading with the Enemy: An Expose of the Nazi-American Money Plot, 1933–1949.* New York: Dell Publishing, 1984.

"Historic UFOs: Anti-Aircraft Guns Blast Mystery LA Invader." *Rense.com.* http://www.rense.com/general28/histla.htm.

"History of Secret Experimentation on United States Citizens." www.global-conspiracies.com/history.htm.

"A History of Secret Human Experimentation." http://www.mindcontrolforums.com/pro_freedom.co.uk/history_secret_experiments.html.

"History of the National Alliance." http://www.natvan.com/what-is-na/na5.html.

"History of the Zapruder Film, A New Look." www.jfklancer.com/History -Z.html.

"A Hoax of Hate: The Protocols of the Learned Elders of Zion." *Anti-Defamation League.* http://adl.org/special_reports/protocols/protocols_intro.asp.

Hochman, John. "Recovered Memory Therapy and False Memory Syndrome." http://www.skeptic.com/02.3.hochman-fms.html.

Hodges, Henry. *Technology in the Ancient World.* New York: Alfred A. Knopf, 1970.

Hoffman, Jim. "Popular Mechanics Attacks Its '9/11' Straw Man." http:// 911research.wtc7.net/essays/pm/index.html.

Hooper, Edward. *The River: A Journey to the Source of HIV-AIDS.* Boston: Little, Brown, 1999.

Hooper, John. "Flirting with Hitler." *Guardian* (UK), November 16, 2002. http://www.guardian.co.uk/weekend/story/0,3605,839755,00.html.

Hopkins, Budd. *Missing Time.* Rev. ed. New York: Ballantine, 1988.

Horowitz, Leonard G. "The CIA and West Nile Virus: What New Viruses, Vaccines, and Lethal Sprayings Have in Common." http://www.healingcelebrations.com/The%20CIA%20and%20the%20West%20Nile%20Virus.htm.

———. *Emerging Viruses: AIDS and Ebola: Nature, Accident or Intentional.* Sandpoint, ID: Tetrahedron Publishing Group, 1996.

HOTT: Hour of the TimeÐVeritas News Service. http://www.hourofthetime.com.

House, Wayne H., and Thomas Ice. *Dominion Theology: Blessing or Curse?* Sisters, OR: Multnomah, 1988.

"Howard Hughes." *Historical Society of Southern California.* http://www.socalhistory.org/biographies/h_hughes.htm.

"Howard Hughes." *Seize the Night.* http://www.carpenoctem.tv/cons/hughes.html.

Howard Hughes Corporation Website. http://www.howardhughes.com.

Howard, Mike. "The Hellfire Club." easyweb.easynet.co.uk/~rebis/ts-artic4.htm.

Howarth, Stephen. *The Knights Templar.* New York: Barnes & Noble, 1993.

Howe, Linda Moulton. *An Alien Harvest: Further Evidence Linking Animal Mutilations and Human Abductions to Alien Life Forms.* Littleton, CO: Linda Moulton Howe Productions, 1993.

———. *Mysterious Lights and Crop Circles.* 2d ed. Jamison, PA: Linda Moulton Howe Productions, 2002.

Hubbard, L. Ron. *Dianetics: The Modern Science of Mental Health.* Los Angeles: Bridge, 1985.

Hughes, Ruth. "The Awful Disclosures of Maria Monk." http://www.english.upenn.edu/~traister/hughes.html.

Hunt, Linda. *Secret Agenda: The United States Government, Nazi Scientists, and Project Paperclip, 1945–1990.* New York: St. Martin's Press, 1991.

Huston, Peter. *Tongs, Gangs, and Triads: Chinese Crime Groups in North America.* Boulder, CO: Paladin Press, 1995.

Hutchinson, Earl Ofari. "Chasing a Katrina Conspiracy." *Pacific News Service,* September 28, 2005. http://www.alternet.org/columnists/story /26126.

Huxley, Francis. *The Invisibles: Voodoo Gods in Haiti.* New York: McGraw-Hill, 1969.

"Hyperdimensional Physics." http://www.mufor.org/hyperd.htm.

"Hypnosis FAQ." http://www.hypnosis.com/faq.

Icke, David. *The Biggest Secret: The Book That Will Change the World.* Bridge of Love, 1999. www.bridgeoflove.com.

"Ignatius of Loyola, Saint: Founding of the Jesuit Order." http://www.encyclopedia.com/html/section/IgnatiusL_FoundingoftheJesuitOrder.asp.

Imperial Klans of America Website. http://www.k-k-k.com.

"Implanted Microchips Common as Cellphones within a Decade." *Propaganda Matrix.* http://propagandamatrix.com/articles/april2005/150405commonascellphones.htm.

Inhofe, Senator James. *The Greatest Hoax: How Global Warming Threatens Your Future.* Washington, DC: WND Books, 2012.

"Inoculations: The True Weapons of Mass Destruction Causing VIDS, Vaccine Induced Diseases." http://educate-yourself.org/cn/vidsgenocide29jan05.shtml.

"Inside Bohemian Grove: The Story People Magazine Won't Let You Read." *FAIR: Fairness & Accuracy in Reporting.* http://www.fair.org/extra/best-of-extra/bohemian-grove.html.

"Institute for Historical Review." *Anti-Defamation League.* http://www.adl.org/learn/ext_us/historical_review.asp.

"Ira Einhorn's Long, Strange Trip." http://www.salon.com/news/feature/2002/10/18/einhorn.

Ireland, Joe. "Who Is Lyndon LaRouche?" Portland State University *Vanguard.* http://www.dailyvanguard.com/vnews/display.v/ART/2004/05/13/40A31AAA061FD?in_archi.

Isikoff, Michael, and Mark Hosenball. "Nixon and Dixon." *Newsweek/MSNBC,* March 23, 2005. http://www.MSNBC.msn.com/id/7276868/site/newsweek/print/1/display mode/1098.

"Is the Trilateral Commission the Secret Organization That Runs the World?" *Straight Dope.* http://www.straightdope.com/classics/a2_295.html.

"Jack the Ripper." http://www.marvunapp.com/Appendix/jtripper.htm.

"Jack the Ripper." *World Wide Serial Killer Homepage.* http://hosted.ray.easynet.co.uk/serial_killers/whitecha.html.

Jackson, Forest, and Rodney Perkins. *Cosmic Suicide: The Tragedy and Transcendence of Heaven's Gate.* Dallas: Pentaradial Press, 1997.

"Jacobinism." http://www.brainydictionary.com/words/ja/jacobinism181198.

Jacobs, David M. *Secret Life: Firsthand Accounts of UFO Abductions.* New York: Simon & Schuster, 1992.

James, William. *Varieties of Religious Experience.* Garden City, NY: Masterworks Program, 1971.

James Stockdale's Website. http://www.admiralstockdale.com.

"Japanese Unit 731: Biological Warfare Unit." *World War II in the Pacific.* http://www.ww2pacific.com/unit731.html.

Jasper, William F. "Conspiracy Realties." *New American,* August 23, 2004. http://www.thenewamerican.com/tna/2004/08-23-2004/realities.htm.

Jeffrey, Jason. "Earthquakes: Natural or Man-Made?" *New Dawn.* http://newdawnmagazine.com.au/Articles/Earthquakes_Natural_or_Man_Made.html.

Jesse Ventura.net. http://www.jesseventura.net.

Jessup, M. K. *The Case for the UFO.* 1955. Reprint Clarksburg, WV: Saucerian Press, 1973.

Jewish Defense League Website. http://www.jdl.org.il.

"JFK: The Kennedy Assassination Home Page." www.mcadams.posc.mu. Edu/home.htm.

"Jim Garrison." http://www.goochinfo.homestead.com/garrison.html.

"John F. Kennedy Jr.: Evidence of a Cover-up." http://www.whatreallyhappened.com/RANCHO/CRASH/JFK_JR/jj.

"John F. Kennedy Jr. Memorial." http://dandalf.com/dandalf/jfkjr.html.

"John Hinckley, Jr.: Attempted Assassin." http://www.who2.com/johnhinckleyjr.html.

"John W. Hinckley, Jr. Biography." http://www.law.umkc.edu/faculty/projects/ftrials/Hinckley/HBIO.htm.

Jones, Adam. "Case Study: The European Witch-Hunts, c. 1450–1750." *Gendercide Watch.* http://www.gendercide.org/case_witchhunts.html.

"Jonestown: Examining the Peoples Temple." http://www.owlnet.rice.edu/~reli291/Jonestown/Jonestown.html.

Joseph, Claudia. "Mystery of 'Copper' Dead Sea Scroll Unravels." http://conspiracycafe.com/news/040102_1.html.

"Judyth Vary Baker." http://jfkmurdersolved.com/judyth.htm.

Kaiser, Robert Blair. *RFK Must Die! A History of the Robert Kennedy Assassination and Its Aftermath.* New York: E. P. Dutton, 1970.

Kaiser, Robert G., and Ira Chinoy. "Scaife: Funding Father of the Right." *Washington Post,* May 2, 1999.

Kantrowitz, Barbara, with Peter Annin, Ginny Carroll, and Bob Conn. "Was It Friendly Fire? In the Bungled Waco Raid, Federal Agents May Have Been Shot by Their Own Men." *Newsweek,* April 5, 1993, 50–51.

Keel, John A. *Our Haunted Planet.* Rev. ed. Lakeville, MN: Galde Press, 1999.

———. *The Mothman Prophecies.* New York: Tor, 2002.

Keith, Jim. *Black Helicopters Over America: Strikeforce for the New World Order.* Lilburn, GA: Illuminet Press, 1995.

———. *Mind Control and UFOs: Casebook on Alternative 3.* Lilburn, GA: Illuminet Press, 1999.

———. *Mass Control: Engineering Human Consciousness.* Lilburn, GA: Illuminet Press, 1999.

———. *Mind Control, World Control.* Kempton, IL: Adventures Unlimited Press, 1998.

Kelly, Edward. *The Stone of the Philosophers.* Edmonds, WA: Holmes, 1990.

Kite, L. Patricia, ed. *Noah's Ark: Opposing Viewpoints.* San Diego: Greenhaven Press, 1989.

Klaber, William, and Philip H. Melanson. *Shadow Play: The Murder of Robert F. Kennedy, the Trial of Sirhan Sirhan, and the Failure of American Justice.* New York: St. Martin's, 1997.

Klass, Philip J. *UFO Abductions: A Dangerous Game.* Buffalo, NY: Prometheus, 1988.

Klimo, Jon. *Channeling: Investigations on Receiving Information from Paranormal Sources.* Los Angeles: Jeremy P. Tarcher, 1987.

Knight, JZ. *A State of Mind.* New York: Warner, 1987.

"Know-Nothing Movement." http://www.infoplease.com/ce6/history/A0827946.html.

Korff, Kal K. *The Roswell UFO Crash.* New York: Prometheus, 1997.

Kouri, Jim. "Police Chiefs Poll Reveals Some Surprises." *PHXnews.com.* http://www.phxnews.com/fullstory.php?article=22621.

Ku Klux Klan Website. http://www.kkk.com.

"Ku Klux Klan." http://www.spartacus.schoolnet.co.uk/USAkkk.htm.

"Ku Klux Klan (KKK)." http://users.skynet.be/terrorism/html/usa_kkk.htm.

Kurtzweil, Paula. "Medical Possibilities for Psychedelic Drugs." *U.S. Food and Drug Administration.* http://www.fda.gov/fdac/features/795_psyche.html.

Lalire, Gregory. "Ghost Dancers' Last Stand." *Wild West,* June 1993, 26Ð33.

Lampton, Christopher. "Wernher von Braun." http://www.germanheritage.com/biographies/atol/braun.html.

Lane, Mark. *Plausible Denial.* New York: Thunder's Mouth Press, 1991.

"LaRouche Calls for Emergency Impeachment Action—Against Vice President Cheney, then Bush." *Executive Intelligence Review.* http://www.larouchepub.com/pr_lar/2005/lar_pac/050707impeachment.html.

"LaRouche: Evil Pundit of Doom!" http://evilpundit.com/archives/006822.html.

LaVey, Anton Szandor. *The Satanic Rituals.* New York: Avon, 1972.

"Lawyers for RFK Assassin Sirhan Say Bullet Was Switched at Trial." FOX News. http://www.foxnews.com/us/2011/11/28/lawyers-for-rfk-ass.

Lea, Henry Charles. *The Inquisition of the Middle Ages.* New York: Citadel Press, 1963.

League of the South Website. http://leagueofthesouth.net.

"A League of Their Own." *Southern Poverty Law Center.* http://www.splcenter.net/intel/intelreport/article.jsp?aid=250.

Leaming, Jeremy, and Rob Boston. "Who Is the Council for National Policy and What Are They Up To? And Why Don't They Want You to Know?" http://www.au.org/site/News2?page=NewsArticle&id=6949&abbr=cs_.

LeBlanc, Pamela. "'Remote Viewing' Keeps Attracting Believers." *Daytona Beach News-Journal,* July 14, 2002.

Lederman, Robert. "Axis of Oil?" http://www.hartford-hwp.com/archives/27c/025.html.

Lee, Martin A., and Bruce Shlain. *Acid Dreams: The CIA, LSD, and the Sixties Rebellion.* New York: Grove Press, 1986.

LeFebure, Charles. *The Blood Cults.* New York: Ace, 1969.

Leone, Richard C., and Greg Anriq Jr., eds. *The War on Our Freedoms: Civil Liberties in an Age of Terrorism.* Hastings: The Century Foundation, 2000.

Lewis, Jon E. *The Mammoth Book of Coverups: The 100 Most Terrifying Conspiracies of All Time.* Philadelphia: Running Press, 2008.

Liberty Lobby Website. http://www.revisionists.com/libertylobby.html.

"Lie of Maria Monk Lives On." http://www.catholicleague.org/research/mariamonk.html.

"The Life of Henry Ford." *The Henry Ford.* http://www.hfmgv.org/exhibits/hf/default.asp.

"Lightning from the East." http://www.factnet.org/discus/messages/3/411.html.

Lin, Rosanne. "China Says Crop Circles Appeared There 3,000 Years Ago." *Shanghai Star,* August 2, 2002. *Rense.com.* http://www.rense.com/general27/crops.htm.

Linder, Doug. "The Charles Manson (Tate-LaBianca Murder) Trial." http://www.law.umkc.edu/faculty/projects/ftrials/manson/mansonaccount.html.

Lindsay, Reed. "Eerie X-File of the Pampas." *Baltimore Sun,* July 23, 2002.

Lindsey, Hal, with C. C. Carlson, *The Late Great Planet Earth.* New York: Bantam, 1978.

"Linkin' Kennedy." http://www.snopes.com/history/american/linckenn.htm.

Lipton, Eric. "Study Suggests Design Flaws Didn't Doom Towers." *New York Times.* October 20, 2004.

Loftus, Elizabeth F. "Searching for the Neurobiology of the Misinformation Effect." https://webfiles.uci.edu/eloftus/Learning%26Memory05.pdf.

———, and Katherine Ketcham. *The Myth of Repressed Memory: False Memories and Allegations of Sexual Abuse.* New York: St. Martin's Press, 1994.

Lomas, Robert, and Christopher Knight. *The Hiram Key: Pharaohs, Freemasons, and the Discovery of the Secret Scrolls of Jesus.* Boston: Element, 1999.

Lopez, Daniel. "Facts on Gun Control." *Hidden Mysteries Conspiracy Archive.*
  http://www.hiddenmysteries.org/conspiracy/facts/guncontrol.html.

Lorenzi, Rossella. "Turin Shroud Older Than Thought." *Discovery News.*
  http://dsc.discovery.com/news/briefs/20050124/shroud.html.

"Louis Beam." *Anti-Defamation League.*
  http://www.adl.org/learn/ext_us/beam.asp?LEARN_Cat=Extremism&LEARN_SubCat=Extremism_in_America&x
  picked=2&item=beam.

"LSD and the CIA."*History House.* http://www.historyhouse.com/in_history/lsd.

Luukanen-Kilde, Rauni-Leena. "Microchip Implants, Mind Control, and Cybernetics." *Illuminati Conspiracy Archive.*
  http://www.conspiracyarchive.com/NWO/microchip_implants_mind_control.htm.

Lyons, Arthur. *Satan Wants You: The Cult of Devil Worship in America.* New York: Mysterious Press, 1989.

———. *The Second Coming: Satanism in America.* New York: Award, 1970.

Maaga, M. McCormick, and Catherine Wessinger. *Hearing the Voices of Jonestown.* Syracuse, NY: Syracuse University Press, 1998.

Macoy, Robert. *A Dictionary of Freemasonry.* New York: Gramercy, 2000.

"Macumba." *Occultopedia.* http://www.occultopedia.com/m/macumba.htm.

Madsen, Wayne. "Exposing Karl Rove." *CounterPunch.* http://counterpunch.org/madsen1101.html.

Mae's Web. http://www.prouty.org/brussell.

"The Majestic Documents: Evidence That We Are Not Alone." http://www.majesticdocuments.com.

Malboa, Wunyabari O. *Mau Mau and Kenya: An Analysis of a Peasant Revolt.* Bloomington: Indiana University Press, 1998.

Malcolm X: A Research Site. http://www.brothermalcolm.net.

"Malcolm X Assassination: The Disappearing Suspect." *Memory Hole.* http://www.thememoryhole.org/deaths/x-suspects.htm.

Malcolm-X.org. http://www.malcolm-x.org.

"Maniacal World Control thru the Jesuit Order: Well-Hidden Soldiers of Satan."
  http://www.conspiracyarchive.com/NWO/black_pope_1.htm.

Manning, Jeane, and Nick Begich. "Angels Don't Play This HAARP: Advances in Tesla Technology."
  www.2012.com.au/HAARP.html.

Mannix, Daniel P. *The Hellfire Club.* London: Four Square, 1961.

Manson, Charles, as told to Nuel Emmons. *Manson in His Own Words—The Shocking Confessions of the Most Dangerous Man Alive.* New York: Grove Press, 1988.

Mantle, Philip. "Alien Autopsy Update." http://ufocasebook.com/alienautopsyupdate.html.

"Marilyn's Death—Undisputed Facts." http://www.crimelibrary.com/notorious_murders/celebrity/Marilyn_Monroe/7.html?sect=26.

"The Marilyn Monroe CIA Memo." http://www.blackmesapress.com/page4.htm.

Marks, John. *The Search for the Manchurian Candidate: The CIA and Mind Control.* New York: Times Books, 1979.

Marrs, Jim. "Anti-gun Hysteria with a Serious Purpose: Globalists Won." *AlienZoo.com.*
  http://archive.alienzoo.com/conspiracytheory/guncontrolconspiracy.html.

———. *Rule by Secrecy: The Hidden History that Connects the Trilateral Commission, the Freemason, and the Great Pyramids.* New York City: Harper Paperbacks, 2001.

———. *War on Freedom.* http://www.conspiracycafe.com/marrs.html.

Martin, Al. "The Ambassador Wilson Affair: The End of Karl Rove—and George Bush?" *Rense.com.*
  http://www.rense.com/general42/rove.htm.

Martin, Rick. "The Biggest Secret: An Interview with David Icke."
  http://www.metatech.org/david_icke_and_reptilians.html.

Masters, R. E., and Jean Houston. *The Varieties of Psychedelic Experience.* New York: Dell/Delta, 1966.

Mayer, Jean Francois. "Apocalyptic Millennialism in the West: The Case of the Solar Temple." *Critical Incident Analysis Group.* http://www.healthsystem.virginia.edu/internet/ciag/reports/report_apoc_intro.cfm.

McAdams, John. "The Kennedy Assassination." http://mcadams.posc.mu.edu/home.htm.

McCarthy, Michael. "Timetable of Global Warming Destruction Unveiled." *Independent* (UK), February 2, 2005.

McClure, Kevin. "Dark Ages." *Fortean Times,* December 1999.

McCommachie, James, and Robin Tudge. *The Rough Guide to Conspiracies.* London, UK: Rough Guides, 2008.

McCormick, Donald. *The Hell-Fire Club.* London: Jarrolds, 1958.

McFadden, Ashley. "The Rosicrucians—A Brief Historical Overview." *R.C. Times,* Summer 1994. http://www.neue_rosenkreuzer.de/quellen/www.arcgl.org/rosie.htm.

McGee, Celia. "'Code' Hot, Critics Hotter." *New York Daily News,* September 4, 2003. http://www.nydailynews.com/entertainment/v-pfriendly/story/114463p-103285c.html.

McGinn, Bernard. *Antichrist: Two Thousand Years of the Human Fascination with Evil.* San Francisco: HarperSanFrancisco, 1994.

McKee, Jennifer. "Montana House Condemns Patriot Act." *Billings Gazette,* April 3, 2005. http://www.rense.com/general63/mont.htm.

McLoughlin, Emmett. *An Inquiry into the Assassination of Abraham Lincoln.* New York: Lyle Stuart, 1963.

McNeil, Donald G., Jr. "U.S. Apologizes for Syphilis Tests in Guatemala." *New York Times.* http://www.nytimes.com/2010/10/02/health/research/02infect.html.

Meacham, Jon. "Sex and the Church: A Case for Change." *Newsweek,* May 6, 2002.

Melanson, Terry. "The Vril Society, the Luminous Lodge, and the Realization of the Great Work." *Illuminati Conspiracy Archive.* http://www.conspiracyarchive.com/NWO/Vril_Society.htm.

Melendez, Albert J. "The World of James Dobson." *Institute for First Amendment Studies.* http://www.buildingequality.us/ifas/fw/9608/dobson.html.

Melton, J. Gordon, Jerome Clark, and Aidan A. Kelly. *New Age Almanac.* Detroit: Visible Ink Press, 1991.

"Men in Black." http://www.crystalinks.com/mib.html.

Metraux, Alfred. *Voodoo.* New York: Oxford University Press, 1959.

Meyer, Marvin, and Richard Smith, eds. *Ancient Christian Magic.* San Francisco: HarperSanFrancisco, 1994.

Michell, John. *Eccentric Lives and Peculiar Notions.* San Diego: Harcourt Brace Jovanovich, 1984.

Middleton, John, ed. *Magic, Witchcraft, and Curing.* Garden City, NY: Natural History Press, 1967.

Miesel, Sandra. "Special Report: Dismantling the Da Vinci Code." *Crisis,* July 8, 2004. http://www.crisismagazine.com/specialreport.htm.

Millard, Joseph. "America's Greatest Unsolved Murder." *True,* February 1953.

Millegan, Kris. "The Order of Skull and Bones: Everything You Ever Wanted to Know, but Were Afraid to Ask." http://www.parascope.com/articles/0997/skullbones.htm.

Miller, Greg. "Cheney Claims al Qaeda link to Hussein: He Also Says Regime Had Program for Prohibited Weapons." *Los Angeles Times,* January 23, 2004.

Monroe, Robert A. *Far Journeys.* Garden City, NY: Doubleday, 1987.

"The Montauk Project." *Lightnet.* http://www.lightnet.co.uk/frontier/montauk.htm.

Moore, James C., and Wayne Slater. *Bush's Brain: How Karl Rove Made George W. Bush Presidential.* New York: John Wiley & Sons, 2003.

Morgellons Data Center. http://www.rense.com/Datapages/morgdat1.htm

Muhammad, Elijah. *The True History of Jesus as Taught by Honorable Elijah Muhammad.* Chicago: Coalition for the Remembrance of Elijah, 1992.

Mullenax, David. "To Look Again." *Augusta Free Press* (Waynesboro, VA), May 31, 2004. http://www.augustafreepress.com/stories/storyReader$22320.

"Murder of Dr. David Kelly." http://www.propagandamatrix.com/murder_of_kelly.html.

"The Murder of John Fitzgerald Kennedy." http://www.reality reviewed.com/JFK%20murder.htm.

Murray, Margaret. *The God of the Witches.* Garden City, NY: Doubleday, 1960.

———. *The Witch-Cult in Western Europe.* Oxford, UK: Clarendon Press, 1962.

Muzhesky, Vladimir. "From Psychotronic Warfare to Biotronic Materials." http://www.ljudmila.org/nettime/zkp4/35.htm.

"*Mystery of the Mitchell Ghost Bomber.*" http://www.surfview.com/mystery.htm.

"Mystery of the Pittsburgh Ghost Bomber." http://pittsburgh.about.com/library/weekly/aa071800a.htm.

MythArc Magazine, May 1, 2005. http://www.mytharc.com/magazine/?cat=36.

National Alliance Website. http://www.natvan.com.

"National Socialist Movement."
   http://www.adl.org/learn/extemism_in_america_updates/groups/national_socialist_movement/default.htm.

"Nation of Islam." http://religiousmovements.lib.virginia.edu/nrms/Nofislam.html.

Nation of Islam Website. www.noi.org.

"Nativism." http://www.history.sandiego.edu/gen/classes/civ/nativism.htm.

Nattrass, Nicoli. *The AIDS Conspiracies: Science Fights Back.* New York: Columbia University Press, 2012.

Naumov, Alex. "Russians Have Psychotropic Weapon to Zombie People." *Pravda Ru.* August 14, 2007.
   http://english.pravda.ru/science/tech/14-08-2007/95965-psychotr.

"Neo-Nazi Skinheads." *Anti-Defamation League.* http://www.adl.org/hate-patrol/neonazi.asp.

Netanyahu, B. *The Origins of the Inquisition.* New York: Random House, 1995.

Neuberger, G. J. "The Great Gulf between Zionism and Judaism." The Tripoli Conference on Zionism and Racism.
   http://www.nkusa.org/AboutUs/Zionism/greatgulf.cfm.

Neville, Leigh. "We Didn't Start the Fire." *Fortean Times,* April 2000, 34–38.

"New Discoveries in Betty Hill's Star Map." http://www.kochkyborg.de/hill05.htm.

"New Nation of Islam." http://noic.ca/home.html.

"New Orleans, and the Garrison Investigation." http://mcadams.posc.mu.edu/garrison.htm.

Newton, Toyne. *The Dark Worship: The Occult's Quest for World Domination.* Vega Books, 2002.

"The New World Order (NWO): An Overview." http://www.educate-yourself.org/nwo.

"New World Order/One World Government." http://www.freedomdomain.com/neworder.htm.

Nichols, Bill, and Jerry Mitchell. "Ex-KKK Member Found Guilty of Manslaughter in '64 Civil Rights Murders." *USA Today,* June 21, 2005.
   http://www.usatoday.com/news/nation/2005_06_20_civil_rights_trial_x.htm?POE=NEWISVA.

Nichols, Preston B., and Peter Moon. *The Montauk Project: Experiments in Time.* New York: Sky, 1992.

———. *Pyramids of Montauk: Explorations in Consciousness.* New York: Sky, 1995.

Nickson, Elizabeth. "A Protocol for Psychic Spies." *National Post* (Canada), July 17, 2002.

"Nikola Tesla, Inventor." http://www.lucidcafe.com/library/96jul/tesla.html.

Niman, Michael I. "The 'Plane Crash' of Senator Wellstone." . http://www.oilempire.us/wellstone.html.

Nimmo, Kurt. "Homeland Security Moves to Man FEMA Camps." *Infowars.* December 19, 2011.
   http://www.infowars.com/homeland-security-moves-to-man-fema-camps/.

"9/11: Debunking the Myths." *Popular Mechanics,* March 2005.
   http://www.popularmechanics.com/science/defense/1227842.html?page=1&c=y.

"Nixon (1995)." http://www.lehigh.edu/~ineng/mac6/mac6-histcontext.html.

"Nobel Peace Laureate Claims HIV Deliberately Created." *ABC News,* October 9, 2004.
   http://www.abc.net.au/news/newsitems/200410/9/216687.htm.

Noe, Denise. "Sirhan Sirhan: Assassin of Modern U.S. History."*Crime Magazine.*
   http://crimemagazine.com/04/bobbykennedy,0527.htm.

Nordland, Rod, and Jeffrey Bartholet. "The Web's Dark Secret." *Newsweek,* March 19, 2001.

Notestein, Wallace. *A History of Witchcraft in England.* New York: Thomas Y. Crowell, 1968.

Offley, Will. "David Icke and the Politics of Madness: Where the New Age Meets the Third Reich." *Public Eye.org.*
   http://www.publiceye.org/Icke/IckeBackgrounder.htm.

O'Grady, Joan. *Early Christian Heresies.* New York: Barnes & Noble, 1985.

"OK City Bombing Timeline." http://historical.disaster.net/historical/ok/timeline.html.

O'Keefe, Theodore J. "The Liberation of the Camps: Facts to Consider." *Journal of Historical Review. Rense.com.*
   http://www.rense.com/general62/camps.htm.

"The Oklahoma City Bombing." www.whatreallyhappened.com/RANCHO/POLITICS/OK/bombs/bombs.html.

Oklahoma City National Memorial. http://www.oklahomacitynationalmemorial.org.

"Order of the Solar Temple." *Religious Movements Homepage Project.* http://religiousmovements.lib.virginia.edu/nrms/solartemp.html.

"Orgone Energy." *Skeptic's Dictionary.* http://www.skepdic.com/orgone.html.

"Osama bin Laden." http://www.adl.org/terrorism_america/bin_l.asp.

Osborn, Andrew. "Bobby Kennedy Assassin Brainwashed by 'Girl in a Polka Dot Dress.'" *Telegraph*, April 29, 2011. http://www.telegraph.co. uk/news/world news/north America/usa/.

Ostrander, Sheila, and Lynn Schroeder. *Psychic Discoveries behind the Iron Curtain.* Englewood Cliffs, NJ: Prentice Hall, 1970.

O'Sullivan, Patrick. *The Lusitania: Unraveling the Mysteries.* New York: Sheridan House, 2000.

"The Other Life of Martin Luther King, Jr.: Commentary from CEO of AmColSo@cs.com." *Rense.com.* http://www.rense.com/general19/mlk.htm.

Ove, Torsten. "Searchers say 'Ghost Bomber' Can Be Found in the Mon." *Pittsburgh Post-Gazette,* April 4, 1999. http://www.post-gazette.com/regionstate/19990404bomber4.asp.

"An Overview of John Wilkes Booth's Assassination of President Abraham Lincoln." http://home.att.net/~rjnorton/Lincoln75.html.

"Paiute—Wovoka—Ghost Dancers." http://www.crystalinks.com/paiute.html.

Parama, Roy. "Discovering India, Imagining Thuggee." *Yale Journal of Criticism* 9:1 (spring 1996): 121–45.

"Paranoia as Patriotism: Far-Right Influences on the Militia Movement." *Nizkor Project.* http://www.nizkor.org/hweb/orgs/american/adl/paranoia-as-patriotism/posse-comitatus.html.

Parenti, Michael. *Dirty Truths: Reflections on Politics, Media, Ideology, Conspiracy, Ethnic Life, and Class Power.* San Francisco: City Lights, 1996.

Patton, Ron. "Project Monarch." http://www.aches-mc.org/monarch.html.

Pearce, Joseph Chilton. *The Biology of Transcendence: A Blueprint of the Human Spirit.* Rochester, VT: Inner Traditions, 2002.

"Pearl Harbor Revelations." http://scribblguy.50megs.com/pearlharbor.htm.

Pease, Lisa. "Sirhan and the RFK Assassination." http://www.webcom.com/ctka/pr398-rfk.html.

The Pentagon Papers (as published in the *New York Times*). New York: Bantam Books, 1971.

The Pentagon Papers: The Defense Department History of United States Decisionmaking on Vietnam. Boston: Beacon Press, 1971.

"A People's Libertarian Index." http://flag.blackened.net/liberty.

Pepper, William. *Orders to Kill: The Truth behind the Murder of Martin Luther King, Jr.* New York: Warner, 1998.

Phelps, Jim. "HAARP Theory and Chemtrails—Research Goals." *Rense.com.* http://www.rense.com/general45/reee.htm.

Pilkington, Ed. "Koch Brothers: Secretive Billionaires to Launch Vast Database." *The Guardian.* November 7, 2011. http://www.guardian.co.uk/world/2011/nov/07/koch-brothers-d.

Pincus, Walter, and Dana Milbank. "Al Qaeda–Hussein Link Is Dismissed." *Washington Post,* June 17, 2004.

Pinkham, Mark Amaru. *Guardians of the Holy Grail: The Knights Templar, John the Baptist, and the Water of Life.* Kempton, IL: Adventures Unlimited Press, 2004.

Pipes, Daniel. *Conspiracy: How the Paranoid Style Flourishes and Where It Comes From.* New York: Touchstone, 1999.

Pitt, William Rivers. "The Most Insidious of Traitors." *Rense.com.* http://www.rense.com/general42/trait.htm.

Plato. *The Timaeus and Kritias.* Trans. Desmond Lee. London: Penguin, 1977.

"Poisoning the Web: Hatred Online." http://www.adl.org/poisoning_web/posse.asp.

"Political Culture: Nativism." http://www.dig.lib.niu.edu/message/ps-nativism.html.

Poole, Patrick S. "ECHELON: America's Secret Global Surveillance Network." http://fly.hiwaay.net/~pspoole/echelon.html.

Posner, Gerald. *Killing the Dream: James Earl Ray and the Assassination of Martin Luther King.* New York: Harvest/Harcourt Brace Jovanovich, 1999.

Posner, Sarah. "Obama the Antichrist and End-Times Doctrine." The Guardian, November 18, 2011. http://www.guardian.co.uk/commentisfree/belief/2011/nov/18/o.

Posse Comitatus Website. http://www.posse-comitatus.org.

Power of Prophecy. http://www.powerofprophecy.com.

Preston, Diana. *Lusitania: An Epic Tragedy.* New York: Berkley Books, 2002.

"Princess Diana: Murder Coverup." *Conspiracy Planet.* http://www.conspiracyplanet.com/channel.cfm?ChannelID=41.

"Princess Diana: The Conspiracy Theories." http://www.londonnet.co.uk/ln/talk/news/diana_conspiracy_theories.html.

Pringle, Lucy. *Crop Circles—The Greatest Mystery of Modern Times.* New York: HarperCollins, 2000.

"Project Silverbug—The Avrocar." http://www.crystalinks.com/silverbug.html.

"Proof Lee Harvey Oswald, Trained by CIA, Worked for ONI." *Rense.com.* http://www.rense.com/general62/Oswald.htm.

"Protestant Paranoia: The American Protective Association Oath." *History Matters.* http://historymatters.gmu.edu/d/5351.

"Protocols of the Elders of Zion." *Seize the Night.* http://carpenoctem.tv/cons/protocols.html.

"The Protocols of the Learned Elders of Zion." http://www.the7thfire.com/Politics%20and%20History/protocols_of_the_elders_of_zion.htm.

Protocols of the Learned Elders of Zion. The complete text. http://aztlan.net/protocols.htm.

Prouty, Fletcher L. *JFK: The CIA, Vietnam, and the Plot to Assassinate John F. Kennedy.* Carol Stream, IL: Carol, 1996.

"Psychotronic War." *Rense.com.* http://www.rense.com/general23/psy.htm.

Public Orgonomic Research Exchange. http://www.orgone.org.

Pullella, Philip. "Cardinal Urges Catholics to Shun Da Vinci Code." Reuters, March 16, 2005.

"Racist Skinheads." *Rick A. Ross Institute.* http://www.rickross.com/groups/skinheads.html.

Raelian Movement Website. http://www.rael.org.

Rainie, Harrison, with James Popkin et al. "Armageddon in Waco: The Final Days of David Koresh." *U.S. News and World Report,* May 3, 1993: 24–34.

Randle, Kevin D. *Case MJ-12: The True Story behind the Government's UFO Conspiracies.* New York: Avon, 2002.

———. *Roswell Crash Update: Exposing the Military Cover-up of the Century.* New Brunswick, NJ: Global Communications, 1995.

———, and Donald R. Schmitt. *The Truth about the UFO Crash at Roswell.* New York: M. Evans, 1994.

———, and Donald R. Schmitt. *UFO Crash at Roswell.* New York: Avon, 1991.

———, Russ Estes, and William P. Cone. *The Abduction Enigma.* New York: Forge, 1999.

Ravenscroft, Trevor. *Spear of Destiny.* New York: Red Wheel/Weiser, 1987.

Ray, James Earl. *Tennessee Waltz: The Making of a Political Prisoner.* St. Andrew's, TN: St. Andrew's Press, 1987.

"Really So Mysterious? 'Strange' and 'Convenient' Deaths Surrounding the Assassination." http://mcadams.posc.mu.edu/deaths.htm.

Reavis, Dick J. *The Ashes of Waco: An Investigation.* Syracuse, NY: Syracuse University Press, 1998.

"Recurring Hate: Matt Hale and the World Church of the Creator." *Anti-Defamation League.* http://www.adl.org/special_reports/wcotc/wcotc_intro.asp.

Redfern, Nick. "In Search of Nazi Saucers." *Phenomena.* http://www.phenomenamagazine.com/0/editorial.asp?aff_id=0&this_cat=Area+51&action=page&type_id=&cat_id=&obj_id=3506.

———. *Keep Out!* Pompton Plains, NJ: New Page Books, 2012.

———. *The NASA Conspiracies.* Pompton Plains, NJ: New Page Books, 2011.

———. "The Roswell Memory Saga." *UFO Iconoclasts.* http://ufocon.blogspot.com/2011/01/roswell-memory-metal-saga.

Reilly, John J. Review of *Dreamer of the Day: Francis Parker Yockey and the Postwar Fascist International,* by Kevin Coogan. http://pages.prodigy.net/aesir/dod.htm.

"Remember the *Maine*." http://www.smplanet.com/imperialism/remember.html.

Reptilian Agenda Website. http://www.reptilianagenda.com.

"Research Topic: Charles E. Coughlin (Father Coughlin)."
http://www.questia.com/library/religion/christianity/catholicism/father-coughlin.jsp.

Revkin, Andrew C. "New Research Questions Uniqueness of Recent Warming." *New York Times,* October 5, 2004.

Rhodehamel, John, and Louise Taper, eds. *Right or Wrong, God Judge Me: The Writings of John Wilkes Booth.* Urbana:
University of Illinois Press, 2001.

Rich, Frank. "The Two Wars of the Worlds." *New York Times,* July 3, 2005.

Richard Hoagland's Website. http://www.enterprisemission.com.

"Richard Mellon Scaife." *Source Watch.* http://www.sourcewatch.org/index.php?title=Richard_Mellon.

Richter, Bob. "Tonkin Incident Might Not Have Occurred." *San Antonio Express-News,* August 3, 2002.
http://www.commondreams.org/headlines 02/0805-09.htm.

"RICO in a Nutshell." http://www.ricoact.com/ricoact/nutshell.asp.

"The Rise and Fall of Richard Nixon." *Modern History Project.*
http://www.modernhistoryproject.org/mhp/ArticleDisplay.php?Article= FinalWarn05-4.

Robbins, Alexandra. *Skull and Bones: The Ivy League and the Hidden Paths of Power.* Boston: Back Bay Books, 2003.

Roberts, J. *Mythology of the Secret Societies.* New York: Macmillan, 1972.

Robinson, B. A. "Santeria: A Syncretistic Caribbean Religion." http://www.religioustolerance.org/santeri.htm.

Robinson, James, ed. *The Nag Hammadi Library.* San Francisco: Harper & Row, 1981.

"Ron Brown." http://www.rotten.com/library/bio/usa/ron-brown.

"Ron Brown: Evidence of a Coverup." http://www.whatreallyhappened.com/RANCHO/CRASH/BROWN/brown.html.

Rosberg, Carl G., and John Nottingham. *The Myth of Mau Mau.* New York: Meridian, 1970.

Ross, Robert Gaylon Sr. *Who's Who of the Elite: Members of the Bilderbergs, Council on Foreign Relations, & Trilateral
Commission.* Privately printed, 1996.

"Rosslyn Chapel." http://heritage.scotsman.com/topics.cfm?tid=542.

Rothmyer, Karen. "The Man behind the Mask." *Salon.com,* April 1998.
http://www.salon.com/news/1998/04/07new.html.

Rove, Karl. *Courage and Consequences: My Life as a Conservative in the Fight.* New York: Threshold Editions, 2010.

Rudden, Liam. "Don't Let New Crusade Ruin Mystery of Chapel." *Edinburgh Evening News,* May 7, 2005.
http://edinburghnews.scotsman.com/print.cfm?id=493402005&referringtemplate.

Ruddy, Christopher. *The Strange Death of Vincent Foster: An Investigation.* New York: Free Press, 1997.

Russell, Jeffrey Burton. *Witchcraft in the Middle Ages.* Ithaca, NY: Cornell University Press, 1972.

Sabeheddin, M. "The Rockefeller-UFO Connection: Shades of an Alien Conspiracy?" *New Dawn,* March–April 1996.
http://newdawnmagazine.com/Articles/Shades%20of%20an%20Alien%20Conspiracy.html.

Sachs, Margaret. *The UFO Encyclopedia.* New York: Perigee, 1980.

Salla, Michael E. "Eisenhower's 1954 Meeting with Extraterrestrials: The Fiftieth Anniversary of America's First
Treaty with Extraterrestrials?" http://www.thewatcherfiles.com/eisenhower.html.

"The Saudi Connection." http://www.cbc.ca/fifth/conspiracy theories/Saudi_printer.html.

Saylor, Frederica. "Radical Religious Movement Breeds Violence and Hate." *Science & Theology News,* January
2004, 1, 32.

Scaife Foundations Website. http://www.scaife.com.

Scheer, Robert. "The 9/11 Secret in the CIA's Back Pocket." *Los Angeles Times.* October 19, 2004.

Scheeres, Julia. "Ervil LeBaron: Renegade Mormon Fundamentalist Wooed Child Brides and Used Them as the Instruments of His Murderous Designs." http://origin-
www.crimelibrary.com/notorious%5Fmurders/classics/ervil%5Flebaron%5Fcult.

Schellhorn, G. Cope. "Is Someone Killing Our UFO Investigators?" *UFO Magazine.*
http://www.metatech.org/ufo_research_magazine_evidence.htm.

Schoch, Robert. "A Modern Riddle of the Sphinx." *Omni,* August 1992.

Schuster, Henry. "An Unholy Alliance: Aryan Nation Leader Reaches Out to al Qaeda." *CNN.com.* http://www.cnn.com/2005/US/03/29/schuster.column/index.html.

Schwortz, Barrie M. "Mapping of Research Test-Point Areas on the Shroud of Turin." http://www.shroud.com/mapping.htm.

"Scientist Murdered after Call for Full BSE Testing." *Rense.com.* http://www.rense.com/general65/murdd.htm.

Scientology (official Church of Scientology Website). http://www.scientology.org/scn_home.htm.

"Secret Memo Shows JFK Demanded UFO Files 10 Days before Assassination." http://www.dailymail.co.uk/news/article-137284/Secret-memo.

"Secret Side of the Tonkin Gulf Incident." *Naval History.* http://www.usni.org/navalhistory/Articles99/Nhandrade.htm.

Seifer, Marc J. *Wizard: Life and Times of Nikola Tesla: Biography of a Genius.* New York: Citadel, 1998.

Seigerfriede, Diarmaid O. "Spanish Authorities Using a New EMP Weapon on Citizens?" *Sovereign Independent.* November 12, 2011. http://www.sovereignindependent.com/?p=29550.

Seligmann, Kurt. *The History of Magic.* New York: Meridian, 1960.

September 11 News.com. http://www.september11news.com/AttackImages.htm.

Shackleford, Martin, updated by Debra Conway. "A History of the Zapruder Film." http://www.jfklancer.com/History-Z.html.

Shanks, Herschel. *The Mystery and Meaning of the Dead Sea Scrolls.* New York: Random House, 1998.

Shannan, Pat. "'MLK Murder Was a Government Plot': Former CIA Participant Says He Was Part of It, Raoul Identified as FBI Agent." *Media Bypass.* http://www.mediabypass.com/archives/may_01.htm.

Sharkey, Matt. "American Dreams: The Matt Hale Interview." *Generator 21.* http://www.g21.Net/amdream9.html.

Shaw, Eva. *Eve of Destruction: Prophecies, Theories, and Preparations for the End of the World.* Chicago: Contemporary, 1995.

Shepherd, A. P. *Rudolf Steiner: Scientist of the Invisible.* Rochester, VT: Inner Traditions International, 1983.

Shermer, Michael. "Fahrenheit 2777." *Scientific American.* http://www.Sciam.com/print_version.cfm?articleID=000DA0E2-1E15-128A-931583411B.

Shinabery, Michael. "Controlled Remote Viewer Takes His Skills to New Sights." *Alamogordo Daily News,* December 5, 1999.

"Shroud of Turin Links." http://www.mysteries-megasite.com/main/bigsearch/shroud.html.

Sieveking, Paul. "Shallow Grave." *Fortean Times,* July 2000, 34–38.

Silva, Freddy. *Secrets in the Fields: The Science and Mysticism of Crop Circles.* Charlottesville, VA: Hampton Roads, 2002.

Singer, Natasha. "'Schindler' vs. the Werewolves: Spielberg Opus Stirs Controversy in Moscow." *Forward,* July 22, 1994.

"Sinking of the USS *Maine,* 15 February 1898." http://www.history.navy.mil/photos/events/spanam/events/maineskg.htm.

Skolnick, Sherman H. "The Murder of John F. Kennedy, Jr.—An Update." http://www.skolnicksreport.com/jfkjr.html.

"Skull and Bones." *CBSNews.com,* June 13, 2004. http://www.cbsnews.com/stories/2003/10/02/60minutes/printable576332.shtml.

Smith, Jerry E. *HAARP: The Ultimate Weapon of the Conspiracy.* The Mind-Control Conspiracy Series. Kempton, IL: Adventures Unlimited Press, 1998.

"Some Frequently Asked Questions about HAARP." http://www.haarp.alaska.edu/haarp/faq.html.

"Some Obama Birth Records Made Public for Years." *New York Times.* April 23, 2011.

Sparrowdancer, Mary. "Fluoride—The Battle of Darkness and Light." *Rense.com.* http://www.rense.com/general45/bll.htm.

———. *The Love Song of the Universe.* Charlottesville, VA: Hampton Roads, 2001.

Spence, Lewis. *An Encyclopedia of Occultism.* New Hyde Park, NY: University, 1960.

———. *The History of Atlantis.* New York: University, 1968.

Spoto, Donald. *Marilyn Monroe: The Biography.* 1993; reprint, New York: Cooper Square Press, 2001.

Springmeier, Fritz. *Bloodlines of the Illuminati.* Frankston, TX: TGS Publishers, 1995.

Starck, Peter. "Are the Holy Grail and Ark of the Covenant Hidden on Baltic Sea Island?" *Rense.com.* http://www.rense.com/general6/baltic.htm.

Starkey, Marion L. *The Devil in Massachusetts: A Modern Enquiry into the Salem Witch Trials.* Garden City, NY: Dolphin/Doubleday, 1961.

Steele, Edgar J. "How Not to Be Interviewed by CNN about the Holocaust." *Rense.com.* http://www.rense.com/general62/cnn.htm.

Steiger, Brad, and Hayden Hewes. *Inside Heaven's Gate: The UFO Cult Leaders Tell Their Story in Their Own Words.* New York: Signet, 1997.

———. *Real Aliens, Space Beings, and Creatures from Other Worlds.* Detroit, MI: Visible Ink Press, 2011.

———. *UFOs Are Here!* New York: Citadel, 2001.

Stevens, Henry. *Hitler's Flying Saucers: A Guide to the German Flying Discs of the Second World War.* Kempton, IL: Adventures Unlimited Press, 2003.

Stoecker, William B. "Suppressed Technologies." August 24, 2008. http://www.Unexplained-Mysteries.com.

Storr, Will. "Morgellons: A Hidden Epidemic or Mass Hysteria?" *The Guardian.* May 6, 2011.

Story, Ronald D., ed. *The Encyclopedia of Extraterrestrial Encounters.* New York: New American Library, 2001.

Stout, David. "Bush Urges Congress to Keep Patriot Act Intact." *New York Times,* June 9, 2005.

Strieber, Whitley. *Communion: A True Story.* Rev. ed. New York: Avon, 1988.

———. *Majestic.* New York: Berkley, 1990.

———. "Rockefeller Obit You'll Only Read Here." *Unknown Country.* http://www.unknowncountry.com/news/?id=3940.

Students for a Democratic Society Website. http://www.sds-1960s.org/index.htm.

Sulzberger, A. G., and Laurie Goldstein. "Bishop Indicted; Charge Is Failing to Report Abuse." October 14, 2011. *New York Times.*

Summers, Anthony. *Conspiracy.* New York: Paragon House, 1989.

———. *Goddess: The Secret Lives of Marilyn Monroe.* New York: Random House, 1987.

Sutton, Anthony. *America's Secret Establishment: An Introduction to the Order of Skull and Bones.* Walterville, OR: Trine Day, 2003.

Swerdlow, Stewart. *Montauk: The Alien Connection.* Peter Moon, ed. New York: Sky, 1998.

Szymanski, Greg. "WTC Basement and Burn Victim Blows Official 9/11 Story Sky High." http://www.articbeacon.com/articles/article/1518131/ 28031.htm.

Targ, Russell, and Harold E. Puthoff. *Mind-Reach: Scientists Look at Psychic Ability.* New York: Delacorte Press/Eleanor Friede, 1977.

Tart, Charles T. *Body Mind Spirit: Exploring the Parapsychology of Spirituality.* Charlottesville, VA: Hampton Roads, 1997.

———, ed. *Altered States of Consciousness.* New York: John Wiley & Sons, 1969.

Taylor, Sid. "A History of Secret CIA Mind Control Research." *Project Freedom.* http://www.mindcontrolforums.com/pro-freedom.co.uk/skeletons_1.html.

Taylor-Perry, Rosemarie. *The God Who Comes: Dionysian Mysteries Revisited.* New York: Algora, 2003.

Temple of Set Website. http://www.xeper.org/pub/tos/infoadms.html.

"10 Most Influential People in the Alternative Media (2011)." http://theintelhub.com/2011/06/13/10-most-influential-people-in-the-alternative-media-2011/.

"Terrorist Organizations: Al-Qa'ida (Al Qaeda)." http://www.terrorismfiles.org/organisations/al_qaida.html.

Tesla, Nikola. *My Inventions: The Autobiography of Nikola Tesla.* Ed. Ben Johnston. Williston, VT: Hart Brothers, 1982.

Thomas, Evan. *The Very Best Men.* New York: Simon & Schuster, 1995.

Thomas, Gordon. *Journey into Madness.* New York: Bantam, 1989.

Thomas, Timothy L. "The Mind Has No Firewall." http://www.tearingdownstrongholds.com.

Thomas, William. "Lab Reports Show 3 Distinct Pathogens." Chemtrails. http://www.geocities.com/Area51/Shadowlands/6583/project367.html?200512.

Tidwell, William A. *April '65: Confederate Covert Action in the American Civil War.* Kent, OH: Kent State University Press, 1995.

———, James O. Hall, and David Winfred Gaddy. *Come Retribution: The Confederate Secret Service and the Assassination of Lincoln.* Oxford: University Press of Mississippi, 1988.

Tourney, Christopher P. "Who's Seen Noah's Ark?" *Natural History* 106:9 (October 1997): 14–17.

Towers, Eric. *Dashwood—The Man and the Myth.* London: Crucible, 1986.

Townsend, Mark, and Jason Burke. "Earth Will Expire by 2050." *Observer* (UK), July 7, 2002. http://www.observer.co.uk/Print/0,3858,4456418,00.html.

———. "2004 Was Fourth-Warmest Year Ever Recorded." *New York Times,* February 10, 2005.

"Traditional Values Coalition." *Southern Poverty Law Center Intelligence Report* 15 (spring 2005): 26.

Tribbe, Frank. *Portrait of Jesus? The Illustrated Story of the Shroud of Turin.* New York: Stein and Day, 1983.

Trifkovic, Srdja. "Pearl Harbor Conspiracy? FDR and the Making of a War." http://www.freerepublic.com/forum/a3a3522a943db.htm.

"Trilateral Commission: World Shadow Government." http://www.geocities.com/CapitolHill/8425/TRI-1SPT.HTM.

Tsoukalas, Steven. *The Nation of Islam: Understanding the "Black Muslims."* Phillipsburg, NJ: P&R, 2001.

Tulsky, Fredric N. "Scientist's Death Haunts Family." *Mercury News,* August 8, 2002. http://www.bayarea.com/mld/mercurynews/news/nation/3822588.htm?template=contentM.

Tunnah, Helen. "NZ Author Suing over Da Vinci Bestseller." *New Zealand Herald,* December 18, 2004.

Turnage, C. L. *ET's Are on the Moon and Mars: The Photographic Evidence.* Santa Barbara, CA: Timeless Voyager Press, 1998.

"The Turner Diaries." http://www.rotten.com/library/culture/turner-diaries.

"The 25 Points of American National Socialism." http://www.nsm88.com/25points/25pointsengl.html.

"UFOs: The Great Airship of 1897." http://ufos.about.com/library/weekly/aa052797.htm.

"UFOs: The Montauk Project." http://ufos.about.com/library/weekly/aa123097.htm.

"The Ultimate Brussellsprout Links to Mae Brussell Articles, Interviews, Tapes and the World Watchers International Series." *NewsMakingNews.com.* http://www.newsmakingnews.com/mblinks.htm.

Underhill, Eveyln. *Mysticism.* 12th rev. ed. New York: Dutton, 1961.

Unterman, Alan. *Dictionary of Jewish Lore and Legend.* New York: Thames and Hudson, 1991.

U.S. Air Force. *The Roswell Report: Case Closed.* Washington, DC: Government Printing Office, 1997.

"U.S. Government Conducts Medical Experiments on Americans without Consent." http://www.worldfreeinternet.net/news/nws192.htm.

"U. S. Government Secret Tests on Humans." http://www.mapcruzin.com/rev_government_secret_tests.htm.

Valiente, Doreen. *An ABC of Witchcraft, Past and Present.* New York: St. Martin's Press, 1973.

———. *The Rebirth of Witchcraft.* Custer, WA: Phoenix, 1989.

Vankin, Jonathan, and John Whalen. *The 70 Greatest Conspiracies of All Time: History's Biggest Mysteries, Coverups, and Cabals.* New York: Citadel, 1998.

"Vatican Assassins: 'Wounded in the House of My Friends.'" http://www.vaticanassassins.org.

"Vatican Paper Set to Clear Knights Templar." Moore, Malcolm. http://www.telegraph.co.uk/core/Content/displayPrintable.jhtml:jsession=DE0ZBA2XT.

Ventura, Jesse, with Dick Russell. *63 Documents the Government Doesn't Want You to Read.* New York: Skyhorse Publications, 2011.

———, with Dick Russell. *American Conspiracies: Lies, Lies, and More Dirty Lies.* Skyhorse Publications, 2010.

Vesco, Renato, and David Hatcher Childress. *Man-Made UFOs 1944–1994: 50 Years of Suppression.* Kempton, IL: Adventures Unlimited Press, 1995.

Vesperman, Gary. "History of 'New Energy' Invention Suppression Cases." June 19, 2006. http://www.rense.com/general72/oinvent.htm.

Villodo, Alberto, and Stanley Krippner. *Healing States: A Journey into the World of Spiritual Healing and Shamanism.* New York: Fireside, 1987.

"Violence against Cults." http://www.americanreligion.org/cultwtch/violence.html.

"Vodun." http://www.religioustolerance.org/voodoo.htm.

von Däniken, Erich. *Chariots of the Gods?* New York: G. P. Putnam's Sons, 1970.

Waite, Robert G. L. *The Psychopathic God: Adolf Hitler.* New York: Basic, 1977.

Walter, Jess. *Every Knee Shall Bow: The Truth and Tragedy of Ruby Ridge and the Weaver Family* New York: Harper-Collins, 1995.

Warwick, Mark. "Mau Mau: Messengers of Misery." http://www.multiline.com.au/~markw/maumau.html.

"Was Spielberg Involved? Last Word on Alien Autopsy Film." http://www.ufos-aliens.co.uk/cosmicaut.html.

"Was There a Conspiracy by the Catholic Church to Murder Abraham Lincoln? Emmett McLoughlin and the Falsification of History." http://www.geocities.com/chiniquy/History.html?200517.

"Weather Underground Organization (WUO) a.k.a. Weatherman." http://www.users.skynet.be/terrorism/html/usa_weather.htm.

Weaver, Randy, Sara Weaver, and Bill Henry. *The Federal Siege at Ruby Ridge: In Our Own Words.* Marion, MT: Ruby Ridge, 1998.

Weber, Mark. "Auschwitz—Myths and Facts." *Journal of Historical Review.* http://www.ihr.org/leaflets/auschwitz.shtml.

Weinberg, Steven Lee, ed., with Randall Weischedel, Sue Ann Fazio, and Carol Wright. *Ramtha.* Eastsound, WA: Sovereignty, 1986.

Weinstein, Joseph. "'Protocols of Zion'—A Non-Zionist Jewish Perspective." *Rense.com.* http://www.rense.com/general66/proto.htm.

Weishaupt, Adam. *The Illuminati.* New York: Hyper Reality, 2011.

Wessinger, Catherine Lowman. *How the Millennium Comes Violently: From Jonestown to Heaven's Gate.* New York: Chatham House, 2000.

West, John Anthony. *The Serpent in the Sky: The High Wisdom of Ancient Egypt.* 2d ed. Wheaton, IL: Quest, 1993.

"West Nile Virus Information." http://www.brainstrain.westnilevirus.iwarp.com.

Weston, Jessie L. *From Ritual to Romance.* Mineola, NY: Dover, 1997.

"What Is Jacobinism?" http://www.bluepete.com/Hist/Gloss/Jacobite.htm.

"What is Zionism?" *Jews against Zionism.* http://jewsagainstzionism.com/zionism/whatis.cfm.

Wheeler, John, Jr. *Earth's Two-Minute Warning: Today's Bible-Predicted Signs of the End Times.* North Canton, OH: Leader, 1996.

White, John, ed. *Psychic Warfare: Fact or Fiction?* Wellingborough, UK: Aquarian Press, 1988.

Whittemore, Katharine. Review of *American Fuehrer: George Lincoln Rockwell and the American Nazi Party,* by Frederick J. Simonelli. http://www.salon.com/books/review1999/07/19/simonelli.

"Who Is Lyndon LaRouche, Jr.?" http://www.larouchepac.com/pages/z_other_files/about_lhl/lhl_biography.htm.

"Who Is MEChA?" http://www.mayorno.com/WhoIsMecha.html.

"Wicca-Witchcraft: Frequently Asked Questions—Straightforward Answers!" *American Wicca.* http://www.americanwicca.com/faq.

Wilford, John Noble. "Debate Erupts over Authors of the Dead Sea Scrolls." *New York Times,* December 24, 2002.

Wilgus, Neal. *The Illuminoids.* New York: Pocket, 1978.

"Wilhelm Reich and Orgone Energy." *Mystical World Wide Web.* http://www.mystical-www.co.uk/reich.htm.

Wilhelm Reich and Orgone Ring. http://g.webring.com/hub?ring=pore.

"William Torbitt: Biography." http://www.spartacus.schoolnet.co.uk/JFKtorbitt.htm.

"Willis A. Carto: Fabricating History." *Anti-Defamation League.* http://www.adl.org/holocaust/carto.asp.

Wilson, Jim. "New Orleans Is Sinking." *Popular Mechanics,* September 11, 2001. http://www.popularmechanics.com/science/research/1282151.html.

Wilson, Lynne. "The Law of Posse Comitatus." http://www.thirdworldtraveler.com/Civil_Liberties/Posse_Comitatus_Law.html.

Wilson, Robert A. *Everything Is under Control: Conspiracies, Cults, and Cover-ups.* New York: Collins, 1998.

Wilson, Traci. "Conspiracy Theories Find Menace in Contrails." *USA Today.* http://www.usatoday.com/weather/resources/basics/2001-03-07-contrails.htm.

Witztum, Doron, Eliyahu Rips, and Yoav Rosenberg. "Equidistant Letter Sequences in the Book of Genesis." *Statistical Science* 9, no. 3 (1994): 429–38.

Wolfe, Donald H. *The Last Days of Marilyn Monroe.* New York: William Morrow, 1998.

Woodward, Bob. *Plan of Attack.* New York: Simon & Schuster, 2004.

"World Leaders Commemorate Death Camp Liberation." *USAToday.com,* January 24, 2005. http://www.usatoday.com/news/world/2005-01-24-camps_x.htm.

"Worldwide Economic Collapse, World War III, New World Order–One World Government." http://nwo-warning.tripod.com/nwo_conspiracies.html.

Wright, Lawrence. "Orphans of Jonestown." *New Yorker,* November 22, 1993, 66–89.

Wu, Tien-wei. "A Preliminary Review of Studies of Japanese Biological Warfare and Unit 731 in the United States." http://www.centurychina.com/wiihist/germwar/731rev.htm.

Wurmser, Meyrav. "Can Israel Survive Post-Zionism?" *Middle East Quarterly.* March 1999. http://www.meforum.org/article/469.

"The X-Files Timeline." http://www.themareks.com/xf.

"The X-Files TV Show." http://www.tv.com/the_x_files/show/61/summary.html.

Yates, Frances A. *The Rosicrucian Enlightenment.* Boulder, CO: Shambhala, 1978.

Yockey, Francis Parker. "On Propaganda in America." http://www.vho.org/GB/Journals/JHR/10/2/Yockey143-147.html.

"Y2K Information and Resources." http://www.y2ktimebomb.com.

Zepezauer, Mark. *The CIA's Greatest Hits.* Tucson: Odonian, 1994.

"The Zeta Reticuli Incident." *Astronomy,* December 1974.

"Zionism." The Jewish Virtual Library. http://www.jewishvirtuallibrary.org/jsource/Zionism/Zionism_Is.

Zuitchik, Alexander. "Meet Alex Jones." *Rolling Stone.* March 2, 2011.

INDEX

CONSPIRACIES AND SECRET SOCIETIES

CONSPIRACIES AND SECRET SOCIETIES